Handbook of Blockchain, Digital Finance, and Inclusion, Volume 1

Handbook of Blockchain, Digital Finance, and Inclusion, Volume 1

Cryptocurrency, FinTech, InsurTech, and Regulation

Edited by

David LEE Kuo Chuen
Robert Deng

Singapore University of Social Sciences, Singapore

ACADEMIC PRESS
An imprint of Elsevier

Academic Press is an imprint of Elsevier
125 London Wall, London EC2Y 5AS, United Kingdom
525 B Street, Suite 1800, San Diego, CA 92101-4495, United States
50 Hampshire Street, 5th Floor, Cambridge, MA 02139, United States
The Boulevard, Langford Lane, Kidlington, Oxford OX5 1GB, United Kingdom

Notices

Knowledge and best practice in this field are constantly changing. As new research and experience broaden our understanding, changes in research methods, professional practices, or medical treatment may become necessary.

Practitioners and researchers must always rely on their own experience and knowledge in evaluating and using any information, methods, compounds, or experiments described herein. In using such information or methods they should be mindful of their own safety and the safety of others, including parties for whom they have a professional responsibility.

To the fullest extent of the law, neither the Publisher nor the authors, contributors, or editors, assume any liability for any injury and/or damage to persons or property as a matter of products liability, negligence or otherwise, or from any use or operation of any methods, products, instructions, or ideas contained in the material herein.

Library of Congress Cataloging-in-Publication Data
A catalog record for this book is available from the Library of Congress

British Library Cataloguing-in-Publication Data
A catalogue record for this book is available from the British Library

ISBN: 978-0-12-810441-5

For information on all Academic Press publications
visit our website at https://www.elsevier.com/books-and-journals

Working together
to grow libraries in
developing countries

www.elsevier.com • www.bookaid.org

Publisher: Nikki Levy
Acquisition Editor: Scott Bentley
Editorial Project Manager: Susan Ikeda
Production Project Manager: Susan Li
Designer: Greg Harris

Typeset by VTeX

Dedicated To
All those who care for the needy

In Memory Of
The late Sim Kee Boon
and
The late Professor Harry Rowen

Contents

List of Contributors

Douglas W. Arner
University of Hong Kong, China

Aleksandra Bal
International Bureau for Fiscal Documentation, Netherlands

Jànos Barberis
Asian Institute of International Financial Law, University of Hong Kong, China
FinTech HK, China

David G.W. Birch
Consult Hyperion, UK

Ross P. Buckley
UNSW, Australia

Cathy Yi-Hsuan Chen
Humboldt-Universität zu Berlin, Berlin, Germany
Chung Hua University, Hsinchu, Taiwan

Shi Chen
Humboldt-Universität zu Berlin, Berlin, Germany

Tan Lee Cheng
Singapore University of Social Sciences, Singapore

Guan Chong
Singapore University of Social Sciences, Singapore

Albert B. Chu
Singapore University of Social Sciences, Singapore

Ding Ding

Singapore University of Social Sciences, Singapore

Christopher Dula

Singapore Management University, Singapore

Hermann Elendner

Humboldt-Universität zu Berlin, Berlin, Germany

Pei Sai Fan

Singapore Management University, Singapore

Andreas Freund

San Diego, USA

Wolfgang Karl Härdle

Humboldt-Universität zu Berlin, Berlin, Germany

Matthew Homer

USAID, USA

David LEE Kuo Chuen

Left Coast, USA

Singapore University of Social Sciences, Singapore

Roy Lai

InfoCorp Technologies, Singapore

Teik Ming Lee

CoinGecko, Singapore

Kelvin F.K. Low

Singapore Management University, Singapore

Ignacio Mas

Tufts University, USA

Alan Megargel

Singapore Management University, Singapore

Loretta Michaels

Copenhagen Consensus Center, USA

Immaculate Dadiso Motsi-Omoijiade
University of Warwick, UK
University College London, Centre for Blockchain Technologies

Njuguna Ndung'u
University of Nairobi, Nairobi, Kenya

Bobby Ong
CoinGecko, Singapore

Salome Parulava
Consult Hyperion, UK

Anju Patwardhan
Stanford University, CA, USA

Srinivas K. Reddy
Singapore Management University, Singapore

Paul Schulte
Schulte Research, Hong Kong, China

Venky Shankararaman
Singapore Management University, Singapore

Ernie Teo
Singapore Management University, Singapore

Simon Trimborn
Humboldt-Universität zu Berlin, Berlin, Germany

Tan Choon Yan
Grab, Singapore

Preface

"Each of us has a vision of good and of evil. We have to encourage people to move towards what they think is good... Everyone has his own idea of good and evil and must choose to follow the good and fight evil as he conceives them. That would be enough to make the world a better place."

– Pope Francis as said to Cultura Oct. 1, 2013.

"To my knowledge, no society has ever existed in which ownership of capital can reasonably be described as "mildly" inegalitarian, by which I mean a distribution in which the poorest half of society would own a significant share say, one-fifth to one-quarter) of total wealth."

– Thomas Piketty, Capital in the Twenty-First Century, 2014.

Background

Financial inclusion and impact investment are not viewed as main stream activities. Recent exodus of senior bankers and financial practitioners to inclusive FinTech companies has changed that perception somewhat. But perhaps it is still not enough to influence the stake-holders in the incumbents due to the lack of understanding of what these companies do, or a lack of good cases that demonstrate a good Returns on Investment (ROI). Increased awareness of "good" disruptive opportunities in digital banking and Internet finance is important for policy makers and investors alike, so that regulation and investment are appropriately aligned to ensure sustainable world growth.

Many are beginning to view the ***sustainability and success*** of both digital banking and Internet finance businesses as closely linked to the degree of financial inclusion and impact investing. Those at the lower end of the wealth pyramid almost always pay higher charges for services, especially financial services. However, businesses are prevented to take advantage of the higher rates because costs remain high to meet the diverse demand at the bottom. This is so until the emergence of FinTech. FinTech has the advantage of lowering cost and being an enabler for new and profitable business models. More recently, ***Blockchain, a technology that*** *originated from cryptocurrency*, is seen as an innovation that may propel financial inclusion to new heights. Blockchain has known to lower business costs, but more importantly, it has the potential to change the way business is conducted. It gives rise to new governance structure and how governance is being executed. It enables transparency in digital business models and may help to generate sustainable new revenue streams.

Besides the awareness and interest in new inclusive financial technology, the mindset of investors is also changing because of the slowdown of the offline economy. This is especially true for businesses that are not fully plugged into the digital economy. They are finding it difficult to grow and are faced with profit margin squeezed. Financial institutions are at the frontline of being disrupted.

Declining Returns on Equity (ROE) of financial institutions have pressured many financial institutions into rethinking their own business models and the ways they engage customers. There is now an increase in willingness to fund technology companies and to search for new business models that are data and computing power intensive. The listing of a peer-to-peer platform Lending Club that raised US$870 million in 2014 has heightened concerns that the use of smart data will further threaten profit margins. The increase in the assets under management of Robo-Advisors such as Wealthfront, Bettlement, and Sigfig have also alerted the wealth managers that some of these services are charged at 10% of current practices. However, what really threatens the financial institutions is not the start-ups that **unbundled** these silo services of the institutions. The real threat is coming from the large technology companies.

Alibaba's Ants Financial (Alipay) and Safaricom's M-PESA, started off as trust agents for the Alibaba e-commerce platform and telecom service provider respectively, have begun to **re-bundle** financial services in a way that no one has done before. They have used data and computing technology to enhance the scope of services with a focus on customers' needs and user experience. They have embraced business models that provide not only financial services originally provided by incumbents, but beyond that into social media, entertainment, crowdfunding, credit rating, insurance, taxi services, delivery services, and other mass market services.

It is important to note that with the new digital business models, not only being scalable is necessary, but the speed of scaling is even more important. Typically, it takes seven years for a tech company to break even. Sustainability is provided mainly by additional funding while building a large Hinternet consisting of hundreds of millions of customers. *Hinternet is a large online or digital platform with a huge number of sticky customers*. World's top FinTech companies are those with the ability to scale fast in large sparsely populated countries. It is not surprising that Ant Financial (Financial Services), Qudian (Qufenqi, Micro Students Loan), Lufax (P2P and Financial Services), Zhong An (Online Insurance), and JD Finance

(Supply Chain Financing) are all originally located in China and among the top ten FinTech Companies in the world. Many of them are serving the underserved micro enterprises, underserved individuals and the unbanked in remote areas via Internet or digital devices. Many successful companies possess the *LASIC characteristics, i.e., Low profit margin, Asset light, Scalable, Innovative, and Compliance easy*. Their strategy was not plainly to take advantage of economies of scales, but also to take advantage of economies of scopes.

Because of QE and after the steep run-up of equities, fixed income, real estate, and commodity prices, investors have also been searching for asset classes that exhibit negative correlation with the market. Digital banking and Internet finance that incorporate financial inclusion and impact investing will be an area worthy of attention. Ant Financial, with USD60b market valuation, is larger than American Express Bank, Morgan Stanley, and Bank of New York. The revenue of Ant Financial was RMB10.2b with a net profit of RMB2.6b in 2016. Profit margin of 26% was higher than Goldman, JP Morgan, Wells Fargo, Bank of America, Citigroup, and Morgan Staley that registered between 18% and 25.6% as at third quarter of 2016. Ant Financial has an annual profit growth rate of 64% from 2015 to 2017. Similar statistics are registered for M-PESA that has 24 million registered customers served by a network of over 100 thousand agents spread over Kenya. There are more M-PESA accounts than formal bank accounts of just over 5 million. M-PESA revenue continues to grow at over 20%.

It is worth taking note of the *4Ds: Digitization, Disintermediation, Democratization, and Decentralization* (see David LEE Kuo Chuen, The 4Ds: Digitization, Disintermediation, Democratization, and Decentralization, 2017, https://www.slideshare.net/DavidLee215/the-deep-skill-of-blockchain-david-lee-27april2017-final, https://papers.ssrn.com/sol3/papers.cfm?abstract_id=2998093). The transformation of the traditional economies will go through the four stages and we are possibly into the second and third stage. Investors and financial institutions seeking for-profit opportunities and higher ROI/ROE in a low-growth environment flushed with liquidity will do well to take advantage of the digital revolution. Both Ant Financial and M-PESA provide good case studies of how businesses are taking a view on combining digitization and inclusion.

Throughout the two volumes, prominent authors will share their technical knowledge, accumulated experiences, business views, political perspectives, and future scenarios. Many of them need no introduction as they are well known academics, practitioners and government officials that were and are still personally involved in the areas that they have written. Topics that are covered are FinTech, Digital Finance, Cryptocurrency, Digital Banking and Insur-Tech, FinTech Regulation, China FinTech, Security, Blockchain, Inclusion and Innovation, and Emerging Technology.

The last few Chapters focus on the 3rd and 4th D: Democratization and Decentralization. The issues of mobile devices and digital identity are crucial to bring on democratization of technology and blockchain is potentially the driver for decentralization. For scalability and sustainability, financial inclusion is key as there are still more than 60% of world population that are still underserved or unserved by the financial system, and excluded from the economic, social, and financial system.

It is therefore the editors' view that it is a right time to publish this two-volume handbook explaining and exploring the important concepts and opportunities in financial inclusion, impact investing, and decentralized consensus ledger.

Purpose

Despite rapid development, few technical papers have been written about blockchain, digital finance and inclusion. It will be interesting to analyze the latest technology and product development in these two areas and their implications. The time seems ripe to bring together economic analysis, financial evaluation, methodological contributions, technology explorations, and findings in the three areas.

This two-volume Handbook will provide a collection of papers by pioneers, academics, and practitioners. The authors are carefully chosen from a pool of established experts in their respective fields. The two volumes will deliver first-hand knowledge about the latest developments, the theoretical underpinnings, and empirical investigations. They bridge the gap between the practical usability and the academic perspective, written in a language assessable to practitioners and graduate students. They will appeal to an international audience that wants to learn not only about their own fields of specialization but also fields related to theirs. Each chapter will review, synthesize, and analyze the topic at hand, acknowledge areas where there are gaps between theory and practice, and suggest directions for future research when appropriate.

Themes

The Handbook has three main themes. The first theme is digital finance, and in specific topics such as the disruption, the function, the evolution, and the regulatory environment (or the lack of it) of digital finance. The idea is to discuss the origins and backgrounds of the digital revolution.

The second theme is financial inclusion. Some explore the sustainability of social enterprises, and examine the potential of e-commerce/telecom companies as future digital entities providing services beyond finance.

The third theme centers on decentralized consensus ledgers and the potential of the blockchain in alternative finance. These chapters will explain the technology while speculating about its use in the future of finance and beyond. The division into three themes is not intended to be hermetic: we expect overlap and links among the chapters of the various parts.

We expect this Handbook to enrich the understanding of the world of blockchain, digital finance and inclusion and be an excellent guide for future work especially in financial inclusion that may bring about sustainable growth. We end the preface with the following quote from Evangelii Gaudium, Apostolic Exhortation by Pope Francis, 2013:

> *"In this context, some people continue to defend trickle-down theories which assume that economic growth, encouraged by a free market, will inevitably succeed in bringing about greater justice and inclusiveness in the world. This opinion, which has never been confirmed by the facts, expresses a crude and naïve trust in the goodness of those wielding economic power and in the sacralized workings of the prevailing economic system. Meanwhile, the excluded are still waiting."*

Hopefully, with a better understanding of how technology can substantially lower operation cost and can create new scalable business models with big data, artificial intelligence, Internet of Things, and computing power, the excluded need not wait too long with technology serving the entire pyramid! With new technology giving hope to achieve a "mildly" inegalitarian distribution in which the poorest half of society would own a significant share (say, one-fifth to one-quarter) of total wealth.

Acknowledgment by David LEE Kuo Chuen

This two-volume Handbook is a project of more than a year dating back to 2015 and two conferences with Stanford University as the beginning and the link. This work would not have been possible if not for the support of the US Treasury for the 2015 Fulbright Visiting Fellowship at Shorenstein Asia–Pacific Research Center at Stanford University. Much of the initial research and understanding of FinTech and inclusion started when the first editor David LEE Kuo Chuen was in Palo Alto researching the Silicon Valley eco system. The mission of the fellowship was to harness Silicon Valley technology to serve the underserved in Asean to be mentored by the late Harry Rowen.

The "SKBI-BFI Smart Nation, Silicon Valley Technology and Connectivity Inclusion Conference" was held on 17th November 2015 at the Bechtel Conference Center, Stanford, California, United States (https://skbi.smu.edu.sg/conference/131141?itemid=611). The late Professor Harry Rowen, who served four US Presidents, was the mentor for the Fulbright Fellowship and scheduled as the first speaker for the conference. Unfortunately, he passed away a few days before the conference. These two volumes are published in memory of both the late Sim Kee Boon and the late Professor Harry Rowen without whom this project would not have started.

> *The late Sim Kee Boon was one of Singapore's pioneer civil servants – men who worked closely with the Old Guard political leaders and played a key role in the success of Changi Airport and turned the fortunes of Keppel Shipyard around. He is among the most versatile of Singapore public servants. He spent all his working life making invaluable contributions in his various roles in Government, particularly in the areas of economic development, trade and investment matters. Mr. Sim dedicated himself fully to serving the country.*

> *The late Henry Rowen was a professor emeritus of Stanford University affiliated with the Graduate School of Business, the Hoover Institution and the Asia/Pacific Research Center of the Freeman–Spogli Institute for International Studies. His non-academic jobs included heading a major non-profit research company (the RAND Corporation) and serving in several Washington agencies under four presidents (two Democratic and two Republican). They have been Assistant Director of the Bureau of the Budget, Chairman of the National Intelligence Council and Assistant Secretary of Defense for International Security Affairs. He published "The Silicon Valley Edge: A Habitat for Innovation and Entrepreneurship" and "Making IT: The Rise of Asia in High Tech" with several other authors, way before the interest in FinTech.*

Special appreciation goes to Prof Tan Chin Tiong and Prof David Montgomery for connection to Stanford as well as the guidance of Acting Director of APARC Prof Takeo Hoshi and Director Professor Gi Wook Shin. Associate Director Huma Shaikh, Center Event Coordinator Debbie Warren, and Executive Assistant Kristen Lee and others at Stanford were most helpful during the initial period of research and the first conference.

I would like to thank Noreen and Herman Harrow for allowing me to stay with them to write some of the chapters while in Monterey; Erika Enos for introducing me to various start-ups and design studios; David Schwartz for going out of his way to assist me in organizing the Smart Nation Conference at Stanford; Ron and Pat Miller, and Barbara Gross for their company and allowing us to play with their dogs.

The following up conference entitled "FinTech and Financial Inclusion: Nascent financial technologies for enhancing access to finance" (https://skbi.smu.edu.sg/conference/142741) was jointly organized with SKBI, IMF, Stanford University, India School of Business, Singapore University of Social Sciences (Formerly UniSIM), Humboldt – Universität zu Berlin, and supported by the Monetary Authority of Singapore and UOB. Other supporting organizations were ChainB.com and Idea Ink, Association of Cryptocurrency Enterprises and Start-ups (ACCESS), Chartered Alternative Investment Analyst Association (both the San Francisco and Singapore Chapters), Economic Society of Singapore, Financial Planning Association of Singapore, iGlobe Partners, Internal Consulting Group, Plug and Play and Singapore Accountancy Commission. Many papers are drawn from this conference.

The Board of Advisors and staff at Sim Kee Boon Institute for Financial Economics (SKBI) are most helpful and the editors are heavily indebted to them. Without the then Provost Rajendra Srivastava and Dean Howard Thomas for "twisting" David Lee's arm to become both the Academic and Executive Director for the Institute, the research would not have taken shape for the two volumes.

Stephen Riady, Chairman of OUE and Lim Chee Oon, ex-Chairman of SKBI, are always great mentors. Special appreciation goes to Jacqueline Loh, Leong Sing Chiong, Mohanty Sopnendu, Roy Teo, Bernard Wee, Stanley Yong and Tan Yeow Seng from the MAS; Auback Kam, Tan Kok Yam, Lee Chor Pharn, Derrick Cham and Jacqueline Poh from the Civil Service, Philip Foo, Priscilla Cheng, and Elaine Goh from SKBI. My special thanks to President Arnoud De Meyer, Provost Lily Kong, Dean Gerry George, Annie Koh, Steve Wyatt, Phil Zerrillo, Christopher Dula, Ernie Teo, Wan Zhi Guo, Yan Li, Pei Sai Fan, Lim Kian Guan, Fock Siew Tong, Francis Koh, Benedict Koh Seng Kee, Chan Soon Huat and others that have helped in many ways. Thanks to those colleagues at Singapore University of Social Sciences, especially Provost Tsui Kai Chong, President Cheong Hee Kiat, Chancellor Aline Wong, Dean Lee Pui Mun, Phoon Kok Fai, Joseph Lim, Linda Low, Ding Ding, Yu Yin Hui, Calvin Chan, Guan Chong, Jason Chiam, and Rubini Nyana. Appreciation also to the support of CAIA, especially William Kelly, Peter Douglas, Joanne Murphy, Scott Nance, Hossein Kazemi, Nelson Lacey, and Wendy Leung. The President of CFA Paul Smith is generous to comment on these two volumes. Without the hard work of Susan Ikeda, Susan Li and the encouragement of Scott Bentley, this project would have been impossible.

My research assistants have been most helpful in collating and preparing the tables and figures, especially Zoey Phee, Yu Xiaoyi, and Dian Fu Research Team consisting of Zhang Han, Chang Su, Chi Ying, and Lin JingXian; the Blockchain Research Team consisting of Wu Yuting, Zhang Mengyu, Sun Ming, Chen Wanfeng, Huang Yiya, Lee Yinhao; the FinTech Research Team consisting of Ng Jing Ying, Kelvin Lim Jia Hui, Abraham Albert Putihrai and Ian Chong Wei Ming; and the Silicon Valley Research Team consisting of Natasha Singhal and Guo Zongren. Many more from my MAF, MWM and GMF classes have helped and I apologize for omitting anyone and not explicitly thanking them.

My family, who always bear with me for spending many nights away in my study room finishing the work, are a force behind these two volumes. Much of the inspiration of this work came from Evangelii Gaudium by Pope Francis and the work of Thomas Piketti. I thank God for guiding me towards a direction of research to serve the entire pyramid that I continue to enjoy. May this book be used in a way to benefit the needy, the excluded and the neglected of this world!

Acknowledgment by Robert Deng

I am very grateful to David LEE Kuo Chuen for initiating this project and for having me as his co-editor. I would like to thank all the authors and everyone else who have contributed to this Handbook and made it possible. My utmost gratitude goes to my family for their unconditional love and support.

17 March 2017

David LEE Kuo Chuen

Robert Deng ed.

CHAPTER 1

Reshaping the Financial Order

Christopher Dula, David LEE Kuo Chuen

Contents

The financial system, which governs and manages the practice of deposits, lending and payments, is in the throes of disruption following the shortcomings of the current regime. Despite US$11 trillion in quantitative easing since 2007, economic growth has been persistently sluggish. The money isn't going where it should be. In 2015, McKinsey reported that global debt had grown by US$57 trillion since 2007. The debt is becoming unsustainable, yet the global debt-to-income ratio continues to rise disproportionally to any deleveraging. The Fed's meandering signaling to nudge up interest rates beyond the near zero range raises concerns that private and even public debt could become unserviceable, reeling the economy back into a serious recession.

Low-interest rates and lack luster growth are likely to persist into the longer term. For example, technological advancements, particularly in computerization, communication and automation, will increasingly displace jobs faster than labor markets can adapt. The result is persistent long-term unemployment. And given the inverse relationship between unemployment and inflation, there will be little rationale for policymakers to raise interest rates. In a low interest rate environment, fractional reserve banking loses its profitability.

At the same time, growing compliance costs and shrinking margins are pushing banks towards greater consolidation. Once Basel III goes into effect in 2018, a percentage of banks' equity must be held in risk-weighted assets, undergoing periodic stress tests. Although this increases solvency, it's also expensive, and may incentivize riskier off-balance sheet activity.

This is bad for economic growth. Consolidation means less competition and a concentration of financial power. The resulting combination of greater rent-seeking behavior and economic fragility puts pressure on governments to underwrite banks' lending practices – which further distorts the financial system. This is all made worse by widespread uncertainty, which favors hedging activity versus real investment. All of this perpetuates income inequality and begs the question, *to whom does the Global Financial Industry serve?*

1.1 Megatrends and New Alternatives

How technology has shifted consumer preferences and opened new doors for greater competition.

The current financial regime is experiencing death by a thousand cuts. New, nimbler competitors are chipping away at the financial industries' bread and butter by offering alternative services better suited for various customer segments. Beginning with payments, these services are expanding more and more into banking's more traditional domains.

Information technology and mobile connectivity have changed everything. The world is merely at the cusp of profound changes wrought by such future shock. These changes will only accelerate as the boundaries between the virtual and physical worlds continue to blur. The commercial implications to this are staggering, and opportunities abound for those who are ready. At the locus of this wavefront is the payments industry, where incumbents and start-ups vie for the fate of money.

The pervasiveness of smartphone technology has fundamentally changed consumer behavior. Amongst myriad other capabilities, these mobiles can be used to advice, influence and consult consumers on purchasing decisions anywhere, at any time. E-commerce – now largely driven by mobile platforms – is rapidly eclipsing face-to-face transactions, growing three times faster than traditional commercial activities.

More than that, most smartphones are now equipped with contactless payment technologies that enable them to be used in the same way as a contactless card, like Visa payWave or MasterCard PayPass, at the point of sale. Smartphones are already absorbing the wallet in the same way they have replaced your music player, camera, GPS device or anything else that can be miniaturized or remotely accessed and operated through a touch-screen.

And cash, the last bastion for anonymous peer-to-peer (P2P) transactions, and the digital payment industry's biggest competitor, is perhaps the next medium to be disrupted. After all, smartphones already contain the means to make such mobile P2P transactions possible.

But it's not just smartphones. There are 10 billion connected devices today, and this number is expected to increase to 50 billion by 2020. Refrigerators, light bulbs, industrial control systems, and clothing – just about any consumer or business product can be equipped with sensors and wireless connectivity features. This means almost anything can be made to communicate and interface with anyone or anything else through, what is called, the Internet of Things.

Digital payments need to be seamlessly and securely integrated into these networks in order for it all to be commercially viable. In that respect, any business model built around managing a network through technology for new entrants and established players – both big and small – is ripe to shake up the status quo. For companies to survive and thrive in this new world, they will need to develop creative solutions and partnerships that leverage the scale and reliability of digital payments to deliver safe, convenient and intuitive experiences to their customers (Lee, 2015a).

1.2 Digital Implications

Considerations to surviving disruption. Managing the network in a hyper-connected world.

Empowered by technology, consumers demand ever-higher levels of responsiveness, immediacy, convenience and customization. They expect instantaneous access to information, entertainment and services. And as a result, market segments are becoming increasingly fractured and finicky. This is happening at all levels of consumer affluence.

There is significant disruption across industries. Most recently, technological convergence has had the most ardent effects on the telecommunications, information technology, consumer electronics and entertainment sectors – which have essentially blended into one and the same. Such convergence has already poured over into banking and finance, and is now beginning to influence fast moving consumer goods and healthcare, amongst other industries. In this environment, interacting and engaging with customers requires a much more integrated and digital approach.

The payment card industry, which stores, processes and transmits cardholder data to facilitate transactions, is essentially an information-communications provider. Decades earlier it was a main disruptor, but now finds itself on the receiving end. It must either innovate or be supplanted by any other more competent network companies. The survival of incumbent firms depends on three essential factors, which must be identified and acted upon.

The first is to clearly define one's core assets; assets that are vital to ensuring scale and relevance as an organization steps into the digital domain. Network effects and trust are key. The second is to identify critical capabilities that enhance and augment these core assets. For example, security functionality and reliability. The third is collaboration and securing where one operates in an ecosystem. Partnerships are vital for establishing network dominance. Ease of integration and having a large degree of openness are important.

Interestingly, there are many similarities with past technological disruption as with today. The idea is to stay abreast of trends by driving disruption as opposed to reacting to it. But most of all, instilling customer stickiness.

1.3 Historical Context

The evolution of finance has followed a clear progression: firms first deploy technological advancement, such as credit and payments, to improve customer stickiness and satisfaction. Once network effects take hold, companies consolidate and become more monopolistic while simultaneously being reined in by regulation.

1950s and 60s

The United States experienced a marked increase in consumerism following World War II. This was facilitated by economic expansion and the increased availability of credit. Credit based payments were nothing new. Retailers like department stores, gas stations and hotels had been offering payment through installment plans on merchant specific credit cards since the early 20th century.[1] A credit manager at Sears Roebuck once said, "A credit customer is yours – a cash customer is anybody's."[2]

In the 1950s, commercial banks significantly expanded credit payments by offering their own credit cards that could be used at a variety of participating retailers.[3] There were several benefits to this.

For instance, credit cards satisfied a consumer's sense of immediacy by realizing purchasing power beyond their cash on-hand. This generated increased turnover for retailers. Moreover, credit transactions for retailers became more secure because banks took on the risk of default. This arrangement was particularly lucrative for banks.

Banks innovated on credit cards through the use of revolving credit, which did not have a structured repayment schedule like the installment plans used by retailers. Instead, banks charged interest on unpaid debt after a period of time and a service fee of 1% to 8% per transaction to retailers.[4] Between 1956 and 1967 personal disposable income increased by 86% and consumer debt by 133% in the US.[5] Banks had seized a "new base of customers who would be bound by debt."[6]

The number of credit card plans flourished in variety and innovation; the personal credit business was booming. Phrases like, *credit card fever*, *credit card nation* and *plastic jungle* entered into the mainstream lexicon.[7] During this period the credit card system was extremely fragmented and local, with little regulation governing credit card lending practices.[8] Rising consumer debt and bank profits soon led to popular concern. In 1968 the Truth in Lending Act put in place standardization and disclosure laws to better protect consumers from dangerous lending practices.

1970s

Consumer protection continued to be a concern. The Fair Credit Reporting Act of 1970 established regulations that demanded greater care in issuing credit cards, limited the liabilities of cardholders and protected the credit information of the consumer.

A nationwide credit system became possible through advances in information and communication technologies (ICT).[9] This enabled large-scale computer networks, which quickly expanded internationally. These networks were expensive and financial institutions had to cooperate in the design and operation of the system.[10] Visa and MasterCard emerged as the dominant payment technology companies that facilitated the use of payment card transactions.[11] By 2005, these two companies accounted for 72% of such transactions worldwide.[12] And today, Visa and MasterCard were accepted by 96% of merchants in the US.[13] Visa alone is accepted in over 150 countries using a hundred different currencies.

Accelerating change

In the 1980s technological advancement in ICT continued to grow exponentially, spurring innovation in financial services. Electronic funds transfers (EFT) became mainstream as more and more people requested their paychecks to be electronically deposited. ATM machines and debit cards made their debut in the mid-1980s. The convenience of debit cards soon began to usurp the role of cash and checks. In 1998 the popularity of debit cards reached a tipping point in which they were used considerably more often than checks.[14]

Non-bank innovation in payments also played a role in the 1980s with the introduction of prepaid phone cards. Closed system, merchant specific, prepaid gift cards entered use in the mid-90s.[15] Shortly thereafter open system prepaid cards appeared. These cards could be more easily topped-up and be used on electronic payments networks, such as those operated by Visa or MasterCard.

Such open system prepaid cards also allowed for anonymity on a payments network and certain types could be topped up with additional funds. Topping up could take place in a number of ways: through an ATM, online, or at a point-of-sale (POS). The unbanked and under-banked were typical users of these cards.[16] However, these cards were also used as gift cards, employee incentives and payroll cards in place of checks and electronic deposits.[17]

1.4 E-commerce and P2P

New entrants from outside the traditional banking and payments space respond to the emergence of Internet-based commerce demands for new methods of payments.

The Internet and the ascent of e-commerce in the late 1990s corresponded with significant growth in non-traditional non-bank P2P payment methods.[18] P2P payment methods traditionally relied on cash or wire-transfers through companies like Western Union. However, these methods were inconvenient for e-commerce activities, like participating in eBay's online auction house. A seamless online intermediary was needed to facilitate P2P payments. PayPal answered this demand by easing the risks and costs of online transactions between buyers and sellers by acting as a middleman for a nominal fee while protecting against fraud through security tokens. In this way a buyer purchased an item using a debit or credit card through PayPal, and PayPal would deposit the payment in either a bank or PayPal account.[19] Customers also had the option to deposit money into their own PayPal account for use as payments in future.

Non-bank intermediaries were similar to banks and were subject to regulation concerning electronic funds transfers. However, non-bank intermediaries did not engage in fractional reserve banking and were therefore not subject to the same stringent financial regulation as banks.[20]

Payment card companies also entered into the e-commerce game in the late 90s to facilitate online merchant transactions.

Online banking had existed in a limited form since the mid-1990s but with extremely modest capabilities. By 2003, however, 53% of commercial banks had online banking websites. By 2011, adoption had reached 90% with much more comprehensive services.

The banks, in partnership with the digital payments industry, entered into the P2P payments market in the late 2000s by creating multibank networks that enabled payments between customers that used different banks. In the mid-2000s commercial banks and non-bank intermediaries expanded their payments capabilities by developing applications for customers to manage accounts and make transactions on mobile devices.

1.5 The Rise of M-commerce

Tech companies and traditional payments companies begin to partner.

In the early 2010s telecom companies all over the world began signing agreements to facilitate payments made on mobile devices that used the Visa, MasterCard, Discover and American Express networks.[21] And major smartphone manufactures, most of which run on Google's Android OS or Apple's iOS, began installing network approved near field communication (NFC) chips for contactless payments onto all of their phones.[22]

Digital payment networks were also partnering and investing in other potentially disruptive payment methods like digital wallets. Digital wallets were mobile device applications that make use of NFC or other communication technology to make wireless transactions. These transactions could potentially be used for e-commerce, P2P, ATM, EFT and POS activities. The extent of these activities was limited to which payment networks could be accessed, including how these networks could be accessed, and the capabilities of those networks.

Google announced *Google Wallet* in 2011, an NFC enabled application that allows customers to pay through MasterCard and Visa wireless POS terminals.[23] It basically transformed a phone into an open loop prepaid card. Google Wallet also involves a partnership between MasterCard, Visa, American Express, Citibank and Sprint.[24] However, this is just one example.

Visa has agreements with Apple's own digital wallet, Apple Pay – launched in late 2014 – which can leverage a customer base comprising 800 million iTunes accounts. There are also 900 app-based start-ups operating in different niches of the mobile payments space. These apps range from customizable money management and mobile banking platforms to e-commerce store fronts and loyalty rewards programs – or just about anything else conceivable.

However, conservative estimates suggest that as eight out of ten of these start-ups will fail. But they bring to the table a cornucopia of new ideas and innovations. In many ways, this current phase is reminiscent of earlier, yet less-wild days of the card payments industry. New frontiers are just now opening up.

1.6 Weapons of Mass Consumption

New means of payments are leading to innovative new business models, most notably in the sharing economy – where network intermediaries peddle in 'trust', 'reliability' and 'convenience'.

Cash is expensive to manage and access to a digital payments network unlocks new markets and increases the velocity of money, all of which are critical to economic expansion. This is why emerging market countries often consider digital payment networks as co-infrastructure in their development strategies.

Consider Alibaba in China: it has empowered millions of SMEs to act globally by linking buyers and sellers from all over the world. Facilitating all these transactions is a digital payments network. Such access simplifies accounting procedures, lowers banking costs and reduces the risks associated with handling cash. It also enables electronic money transfers – remittances – which is the single largest FDI flow for some countries. But these networks directly accelerate local economic activity as well, especially in retail.

Plastic cards create a frictionless payment experience that is fast and convenient. It helps merchants to minimize queues; speeds up cashier efficiency and makes them less prone to error. This improves the shopping experience of customers, and that drives loyalty. Contactless cards take this experience even further.

However, credit card penetration is a lot lower in emerging markets versus their more developed counterparts, but in almost every market, rich or poor, smartphone penetration is nearly complete. It's not a privilege for the affluent anymore. So, while Visa may have around two billion cards in circulation, there are some 7–8 billion smartphones actively being used. What we are witnessing is a democratization of access.

Consumers that were previously unbanked can now receive banking services through their smartphones via mobile communications networks. And with NFC technology, these mobile devices can be used as a contactless card, an e-commerce platform, or a location-based payments service, à la Uber, which uses a combination of mobile broadband and GPS to facilitate digital payments transaction in ride-sharing – a business model that is disrupting traditional taxi services in irreversible ways.

There is an active drive to create an effortless consumer experience that is indistinguishable to face-to-face and remote commerce. And it is the role of players in the digital payments industry to create an ecosystem that connects banks, merchants and consumers through a real-time and secure global network that makes all this possible.

Merchants and consumers that rely only on cash are penalized to just one, single limited form of payment. However, cash *does* have certain advantages. It is universally accepted (practically), anonymous and versatile. And for companies like Visa, MasterCard and American Express – a viable cash replacement continues to be their greatest market opportunity in the small transactions and P2P payments space, which is growing in-step with the rapid growth of the peer-to-peer sharing economy.

Moreover, the peer-to-peer sharing economy is quickly making traditional corporate models obsolete. Crowdfunding (Kickstarter), ridesharing (Uber), apartment/house sharing (Airbnb), co-working (The Coop), reselling and trading (Craigslist), knowledge and talent sharing (TaskRabbit) are just a handful of companies doing revolutionary work that is driving change across the spectrum. These companies are transcending national boundaries and innovating faster than regulation can contain them.

In the new economy trust is the currency that matters more than ever.

1.7 Banking 2.0

Inclusive business models are the new frontier in banking – but traditional banks may struggle to compete against new entrants.

Acquiring customers is key to growing new business for banks, which further stimulates the global economy. More than two billion people in the world remain unbanked or under-banked. Traditional banks, however, have been reluctant to cater to this segment given the unknown risk profile, low income, limited wealth and geographic dispersion of their potential customers. They are simply too expensive to service, the returns too low for them to bother. Financial technology, or FinTech, is disrupting the established regime.

The reach and scalability necessary to service those at the bottom of the pyramid is not only economically possible, but profitable. The market potential is huge, and it's not limited to emerging markets. There is significant latent demand in the advanced economies as well. According to the FDIC, around 20 percent of US households are under-banked as of 2016. Without access to banking and financial services, these people are hard pressed to build equity and engage in entrepreneurship.

Inclusivity is the next growth frontier in banking and finance. Indeed, such inclusivity is already part of a wider economic trend, such as frugal innovation, which aims to serve previously neglected consumer segments. By ignoring those neglected by the financial system, banks have made room for tech companies and their ilk to make financial inclusion a viable business model. It is thus the Internet companies, telecoms and start-ups (not banks) that were among the first to seize the opportunity and develop alternative, more efficient systems, to provide banking and financial services at scale to the un-banked. Starting with payments, they have moved into other financial services like savings, loans and investments – slowly chipping away the bread and butter of traditional banking. Transferwise, Ant Financial, Lending Club and M-Pesa are just a few notable companies in this space.

According to Accenture, global investment in FinTech has tripled within a year to US$12.2 billion in 2014 from US$4.05 billion in 2013. Banks have since taken notice, and are now vigorously acquiring FinTech start-ups to get in on the action. But this approach may not work for banks in the same way it has worked for telecoms and Internet companies. There are obvious reasons for this.

1.8 Understanding the Model

In FinTech, disruptors exhibit five common traits defined by the LASIC model: Low margin, Asset light, Scalable, Innovative and Compliance easy (Lee and Teo, 2015).

Alternative banking and financial services have far fewer compliance obligations and lower operational costs because they do not engage in fractional reserve banking, and can conduct cross-border transfers without relying on inter-bank clearing. In addition, the capital requirements imposed by Basel III does not apply to them. And the revenue stream for FinTech alternatives has thus far been based on small facilitation fees, which does not make economic sense for banks, given their higher operating costs.

Another reason that banks may struggle in the FinTech space is that they suffer from massive legacy systems that make it difficult to incorporate new technology into their infrastructure. Even if a bank acquires a FinTech company for its technology, it may lack the tools to integrate that technology into its system – or at least not quickly enough to matter. The necessary digital overhaul and talent would be hugely expensive. Besides, the culture within banks and other financial service companies may lack the speed and scalability, which have made tech companies so successful in this space.

Internet companies – particularly in the social media, e-commerce and logistics space – are much better positioned to incorporate FinTech into their digital infrastructure. What's more, these companies already have millions of active users and are at an advantage in terms of how they interact and engage with them. Many Internet companies are completely immersed in consumer lifestyles – where they generate enormous amounts of data that can be analyzed to better understand customer context.

This helps these companies paint a more accurate picture of a customer's potential financial risk versus what their more traditional peers can perceive. Because of this, these companies can disrupt the financial sector by lending and insuring at a lower cost. And given their inherent scalability with no need for brick and mortar branches, these reduced costs can be multiplied and passed on to millions of previously untapped consumers on a low margin fast-moving model.

Profit, as Amazon has demonstrated, is becoming secondary. FinTech companies grow by reaching out to the masses, diversifying service offerings and disrupting further up the value-chain. Thus, they attract more capital.

Alibaba has been offering low-cost loans to merchants for years. They have since branched out into micro-loans for consumers. Because transactions between buyers and sellers take place through an e-wallet like Alipay, Alibaba is able to quickly assess a company or individual's cash cow in real time. Low-interest rate loans of 30 days to a year are approved within 24-hours. A traditional bank would struggle to do that.

Consumer credibility can be analyzed in fine detail. Loan approvals can look through historical data where years of spending patterns can be observed. Not only that, but social networks in collaboration with FinTech companies can even evaluate the creditworthiness of applicants based on whom they associate with – and maybe, even what kind of content they search for and consume. This has mostly been used for small, short-term low-rate loans – but so far, default rates have been very low.

When services run on servers and software, they can be quickly scaled. When an app's functionality is dependent upon users being part of a group or community, where access to content requires user commitment, the switching cost for consumers becomes very high. The 'stickier' the app, the richer the data it collects. Digital services like iTunes, Skype and WhatsApp can create huge, captive user bases that generate enormous amounts of data. There is extraordinary value in this. In 2013, Facebook bought the start-up messaging service WhatsApp, with its 400 million active users, for US$22 billion, despite the acquired company earning a net loss of US$138.1 million that same year. However, this also represents 400 million users that could potentially be integrated into a FinTech platform. Logistics companies, which facilitate commerce and manage large swathes of valuable data, are being acquired for huge sums as well. In the new economy, data is money.

Any such digital service has the capacity to offer payments, peer-to-peer lending, and integrate into new media and the sharing economy. There are thus hitherto unknown business models that could usurp traditional banking and finance in ways not yet imagined. What is happening now is merely the beginning.

Since 2012, the growth in mobile transactions has been impressive. Some e-commerce companies are moving beyond simple payment, delivery and settlement services. They are partnering with social media companies to provide lending, microcredit, investment products and more – they are even getting into insurance.

Alipay – originally a payment platform in China's Alibaba Group and the largest e-commerce company in the world – has over 450 million mobile users; just under half of the total Chinese online payments market. The Tencent Group, owner of TenPay, another large competitor in the Chinese payments space, has subsidiaries in social media, digital entertainment, and mobile services. In February 2013, China's insurance regulator approved a joint venture between Alibaba and Tencent in a partnership with the country's top insurer, PingAn, to launch an online-only insurance company, ZhongAn. Less than two years later, on November 11, 2014, these giants would set an unprecedented record.

That record was set on China's biggest retail shopping day of the year, Singles Day. In that one day, Alibaba recorded sales of more than US$9 billion, over half of which was facilitated by Alipay. Bolstering these numbers were a total of RMB100 million (US$16 million) in online insurance premiums, from companies like ZhongAn, which sold 50-cent insurance policies covering package delivery. At such large scales, even the smallest margins become lucrative.

Overall, what has happened is that profit margins are so low that potential competitors find no incentives to go after new entrants. With negligible margin cost, these disruptors grow the business exponentially with a very light balance sheet of liabilities and assets i.e. the have very low overhead and are highly automated. They scale to achieve economies of scale with few resource via the Internet and mobile technology, which enables them to reach out to a large number of unbanked and underserved in emerging markets. The needs of these newly acquired customers are varied making it easy to introduce a wider scope of innovative services. At the moment, it remains to be seen how or if these services can be regulated – until such regulations do arise – compliance costs are low.

1.9 The Democratization of Banking and Finance

Technology is making centralized organizations obsolete. This has the potential to erode entrenched financial powers and better distribute both risk and reward.

Lending Club, an online peer-to-peer (P2P) lending service based in San Francisco, facilitates unsecured personal loans of up to US$35,000. Initially launched on Facebook as a social networking service, the company developed an algorithm to match potential lenders and borrowers based on social affinity factors like education, geography, professional background and social media connectedness. It has since incorporated more conventional risk assessment metrics such as credit history and debt-to-income ratios, and today has a default rate of 3.39%. The U.S. Federal Reserve reports an average consumer loan default rate of around two percent. Despite a slightly higher risk of default in P2P lending, Lending Club reports solid returns to lenders. Borrowers make monthly principal and interest payments for short-term loans, while investors have risk spread across multiple borrowers by lending in small US$25 tranches. The average net-annual returns to lenders yield six percent for 36-month B-grade notes.

Once again, compliance costs are low because Lending Club is not engaged in fractional reserve banking. Instead the lending process has been democratized. Borrowers get access to credit within hours and lenders earn returns in excess of most coupon rates. Lending Club profits through small origination fees of half a percent to one percent of the loan amount. As of 2015, it had issued 880,000 loans amounting to US$11 billion.

This has proved to be an attractive model for capital investment. In December 2014, Lending Club raised US$900 million in the largest tech IPO of 2014. In 2015 the company signed a partnership agreement with Google to expand lending services to small companies using Google's business services. It is also entering into partnerships with other companies to further expand into services such as car loans and mortgages.

A similar service, Capital Match, exists in Singapore and matches individual lenders to small and medium-sized enterprises. And companies like Estonian-developed, U.K.-based Transferwise are facilitating cross-border remittances for fees as low as half a percent whereas typical money transfer services charge fees of around five percent.

Transferwise can achieve much lower rates by crowdsourcing the funds flow, and in the process it bypasses traditional banking and payment networks. Instead of facilitating a direct transfer from a sender to a recipient, which involves a currency conversion, Transferwise reroutes payments from a sender to a recipient of another transfer, which is simultaneously taking place but going in the opposite direction. The disruption is happening from the bottom up (Lee and Dula, 2016).

1.10 The Incumbents

Even amongst incumbents, there is a shift in thinking towards transforming their legacy networks and partnerships into more open and inclusive systems. However, this must not degrade security and reliability.

In 2013 Visa, MasterCard and American Express began co-developing a new technology to supplement digital payments security. 'Tokenization' as it is called replaces a payment cards 16-digit number with an encrypted digital proxy, or token, that adds an additional layer of security that shields the personal account number – keeping the account itself pristine in the event of fraud.

It allows payment issuers to directly send account credential (tokens) in real time to customers through any device or application through any means of connection to make payment.

This technology enables partners and clients to secure payment authorization over the cloud through the device. Where payment can also be guaranteed upon delivery and perhaps satisfaction of the service, depending.

This additional layer of security works on top of biometric verification built into the device (a common feature on current generation smartphones) along with conventional network security. It also has the possibility of anonymity options between buyer and seller since the transaction takes place through encrypted tokens via the cloud.

The fact of the matter is that the way in which payment networks are currently accessed has not changed much in fifty years. Paying with smartphones using debit or credits cards loaded on them is not much different from using a plastic card – more convenient, yes, but not particularly groundbreaking.

What is different about tokenization is that digital payments companies are opening up their networks to app developers. In the past, these networks have been closed. This means that people around the world can develop applications and services with tailor-made payment experiences that utilize an established global payments network. This is a clear signal that the traditional network payment companies are preparing for the total pervasiveness of the Internet.

This pervasiveness is driving technological convergence and is causing ever-increasing levels of integration between industries, and online/off-line experiences are coalescing. FinTech will play a fundamental role in enabling 'global interoperability and reliability'. It is opening the network to new partners and enabling them to design new, unique customer experiences while ensuring safe and secure payment. This has the potential to transform commerce in truly unforeseen ways.

The most successful players will be the ones that dream big and create new solutions that impact the lives of billions of consumers and merchants around the world that leverage the scale, reliability and network security.

1.11 Cryptocurrencies and Blockchain

What does the future hold? Perhaps a wholesale transition to secure distributed and automated systems built around cryptocurrencies and Blockchain. This would entirely circumvent legacy networks and remove the need for any centralized ownership of any network, and creates mechanisms to conduct 'asset sharing'.

The most exciting applications are found in FinTech platforms built on cryptocurrencies like bitcoin and other Blockchain technologies, which are typically open access and have extraordinary potential to automate banking services while improving security and transparency. For example, in a Blockchain, a transaction is transparently recorded simultaneously across an automated peer-to-peer computer network. Transactions take place across numbered accounts, which are public. Every transaction is verified through a distributed process that records the date, time, account number and amount for the transaction, where each network node (and there are thousands), contains a full copy of the ledger (Lee, 2015b).

A transaction is only approved once the nodes reach a consensus on the state of the ledger. This keeps the system synchronized, and – in all practical terms – it is almost impossible to defraud. A Blockchain based cryptocurrency can also be programmed to represent anything of value: a company share, tax or environmental credits, vouchers, cash, votes... whatever. Embedded instructions can be programmed to perform any transaction determining how, when and where a transaction can take place. This has critical importance in building the necessary infrastructure to support the Internet of Things. It also has extraordinary implications for banking systems, including the potential to better automate processes and thereby reduce operational and compliance costs.

Banks, however, have been reluctant to adopt technologies like Bitcoin, given its nefarious press and association with illicit money transfers. This is changing. USAA, an influential American financial services and insurance company, has openly embraced Bitcoin for its members and is looking into Blockchain technologies to improve operations. Still, distributed ledger technologies and peer-to-peer lending is alien to the banks' middleman business practices and highly centralized nature. The better gambit is with the telcos, Internet and tech firms.

There are attempts by banks using blockchain or decentralized ledger technology to serve only the existing clients in order to strengthen their oligopoly or monopolist position. The attempt by Wall Street, to engage banks with a 'permissioned Blockchain' technology – meaning it seeks to establish a closed private network of distributed ledgers amongst banks – is interesting, but misses the point in that it lacks inclusivity. Such a collaborative consortium would likely result in non-competitive behavior, leading to even greater market concentration and centralization. As a non-permissioned and open distributed ledger, bitcoin's Blockchain technology better reflects the philosophic roots of the Internet.

Contrary to some interpretations, Blockchain adoption is more likely to originate in a decentralized trustless environment through the sharing of initially low value assets before scaling exponentially – not through a centralized financial market that transacts in high-value smart contracts, such as those from the derivative market.

The *openness* of bitcoin is its most powerful feature; a distinction overlooked by many in the business of distributed networks. For example, the greater vastness of a non-permissioned Blockchain serves as a deterrent to hackers because the cost of obtaining private keys increases with the number of nodes in a distributed network.

Moreover, a non-permissioned Blockchain like Bitcoin is designed to enable asset sharing. This is a key point. As the sharing economy expands, companies like Uber and Airbnb will accumulate greater influence and wealth. It is not the sharing of services, but the sharing of assets that matters. A sharing economy without asset ownership sharing is serfdom. If data is an asset, why should Mark Zuckerberg profit disproportionately off the data one sows?

Gems, for instance, is a social networking and messaging app that rewards users with cryptocurrency based on their relative contribution to the network. Contribution is measured in terms of the number of active daily users that a user introduces to their network. Each user has a unique e-wallet from which currency can be freely transferred exchanged. While sharing user-generated content between friends in a network is free, advertisers must either buy or trade the Gems currency and pay that currency to individuals in order to advertise to them. Users thus take ownership and partake in the gains of the network in accordance with their own contribution.

Perhaps one day the global financial system could become indistinguishable from the Internet itself: an open access distributed network of computer systems built on communication protocols with no centralized ownership or governance. Nonetheless, there is still a long way to go before arriving at such utopian visions.

1.12 The FinTech Promise

Considerations for reshaping the Global Financial System.

Harnessing technology to provide financial and basic services to the masses is a key step towards reducing inequality and economic growth. But beyond sharing services, asset sharing services are even more inclusive. What is needed is the widespread adoption of Blockchain technology to enable collaboration that supports a register for asset sharing at low cost (Lee, 2016).

For this to occur, investments must be made into soft and hard infrastructure in connectivity, for all people and enterprises to compete, collaborate, scale and grow in. An open platform with open API and open data remains the key to a successful collaborative, innovative sustainable financial system. Governments take note; these developments should not be hindered and instead supported by experimental initiatives like sandbox regulations.

The major fault of the current financial system is overinvestment into the overserved segment resulting in rent seeking in a monopolistic environment protected by regulation. But financial inclusion itself does not automatically attract non-rent seeking participants. Those that eventually go out of the box must be those that seek to serve the unserved and underserved rather than those that seek to rule within partitioned portions of the Internet. That should form the underlying principle of regulation: *a system that serves rather than rules.*

References

Lee, David Kuo Chuen, 2015a. On the edge of disruption. Asia Management Insights 2 (2), 78. http://ink.library.smu.edu.sg/lkcsb_research/4870/.

Lee, David Kuo Chuen, 2015b. Handbook of Digital Currency: Bitcoin, Innovation, Financial Instruments, and Big Data. Elsevier, Academic Press. https://www.elsevier.com/books/handbook-of-digital-currency/lee-kuo-chuen/978-0-12-802117-0.

Lee, David Kuo Chuen, 2016. The fintech promise. The European Financial Review. http://www.europeanfinancialreview.com/?p=6093.

Lee, David Kuo Chuen, Teo, Ernie, 2015. Emergence of fintech and the LASIC principles. Journal of Financial Perspective 3 (3). https://fsinsights.ey.com/thejournal.

Lee, David Kuo Chuen, Dula, Christopher, 2016. How the internet is democratizing global finance. The Straits Times. 23 Feb. http://www.straitstimes.com/opinion/how-the-internet-is-democratising-global-finance.

Notes

1. Zumello, Christine. *The "Everything Card" and Consumer Credit in the United States in the 1960s*. Business History Review. 85. Autumn 2011. The President and Fellows of Harvard College. p. 552.

2. Ibid. p. 554.

3. Zumello, Christine. *The "Everything Card" and Consumer Credit in the United States in the 1960s*. Business History Review. 85. Autumn 2011. The President and Fellows of Harvard College. p. 552.

4. Ibid. p. 558.

5. Ibid. p. 555.

6. Ibid. p. 554.

7. Ibid. p. 574.

8. Ibid. p. 571, 572 & 574.

9. Ibid. p. 574.

10. Ibid. p. 574.

11. The Federal Reserve Bank of St. Louis. *Cards, Cards and More Cards: The Evolution of Prepaid Cards*. Inside the Vault. An Economic Education Newsletter from the Federal Reserve Bank of St. Louis. Vol. 16. Issue 2. Fall 2011. p. 1.

12. Zumello, Christine. *The "Everything Card" and Consumer Credit in the United States in the 1960s*. Business History Review. 85. Autumn 2011. The President and Fellows of Harvard College. p. 574.

13. Euromonitor. Passport: *Financial Cards and Payments in the US*. Euromonitor International. November 2011.

14. Ibid. p. 1.

15. Ibid. p. 3.

16. Ibid. p. 3.

17. Ibid. p. 3.

18. Bradford, Terri & Keeton, William R. *New Person-to-Person Payment Methods: Have Checks Met Their Match?* Payments System Research at Department of the Federal Reserve Bank of Kansas City. Economic Review. Q3 2012. p. 43.

19. Bradford, Terri & Keeton, William R. *New Person-to-Person Payment Methods: Have Checks Met Their Match?* Payments System Research at Department of the Federal Reserve Bank of Kansas City. Economic Review. Q3 2012. p. 44.

20. Sawers, Paul. *The Future of Online Banking*. TNW: The Next Web. 1 March 2012. Retrieved from: http://thenextweb.com/insider/2012/03/01/the-future-of-online-banking/.

21. Hachman, Mark. Isis Carrier Venture Signs Payment Deals with Visa, MasterCard, Others. PC Magazine. 19 July 2011. Retrieved from: http://www.pcmag.com/article2/0,2817,2388712,00.asp.

22. Euromonitor. Passport: *Financial Cards and Payments in the US*. Euromonitor International. November 2011.

23. Euromonitor. Passport: *Financial Cards and Payments in the US*. Euromonitor International. November 2011.

24. Ibid.

CHAPTER 2

From Ant Financial to Alibaba's Rural Taobao Strategy – How Fintech Is Transforming Social Inclusion

Ding Ding, Guan Chong, David LEE Kuo Chuen, Tan Lee Cheng

Contents

2.1 Introduction

With estimated two billion individuals and 200 million micro, small and midsize businesses (MSMEs) in emerging economies considered as unserved or underserved by the formal financial system (Manyika et al., 2016), financial inclusion has emerged as a critical challenge to economic development. Many transact exclusively in cash, with no secured way to savings and investments, and limited access to credit beyond informal lenders and personal networks.

As new platforms and technologies are introduced to the market, the boundaries of traditional business models are challenged. Digital financial services (or Fintech) can be provided with greater accountability, efficiency and accessibility. Using digital channels rather than brick-and-mortar branches can also dramatically reduce costs for providers, providing financial solutions to individuals at all income levels and MSMEs in rural areas.

Ant Financial, China's largest Fintech company under Alibaba, is set to revolutionize China's financial network, including digital payment, digital wealth management and loans. It leverages on Alibaba's well-established ecommerce platform – Taobao, along with Alibaba's rural Taobao Strategy. Focusing on the underserved markets by the major Chinese banks, Fintech can erase huge inefficiencies, unlock significant economic opportunity and accelerate social development.

In this chapter, we review the current progress of e-commerce and digital finance in China and summarize their implications on rural villages, focusing on Alibaba as a successful case. The remainder of the chapter is organized as follows. In the next section, we briefly review the issues and concerns that have emerged in rural China. This review highlights the need to reconsider the underlying linkages between urban areas and rural villages. Then, we introduce Alibaba's rural strategies, including Taobao Rural Service Centers and Taobao Villages. Subsequently, we review the Fintech development in China, and summarize how e-commence and digital finance can help address some of the issues in rural China and promote social inclusion.

2.2 Issues in Rural China

China's development in the last four decades was characterized by a rapid transition from a rural-dominant society to a continuously enlarging urban society. China crossed over from a majority rural to a majority urban country in 2011, when the urban population officially represented 51.27 percent of the total population (Preston, 2012). By the end of 2015, 53.86 percent of the total population lived in urban areas, a rate that rose from 26 percent in 1990. The ratio is close to developing countries with similar per capita income levels as China (60 percent), but still lower than developed nations' average of 80 percent (NBSC, 2015).

As China evolves into a majority urban country, it presents a number of challenges to the continuing rural population, who have been confronted with significant changes in demographic structures, employment opportunities, lifestyles and standards of living, accessibility and rural culture. The key trends include mass migration from rural villages to urban areas and the emergence and development of 'villages-in-the-city' (Cheng Zhong-cun) of rural migrant workers (Chan, 2010; Chung, 2010; Liang et al., 2002; Song et al., 2008); the growth of urban sprawl and the loss of agricultural land (Lin, 2006; Liu et al., 2010; Wang and Scott, 2008; Wei and Zhao, 2009; Yu and Ng, 2007); and rural industrialization, especially in districts close to cities with highly liberalized economies (Peng, 2007).

2.2.1 "Hollowed Villages"

The current definition of urban residents includes migrant workers who have worked in cities for more than six months, however, migrants might not benefit from the urbanization process in the same way as the original urban residents do. A distinctive feature of China's urbanization is the *hukou*, or household registration system, which links receipt of social services (from healthcare to education) to a residence permit. This system has created a bias against settling rural-to-urban migrants in the cities by keeping migrants' access to local public services restricted (Guan et al., 2016). By March 2014, 269 million Chinese migrant workers and their families live in places where they are not registered and are thus legally excluded from some local public services.[1]

The migrant workers without *hukou* have difficulty integrating themselves into the urban societies and their welfare is concerning. This means that there are millions of children of urban workers who live in rural villages apart from their parents because they are legally excluded from the schools in the city. Likewise, many migrants must return to their home villages for health care because they have limited access to these services in the places they live and work. These migrants often return to their villages if they lose their job in the city.

As large number of rural workforces migrated to cities and towns to earn a living, many dwellings were left behind in the inner village unoccupied either seasonally or permanently. The rapid depopulation caused massive outflow of rural investment and industries and further created a unique phenomenon known as "hollowed village" (Liu et al., 2010). "Hollowed villages" are communities in which depopulation and housing modernization has led to the abandonment of a significant number of properties, spread throughout the settlement (Liu, 2009; Liu et al., 2010; Long et al., 2009). Since early 1990s, many villages in China have seen an increasing number of deserted houses, which is not only a waste of land, but also an impediment to urbanization and the development of rural villages. Homes that are unoccupied may even become public dumps. Statistics show that hollow villages now account for 20 to 30 percent of the villages in Shandong province (China Daily, 2015). According to 2010 census figures, China's migrant population number was 221 million or 16.5 percent of all citizens in 2010. The number is expected to surpass 300 million and maybe reach 400 million by 2025. A government report issued in 2011 said more than 100 million more farmers would move to urban areas over the next decade. Between 2000 and 2010 an estimated 116 million people from China's hinterlands migrated to the booming coastal cities in the hope of finding better lives (China Labor Bulletin, 2011).

Since farming doesn't bring much profit, most young men leave home seeking jobs in the cities. Once they have left their village many of them don't want to return to their home to live. They find their villages' economic and social conditions depressing. They also worry about their children because village schools are of lower quality than schools found in the cities. A study of 2,749 villages in 17 provinces found that 74 percent of these villages had no one left behind who was fit to go work in city factories as migrant workers (Bradsher, 2010). During the busy farming season, the elders, women and children are seen as the main labor force in fields across most Chinese rural villages.

The process of rural hollowing has obviously caused a series of problems, such as low efficiency of rural residential land use, and lateral expansion of rural dwellings at the expense of farmland loss, decrease in the ability of rural inner development, and deterioration of rural residential environment (Liu et al., 2010; Wang, 2010). As such, rural hollowing is a holistic degradation of rural functions, and becomes a major problem facing China's agriculture and rural development (Long et al., 2012).

2.2.2 The "Left-Behind" Children

Besides the "hollowed villages," another major challenge that China faces is the rural "left-behind" children. With parents gone searching for jobs, many children are left behind to be brought up by grandparents or other relatives. The only time the children meet their parents is when they return home over the Chinese New Year holiday. Often, some don't make it home because they are required to work overtime at their factory or construction site.

According to the census conducted in 2005, 58 million children, accounting for 21.7% of the 0–17 age cohort of children, were left in villages by their migratory parents (NBSC, 2005). The Sixth National Population Census indicated that this number increased again from 3 million to 61 million in 2010, which represents 37.7% of rural children (NBSC, 2011). At the compulsory education stage (elementary and junior high school), the number of children who are left behind is 22.7 million (MOE, 2011).

Under constraints from institutional arrangements, such as the Household Registration System (*hukou*), in China, rural migrant families who live in cities benefit little from the available human resource service programmes that fund education and health. One example of these families' problems is that their children cannot be enrolled in urban public schools without them having to pay more than the parents of the children who have urban *hukou*, and they usually cannot afford this cost (Lai et al., 2009). The latest research indicates that migrant students who are unable to enroll in public schools perform significantly worse than their more fortunate counterparts (Chen and Feng, 2013). Although there are a number of private and for-profit schools that the children of migrant workers can attend in some cities, the high tuition fees of these schools are usually accompanied by poor facilities and underqualified, demotivated teachers. Furthermore, most of these schools, which are not certified by the government, have the risk of being shut down. Thus, in most cases, these families' school aged children are left behind in villages when the parents move to the city for work (Wu et al., 2004).

Many studies, including the ones by Lee (2011), Meyerhoefer and Chen (2011) and Wen and Lin (2012), Liang and Chen (2007) indicated that temporary parental migration into cities or suburban areas significantly decreased children's school enrollment rate. The left-behind children are usually looked after by poorly educated grandparents who are unable to substitute the roles of the parents (Biao, 2007). Grandparents may either spoil the children or fail to provide enough emotional care (Wang et al., 2006). Furthermore, living with grandparents is often correlated with certain negative health outcomes (Gao et al., 2010).

2.3 Alibaba's Rural Taobao Strategy

By the end of 2015, 46.14 percent of the total Chinese population was still living in rural areas (NBSC, 2015). Providing access to e-commerce and digital financial services to millions of the country's poorer residents and MSMEs can help raise the living standards in China's countryside. It could also be translated into a lucrative opportunity for the e-commerce giants like Alibaba. Alibaba seized this vast and largely untapped growth opportunity. "We're really hoping to bring e-commerce to all of China's village, so that rural people can get a taste of the city life and sell their own products in the cities," said Jack Ma, Alibaba Chairman (Wang, 2014).

Alibaba Group was listed in New York Stock Exchange on September 19, 2014. After its IPO, it announced the three major strategies, "e-commerce in rural areas, globalization and big data" (Aliresearch, 2015). Thereafter, the rural strategy of Alibaba Group began to officially come into being. Taobao is Alibaba's e-commerce arm, China's largest e-commerce website with a consumer focus. Alibaba's Rural Taobao Strategy comprises of "dual cores", namely, Rural Taobao and Taobao Villages. The two core strategies are discussed in detail in the following section.

Table 2.1: Internet penetration in China's urban and rural population in year 2006–2014 (in thousands).

Year	Urban Population	Urban Internet User	% of Internet Users in Urban Population	Rural Popula-tion	Rural Internet User	% of Internet Users in Rural Population
2014	749160	470280	62.77%	618660	178460	28.85%
2013	731110	440950	60.31%	629610	176620	28.05%
2012	711820	408340	57.37%	642220	155660	24.24%
2011	690790	377130	54.59%	656560	135790	20.68%
2010	669780	332460	49.64%	671130	124840	18.60%
2009	645120	277190	42.97%	689380	106810	15.49%
2008	624030	213400	34.20%	703990	84600	12.02%
2007	606330	157830	26.03%	714960	52620	7.36%
2006	582880	113890	19.54%	731600	23110	3.16%

Source: CNNIC (2015) 农村互联网发展状况研究报告; National Bureau of Statistics of China (NBSC) (2015) 中国统计年鉴

2.3.1 Taobao Rural Service Centres

At the end of 2014, the internet penetration rate in China's rural areas was only 28.85 percent compared with 62.77 percent in the cities (CNNIC, 2015). Table 2.1 presents the Internet penetration rates among China's urban and rural population between 2006 to 2014.

Alibaba aims to bring convenient and affordable goods and service to rural areas so that the rural residents can fully enjoy the benefits of the information society. Since about three quarters of the China rural population does not have access to Internet, Alibaba decided to take the services to the customer's doorsteps.

To better serve the rural residents and to support agricultural innovation and economic development in rural areas, Alibaba Group released the "1,000 counties and 10,000 villages" programme (namely the rural Taobao mode) in October 2014. This programme brings forward 10 billion RMB (about 1.48 billion USD) of investment on logistics, hardware, and training in the next three to five years to establish 1,000 county-level Service Centers and 100,000 service stations in rural areas (Aliresearch, 2015). The programme would develop rural Taobao by building county-level operations centers in county seats and village-level service stations in villages as parts of a rural e-commerce service system. It would build information and logistic channels to "bring consumption goods to the countryside" and explore the ways of selling rural products online.

Many Taobao Rural Service Centers are located at the local convenience store, where computers, wall-mounted flatscreen monitors are provided, with well-trained villagers serving as representatives. In the service centers, villagers can check out the latest Taobao online deals

Table 2.2: Best-selling product categories.

Ranking	Best-selling Product Categories Sold through Taobao Rural Service Centers	Sold by Taobao Village Merchants
1	Home appliances	Apparel
2	Mobile top-up	Furniture
3	Women's apparel	Shoes
4	Kitchen appliances	Automobile accessories
5	Men's apparel	Bags, luggage and leather products
6	Mobile phones	Toys
7	Cleansers/feminine hygiene products /tissues/air fresheners	Home products
8	Flower deliveries/artificial flowers/plants	Bedding products
9	Women's shoes	Outdoor products
10	Furniture	Home improvement materials

Source: Alizila (2016a, 2016b) An Introduction to Taobao Villages, Retrieved from http://www.alizila.com/an-introduction-to-taobao-villages/; Wang (2015) E-commerce Gaining Traction in Rural China; Retrieved from http://www.alizila.com/e-commerce-gaining-traction-rural-china-2/

on mobile phones, toothpaste, pesticide dispensers, and many more. They can get accustomed to making purchases and paying bills online, as well as picking up items they purchased from Taobao. By September, 2016, more than 16,000 Taobao Rural Service Centers were already in place (Alizila, 2016a, 2016b). To ensure timely delivery of purchases, Alibaba is opening warehouses and working with delivery companies and local officials.

Historically, with low incomes, dispersed populations, and poor logistic infrastructure, the rural areas haven't attracted many brick-and-mortar stores. Thus, shopping in rural China had been characterized by limited choice, inflated prices, and poor quality in the past. With the help of Taobao Service Centers, it takes little time for the rural consumers to realize that the price is cheaper, the choice is better, and it is far more convenient to shop online, noting that they no longer need to make a half-day trip to the dealers. In 2015, the best-selling items sold through Taobao Rural Service Centers were home appliances, mobile top-up and women's apparel (Wang, 2015). Table 2.2 presents the best-selling product categories of both items sold through Taobao Rural Service Centers and those sold by Taobao Village merchants. In this process, Alibaba is nurturing the culture and habit of shopping online among the rural population.

In addition, the centers have provided other innovative services. By working with local branches of Railcom, China Unicom, Telecom and other operators, the centers provide recharging services and Internet access; through collaboration with Ali Trip, they provide services such as train ticket, air ticket and hotel booking to villagers; through cooperation with Alipay, it grants credit to rural Taobao partners and provides services such as living expenses payment and cash withdrawing in small sum to villagers. It will soon rely on the platform of AliJK in the future and provide service such as registration, medicine pick-up and remote diagnosis. On the November 11 shopping festival in 2015, service centers of rural Taobao in the whole country accomplished the turnover of 293 million RMB (about 43.4 million USD) in a single day, more than 30,000 RMB (about 4,440 USD) in each village on average, which demonstrated the huge consumption potential of rural areas in e-commerce (Aliresearch, 2015).

2.3.2 Taobao Villages

Besides bringing consumption goods to the countryside, Taobao Service Centers also serve another important function – selling the agricultural products to cities. Since 2009, clusters of rural online entrepreneurs who have opened shops on Taobao began to emerge in China. These clusters are often referred to as "Taobao Villages". The number of Taobao Villages has been on the rise since then. According to AliResearch, a "Taobao village" is defined as a village with a large number of online merchants who adopt Taobao as the key trading platform, relying on the Taobao e-commerce ecosystem and forming a scalable cluster. The criteria of Taobao villages include the following three principles (Aliresearch, 2015):

1. The trading places are mainly rural areas;
2. The annual turnover in e-commerce reaches 10 million RMB (about 1.48 million USD) or more;
3. The number of active online merchants in the village reaches 100 or more, and/or active online shops account for 10% or more of the local households.

In May 2015, Taobao Villages launched the "2.0 mode". Its partners changed from owners of traditional village convenience stores to specialized "rural Taobao partners". The rural Taobao partner programme targets the local villagers who are open-minded, familiar with the Internet and online shopping, especially young migrant workers who are returning to their hometown from the cities. A total of 1311 Taobao villages widely distributed in 18 provinces were founded in China as of the end of August, 2016 (Ali Institute and the New Village Research Center, 2016). Apparel, furniture and shoes are the best-selling products categories sold by the Taobao Village merchants. The list of top ten product categories in terms of 2015 sales is presented in Table 2.2.

With the help of more and more rural Taobao partners, many traditional farming communities have gradually transformed into e-commence clusters with many new job opportunities, including both Internet-based jobs and logistics related positions. The drain of young workforce in the countryside used to pose a great threat to the economic and social development of the rural areas. By attracting more and more young migrant workers to come back to Taobao

Villages from the cities, Alibaba's rural strategy not only promotes business start-up opportunities, employment and economic development, but it may also mitigate many of the issues caused by rapid urbanization.

The connection to urban consumers through Taobao Villages is also changing the farmers' attitudes towards the goods they produce and their agricultural practices. They earn more by removing the middlemen and cutting short the supply chain, going straight to the consumers. Their consumers are mostly urban residents who are concerned about food quality and safety. Thus, villagers are focusing more and more on producing quality goods rather than cutting cost and compromising on quality.

To support the Rural Taobao Service Centres and Taobao Villages, Alibaba has helped rural areas build the infrastructure of e-business, including trade, logistics, digital payment and financing, cloud computing, data analytics and so on. Other business entities and entrepreneurs outside of the Alibaba ecosystem can also make use of the infrastructure in the future and contribute to the rural economy. Alibaba is working with third-party logistic service providers to set up the logistic channels in rural areas through subsidy and other means; Cainiao network built the "distribution network for big household appliances," covering 95% districts and counties in the country and 500,000 villages; Mantianxing programme had incorporated 51 counties in the country by December 2015 and traced the sources of high-quality agricultural products; Ant Financial had connected more than 2,300 rural financial institutions, served more than two million rural e-businesses and provided business loans to 180,000 small and micro corporations in rural areas, lending 30 billion RMB (about 4.43 billion USD) in total (Aliresearch, 2015).

2.4 Digital Financial Services and Fintech Platforms

One crucial factor that helped spur the fast growth of Taobao Villages in China is the rise of new technology enabled financial services for the rural residents and micro businesses (Lee and Teo, 2015). According to the most recent Financial Inclusion Index reported by Peking University,[2] from 2011 to 2015, the gap between different regions in China in terms of financial development has substantially narrowed due to the availability of digital financial technology. For example, in 2011 the financial inclusion index showed that Shanghai ranked No. 1 in financial development in China and the figure was 4.9 time of that for Tibet, which ranked the lowest. However, this gap has dropped to 1.9 times in 2013, and 1.5 times in 2015.

Furthermore, in a subsector ranking in terms of level of support through digital services, cities and small towns in central and western China showed surprising results. Most of the top 10 ranked cities are from central and western China, for example, Guoluo region in Qinhai Province, Tacheng region in Xinjiang Province, and Ali region in Tibet. The measurement of level of support through digital services included factors such as mobile payment and loan interest rate. This showed that although lagging behind in terms of financial inclusion, western regions in China have surpassed the more developed areas in eastern China in terms of usage of mobile payment.

When it comes to mobile payment, there are two leading companies in China, namely, Alibaba and Tencent, each with their own financial services subsidiaries. These two giant companies have shifted the entire financial services sector with their digital financial solutions in the past few years, not only changing the way that businesses are conducted, but also the way people live.

2.4.1 Ant Financial Serveries Group

Ant Financial Services Group (Chinese: 蚂蚁金服), founded in 2004 and based in Hangzhou, is an affiliated company of the Chinese Alibaba Group. Formerly known as Small and Micro Financial Services Company, Ant Financial initiated its formation process in early 2013 and is now comprised of six financial services entities that are affiliated with Alibaba. The name 'Ant' was chosen to symbolize the potential strength of a number of smaller brands working together. The new Ant Financial Services Group oversees six financial service entities that are affiliated with Alibaba, including: Alipay; Alipay Wallet; Yu'e Bao, a money market fund with 570 billion RMB (about 84.15 billion USD) under management; Zhao Cai Bao, a third-party financial services platform; micro-loan provider Ant Micro; and MYBank, a private bank (Zhou et al., 2015).

1. **Alipay** Alipay is the world's leading third-party payment platform. As of the end of 2013, the number of Alipay registered users reached 300 million and the number of partnering financial institutions exceeded 200. Due to Alibaba's dominant market position in e-commerce, Alipay has emerged as the online payment processing market leader in China. It clears 80 million transactions per day, including 45 million transactions through its Alipay Wallet mobile app (Shih, 2014). Data show that among all the new Alipay users in 2014, 48% were from first- and second-tier cities, with third-tier cities accounting for the remaining 52%. Forty-nine percent of new Alipay wallet users were from first- and second-tier cities, with 51% from third- and fourth-tier cities (Business Wire, 2014).

2. **Alipay Wallet** Alipay Wallet has operated as an independent brand since November 2013. As of October 2014, there were 190 million annual active users (Lee, 2014). In addition to provide basic services such as shopping payment, credit card repayment, money transfer, and utilities bill payment on mobile phones, Alipay Wallet is expanding its offline applications to shopping malls, convenience stores, taxis and hospitals.

3. **Yu'e Bao** Yu'e Bao was launched in June 2013 jointly by Alipay and Tianhong Asset Management. According to Tianhong, as of the end of June 2014, Yu'e Bao had attracted approximately 570 billion RMB (about 84.16 billion USD) in assets under management and nearly 125 million Yu'e Bao users. Zeng Libao, Yu'e Bao's money market fund, became the largest individual money market fund in China, according to Tianhong Asset Management's Q3 2013 Financial Report. At the end of May 2014, Ant Financial gained approval from the China Securities Regulatory Commission to acquire a 51% stake in Tianhong Asset Management (Business Wire, 2014).

4. **Zhao Cai Bao** Zhao Cai Bao launched in April 2014 as an open platform for investment and financial products and services. Zhao Cai Bao is open to third-party financial institutions and provides convenient and safe Internet finance services for individuals and MSMEs. Products offered on the platform include loans for small and medium enterprises, individuals, universal insurance and structured funds.

5. **Ant Credit** Ant Credit provides micro online loans to small and micro enterprises and individual online entrepreneurs, evaluated based on data. The products include credit loans, online merchant loans and loans for Taobao sellers.

6. **MYBank** Ant Financial received approval from China Banking Regulatory Commission on September 29, 2014 to set up a private bank called MYBank together with Shanghai Fosun Industrial Technology, owned by Fosun International; a subsidiary of Wanxiang Group, and Ningbo Jinrun Asset Management. MYBank is part of a pilot programme launched earlier that year and the first tentative step by the country to open its closely guarded banking sector to private investors. MYBank will fully utilize online and big data analytics to serve the financial needs of small and micro enterprises, as well as individual consumers.

Ant Financial is a financial services provider, rather than a financial institution with major financial holdings. It focuses on serving small and micro enterprises, as well as individual consumers. Building on Internet-based solutions and technology, it works with financial institutions to create an open ecosystem, as well as provides support to the financial industry to realize its vision 'To turn trust into wealth'. Ant Financial Chief Financial Officer Eric Jing said in 2015, "In the future, the financial ecosystem will be characterized by collaboration rather than competition". Like Alibaba's ecosystem in the e-commerce industry, a similar ecosystem will emerge in the financial industry. This ecosystem will be supported by cloud computing, big data and credit systems that enable payment, financing, wealth management, insurance (InsurTech) and banking platforms and services (Tan et al., 2016). We believe that Ant Financial will play a key role in leading the development of this ecosystem for the benefit of small and micro enterprises and individual consumers. As mobile commerce continues to gain ground in China, the products and services offered by Ant Financial are increasingly part of entrepreneurs' and consumers' daily lives.

2.4.2 Technology Behind the Services

The various business operations of Ant Financial are supported by cloud computing, big data and credit systems. Ant Financial opens up these supporting platforms to partners to create a new financial ecosystem.

Big Data Analytics Ant Financial has utilized big data technologies in many of the services in their new financial ecosystem. For the past few years, the MYBank and the former "Ali Small Credit" have been giving out small and micro loans using a model based on big data analytics. Using their clients' data and relevant predictive modeling, they could conduct credit analysis, and approve loans in a "310" standard, namely, 3-minute application, 1-second approval, and 0 human intervention. In five years, they have given out more than 4 million loans to small and micro business with a total loan amount of more than 700 billion RMB (about 103.4 billion USD). It provided the dearly needed capital to those small and micro businesses to help them survive and develop, so that they could create more jobs in the rural regions.

Similarly, the application of big data is also fully reflected in the Ant Financial's third-party credit rating service – sesame credit. "Sesame credit" is the credit rating computed using massive data mainly from five dimensions, including: user's credit history, behavior preferences, performance of contract, identity features, and personal connections. Sesame credit is built on Alibaba's e-business data and Ant Financial Internet finance data, and collaborates with public security networks and other public institutions and partners. Differently from the traditional credit rating process, the Sesame credit data covers more information such as credit card repayment, online shopping, online transfer, water and electricity payment, rental information, changes in addresses, social relations and so on. Through the analysis of a large number of network transactions and behavioral data, Sesame credit can provide users' credit assessment, which in turn helps the Internet financing companies to evaluate users' willingness and ability to repay the loans, so that they can provide users with fast credit and installment services.

Face Recognition Technology Ant Financial Services has been working on the development of biometric technology and its application in the field of Internet identity authentication, to achieve higher security and better user experience. Based on the leading face matching algorithm, they developed the interactive face detection technology and the image desensitization technique and designed the system security architecture with high concurrency and high reliability. These technologies have been successfully applied in products and services in the MYBank and Alipay identity authentication and other applications. Among them, the core algorithms are in vivo detection algorithm, image desensitization algorithm and face alignment algorithm. According to a study conducted by the Chinese University of Hong Kong in 2014 using the international public face database LFW, the accuracy of the face recognition algorithm (99.6%) has exceeded that of the naked eye (97.2%) (Uwechue and Pandya, 2012).

Cloud Computing Technology Ant Financial Cloud is Ant Financial's cloud computing service. Built on Alibaba and Ant Financial's cloud computing technology, rich experience and consolidated resources, Ant Financial Cloud is tailored for the needs of the financial industry research and development. As an integral part of the "Internet Thruster" program, the Ant Financial Cloud is an open cloud platform that promotes financial innovation and helps financial institutions to upgrade their IT infrastructure to build safe, low-cost and innovative financial applications, so that financial institutions can better serve their customers. After several years of efforts, Ant Financial Cloud now has the achieved following capabilities: high availability disaster recovery (99.99% availability), secured funds management (billions of funds / daily changes), high concurrent transactions (85,900 transactions per second processing power), real-time security control (millisecond risk defense capability), and low-cost transactions (a few cents for single transaction).

Risk Management Technology The core to mobile payment is to meet the users' needs and provide fast and secure transfer of money. How to control risk becomes the industry's top priority. Founded in December 2004 and with years of exploration, Alipay has achieved intelligent and remarkable control and prevention of risk. Alipay risk control system uses the original historical transaction data for personalized verification to improve account security. About 80% of the risk events can be solved in the intelligent control process. In addition to the ex post audit and pre-prevention, monitoring is also very important: classification of the account to ensure different accounts corresponding to different risk levels; conduct strategic risk assessment and monitoring review on the new online products.

Among all the 7000 employees in Ant Financial Services Group, more than 1,500 employees are dedicated to risk monitoring, analysis and management. At present, Ant Financial is working with the public security organizations such as the Police Force and the Court to stop the Internet financial fraud cases, and to combat financial crime. In addition, Ant Financial is also actively working with banks, third-party payment companies, risk management related hardware and software vendors, Alipay merchants and users, universities and research institutions and other sectors of the community to enhance the security and capability of whole payment industry.

Artificial Intelligence Technology Artificial intelligence technology is used by Ant Financial in the area of "smart customer service". Ant Financial uses data mining and semantic analysis technology to achieve the automatic judgment and prediction. It can identify the user's identity information, apply user's behavioral logic, and predict what problem the user has encountered, and summarize the common problems faced by many users. In the process of communication, "My Customer Service" applies semantic analysis and other techniques to obtain critical information and then conduct the match. In addition to "smart customer service", Ant Financial also has the smart quality control and refund ability. In the past, companies needed to go through research to evaluate the quality of service, and sampling coverage was about 2%. Now the robot can be real-time customer service personnel to achieve intelligent automatic quality control for all transactions. The other feature is smart payouts. In the insurance business, "My Customer Service" already has professional audit capability to complete the payment in an average of 24 hours, of which 32% claims can be completed within one hour directly, and 50% of complex claims can be completed within 6 hours.

2.4.3 Tencent Holdings and WeBank

Ant Financial in not the only player in China's hot market of internet finance. Rival Chinese Internet giant Tencent Holdings Ltd. also operates a competing payments platform known as WePay. Moreover, it has launched China's first private bank – WeBank, which happens to be an entirely online operation. WeBank is notable for being the first bank not entirely controlled by the Chinese government. Yet, perhaps more importantly, it has no brick-and-mortar presence, which means customers do all their banking online, from depositing and transferring funds to securing loans.

Tencent is a major player in China, providing a wide range of services, including its own social network, an instant-messaging platform known as QQ and the mobile app WeChat. China's closest equivalent to Facebook, the WeChat social network is used by 600 million people, and the company also owns an e-commerce company and is a major force in online gaming.

WeBank, a joint venture led by Chinese gaming and social network group Tencent Holdings, became the first private bank to start operations under a pilot, after the banking regulator granted licenses to six such institutions in 2015. Its name comes from WeChat, Tencent's popular instant messaging and social networking app. WeBank's scope covers personal banking, corporate banking, and international banking. Given its diverse portfolio of companies, it's perhaps no surprise that it added banking to the mix. By jumping into banking, Tencent puts itself in direct competition with government-sponsored banks across China. However, the charter for private banks allows WeBank to focus on individuals and small businesses, rather than large corporations. Private, online banks can issue small loans, collect deposits and perform other standard banking tasks.

WeBank is actively seeking to expand its personal-loan service called Weilidai—"a tiny bit of loan" in English—which allows users to borrow up to 200,000 RMB (approximately 29541.88 USD) without providing a guarantee or collateral. No traditional credit checks and no wait. In September 2015, Tencent's popular WeChat messaging app, which has 650 million users, added the Weilidai service as an additional feature for a limited number of creditworthy users. The new loan service relies on bank account information as well as data gleaned from a user's social network history to gauge a person's creditworthiness in seconds. How much you spend on restaurants and cabs, which are also part of WeChat's web of e-commerce, might help determine your creditworthiness. The loans can extend up to 20 months and carry interest rates staring at 0.05% a day. How fast WeBank can expand will depend in part on Chinese regulators. Still, China has enlisted the Internet companies in part because their expertise in online services could help make the country's financial sector – long dominated by state-owned banks – more competitive and responsive to private customers.

2.5 Conclusion

The ultimate goal of Alibaba Rural Strategy is the realization of increase in farmers' income, growth of rural economy, upgrade of agriculture and new urbanization through the "popularization of Internet" in rural areas. These principles have provided guidance and direction for the in their efforts to promote e-commerce opportunities and digital financial services for the rural residents. They have made remarkable achievements along the way and transformed the lives of people in the rural areas. Although there are still many challenges ahead, these innovative companies will strive on and continue to reshape the landscape of e-commerce and financial industries in future. Ensuring a level playing field for consumers that live in rural locations or regions without the structures of an urban economy is vital in achieving full financial and social inclusion.

References

Ali Institute and the New Village Research Center, 2016. China's Taobao Village Research Report. Retrieved from http://www.bestchinanews.com/Domestic/4379.html.

Aliresearch, 2015. Research Report on China's Taobao Villages. Retrieved from http://i.aliresearch.com/img/20160126/20160126155201.pdf.

Alizila, 2016a. Mapping Alibaba's Rural China Drive. Retrieved from http://www.alizila.com/rural-taobao-success-stories-map-video/.

Alizila, 2016b. An Introduction to Taobao Villages. Retrieved from http://www.alizila.com/an-introduction-to-taobao-villages/.

Biao, X., 2007. How far are the left-behind left behind? A preliminary study in rural China. Population. Space and Place 13, 179–191.

Bradsher, Keith, 2010. Defying global slump, China has labor shortage. The New York Times. Retrieved from http://www.nytimes.com/2010/02/27/business/global/27yuan.html?_r=0.

Business Wire, 2014. Official launch of ant financial services group brings new financial ecosystem to China. Retrieved from http://www.businesswire.com/news/home/20141016005260/en/Official-Launch-Ant-Financial-Services-Group-Brings.

Chan, K.W., 2010. Fundamentals of China's urbanization and policy. China Review 10, 63–93.

China Daily, 2015. Hollow villages. Retrieved from http://usa.chinadaily.com.cn/epaper/2015-05/07/content_20648746.htm.

China Labor Bulletin, 2011. Retrieved from http://www.china-labour.org.hk/en/node/100259.

CNNIC, 2015. 农村互联网发展状况研究报告. Retrieved from http://www.cnnic.net.cn/hlwfzyj/.../ P02015062346645 8430466.pdf.

Chen, Y., Feng, S., 2013. Access to public schools and the education of migrant children in China. China Economic Review 26, 75–88.

Chung, H., 2010. Building an image of villages-in-the-city: a clarification of China's distinct urban spaces. International Journal of Urban and Regional Research 34, 421–437.

Gao, Y., Li, L.P., Kim, J.H., Congdon, N., Lau, J., Griffiths, S., 2010. The impact of parental migration on health status and health behaviours among left behind adolescent school children in China. BMC Public Health 10, 56.

Guan, Chong, Ding, Ding, Yu, Yinghui, 2016. The urbanisation of rural villages in China. In: Rappa, Antonio L. (Ed.), The Architectonics of the Village. Singapore Management University and Ethos Press.

Lai, F., Liu, C., Luo, R., Zhang, L., Ma, X., Bai, Y., Sharbono, B., Rozelle, S., 2009. Private Migrant Schools or Rural/Urban Public Schools: Where Should China Educate Its Migrant Children. Stanford REAP working paper, 224.

Lee, David Kuo Chuen, Teo, Ernie, 2015. The rise of chinese finance: the game of Dian Fu. Presented at the Sim Kee Boon Institute for Financial Economics: Seminar Series, 17 Aug 2015. Retrieved from http://skbi.smu. edu.sg/sites/default/files/skbife/pdf/The%20Rise%20of%20Chinese%20Finance%20%E9%A2%A0%E8 %A6%86.pdf.

Lee, M.H., 2011. Migration and children's welfare in China: the schooling and health of children left behind. The Journal of Developing Areas 44, 165–182.

Lee, Melanie, 2014. Alipay targets rural and overseas users. Retrieved from http://www2.alizila.com/alipay-targets-rural-and-overseas-users.

Liang, Z., Chen, Y.P., Gu, Y., 2002. Rural industrialisation and internal migration in China. Urban Studies 39, 2175–2187.

Liang, Z., Chen, Y.P., 2007. The educational consequences of migration for children in China. Social Science Research 36, 28–47.

Lin, G.C.S., 2006. Peri-urbanism in globalizing China: a study of new urbanism in Dongguan. Eurasian Geography and Economics 47, 28–53.

Liu, L., 2009. National market location, income levels and urban–rural inequality in China. International Development Planning Review 31, 397–421.

Liu, Y.S., Liu, Y., Chen, Y.F., Long, H.L., 2010. The process and driving forces of rural hollowing in China under rapid urbanization. Journal of Geographical Sciences 20 (6), 876–888.

Long, H.L., Zou, J., Liu, Y.S., 2009. Differentiation of rural development driven by industrialization and urbanization in eastern coastal China. Habitat International 33, 454–462.

Long, H.L., Li, Y.R., Liu, Y.S., Woods, M., Zou, J., 2012. Accelerated restructuring in rural China fuelled by 'increasing vs. decreasing balance' land-use policy for dealing with hollowed villages. Land Use Policy 29, 11–22.

Manyika, James, Lund, Susan, Singer, Marc, White, Olivia, Berry, Chris, 2016. Digital Finance for All: Powering Inclusive Growth in Emerging Economies. McKinsey Global Institute, McKinsey & Company. Retrieved from http://www.mckinsey.com/mgi.

Meyerhoefer, C.D., Chen, C., 2011. The effect of parental labor migration on children's educational progress in rural China. Review of Economics of the Household 9, 379–396.

MOE, 2011. 2010 National Educational Development Statistics Bulletin. Ministry of Education, Beijing.

NBSC, 2005. 1% of the Population Nationwide Sample Survey Data. China Statistics Press, Beijing.

NBSC, 2011. 2010 Sixth National Population Census Data Bulletin. China Statistics Press, Beijing.

NBSC, 2015. 中国统计年鉴, National Bureau of Statistics of China.

Peng, Y.S., 2007. What has spilled over from Chinese cities into rural industry? Modern China 33, 287–319.

Preston, Dale, 2012. Urban China is growing, but rural China's 650M consumers can't be ignored. Consumer. The Nielsen Company. Retrieved from http://www.nielsen.com/us/en/insights/news/2012/urban-china-is-growing-but-rural-chinas-650m-consumers-cant-be-ignored.html.

Song, Y., Zenou, Y., Ding, C., 2008. Let's not throw the baby out with the bath water: the role of urban villages in housing rural migrants in China. Urban Studies 45, 313–330.

Shih, Gerry, 2014. Alibaba affiliate Alipay rebranded Ant in new financial services push, Reuters. Retrieved from http://www.reuters.com/article/us-china-alibaba-idUSKCN0I50KJ20141016.

Tan, Choon Yan, Schulte, Paul, Lee, David Kuo Chuen, 2016. InsurTech and FinTech: Banking and Insurance Enablement. Working paper.

Uwechue, Okechukwu A., Pandya, Abhijit S., 2012. Human Face Recognition Using Third-Order Synthetic Neural Networks. Springer.

Wang, M., 2010. Impact of the global economic crisis on China's migrant workers: a survey of 2700 in 2009. Eurasian Geography and Economics 51, 218–235.

Wang, Susan, 2014. "Taobao villages" in rural China grow tenfold in 2014. Retrieved from http://www2.alizila.com/report-taobao-villages-rural-china-grow-tenfold-2014.

Wang, Susan, 2015. E-commerce gaining traction in rural China. Retrieved from http://www.alizila.com/e-commerce-gaining-traction-rural-china-2/.

Wang, Y.M., Scott, S., 2008. Illegal farmland conversion in China's urban periphery: local regime and national transitions. Urban Geography 29, 327–347.

Wang, L., Zhang, S., Sun, Y., Zhang, X., 2006. The current situation of loneliness of left behind children in countryside. Chinese Journal of Behavioral Medical Science 15, 639–640 (in Chinese).

Wei, Y.P., Zhao, M., 2009. Urban spill over vs. local urban sprawl: entangling land-use regulations in the urban growth of China's megacities. Land Use Policy 26, 1031–1045.

Wen, M., Lin, D., 2012. Child development in rural China: children left behind by their migrant parents and children of nonmigrant families. Child Development 83, 120–136.

Wu, D.J., Tang, Y., Fang, M., Qin, X., Yang, X., et al., 2004. The study on the migrant children (in Chinese). Educational Research 10, 15–18.

Yu, X.J., Ng, C.N., 2007. Spatial and temporal dynamics of urban sprawl along two urban–rural transects: a case study of Guangzhou, China. Landscape and Urban Planning 79, 96–109.

Zhou, Weihuan, Arner Douglas, W., Buckley Ross, P., 2015. Regulation of digital finance services in China. Tsinghua China Law Review 8 (25), 25–62.

Notes

1. Press conference held on March 19, 2014 on the National New-type Urbanization Plan (2014–2020) by the State Council Information Office of the People's Republic of China.

2. <北京大学数字普惠金融指数 2011–2015>, Institute of Internet Finance, Peking University, July 2016.

CHAPTER 3

The M-Pesa Technological Revolution for Financial Services in Kenya: A Platform for Financial Inclusion

Njuguna Ndung'u[#]

Contents

3.1 Introduction

In March 2007, following a pilot project, the M-Pesa technological platform was launched. The M-Pesa platform enabled users to store value on the SIM cards of their mobile phones or mobile account in the form of electronic currency that could be used for multiple purposes including transfers to other users, payments for goods and services, and conversion to and from cash. It was first developed as a bank product in partnership with Safaricom, a telecommunication (Telco) company and the Commercial Bank of Africa (CBA), a commercial bank in Kenya. The M-Pesa product developed further as a platform of

---

[#] On Leave of Absence from the University of Nairobi and the immediate former Governor of the Central Bank of Kenya, 2007–2015.

financial services that provided virtual savings accounts in commercial banks and further into a source of credit supply among other financial services where other commercial banks, microfinance institutions and SACCOs have since integrated with this platform. It can as such be described as a technological platform that has allowed Kenyans to access a menu of financial services in the comfort of their homes, workplaces or locations they choose for themselves, without a trip to the bank or a financial services touch point. It has become an important instrument to push financial inclusion space in Kenya.

The M-Pesa platform represents a revolution in financial inclusion that has enhanced convenience, security, management of low transactions at affordable prices and offered these services in real time. This is beyond the success of other financial inclusion instruments like microfinance, SACCOs or even the Agency Banking model in Kenya. What has been evident in Kenya is that M-Pesa has helped these other financial inclusion instruments to be mutually reinforcing on the final outcomes of financial inclusion observed between 2007 and the present. A lot of interest to study this product has emerged in the recent years, first driven by anxiety to understand the workings and the processes and, second, to explain how easily it has worked and has stood the test of time. But more importantly, from a public policy point of view, the success to push the financial inclusion frontier as well as endogenous demand to complete the financial infrastructure and to design an appropriate regulatory technology and capacity has perhaps been the most celebrated outcome in Kenya. For example, Hinz (2014) demonstrates its ease of access in terms of converting electronic money into cash, the large network of agents who act as "human ATMs" who have proved to be cost effective and convenient to millions of Kenyans hence boosting their confidence in the M-Pesa platform. In addition, Klein and Mayer (2012) argue that the M-Pesa platform has demonstrated that liquidity distribution can take place effectively, efficiently and in real time outside the banking halls. In an effort to document the M-Pesa evolution and the technological platform that has emerged, we start by showing its developments in four innovative but also virtuous generations. First, the digital financial services platform in Kenya has entailed four generations of virtuous developments: The **First Generation** is where the mobile phone technological platform was used for transfers between users and later payments and settlement. This was made easier in 2006 for M-Pesa type of products to be rolled out in the market when the Government amended the communication law to recognized electronic units of money. It was thus easy and practical to develop a Trust Account that became the payments solution – or a transactions platform, in the absence of a national payments and settlement law. The **Second Generation** followed with virtual savings accounts using the same M-Pesa technological platform – a virtual banking service (costless to transfer from M-Pesa to savings account). This now acquired a new definition of digital financial services, as it developed, but more importantly, it started to impact on the banking intermediation process. The **Third Generation** that followed was a development and application of information capital for participants in this technological platform. This is where transactions and savings data were used to generate credit scores for use as the basis to evaluate and price micro credit. The celebrated M-Shwari type of products in Kenya (others include M-Kesho and KCB-Pesa in Kenya with other commercial banks, and M-Pawa in Tanzania). The **Fourth Generation** is now where **currently** these developments allow for cross-border payments and international remittances based on the M-Pesa technological platform. This is what has given Kenya a name in the financial inclusion policy success. From these developments spanning almost ten years, the M-Pesa technological platform today has revolutionized financial inclusion in Kenya to reach over 75% of the population, improved financial access touch points – 76.7% of the population are within 5 km of a financial access touch point and there are 161.9 financial access touch points per 100,000 Kenyans compared to 63.1 for Uganda, 48.9 for Tanzania and 11.4 for Nigeria.

The rest of the chapter is organized as follows: the next section provides a background to the M-Pesa revolution. Section 3.3 discusses how M-Pesa has provided a platform for financial inclusion in Kenya. Section 3.4 discusses the impact of the M-Pesa technological platform on financial inclusion in the country and Section 3.5 concludes.

3.2 Background

In October 2005, Vodafone and Safaricom, telecommunication companies and mobile network operators (MNOs), initiated the M-Pesa pilot program in Kenya consisting of eight agents in Nairobi Central Business District, Mathare slums in Nairobi and Thika town (Buku and Meredith, 2013). M-Pesa was conceived of as a means for micro-credit disbursement and repayment. In order to achieve this objective Safaricom partnered with Faulu Kenya (a local micro-finance institution), enrolled five hundred Faulu Kenya clients, provided them with M-Pesa ready phones, and instructed them on how to use them to repay their loans. The initial idea was to use pre-paid air time as a basis for the repayment of loans and Safaricom would use its agents who dealt with air-time sales as 'aggregators' of such airtime and then converted to cash that would prepay the micro loans. During the pilot program, it was observed that the M-Pesa technological platform could be used for other financial services such as payment for trading between businesses, as an overnight safe since banks closed earlier than M-Pesa agent shops, people depositing cash in one pilot area and withdrawing in another and people sending airtime purchased by M-Pesa directly to their relations up country as a kind of informal remittance (Buku and Meredith, 2013). When the pilot ended in May 2006, the initial concept of M-Pesa as a means for micro-credit disbursement and repayment took a back seat and more focus was placed on its new capabilities realized during the pilot program. This was made possible by the amendment of communication law which recognized electronic units of money. Therefore, in March 2007, Safaricom fully launched the M-Pesa technological platform but now the product can use electronic units of cash stored in the SIM card and the role of the agents was now to transform cash into electronic units of cash and vice versa. Before the launch, Safaricom recruited about 750 M-Pesa agents and invested in a nationwide advertising campaign to provide customer training in the use of mobile phone technology and the M-Pesa service.

The M-Pesa model together with the legal definition and risk mitigation forms an interesting set of regulatory innovativeness. From the outset, the Central Bank of Kenya (CBK) argued that M-Pesa was a bank product that was unique in that it was a partnership between a Telco and a commercial bank. The Telco (Safaricom) provided the transmission function of funds via the mobile phone. The funds would be held in a Trust account in the bank and it formed the transactions platform. This would work as a pay-in and pay-out platform and the only concern would be residual balances in the individual micro-accounts. This M-Pesa model allowed Safaricom to issue electronic money in exchange of cash at par value and was stored in the SIM card for the customer. The way it worked was that once the electronic money was stored in the SIM card, it was simultaneously loaded into the trust account at the Commercial Bank of Africa and this account was under the custody of trustees. So, the trust account was not a Safaricom business account. The funds were held in trust and were separated from the funds of Safaricom and so Safaricom could not access the funds and in addition the funds in the trust account were not part of the Safaricom balance sheet. So, if Safaricom were to be bankrupt, the funds were still safe from any Safaricom creditors. Trust accounts thus became the payments system platform in a commercial bank, thus separating regulatory issues for Banks and Telecommunication Company and this provided the market with confidence. In addition, the trust account being a payments platform allowed layers of insurance that would protect the platform to be developed.

The literature on M-Pesa revolution has developed in a three-dimensional approach; the policy question, the requirements for a supporting legal framework and the operational environment where risks were mitigated to boost confidence in the market place. First, the policy question or the quest for a policy solution starts by the time M-Pesa product was rolled out into the market, the outreach issues via a network of Safaricom agents had been resolved, but then the outcomes and the dynamics of market developments that took place after the roll-out endogenously forced the Central Bank of Kenya (CBK) not only to adopt policies that were not consistent with M-Pesa growth and support, but also those that would provide an array of instruments and solutions to support the innovations in the market that demanded more and more from the CBK. This means enhancing a public policy for financial inclusion as well as developing appropriate technical capacity for regulation. The layout was that M-Pesa was first a money transfer product dominated by person to person (P2P) money transfer. But this required a national payments and settlement legal framework and guidelines for the market. The legal framework was not in place, this is what made M-Pesa in Kenya very noble and novel, that it was operationalized without a direct legal framework to regulate it. Second, to overcome the legal vacuum, the Trust Law was invoked. This required the payment solution/platform to be developed as a Trust account owned by Trustees and the Central Bank of Kenya provided guidelines on how it would be operated. Third, the guidelines to be followed by the Telco agents had to be developed and agreed. These guidelines had to be agreed between the Communication Commission of Kenya (CCK), the regulator for Telcos, and the Central Bank of Kenya (CBK). Finally, once all these technical issues were resolved, the next issue was confidence boosting and showing how the risks would be mitigated. These dimensions of the market development, policy response and the reactions to the existing conditions in the financial market allowed the innovations to take root with a 'test-and-learn' approach and at the end the platform was developed and was operational. This platform, the M-Pesa technological platform, has enabled millions of Kenyans to make payments and send remittances. The Central Bank monitored the average residual balance in M-Pesa accounts. This whole setup provided the payments platform and also liquidity distribution among agents that was efficient, effective and transparent. Safaricom supervised and regulated its agents. The network of agents formed the point of service countrywide. This formed the backbone of investment for M-Pesa technological platform to work and serve the Kenyan population. Having shown the initial developments of M-Pesa, it now becomes easier to dwell on its dynamic nature and the impact on financial inclusion.

3.3 M-Pesa as a Platform for Financial Inclusion

The M-Pesa technological platform provides a firm foundation for mobile phone financial transactions, mobile phone based banking and access to financial services in general. Among the binding constraints that sustained financial exclusion in Kenya were levels of income, the irregular flow of that income and the physical distance to a bank branch or financial service point. In one stroke, M-Pesa seems to have solved these binding constraints and turned tables from financial exclusion to financial inclusion. Fig. 3.1 shows how different financial services have used the M-Pesa platform to enlarge the space and improve accessibility of the financial markets. Three types of financial services are shown. At the center is mobile payment. Initially, the M-Pesa platform was used for money transfer and quickly developed into a platform for payments of goods and services. Then over time mobile banking and finance have been incorporated.

Most participants who entered this ecosystem did not have or did not need a bank account. It was an easy access for them as the mobile phone number became the account number. For those with bank accounts, they were integrated with their bank accounts and could withdraw money directly from their accounts using their mobile phones. All M-Pesa account holders

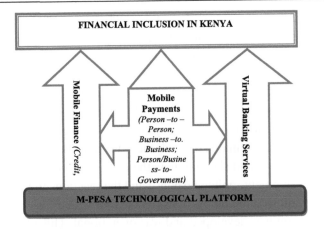

Figure 3.1: The M-Pesa platform and financial services products.
(Source: Author)

would then benefit from a range of financial services and this has pushed the frontier of financial inclusion in Kenya. Other financial service providers have also increased their range of financial services and products by using the M-Pesa platform. Currently most of the commercial banks and Savings and Credit Co-operatives (SACCOs) are offering services through mobile phone platforms. New types of financial services are emerging as individuals transact using mobile phone financial services leaving valuable digital data trails (Manyika et al., 2016). Additionally, other financial subsectors like insurance, pensions and capital markets have found the platform useful to roll out their products (Jones et al., 2016). Generally, the mobile phone platform presents a full menu of financial services at the comfort of Kenyans' homes. Through the M-Pesa platform, millions of Kenyans can now receive and send money, buy airtime for themselves or transfer to others, receive wages, save, pay school fees, pay utility bills, among other services.

M-Pesa has also led to increased efficiency in financial transactions. This has led to increased use and participation in the financial system which has consequently lowered the transactions unit costs. Consequently, the general transactional costs of financial services in the country have been substantially reduced. Use of M-Pesa technological platform has lowered the cost of physical distance to financial access touch points that was previously provided by the bank branches, micro-finance institutions or SACCOs. In Africa, given its terrain and geography, physical distance to a financial access touch point was perhaps one important barrier to formal financial services. The M-Pesa technological platform seems to have solved that major handicap and its associated costs. Additionally, M-Pesa has enabled the financial service providers to develop new business models, offering expanded services to customers leading to potential new revenue streams to providers. The mobile phone financial services platform has enabled providers to serve customers who transact frequently and in small amounts cost effectively (Manyika et al., 2016). In addition, there is evidence of an increase in savings. Whether these savings have been invested or have been used for consumption smoothing will require further data points and analysis in the future. Finally, it is rare in Africa to find a financial product that transcends across market segments. Markets in Africa are segmented by different factors, but levels of income and physical location/distance stand out. M-Pesa transcends all these market segments.

3.3.1 Strong Banks Have Emerged With Strong Intermediation Capacity

The M-Pesa technological platform has supported the development of financial markets through four innovative and endogenous developments. From money transfers to payments and to virtual savings services and to virtual credit supply/provision and to cross-border payments and international remittances. These four innovative and virtuous generations of the M-Pesa technological platform have shaped the financial market and the developments in the banking sector in Kenya. New products have been introduced in the market that have allowed the poor and the middle-income groups to benefit from the financial services at affordable prices and within reach. Such products include: Savings products such as M-Shwari, introduced three years ago, which has over 15 million customers out of which 67% are aged between 18 and 34 years. There are also KCB – Pesa and M-Kesho. These products have led to increased savings in the country. The same products have moved from virtual savings platforms to provide affordable short-term credit platforms propelled by generated information capital of market participants. This has revolutionized the banking system in Kenya in two fronts. First, the M-Pesa technological platform has provided a means of managing bank accounts, including micro-accounts especially for banks that had no appropriate technology for managing small value accounts that had irregular flows. The Kenyan banks have used this platform to reach to more Kenyans and this has created mountains of deposits. Fig. 3.2 shows the number of bank branches and the distribution across rural and urban areas in Kenya. The branch outlets have increased from 534 in 2005 to 1443 in 2015. The rural branch network has not been left behind either, growing from 181 branches in 2005 to 660 in 2015. The acceleration of branch outlets seems to start in 2007/2008 period. In addition, 11 Kenyan banks have expanded to Eastern Africa region, with over 310 branch outlets.

Second, M-Pesa technological platform has provided an important avenue to generate credit scores for use in pricing short term credit. It has thus developed into a platform for short-term credit provision. These credit scores generated from savings and transactions data can change the environment for credit provision in Kenya by solving the information asymmetry problem that will in turn revolutionize the collateral technology that has worked as major handicap for credit market development in Africa.

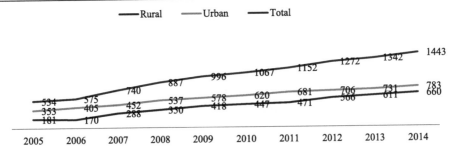

—Rural   —Urban   —Total

Figure 3.2: Growth in branch network in Kenya.
(Source: Central Bank of Kenya)

Figure 3.3: Growth in bank accounts in Kenya.
(Source: Central Bank of Kenya)

Fig. 3.3 shows the growth of deposit accounts in the same period, 2005–2015. Deposit accounts have increased from 2.55 million in 2005 to nearly 34 million in 2015 with over 90% of these deposit accounts being micro accounts and now at 29% and 94% are micro savings accounts. The number of micro accounts has increased more than twelve-fold from about 2.14 million accounts in 2005 to over 32 million accounts in 2015. This growth is attributable to reduced costs of maintaining micro accounts and introduction of innovative instruments targeting lower tier market segments – using the M-Pesa platform to open savings accounts like M-Shwari, KCB-Pesa and other products.

Looking closely at the growth of micro-accounts, the acceleration seems to start in 2007, from 4.12 million accounts to 8 million accounts in 2009. The operationalization of microfinance banks through enactment of the Microfinance Act, 2006 and the subsequent Microfinance (Amendment) Act, 2013 has enhanced the outreach of financial services targeting mainly SMEs that are key drivers of economic growth in Kenya. The progression from then on is driven by the dynamics in the market and it is a period that approximately 10,000 accounts were being registered on the M-Pesa technological platform daily. By 2010, one of the complementary additions to the branch network was the successful launch of the Agency Banking. Two banks started to appoint agents in 2010 and, so far, 16 banks have appointed over 3,500 agents. The pattern of branch networks, the success of the agency model and the success of

M-Pesa, all seem to corroborate the pattern of deposit accounts and the vibrancy of the banking sector in Kenya over this period.

The ease of collecting large deposits provides banks with capacity to grow and intermediate. Most micro savers are 'target savers', they save for a targeted investment and so the deposits/savings stay in the bank accounts for a period (that is why affordable credit can minimize the savings-investment cycles for such savers). Kenyan banks have seized this opportunity as well as used the M-Pesa platform to manage micro accounts. The M-Pesa technological platform has therefore led to the emergence of strong banks with the commercial banks and microfinance banks leveraging on the platform to manage micro-accounts, build deposits and extend financial services to previously unbanked and underserved population. The Kenyan banks have invested heavily on this technological platform and this has allowed them to develop capacity to grow and serve their market niches – strong banks can weather shocks and roll out competitive products for their market niches. From the data analyzed and from the time M-Pesa hit the Kenyan financial market, we can conclude that M-Pesa technological platform has driven financial inclusion with speed and dynamism. It has supported strong banks to emerge, by providing a technological platform not only to manage micro accounts but also transactions in general that take place any time of the day and night. In this regard, branch outlets, bank deposits and loans accounts have increased. This has provided banks with a large deposit base and capacity for growth.

3.3.2 Financial Inclusion Has Improved the Environment for Monetary Policy in Kenya

The role of the Central Bank is to conduct monetary policy which works more efficiently when financial markets are fairly developed. In Kenya, perhaps the starting point is participation in the bank-dominated financial sector. Most of the population were financially excluded and over time with declining economic opportunities, most commercial banks had withdrawn their branch networks from the rural areas and poor peri-urban centers. Secondly, most transactions were taking place in cash and a large proportion of currency outside the banking system. The introduction of M-Pesa platform changed the traditional holding of currency outside of banks and the preference of cash. These developments affected the velocity of money and the money multiplier, the basic pillars of monetary policy framework at the time.

As soon as M-Pesa hit the ground, currency outside the banking system started to decline and the velocity of money started to decline. Since 2009, velocity of money and proportion of currency outside banks have declined significantly reflecting financial deepening and increased financial innovation. The declining currency outside banks and the significant velocity decline reflect changes in behavior of holding cash – people are keeping less and less money outside of banks and prefer less cash in their daily transactions. The monetary policy framework at

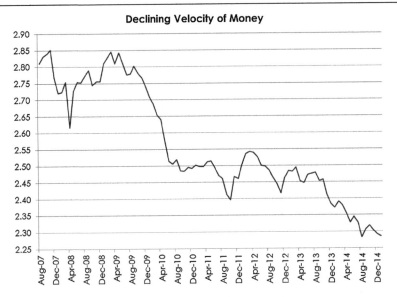

Figure 3.4: Declining velocity of money.
(Source: Central Bank of Kenya)

the time relied on the assumption that velocity of money was constant and the relationship be-tween base money and broad money, the multiplier, was stable and predictable. From 2007, the picture changed as Figs. 3.4–3.6 show and the monetary policy framework had to be re-vised to incorporate these changing dynamics.

In addition, due to innovations taking place in the banking sector through the M-Pesa techno-logical platform, the money multiplier has been rising, see Fig. 3.6.

Declining velocity and rising money multiplier reflects the fact that money demand function has shifted and thus became unstable. This provided a chance to revise the monetary policy framework to a forward-looking framework. This has created an environment for monetary policy signals to work through the market effectively and efficiently. Monetary policy works through signals in the market: these signals cannot be processed by market agents if they are not included in the financial system. In this case, financial inclusion allows access and partic-ipation in the financial system and this has provided a better environment for monetary policy to influence the market.

3.3.3 Financial Inclusion and the Digital Financial Platform Has Improved the AML/CFT Regime in Kenya

During this time, 2007–2014, even with all these developments and innovations taking place in Kenya, the Anti-Money Laundering (AML) and Combating Financing of Terrorism (CFT),

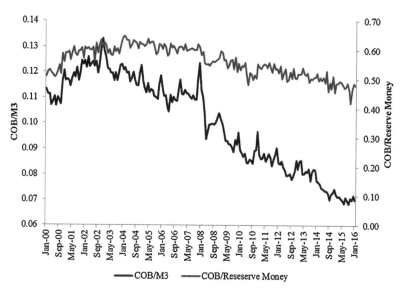

Figure 3.5: Decline in cash outside bank in relation to broad and reserve money.
(Source: Central Bank of Kenya)

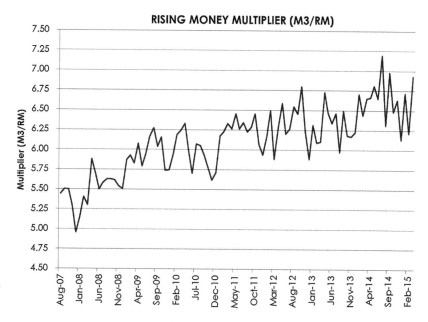

Figure 3.6: Rising money multiplier.
(Source: Central Bank of Kenya)

the AML/CFT regime in Kenya as per the Financial Action Task Force (FATF) classification was considered inadequate (in subsequent years Kenya was placed under the 'dark gray' list with possibilities of counter measures). One of the misunderstandings was that M-Pesa would lead to a massive money laundering in the economy. My argument in FATF meetings was that financial exclusion was more dangerous for AML/CFT regime in Kenya and M-Pesa was supporting financial inclusion and so a better environment to monitor financial transactions. In order to enhance AML/CFT on this micro transaction platform, stringent measures were put in place at the time to adhere to AML/CFT requirements at the bank and at the M-Pesa platform levels. The Central Bank of Kenya (CBK) ensured that regulations were in place to ensure that the M-Pesa platform remains a low risk money transfer system. The CBK has maintained a ceiling on transactions threshold as well as how much money can be stored in the SIM card. These included limiting the size (value) of mobile transaction which was set at Kshs 35,000 (then about $500) per transaction at any one time (now set at Kshs 70,000 per transaction with a maximum transaction amount of Kshs 140,000 per day) and maximum limit of Kshs 50,000 that a SIM card could hold (about $700) at any one time (now set at a maximum limit of Kshs 100,000). The maximum limit discourages the SIM card holders from making it look like an alternative bank or holding account. These regulations mean that the M-Pesa transactions are keenly monitored, hence improving environment for AML/CFT regime in Kenya. The point that should be appreciated is that AML/CFT regime worsens with financial exclusion and in a high cash transaction economy. With increasing and successful financial inclusion, transactions and cash movements in banks can be monitored. In addition, a technological platform like M-Pesa provides a versatile and dynamic platform for data generation and monitoring. This further improves the AML/CFT regime for the economy. This has allowed the FATF to upgrade Kenya's AML/CFT regime to a 'Grey List' – that is, Kenya has a satisfactory AML/CFT regime.

3.3.4 A Game Changer for a Variety of Opportunities for Kenyans

The M-Pesa platform has enabled m-commerce and on-demand services to thrive in Kenya. The platform has enabled increased person to person, person to business, business to person, citizens to government, government to citizen payments. In 2009, Safaricom launched its pay bill service on the M-Pesa platform. Since then, Safaricom has partnered with 25 banks and over 700 businesses to facilitate fund deposits, bank transfers and the regular payment of utility bills, insurance premiums, and loan installments (Buku and Meredith, 2013). Currently, there are several businesses using the online shopping platform to reach customers who eventually make their payments through the M-Pesa platform. Additionally, most of the utility companies have embraced M-Pesa payments which allows many Kenyans pay their utility bills via M-Pesa. This has given a boost to the M-Pesa technological platform in the country which has opened the door to more businesses embracing the "Pay with M-Pesa" mode of transaction. For example, Manyika et al. (2016) presents an example of a cashless "academy in a box" launched by Bridge International Academies where the school administration is run entirely on tablets and smart phones, eliminating the need for accounting and finance functions and their associated costs. In this new business model, enabled by the M-Pesa platform, school fees and teachers' salaries are paid monthly using M-Pesa. This consequently means that the parents, teachers, and even the suppliers associated with the schools should be on the M-Pesa platform hence increased financial inclusion. M-Pesa has also had an impact on the ability of individuals to share risk. By expanding the informal risk-sharing networks, M-Pesa platform allows for more efficient risk sharing since it facilitates timely transfer of small amounts of money before conditions worsen to levels that cause long-term damage (Jack and Suri, 2011).

Moreover, the expanded reach of M-Pesa technological platform across the country has offered an opportunity for the government to develop the *eCitizen* platform (an e-government platform) where the citizens can apply for government services and pay via mobile money. This has significantly reduced the red tapes in access to government services and has been consequently embraced by many Kenyans who no longer must pay brokers to access government services. In addition, the government has used the M-Pesa platform to support its social protection programs. For example, Jones et al. (2016) has shown that the government of Kenya has used the M-Pesa platform to target the old and physically disadvantaged in a social protection program. These government initiatives have further improved the financial inclusion frontier in the country since the government services are on demand all over the country.

3.4 Impact of M-Pesa Revolution on Financial Inclusion

The M-Pesa technological platform has made it easier for Kenyans to access financial services. Starting with transactions then virtual banking services, the M-Pesa platform supports a menu of financial services with significant effect on financial inclusion outcomes. Ten years of data points tracking reveal some interesting results for financial inclusion in Kenya. We use the available four financial survey data from 2006: before M-Pesa to 2009, after M-Pesa was introduced in Kenya, and two subsequent surveys in 2013 and 2016. A vivid picture on financial inclusion seem to emerge as Table 3.1 shows.

- The proportion of the adult population included in both formal and other formal financial services has increased from 26.4% in 2006 to 75.3% in 2016. Those preferring the informal financial services have declined from 35.2% in 2006 to 7.2% in 2016.
- The proportion of the adult population totally excluded from the financial services has declined from 38.4% in 2006 to 17.4% in 2016.

Table 3.1: Financial inclusion profile in Kenya 2006–2016 (percentage of the adult population).

Financial Access Category	Total%	Urban%	Rural%	Male%	Female%
2006					
Formal	18.9	32.0	18.9	23.8	14.3
Other Formal	7.5	22.8	8.5	9.2	5.9
Informal	35.2	3.5	39.2	29.5	40.5
Excluded	38.4	41.6	37.4	37.5	39.3
2009					
Formal	21.0	40.3	15.9	25.7	16.7
Other Formal	19.5	22.1	18.7	22.4	18.0
Informal	26.8	16.5	29.5	19.5	33.3
Excluded	32.7	21.1	35.9	32.4	33.0
2013					
Formal	32.4	46.6	24.9	39.1	26.1
Other Formal	34.5	33.4	34.9	32.1	37.3
Informal	7.8	4.3	9.7	4.7	10.7
Excluded	25.3	15.8	30.5	24.1	26.5
2016					
Formal	42.3	59.9	32.1	50.4	34.6
Other Formal	33.0	26.4	36.9	29.3	36.6
Informal	7.2	4.1	9.0	4.1	10.2
Excluded	17.4	9.5	22.0	16.2	18.6

Source: Various FinAccess Surveys: 2006, 2009, 2013, 2016

- The proportion of women excluded has declined from 39.3% in 2006 to 33% in 2009, to 26.5% in 2013 and further to 18.6% in 2016. The acceleration seems to coincide with M-Pesa and a whole range of accessibility to the financial system between 2009 and 2016 where data points are comparable.
- The men's profile of financial inclusion has been relatively better. Those excluded have declined from 37.5% in 2006 to 24.6% in 2013, and drastically declined to 16.2% in 2016.
- In terms of rural–urban divide, financial exclusion has followed the national average, but urbanites have a better financial access than their rural counterparts. By 2016, only about 9.5% of the urban adult population was financially excluded compared to 22% of the rural population. The preference of mobile phone financial services across rural/urban and across gender and age cohorts seems to explain the financial inclusion and accessibility of financial services.

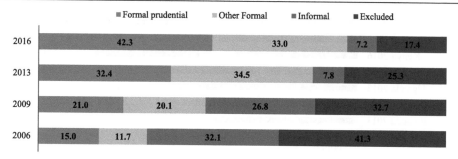

Figure 3.7: Kenya's financial inclusion profile: 2000–2016.
(Source: Various FinAccess Surveys)

- An important and striking result is the significant decline on the preference of informal financial services. This has declined from 35.2% of the adult population in 2006 to 26.8% in 2009, and further drastically to 7.8% and 7.2% in 2013 and 2016, respectively.

In a sense the introduction of M-Pesa and other financial services products has provided a framework for a bankable population to emerge since 2007 that led to 27.9% of bankable population accessing money transfer services by 2009. The 2013 and 2016 FinAccess surveys show even more spectacular results on financial inclusion as well as use of financial services. The results of financial inclusion profile in Kenya between 2006 and 2016 attest to this success.

The results in Table 3.1 have can also be replicated by a summary set of results provided in Fig. 3.7 that can be summarized as follows:

- Those being served by the formal financial services providers have increased to 75.3% of the adult population in 2016 compared to 66.9% in 2013 and 30.5% in 2009 and 27.4% in 2006.
- The informal financial channels were serving only 7.2% of the adult population in 2016 having declined from 35.2% in 2006 to 26.8% in 2009, and further to 7.8% in 2013.
- Even though the financially excluded population is still high, however, there has been a successful drive to inclusion from 41.3% in 2006, declined to 32.7% in 2009, further down 25.3% in 2013 and now declining further to 17.4% in 2016. This has been quite a dramatic decline on the proportion of the financially excluded population.

In the last 10 years, Kenya has accelerated financial inclusion to surplus its comparators as evidenced in Fig. 3.8. Kenya appears to have come a long way, it is ranked third taking after Mauritius and South Africa on financial inclusion indicators.

The financial inclusion picture that has emerged is consistent with the fact that the M-Pesa revolution has allowed accelerating financial inclusion in Kenya where new financial services

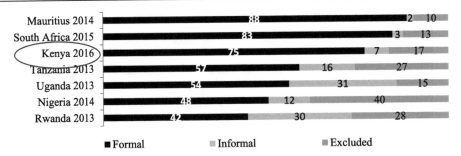

Figure 3.8: Financial inclusion comparisons in some successful African countries.

and products have emerged: encouraged by innovation and sound regulation, new delivery channels have been developed and these channels are effective, transparent and efficient and that a payments system has emerged that has reached the poor as well as the wealthy in the same speed. Other financial services seem to have been complemented by the M-Pesa financial services:

- The proportion of the adult population using banks has increased to 38.4% compared to 29.2% in 2013 and 14% in 2006 before the M-Pesa technological platform was launched in Kenya.
- Insurance is serving 23.2% of the adult population using the 2016 survey compared to 4.9% in 2006.
- Savings products in the banking sector, M-Shwari and KCB-Pesa have attracted 18% of the adult population – this is virtual banking service. The survey results show that more Kenyans are now using mobile financial services and mobile banking on a daily basis.

The M-Pesa revolution has also led to an increase in financial access touch points across the country. The strong growth in mobile money transfers in Kenya has been supported by an expanding Agent network across the country, dominated by M-Pesa agents. The successful growth of M-Pesa agents' network across the country, handling substantial amount of money, made the commercial banks confident in pursuing agency banking. This has led to a significant increase in financial services providers' outlets across the country hence enhancing financial inclusion. The agency banking model has allowed banks to locate non-traditional outlets in remote areas where "brick and mortar" branches and other outlets are not financially feasible. The introduction of agency banking in May 2010 has propelled growth in the levels of formal financial inclusion cost-effectively. In most of the cases, the agents for the mobile phone financial service providers had a dual role as agents of banks and M-Pesa agents. This implies that the penetration of bank agents has leveraged on the mobile phone financial service providers' network across the country. Consequently, financial access touch points in Kenya have continued to expand. These include an increase in bank branches, Automated

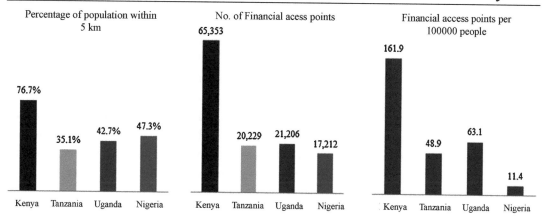

Figure 3.9: Comparison of financial access touch points.
(Source: Country Geospatial Surveys, 2013)

Teller Machines (ATMs), Telco agents and Agency network for banks that have increased to over 35,000 since their inception in 2010.

Financial access touch points have expanded in Kenya and it does appear that the country is ahead of its peers on financial inclusion profile. It is seen from Fig. 3.9 that 76.7% of the population are within 5 km of financial access points – compared with 35.1% in Tanzania, 42.7% in Uganda and 47.3% in Nigeria. In addition, financial access points per 100,000 people stands at 161.9 in Kenya, compared with 48.9 in Tanzania, 63.1 in Uganda and 11.4 in Nigeria.

In addition to increasing the financial access touch points across the country, M-Pesa technological platform has played a critical role as an entry point into the financial system for the bottom 40% of the Kenyan population who are poor (with low levels of education and capital accumulation) and mostly unbanked. In the past, financial markets have failed to meet the needs of the poor majority, especially the poor living in rural areas and poor peri-urban locations in a way that is affordable, convenient, and safe.

3.5 Conclusion

The conclusion that can be drawn from the sections of this chapter is that the M-Pesa technological platform has been a catalyst and a driver for financial inclusion in Kenya. First, M-Pesa platform has been an important tool for revolutionizing the payments and settlement system in the country. The platform has supported the national retail payments evolution and revolution – transactions per day are now close to 4.5% of annualized GDP. The payments and settlements through the M-Pesa platform are in real time, efficient, effective and transparent. The M-Pesa platform has ensured that the poor and SMEs can access the financial system, they are transaction heavy. The M-Pesa platform transcends across all market segments in Kenya and has supported the development in other financial markets like micro insurance, capital markets and pensions, as well government's social protection program. As an efficient and effective payments platform, M-Pesa has been useful for government's targeted social protection for poor households and physically disadvantaged persons for financial transfers. Additionally, the M-Pesa platform has been useful to track fraudulent flows into personal accounts. Financial inclusion as well as the ease in monitoring the M-Pesa platform has improved the regulatory environment in Kenya and improved the AML/CFT regime.

Second, the M-Pesa technological platform is an effective tool for financial inclusion and has supported banks as a platform to manage micro accounts – brought the unbanked into the banking system in Kenya. Most of the Kenyans were unbanked due to a combination of factors, the most prominent ones are low income levels, irregular flows of such income and inhibiting physical distances to a bank or a financial service point. This technological platform has allowed banks to develop capacity to grow and to serve their market niches – strong banks can weather shocks and roll out competitive products for their market niches. The M-Pesa revolution has also led to an increase in financial access touch points (growth in M-Pesa agents' network and agency banking) across the country. Majority of Kenyans can now receive financial services at their door step. Almost 77% of Kenya's adult population live within 5 km of a financial service point. Between 2007 and 2016, branch networks of Kenyan banks have expanded from about 575 to 1443 branches. The rural branches have even expanded faster from about 170 in 2007 to 660 in 2016 and the microfinance institutions have also equally increased. In addition, Kenyan banks have expanded to Eastern Africa region, with over 310 branch outlets. Consequently, strong banks have emerged – branch outlets, bank deposits and loans accounts have increased. The customer base has also increased. Deposit accounts have increased from about 4.72 million accounts in 2007 to over 35 million accounts in 2015. This has provided banks with a large deposit base and capacity for growth.

Third, M-Pesa technological platform allows an efficient platform for savings and has supported the evolution of credit market development. The developments in credit markets using credit scoring procedures have the potential to change the collateral technology in the credit market. This is in addition to the Credit Reference Bureaus (CRBs) that have provided the base of credit information and information capital will in future transform the credit market in Kenya. The celebrated M-Shwari and KCB Pesa types of products (and M-Pawa in Tanzania) provided short-term credit and pricing related to individual risk profile, have been the natural development from the virtual banking system. The collateral technology has been a major barrier to affordable credit and financial sector growth in many African countries, the transformation will open avenues for further financial inclusion and now household investments.

Fourth, the M-Pesa technological platform has boosted financial deepening in Kenya. There have been increased financial products and product diversification and this has changed the profile of financial depth. In addition, there has also been a sustained endogenous demand to complete and strengthen the financial infrastructure – deposit insurance, information capital, and financial intelligence unit. M-Pesa type of products have pushed financial inclusion profile and with it an endogenous demand for regulatory reforms, regulatory capacity and regulatory technology. The Kenyan economy has also witnessed new institutions and policy reforms/designs that will in future protect and support the development of the market.

Finally, the M-Pesa technological platform has induced a digital financial services evolution that has improved the environment for monetary policy. A vibrant financial market in Kenya that has improved the profile of financial inclusion and financial market development has appropriately improved the monetary policy environment. Currency outside the banking sector as a ratio of broad money has declined – a signal for less money being held in "unsafe" places. This means that outside money is declining and inside money increasing – much easier for economic agents to process monetary policy signals – which leads to an improved environment for monetary policy. We can then conclude that the M-Pesa technological platform has supported the development of a better environment for forward-looking monetary policy to replace years of financial repression and reactive policies. In addition, it is rare to find a product like M-Pesa in Africa that transcends across market segments and seems to coordinate all markets. In Kenya, you can use your M-Pesa account to pay for a meal in a five-star hotel, shop at a high-end mall, pay for goods to a rural shopkeeper and pay for a cup of tea in a roadside kiosk.

References

Buku, M.W., Meredith, M.W., 2013. Safaricom and M-Pesa in Kenya: financial inclusion and financial integrity. Washington Journal of Law, Technology & Arts 8 (3). Mobile Money Symposium 2013.

Hinz, M., 2014. M-PESA: the Best of Both Worlds, Financial Inclusion Flash. BBVA Research Department. Available at https://www.bbvaresearch.com/en/publicaciones/M-Pesa-the-best-of-both-worlds/ (accessed on 15th October, 2016).

Hughes, N., Lonie, S., 2007. M-PESA: mobile money for the "unbanked" turning cell phones into 24-hour tellers in Kenya. Innovations 2 (1–2), 63–81.

Jack, W., Suri, T., 2011. Mobile Money: The Economics of M-Pesa. NBER Working Paper 16721, National Bureau of Economic Research, Cambridge, MA.

Jayamaha, R., 2015. Innovate to win: innovate for financial inclusion, 27th Anniversary Convention 2015. Available at http://www.apbsrilanka.org/articales/27_ann_2015/2_7th_Dr.Ranee_Jayamaha.pdf (accessed on 15th October, 2016).

Jones, E., Ngaire Woods, N., Ndung'u, S.N., 2016. Consolidating Africa's Mobile Banking Revolution, May 2016 Conference Report. Global Economic Governance Programme and Blavatnik School of Government, University of Oxford.

Klein, M., Mayer, C., 2012. Banking and Financial Inclusion: The Regulatory Lessons. World Bank Policy Research Working Paper 5664, Washington.

Manyika, J., Lund, S., Singer, M., White, O., Berry, C., 2016. Digital Finance for All: Powering Inclusive Growth in Emerging Economies. September 2016, McKinsey Global Institute, McKinsey & Company, San Francisco.

Morawczynski, O., Pickens, M., 2009. Poor People Using Mobile Financial Services: Observations on Customer Usage and Impact from M-PESA, CGAP Brief. Available at https://www.cgap.org/sites/default/files/CGAP-Brief-Poor-People-Using-Mobile-Financial-Services-Observations-on-Customer-Usage-and-Impact-from-M-PESA-Aug-2009.pdf (accessed on 15th October, 2016).

Muthiora, B., 2015. Enabling Mobile Money Policies in Kenya: Fostering a Digital Financial Revolution. GSMA.

Mwangi, S. Kimenyi, Njuguna, S. Ndung'u, 2009. Expanding the Financial Services Frontier: Lessons from Mobile Phone Banking in Kenya; Brookings Institution, October 16, 2009.

CHAPTER 4

Financial Inclusion in the Digital Age

Anju Patwardhan

Contents

DOI: 10.1016/B978-0-12-810441-5.00004-X

4.1 Financial Inclusion

Financial inclusion is defined as means having universal access to reasonably priced financial services, provided by sound and sustainable institutions. It includes saving, investing, borrowing and insurance. The market for the financially underserved includes those who are traditionally defined as unbanked and underbanked.

In recent years, a lot of progress has been made in promoting financial inclusion through basic account ownership for individuals but billions of people in developed and emerging markets remain financially underserved. There are over two billion unbanked adults in the world who do not have access to basic financial services. Several billion more are underbanked i.e. they may have basic accounts but are underserved by the financial services industry in areas related to savings, insurance and access to credit.

Many of the unbanked and underbanked individuals are financially unhealthy and insecure. Financial insecurity is not just a low-income bottom-of-the-pyramid problem in the unbanked population in developing countries. It has been democratized. It is an equal-opportunity problem impacting many in developed markets too and that includes nearly half the American population.

Achieving financial inclusion and financial security are not an end but a means to an end. They are broadly recognized as critical to reducing poverty and achieving inclusive economic growth. Studies show that financial inclusion enables individuals to start and expand businesses, invest in education, manage risks better and absorb financial shocks.

It also has positive effects on consumption, employment status and income and on some aspects of physical and mental health. For both individuals and small firms, greater access to financial services including access to credit, helps reduce income inequality and accelerates economic growth.

Under the United Nations' Sustainable Development Goals, greater financial inclusion is a key goal as it enables poorer households and informal economies to increase resilience and capture economic opportunities.

There is increasing awareness of this need and opportunity across the private, public, and social sectors. Policy makers and regulators are beginning to making financial inclusion a priority in financial sector development. Several governments are introducing comprehensive measures to improve access and usage of financial services. International organizations, including the G-20 and the World Bank, are beginning to formulate strategies to promote financial inclusion. More than 50 countries have set formal targets and ambitious goals for financial inclusion.

The progress in financial inclusion has been slow but momentum has picked up significantly in the last few years. This has brought in several new players from the private sector who are interested in 'for-profit' impact investing. Technology has become a key enabler for promoting financial inclusion in a commercially viable manner in both developing and developed markets. A consumer financial services revolution is taking place around the globe, powered by mobile phones, technological innovations and changing consumer mindsets. Several countries have started to benefit from harnessing digital financial services as a developmental tool to support inclusive economic growth and reducing income inequalities.

China and India are taking the lead in this aspect and becoming role models for other countries in supporting inclusive growth.

4.2 The Financially Underserved Consumer

For the unbanked, account ownership as per the World Bank Global Findex[1] database is the most widely used definition of financial inclusion. It is defined as having an account either at a financial institution (such as a bank, credit union, cooperative, or microfinance institution) or through a mobile money provider (for phone-based services used to pay bills or to send or receive money).

The other commonly used definition is the one provided by the World Economic Forum which defines full financial inclusion as providing convenient access to a full range of quality, affordable financial products and services to everyone around the world in ways that are economically sustainable.[2]

In recent years, a lot of progress has been made in promoting financial inclusion for unbanked individuals for their saving needs through new mobile payment systems and increased access to bank accounts. World Bank research[3] indicates that in the three years leading up to 2014, the number of unbanked adults globally has dropped 20 percent from 2.5 billion to 2 billion, increasing the percentage of account owners from 51 percent to 62 percent.

In developing economies, this represents an increase of 13 percent in account ownership to 55 percent during this period. Nearly half the unbanked adults live in Asia-Pacific region and their numbers are dropping rapidly supported by improvements in mobile infrastructure, increasing smartphone penetration, launch of easy-to-use products by financial technology ("fintech") companies and government initiatives. In the three years to 2014, account ownership has improved from 64 percent to 79 percent in China and from 35 percent to 53 percent in India.

Innovations in technology, particularly mobile money, have helped with rapid expansion in Sub-Saharan Africa. Mobile wallets are being increasingly used for sending and receiving money, for making payments such as utility bills and school fees, for online shopping and for various other services.

As of 2014	Number of adults (in million)	Account ownership	Unbanked adults	Unbanked adults (in million)
World	5231	62%	38%	2014
Emerging Countries	4354	55%	45%	1961
OECD countries	977	94%	6%	53
India	888	53%	47%	416
China	1113	79%	21%	235
Indonesia	178	36%	64%	114
Bangladesh	110	31%	69%	76
Mexico	87	39%	61%	53
Brazil	152	68%	32%	49
United States	254	94%	6%	16

Source: World Bank Global Findex database, 2014

The 2 billion unbanked, representing 38 percent of all adults globally, remain excluded from accessing financial services. It may seem incredible in this digitally connected and technologically advanced world that 38 percent of adults in the world exist as financial nomads. They don't have basic bank accounts or mobile wallets, earn in cash and transact exclusively in cash. Many of them live in poverty across Africa, Asia, and Latin America. If you think of the world as a financial pyramid, these two billion adults are at the bottom of it.

At the top of the pyramid are five percent of adults that consist of wealthier people living mostly in developed countries with easy access to banks and abundant financial services. The middle of the pyramid includes 57 percent of adults globally who are underbanked. They have basic accounts but many may not have access to full range of other financial services such as insurance, investing or borrowing.

Globally, big gaps also remain in financial inclusion amongst women, poor people and those living in rural areas. Nearly 20 percent of unbanked adults live in low-income countries in extreme poverty, earning less than two dollars per day. Fifty-five percent of unbanked are women.

The unbanked rely on informal financial solutions that are often less flexible and more expensive than formal alternatives—and frequently fail to deliver when needed the most. They do not have a safe way to save or invest money and often save in the form of livestock, gold, or through informal saving groups. They do not have access to credit and end up borrowing from personal network of family and friends, or from money lenders or payday lenders at very high interest rates.

Account ownership is a good measure of financial inclusion for the unbanked but is not an accurate measure of full financial inclusion for most of the global population that belongs to the underbanked category. While accurate global data for the underbanked is not available, the Federal Deposit Insurance Corporation ("FDIC") in the United States publishes information on unbanked and underbanked households. As per this, 16 million adults in the United States are unbanked (similarly to the World Bank numbers) and another 51 million adults are underbanked.

The numbers stated above are for individuals. The percentage of small businesses globally that do not have access to credit is even higher. Amongst the micro-enterprises, 70 percent have a bank account but less than 5 percent have access to term loans from banks and only 1 percent to working capital facilities. In ASEAN alone (Anon, 2014a), Small and Medium Enterprises ("SMEs") account for over 90 percent of all firms, and for over two-thirds of all employment, but fewer than 15 percent have access to credit.[4] This inability to raise working capital is particularly a problem for micro and small businesses, including technology start-ups and professionals branching out into entrepreneurship.

4.3 Consequences of Being Financially Underserved

The unbanked and underbanked consumers and businesses are not able to fully participate in the formal financial system due to various constraints.

They are financially fragile and have limited financial resilience. They are ill-prepared for financial disruptions and emergencies. This detracts them from exploring opportunities for establishing a cushion for financial resilience or positioning themselves for financial security and mobility. Financial insecurity impacts their physical health and is also associated with mental health problems such as depression and anxiety.

The financially underserved use alternate channels for meeting their financial needs and face exorbitant pricing. One of the services most frequently used by the unbanked migrant workers is international remittances. They typically send small amounts of a few hundred dollars to their families. Being able to accept remittances and use those funds immediately upon receipt is important for the family members. The cost of sending these remittances through informal channels is expensive relative to the amounts being sent but due to lack of options, the under-banked still use them.

As per the World Bank 2016 fact base, on a global basis, average cost of sending a remittance as of third quarter of 2016 is eight percent of the amount sent. Thus, sending $200 from one place to another in the world will cost $16 on average. But that is just an average. The fact base lists the remittance cost for hundreds of international payment corridors and some examples are in the table below.[5] The cost has been improving over the years but is still way higher than the three percent target as per the United Nations' Sustainable Development Goals.

Remittance corridor	Average cost to send $200	As %age of amount sent
Australia to Vanuatu	$41.40	20.7%
South Africa to Zambia	$38.00	19.0%
Singapore to Pakistan	$34.00	17.0%
Japan to China	$31.80	15.9%
Spain to China	$29.20	14.6%
Global Average	**$16.00**	**8.0%**
United States to India	$6.00	3.0%
UAE to Pakistan	$3.40	1.7%

Remittance charges vary depending on the provider selected but most unbanked do not have the means or the ability to do pricing comparisons. An efficient funds transfer mechanism that uses technology to reduce the price of remittances will provide significant savings for migrant workers and their families. Several fintech companies have started offering such services in recent years in the high remittance volume corridors and are cheaper than the traditional options.

Another example of the underserved customers paying significantly higher charges is for rent-to-own services. A report published in the United Kingdom in March 2016[6] revealed that several consumers who rented consumer goods and appliances ended up paying several times the actual cost. The cheapest washing machine sold by one the largest suppliers of rent-to-own appliances was costing the customers £936 based on prevailing interest rates for the weekly repayment plan. A similar model on high street was priced at £350 for an outright purchase and £491 using a weekly loan from a credit union. The rent-to-own lending groups justified that their high interest rates were to compensate for the borrowers' default risk and the people intensive nature of their weekly rent collection process.

The UK financial watchdog – the Financial Conduct Authority – is reviewing such high-cost products that are generally used by the financially vulnerable customers. This kind of lending is an example of an area where use of technology to automate some of the processes can reduce the distribution and collection costs and help provide the services at a lower price.

4.4 Financial Exclusion Affects the Middle Class Too, not Just the Poor

Nineteen percent of unbanked adults globally are from low-income economies[7] like Rwanda, Malawi and Sierra Leone which have average per capita income of less than two dollars per day. In these countries, financial exclusion is very high at 72.5 percent of all adults.

Close to 77 percent of unbanked adults are from middle-income economies such as India, China, Indonesia, Mexico, Philippines and Brazil.

The above are percentages from the two billion unbanked adults globally. In addition, many middle-income people are also underbanked. They have limited product choices and / or face high fees as explained earlier.

4.5 Financially Underserved in Developed Countries

One of the common misconceptions is that financial exclusion is a problem only in the emerging economies. It is true that a large majority of unbanked adults live in emerging markets but financial exclusion is also a challenge in the developed countries, albeit to a lesser extent.

The World Bank database reveals that 53 million people (six percent of unbanked adults) are from high-income developed countries. A much larger proportion of population in developed countries is in the underbanked category. Their exclusion creates similar challenges as in emerging markets while their inclusion offers the same opportunities to local economies as in other parts of the world.

Financial inclusion in Europe is a tale of two regions. About five percent (17 million) of all adults in the Eurozone are unbanked. While countries such as Denmark, Norway, Sweden and Finland have zero unbanked, the numbers in central and eastern European countries are more akin to those of Africa and Latin America. Almost 40 percent of all adults in Romania and 43 percent in Turkey are unbanked.

As per the World Bank report, the United States has 16 million unbanked adults (6.4 percent) who do not have a checking, savings, or money market account.

The FDIC sizes the United States underserved[8] market at 27 percent of all households (67 million adults). These include seven percent unbanked households (16 million adults) and 20 percent underbanked households (51 million adults). The FDIC defines underbanked households as those who have basic accounts but are also using at least one alternative financial service. They may find access to a full range of conventional financial products limited by their low-to-moderate household income or income volatility and may lack access to credit from financial institutions due to subprime credit scores or thin or no credit bureau files.

The most common groups of unbanked in the United States are low-income individuals and families, less-educated, young adults and immigrants. One of their biggest challenges is the high cost of using financial alternatives that prevents them from saving money and climbing out of poverty. A household with annual net income of $20,000 may end up paying as much as $1,200 annually as fees for alternative services – substantially more than the expense of a checking account in a bank.

Alternate financial services used by the underserved segments broadly fall into three categories - money transfer services, check cashing services and borrowing. Money transfer services include remittances and prepaid cards and are used most frequently by underserved households, with 54 percent using this service to send a money order within the United States or internationally.

Borrowing includes loans from pawn shops or payday lenders, rent-to-own services, pay check advances and tax refund anticipation loans. It is the second most commonly used service, used by 33 percent of underserved households.

A survey published by the US Federal Reserve in 2014 highlighted the skewed distribution of income and wealth in the United States. Top three percent of the families received 31 percent of income and held 54 percent of wealth in 2013.[9] Ninety percent of the families that represent bulk of America received 53 percent of income and their share of wealth was just below 25 percent.

	Share of income	Share of wealth
Top 3% of families	31%	54%
Next 7% of families	17%	21%
90% of families	53%	25%

The average net worth of a family in the United States is USD 535,000. But averages do not provide the full picture. The average net worth of top ten percentile is over USD 4 million. For the bottom quartile, the average net worth is negative USD 13,400, i.e. they are in debt, and the next quartile's average net worth is USD 36,000.

4.6 Financial Health and Financial Security

Financial health, like physical health, is necessary to lead a happy and productive life. A sound financial present is connected to a better financial future. People with reasonable debt today, for example, are more likely to avoid bankruptcy, build wealth and plan for retirement. Financial health means that an individual's daily financial system functions well, increases the likelihood of financial resilience in the face of ups and downs, and provides the capacity to seize opportunities that may lead to enhanced long-term financial security and upward mobility.[10]

Like physical health, financial health is not a one-time result that can be achieved and then ignored. Physical health requires an individual's discipline in eating habits and exercise, healthy and clean external environment, good insurance plan and good medical care infrastructure. Similarly, financial health also needs to be cultivated over time and requires persistence and financial discipline, financial literacy, a supportive economic environment and job market, and access to suitable financial products and services.

Pursuing and maintaining financial health should be a vital goal for all individuals.

A 2016 survey across the European Union highlighted that Europeans' financial well-being has deteriorated over the last few years, with 29 percent responding that they did not have enough money for a dignified existence and 39 percent were worried that after paying their bills, money that was left each month would not suffice. Nearly 25 percent, or one in four adults, missed paying their bills on time on at least one occasion in the past 12 months due to inability to pay, i.e. that they did not have the money to pay.[11]

Most Europeans recognize the need for saving to have funds for unexpected expenses. An interesting observation is that the Europeans primarily hold their savings in a saving accounts (69 percent) and in cash (26 percent) rather than in an investment account - an indication that most people save money to have a buffer and not to make it grow.

Data from the United States suggests similar challenges related to financial health of consumers. A US Federal Reserve report published in May 2016 highlights that nearly half the Americans adults are living in a continuous state of financial insecurity or financial distress. They are ill-prepared for a financial disruption and would struggle to cover emergency expenses should it arise. Many of these people are not low income or poor but middle class.

When asked how they would pay for a $400 emergency, 46 percent of American adults said that either they would cover the expense by borrowing or selling something, or they would not be able to come up with the $400 at all.[12] The answer was shocking and astonishing. Nearly half the population said they could not come up with four hundred dollars. When costly emergencies arise, nearly 37 percent are not confident they can come up with $2,000 within the next month for an unexpected need.

One can think of this as a liquidity problem as people may not have enough cash in their checking or saving accounts to meet an unexpected expense, but looking at the net worth data quoted earlier suggests that the problem is real. A quarter of American households have a negative net worth and the sum of their assets, including the retirement accounts, is less than the debt.

Other studies in the United States in recent years, including the 2014 Bankrate survey and reports by Pew Charitable Trusts, have highlighted similar challenges that households do not have enough liquid savings to replace even a month's worth of lost income.

The World Bank Findex database shows that 94 percent of Americans are financially included. What is not obvious from these numbers is that while they may have basic accounts and access to some of the financial services from banks or alternative financial services providers, nearly half of them are struggling financially. A report published in 2015 by the Center for Financial Services Innovation highlighted that 57 percent of American adults – approximately 138 million – are struggling, to varying degrees, with managing their day-to-day financial lives, establishing a cushion for financial resilience, and positioning themselves for financial security and mobility.

It underscores how widespread the consumer challenges are.

Until recently, most economists published statistics on unemployment rates, income and wealth inequality, and savings and debt. But none of these statistics captures what is happening in households trying to make ends meet daily. This concept that people aren't making ends meet or the idea that if there was a shock, they would not have the money to pay, is a new insight.

The key point here is that financial insecurity is not just a low-income bottom-of-the-pyramid problem in the unbanked population. It is an equal-opportunity problem impacting nearly half the American population that includes middle class professionals. These individuals are financially included and but are not financially healthy. This explains some of the deep economic discontent that was often a topic of discussion in the presidential elections in 2016.

As mentioned earlier, financial insecurity impacts people beyond their physical health and is associated with depression, anxiety and a loss of personal control. Better financial health helps reduce physical and mental stress for the individuals and reduces the strain on local governments and agencies. It can help lower social security payouts, and provide a win-win for governments and individuals.[13]

4.7 Financial Inclusion and Financial Literacy

Financial inclusion and financial literacy go hand in hand. Financial education about household economy is critical in ensuring households do not get overly indebted and fall into a negative debt behavior. While financial products have become increasingly sophisticated in the last decade, they are too complex for most people whose knowledge of finances has not kept pace. This financial illiteracy correlates with financial distress. People make financial choices without thinking through the implications fully, due to lack of knowledge or interest or both.

It is important to understand some of the reasons behind the current financial health challenges in the United States. Have the consumers started taking on more deby than before? Data suggests that consumer behavior today on incurring debt through credit cards or home equity loans is not significantly different from the previous decade, but what has changed is that they are not earning enough. Most people in their late 20's or early 30's assume that their income will continue to grow steadily over the next couple of decades the way incomes used to grow in America. But the new reality is different.

Since 2000, inflation-adjusted household incomes have increased for the top quartile of the American population but have declined for the other quartiles.[14] While people are living beyond their means chasing the American dream, the means also seem to be dwindling.

Savings is an essential part of consumer financial health anywhere in the world. Saving products are beneficial and even a small amount of saving can cushion an income disruption that can stop families from missing bill payments. It can also help consumers manage liquidity challenges, cover unexpected expenses and reach long-term financial goals. Consumers with a planned saving habit are four times more likely to be financially healthy than those without.[15]

An additional way that individuals can insulate themselves from negative repercussions of a financial shock is through insurance policies that cover specific economic risks. Most American adults have health insurance, auto insurance, and homeowners' insurance among those who own their home. However, just over half have life insurance and only one-quarter have disability insurance.[16]

Saving rate for individuals tends to be higher in countries that do not offer social safety nets or a welfare system. Household saving rates in China and India are over 40 percent and 30 percent respectively compared to 5.1 percent in the United States.

While many households may find saving for emergencies to be a challenge, it is not impossible. Currently, there is a dearth of financial services and financial education for the underserved segments. This highlights a vast market opportunity for banks and fintech companies to offer products that support financial health and address the needs of underserved consumers. With access to high-quality micro-savings and micro-insurance products designed to effectively engage account holders, consumers can build saving habits and hence improve their financial health. In addition, the necessary awareness about financial products and systems through financial tools can go a long way in improving financial health by helping consumers make better financial choices.

Several fintech firms have emerged in recent years that are supporting this vision. Some offer financial literacy through a comparison of financial products and services in a transparent manner with information on fully loaded pricing and key terms and features. These include firms for retail consumer products, for insurance products and for small businesses. Others help consumers gradually pay down their expensive credit card debt through cheaper lines from community banks, develop a savings habit or help consumers save or cut down on expensive and / or unused subscriptions and other services by canceling or suggesting lower cost providers.

4.8 Financial Inclusion for Micro, Small and Medium Enterprises (SMEs)

Micro, small and medium enterprises (SMEs) are a major driver of economic growth and job creation. They account for more than half of the GDP in high-income countries and two-thirds of the formal work force.[17] And yet, these companies have difficulty securing financing which limits their ability to grow and thrive. Access to financing by SMEs is an area that challenges almost every government.

The situation in emerging markets is no different, with more than 200 million SMEs lacking access to finance.[18] The International Finance Corporation (IFC) estimates that 55 percent of SMEs in developing countries do not have access to credit at all, or not have enough credit to grow their business and estimates a significant credit gap of over USD 2.1 trillion[19] for such financially excluded SMEs. This credit gap also represents a huge missed revenue opportunity for the financial sector. The financing needs of SMEs so far are met largely by informal service providers, governments, state agencies, development organizations and non-governmental organizations. Most SMEs end up borrowing from family and friends, or at exorbitant rates from money lenders and payday lenders.

SMEs need financial products and services that are appropriate for them, at the right price and design, with ease of access and fast processing. Their credit needs can be summarized as high in complexity and low in scale, leading to the traditional banking view that MSME financing is low-end and unprofitable. The credit underwriting process is time-consuming and expensive for a variety of reasons, such as a lack of credit bureaus, stringent regulatory know-your-customer requirements and the fact that many SMEs lack an audited financial history. SME credit risk is assessed manually as most financial institutions do not have credit scoring models for underwriting. The process tends to be similar to that for the large corporates but with smaller credit facilities and hence lower revenues. Also, the high intrinsic risk of SMEs often exceeds banks' risk appetite.

Small businesses are the Goldilocks of digital banking: corporate apps are too complex for them, but retail ones are way too simple. They often end up being offered retail credit products, though their diverse needs call for a more customized service. Banks often pursue lending in this area under regulatory pressures or as part of philanthropic ambitions.

The global financial crisis of 2008 threw the SME finance sector around the world into disarray, making it even more difficult for SMEs to secure financing. Banks have reduced their lending exposure to SMEs. In the United States, SME loans as a percentage of all bank business loans have fallen from 35 percent to 24 percent since the financial crisis. In the United Kingdom, bank lending to SMEs has declined year on year since 2009. The risk-return equation has been further worsened by increased regulation and higher capital costs under Basel III regulations for (riskier) small business loans. As of November 2016, the European Commission is reviewing the banking regulations that will lower the capital requirements for small businesses to make the regulation "more proportionate and growth friendly."

Widening access to financing for SMEs is top of almost every government's agenda, given the sector's importance for jobs and economic growth. In the United Kingdom, as the banks pulled back from SME lending, the government realized that a more diversified and resilient financial services sector was needed and started enabling this through various options. It issued a new category of banking licenses called challenger bank licenses and created the British Business Bank. Within the Small Business, Enterprise and Employment Act, it proposed legislation to mandate banks to refer to other providers when they decline finance for SMEs. All these actions have created an environment in which the SME alternative finance sector in the UK has flourished in recent years.

Several other governments have introduced specific programs to support SMEs through favorable taxation policies and other incentives. China has issued new banking licenses to technology companies to promote financial inclusion. The US JOBS (Jumpstart Our Startups) Act of 2012 has had positive impact for meeting credit needs of individuals and small businesses.

Governments have a key role in the future of alternative finance in the SME sector. Many are seeking to work with the fintech companies to facilitate development of the industry and get capital into the hands of businesses that can then create economic growth and jobs. However, while the efforts have shown some positive results, and momentum is building, a vast funding gap remains.

Banks and alternative financial service providers can meet the credit needs of underserved segments by using technology to offer commercially viable solutions. The global financial crisis has resulted in rapid growth of several fintech companies that are using innovative business models and partnerships to enable individuals and SMEs to secure credit profitably, with low-cost, scalable services. They are using predictive credit models, advanced analytics based on existing and new data sources and machine learning algorithms, to assess credit risk and offer digital solutions. In addition to using existing credit bureau and financial data better, they are increasingly using alternative data sources such as smartphone usage data, utility bills payment history, invoice data and shipment data to assess creditworthiness. Many are targeting specific underserved segments such as self-employed individuals, small businesses, students, immigrants, Hispanics and others. All of them are helping their customers get access to financing and build credit history.

The alternative lending platforms have a lower cost structure than banks, and lighter regulatory scrutiny. The diverse financing needs of SMEs can be met through digital solutions, a network of agents and correspondents, and partnerships with the development sector.

4.9 Financial Inclusion Matters and Can Be Profitable

Financial inclusion is not an end but a means to an end. While financial inclusion starts with account ownership, it doesn't stop there. Regular use of such accounts by consumers is what helps in economic growth.

A report published by McKinsey in September 2016 quantifies the huge economic benefit of digital financial services targeted at 1.6 billion unbanked adults in emerging economies. An estimated USD 4.2 trillion in deposits could flow into the financial system as digital finance enables more people to open accounts and shift their savings from informal mechanisms. It could increase the volume of loans to individuals and businesses by USD 2.1 trillion and allow governments to save USD 110 billion per year by reducing leakage in spending and tax revenue. The government savings are estimated at USD 32 billion in South Asia, USD 27 billion in South East Asia, USD 20 billion in China and USD 12 billion in Africa and Middle East.

Lending to small businesses is also financially attractive. A study by CARE International and Accenture estimates that bringing today's excluded small businesses into the formal banking sector could generate annual revenues of USD 270 billion[20] for banks by 2020, by closing the credit gap at average lending spreads and adding fee-based services.

Governments are playing an important role in digitizing payments such as public sector salaries, pension and social benefit payments. Digital operations can create significant cost savings for governments. Identifying large opportunities to promote greater use of transaction accounts to support digital payments, such as paying utility bills and taxes, in an easier, more affordable, and more secure way is critical for reaping the benefits of financial inclusion.

The benefits for governments go beyond financial inclusion. In many emerging markets, the shadow economy or "black" economy is pernicious. For governments, the predominance of cash creates a leaky pipeline for expenditure and tax revenue.[21] Several governments also provide social programs such as fuel subsidies and food staples which are built on cash payments and subsidized goods but it is challenging to target aid and subsidies effectively. The International Monetary Fund (IMF) estimates that 43 percent of the benefit of fuel subsidies worldwide goes to the wealthiest quintile and only 7 percent to the poorest quintile.[22] India's financial inclusion journey covered later in this chapter explains how technology and government determination can help solve this. Shifting social programs such as government benefits and subsidies from cash to digital payments linked to transaction accounts can improve outcomes through better targeting of intended recipients.

4.10 Fintech Revolution Enabled by Smartphones

As the world becomes increasingly interconnected, both economically and socially, technology adoption has become one of the defining factors in human progress.

Digital financial services – delivered via mobile phones or the Internet – offer several benefits including expanding access, driving down costs, and increasing the convenience of transactions. Digital channels have become pervasive everywhere and are being used actively for financial products. They have created an opportunity to provide financial services to the underserved segments at scale at a much lower cost.

Smartphones are playing an increasingly important role in the next generation of digital financial services. Cheaper mobile devices, innovative pricing models and data-ready mobile networks are contributing to an accelerated pace of smartphone adoption.

There are over 7.5 billion mobile subscriptions globally from 5.1 billion subscribers as of September 2016.[23] In contrast, there are 1.6 billion home Internet users accessing Internet from PCs or laptops and 1.4 billion fixed line phones (the numbers peaked in 2005 and have been declining since then).

Mobile phone penetration is at over 96 percent of adult population and several users have more than one mobile device. Smartphones make up 55 percent of all phones in use and accounted for 80 percent of all new phones sold during the third quarter.

In emerging markets like India, China, Indonesia and Myanmar, the population has leapfrogged from no fixed line phone or home Internet directly to mobile phones and smartphones. India and China have over 1 billion mobile subscribers each and smartphone penetration is growing rapidly.

There are 2.5 billion smartphone users globally of which 52 percent are in Asia-Pacific. This region also has nearly half the unbanked adults globally. Almost all the new fintech solutions being launched in emerging markets have a mobile option.

Increasing penetration of smartphones is creating opportunities for banks, telcos and fintech companies to offer financial products and services via the mobile platforms. Mobile technology in countries like Kenya has become a game changer for financial inclusion and has shown that a bank account is not necessarily needed for basic banking services.

Even in the United States, mobile phone penetration has been increasing and smartphone ownership among the underserved segments now exceeds home Internet access. In the unbanked segment, 28 percent of the households have internet access at home but 43 percent have smartphones.

Mobile phone, smartphone and home internet access for US households				
Distribution in US households	% of households	Mobile phone	Smartphone	Internet at home
Unbanked	7%	69%	43%	28%
Underbanked	20%	91%	76%	73%

Source: 2015 FDIC National Survey of Unbanked and Underbanked Households (for 5% of households, status on banked or unbanked is unknown)

Mobile solutions can also lower the cost of providing financial services by 80 to 90 percent, enabling providers to serve lower income customers profitably. The digital data trail these technologies create enables lenders to assess the creditworthiness of borrowers. Already, over 1.7 billion adults who were unknown to formal credit bureaus are becoming 'digitally discoverable' by the financial sector and fintech firms through their mobile phones.

Financial institutions as well as alternative financial services providers are increasingly seeking to interact with customers through the mobile phones and support financial inclusion.

4.10.1 Digital Payments and Mobile Money

Digital disruptions have revolutionized the way we pay and manage our finances. As a society, we are reducing usage of cash or cheques for payments and leaning towards debit or credit cards, Internet banking and online shopping. The range of secure digital payment options available to consumers include mobile wallets, Quick Response (QR) codes, Near Field Communication (NFC) technology, sound wave systems, virtual cards and more.

Like electricity or roads, a digital-payment network acts as the basic infrastructure of an economy that enables individuals and businesses to transact with one another seamlessly. It gives consumers maximum convenience and confidence in making payments; and enables firms to increase productivity through payments integrated with business processes.

Several business innovations are already apparent in emerging economies using the digital infrastructure. India and Africa are creating new ways of storing and transferring money, and are creating value through electronic payments. Digital payments also allow small value transactions in a profitable manner and that has created new business opportunities based on micro-payments. Examples in Africa include pay-as-you-go solar power for households, irrigation systems purchased on layaway plans, and school tuition fees broken into small, frequent payments.

In 2006, 80 percent of the adult population in Kenya worked with cash alone and less than 10 percent had bank accounts. Over 75 percent of the population lived in rural areas but majority of bank branches and ATMs were in urban areas. The cities had many workers whose families lived in the villages. To send money home, a city worker had to seal his wages in an envelope and pay a courier to travel for hours to the village.

When the telecom operators Safaricom and Vodafone launched M-PESA in Kenya in 2007, it was intended to be a money-transfer application residing on a phone's SIM card that could be used as a tool for microfinance organizations to collect loan payments. They soon realized that it was being used by urban workers to send money home. They used their distribution channels of thousands of master distributors and retail agents to provide coverage all over the country. The retail agents provided the last mile customer connectivity to send or receive cash. By 2015, nearly 80 percent of Kenyans had made the transition to having either a bank or a mobile money account.[24]

The degree to which mobile money is capturing the unbanked market varies across countries. This may reflect the diverse and evolving public policies and regulations surrounding mobile money. Mobile money has achieved the broadest success in Sub-Saharan Africa. As per World Bank 2014 report, only 2 percent of adults globally have a mobile money account. For Sub-Saharan Africa, this is at 12 percent and 45 percent of them have only a mobile money account.

Mobile money has significantly contributed to changing the financial inclusion landscape in Sub-Saharan.[25] Africa where people in 19 countries have more mobile money accounts than accounts with a financial institution.

The mobile money account prevalence also reflects that the intended consumers do not necessarily want bank accounts; they just want an effective mechanism that meets their money transfer needs. This is an important insight. Understanding and meeting the real needs of the unbanked is important. It cannot be assumed that they need the same types of services as the underbanked. Many of them live in a different ecosystem and may be on weekly or daily wages and their family circumstances may be different.

Tanzania, Ghana and Uganda have also been pushing mobile money capabilities with government support. People in these countries can buy and sell goods, send and receive cash, and build their credit history using their mobile phones.

Mobile money accounts are becoming central to the lives of financially excluded and underserved customers. These are available in 93 countries and in December 2015, over a billion mobile money transactions worth USD 19 billion were processed.[26] That is close to 33 million transactions per day from 411 million registered mobile money users and is more than double of what PayPal processed globally.

Africa started the mobile money revolution but it is now picking up momentum in South Asia and Latin America. Agents remain the backbone and face of mobile money to digitize and disburse cash in most countries, compared to ATMs and branches for banks, and represent more than 90 percent of cash-in and cash-out footprint.

The cross-border mobile money services are also expanding to serve the remittance needs of economic migrants and for cross-border trade. In 2015, there were 29 cross-border mobile money initiatives connecting 19 countries.

Several fintech lending platforms have emerged that use digital data and match middle class and wealthier savers with small businesses and households looking for credit. They use digital data to assess creditworthiness. New apps and digital tools have also emerged to help SMEs analyze their sales to build cash flow statements, improve operations and gain access to working capital facilities.

Digital payment options also support development of online e-commerce or mobile commerce. Today, although most online shopping in emerging economies is done via smartphones, they still rely on payment by cash when goods are delivered. That is changing rapidly as digital payments are becoming more prevalent and providing greater convenience.

4.11 Financial Inclusion in China – World's Largest Fintech Market

China has become the world's largest financial technology market and is a global leader in fintech in product innovation, market size and consumer adoption. The main drivers behind this revolution are a large population underserved by the banking sector, transition into a domestic consumption economy, a very high smartphone penetration rate and a large e-commerce ecosystem.

The market in China is dominated by three technology giants – Baidu, Alibaba and TenCent – collectively referred to as BAT.

In China, the fintech companies are referred to as "internet finance" companies. Their evolution has been different from that of fintech companies seen in Europe or the United States partly because the consumer financial markets in China have developed over the last couple of decades and most fintech solutions have been created without any legacy retail banking platforms. The fintech revolution has been similar to that for phone usage where most of the current generation has leapfrogged from no fixed landlines to smartphones.

The three BAT companies are at the core of China's Internet finance revolution. They dominate the Internet ecosystem and together generated USD 39 billion of revenue during the 12 months' period ending June 2016. They have a significant advantage over incumbent banks and other players as they own proprietary third-party payment systems and generate voluminous transaction data sets that enable advanced analytics. All three are leveraging mobile technology to offer a range of financial products and services such as mobile payments, mobile commerce, credit scoring, wealth products, loans and more.

Alibaba's affiliate Ant Financial has established AliPay as China's leading online payments system by building on its hugely successful business-to-business platform (Alibaba.com) and consumer/ business to consumer platforms (Taobao, Tmall). TenCent, owner of China's dominant instant messaging service WeChat, has capitalized on the scale of its social network WeChat to establish a digital payments presence through TenPay and a lead in the online banking through WeBank, China's first mobile banking service. Baidu, China's leading online search engine, lacks a similar flagship financial product but has invested heavily in other Internet finance companies and has built partnerships with traditional financial institutions.

Alibaba has consumer spend behavior data of over 420 million customers which has been used to build its proprietary Sesame credit score. In comparison, National Credit Bureau, run by People's Bank of China has data on 300 million people. Sesame Credit uses a number of factors into its algorithms, including online shopping behavior, traffic fines, tax payment information and more.

4.11.1 Digital Payments in China

China has been a hotbed for payments innovation and the integrated solutions have made themselves an indispensable part of their users' daily lives. Mobile payments are the largest and fastest growing segment of Internet finance in China. The transaction volume triple in 2016 to USD 5.5 trillion in 2016.[27] In comparison, mobile payments in the United States increased 39 percent to USD 112 billion.

With 380 million smartphone users shopping online in China with their phones, mobile commerce has seen rapid growth. Nearly 200 million people use their phones as a wallet for in-store payments.

The digital payments market in dominated by AliPay and TenPay, processing 70 percent and 20 percent of all payments respectively. Currently, no other payment solution in the world offers the versatility and comprehensiveness of AliPay or TenPay. The customer-friendly and easy to use features have enabled the market to leapfrog from cash transactions to mobile and digital payment systems, enabling the move towards a cashless and checkless society.

The type of innovation and the size and scale of online transactions in China is much more sophisticated than any developed market. AliPay processed transactions worth USD 1.7 trillion in 2016, nearly double of USD 931 billion in 2015, and nearly five times PayPal's global payment volume of USD 354 billion.[28]

TenCent has integrated WeChat and payments to let users make seamless peer-to-peer payments, shop online, and even pay at physical merchants.

The Singles' Day sale by Alibaba is one of the most successful examples of innovation in mobile commerce and digital payments. Singles' Day started in China as an obscure "anti-Valentine's" celebration for single people back in the 1990s. It was adopted by Alibaba in 2009 and has since become the world's biggest online shopping day that takes place on November 11 every year.

In 2015, Alibaba recorded online sales of USD 18 billion on Singles' Day, 25 percent higher than prior year, and 84 percent of sales were from mobile devices. This is more than the combined sales of on Black Friday and Cyber Monday in the United States across all stores and online shopping sites. The company's systems processed 120,000 transactions per second. The volumes reflect the strength and resilience of Alibaba's infrastructure that can support such transaction volumes.

4.11.2 Savings and Investments

China has a high consumer savings rate of over 40 percent resulting in over USD 7 trillion of investable wealth. A relatively closed capital account and low interest rates on bank deposits have resulted in a large unmet demand for savings and investment products in the underserved segments.

In June 2013, Alibaba launched the investment product Yu'E'Bao, a money market mutual fund through its online payment platform AliPay. It allows customers to invest their money in a flexible manner into short-term products such as central bank bills, negotiated deposits and certificates of deposit. Within ten months, Yu'E'Bao grew into China's largest money market fund with 554 billion yuan or USD 90 billion, making it the fastest growing mutual fund of all-time, anywhere. In the three years since launch, Yu'E'Bao, which means 'leftover treasure' became the third-largest money market fund in the world, after Vanguard and Fidelity. In April 2017, in less than four years since its launch, it became the largest such fund in the world with USD 165 billion in assets.

One of the key attractions of this fund is its easy user interface and customer-friendly product features. Customers can start investing with as little as 1 RMB and can transfer funds easily between Yu'E'Bao and their bank accounts using a smartphone or personal computer with one click. There is no fee and funds can be withdrawn at any time without a penalty.

Other leading players in China in savings and investments are TenCent's Licaitong and Baidu's Baifu. For wealth management and asset management, firms such as CreditEase are taking the lead and have become significant players.

The Internet finance companies in China have proven that unmet consumer demand, combined with easy to use technology platforms and suitable high-quality financial products, can support financial inclusion and result in profitable growth.

4.12 Financial Inclusion in India – A Success Story

India is setting a new global standard in using financial technologies to support financial inclusion. The country has become a giant testing ground for financial inclusion and innovation that may become a role model for other emerging economies.

The government is laying down the foundations for a national infrastructure that will enable the country to leapfrog to the next generation of financial services. It is providing critical enablers that have set the stage for a financial inclusion revolution: a national biometrics digital identity program (Aadhar), a financial inclusion program which has added over 250 million new accounts (Prime Minister's Jan Dhana Yojana) and a national payment network.

A slew of new "light" banking licenses in payments and SME finance have been issued to encourage new entrants. Most of these licenses were not given to traditional banks, but primarily to telecom, software and technology companies — most of whom have a strong track record of scaling by dramatically lowering operating costs and disrupting existing business models.

The three key enablers for financial inclusion in India are often referred to as JAM trinity – standing for **J**an Dhana Yojana, **A**adhar and **M**obile phones.

4.12.1 Aadhar: Billion-Person Digital Identity Database

Aadhar, which means foundation, is a unique digital identity number issued by a central government agency to all Indian residents. The identity number is linked to demographics and biometrics (finger prints and iris scans) and covers over 1.1 billion residents. It serves as proof of identity and address anywhere in the country, allowing verification of a person's identity in real time, subject to consent of course, without relying on paper evidence.

Aadhar is one of the few databases in the world that covers more than one billion people, the others being Facebook and Google. It is expected that the next version of Apple and Google phone operating systems will have Aadhar authentication technology embedded in the devices.

Aadhar is a means to an end and its usefulness depends on the convenience it provides to users in their daily lives. The government has created several avenues for its use. Aadhar is now used as the official document for Know Your Customer (KYC) authentication for bank accounts, insurance policies, demat accounts for securities, mutual fund schemes, landline and mobile phone applications, vehicle purchases and new gas connections.

4.12.2 Jan Dhana Yojana: Bank Accounts for the Financially Excluded

One of the biggest initiatives launched in India was the Prime Minister's Jan Dhana Yojana (PMJDY) program. PMJDY is India's National Mission for Financial Inclusion to ensure access to financial services for all, namely bank accounts, remittance services, line of credit, insurance and pension in an affordable manner. Its literal meaning is Prime Minister's People's Money Scheme. Under this, the banks were mandated to open accounts for several hundred million citizens who had been financially excluded.

The program was launched in August 2014 and 15 million accounts were opened on the first day. As of November 2016, over 258 million new bank accounts have been opened.[29] Another 140 million existing bank accounts have been linked to Aadhar number. There is no other example of this kind in the world where the financial institutions have opened so many bank accounts in just over two years. The key enabler was the Aadhar card which facilitated simplified Know-Your-Customer process for account opening and reduced the cost of account opening from USD 15 to USD 1.

4.12.3 Promoting Usage and Reaping Benefits

As mentioned earlier, opening bank accounts in a consumer-friendly way is a means to the end and not the endgame for financial inclusion. Account opening must be paired with products and services that are immediately useful and can foster continued engagement and account usage.

The hundreds of millions of new bank accounts that have been created in India need to be used to support financial inclusion. One of the ways to promote usage is to convert government payments away from cash and send them digitally into Aadhar linked bank accounts. But even that does not ensure that the previously unbanked will start using that account and other products more frequently. Instead, the recipients may simply withdraw cash and go back to living in a cash world until the next payment. Specific products need to designed and actions taken to build financial tools that are useful for them.

In India, bank account penetration increased from 35% to 53% between 2011 and 2014 but initial data showed 43% of all bank accounts to be dormant and others had negligible balances. That led to State Bank of India, one of the largest state owned banks, and others to undertake a major effort to encourage the utilization of the newly opened accounts. In 18 months, the accounts with zero account balances fell from 90% to 40%.[30]

As of November 2016, the 258 million new banks accounts opened under PMJDY have an aggregate balance of USD 11 billion and are being used. Less than 25 percent of accounts have zero balance.[31]

4.12.4 Digital Payments and Direct Benefits Transfers

To promote digital payments and account utilization, the Indian government has started making payments for salaries for government employees, pensions and other government benefits directly to the Aadhar-linked accounts.

Aadhar is also being used to provide government subsidies. Indian government runs an enormous financial network that disburses an estimated USD 45 billion – over 3 percent of India's GDP – as social benefits to the poor. These include programs such as guaranteed employment benefits to the rural poor, scholarships for education, cash assistance for expectant mothers and health workers, and pensions to the elderly, widowed and disabled.

The government has launched a subsidy reform program called the Direct Benefit Transfer (DBT) program under which subsidies are transferred directly to the people through their Aadhar linked bank accounts instead of going through various intermediaries. It is hoped that crediting subsidies into bank accounts will reduce delays, bring transparency and eliminate pilferage from distribution of funds sponsored by the Central Government.

The goal of the government in subsidy reform is not to do away with subsidies, but instead target them effectively to the intended beneficiaries. Such targeting of subsidies is extremely problematic when the subsidy is embedded in the physical delivery of a product at a price that is below the open market price. This price gap distorts the market, providing opportunities for arbitrage, diversion of supplies and profiteering in the black market. An elaborate administrative apparatus must be maintained at huge cost to manage the process. Despite this, problems of product adulteration, leakages, and harassment of beneficiaries remain endemic.

One such subsidy program that was targeted by the government for direct benefit transfer scheme was for liquefied petroleum gas (LPG). The LPG subsidies cover over 150 million registered users in the country and benefits were previously administered by providing gas cylinders through the various distribution agents at below market subsidized rates. After a successful pilot in 2014, the direct credit of LPG subsidy to Aadhar linked accounts went national in January 2015. Under these changes, the LPG cylinders are now sold by the distribution agents at market prices (not subsidized rates) and the subsidy amount is credited directly to Aadhar linked bank account of the intended beneficiary.

Benefits of this reform have been huge and the government has saved USD 2.5 billion in the first year.[32] Benefits have been realized by identifying and eliminating areas of pilferage such as duplicate LPG connections, people claiming kerosene and LPG subsidies (only one is allowed) and unofficial routing of subsidized domestic gas connections to commercial enterprises which are supposed to pay the market prices.

The government has now linked all pension benefits to Aadhar and significant savings are expected in this area too.

4.12.5 Unified Payments Interface (UPI)

Making funds transfer transactions simpler and cheaper is fundamental to promoting financial inclusion. Last mile electronic connectivity is important.

The interbank payment systems in India are quite advanced and charge low transaction fees. Most customers in India with bank accounts can use online channels for instant money transfers across banks, free of charge. While online banking enables near real-time transfers anywhere within the country, the sender is required to provide recipient's full name, bank account details and routing code which is a cumbersome process.

In September 2016, India launched a new online payments system called "Unified Payment Interface" or UPI, tied to Aadhar. The UPI is unlike anything available in China or the United States or any other large country. It is intended to enable secure, real-time funds transfers from one person to another, or to a business / company, through one common UPI app using Internet or smartphones.

UPI is a single app that can enable individuals and businesses to manage funds held across multiple accounts at various banks, mobile wallets, merchants and billers. In additional to money remittances, UPI will enable faster transactions for merchants and faster loading of cash into consumer wallets. It will allow a user to pay a street vendor for vegetables as well as for goods bought online. It is a secure payments infrastructure that will be interoperable across banks, telco and merchants.

The new payments platform could enable the country to skip traditional payment channels like cash machines, debit cards and point-of-sales terminals and move rapidly towards a cash-less economy. The platform caps single transactions at 100,000 rupees – around USD 1500 and the transaction cost is almost negligible at 50 paisa or less than 1 cent per transaction.

India's payments innovation stands out for two reasons. The first is that UPI relies on Aadhar, which allows verification of a person's identity in real time. The second is that UPI is not controlled by the government or a large private enterprise. It is part of a not-for-profit organization called National Payments Corporation of India (NPCI) which was championed by the Reserve Bank of India (the country's central bank) and the Indian Banks' Association to facilitate affordable payments and compete against Visa and MasterCard.

In countries like India, debit and credit card penetration is very low. Cash still accounts for nearly 95 percent of consumer payments but digital payments supported by initiatives like UPI can expedite the efforts to reduce cash in the economy.

4.12.6 Demonetization

The issue of 'black' economy and its negative impact on governments' tax revenues was highlighted earlier. The Indian government has taken significant steps in 2016 to reduce black money in the economy and get more money into tax coffers. It introduced a tax amnesty scheme until September 2016 which brought in close to USD 10 billion in undeclared income.

In November 2016, the government announced the withdrawal of existing large-denomination currency notes (Rupees 500 and Rupees 1000), making 86 percent of the country's bank notes invalid overnight. While the pros and cons of the move are being debated endlessly, the resultant cash shortage pushed consumers towards digital payments in a big way. Demand for digital payment solutions and mobile wallets increased exponentially by several hundred percent within days of the announcement.

India has USD 265 billion of cash in circulation, of which 86 percent (USD 212 billion) was in high-denomination notes that were banned. It is estimated that USD 127 billion has been returned to the banks in four weeks since the ban was announced.[33] This will help bring more individuals under the tax fold and help reduce India's fiscal deficit which stood at close to USD 80 billion in 2015.

4.13 Fintech Revolution Examples From Other Countries

From Silicon Valley to Singapore, the fintech revolution is gathering momentum as venture capitalists continue to invest money in this sector. The real proving ground for fintech for financial inclusion lies in emerging markets like India, China, Bangladesh, Indonesia, Vietnam and Nigeria. Embracing secure, low-cost, large-scale digital financial services has clear economic benefits in these markets.

India and China have been two of the biggest success stories in financial inclusion in recent years. While the fintech revolution in China has been led mainly by the local Internet finance companies, growth in India has been driven through government efforts in partnership with the private sector. In India, banks have been active participants in supporting financial inclusion and financial health while in China, technology companies have taken the lead and banks have remained on the sidelines. The two countries have followed very different models but both have produced great results.

M-Pesa in Kenya and bKash in Bangladesh are the other obvious examples of businesses that have grown fast by serving the unbanked and have been commercially successful.

Thailand has built a national payment infrastructure that allows consumers to pay each other using their mobile phone numbers as identifiers. Some banks in India offer features that enable individuals to pay each other using mobile phone numbers and social media platforms such as WhatsApp, Messenger and Twitter as identifiers.

Singapore has a payments system called FAST, an acronym for Fast and Secure Transfers. It enables near-instant secure online payments in the country. But FAST is grossly underutilized and one of the key barriers is that making a payment through FAST requires bank account details of the recipient. Most people do not remember their own bank account number, let alone knowing the account number of those they want to send money to. To solve for this, Singapore is building a national Central Addressing Scheme (or CAS) that will allow payments to be made through FAST using only a recipient's mobile number, or national identity number for individuals, or the unique business entity number for SMEs.

Debit and credit cards are widely used by Singaporeans but interoperability at the acceptance points in the retail outlets and restaurants needs to be enhanced. Not all cards can be used everywhere, and customers have to often ask merchants if some specific cards are accepted. A common sight in Singapore stores, and in almost every other country in the world, is the array of multiple point-of-sale terminals cluttering up cashiers' counters. This is confusing for customers and unproductive for counter staff. Singapore has tapped on the payments industry to develop a unified point-of-sale terminal or UPOS, which can accept all major card brands, including those that are contactless or embedded in smartphones. UPOS terminals are already being rolled and over 1000 of them have already been deployed in 2016[34] at convenience stores such as 7-Eleven and other retailers. Full nationwide coverage is expected in the next two years.

Singapore is also building a national utility leveraging existing government identity database to support Know-Your-Customer requirements for financial institutions. This will help improve productivity for financial institutions as well as consumers. A pilot launch with four of the largest banks in Singapore is scheduled for mid-2017.

Several other countries are starting to look at similar solutions and learning the benefits of collaboration to build shared financial infrastructures that are secure, resilient and scalable, and support financial inclusion and financial health.

4.14 Potential Risks With the New Business Models

New providers are emerging globally for serving the unbanked and underbanked profitably. Limited-service fintech companies and their partners are gaining traction around the world and handling a significant part of public's funds. Most of these are not regulated or supervised the way banks or telcos are. These new business models introduce new risks that need to be monitored and managed.

Agents or correspondents are an integral part of the financial services industry in developing countries. They serve as a primary connection between remote population in rural areas and basic financial services. While this mechanism helps reduce distribution costs, agent-based services also carry significant risks and lack of adequate oversight can result in fraud, theft and lack of transparency.

Digital delivery of financial services through partnerships involves multiple providers who have access to some or all of customer data. Data privacy and security are other potential areas of concern that need to be monitored.

Multiple partners in the delivery process also means increased risks of data security breaches or hacking, including the vulnerability of cheap smartphones to malware. Several customers in emerging markets are illiterate and that can cause an accidental exposure of sensitive information to third parties with all the worrying outcomes.

None of these risks is insurmountable but most need careful due diligence of partners and require ongoing monitoring.

As mobile money usage increases around the globe, mobile apps security is another area that is becoming critical. Apps in a smartphone increase the risk of malware and hacking and can potentially compromise user data. Mobile money providers around the globe must take customer data security very seriously and deign apps that provide great user experience but also adequate security.

4.15 The Path Ahead: Creative Collaboration Between Policymakers, Banks, Telcos and Technology Firms

Financial inclusion has been listed by the World Bank as the number one priority. It also has the attention of local governments and philanthropic organizations such as Bill and Melinda Gates Foundation and the Omidyar Group but this cannot be done by government and foundations alone. It needs the active support of banks, capital markets, mobile network operators, technology firms and regulators.

New technologies have become a game changer for financial inclusion, as new solutions can be customized, effective and profitable at lower scale. Previously, servicing these segments using brick and mortar infrastructure was not commercially viable or the services were offered at exorbitant fees. Most banks stayed away from serving the unbanked segments due to lack of adequate returns while some made commitments to tackle financial inclusion through microfinance and the philanthropic efforts of their corporate foundations.

Now with digital technology that can scale quickly, tailored services – such as micro-savings, insurance, working capital finance and online supply chain finance – which are normally out of bounds for the underserved consumers can be offered to gain significant market share and revenue. The unbanked and underbanked segments are an important new opportunity for banks and financial technology companies.

Impact investing has become a promising new field that strives to achieve philanthropic goals through innovative forms of return-seeking investment. The vital question that comes up regularly is whether it is possible to achieve both market-rate financial returns and meaningful social impact. For those living in poverty and earning less than two dollars per day, the commercial model is still to work. But the success stories from China and India have proven that it is possible to build viable commercial businesses targeting the unbanked and underbanked in middle-income countries.

The debate has evolved from just asking broad questions to actually seeking specific solutions using technology to help maximize both expected returns and expected impact. Distances are no longer insurmountable. Transaction sizes are no longer too small. Data can now be used and collected to create credit profiles more easily.

Banks have a critical role to play in this digital future. Inherently banks have a funding advantage because of their access to low-cost deposits. They also know financial products, have a key competitive advantage of managing risks better and possess the required scale, capital and consumer trust. Technology firms bring innovation, new customer segments and new distribution channels. Collaboration between banks and technology firms can clearly benefit the unbanked and underbanked.

Governments and regulators also need to be supportive and more is being done through regulatory reforms and co-funding schemes. Governments in many emerging markets are anxious to promote economic development and financial stability, while promoting financial inclusion and balancing regulations. The linkages between economic growth, financial stability and innovation are clear.

Banks and financial technology firms have a complex relationship that wavers between working as partners and seeing each other as potential rivals. However, together, they can solve the industry's one-size-fits-all problem for small business needs and create profitable technology driven business models for the underserved segments. Partnerships are important in reaching those who have been excluded.

Financial inclusion is a bigger problem in the emerging economies and it is not surprising that most of the innovative solutions are emerging from countries like India, China, Bangladesh and Kenya. Governments and regulators are actively supporting innovations that promote financial inclusion in a coordinated manner. These countries are leapfrogging to the next generation of financial services to support inclusive growth while countries like the United States are starting to lag in offering reasonably priced basic financial services.

In the developed countries, financial inclusion for the unbanked may not be a big problem but financial well-being of the large underserved segment is a significant challenge. Several large incumbent banks have been slow to adapt for a variety of reasons. They need to take interest and become more involved in offering products and services suited for these segments. Adopting some of the innovative solutions from emerging markets may be beneficial and will help reduce the overall transaction cost for the underserved globally. This will need significant support from regulators and policymakers too.

Banks are increasingly realizing that they need a license to operate – not just from regulators, but from society. They have to be a force for good.

With mobile platforms being provided by the telcom companies, low-cost scalable technology solutions by technology companies, policy support by governments and solid partnership by banks, the prospects for financial health and financial inclusion are looking bright.

References

Anon, 2014a. ASEAN SME Policy index 2014 – Towards competitive and innovative ASEAN SMEs [online]. Economic Research Institute for ASEAN and East Asia (ERIA). Available at: https://www.oecd.org/globalrelations/regionalapproaches/ASEAN%20SME%20Policy%20Index%2014.pdf [Accessed 11 Oct. 2015].

Anon, 2014b. Changes in U.S. Family Finances from 2010 to 2013: Evidence from the Survey of Consumer Finances. Federal Reserve Bulletins [online]. The Federal Reserve Board. Available at: https://www.federalreserve.gov/pubs/bulletin/2014/pdf/scf14.pdf [Accessed 10 Sep. 2016].

Anon, 2015a. Global Findex [online]. Worldbank.org. Available at: http://www.worldbank.org/globalfindex [Accessed 11 May 2016].

Anon, 2015b. Understanding and Improving Consumer Financial Health in America [online]. The Center for Financial Services Innovation (CFSI). Available at: https://www.metlife.com/assets/cao/foundation/understanding-and-improving-consumer-financial-health-in-america.pdf [Accessed 11 Aug. 2016].

Anon, 2016a. An Electronic Payments Society – Speech by Ravi Menon Managing Director, Monetary Authority of Singapore.

Anon, 2016b. Banks can profit from financial inclusion – Accenture [online]. Accenture.com. Available at: https://www.accenture.com/us-en/insight-banks-grow-profitably-emerging-economies [Accessed 11 Sep. 2016].

Anon, 2016c. Don't Show me the money. Business Today [online]. Available at: http://www.businesstoday.in/magazine/money-today/banking/dont-show-me-the-money/story/238070.html [Accessed 2 Sep. 2016].

Anon, 2016d. Ericsson Mobility Report, November 2016. Ericsson Mobility Report [online]. Ericsson. Available at: https://www.ericsson.com/assets/local/mobility-report/documents/2016/ericsson-mobility-report-november-2016.pdf [Accessed 24 Nov. 2016].

Anon, 2016e. Pradhan Mantri Jan-Dhan Yojana | Department of Financial Services | Ministry of Finance [online]. Available at: http://pmjdy.gov.in [Accessed 5 Dec. 2016].

Anon 2016f. Regulation – Effects and Outcomes – Keynote Address by Mr Ravi Menon, Managing Director, Monetary Authority of Singapore.

Anon 2016g. Singapore's FinTech Journey – Where We Are, What Is Next Speech by Mr Ravi Menon, Managing Director. Monetary Authority of Singapore.

Anon, 2016h. 2016 FinAccess Household Survey [online]. FSD Kenya. Available at: http://fsdkenya.org/dataset/finaccess-household-2016/ [Accessed 11 Sep. 2016].

Bhat, S., Bhatia, R., 2016. While India plugs black money holes, Indians find leaks [online]. Reuters India. Available at: http://in.reuters.com/article/india-modi-corruption-taxes-bank-notes-idINKBN1360UH [Accessed 14 Nov. 2016].

FDIC, 2016. FDIC National Survey of Unbanked and Underbanked Households. National Survey of Unbanked and Underbanked Households [online]. FDIC. Available at: https://www.fdic.gov/householdsurvey/2015/2015report.pdf [Accessed 15 Nov. 2016].

Financial Inclusion Center, 2016. Better and Brighter? Responsible RTO alternatives [online]. London: Financial Inclusion Center, p. 4. Available at: http://inclusioncentre.co.uk/wordpress29/wp-content/uploads/2016/03/Better-and-Brighter-Responsible-RTO-Alternatives-Summary-150316.pdf [Accessed 3 Aug. 2016].

Gabler, N., 2016. The Secret Shame of Middle-Class Americans Living Paycheck to Paycheck [online]. The Atlantic. Available at: http://www.theatlantic.com/magazine/archive/2016/05/my-secret-shame/476415/ [Accessed 1 Dec. 2016].

Galani, U., 2016. India lays foundation for a fintech revolution. [Blog] Reuters Breakingviews. Available at: http://www.reuters.com/article/idUS312992507220160914 [Accessed 13 Oct. 2016].

Gareth, E., Christine, A., 2016. Better-and-Brighter-Responsible-Rent To Own-Alternatives-Summary-150316 [online]. London: The Financial Inclusion Centre. Available at: http://inclusioncentre.co.uk/wordpress29/wp-content/uploads/2016/03/Better-and-Brighter-Responsible-RTO-Alternatives-Summary-150316.pdf [Accessed 17 Oct. 2016].

International Finance Corporation, 2013. Closing the Credit Gap for Formal and Informal Micro, Small, and Medium Enterprises [online]. IFC ADVISORY SERVICES. Available at: http://www.ifc.org/wps/wcm/connect/4d6e6400416896c09494b79e78015671/Closing+the+Credit+Gap+Report-FinalLatest.pdf?MOD=AJPERES [Accessed 8 Oct. 2015].

International Monetary Fund, 2010. The Unequal Benefits of Fuel Subsidies: A Review of Evidence for Developing Countries [online]. International Monetary Fund. Available at: https://pdfs.semanticscholar.org/d7fe/d5ccd0c8e6af1ff664442325b11ef095812f.pdf [Accessed 9 Sep. 2015].

Intrum Justitia, 2016. European consumer payment report 2016. European consumer payment report [online]. Intrum Justitia. Available at: https://www.intrum.com/globalassets/corporate/publications/ecpr/intrumjustitia_ecpr2016_en.pdf [Accessed 5 Aug. 2016].

McKinsey & Company, 2016. Digital finance for all: powering inclusive growth in emerging economies [online]. McKinsey Global Institute. Available at: http://www.mckinsey.com/global-themes/employment-and-growth/how-digital-finance-could-boost-growth-in-emerging-economies [Accessed 6 Oct. 2016].

Patwardhan, A., 2016. Financial Inclusion: Is SME lending the Goldilocks of digital banking? [online]. LinkedIn. Available at: https://www.linkedin.com/pulse/financial-inclusion-banks-ready-support-sme-lending-anju-patwardhan?trk=mp-author-card [Accessed 7 May 2016].

Peric, K., 2016. Welcome to Euromoney [online]. Euromoney. Available at: http://www.euromoney.com/GatewayAd.aspx?Redirect=http%3a%2f%2fwww.euromoney.com%2fArticle%2f3547134%2fEmerging-markets-Fintech-for-the-unbanked.html [Accessed 7 Jun. 2016].

Rogoff, K., 2016. The Curse of Cash, 1st ed. Princeton University Press.

The World Bank Group, 2015. The Global Findex Database 2014. The Global Findex Database [online]. Available at: http://documents.worldbank.org/curated/en/187761468179367706/pdf/WPS7255.pdf [Accessed 6 Aug. 2015].

US Federal Reserve, 2014. Changes in U.S. Family Finances from 2010 to 2013: Evidence from the Survey of Consumer Finances, pp. 3, 10–12, 16–18.

US Federal Reserve, 2016. Report on the Economic Well-Being of U.S. Households in 2015. Board of Governors of the Federal Reserve System, Washington, DC, pp. 15, 23, 28, 37–38.

World Bank Group, 2016. Migration and Remittances Factbook 2016 [online]. World Bank Group. Available at: http://siteresources.worldbank.org/INTPROSPECTS/Resources/334934-1199807908806/4549025-1450455807487/Factbookpart1.pdf [Accessed 5 Oct. 2016].

Notes

1. 2014 edition of World Bank Global Findex database provides more than 100 indicators on topics such as account ownership and use, payments, saving, credit, and financial resilience.

2. World Economic Forum Principles for Achieving Full Financial Inclusion: Encouraging and enabling private sector innovation and investment at scale.

3. http://www.worldbank.org/globalfindex.

4. ASEAN SME POLICY INDEX 2014 – TOWARDS COMPETITIVE AND INNOVATIVE ASEAN SMES. Edited by ERIA SME RESEARCH WORKING GROUP, JUNE 2014.

5. file://World Bank Migration remittances Factbook part1 2016.pdf.

6. http://inclusioncentre.co.uk/wordpress29/wp-content/uploads/2016/03/Better-and-Brighter-Responsible-RTO-Alternatives-Summary-150316.pdf.

7. The World Bank classifies economies using gross national income (GNI) per capita. As per 2013 data, countries with GNI per capita of $1,045 or below are Low-income economies, with $12,746 or more are High-income economies, and from $1,045 to $12,746 are Middle-income economies.

8. https://www.fdic.gov/householdsurvey/2015/2015report.pdf.

9. https://www.federalreserve.gov/pubs/bulletin/2014/pdf/scf14.pdf (page 10).

10. As defined in CFSI report on Understanding and Improving Consumer Financial Health in America.

11. https://www.intrum.com/globalassets/corporate/publications/ecpr/intrumjustitia_ecpr2016_en.pdf.

12. https://www.federalreserve.gov/2015-report-economic-well-being-us-households-201605.pdf.

13. Research funded by JPMorgan Chase at the Urban Institute.

14. Article in The Atlantic – the Secret Shame of Middle-Class Americans – by Neal Gabler in May 2016.

15. CFSI's study of consumer behaviors, Understanding and Improving Consumer Financial Health in America.

16. https://www.federalreserve.gov/2015-report-economic-well-being-us-households-201605.pdf (pg 32).

17. http://www.ifc.org/wps/wcm/connect/4d6e6400416896c09494b79e78015671/Closing+the+Credit+Gap+Report-FinalLatest.pdf?MOD=AJPERES (page 11).

18. SME Finance Forum.

19. http://www.ifc.org/wps/wcm/connect/4d6e6400416896c09494b79e78015671/Closing+the+Credit+Gap+Report-FinalLatest.pdf?MOD=AJPERES.

20. Report "Within Reach" https://newsroom.accenture.com/news/banks-have-a-380-billion-market-opportunity-in-financial-inclusion-accenture-and-care-international-uk-study-find.htm.

21. Kenneth S. Rogoff, The curse of cash, Princeton University Press, 2016.

22. Arze del Granado, Javier, David Coady, and Robert Gillingham, The unequal benefits of fuel subsidies: A review of evidence for developing countries, IMF working paper number 10/202, September 2010.

23. Ericsson Global Mobility Report, November 2016.

24. 2015 FinAccess Survey.

25. http://www.gsma.com/mobilefordevelopment/wp-content/uploads/2016/04/SOTIR_2015.pdf, page 30.

26. http://www.gsma.com/mobilefordevelopment/wp-content/uploads/2016/04/SOTIR_2015.pdf.

27. https://www.statista.com/statistics/278524/online-payment-transaction-volume-in-china/.

28. https://www.statista.com/statistics/419783/paypals-annual-payment-volume/.

29. http://pmjdy.gov.in/.

30. http://www.euromoney.com/Article/3586642/How-financial-inclusion-will-change-the-face-of-banking.html?single=true&copyrightInfo=true.

31. http://pmjdy.gov.in/.

32. https://www.iisd.org/gsi/news/estimating-impact-indias-aadhaar-scheme-lpg-subsidy-expenditure.

33. https://www.ft.com/content/e52dab06-b093-11e6-a37c-f4a01f1b0fa1.

34. https://www.gov.sg/~/sgpcmedia/media_releases/mas/speech/S-20160819-1/attachment/Speech%20by %20Mr%20Ravi%20Menon_An%20Electronic%20Payments%20Society,%2019%20Aug%202016.pdf.

CHAPTER 5

Using Broadband to Enhance Financial Inclusion

Ignacio Mas[#]

Contents

[#] The author is Executive Director of the Digital Frontiers Institute and Senior Fellow at the Fletcher School's Council on Emerging Market Enterprises at Tufts University. This work was funded by the Inter-American Development Bank, and was circulated as Inter-American Development Bank, Discussion Paper No. IDB-DP-427, January 2016. The author would like to thank the following people who shared particularly useful insights and information for this study: Gabriela Andrade, Frank Nieder and Fermín Vivanco of the Interamerican Bank, Claire Alexandre of Vodafone Group, Mireya Almazán of the GSMA, Marcos Bader formerly with Bradesco, Camille Bemerguy of Fundación Capital in Brazil, Johann Bezuidenhout and David Porteous of Bankable Frontier Associates, Jean Boudeguer of Cumplo, Paul Breloff of Accion Venture Lab, César Buenadicha, Mike Catalano of Pmt-Americas, Edrizio de la Cruz of Regalii, David del Ser of Frogtek, Lynn Eisenhart and David Lubinksi of the Bill & Melinda Gates Foundation, Innocent Ephraim of Vodacom, Mariana Escobar of Citi Colombia, Xavier Faz and Yanina Seltzer of CGAP, Dan Gertsacov of Lenddo, John Gitau of the Financial Education Centre, Pia Giudice of ideame, Reza Jalili of Adobe, Raunak Kapoor of MicroSave, Carlos López-Moctezuma of BBVA-Bancomer, Ben Lyon of Kopo Kopo, Jojo Malolos of Cignify, Xavier Martín (independent consultant), Beatriz Marulanda of Marulanda Consultores, Jordi Mas of Cambridge University, Amolo Ng'weno of Digital Divide Data, Francisco Noguera of Compartamos con Colombia, Tonny Omwansa of the University of Nairobi, Ana Pantelic of Fundación Capital in Colombia, Jean-Claude Rodgriguez-Ferrera of Puddles, Avijit Saha of ICICI Bank, Prateek Shrivastava of Accendo Associates, John Staley of Equity Bank, Evelyn Stark of MetLife Foundation, Scott Stefanski of Maana Mobil, Shiv Vadivelalagan of Stanford University, Kim Wilson of the Fletcher School, and Gabriela Zapata (independent consultant).

5.1 Introduction: The Potential of Broadband Solutions to Enhance Financial Inclusion

5.1.1 Motivation

The progress of financial inclusion in the Latin America and Caribbean (LAC) region is constrained by the high costs involved in providing and accessing financial services. On the client side, micro- and small-sized firms and lower-income households face high transaction costs due to the difficulty of getting to the points of service and in meeting documentation requirements. On the provider side, the lack of economies of scale for financial service transactions and the difficulty of obtaining reliable information on these types of clients create high operational costs. These high costs undermine profitability in serving these market segments, and this in turn results in a weak competitive environment.

Using broadband to deliver financially services has the potential to address fundamentally the above cost factors. In most countries in LAC, broadband coverage extends over areas where 90% of the population lives and is available 24/7. The falling costs of broadband access and smartphones makes it possible to envision a rapid rise in take-up and usage of mobile broadband over the next few years.

At the same time, the eventual mass use of broadband data-enabled mobile devices will also significantly diminish mobile operators' control over the services that flow through their mobile channels. This will result in a more level playing field among financial service providers

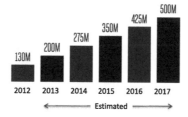

Figure 5.1a: Mobile and fixed broadband penetration by country (as percent of population, 2012).

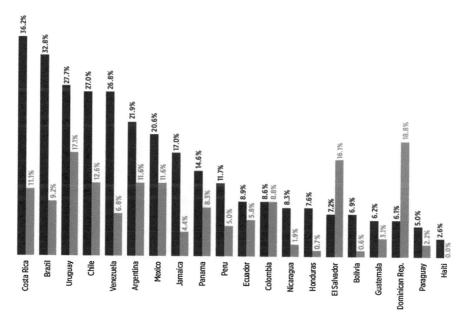

Figure 5.1b: Expected growth in the number of mobile broadband connections in LatAm.

(particularly between those that are associated with a mobile operator and those that are not), and ought to make it easier for new financial players with innovative offers to enter the market.

The GSMA (the global mobile trade association) estimates that the number of mobile broadband subscriptions in LAC will rise to 500 million by 2017, compared to 200 million in 2013 and a total population of 610 million (see Fig. 5.1b). Smartphone penetration was close to 20% of the population at the end of 2013, marginally below global averages; it is forecast to rise to 44% by 2017, which would bring mobile broadband access close to the current level of cell phone access in the region. Mobile broadband penetration is already far outstripping fixed broadband penetration in most countries in the region (see Fig. 5.1a). Combining this growth

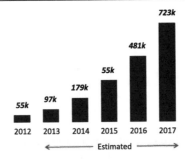

Figure 5.1c: Recent evolution in the average cost of mobile broadband plans in LatAm (USD/month).

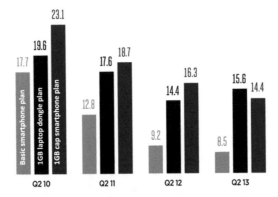

Figure 5.1d: Mobile data traffic in Latam (Terabytes/month).
(Source: GSMA, "Mobile Economy Latin America 2013")

in mobile broadband penetration with the expected increased data usage per subscriber, the total volume of mobile broadband data is expected to grow at a 67% per annum over the same period (see Fig. 5.1d). The GSMA also expects monthly mobile broadband data plan prices to continue to show a significant downward trend, especially for the smaller smartphone plans (see Fig. 5.1c).

Despite the falling prices of smartphones and mobile data plans, the penetration within the population will continue to be limited by the coverage of mobile services across the territory. Mobile services are likely to remain unavailable to a significant proportion of the rural population – accounting for roughly 25% of the region's total population – who live beyond reach of mobile services.[1] Thus, mobile broadband may not help where the financial inclusion gap is widest: in deep rural areas.

Increasing universality of broadband access can broaden the range of financial services that can be provided digitally, and deepen the relationships between clients and providers. As many types of transactions no longer need to be conducted within the physical facilities of financial institutions, transaction costs can be reduced sharply for both clients and providers. Digital service provision should also enhance access to relevant information, about clients as providers evaluate them for credit decisions, as well as about alternative service providers as customers evaluate offers from competing providers. All this should create opportunities for financial service providers to, on the one hand, drive greater scale and reap falling average unit costs, and on the other to develop more specialized service and business models. Specialization and scale should enhance competition by making the potential market larger and more profitable.[2]

There are numerous web-based financial services directed to moderate income households and smaller firms in advanced economies, which demonstrate the potential of this modality of delivery to serve those currently financially excluded. In LAC, however, there are currently only a small number of start-ups in this space. But the expected relatively high use of smart phones in the region gives LAC the potential to leapfrog over other developing country regions, which have relied on SMS-based systems for rapidly expanding access to financial services.

This paper seeks to provide a source of basic information on the potential and constraints for using broadband channels and applications to increase financial inclusion in LAC. It is expected to be a resource for policymakers, financial institutions and the broader development community in the region.

5.1.2 Classifying the Potential of Broadband on Financial Service Delivery Models

Fig. 5.2 presents the framework we will use to understand the potential of broadband in transforming the nature and delivery of financial services (see table below). The first column distinguishes between new broadband-enabled service concepts by the type of innovation they embody:

- Under the *product innovation* category, we include new service concepts that either offer new service elements to customers or present existing services in a more user-friendly, personalized fashion. These can be introduced by new players seeking differentiation, or by existing players seeking to deepen their customer relationships.
- Under the *model innovation* category, we include new business models that challenge traditional intermediation roles of financial service providers. These new players seek to facilitate financial services by building online marketplaces and transaction management systems, but without getting into the transaction flows themselves.

- Under the *process innovation* category, we include specialized players who use broadband channels to present and deliver existing financial services more efficiently and widely than traditional financial institutions, by lowering transaction costs and reducing information asymmetries.

The final row in Fig. 5.2 covers how broadband can help in the dissemination of financial education content and tools – rather than the financial services themselves.

Note that this paper is intended to look at how broadband channels can be used to enhance customer experiences, and hence the focus is at the end-service level. We do not look at innovations that address specific infrastructure or service component challenges, such as identity, core banking platforms or customer care engines. Equally, we do not look at productivity solutions for front-line staff, such as the use of smartphones by loan officers or for streamlined account opening.

Each of the three types of innovation categories described above is further broken down into three specific opportunity areas (see column 2 in Fig. 5.2). We therefore consider ten different opportunity areas in this paper. Column 3 in Fig. 5.2 lists the key financial services involved in each case. Each of the ten opportunity areas is described with reference to an illustrative prototypical example, which is mentioned in the fourth column in the table. Nevertheless, under each opportunity area we will note the range of experiences that are being experimented with globally and in Latin America.

It should be noted that the opportunities listed in table and considered below may not all end up having a positive impact for financial inclusion. For instance, instant on-line loans could possibly have deleterious consequences, given the high interest rates applied and the history of abusive practices of payday of similar off-line lenders.

The structure of the remainder of the paper is as follows. The next four sections develop the ten opportunity areas, based on the classification in the table. In each case we describe how they are working today with reference to concrete examples; we look briefly at the prevalence of similar experiences globally and in Latin America; we identify the specific opportunities they raise for financial inclusion, with reference to potential benefits for clients and/or providers; and discuss any specific policy and regulatory issues they raise.

5.2 Deepening Customer Engagement Based on Mass Customization

In this section we review some ways in which the availability of broadband delivery channels can enhance the service proposition offered by traditional types of service providers. We first consider how banks can redesign their basic savings offering so as to increase the scope of personalization and hence service relevance for their customers. We then look at how

Broad area of impact	Nature of opportunities	Financial services involved	Sample global experience
PRODUCT INNOVATION Deepening customer engagement based on mass customization *(Supporting product innovation by existing or new players)*	Enhanced functionality and personalization of savings accounts	Goal-based savings, recurring deposits, savings reminders	iWish by ICICI Bank in India
	Working capital loans for businesses that digitize their transactions	Loans automatically repayable from online merchant payments	Grow by Kopo Kopo in Kenya
	Financing based on connections to cloud-based business applications	More flexible business loans (installment, term, line of credit)	Frogtek in Mexico & Colombia
MODEL INNOVAITON Digital marketplaces supporting new (dis-) intermediation models *(Disruptive model innovation by new players)*	Direct peer-to-peer (P2P) lending platforms	Short- to medium-term loans for individuals and small businesses	Cumplo in Chile
	Project-based crowdfunding platforms	Equity, rewards-based financing	Ideame in Argentina
	Platforms for managing savings & loan groups	Savings & loans within closed user groups (ROSCA, ASCA)	Puddle in the United States
PROCESS INNOVATION Specialized online service delivery models *(Disruptive process innovation by new streamlined players)*	Online international remittance services	International remittances & bill presentment/payment	Regalii in the Dominican Republic-US corridor
	Instant online personal loans	Short-term unsecured consumer loans, payday loans	Lenddo in Philippines, Mexico and Colombia
	Price comparison sites and service aggregators	Information on and channel for all financial services	Money Super Market in the United Kingdom
INFORMATION *(Existing or new players)* Delivery of financial information and education		All financial services, and beyond	Colombia LISTA by Fundación Capital

Figure 5.2: Framework for broadband financial services.

merchant acquirers can add a credit component to their digital payment processing function. Lastly, we examine how cloud-based business applications can be leveraged to increase the benefits for businesses from engaging in digital payments, and as a source of information for credit risk analysis and decisions.

5.2.1 Enhanced Functionality and Personalization of Savings Accounts

Motivation. A key challenge for banks and other financial service providers is to increase the frequency and range of interactions they have with their clients, and through that to gain deeper knowledge of their clients. This in turn should allow them to make more tightly-priced and more responsible credit decisions, cross-sell new services to existing customers so as to meet more of their needs and increase loyalty, acquire new customers by targeting their offers to defined segments, and drive more relevant product development.

Opportunity. By freeing up client–bank interactions from necessarily taking place within the confines of traditional physical banking infrastructures, digital broadband channels can make banking services available immediately, around the clock, from (almost) anywhere.

These services can be accessed at very low cost, both by reducing direct transaction costs and by wiping out the transport costs and dead time previously involved in accessing banking premises.

Moreover, digital broadband services make it possible for banks to present targeted offers to each client or segment, and to position new services in a dynamic and contextualized way; conversely, they let customers discover, learn about and experiment with new services at their own pace and in their own time. The objective is a much higher level of customer engagement. As argued in the MIF's ProSavings report, the financial education gap that has traditionally separated banks from their client base can more easily be bridged if services that embody notions and use language are more familiar with customers and incorporate easy follow-up mechanisms.[3]

Banks have extended banking service via the Internet and mobile apps for many years now, but most have conceived their Internet/app banking merely as a new channel. Most Internet banking sites and apps are designed to replicate the experience that would otherwise take place face-to-face at a branch. However, a new breed of service providers is developing novel service concepts and user interface designs that more fully exploit the possibilities of digital broadband service delivery. This includes:

- Giving customers more opportunities to adapt or personalize the service to their own needs and circumstances. This is achieved, for instance, by letting customers classify their money as user-defined goals rather than accounts with pre-defined characteristics.
- Providing customers with more feedback on their financial behavior and reinforcement on their goals through targeted reminders, iconic depiction and visualization of savings goals and balances, and intuitive spending analysis tools.
- Putting people's financial management in the context of their social relationships. By bridging digital financial management tools with online social networking, users can for example request contributions to goals from their friends, or use peer pressure devices to build self-discipline.

Global experiences. A number of new players are experimenting with this sort of enhanced Internet/app banking experiences. Early innovators in this space were savings goal-oriented start-ups such as Smartypig and Goalmine in the US, and these have been followed by newer entrants such as Simple and Moven (also in the US) which have created fuller banking propositions. These firms see to control the presentation layer of financial services on the web, and their partner banks serve primarily as the custodian of the savings funds.

In the US, American Express, in partnership with Walmart, has created a very flexible form of prepaid account called Bluebird. It allows users to create instantly any number of goal-based subaccounts ("SetAside accounts"), into which they can move money on a one-off or recurrent basis; users need to move the money back into their main account to access the funds. It also allows users to associate up to five subaccounts for family members ("Family Accounts") on which the user can exercise various degrees of control over the financial actions of their family members (setting daily spending limits, receiving alerts, issuing debit cards, or turning ATM access on/off).

SaveUp of the US is a rewards program that works in partnership with a large number of financial institutions. SaveUp seeks to promote good financial decisions among its registered users, who receive points every time they save money or make a loan or credit card repayment. With these points users can win prizes through raffles organized by SaveUp.

Banks are now incorporating this type of service into their own Internet banking offerings, either by licensing the platforms of these early entrants and creating their own service or buying them outright. A notorious early mover who developed its own systems was ING Direct, a subsidiary of ING Bank that was subsequently sold to Capital One of the US. In contrast, Old Mutual in South Africa bought one year old start-up 22seven in 2013, and BBVA of Spain bought the US-based Simple in 2014.

Another leading example is ICICI Bank, a private bank in India, which created a goal-based, flexible recurring deposit service called iWish in 2012, based on the Smartypig platform. iWish is marketed as the "wish fulfilling deposit." Users can define their own goals, and can contribute flexibly to them without having to commit to a particular savings frequency. They can optionally set up an automated recurrent payment scheme to fund their iWish account from their checking account, but even in this case there are no penalties if installments are skipped or contributions vary from the originally planned amount. A system of SMS reminders is designed to keep people on their savings track. Goals can be canceled at any time, but there is a small penalty for early cancellation. There are now around 2.5m iWish accounts and the average saved balance is around USD 300, though many are largely inactive.

In Latin America, a number of specialized players are moving in this direction with certain elements of this kind of experience, albeit for the time being with simple mobile phones. In Mexico, Kiwi is a start-up that helps users set up their own layaway plan for purchases they intend to make at participating stores. Juntos Finanzas operates a savings reminder platform by SMS with partners in several Latin American countries, which is designed to enhance people's savings culture and discipline. Juntos Finanzas does not itself provide savings services: it can be used to support savings at partner banks or informal savings by people themselves.

Potential for financial inclusion. Most of these players are currently targeting younger, more tech-literate people who are under-banked rather than unbanked – people who have a banking relationship but do not find it so useful or user-friendly. However, the potential for meeting the needs of the unbanked is significant, as they increasingly get access to, and become more familiar with, its use. Beyond reducing transaction costs, the new service presentation methods can make financial services much more intuitive and relevant to people who are not at all familiar with banking concepts. At the same time, these sites provide self-discipline and peer pressure tools which are particularly valuable to poorer people, and which are much closer to the kind of money management they already do informally. This type of money management tools can result in higher savings balances, which in turn can drive higher credit ratings for its users.

On the other hand, given the short experience with this type of solutions, there are still many questions around their fit for base-of-the-pyramid users. Less tech savvy users may take a long time to accept these solutions as it may be harder to build their intuition of how they work and they may inherently distrust technology-mediated solutions. It is not clear how effective reminders can be in stimulating savings on a longer-term basis, once they came to be expected by users, especially if reminders are used more persistently by a broader range of service providers. And the effectiveness of sharing goals on online social networks is still unclear.

Regulatory issues. This type of service does not present special regulatory issues, as long as it is provided by regulated deposit-taking institutions or in partnership with them. Banking authorities could consider opening up this sort of activity to specialized players with an appropriate e-money license, which would allow them to handle customers' savings balances but not to intermediate their funds.

5.2.2 Payment Systems and Working Capital Loans for Businesses That Digitize Their Transactions

Motivation. The share of goods and services that are paid for electronically is likely to grow markedly, driven by several related factors:

- New technology-enabled models for financial inclusion are lowering the cost of issuing digital payment instruments to mass-market consumers, whether they are card-based (such as with most banks in Latin America) or mobile-based (such as with M-PESA in Kenya or Tigo Money in El Salvador, Guatemala, Honduras and Paraguay). Under these systems, the sender typically pays the cash in and the recipient retrieves the cash at a local participating store (termed an *agent*). Tigo Money operates as a cash-to-cash money transfer system, where the sending customer pays cash to the agent to fund the transfer, and a unique code (technically: a one-time password) is sent automatically to the recipient's phone via a text message. The recipient can then go to an agent and claim the cash on presentation of this unique code. While Tigo Money doesn't work on the basis of a customer account, in the case of M-PESA the transfer flows between the sender's and the recipient's account. The sender must first deposit money into his account at the agent, and then he can issue a money transfer instruction from his mobile phone; the recipient can keep the money in his account, transfer it to someone else, or go to an agent to withdraw it.

- Moreover, the spread of smartphones and the emergence of simple card readers attachable to the audio jack of smartphones (originally conceived by Square in the US) have spawned the development of low cost electronic payment systems for small shops wishing to receive card-based payments from their clients. The built-in camera on smartphones can also be used as an automated payment input device. In this regard, a smartphone app by Mitek (US) automatically extracts relevant data from a bill that has been photographed and automatically fills in the fields required to make a mobile payment. In Mexico, start-ups like Clip, PagoFácil and Sr.Pago are helping small businesses receive electronic payments with low-cost mobile point-of-sale system that include a Square-like card reader, mobile apps for managing payments they receive, and a prepaid debit card that gives merchants instant access to funds that they're paid.
- A number of low-cost, cloud-based solutions are emerging that are designed to help small businesses and traders keep track of their business. These create incentive for businesses to want to capture their transaction information electronically at source, i.e. at the point of payment. For instance, Frogtek in Mexico (see next section) is a smartphone app that keeps track of store's inventory levels and offers check-out services at point of sale.
- The growth of e-commerce platforms directly feeds into demand for online payment solutions by third parties, such as PayPal (US).

Opportunity. As transactions are recorded digitally via smartphones at the point of sale – whether as a store check-out or customer bill payment – valuable information accumulates which can be harnessed by financial service providers to offer working capital loans to those businesses. By gaining visibility of detailed, real-time sales data, credit providers can offer terms that would not be feasible otherwise. This data may be enhanced by also collecting information about merchants from their social media profiles and online accounting software.

Moreover, by inserting themselves in the merchant payment flow, loans can be repaid automatically from future card/electronic payment receipts processed from the merchant. This aligns the interest of both merchant and the credit provider around business growth. However, the automatic repayment rate cannot be too high as otherwise the merchant would be disincentivized from collecting payment from its customers electronically (which would trigger automatic loan repayment) rather than cash.

Global experiences. This space is now being developed aggressively by online merchant acquirers (specialized companies that help retailers accept and process electronic payments from their customers), which are adding credit support to their range of merchant solutions. Capital Access Network (CAN) of the US pioneered the notion of merchant cash advances, and is now the leader. PayPal started its SME lending facility, Working Capital, in the US in September 2013 and then in the UK in July 2014. Square launched its lending program, Capital, in the US in May 2014.

This experience is now spreading to emerging markets where digital, and especially mobile, payments are making deeper inroads. Kopo Kopo, the leading M-PESA merchant acquirer in Kenya, launched Grow in May 2014, and in four months has provided merchant cash advances to around 500 stores. Retailers who have received merchant payments through Kopo Kopo for at least three months can apply loans for a value of up to USD 60,000. Loans get repaid automatically based on an agreed share of daily electronic merchant payment receipts that are automatically set aside by Kopo Kopo to repay the loan. Loans are unsecured beyond this automatic repayment rate. While the mobile payments supported by M-PESA run on simple mobile phones through SMS, merchants can apply for more advanced online access and get instant credit decisions. Kopo Kopo sees Grow as a key service to induce their merchants to migrate from simple mobile phones to smartphones that offer more functionality and a faster and more convenient merchant experience.

In Latin America, Banco Estado in Chile is conducting pilots to starting to experiment with this type of merchant working capital loans.

Market sizing. According to one estimate, the value of merchant cash advances to small businesses in the US was $3 billion in 2013.[4] This includes purchases of future credit card sales, online lenders that provide revenue-secured loans such as Kabbage and OnDeck (discussed further below), and other lending mechanisms to businesses whose repayment is based on daily capture of funds. Just three online lenders (CAN, OnDeck and Kabbage) accounted for half of this volume, though not all of it fits the description of daily capture of funds.

Potential for financial inclusion. These types of digital credit solutions based on digitized transactions are efficient relative to standard SME working capital sources for two reasons. First, they reduce the information asymmetry between the merchant and the credit provider, thereby making credit risk more assessable and monitorable. Second, by directly linking customer merchant payments with credit repayments, transaction costs of servicing the loans vanish and the credit can be offered on an automatic rollover basis, which reduces transaction costs for all parties.

Moreover, such credit solutions can become a valuable element of digital financial inclusion programs in developing countries because they address one of the toughest issues in building digital payment ecosystems: convincing everyday stores to accept merchant discounts. The possibility of getting instant working capital loans can become a strong incentive for stores everywhere to promote digital payments with their customers. The ability to make digital payments at everyday stores can in turn enhance the value proposition from banking for the general public. In so doing, they can in turn be a strong driver for business formalization, by providing incentives for business owners to report their business activities and transaction flows more accurately.

Regulatory issues. Merchant credit offered on this basis is effectively collateralized by future (electronically received) revenues. However, regulators often treat them as uncollateralized loans, since there is no constituted collateral at the time the credit is extended. As a result, the mandated risk rating and provisioning requirements are set at higher levels than might otherwise be the case, which makes this form of credit more expensive.

5.2.3 Financing Based on Connections to Cloud-Based Business Applications

Motivation. Access to broadband presents an especially significant opportunity for small businesses to harness financial information linked to a variety of business contacts, processes and workflows. Broadband, along with the proliferation of mobile devices, allows much more information to be captured, processed, analyzed and deployed in value-enhancing ways. This results in a stronger sense of business control and faster business reaction times to market conditions or events.

Moreover, the growing trend in providing access to software as a service (SaaS) rather than as localized company-specific installations has massively reduced technology adoption costs. Small business can now access shared services that previously were only available if they belonged to larger industrial groups. Businesses can now avail themselves of the latest software services without needing business-specific IT support staff. Cloud-based services are generally designed to upgrade easily, as business needs grow and evolve, and hence are more flexible than traditional shrink-wrapped software. The solutions are available through a browser "anywhere, anytime," which facilitates collaboration among business partners and employees and better supports remote or field workers. They can also be implemented through an app downloaded on the user devices, which offers a faster, more convenient experience to users.

Opportunity. In general, digitizing business information allows various stakeholders to hold relevant information on structured databases, and this in turn lets providers offer businesses more services in a less risky way. But resistance to this path of increasing digitization of business information is often high, as it often involves changing business practices, incurring new fees to new service providers, and potentially exposing more information to tax authorities. Therefore, providers need to make sure that they can make the value embedded in the business information more relevant to the business so that it has an incentive to collect it.

Global experiences. There are now many cloud-based services that allow businesses to structure and access information linked to their transactions for a variety of purposes. Good examples are US-based Intuit's general database management software QuickBase and accounting software QuickBooks, which can be used to manage database access permissions and automate notifications, perform standard analytics, and link the databases to business apps in a number of categories. Another leading example is the customer resource management (CRM) solution Salesforce.com, also of the US, which helps businesses to maintain a full life-cycle view of their customers, from prospects through to sales and service. There are also more specific solutions such as the time tracking software OfficeTime (US) that helps contractors keep track of billable time and generate invoices, and the Maana Mobile (US) loan management system that automatically reports payments to update both borrower and lender records.

Some applications are particularly focused on retailers in emerging markets, who are likely to become transaction acquirers for the new breed of mass-market digital/mobile payments. For instance, FrogTek offers store check-in/out services based on a tablet and a barcode scanner. This system provides retailers (and potentially their distributors) with detailed reporting on inventory, sales and profitability right on their smartphone.

Kabbage.com of the US is a service that offers a line of credit to SMEs who are willing to share with them the data from these types of online business support applications, as well as other online relationships such as bank or PayPal account. By using real-life business data from these sources, Kabbage is able to approve funding in minutes for businesses that might not have an established credit score or who might not have a significant digital merchant payment stream. Kabbage therefore goes beyond the merchant cash advances discussed in the previous subsection.

Market sizing. (See the corresponding entry in the previous section, into which this market segment has been subsumed.)

Potential for financial inclusion. These types of business control services can play a significant role in financial inclusion by enhancing the value proposition to businesses of formalizing and digitizing their financial management practices. By providing a direct business benefit beyond the sheer payment function, these services make it more attractive for businesses to entertain the risk of disruption involved with switching to formal financial services. They can also alleviate the concerns over the higher explicit fees and exposure to taxes that are often perceived to come with formal finance.

These types of digital transaction recording solutions can be particularly effective in supporting financial inclusion if they are directed specifically to drive the business case for cash in/out agents. They can drive a store loyalty scheme that incentivizes frequent customer use of cash in/out services or digital payment for goods. They can also drive mobile advertising campaigns (e.g. via SMS) that can be either localized (broadcast to all mobile users within a cell) or targeted (e.g. to previous customers who have paid with their mobile phone). They can also make it easier to expand their business to digital purchases under electronic voucher systems.

Regulatory issues. The main regulatory issues that arise relate to the legal standing of electronic documents and signatures in contracts and legal procedures, and the privacy of business information gleaned from borrowers. In addition, to the extent that having greater visibility of the borrower's business transactions on an ongoing basis permits closer monitoring of the borrower, it may be justified to classify these types of loans under a lower risk weighting.

5.3 Digital Marketplaces Supporting New (Dis-)Intermediation Models

More widespread access to broadband has the potential for enabling much more meaningful and direct interaction between end-users and a host of market participants, thereby eroding the central importance of traditional financial institutions – and potentially bypassing them altogether. The next set of global experiences we will look at are much more challenging of traditional intermediation because they use broadband channels to build trust and achieve more decentralized matching between transacting parties. They replace the notion of the financial intermediary (which transacts separately with the borrower and the provider of funds, such as depositors). Rather, with these systems the parties to the transaction agree on the terms and conduct the transaction independently, via a third party which puts them into contact.

We will first look at online marketplaces for individual loans; then we will look at online marketplaces for syndicated project funding; and lastly we will look at online tools that can bolster the trust in and reach of traditional lending circles or savings groups.

5.3.1 Direct Peer-to-Peer Lending Platforms

Motivation. Formal financial services tend to be based on specialized entities intermediating the trust between debtors and creditors. These intermediating agencies have a certain comparative advantage in absorbing credit risk because they can: (*i*) impose specific selection, screening and monitoring mechanism on borrowers; (*ii*) pool risks across many borrowers who face idiosyncratic (i.e. uncorrelated or non-market) risks; (*iii*) invest in appropriate hedging strategies to handle market risks; and (*iv*) invest the necessary resources in legal enforcement mechanisms to maintain the validity of their claims.

But this intermediation comes at a price, which can either take the form of high administration fees or a wide margin between lending and borrowing rates. It also leaves savers with residual credit risk on the intermediating agencies themselves (unless there is a government-sponsored deposit insurance scheme), one that is hard to assess by creditors because the financial condition of intermediaries is notoriously non-transparent. At the same time, traditional intermediation leaves savers with no control over how their resources are redeployed (i.e. who is funded), which may be hard to accept by more socially-conscious investors.

Opportunity. In finance as in many other areas, the Internet is powering new business models of a much more decentralized nature that promise unprecedented levels of customer choice with much reduced transaction costs. A new class of peer-to-peer (P2P) lending sites is emerging which are more akin to a "financial eBay" than to a traditional bank. P2P sites are marketplaces that enable prospective borrowers to post their financial requirements online and thereby attract lenders who are willing to fund them directly.

Online P2P loans are mostly unsecured personal loans between people who don't know each other, though there are now versions that cater to business lending or more specialized needs such as student loans, invoice factoring or real estate loans. P2P websites generally contain a description of a large number of borrowers and the intended purpose of the loan. Prospective lenders can go to the website and choose whom among them they wish to fund. Some sites have a voting mechanism through which borrowers can build up a public score, and a few link to social networks as a further trust-building mechanism. Loans can be resold to other lenders on the same site, though liquidity tends to be very low.

P2P sites usually perform borrower verifications (such as identity, bank account, employment and income) and credit checks, they process payments between borrowers and lenders, and may also take action to collect payments from delinquent borrowers – but they do not intermediate the loans themselves and hence carry none of the credit risk. Interest rates are usually set by lenders who compete for the lowest rate on a reverse auction basis. In some cases, though, P2P sites include credit models for loan approvals and pricing.

Global experiences. The leading countries in terms of development of P2P platforms remain the US and the UK, where this model originated. The first P2P site was Zopa in the UK, launched in 2005, followed by Prosper in the US a year later. The model has now spread to many countries, including China (Creditease and SinoLending), France (Prêt d'Union) Germany (Auxmoney) and Spain (Comunitae).

Cumplo of Chile was launched in May 2012 as the first person-to-person lending site in Latin America, and is now focused on enabling P2P loans to SMEs. The growth in SME loans has been spurred by the fact that they can tap into a government loan guarantee scheme for eligible SMEs. A smaller proportion of posted enterprise loans are backed by the enterprise's invoices for collection and are therefore akin to factoring. As of early September 2014, Cumplo had over USD 32 million outstanding in 700 loans.

Other examples of P2P lending platforms in Latin America are Afluenta in Argentina, and Prestadero and Ku-bo Financiero in Mexico.

Market sizing. The leading platform in the US, Lending Club, has facilitated more than USD 5 billion in loans, to almost 300,000 individuals, from its inception in 2007 to end-June 2014. Of this amount, USD 1 billion was in the second quarter of 2014 alone, demonstrating a phenomenal growth rate of almost 100% year-on-year.[5] During the month of September 2014, US-based Prosper facilitated USD 136 million in loans, an increase of 421% over the same month a year earlier. In the same month, UK-based Funding Circle and Zopa, two market leaders, facilitated a combined USD 66 in loans, an increase of 90%.[6] In the UK, peer-to-peer lenders have collectively lent almost USD 1 billion in 2013, of which half was lent to individuals and half to small businesses; of the USD 500 million that went to businesses, two-thirds were in direct loans and one third took the form of invoice trading.[7]

New loans worldwide processed through P2P sites in the month of July 2014 are estimated to have been around USD 250 million.[8] An investor in the space expects that one trillion dollars in loans will be originated through P2P platforms globally, accounting for 10% of all consumer and SME lending.[9]

Potential for financial inclusion. Most informal financial practices contain an element of trust among peers, either on a personal basis (as when money is given to a money-guard or loaned out to a friend) or through a group solidarity process (as in rotating savings schemes and self-help groups). Online P2P lending platforms may therefore be culturally and practically closer to what people are familiar with, since they preserve greater personal discretion over the destination of the funds and incorporate a social element. P2P sites could be a useful way to induce greater formalization of lender/borrower relationships, without implying a large transfer of responsibility to physically and culturally distant financial institutions.

Regulatory issues. The main regulatory issues surrounding P2P lending concern: (*i*) the legality of soliciting investments from the general public, and (*ii*) the reporting requirements on the marketplace players. These are concerns because, unchecked, these platforms can lead to overindebtedness as individuals gain such easy, direct access to borrowing.

There are questions as to whether individual loans sold online constitute securities, and hence are subject to registration and fuller documentation.[10] Due to their short history, it is not clear how P2P lending will perform in a downturn, and there have already been a few isolated cases of a platform closure.[11] There could also be many potential consumer protection pitfalls associated with unscrupulous P2P platforms misleading lenders on lending terms, and unscrupulous borrowers misrepresenting themselves. We can therefore expect that in the future P2P platforms will be increasingly regulated by financial authorities, and may be require special licensing.

In March 2014, the UK passed the most comprehensive regulatory framework around P2P lending platforms. The Financial Conduct Authority (FCA) imposed a minimum capital requirement on platforms based on their volume of loans outstanding, starting at 0.2% for the first GBP 50 million pounds in lending, with a declining rate with larger volumes. The FCA requires that platforms not comingle client funds and that they perform proper reconciliations. The FCA extended certain consumer protection obligations on platforms, such as providing cancellation rights to investors under certain conditions and within certain timeframes, providing adequate disclosures, and instituting proper complaints and dispute resolution processes. Platforms must ensure they have a robust back-up plan in place to service loans in the event they go out of business or otherwise cease to operate. The FCA also imposed regular reporting requirements such as disclosing their prudential and financial position, notification of a change in total value of loans outstanding of 25% or more, client money positions, investor complaints, and loans arranged over the previous quarter.[12]

In contrast, in the US, P2P platforms "fall between the cracks for federal regulators. Because they are not banking entities, the traditional regulators – particularly the Federal Deposit Insurance Corporation, the Federal Reserve and the Office of the Comptroller of the Currency (OCC) – have been less involved."[13] The Securities and Exchange Commission (SEC) determined in 2008 that loans traded on P2P platforms are indeed securities, and that the platforms that promote them ought to be treated as brokers or dealers, with specific rules attached to them. Accordingly, P2P platforms must register their offerings as securities with the SEC as well as in every state in which the securities are offered for sale to the public. However, the US has not passed a unified regulatory framework for consumer protection around P2P platforms, so rules are fragmented between various agencies at the federal and state levels.

No country in Latin America has yet established a regulatory framework for P2P lending, though the authorities in many countries such as Chile are letting such platforms develop undisturbed. To avoid the kind of legal vacuum that Cumplo is operating in, Ku-bo Financiero in Mexico has already taken the step of getting a *Sociedad Financiera Popular* (SOFIPO) license.

5.3.2 Equity Crowdfunding Platforms

Motivation. Crowdfunding sites are online marketplaces that facilitate the pooling of money from a diverse collection of investors to fund specific business projects, including start-ups which cannot get access from other sources such as venture capital funds or which want to maintain greater independence. Funds can be raised as pure donations (based on affinity with purpose, with some level of recognition), in exchange for rewards (such as getting access to early version of the product, or price discounts), against equity, or as lending. The concept of crowdfunding is therefore a generalization of the direct funding solicitation concept pioneered by P2P lending platforms.

Opportunity. Equity crowdfunding platforms offer the means to smaller investors to take direct equity positions in companies and to provide smaller and newer firms with additional and usually lower-cost sources of financing. Their equity investments are protected by the statutory provisions afforded to ordinary shareholders by the funded companies, though as private equity funding they enjoy much less protection than publicly traded shares. Some platforms offer additional protection to investors, in the form of subscription agreements with the funded companies, which contain protections such as consent and pre-emption rights on the issue of new securities, and tag-along rights in the event of the sale of shares by a major shareholder.

As with P2P lending sites, equity crowdfunding sites handle the payments involved but do not get involved in the transaction itself. Each site has rules as to the conditions under which money pledged by investors must be paid up: some sites collect investor funds only if a minimum amount pre-specified by the investee has been pledged within a defined fund-raising period, whereas other sites collect all pledged amounts from investors and leave it up to the investee to determine whether the amount raised is sufficient to complete the project or whether the pledged funds should be returned to the investors. Because crowdfunding tends to cater more specifically to entrepreneurs and innovators, the platforms may also provide services such as media hosting, social networking, and facilitating contact with contributors.

Global experiences. The earliest crowdfunding sites were donor and reward-based. The first online crowdfunding platform was ArtistShare, launched in 2003 in the US. Since then, most have been commercially oriented in the US (including KickStarter, Indiegogo, Profounder and Microventures) as elsewhere, such as FundRazr in Canada, DemoHour in China, Fundedbyme in several Europe countries, Headstart in Israel, Sellaband in Germany, and Goteo in Spain. Some crowdfunding sites have a social and charitable purpose: for instance, Handup is a site specifically for helping homeless people in the US.

Equity-based crowdfunding platforms, understood as the sale of registered securities by mostly early-stage firms to investors, started in the US in 2010 with RockThePost (subsequently merged into OneVest). Currently the largest platform is US-based AngelList, which supports both equity and debt investments for start-ups, but it only allows accredited investors to invest. Other leading US-based equity crowdfunding platforms in the US are Early Shares, Fundable, CircleUp, and Crowdfunder. The two leading UK-based equity crowdfunding platforms employ different investment mechanisms: while CrowdCube allows individual investors to acquire shares directly in start-up companies, Seedrs pools the funds to invest in new businesses as a nominated agent.

Mirroring the international experience, the majority of emerging crowdfunding platforms in Latin America are grant/reward-based, and many focus on creative or artistic projects. Such is the case with ideame, which was launched in Argentina in 2011, acquired the Movere crowdfunding service in Brazil in 2012, and has now spread to four other Latin American countries; Catarse, the market leader in Brazil; Fondeadora in Mexico;

However, a number of equity-based crowdfunding platforms are also emerging. US-based Crowdfunder opened up a Mexican subsidiary platform in December 2012. Broota was founded in Chile in 2013 but remains small: it claims to have closed USD 200,000 in financing from 68 investors. Beyond financing, its aspiration is to become a social network for entrepreneurs. Vakita Capital was founded in Mexico in April 2013, but has not yet started operations.[14]

Market sizing. The volume of equity crowdfunding globally was estimated to be USD 116 million in 2012; this is still a tiny percent of the USD 2.7 billion that was raised through crowdfunding globally.[15] It is estimated that in the UK alone in 2013 the volume of equity deals closed through crowdfunding platforms was USD 45 million, and a further USD 2 million was in revenue or profit-sharing deals.[16]

Potential for financial inclusion. As with P2P lending, crowdfunding could become an effective funding mechanism for start-ups and small companies in emerging markets as it provides the potential for smaller firms to expand their access to finance and at more favorable terms from financial intermediaries. In addition, it can exploit the more collaborative, community-oriented practices prevalent in the informal economy. Crowdfunding platforms can also be a powerful channel for socially minded investors to contribute to socially- and development-oriented projects. In particular, they could become a particularly useful mechanism for diaspora communities to invest in a diversified set of projects in their home country.

Regulatory issues. Many governments recognize the value of crowdfunding as a mechanism for funding entrepreneurship and innovation, but are concerned about the overt public investment solicitation it represents. A key concern is whether investors understand the kinds of risks that are involved in funding start-ups, which have a notoriously high failure rate. Regulators are therefore grappling primarily on what restrictions need to be placed on non-accredited investors seeking to invest through public crowdfunding platforms, and the disclosure and transparency rules that apply to the platform itself.

The US took the lead in promoting crowdfunding through the passage of the JOBS act in 2012, which introduced requirements on all the players involved. Crowdfunding sites must be registered with the Securities and Exchange Commission (SEC). On the investor side, only accredited investors (individuals with a net worth exceeding $1 million excluding their home, or earning more than $250,000 per year) can invest through equity crowdfunding, and they are only permitted to invest a certain amount per year (the lower of USD 100,000 or 5% of assets). On the investee side, there is a cap on how much each investee can raise per year (up to USD 1 million dollars), and their financial statements must be reviewed or audited independently if they have raised more than USD 100,000.

In Europe, Italy became the first country to regulate equity-based crowdfunding when the Italian financial securities regulator, CONSOB, issued two rules in July 2013. Only companies that are specifically designated as "innovative start-ups" by the Chamber of Commerce can solicit equity through crowdfunding platforms, and the maximum amount that a start-up can raise is set at €5 million. Such start-ups are required to: (*i*) have a professional investor, a bank foundation, a financial corporation or an incubator that subscribes at least 5% of the capital offered; and (*ii*) insert a clause in their statutes which guarantees to crowdfunding investors the right sell their shares in case the major shareholder sells its stake to a third party. CONSOB did not limit who can invest through crowdfunding platforms, beyond requiring that they take a test to demonstrate that they are aware of the risks they are taking when investing, and that they can afford the possible loss of the amount invested. CONSOB also imposed some fit and proper restrictions on promoters of equity crowdfunding platform, and placed certain information transparency obligations on them.[17]

Like Italy, France does not impose restrictions on investors in crowdfunding platforms. The UK regulator is taking a tougher line: in March 2014 the Financial Conduct Authority (FC) required that inexperienced investors in equity schemes must certify that they will not invest more than 10% of their portfolio in unlisted businesses.[18]

5.3.3 *Platforms for Managing Savings & Loan Groups*

Motivation. Informal financial solutions tend to have a strong social dimension. It is very common to find basic rotating savings and loan schemes (generically called ROSCAs) into which members contribute a fixed amount at each regular meetings, and take turns in taking the sum collected at each meeting. There are more flexible schemes (generically called accelerating savings and loan schemes, or ASCAs) under which members can apply for loans at a meeting, which they repay in fixed installments in subsequent meetings; any excess of funds raised over borrowings outstanding are saved in a communal pot which typically takes the form of a lockbox or a bank account. Sometimes savings groups come together in an *ad hoc* fashion for a particular fundraising purpose, such as to pay for a wedding, hospital bill or funeral of someone in the community; these groups dissolve once the target amount is raised.

These informal grassroots financial solutions rely heavily on trust between the members. This presents several limitations. These groups tend to be geographically constrained, as the mechanics of trust building and monitoring require that people meet physically on a regular basis, and monitor each other between meetings. These services are also not portable when a member migrates to a different village, as the groups at the new location will be entirely unaware of the member's history with groups at the location of origin. And when trust is broken, which happens not infrequently, it is wrenching and it takes a long time to rebuild trust.

Opportunities. There are two approaches to leveraging broadband solutions to support savings & loan groups, without changing the core proposition of direct (non-intermediated) trust between group members. One approach is to incorporate broadband solutions into the basic mechanics of traditional groups in a way that helps mitigate some of the limitations mentioned earlier but without displacing physical group meetings. These solutions tend to be focused on maintaining proper accounting and managing the group's information transparently. Under the second approach, smartphone-based apps can be used to organize "virtual groups" which need not come together physically. The service therefore replicates, rather than complements, the experience of physical group meetings. The app can contain tools to invite group members, solicit (electronic) contributions from members, handle loan requests by individual members, and push regular information back to all members.

Global experiences. Kenya-based eRecording is an Android app freely downloadable from Google Play that contains all the necessary accounting tools to maintain proper monitoring of savings and credit groups. It can be used at physical group meetings to record all the transactions that occur, and a summary can be automatically sent to each member of the group by SMS into their personal phone. E-kulki of Colombia has been developing a similar application.

Mission Asset Fund of the US reports the savings and borrowing activity of members of its groups to credit bureaus, so that group members can begin to nurture a credit rating through their informal financial activities. By enhancing transparency and making more information available to all members at any time, it may be less tempting for the group leader/treasurer to cheat or manipulate the accounts. Trust can become stronger and build up faster than otherwise.

Tutanda of Mexico is a web-based platform for setting up and managing ROSCAs ("tandas," in Spanish), as is eMoneyPool and Yattos in the US.

Puddle of the US is a web-based platform for setting up and managing lending circles or ASCAs, which offer more flexibility on the timing and amount that members can borrow against group contributions. Individual borrowings are not in fact approved by the group, but are extended automatically by Puddle as long as the group has positive net funds (i.e. contributions larger than borrowings outstanding). In addition to the group management and accounting tools, it lets people find groups they may want to join, or meet other people with whom they might form a new group.

This sort of tools is likely to be particularly useful for shorter-term, specific-purpose groups formed around particular events such as a wedding, local festivities, or hospitalization of a community member. Safaricom in Kenya has built a tool, called Changa na M-PESA, essentially as a temporary bill-pay number which allows money to be collected easily. M-Changa, a start-up in Kenya, has built a dedicated app, also available in Google Play, which has more sophisticated tools to communicate with group members.

Potential for financial inclusion. These solutions can be a powerful component of financial inclusion strategies because they tap more directly into the psyche and the current practices of most people in the informal sector. They can be a complement to formal financial services, but more importantly they can act as a stepping stone into personal financial services.

Regulatory issues. There are no additional regulatory issues with broadband solutions that merely support the accounting and communication within existing, traditional savings & loan group structures – beyond those that already apply to such structures. Insofar as they build transparency, they are aligned with generally accepted consumer protection policies.

However, sites that seek to facilitate the creation of virtual groups share some of the issues of P2P and crowdfunding sites mentioned above (such as consumer protection and reporting requirements), insofar as they bring together people who are in a position to fund each other. However, savings & loan groups constitute closed user groups based on a longer-term relationship, and hence present far smaller issues than the more open, transactional P2P and crowdfunding sites. In August 2014, the State of California has passed a pioneering law which formalizes the treatment of these services if they are run by non-profit organizations, granting them exemptions from certain restrictions that normally apply to lenders.[19]

5.4 Specialized Online Service Delivery Models

The next set of experiences cover how broadband channels may disrupt traditional financial service providers not by changing the fundamental intermediation logic of the market but simply by streamlining operations in a way that reduces transaction costs and information asymmetries. They generally involve new narrowly specialized players who are able to gain an informational or marketing advantage over more established players by virtue of their focus.

We first look at how purely online players are seeking to break into the high-margin international remittance market. We then look at online lenders that leverage electronic information resources for credit scoring. Lastly, we look at online aggregators: companies who do not offer their own financial services but collect pricing information on multiple providers and act as conduits for consumers seeking the best deals they can find.

5.4.1 Online International Remittance Services

Motivation. International remittances are notoriously expensive, especially into developing markets. This is a result of a number of cost factors which have in the past resulted in high entry barriers, such as: (*i*) the need to develop granular distribution across multiple markets, on both the sender and receiver side; (*ii*) high compliance costs due to regulatory concerns with anti-money laundering and the combating of terrorist financing, which differ country by country; and (*iii*) the high cost of moving money across borders through official banking channels, and the financial infrastructure that requires.

Opportunity. Given the perceived high margins in this market, there are a large number of players who have sought to use electronic means to deliver international remittances at a much lower cost. Broadband solutions have proven particularly useful on the sending side, because that tends to take place in developed countries where broadband is more ubiquitous and more commonly used, and senders are often more educated and experienced than the people they send money to. Many services attract senders through web-based interfaces, on which the necessary transaction information can be captured (including relating to identity).

Global experiences. Examples of pure-play online remittance services are US-based Xoom, which claims 30 country destinations, and Remitly, which specializes in transfers to the Philippines. Generally these remittances are terminated into existing (non-broadband-based) licensed agent-based systems (Western Union, mobile money, bank branches, etc.) in the receiving country.

Regalii, which currently focuses on the US-Dominican Republic corridor, specializes on helping immigrants in the US pay local utility and telecoms bills on behalf of their family members back home. Remittances are therefore paid into corporates' accounts, obviating the need for a network of local agents on the receiving side. Regalii does not need to conduct its own Know Your Customer (KYC) procedures on senders because their identity is already established by the bank or credit card issuer they use to fund the remittance, and the destination and purpose of the funds is restricted to paying an identified corporate biller.

Quippi, which currently focuses on the US-Mexico corridor, has a similar concept but based on gift cards. Users in the US purchase international Quippi gift cards online and communicate the PIN to the intended recipients back home, who can then redeem them with local retailers. Quippi has four retail partners in Mexico listed on their website. The service is free to users, as Quippi gets a discount from the retailers.

These services require the sender to have a bank or prepaid account (or access to a pay-by-cash e-voucher system such as PayNearMe in the US) in the sending country from which they can fund their remittance; the provider must also have a bank account in each country they operate in order to receive these payments. Some providers, such as Bitpesa in Kenya, are now using Bitcoin as a way for senders to fund their remittances. Bitpesa can then receive bitcoins from anywhere without having to be paid into local bank accounts (subject to applicable regulatory restrictions on the use of crypto-currencies in each country). The sender would likely still require a bank account in order to be able to purchase the necessary bitcoins at a local bitcoin exchange, but it reduces the financial infrastructure that the remitter needs to put in place on the origination side.

Market sizing. In terms of volumes, the World Bank estimates that 13% of all international remittances were being sent online as of March 2014, and that USD 436bn will be sent overseas in the course of 2014.[20] Thus, the volume of online remittances may well exceed USD 60 million annually (=13% of 436bn).

To sum up, broadband channels have so far played a much lesser role on the termination side than on the origination side because they need to be linked into existing cash-out mechanisms. This could change as broadband becomes more ubiquitous in developing countries and hence more accessible and convenient, and transactions are increasingly digitized thereby obviating the need for cashing out.

Potential for financial inclusion. Facilitating international remittances through broadband channels can support financial inclusion in several ways. Lower remittance costs and easier access would be the most direct and important benefits. But other benefits might arise as well. First, the higher and more stable incomes propitiated by remittances can itself be a driver for switching from informal to formal solutions. Second, remittances may be a hook for recipients to open and use accounts at the institutions through which they receive the money. Third, a regular flow of international remittances can substitute for a regular job in credit applications, and the pattern of remittances received can feed into alternative credit scoring algorithms. Fourth, there are opportunities to link the payment of the remittance with a money management solution, for instance, if the remittance is earmarked by the sender for a particular purpose (such as paying for school fees or the rent of the family home) or if the receiver creates an automatic set-aside rule on incoming remittances to fund some purchase on a lay-away basis. Fifth, remittances processed online are significantly cheaper; the World Bank estimates that online services have an average cost of 6.06% of remitted value, against an average cost of 8.36% across all remittance channels.[21]

Regulatory issues. Online remittance services do not present any special regulatory issues, as long as they comply with existing financial integrity rules regarding identification of the transacting parties and reporting of larger or unusual transactions. These can be quite tough in some markets, and this can hinder the development of new remittance solutions.

5.4.2 Instant Online Personal Loans

Motivation. The microcredit experience over the last thirty years has shown that there is a strong demand for credit among a large segment of the population for whom formal credit options have traditionally not been accessible. Moreover, the overwhelming experience has been that uncollateralized microloan programs can experience high repayment rates if they are properly structured. However, the sector has struggled with: (*i*) high interest rates resulting from the high cost of handling small loans through field loan officers, and (*ii*) evolving away from group loans which are based on rigid cycles and undesired and often unclear joint borrower liabilities.

Opportunity. There are many pure-play online lenders who leverage the Internet in four main ways. First, they use it to collect new types of information on, and verify information provided by, prospective borrowers. This disparate information can then feed sophisticated analytical models for credit evaluation. Second, they use Internet communications and automated credit decision engines to deliver instant loan processing to customers. Third, they use social media to promote their services and reach a target market that is technologically included but financially excluded. Finally, some use the Internet, and in particular social networks, effectively in their credit recovery process when loans fall overdue in order to "shame" bad debtors.

By combining these capabilities, online lenders are able to cater to a segment of the population that would have traditionally been denied access to credit or faced burdensome and lengthy documentation processes. However, online lenders do not necessarily go to the base of the pyramid, since they seek customers who: (*i*) have demonstrably stable income streams (e.g. salary or remittances), (*ii*) are sufficiently tech savvy to feel comfortable using online tools and have sufficient web presence, and (*iii*) have electronic accounts through which they can make and receive payments. Online lenders require at least proof of identity, a mobile phone and a bank account (into which loans are paid), they may require proof of employment, and some insist on having visibility of users' presence on social networks.

Loans are unsecured – they typically don't require guarantors or collateral – and as a consequence they tend to carry a fairly steep interest rate. The immediacy of credit often trumps the high cost under which the credit is offered in the minds of many customers.

Global experiences. The online consumer and payday lending business has burgeoned online. One of the largest online lenders is UK-based Wonga, which offers online payday loans in its home market plus South Africa, Canada, Spain, Germany and Poland. Boodle and Wanna Loans are similar providers in South Africa, and GetBucks offers instant loans online in five south and east African countries and Spain. Oakam in the UK has added a reward structure to its online lending operation, with cash-back rewards for on-time repayments. In Mexico,

Kueski and Mimoni offer general personal loans, whereas Micel offers online financing for mobile handsets.

An early example of online lender that exploited the social graph in credit evaluations was Lenddo, which operates in the Philippines, Colombia and Mexico. Marketed as "credit based on community trust," Lenddo seeks to extend the traditional trust based on personal reputation and social relationships that have underpinned personal credit for centuries (e.g. by the local store, local credit circle or money-lender) with trust based on online communities.

US-based FinanceIT uses a different loan solicitation model. Instead of acquiring borrowers directly, it offers retailers the opportunity of giving financing terms to their customers. Both retailers and individual customers need to be preapproved by FinanceIT, but once they are a retailer they can offer customers affordable monthly payments on large purchases. This process is paperless: it is handled digitally through the retailer's smart devices.

DealStruck and OnDeck in the US offer a range of lending product to the small business segment in the US, including revenue-secured term loans and asset-based lines of credit.

As more and more banks offer their services online, the key competitive advantage of these online lenders remains their credit analysis models. Some are therefore concentrating on credit origination, and pass the credit risk onto mainstream lenders. Lenddo is moving from direct online lending to analytics provider, and is therefore becoming more akin to alternative credit score providers Cignifi and Experian MicroAnalytics, both based in the US.

Market sizing. The market for online lending is vibrant but still small in relation to the entire lending market. Business loans outstanding from online lenders in the US are estimated to be currently in the order of up to ten billion, compared to the USD 1.7 trillion in business loans outstanding from commercial banks.[22]

Potential for financial inclusion. There is some controversy about online lenders due to the high interest rates they apply on their unsecured loans, and the risk that they may lead customers into overindebtedness. Expensive consumer lenders have always been around, so there is nothing intrinsically new about the general business model of this latest crop of lenders. But taking the activity online could arguably accelerate overindebtedness cycles. There is therefore a need to regulate and monitor their activities closely.

Regulatory issues. Online lenders present consumer protection risks similar to more traditional consumer and payday lenders. Because they cater to a market with less access to information and fewer options, they may be more vulnerable to abusive terms and irresponsible lending practices. Regulators need to ensure that loan terms are presented transparently, and that they contain appropriate error resolution and cancellation rights. There need to be limits to rolling over of loans, in order to protect against debt distress. Regulators also need to remain vigilant to ensure that the collection practices they employ are fair and proportionate.[23]

While these principles are common to traditional unsecured lenders; adapting existing consumer protection to a purely online environment can present particular challenges. For instance, online lenders in South Africa argue that the requirement of conducting affordability test in South Africa may be hard to do online.

5.4.3 Price Comparison Sites and Service Aggregators

Motivation. Customers are drawn to price comparison sites in order to be able to make informed purchase choices. They might use them to discover who the available providers are, and the terms of their offers.

Price comparison sites have long been particularly popular in the travel sector, mainly because of the complex yield management techniques that transport companies use to optimize the use of their infrastructure. They have also increased in popularity in the telecoms space, because operators have increasingly sought to differentiate their offers and proliferate their promotions in order to combat the prevailing high levels of customer churn. In banking, churn has been traditionally low, but as financial services go digital customer loyalty will likely tend to decrease and price sensitivity will inevitably rise. In this new environment, consumers of financial services are likely to find increasing value in sites that compare the price (as well as the key features) of competing offers in the marketplace.

Opportunity. Price comparison sites are designed to strengthen the power of consumers in front of providers by exposing relevant information to them with which they can make better-informed decisions. Price comparisons are useful any time there are multiple providers, but they become particularly relevant in markets where providers use complex pricing structures presented in a partial, non-transparent, confusing or misleading way, so as to preclude customers from exercising direct cost comparisons. The purpose of price comparison sites is then to "undo" this complexity, by expressing the terms of disparate offers in a consistent way, re-instituting direct comparability across offers and providers.

While structuring price comparisons sounds simple, in practice there are many ways of calculating common metrics and presenting the resulting information. For instance, if there are flat fees, customers may make different inferences if the cost or return information is presented on an absolute money or annual percentage basis. Discrepancies between price comparison sites may be due entirely to methodological differences, which can undermine the transparency objective of these sites.

Moreover, while pure price comparison sites are meant to be essentially information tools for buyers, some sites act as a channel into the online properties of various service providers and hence act more as aggregators than pure information providers. Their incentives can become biased if they receive placement or brokerage fees from online providers they bring customers to.

In a further twist, some providers of price comparison information sell their service on a unbranded (or white label) basis to other sites, including financial service providers who want to show on their website that they are the cheapest. Thus, not only is their funding non-transparent to users of the sites they power but they also do not have a visible brand to protect.

Because prices are easier to compare relative to other elements of service (such as product quality, customer care levels, etc.), comparison sites tend to focus the attention on price. However, they typically include a comparison of the various features associated with each product. Service quality issues are usually relegated to voting by and comments from other users on price comparison websites rather than being independently assessed. In some cases, this could lead to overly aggressive price-based competition as other elements of service are under-reported on the website and hence undervalued by its users. However, they can still be a useful tool for discriminant customers who wish to assess the extent to which a given price differential is justified on the basis of brand or service quality.

Global experiences. Financial price comparison sites are particularly prevalent for insurance and mortgage contracts that entail more small print. Price comparison sites are used heavily in the UK[24]; examples are Moneysupermarket.com, GoCompare, Beatthequote (recently acquired by Google), and OMG (which sells access to its engine to service providers on an unbranded basis). Examples in other countries include Bonkers in Ireland, Wheretobank in South Africa, and ComparaOnline in Chile.

Rocket in Colombia is a web-based service that has a comparison engine at its heart, but rather than exposing the different providers' offers on a standardized table, it surfaces what it deems to be the right product for each user based on a series of online questions about the user's needs and circumstances. It therefore acts more as an online financial advisor than an information resource.

Some price comparison information resources are made available by public institutions and NGOs as part of a broader mission to put downward pressure on prices at the overall market level and instill pricing transparency, and not just to surface the better deals. The World Bank has a web-based resource called Remittance Prices Worldwide covering 226 international remittance corridors which lists the various available product/provider options and ranks them according to fee, exchange rate margin and transfer speed (on two standard remittance sizes).

Microfinance Transparency lists microcredit pricing for over 530 institutions in 29 countries in a transparent and comparable fashion.

Potential for financial inclusion. If price comparison and aggregator sites are governed appropriately and truly represent the interests of consumers rather than providers, they can play a very useful role in financial inclusion. Their primary benefit would be to enhance competition, resulting in potentially lower cost services and easier access. They can be particularly helpful for new-to-finance consumers find the best offers for them, and in so doing they can help build public trust in the financial system as a whole.

Regulatory issues. Regulatory policy towards price comparison sites needs to focus on ensuring that they fulfill their role of informing and empowering consumers. Key concerns are that they: (*i*) express the relevant information with enough accuracy, completeness and clarity, and (*ii*) disclose what role they play, if any, in distributing the products evaluated on their site, including what contractual institutional links they might have, if any, with the providers of those products.[25]

In addition, sites that act as aggregators through which financial services are sold should be subjected to the same codes of conduct that applies to the companies operating in the segment(s) on which they report. Regulators might complement this with guidance on how to present and sell services through price comparison sites, as the UK's Financial Services Authority did in 2011. This guidance should provide clarity on what types of activities and under what circumstances the operation of price comparison sites constitutes mere information dissemination, giving financial advice, or providing a brokerage service.

5.5 Delivery of Financial Information and Education

Motivation. In a last category of experiences, we look at financial education resources that are available over broadband channels. While price comparison sites aim to shed light on the available offers across a broad range of financial services and institutions, other websites aim to strengthen the awareness of consumers on how to they can best take advantage of those services within the context of broader means, aspirations and needs. Thus, price comparison sites offer entirely a supply-side view, whereas financial education content seeks to bridge supply-side offers with demand-side perspectives.

Opportunity. Broadband is of course a particularly useful medium to transmit information, and therefore could become a prime channel to deliver financial education material. The opportunity is not just to increase the volume of information that is available to users, but also to make financial education more interesting and exciting for users through the use of multimedia formats.

There is a plethora of financial education material online, though most is from developed countries. For the US alone, the American Association of Family and Consumer Sciences (AAFCS) lists over 200 websites. The content available can be broadly categorized as follows.

- General information resources, such as the sites of financial authorities and consumer protection agencies containing benchmark rate information, contact information, general advice and FAQs. Examples are a consumer guide by the Federal Reserve Bank, and factsheets and glossaries by industry associations and watchdogs offering reports such as Consumer Action and AM Best.
- Planning tools and calculators, such as for college financial planning (e.g. by NCES); whether to buy or rent a home (e.g. by Yahoo); to estimate savings based on savings rates and yields (e.g. by Dinkytown); eligible deposit insurance coverage (e.g. by FDIC); college costs (e.g. Rutgers); the cash value of life insurance contracts (e.g. by CFA); and investment returns (e.g. by AARP).
- Public access sites, such as for free credit reports (e.g. in the US); official listings, of licensed financial institutions, registered financial planners (e.g. by CFP); and provider ratings (e.g. by AM Best).
- Video explanations on a wide range of specialized topics, such as on balancing the checkbook, types of bankruptcy, protecting against identity theft, buying homeowner insurance, and retirement planning.
- Structured financial education courses, such as paid courses (e.g. by Financial Avenue); free ones targeted at young people (e.g. by Moneyskill); and specialized courses such as on retirement planning (e.g. by Perdue University). There are also educator materials and lesson plans (e.g. by University of Arizona and VISA).

Global experiences. There are a number of online sites which act as portals or gateways to a range of relevant financial education materials. Brazilian Banking Association, FEBRABAN, launched a financial inclusion portal called Meu bolso em dia, which has already received 900,000 *likes* on Facebook. Bússola do Investidor is a Brazilian finance information platform launched in 2010 that contains a mix of news and tools and calculators. It also recently introduced a monitoring investment dashboard that users can access for free with a 15-minute delay, and which becomes available in real-time for paid subscribers. In the US, Revolution-Credit is an interesting web resource that combines a responsible credit decision engine for providers with financial education content for their users.

Web resources such as these are easily available to those with a broadband connection. Financial education that is aimed at poorer and more rural people in developing countries needs to find appropriate distribution platforms that bring together the content and the device. Fundación Capital's Colombia LISTA program claims to be the world's first tablet-based financial education program, which targets social welfare recipients. Their content is designed to be highly interactive, and through learning-by-doing apps such as the "ATM simulator" it seeks to make it both fun and directly useful. By placing the materials in a device that users can use on their own, at their own pace, in their own way, LISTA aims to provide a more personalized experience around financial education. Fundación Capital's vision is that their app and expertise in creating digital learning experiences can be leveraged by other private and public organizations wishing to distribute educational materials for the base of the pyramid in sectors beyond finance.

Regulatory issues. This type of information resources does not present any salient regulatory issues, but there are opportunities for financial authorities to align this content with national financial education objectives and strategies.

5.6 Prospects: Globally and in Latin America

In this concluding section we bring the main themes of this paper together. First we summarize the main market opportunities and challenges presented by broadband channels. Then we draw some inferences on how broadband will change the nature of and market for financial services. Finally, we look at the key regulatory issues and potential role of government in promoting these solutions.

5.6.1 Assessment of Market Opportunities and Challenges

The availability of broadband delivery channels represents an increase in the degrees of freedom that financial service providers have to piece together customer experiences. Relative to traditional brick-and-mortar infrastructure, broadband channels can offer: (*i*) a much greater sense of immediacy and ubiquity; (*ii*) a shift from large fixed costs to smaller and variable unit transaction costs; and (*iii*) automated collection of a much larger set of data on customers and transactions. Relative to first-generation mobile money solutions, broadband channels can offer: (*i*) much greater interactivity and usability through the use of graphical elements in the user interface, larger screens that can support richer menus, and a range of personalization and contextualization option; (*ii*) lower incremental connectivity costs per megabyte or per transaction; and (*iii*) less dependence on the mobile operators for security and authentication. All this should result in the development of more customer-centric service concepts that better meet the needs of the financial inclusion target populations.

Making broadband accessible and affordable to the entire population ought to have a significant impact on financial inclusion. Broadband delivery channels can make interactions between customers and providers much more frequent, engaging (through use of graphical user interfaces and personalization tools) and data rich (through more information provision, capture and analysis). This combination of enhanced service quality and much deeper customer understanding can help drive a case for financial inclusion for both providers and their customers.

On the supply side, more data-rich, broadband-mediated services can help providers better assess risks using more powerful analytical tools, as well as to develop more targeted customer-centric service concepts which fit more tightly the needs of individual customers.

Latin America seems well poised to become a vital testing and development ground for financial services delivered through broadband channels for a number of reasons. The region enjoys relatively higher education and infrastructure levels than other developing countries. It has a dense fabric of micro and small enterprises, operating within a relatively developed microfinance sector. Two large common languages make it easier to port apps and services across countries in the region. All this in the context of levels of formal financial exclusion that are not commensurate with most other indicators of socioeconomic development in Latin America.[26]

However, some factors may militate against the development of broadband-based solutions in Latin America. Telecoms pricing remains relatively high, and many people may have smartphones but no data plans. There are very high business informality rates, and businesses have an inherent suspicion of recording their activities digitally.

This suggests some clear key enablers for the spread of such services through Latin America:

- The continued spread of smart mobile devices, the creation of affordable mobile data plans that turn smart devices into connected devices, and the extension of cellular coverage deeper into rural areas so that broadband is available to all.
- The development of easily deployable apps-on-the-cloud, which have common standards and APIs, are robust to network speed and quality, and adapt gracefully to various types of mobile devices. Fragmentation of the solution space, based on mobile screen sizes, device operating systems and back-end platforms could push many players to sit the digital trend out as early adopters confront the pain of piecing together their digital service environment. This is a difficult area for Latin American regulators to address on their own: any set of standards that governments may wish to create may end up being suboptimal, quickly superseded by newer technologies, or not backed by regulators in other regions of the world.
- The effective selling of the business benefits of these digital services, so that small local businesses see a compelling case for adoption despite the necessary business formalization and taxation visibility that they imply.

- The development of fraud management systems, based on sophisticated analytics and strong operational processes. Many institutions will incur much pain, and will need to go on steep learning curves, as they confront a growing tide of online fraud.

5.6.2 Three Major Implications for Financial Service Models and Market Structure

A first major implication is that widespread access to broadband, and hence to the Internet, will enable the development of new financial service concepts and delivery models. We can distill the key characteristics of the new digital financial landscape from the global experiences reviewed above. Thus we can predict that:

- Services will embody an increased range of customer choices. Customers will be guided through these choices by increasingly sophisticated customer analytics and personalization tools.
- Providers will invest heavily to develop sophisticated customer engagement models in order to capture as much information as possible from their customers. The sheer quantity of customer information collected will become a key competitive tool among providers.
- Credit providers will tap into an increasing range of relevant information sources with which to make credit decisions, especially from social graphs and online reputations. Credit providers will be increasingly focused on mediating online information sources and online referral opportunities, and not just soliciting information from customers themselves.
- There will be a shift from marketing specific products to constructing and managing more integrated and seamless customer experiences. Thus, the boundaries between product categories will get increasingly fuzzy.
- By enabling services that are more personalized, take greater account of social context, and are consumable in smaller, more frequent transaction amounts, formal services will increasingly emulate what people already do today. There will be a range of new service offers and business models that seek to fill in the gap between informal and formal financial services, and this will in turn reduce the need for customer education for first-time users.

A second major implication is that the competitive nature of financial markets will shift significantly. There will be an increasing range of specialized providers, who will achieve very low cost and large scale by developing specific reputation and expertise in particular service segments. This fragmentation will in turn will give rise to a class of aggregators who do not sell their own services but position best-in-class services or those of partners.

As a result, traditional barriers to entry based on control over retail footprint, communications channels and advertising muscle will tend to erode. Broadband will, in particular, undermine mobile operators' control over mobile financial services. The source of scale advantages will shift from being based on physical infrastructure to aggregation of customer information. In a digital information world, sheer customer numbers can be the strongest competitive advantage.

A third major implication as financial services migrate to broadband channels will be a much sharper of focus of financial inclusion on businesses. Over the last decade, financial inclusion policies have tended to be focused on individuals and households, as it has been deemed to be a useful way of reducing socioeconomic vulnerability. But as financial services migrate to broadband channels, opportunities are likely to be relatively much larger for micro and small enterprises who will see increasing business benefits from recording and transacting more of their business digitally. Leaving a greater digital footprint will result in expanded access to credit for working capital – from online specialists with sophisticated analytical tools, from business peers or upstream value chain players they are networked with, as well as from non-intermediated P2P online credit marketplaces. It will also lead to business efficiencies and greater sense of financial control, which ought to make them more receptive to growth.

As smaller, informal businesses avail themselves of more digital financial services, there will be a knock-on increase in access to finance for those living in the communities these businesses serve. As they formalize and create more jobs, their employees will naturally have access to credit. And these businesses will be in a better position to offer credit terms to their customers who may find it difficult to tap into affordable credit sources themselves.

5.6.3 Key Regulatory Issues and Potential Role of Government in Promoting These Solutions

Financial regulators can expect five sets of issues to take center stage as digital financial services delivered on broadband channels develop:

- **Transparency and disclosure**. The proliferation of online lending sources may make it more difficult for borrowers to correctly assess the benefits and risks of each. There need to be clear rules on transparency and disclosure of terms by online lenders, so that individual and small business borrowers can easily understand the terms of the transaction. There may be a need for greater standardization of how terms are expressed to make it more easily digestible for borrowers and comparable across lenders.
- **Borrower education and awareness**. These disclosure rules will need to be supported with effective programs for financial education and borrower awareness so that individuals and small business borrowers who are not accustomed to having ready access to formal credit engage with the new online borrowing sources responsibly, and are informed about the various choices they have.

- **Client data protection**. The new breed of online lenders will rely on trawling a much broader set of information from public registries, social networks and other Internet services in order to ascertain the creditworthiness of new classes of borrowers who do not have an established credit record. Clear data protection rules need to be in place in order to ensure that this information is accessed, stored, used and discarded appropriately. Users should be able to exercise some form of control over what information providers are accessing. Data should only be used for the purposes that it had specifically been collected for (as notified to the user), and client confidentiality rules should limit how data may be shared between various service providers.

- **Regulatory reporting and oversight**. General indebtedness levels will need to be monitored carefully as people and businesses gain much faster access to new forms of credit from a broader range of players. There is little experience on how these services will respond in the event of an economic downturn, and some online lenders already offer unsecured consumer credit at very high interest rates. There need to be clear reporting requirements on online lenders and financial marketplaces so that regulators and policymakers can monitor macro-prudential risk across the financial system. These agencies will need to ensure that sufficient resources are devoted to analyzing credit levels on an increasingly finer segmented basis.

- **Regulation and supervision of digital marketplace platforms**. There is already increasing recognition of the unprecedented opportunities for entrepreneurs and microbusinesses – segments which traditionally have suffered from credit and capital constraints in emerging markets – to get direct funding through managed online marketplaces on a peer-to-peer or crowdfunding basis. Regulators will need to be increasingly pragmatic in allowing some degree of public solicitation for funding through these channels, unencumbered by disproportionately burdensome securities regulations. However, these platforms will need to be regulated, to ensure that: (*i*) they are managed in a responsible and professional manner, and have the necessary financial resources to be sustainable; (*ii*) they take all the necessary steps to protect any client funds they hold or process in the course of their business; (*iii*) they make sure that investors are aware of the terms of their investment and that only those who have the capacity to understand the risks involved are accepted; and (*iv*) they impose appropriate disclosure and reporting requirements on those who are funded (via debt or equity) through their platforms.

Of these financial regulation issues, only the last is new in a significant way; the others are traditional regulatory issues that will only become more important over time as the range of providers broadens and their offerings become more diverse and differentiated. As a result, policy tools will increasingly tend towards provider registries rather than licenses, industry codes of conduct rather than prescriptive regulations, regular information audits rather than legal challenges, and proactive information provision by public entities rather than reliance on disclosures by private providers.

Beyond regulation, there are certain steps that financial regulators and policymakers can take to promote the take-up and use of these broadband-enabled solutions for financial inclusion:

- **Promoting digital payments solutions**. All the services mentioned above rely on the customer having a digital payment capability through which it can make the necessary contributions and repayments and collect any moneys do. In Latin America, today, this is mostly done through interbank transfers, or using debit cards, credit cards and online payment services (such as PayPal) that are linked to bank accounts. However, the penetration of these services remains limited, and this by definition limits their potential for addressing the needs of the unbanked. Policymakers need to make sure that low-cost digital payments emerge that are suitable for the mass market, especially the informally-occupied majority. These solutions will need to be based on proportionate Know Your Customer (KYC) requirements, flexible cash in/cash out mechanisms that leverage the retail infrastructure in the country, and a broader range of authorized non-bank (e-money, prepaid or narrow bank) account issuers who do not intermediate funds. Their development would also be supported by interoperability between the various payments service providers, both in terms of platform interconnection and merchant acquiring.
- **Public promotion and use**. The new types of digital financial marketplaces, and the so-called "sharing economy" (or "*economías colaborativas*," in Spanish) movement within which they are developing, are so far reaching a certain segment of early adopters – mostly young, well-educated, tech savvy, highly socially minded and connected individuals. In order to break out into the mass market, these emerging platforms would benefit from more explicit public support from government agencies. This would serve to give them a sense of legitimacy in the public's mind that has so far been lacking, and to allay fears about their propriety and legal status given their newness. This support can be in the form of news reports and events that explain how these platforms can complement more traditional financial options, showcase enterprises that have benefited from these platforms, and discuss the issues and risks involved. This support can also take the form of public agencies using these platforms from time to time to meet their own policy objectives, for instance to fund smaller projects involving public and private participation.

To this list of financial policy and regulation issues, we need to add of course the telecoms policy requirement of securing universal broadband access at an affordable cost for all. The digital-broadband divide will be particularly nefarious if in addition to all the benefits that come with having access to the Internet today one adds preferential access to low-cost financial services. This includes the following two key types of policies:

- **Universal access.** There will need to be very large investments to push broadband telecoms infrastructure ever deeper into rural areas. These will need to be funded from fiscal sources or through an industry cross-subsidization scheme.
- **Equal access.** The providers of telecoms services should not be in a position to extend their control over the communications access of their clients into effective control over the financial services enjoyed by their customers. They should be held to equal access standards requiring them to offer their communications channels to all financial service providers on a non-discriminatory basis. This should happen naturally as services migrate to broadband mobile data channels, but regulators need to remain vigilant to potential abuses of mobile operators' control over the mobile channel.

Notes

1. For detailed information on the state of mobile coverage in rural areas across Latin America, and the initiatives taking place around that, see the IDB's Digilac website.

2. For a general elaboration of the implications of the spread of smartphones and scenarios for future development of mobile money, see Mireya Almazán and Eliza Sitbon, "Smartphones and Mobile Money: The Next Generation of Digital Financial Inclusion," GSMA Discussion Paper, July 2014.

3. See "Note 4: Expanding Commitment Savings: A Menu of Challenges," March 2014. In Xavier Martin (2014), "Inclusive Commitment Savings in Latin America and the Caribbean," Multilateral Investment Fund, available in www.pro-savings.org.

4. Source: Sean Murray in DailyFunder, Issue 1, January 2014. One interprets the estimate to be for the US alone, but not specified in the report.

5. Source: Lending Club website.

6. Source: P2P-Banking.com, post dated 1 October 2014 by wiseclerk.

7. Source: Financial Times; and "The rise of future finance: The UK Alternative Finance Benchmarking Report," By Liam Collins, Richard Swart, and Bryan Zhang, December 2013.

8. Source: P2P-Banking.com.

9. "A trillion dollar market by the people, for the people: How marketplace lending will remake banking as we know it," by Charles Moldow of Foundation Capital.

10. In July 2013, Prosper in the US paid USD 10 million to settle a claim that it had sold unregistered securities (source: P2P-Banking.com).

11. One example was Quakle in the UK in 2011, which experienced exceedingly high default rates. P2P sites need to be designed very carefully so that they don't end up attracting an undue proportion of high-risk borrowers for whom this is their only option.

12. See FCA Policy Statement Ps14/4, "The FCA's regulatory approach to crowdfunding over the Internet, and the promotion of non-readily realizable securities by other media," as summarized by Georgia Quinn in Crowdfund Insider.

13. Source: "The State of Small Business Lending: Credit Access during the Recovery and How Technology May Change the Game," By Karen Gordon Mills and Brayden McCarthy, Harvard Business School Working Paper 15-004, 22 July 2014.

14. Source: Venturamexico.com, on 27 August 2014.

15. Source: "Crowdfunding industry report 2013," by MasSolution. There is no regional breakdown of the equity crowdfunding total. But if one looks at the total crowdfunding volumes, 60% were in the US and 35% in Europe, and only a tiny USD 0.8 million of this amount were raised in Latin America.

16. Source: "The rise of future finance: The UK Alternative Finance Benchmarking Report," By Liam Collins, Richard Swart, and Bryan Zhang, December 2013.

17. Source: Irene Tordera, in CrowdValley, 22 July 2013.

18. Specifically, "any person can invest, but must keep each of their first two investments under 10% of their net assets (money that does not affect their house, pension, or life insurance). After this, the investor can choose to self-certify as a sophisticated investor and put up as much money as they desire." Source: Freddie Dawson in Forbes.com, 29 April 2014.

19. This refers to California Law SB896. For a summary of the provisions, see: Jose Quinones's post of 20 August 2014 in the Mission Asset Fund blog.

20. Sources: World Bank, "Remittance Prices Worldwide," Issue No. 9, March 2014; and Mark Andersen in the Guardian's Global Development website, 18 August 2014.

21. Source: World Bank, "Remittance Prices Worldwide," Issue No. 9, March 2014.

22. Sources: Ronald Fink in Crain's New York Business, 27 April 2014; and "The State of Small Business Lending: Credit Access during the Recovery and How Technology May Change the Game," By Karen Gordon Mills and Brayden McCarthy, Harvard Business School Working Paper 15-004, 22 July 2014.

23. Wonga was recently ordered to pay compensation by the UK authorities, after it threatened overdue borrowers with fake letters from legal firms.

24. For instance, one third of the motor policies written in the UK during 2013 were sold through these sites, according to the UK's Financial Conduct Authority.

25. The assessment of 14 price comparison sites conducted by the UK's Financial Conduct Authority in 2014 found serious shortcomings on both aspects with a number of providers.

26. According to the global Findex survey of financial inclusion, Peru and Indonesia had a similar share of adults with an account at a formal financial institution in 2011 (around 20%). This share is smaller in Peru, Bolivia, Mexico and Colombia than in India, Kenya or South Africa (35% or more).

CHAPTER 6

Mobile Technology and Financial Inclusion

Albert B. Chu

Contents

6.1 Introduction

This chapter describes how mobile technologies are expanding digital financial inclusion, defined as providing access and delivery of basic banking services, savings, lending, insurance and other financial services to everyone in the population—especially those who live under the poverty line. The World Bank estimates that over 38 percent of adults in the world, or about two billion adults are unbanked, have no access to formal banking services (Demirguc-Kunt et al., 2015). Financial inclusion helps those unbanked and underbanked bridge the gaps between the physical, digital and psychological use and access to money (Mas, 2012). In today's digital world, physical cash is rapidly becoming a remnant of traditional societal mores and legacy financial systems that have disadvantaged the unbanked. By combining digital financial tools (such as mobile remittances using blockchain technology) with psychological tools (such as financial education), the unbanked can attain financial services and break out of the poverty cycle (Pande et al., 2012).

At the turn of the 21st century, the number mobile phone subscribers increased 700 percent, from 750 million in the year 2000 to 6 billion globally in 2011 (Yanofsky and Mims, 2012). In about a decade's time, mobile technologies delivered the vision of mobile inclusion, providing billions of people access to communications services through the use of mobile phones that enabled people to communicate with each other around the world at an affordable cost. Mobile phones reached an unprecedented 93 percent global penetration in 2013 (Yoon, 2015). These mobile devices provide basic telephony services, such as voice and text messaging, though not all of them provide mobile Internet access.[1] In addition, mobile Internet access globally is expected to reach 63 percent by 2019 (Statista, 2016).

This global mobile inclusion is the gateway to universal financial inclusion. As access to affordable and advanced mobile technologies continues to proliferate, innovations in mobile-based financial services are being developed and deployed. Typical problems in developing countries, such as lack of access to financial services in rural areas, are now being solved with mobile financial technology solutions. For example, instead of relying on in-person cash transactions, farmers in Kenya can now sell and buy products using mobile payments. Instead of being charged high fees by traditional money transfer services, Filipino workers overseas can now remit their savings to their families back home via their mobile phones conveniently and affordably. And in China, millions of rural residents who did not have access to banking services can now invest their savings and participate in financial investment tools using their mobile phone. Digital financial services have created a sea change for the unbanked and underbanked populations, providing them access and participation in an inclusive digital economy.

To be clear, there are challenges in delivering digital financial services, depending on the region, local needs of populations and the types of financial services needed. In addition to those in the developing countries, there are still unbanked and underbanked populations in the developed world.

The good news is that financial inclusion has become a development priority of governments and non-governmental organizations (NGOs). On a local level, governments are working with banking, telecom and software companies to expand access to financial services. On a global level, the United Nations, the World Bank Group, and the G20, all have a focus on global financial inclusion efforts. The World Bank Group, for example, has stated:

"The aspiration to achieve universal financial access should force "our whole team" at the World Bank Group to "take responsibility and think about what we need to do differently to get there" by 2020.... . Financial inclusion is an enabler and a catalyst for achieving the Bank Group's goals of ending extreme poverty by 2030 and boosting shared prosperity for the bottom 40 percent of the population

in all developing countries."—Jim Kim, World Bank Group President (The World Bank, 2013)

The number of unbanked adults worldwide has decreased from 2.5 billion in 2011 to 2 billion in 2014—a 20 percent decline in three years (The World Bank, 2016). Even more promising, the greatest segments of financial inclusion are taking place in the poorest and most rural regions of the developing world, including China, India and Sub-Saharan Africa. In some cases, emerging markets have leapfrogged developed countries in digital financial innovations. For example, an off-grid household in Tanzania goes straight to solar power and mobile communications rather than to gas energy and landline phones because they do not have much of a choice. However, there is still much to accomplish to achieve universal financial inclusion and mobile technologies will play a key role in reaching this goal.

The thesis of this chapter is that mobile inclusion is the gateway to digital financial inclusion. Thus, it is instructive to understand how the key success factors driving mobile inclusion— accessibility, affordability and availability of an open ecosystem—can also be drivers for success in digital financial inclusion.

This chapter was written after consulting with industry innovators and entrepreneurs. With the use cases and examples of technologies and projects, the reader must understand that this information can become quickly outdated because the fields of mobile technology and digital financial inclusion are progressing rapidly.

6.2 The Current Landscape

There is no precedence in modern world history for a technology diffusion that is as rapidly and widely adopted as mobile technology. While different countries have had different adoption rates, the average global mobile phone penetration in 2013 was 93 percent—more than any other consumer technology in recent history. In a little over ten years after the mainstream market launch of the mobile phone, the total number of mobile devices shipped worldwide outpaced the total number of television sets or the total number of personal computers shipped worldwide (Meeker, 2014).

This rapid deployment of mobile technology accelerated global mobile inclusion and has created a significant impact to expanding digital financial services, both in developed and developing countries. Therefore, it is instructive to understand the key success factors that led to mobile inclusion, as these same enablers foreshadow how mobile technology can have a similar impact on digital financial inclusion.

It may not be immediately obvious, but communications services and financial services have many business model similarities. Prior to the advent of mobile technologies, providing access to communications services meant high capital investments to deploy central offices with expensive networking equipment, high labor costs to lay fiber optic cables and telephone lines to deploy the "last mile" phone line to the home or business, and high maintenance costs to run and upgrade the phone service. Similarly, providing access to financial services requires significant capital investments to build out bank branches and ATM locations in densely-populated cities and rural villages and significant maintenance costs for staffing and for the operations of a secure and trusted banking network.

Universal communications access, much like universal financial inclusion, was a vision that seemed costly and difficult to attain. Legacy banking largely fails to offer services to the unbanked or underbanked mostly because it is not financially viable. The cost of building out bank branches in remote villages, staffing them, providing needed security and infrastructure does not justify a return on investment when the customers cannot even afford to pay the banking service fees.

Mobile technologies changed the communications services landscape. Mobile phones provided basic communications services—voice and text messaging services—to billions of mobile phone subscribers around the globe with a faster deployment and cheaper service costs compared to traditional fixed-line communication services. In addition, with the introduction of smartphones almost ten years ago, mobile phone users who had smartphones could also access advanced communications services, such as Internet services. The number of people using mobile Internet will grow 280 percent, from 2.5 billion people in 2015 to a projected 3.8 billion people in 2020, with this growth driven primarily in developing countries (GSM Association, 2016). It may be hard to imagine, but a smartphone user today has "more computer power than all of NASA back in 1969, when it placed two astronauts on the moon." (Kaku, 2011)

6.2.1 Accessibility, Affordability and an Open Ecosystem

The key factors driving the rapid proliferation of mobile technologies include accessibility, affordability and availability of an open and robust ecosystem.

Accessibility means that the mobile network has to be accessible anywhere, anytime. It also means that the network has to be standards-based so that it can interoperate with different mobile network operators and mobile phone models. The mobile phone itself also has to be accessible; it has to be network standards compliant, portable and easy to use. Mobile accessibility has led to mobile phones overtaking personal computers as the preferred method to access the Internet in many developing countries, including China and India (Meeker, 2012).

Affordability is another key factor that led to the proliferation of mobile technology. The technology has to be affordable both for mobile network operators to install and operate the network infrastructure and services, and for the end user to afford the costs of a mobile phone and service plans. The average cost of smartphones continues to drop. While today the average price of a smartphone device is around US$100, some models expected to be priced sub-US$20 for emerging markets (GSM Association, 2016a).

A final key factor to the rapid proliferation of mobile technology is the availability of an open and robust ecosystem of services. This open ecosystem needs to support a diverse set of partners who can develop and deploy financial services based on open standards and programming interfaces. This ecosystem needs to be cost effective, trusted and accountable. As mobile networks are becoming faster and mobile phones support more advanced processors and operating systems, the ecosystem needs to continue to expand to take advantage of these innovations. Mobile technology platforms, such as Google Android and Apple iOS, are creating a trusted foundation so that digital financial services and apps can be reliably and easily deployed.

Services built on mobile ecosystems have disrupted traditional industries and improved the daily lives of mobile users. Some examples include:

- Uber and Didi Chuxing disrupted the traditional taxi industry with ride-sharing services that rely on mobile technology.
- Amazon and Alibaba changed the retail industry and continue to use mobile technology to expand their services beyond retail into other industries, including financial services.
- M-Pesa, launched in 2007, changed the way Kenyans do money transfers and transactions using their mobile phones. By the end of 2015, there were over 270 mobile money services in over 90 markets (GSM Association, 2016b).

In the coming decade, the mobile Internet, along with innovations including blockchain technology, big data analytics and the Internet of Things, is poised to disrupt the legacy banking industry. This traditional, vertically-aligned industry will be unbundled by mobile and other financial technology solutions (CB Insights, 2015). According to a McKinsey study, the impact of mobile Internet for developing countries could reach over $2 trillion by 2025, with first-time mobile Internet users contributing most of this value (Manyika et al., 2013).

6.3 Mobile Inclusion Leads to Financial Inclusion

Financial inclusion looks different in developed economies than in emerging ones. But because mobile inclusion is a global phenomenon, mobile technologies can adapt to the different financial inclusion requirements of developed and developing economies at a very local level.

The key factors of accessibility, affordability and open ecosystem will need to not only address these local market and cultural requirements, but also incorporate new technologies such as blockchain and big data analytics.

6.3.1 Addressing Local Market Needs

Availability and affordability of mobile financial technologies for the underbanked populations in developing countries will undoubtedly have a different flavor than in developing countries. In the United States, for example, it is commonplace to see mobile financial apps used, like Venmo, Square Cash and other mobile apps to send and receive money and pay bills; Apple Pay, Facebook Payments and other mobile wallet apps to transact with individuals and merchants; and Personal Capital, Acorn and other financial apps to manage money, obtain loans and financial advice.

In emerging markets and developing countries, the needs are different for those who are unbanked. Yet, because of the significant market penetration of mobile phones even in developing countries, mobile solutions can be deployed to address the local needs. M-Pesa in Kenya is an archetypical example of how mobile technology is used to bring financial services to the unbanked.

M-Pesa is a short message service (SMS, or text messaging service) mobile money system launched by Safaricom and Vodafone Group and aided by the UK Department for International Development in 2007 (The Economist, 2013). M-Pesa allows users to send, receive and withdraw money—from purchasing food at local markets or airtime minutes for their mobile phone to ATM withdrawals or paying utility bills. A user can deposit and withdraw cash via M-Pesa and Safaricom agents, who are well-distributed throughout the country and can be found in large shopping malls as well as small, rural shops.[2] Users withdraw and deposit funds via a three-factor authentication process which requires an identification card, SIM card (present in the mobile phone) and PIN when with an agent (Alexander, 2010). This is an example of how commodities, such as mobile airtime in Kenya with Safaricom, can be used as a vector for actual cash.

According to the International Finance Corporation of the World Bank Group, M-Pesa's key success factor centers around availability: the availability of mobile phones, which was at 39 percent market penetration when launched and now at 88 percent as of Q1 2016 (Communications Authority of Kenya, 2016), and the ability for M-Pesa to function on any type of mobile phone (International Finance Corporation and World Bank Group, 2016). As a mobile network operator, Safaricom had built customer trust in Kenya prior to launching M-Pesa and further encouraged trust through increased mobile network efficiency, customer service and education efforts that their M-Pesa agent network provided to customers. This ecosystem was also supported by a unique partnership between the Safaricom/Vodafone Group and the Central Bank of Kenya: Vodafone was allowed to perform mobile transactions without partnering with a bank.

Affordability is key, as well. Traditionally, cash would be held and transported by individuals via buses and public transportation. For example, a man working in Nairobi would save money to bring back home to his family in rural Kenya. With mobile money, cash can be sent directly home at a more affordable cost than the time spent storing and transporting cash (International Finance Corporation and World Bank Group, 2016). Mobile money remittance is the "killer app" and Safaricom leveraged this use case to market M-Pesa by advertising "send money home" when launching the project (The Economist, 2013).

M-Pesa shows how mobile inclusion can provide the gateway to digital financial inclusion at scale. A 2013 report by the Central Bank of Kenya states that the most widely-used financial service in Kenya is mobile financial services—used by 11.5 million adults (out of 18.5 million), or 62 percent of the adult population. This same report also noted that the proportion of financially excluded adult population in Kenya decreased from 39.3 percent in 2006 to 25.4 percent in 2013 (Alliance for Financial Inclusion, 2013). Kenya is showing by example how mobile financial services are a gateway to universal financial inclusion.

Another example of how mobile technologies can address uniquely local problems is in providing pay-as-you-go (PAYG) mobile payments options for energy and water bills in developing countries. Energy is a critical local need for those living off-grid in rural East Africa. Without access to energy, a family does not have a light to do homework at night, a plug to power a radio to get market information on when to sell and how much to price crops or a way to charge a mobile phone. These local needs, which people in developed economies might take for granted, are the main vectors in which financial inclusion can emerge in less developed economies.

M-Kopa, a Kenyan solar energy company founded in 2011 (Wikipedia, 2016), has sold over 300,000 solar systems (Bright, 2016) in East Africa. They are able to sell solar-powered systems because they implement a rent-to-own financing system for customers using their solar products. The M-Kopa IV Solar Home System includes an 8-W solar panel, two LED light bulbs, a rechargeable LED flashlight and a mobile phone-charging USB with five standard connections. Customers deposit 3,500 KES (about US$35) and pay a daily (PAYG) fee of around 45 KES (around US$0.45) per day—via M-Pesa—until they own the unit (the price also includes maintenance and instruction on how to use the system if needed) (Shapshak, 2016; M-KOPA Solar corporate website, 2016). The payment plan allows low-income customers in rural areas to own their system within two years (Mulligan, 2016). This is important because high, upfront costs are major inhibitors for those who cannot afford products and utilities.

6.3.2 Incorporating New Technologies Into an Open Ecosystem

In the coming years, there will be significant enhancements in mobile technology that will further advance digital banking and financial services. Some companies are already starting to leverage the Internet of Things (IoT) for data collection on their products. The sensors on their products deliver real-time data to companies that enable them to implement PAYG systems and better maintenance services with their products. Angaza, for example, creates software for both manufacturers and distributors of off-grid solar products that allows them to collect data remotely on customer payments and maintenance needs for solar systems (Angaza corporate website, 2016). M-Kopa also leverages the IoT in their products to collect data on customer payments and monitor battery information (Fehrenbacher, 2014). Once a household pays for their electricity remotely via M-Pesa or Airtel minutes, M-Kopa can remotely turn on their system.

Blockchain technology, best known as the platform behind cryptocurrencies such as bitcoin and ether, will also be a driving force behind advanced digital financial services.

One current example of the use of blockchain is Coins.ph, a Philippine-based start-up that provides money transfers to users without the need for a traditional bank account. Starting in the Philippines, Coins.ph has the goal to accelerate financial inclusion using blockchain technology throughout Southeast Asia. Similarly to M-Pesa, Coins.ph partners with small, government-regulated stores and individuals who act as local agents or tellers. The user sends money, in the form of cryptocurrency, to someone else via a smartphone. When the person receives the cryptocurrency, they go to a local teller who exchanges the cryptocurrency into cash for a small fee. The key technology to move the cryptocurrency without the need of a traditional bank is the blockchain. Blockchain effectively removes the need and cost of an intermediary, such as Western Union (Balea, 2015).

The driving use case for Coins.ph is remittances. According to Ron Hose, founder of Coins.ph, nearly 10 percent of Filipinos work abroad and send over US$26 billion home annually. If they use Western Union, they can lose seven to eight percent just in fees. But if they use Coin.ph, the cost to send money is reduced. The only cost is the fee a customer pays to exchange bitcoins into Philippine pesos. Each person or store acting as a teller for Coins.ph competitively prices their exchange rate, which ends up being much less than the Western Union fee. Furthermore, the recipient does not have to take public transportation to a city hub and wait in line at a bank or a Western Union branch to receive the remittance. With over 25,000 local and mobile tellers throughout the Philippines, Coins.ph makes it cost effective and convenient for their users and can scale their infrastructure easily. "Over a third of municipalities in the Philippines still don't have any form of banking facilities and even in big cities, retail banks are only able to serve a small percentage of the population," notes Hose.

As Coins.ph demonstrates, mobile becomes a platform for blockchain-based solutions that removes much of the costs of a third-party intermediary while still providing security and trust in the transaction.

Another, perhaps initially unintended, consequence of mobile technology in advancing digital financial inclusion is the use of big data analytics. Traditional methods of data collection to determine individual identification, purchase history and credit ratings can now be done via mobile technologies. For example, smartphones have encrypted biometric identification input, such as fingerprint scanner, which, when combined with passwords and other security methods, can provide a unique identity for use with financial transactions.

In addition, mobile technologies can help aggregate or crowdsource data that provide input for government and financial institutions. This data, which can range from mapping where financial services are located to taking photos of real-time pricing of commodities in local markets, can supplement or supplant the traditional methods of data collection—often with more accuracy and timeliness.

Premise, a San Francisco-based information technology start-up, has created mobile technology that allows individuals to take photos of products, prices and buildings, in places that do not have sufficient local infrastructure and uploads the photos to a central server for analysis. While the concept seems simple, the results are powerful—ranging from mapping where critical financial and utility services are to providing near-realtime consumer price index and getting early warning signs of inflation in developing countries (Premise corporate website, 2016). For example, Premise partnered with Standard Chartered Bank in Nigeria and Ghana to get a real-time read on prices of food in local markets so Standard Chartered could better manage risk in foreign investment in the region. They know right away when there is a shortage of food. Now Premise is in more than 30 countries and collecting all sorts of valuable local data points that enable people to make better decisions—mapping where products are available and how far away services are, including banking services (Lidow, 2014).

As Luís Garcia, Brazil country manager at Premise, states, "Brazil is the face of inequality and the [mobile] phone is a great equalizer." Premise recruits locals and pays them to capture prices of products, which gives the locals extra income and Premise's clients better information of what is happening on the ground (Baker, 2016). Using crowdsourcing and big data analytics, mobile technologies can contribute to financial data gathering which can lead to more informed financial policy making and better decision-making for banks.

Big data can also provide the farmer in a rural village with the latest market and pricing information so that his crops or livestock can be sold at a fair market price—addressing an aspect of financial inclusion that goes well beyond basic banking transactions. Smallholder farmers can also benefit from big data analytics. Ignitia (Ignitia corporate website, 2016), a Sweden-based start-up, collects weather data in partnership with institutions such as NASA to democratize valuable information to more than 12 million farmers in West Africa (Executive Agency for SMEs and European Commission, 2016). This information can double crop yields for farmers giving them greater purchasing power in the market.

6.3.3 It Takes an Open Ecosystem

As seen with M-Pesa in Kenya, a robust and secure ecosystem must exist for mobile financial inclusion projects—addressing local market needs—to scale and have tangible impact. That means government and regulators, banks and business enterprises, NGOs and start-ups—all the players in the ecosystem—must work together to add value towards providing financial inclusion solutions. Mobile technology may provide the base platform, but it takes an open and inclusive, secure and trusted ecosystem to deliver a complete set of financial inclusion solutions—from basic banking services to credit and insurance.

In some cases, it takes government initiatives to bring telecom companies, banks and startups to work together. Similarly to the case of Safaricom and M-Pesa in Kenya, Peru's government is creating a healthy legislative framework to encourage financial inclusion through the creation of Peruvian Digital Payments (PDP), which is co-owned by the Association of Banks of Peru (ASBANC) (Center for Financial Inclusion Blog, 2016). Less than one-third of Peruvians have bank accounts, but the public–private partnership is creating an SMS mobile wallet services, called BiM, to serve underbanked and unbanked populations, using smartphones. After the legislative environment was created, PDP and ASBANC could get major banks and telecom providers on board, which enabled Peruvians without a bank account to participate, using mobile carriers and financial providers to create an inclusive, secure cross-platform environment for end users. Launched in early 2016, BiM has buy-in from 32 banks, creating the interoperability necessary for this ecosystem to thrive. BiM has over 23,000 users and expects to scale to five million users within five years (Mendoza, 2016).

While BiM in Peru is a new case study emerging as this chapter is being written, there are other, more developed digital financial ecosystems today, like what the Ant Financial Group is deploying in China.

Ant Financial Group is an example of what a scalable, trusted financial ecosystem might look like in the future. In 2004, Alibaba, an e-commerce platform, created AliPay, a trusted system between merchants and buyers by holding payments in escrow. AliPay rapidly grew to become China's largest online payments platform with 400 million real-name users and about 82 percent market share in 2014 (Tian, 2015). Alibaba spun off AliPay in 2011, which was rebranded as Ant Financial Group in 2015. Today, Ant Financial provides a portfolio of financial services ranging from access to a mobile wallet and payments platform through AliPay, to money market funds via Yu'e Bao, to credit ratings via Sesame Credit.

The high infrastructure, transportation and risk management costs of brick-and-mortar banks have made banking services unaffordable and inaccessible for individuals with low incomes. Ant Financial is cutting transportation costs through AliPay's mobile wallet, which allows people to send and receive small payments via their smartphone. Ant Financial is also lowering infrastructure costs through their financial cloud computing network called MYBank. Over the past few years, Ant Financial has been has been providing small businesses with loans of around US$160,000. MYBank is Ant Financial's effort to expand their small business loans program through partnerships with private banks in China. Furthermore, AliPay Wallet app allows users to invest in the Yu'eBao money-market fund, which offers higher interest rates than traditional banks.

Access to Alibaba's e-commerce data of over 400 million users and 37 million small businesses, along with the data collected from the many services Ant Financial provides, allows users and businesses to build an identity and financial history. Since people's transaction histories and data are known, this lowers risk management costs and allows them to build more accurate credit rating systems through Sesame Credit (Tsang, 2016). Users also build credit via their AliPay wallet. So, for example, when someone pays a utility bill via AliPay, purchases a phone and data plan via Alibaba, or pays back a small business loan to Ant Financial and MYBank, they build credit.

Alibaba and Ant Financial Group exemplify how mobile technologies, together with cloud computing and big data analytics, can create a robust and trusted ecosystem for advancing financial inclusion. In 2014, AliPay was processing 120 million transactions per day, compared to all the banks in China processing a combined 170 million non-cash transactions per day on average. With this scale and growth, Ant Financial is already one of the world's largest digital financial inclusion success stories.

This open ecosystem approach is the modern pathway to closing the digital financial inclusion gap. Once basic mobile technologies are deployed, an open ecosystem of digital financial services can be deployed so that the unbanked can access a full range of digital financial services. Similarly to the open ecosystem approach for mobile technologies, where a full range of apps and services have proliferated for just about every use imaginable, an open ecosystem approach for financial technologies will help address the financial services needs for the diverse use cases in both developing and developed countries.

6.4 Conclusion

Today, two billion people in the world are unbanked and do not have access to financial services. But through the use of mobile technologies, the unbanked will be able to have access to digital financial services. That is why mobile penetration has become intimately attached to digital financial inclusion. Mobile phones can be used to help address and solve local problems and needs of the unbanked and underbanked. Mobile technologies can help the unbanked with basic access to a bank account or somewhere to store and transact their money safely, with access to credit and the ability to build it and access to insurance and other financial management tools. Thus, it makes perfect sense that a country's mobile capacity and penetration is used as one of four major scoring criteria when the Brookings Institution compiled its most recent financial inclusion report (Villasenor et al., 2016).

While mobile phones solve issues and costs around distance and transportation, IoT, blockchain and big data analytics solutions will further accelerate financial inclusion by giving people identity and security in their transactions. There are still many challenges facing digital financial services, including the risks of digital fraud and identity hacking, cyberattacks and digital security. However, there is no doubt that the trend of continued innovation and advances in mobile financial technologies will make the vision to provide universal digital financial services an achievable goal.

Technology itself is useless without an open and robust ecosystem. Government institutions, private and public banks, telecom providers, and for-profit and nonprofit players must all work together to upgrade the current financial systems into a more affordable and accessible one that can serve everyone. This is not an easy task. There is no one-size-fits-all or silver bullet as this change is often happening from the ground up in local communities and nation states. What works for one place does not mean it works exactly the same in another—an important note for practitioners and graduate students as they move into this field.

References

Alexander, C., 2010. The consultative group to assist the poor, 10 things you thought you knew about M-PESA, November 22, 2010. https://www.cgap.org/blog/10-things-you-thought-you-knew-about-m-pesa (accessed 23 October 2016).

Alliance for Financial Inclusion, 2013. Dramatic changes in Kenya's financial inclusion landscape, November 21, 2013. http://www.afi-global.org/news/2013/11/21/dramatic-changes-kenyas-financial-inclusion-landscape (accessed 23 October 2016).

Angaza corporate website, 2016. www.angaza.com (accessed 23 October 2016).

Baker, D., 2016. Photos are creating a real-time food-price index, Wired, April 5, 2016. http://www.wired.co.uk/article/premise-app-food-tracking-brazil-philippines (accessed 23 October 2016).

Balea, J., 2015. Uber for banking? Coins.ph turns people into ATMs, Rappler, July 21, 2015. http://www.rappler.com/technology/features/99996-coins-ph-people-into-atms (accessed 23 October 2016).

Bright, J., 2016. Solar startup M-KOPA leapfrogs Africa's electricity grid, TechCrunch, April 28, 2016. https://techcrunch.com/2016/04/28/solar-startup-m-kopa-leapfrogs-africas-electricity-grid/ (accessed 23 October 2016).

CB Insights, 2015. Disrupting Banking: The Fintech Startups That Are Unbundling Wells Fargo, Citi and Bank of America, November 2015. https://www.cbinsights.com/blog/disrupting-banking-fintech-startups/ (accessed 23 October 2016).

Center for Financial Inclusion Blog, 2016. BiM – The First Fully-Interoperable Mobile Money Platform: Now Live in Peru, February 17, 2016. https://cfi-blog.org/2016/02/17/bim-the-first-fully-interoperable-mobile-money-platform-now-live-in-peru/ (accessed 23 October 2016).

Communications Authority of Kenya, 2016. Kenya's mobile penetration hits 88 per cent. http://www.ca.go.ke/index.php/what-we-do/94-news/366-kenya-s-mobile-penetration-hits-88-per-cent (accessed 23 October 2016).

Demirguc-Kunt, A., Klapper, L., Singer, D., Van Oudheusden, P., 2015. The Global Findex Database 2014: Measuring Financial Inclusion Around the World. World Bank Policy Research Paper 7255, World Bank Group, pp. 4–5, April 2015.

Executive Agency for SMEs, European Commission, 2016. Ignitia profile. https://ec.europa.eu/easme/en/sme/4321/ignitia (accessed 23 October 2016).

Fehrenbacher, K., 2014. How M-KOPA unlocked pay-as-you-go solar in rural Kenya, Gigaom, April 10, 2014. https://gigaom.com/2014/04/10/how-m-kopa-unlocked-pay-as-you-go-solar-in-rural-kenya/ (accessed 23 October 2016).

GSM Association, 2016. The Mobile Economy 2016. http://www.gsma.com/mobileeconomy/global/2016/ (accessed 23 October 2016).

GSM Association, 2016a. The Mobile Economy 2016. p. 41. http://www.gsma.com/mobileeconomy/global/2016/ (accessed 23 October 2016).

GSM Association, 2016b. The Mobile Economy 2016. p. 44. http://www.gsma.com/mobileeconomy/global/2016/ (accessed 23 October 2016).

Ignitia corporate website, 2016. www.ignitia.se (accessed 23 October 2016).

International Finance Corporation, World Bank Group, 2016. M-Money Channel Distribution Case—Kenya. http://www.ifc.org/wps/wcm/connect/4e64a80049585fd9a13ab519583b6d16/tool+6.7.+case+study+-+m-pesa+kenya+.pdf?mod=ajperes (accessed 23 October 2016).

Kaku, M., 2011. Physics of the Future: How Science Will Shape Human Destiny and Our Daily Lives by the Year 2100. Doubleday, New York.

Lidow, N., 2014. Holiday Feasts in Nigeria, Premise blog, August 6, 2014. http://blog.premise.com/data/science/2014/08/06/holiday-feasts-in-nigeria/ (accessed 23 October 2016).

M-KOPA Solar corporate website, 2016. http://www.m-kopa.com/products/ (accessed 23 October 2016).

Manyika, J., Chui, M., Bughin, J., et al., McKinsey Global Institute, 2013. Disruptive technologies: advances that will transform life, business, and the global economy, p. 5.

Mas, I., 2012. Payments in developing countries: breaking physical and psychological barriers, December 2012.

McKay, C., Mazer, R., 2014. The consultative group to assist the poor, 10 myths about M-PESA: 2014 update, October 1, 2014. http://www.cgap.org/blog/10-myths-about-m-pesa-2014-update (accessed 23 October 2016).

Meeker, M., 2012. Internet Trends 2012, Kleiner Perkins Caulfield Byers.

Meeker, M., 2014. Internet Trends 2014, Kleiner Perkins Caulfield Byers, Slide 95. http://www.slideshare.net/kleinerperkins/internet-trends-2014-05-28-14-pdf/95-95Global_TV_vs_PC_Desktop (accessed 23 October 2016).

Mendoza, N., 2016. Anatomy of a mobile banking collaboration, Devex Impact, February 26, 2016. https://www.devex.com/news/anatomy-of-a-mobile-banking-collaboration-87799 (accessed 23 October 2016).

Mulligan, G., 2016. M-KOPA Solar launches solar-powered digital TVs, Disrupt Africa, February 19, 2016. http://disrupt-africa.com/2016/02/m-kopa-solar-launches-solar-powered-digital-tvs/ (accessed 23 October 2016).

Otieno, D., Daily Nation, 2015. Banking sector has plenty of room for growth, November 22, 2015. http://www.nation.co.ke/newsplex/Newsplex-overbanked/-/2718262/2963604/-/fkndupz/-/index.html (accessed 23 October 2016).

Pande, R., Cole, S., Sivasankaran, A., Bastian, G., Durlacher, K., 2012. Does Poor People's Access to Formal Banking Services Raise Their Incomes? EPPI-Centre, Social Science Research Unit, Institute of Education, University of London.

Premise corporate website, 2016. www.premise.com(accessed 23 October 2016) .

Shapshak, T., 2016. How Kenya's M-Kopa Brings Prepaid Solar Power to Rural Africa, Forbes, January 28, 2016. http://www.forbes.com/sites/tobyshapshak/2016/01/28/how-kenyas-m-kopa-brings-prepaid-solar-power-to-rural-africa/#653863bc70f4 (accessed 23 October 2016).

Statista, 2016. Mobile phone Internet user penetration worldwide from 2014 to 2019. https://www.statista.com/statistics/284202/mobile-phone-internet-user-penetration-worldwide/ (accessed 23 October 2016).

The Economist, 2013. Why does Kenya lead the world in mobile money? 27 May 2013. http://www.economist.com/blogs/economist-explains/2013/05/economist-explains-18 (accessed 23 October 2016).

The World Bank, 2016. Global Findex. http://www.worldbank.org/en/programs/globalfindex/overview (accessed 23 October 2016).

The World Bank, 2013. Achieving Universal Financial Access by 2020 Requires the World Bank Group to 'Think About What We Need to Do Differently', November 2013. http://www.worldbank.org/en/news/feature/2013/11/07/achieving-universal-financial-access-by-2020-requires-the-wbg-to-think-about-what-we-need-to-do-differently (accessed 23 October 2016).

Tian, M., 2015. Can Alibaba's Ant Financial Disrupt China's Financial Industry? CKGSB Knowledge, August 5, 2015. http://knowledge.ckgsb.edu.cn/2015/08/05/finance-and-investment/can-alibabas-ant-financial-disrupt-chinas-financial-industry/ (accessed 23 October 2016).

Tsang, T., 2016. How New Credit Scores Might Help Bridge China's Credit Gap, Center for Financial Inclusion Blog, June 6, 2016. https://cfi-blog.org/2016/06/06/how-new-credit-scores-might-help-bridge-chinas-credit-gap/ (accessed 23 October 2016).

Villasenor, J., West, D., Lewis, R., 2016. The 2016 Brookings Financial and Digital Inclusion Project Report: Advancing Equitable Financial Ecosystems. Brookings Institution, Washington, D.C.

Wikipedia, 2016. M-kopa. https://en.wikipedia.org/wiki/M-kopa (accessed 23 October 2016).

Yanofsky, D., Mims, C., 2012. Since 2000, the number of mobile phones in the developing world has increased 1700%, Quartz, October 2012. http://qz.com/9101/mobile-phones-developing-world/ (accessed 23 October 2016).

Yoon, S., 2015. The Rise of Mobile Phones: 20 Years of Global Adoption, Cartesian Insights, June 2015. http://www.cartesian.com/the-rise-of-mobile-phones-20-years-of-global-adoption/ (accessed 23 October 2016).

Notes

1. There is still a wide divide between developed and developing markets when it comes to mobile internet access: 60% of the population in developed markets have mobile Internet access, compared 40% in developing markets (GSM Association, 2016).

2. As of 2014, there are 81,000 M-Pesa agents (McKay and Mazer, 2014), compared to 1,443 bank branches (Otieno and Daily Nation, 2015).

The Cross-Section of Crypto-Currencies as Financial Assets[1]

Investing in Crypto-Currencies Beyond Bitcoin

Hermann Elendner, Simon Trimborn, Bobby Ong, Teik Ming Lee

Contents

146   Chapter 7

A.2	Portfolios	171
A.3	Power Law	172

References 172

Note 173

Chapter Points

- Hundreds of crypto-currencies have been created following Bitcoin and form an asset class for alternative investments.
- Returns on crypto-currency investments exhibit high expected returns with very high volatilities; however, their returns show very little correlation with those of standard financial assets, or with each other.
- Portfolios of crypto-currencies therefore provide diversification benefits.

7.1 Introduction

With Bitcoin, Satoshi Nakomoto permanently changed the world's investment universe to include purely virtual assets: in 2008 he invented the first digital currency. Less than a decade later, not only the original Bitcoin technology has evolved from a technical proof-of-concept to a serious and dependable investment asset: the underlying blockchain technology has spread and gained recognition, and several hundred of different crypto-currencies have been created and are actively traded. Virtual assets are no longer *one* alternative investment: cryptographic claims nowadays form an entire asset class for alternative investments, with a large cross-section to choose from.

The wide and fast proliferation of the blockchain technology owes to the open-source nature of Bitcoin, with its source code publicly available at `github.com` and a free-software license that allows derivative works. Computer programmers worldwide can copy, modify and experiment upon the Bitcoin concept, thereby creating many alternative crypto-currencies (altcoins). This has brought about a vibrant ecosystem that allows for diverse experimentation in the development of digital currencies.

Crypto-currency traders worldwide have seized upon the altcoin growth to invest in an alternative asset free from direct government intervention, or to speculate on the often volatile values of these crypto-currencies. Some altcoins have led to significant improvements to the development of digital currencies as a whole, such as Ethereum, Ripple, Dash (formerly

www.elsevierdirect.com

Darkcoin), Namecoin and others. For example, Ethereum is a crypto-platform that introduces a Turing-complete scripting language allowing for the creation of smart contracts; Dash
allows for anonymity of blockchain transactions; Namecoin implements a decentralized Domain Name System.

Many altcoins, however, have been created as a simple clone of Bitcoin with minimal changes
(see `dillingers.com/blog/2015/04/18` for a how-to): some due to a belief of different parameters being preferable; some with little other purpose than to pump-and-dump the
market for a quick return.

There exist altcoin developers who have conducted outright scams via Initial Coin Offerings, with the creators disappearing after crowdsourcing bitcoins from the community.
An example of an Initial Coin Offering (ICO) scam is Edgecoin, where the organizers
changed their original ICO announcement to one informing that they had been hacked, see
`bitcointalk.org`. Meanwhile, some altcoins have also been created with illegitimate
aims such as stealing users' personal details or bitcoin private keys through the installation of
malware and trojans onto altcoin wallets.

The presence of free-riders and fraudsters, however, does not imply a fundamental weakness
of the asset class; it stems from the sudden growth in the early stages of a new market and
from the presence of many unknowledgable participants (Böhme et al., 2015). After all, in the
early days when the first joint-stock corporations publicly floated their shares, stock scams
were widespread, and physical currencies are plagued by counterfeiting to this day. Yet who
would exclude stocks and currencies from investment considerations?

These nuisances should not distract from the fact that crypto-currencies are a new asset class
that is here to stay. The cryptographic claims are based on a strong, highly competitive and
remarkably resilient technology: the blockchain. As the economy is becoming more and more
digital, the role of digital assets in investment decisions will also grow. To exclude digital assets from investment choices, in particular in light of their properties this chapter will point
out, will become as restrictive as excluding entire other asset classes.

This chapter serves as an introduction to crypto-currencies as alternative investments: We
consider their properties as financial assets, with a particular focus on their returns, as well
as their diversification effect in investment portfolios. We investigate the movements of the
crypto-currencies, analyze the co-movements of the altcoins and Bitcoin and compare their
relation with established assets like stock indices, real estate, gold and US Treasury Bills.

7.2 The Dynamic Environment of a Multiplicity of Crypto-Currencies

While Bitcoin still is the most valuable crypto-currency, the investment universe of block-chain-based crypto-currencies has seen higher than proportional growth for alternative implementations, so-called *altcoins*.

At the time of writing (31 August 2016), `coinmarketcap.com` lists 767 active altcoins. This list is not exhaustive: many more have been and are being created; only the most liquid ones are traded on altcoin exchanges and listed on Coinmarketcap. The others are deemed too illiquid. However, the existence of many insignificant crypto-currencies must not detract from the fact that the importance of altcoins as alternative investment vehicles is growing: Altcoin market capitalization as a percentage of total market capitalization of crypto-currencies including Bitcoin has already reached 19%.

One major factor enabling such growth has been the relative ease of setting up new crypto-currencies.

7.2.1 Starting Yet Another Crypto-Currency

In 2014, altcoins were rapidly being created each day, with the number of altcoins listed on Coinmarketcap increasing from 69 in January 2014 to 590 by December 2014, see `web.archive.org`. Growth in active altcoins has since tapered off and the number of active altcoins has been hovering between 650 and 770 since June 2015.

There are two types of altcoins listed on Coinmarketcap, namely crypto-currencies and crypto-assets. Crypto-currencies have their own blockchain and require their own time-stamping mechanism. Examples of crypto-currencies are Litecoin, Peercoin, Ether, Dogecoin, Stellar, etc.

Crypto-assets do not have their own blockchain or timestamping mechanism but instead are created off crypto-currency platforms and rely on the main crypto-currency's blockchain. Examples of crypto-currency platforms (which also serve as a crypto-currency) are Counterparty, NXT, Ethereum, Omni (previously Mastercoin), and Bitshares. Some examples of crypto-assets that are based on these crypto-currency platforms are MaidSafeCoin (a crypto-asset of Omni), DigixDAO (a crypto-asset of Ethereum), Storjcoin X (a crypto-asset of Counterparty), SuperNET (a crypto-asset of NXT) and others.

It requires technical knowledge to create or even to clone an existing crypto-currency. Creating a crypto-asset on the other hand is relatively simple and does not require strong technical expertise.

7.2.2 A Brief History of Altcoins and Approaches to Generate Value

The first altcoin ever created was the Bitcoin Testnet 1, created by Gavin Andresen (see `reddit.com`); it has by now been abandoned. One of the earliest crypto-currencies still in active use is Ripple, an exceptional altcoin with respect to its development, which to a large degree is independent of Bitcoin's. Not only do these two crypto-currencies employ different timestamping models, with Ripple using the Consensus protocol, see Schwartz et al. (2014), against Bitcoin's SHA-256 Proof-of-Work: Ripple is also implemented with an entirely different source code – a rarity, since most crypto-currencies are built as edited versions of Bitcoin's source code.

Namecoin was one of the earliest designs of innovative altcoins, in the sense that it was created with the aim of functionality beyond coin transfers, i.e., for a different use-case: Namecoin was built to improve decentralization by serving as an alternative decentralized Domain Name System (DNS) system and identity storage. DNS servers, the machines which store the look-up information to link internet domain names to those computers effectively serving the associated content, are until today controlled by governments and large corporations – an infrastructure setup that allows for certain websites to be censored. Namecoin enables the creation of `.bit` websites which cannot be censored. Furthermore, Namecoin also allows for the storage of key/value data, which proves useful for identity management. For instance, the startup Onename used to store information on individual identities on the Namecoin blockchain (but has since moved to the Bitcoin blockchain due to security reasons, `blog.onename.com`). Namecoin is also noteworthy for being the first fork of Bitcoin and the first altcoin to implement merged mining with Bitcoin on the SHA-256 Proof-of-Work algorithm, see `namecoin.info`.

The first major altcoin to make use of a different hashing algorithm was Tenebrix, which used the Scrypt Proof-of-Work algorithm. However, likely due to an excessive pre-mine of 7.7 million coins out of a cap of 10.5 million, Tenebrix did not survive. Pre-mining refers to mining before the general public is invited to participate in the operation of the blockchain, and hence before anybody but the developers can participate in the seignorage, obtaining newly created coins. Naturally, large pre-mining is perceived very critically by potential altcoin investors, as it effectively allocates a significant fraction of the aggregate (also long-run) money supply to the developers before the coin's launch.

In the early days of altcoin creation, however, debates about altcoin designs centered mostly on the concrete parameterization of the blockchain. Parameters such as total coins available for mining, transaction time and distribution period were pivotal in arguments about pros and cons of an altcoin. Hence, many altcoins were purely a reincarnation of the Bitcoin blockchain with a different set of parameter choices. A classical example of such parameter

Table 7.1: Comparison of parameters of Bitcoin and Litecoin.

	Bitcoin	Litecoin
Coin Limit	21 million	84 million
Timestamping	proof of work	proof of work
Proof-of-Work Hashing Algorithm	SHA-256	Scrypt
Block Time	10 minutes	2.5 minutes
Difficulty Retarget	2,106 blocks	2,106 blocks
Block Reward Halving	every 210,000 blocks	every 840,000 blocks
Initial Block Reward	50 BTC	50 LTC
Created By	Satoshi Nakamoto	Charlie Lee
Creation Date	3 January 2009	7 October 2011

Source: coindesk.com

tweaking to "improve" Bitcoin is Litecoin. Table 7.1 compares the parameters of Bitcoin and Litecoin.

Following the trend of tweaking parameters for altcoins, developers started innovating on the *proof-of-work* concept. In order to prevent adversaries from undermining the network, the blockchain requires every new block to contain proof that a certain (expected) amount of effort has been invested. This proof of work is rewarded with newly created coins (seignorage) and transaction fees (if any). The proof is delivered in the form of a number that solves a computational problem which is hard to solve but very easy to verify. In this context, "hard to solve" means that the only way to come up with a solution is a trial-and-error approach that requires sizable computational resources ("number crunching;" the difficulty of the problem is re-set periodically so that on average a new block is found after a given block time).

This proof-of-work approach makes the propagation of a fraudulent continuation of the blockchain prohibitively expensive ("51% attack"), but it does imply that sizable amounts of computational power (and hence electricity) are used to ensure the blockchain's operation. While the frequently voiced position that this energy be "wasted" certainly overlooks the fact that other payment systems also require far from negligible expenses to operate and maintain, even if they do not achieve independence from a trusted third party, it led to the development of an alternative approach to ensure the blockchain cannot be extended illegitimately: *proof of stake.*

The proof-of-stake idea was first mooted by the Bitcointalk user QuantumMechanic in July 2011, see `bitcointalk.org`. Sunny King, the founder of Peercoin (previously known as PPCoin) was the first to implement a proof-of-stake altcoin, see King and Nadal (2012). The aim the proof-of-stake design was to remove the need to expend computational resources in securing the blockchain. The right to extend the blockchain is not obtained by providing the solution to a computational riddle, but rather requires a party to prove ownership of a certain amount of coins. In order to attack a proof-of-stake altcoin, an attacker would not need to surpass the entire remaining community in terms of computational power, but rather buy a significant portion of the coins outstanding. In this case, however, attacking the coin (and thus destroying its value) will no longer be incentive compatible; at least unless the threat to do it anyway is credible (Houy, 2014). For more information, see the article of Vitalik Buterin, the founder of Ethereum, explaining the differences between Proof-of-Work and Proof-of-Stake, in bitcoinmagazine.com.

The debate about the relative merits of proof of work vs. proof of stake is still active, however, and development of proof-of-work altcoins has kept progressing. For instance, tweaking Bitcoin's SHA-256 algorithm allowed more individual miners to participate in the network in order to keep it decentralized. As a result of these innovations, we see many altcoins launching with algorithms such as Scrypt, X11, X13, X15, Blake-256, Groestl and more. Developers also started launching altcoins using multiple hashing algorithms, such as Myriadcoin which uses five hashing algorithms: SHA256d, Scrypt, Myr-Groestl, Skein, and Qubit.

The third approach to ensure the integrity of a blockchain is *proof of burn,* first used by Counterparty. The Counterparty tokens, XCP, were distributed proportionately to everyone who destroyed bitcoins by sending them to an unrecoverable address during the proof-of-burn period in January 2014, see counterparty.io. The proof of burn was used by the team launching Counterparty to ensure the legitimate distribution of coins. This process helped the Counterparty team establish credibility as the developers do not gain anything from the bitcoins "burnt."

Another trend that started in 2014 was altcoin developers launching sovereign altcoins, associated with particular countries. The first such sovereign altcoin was Auroracoin, created in February 2014 to serve as the crypto-currency for the nation of Iceland. Like most of these sovereign altcoins, Auroracoin distributed the coins to residents via an airdrop: Icelandic residents entered their resident ID on Auroracoin's official website, and received their reserved 50% of the total supply of Auroracoin, see coindesk.com.

A sizable hype ensued, making Auroracoin the second-largest crypto-currency in terms of market capitalization in March 2014, see blogs.wsj.com. The success of Auroracoin inspired other developers to launch similar sovereign altcoins for other nations or territories such as Pesetacoin (Spain), Scotcoin (Scotland), eGulden (Netherlands), Mazacoin (Lakota Nation – a Native American territory in USA) and others. For a list, see coindesk.com.

Next, development efforts were directed at altcoins with anonymity as a design goal. The pseudonymous nature of Bitcoin was sufficient to attract transfers for illegitimate or illegal purposes, but the public and unalterable trace of all transactions also provided the basis for successes by law enforcement in identifying the agents behind certain transactions. Altcoins such as Dash (previously known as Darkcoin), Monero, ShadowCash and others aimed at providing the possibility of transferring coins without disclosing one's identity. Dash, for example, has a PrivateSend (previously known as DarkSend) implementation that extends the idea of CoinJoin, first proposed by Bitcoin core developer Gregory Maxwell as a way to improve bitcoin transaction anonymity by combining bitcoin transactions with another person's transactions, see `bitcointalk.org`. Duffield and Diaz (2015) in their Dash whitepaper point out three methods in which bitcoin transactions can be de-anonymized: through linking and forward linking via identified exchanges, and also CoinJoin amount tracing. PrivateSend requires at least three participants and for it to work each participant needs to submit transaction inputs and outputs in common denominations of 0.1DASH, 1DASH, 10DASH and 100DASH.

Potentially the most important developments, however, were those to add *smart-contract* capabilities onto the blockchain. Some platforms that are built on top of the Bitcoin blockchain to add this functionality include Omni (previously Mastercoin), Counterparty and Rootstock. Other developers have created new platforms such as Ethereum, Bitshares and NXT. Platforms such as Ethereum introduced new concepts into the protocol such as a Turing-complete programming language, allowing to create arbitrarily complex smart contracts.

These platforms allow for the creation of crypto-assets and supported the growth of crypto-assets. For example, Counterparty has a total of 50,520 assets (according to `blockscan.com`), NXT has 685 assets (`nxtreporting.com`), and Bitshares has 198 active assets (`cryptofresh.com`), at the time of writing. Despite the high number of crypto-assets, most of these are not actively traded. CoinMarketCap lists only 59 actively traded crypto-assets, see `coinmarketcap.com`. The most successful crypto-asset is the DAO: it raised USD 162 million worth of tokens; however, on 17 June 2016, a vulnerability in the code resulted in the loss of 3.6 million ethers worth USD 60 million, see `coindesk.com`. The resolution of this problem by re-defining the blockchain led to a fork and heated debate.

Finally, the growth of enthusiasm about Bitcoin has been reflected in the growth of bitcoin transactions, to the point that today developers are discussing how to ensure the protocol can accommodate such high growth rates well into the future. To this end, the blockchain itself will likely need to be decentralized, and work is progressing on so-called *pegged sidechains* (Back et al., 2014). To get onto a sidechain, a user will send bitcoins to a specially-formed Bitcoin address. Bitcoins sent to the address are immobilized (not within anyone's control). Once the transaction is confirmed, tokens on the sidechain are released so that they can be controlled by the same user. The reverse can happen once the tokens in the sidechain are no longer needed. Sidechains are essentially altcoins in a Bitcoin ecosystem. There are numerous interesting applications that can take place once this proposal goes live and may well be the future direction of crypto-currencies.

7.2.3 Altcoin Trading Platforms

Both the desire to innovate and the ease of building on the Bitcoin implementation have thus led to the breadth of various altcoins available for investment and as media of exchange. They are traded online with huge discrepancies in liquidity.

Trading activity of popular altcoins is conducted at online crypto-currency exchanges. Similarly to exchanges trading BTC for sovereign currencies, these exchanges commonly operate continuously, i.e., 24 hours per day, 7 days every week. The complete alignment of trading hours with calendar time provides an aspect of liquidity that the world's largest stock exchanges do not provide.

Altcoin exchanges operate one order book per currency pair, where prices are determined from active trading. Most altcoins are thereby traded against bitcoins, effectively making it the virtual reserve currency. Only the most popular altcoins sometimes have trading pairs with fiat currencies such as the US Dollar, the Euro, the Chinese Yuan, or the Russian Ruble.

One of the largest altcoin exchanges by trading volume at the time of writing is `poloniex. com`. Poloniex is a US-based exchange that does not support fiat-currency trading. Poloniex supports trading of 115 altcoins across 135 market pairs with 4 base currencies of bitcoin (BTC), ether (ETH), monero (XMR) and tether (USDT). Poloniex's 24-hour trading volume on 24 July 2016 was 67,906 BTC.

Most trading volume occurs on the BTC base currency. There are 108 markets with bitcoin, 15 markets with monero, 8 markets with tether and 4 markets with ether as base currency. The most popular market pair on Poloniex is ETH/BTC with 24-hour trading volume of over 41,000 BTC. This is followed by ETC/BTC, NXT/BTC, LSK/BTC, DAO/BTC and STEEM/BTC.

One of the oldest altcoin exchanges is `btc-e.com`. Btc-e has been in operation since July 2011. Its owner and location, however, are uncertain, with its terms of use claiming that it is bound by the laws of Cyprus, website description claiming it is operating from Bulgaria, and the website having a strong Russian language design. Despite its shady circumstances, btc-e has been in operation for a long time and has withstood many competitors who have since ceased to exist.

Currently, btc-e supports trading of 7 altcoins across 18 market pairs with 5 base currencies of US Dollar, Euro, Russian Ruble, bitcoin (BTC) and litecoin (LTC). Btc-e's 24-hour trading volume on 24 July 2016 was 4,721 BTC; a small number compared to Poloniex.

Yobit, Bittrex, C-Cex are exchanges which offer support for many altcoins. Yobit supports 618 altcoins, Bittrex supports 205 altcoins and C-Cex supports 143 altcoins, and these three exchanges offer traders more opportunities in trading their altcoins when the altcoins are not listed on Poloniex.

It is quite common for altcoin exchanges to disappear overnight in this industry with the most popular narrative being that the exchange has been hacked. Without proper security precautions in place, hackers can run away with funds in an exchange making it insolvent. Users are advised to not store any altcoins on the exchanges to reduce counterparty risk. Some of the popular altcoin exchanges that have disappeared with users' funds over the years are Cryptsy, Mintpal and Vircurex.

7.2.4 Altcoin Information Platforms

There are many sources of information that can be used to analyze the crypto-currency ecosystem. One of the primary sources of information is to use blockchain data. The `blockchain.info` provides online Bitcoin wallets and also data such as price, mined blocks, number of transactions and various others statistics.

Alternative block explorers providing blockchain information for Bitcoin are `kaiko.com` and `blockr.io`. Since each crypto-currency has its own blockchain, the information for each altcoin needs to be obtained from each individual altcoin's block explorer. `BitInfocharts.com` provides statistics for selected altcoins.

While block-explorer services are suitable for the average user to obtain information related to the blockchain, application developers prefer more flexibility in interacting with the blockchain and may opt for Application Program Interface (API) services such as `BlockCypher.com` and `BitGo.com`. Traditionally, developers need to host a bitcoin node in order to obtain the latest transactions and blocks. With these services, the barriers to entry for developers to build apps on top of the bitcoin blockchain are reduced.

To get more information on the level of decentralization in Bitcoin, one can use Bitnodes (available at `bitnodes.21.co`). Bitnodes attempt to estimate the size of the Bitcoin network by finding reachable Bitcoin nodes in the network.

To get information on the latest price for bitcoin, it needs to be obtained from the dozens of exchanges operating worldwide. Each of these exchanges has its own market and order book, and due to differences (including transaction volume) each exchange will quote somewhat different bid/ask prices. So far, there has not been a global standard in determining the bitcoin "spot price." There are several initiatives to identify the true spot price of bitcoin such as the CoinDesk Bitcoin Price Index and the Winkdex.

In September 2013, the CoinDesk Bitcoin Price Index (BPI) was launched by CoinDesk. The aim of BPI is to establish the standard retail price reference for industry participants and accounting professionals. Due to the growing importance of the bitcoin market in China, a specialized BPI for the Chinese Yuan market was introduced in March 2014. At the time of writing, the following exchanges are included in the USD index: Bitstamp, Bitfinex, GDAX, itBit and OKCoin while the following exchanges are included in the CNY index: BTC China, Huobi and OKCoin. The minimum criteria for a Bitcoin exchange to be included in the BPI are the following, see `coindesk.com/price` and `coindesk.com` for reference:

1. USD exchanges must serve an international customer base.
2. The exchange must provide bid–offer quotes for an immediate sale (offer) and an immediate purchase (bid).
3. Minimum trade size must be less than 1,500 USD (9,000 CNY) or equivalent.
4. Daily trading volume must meet minimum acceptable levels as determined by CoinDesk.
5. The exchange must represent at least 5% of the total 30-day cumulative volume for all of the exchanges included in the XBP.
6. The stated and/or actual time for a majority of fiat currency and bitcoin transfers (whether deposits or withdrawals) must not exceed two business days.

In July 2014, the Winkdex price index was launched by Cameron and Tyler Winklevoss. The Winkdex formula is calculated based on the top three highest-volume Bitcoin exchanges in the previous two-hour period using a volume-weighted exponential moving average. Transactions executed on exchanges with higher volumes and most recent by time would provide a higher weight to the Winkdex formula, see `winkdex.com`.

Finally there is `BitcoinWisdom.com`, a real-time bitcoin market chart website. BitcoinWisdom offers real-time price charts allowing users to apply technical analysis onto Bitcoin and selected altcoin markets. BitcoinWisdom gives a real-time overview on what is happening in major bitcoin exchanges by streaming data on order books and executed trades.

For altcoin pricing, volume and trading data, one will have to refer to other online services such as `CoinMarketCap.com`, `CoinGecko.com`, and `CoinHills.com`. CoinMarketCap is a website that tracks the market capitalization of all active crypto-currencies using the following formula: weighted average price multiplied by total available supply.

CoinGecko is a website that tracks crypto-currencies beyond market capitalization. The website ranks crypto-currencies based on several other metrics such as liquidity, developer activity, community and public interest, see `coingecko.com`. CoinGecko was based on the premise that a strong community and developer team form the foundation of a crypto-currency with good growth.

CoinHills is a website that tracks the price and trading activity of various crypto-currencies from different exchanges. CoinHills does not rank altcoins but provides insights on the exchanges and altcoins with the most trading volume on a real-time basis. Using CoinHills, traders can learn more about unusual activities in the crypto-currency markets and obtain potential trading ideas.

To capture the evolution of the values of crypto-currencies in the cross-section, `crix.hu-berlin.de` offers an index which tracks the average price movement of the most representative altcoins, similar to a stock-market index. CRIX determines the coins included via an information criterion and weighs their return contributions by the respective amounts of coins at the start of each month. Thus, CRIX mimics a monthly rebalanced portfolio. While S&P500 and the CSI300 provide a summary statistic about the current state of the US and Chinese markets, respectively, CRIX does the same for the crypto-currency market. CRIX was proposed by Härdle and Trimborn (2015) and further investigated by Trimborn and Härdle (2016). The first publication proposes a first version of CRIX and compares the dynamics of the index against other markets. The latter further develops the methodology of CRIX and evaluates the performance of the methodology on other markets.

7.3 Properties of Crypto-Currency Dynamics

While there is ongoing debate about whether altcoins should legitimately be characterized as *currencies* or rather as *digital assets* (Yermack, 2015), indisputably they represent an alternative investment with the evolution of their value of key importance. From the perspective of their owner, next to their usefulness as media of exchange, their capabilities as stores of value are critical; or put differently: the financial returns to holding the digital coins. The emergence of a broad cross-section of different coins has prompted the necessity to assess the risk and return profiles of hundreds of different assets, as well as considerations of diversification and portfolio management.

This section provides an overview of the returns to the price processes of crypto-currencies in general from the perspective of an altcoin investor. While it cannot claim completeness, it is aimed to characterize the cross-section broadly.

7.3.1 The Universe of Crypto-Currencies

There currently exist 767 crypto-currencies while our data set consists of 327. Some altcoins have effectively already gone extinct, while permanently new ones emerge. This nascent market constantly exhibits substantial changes.

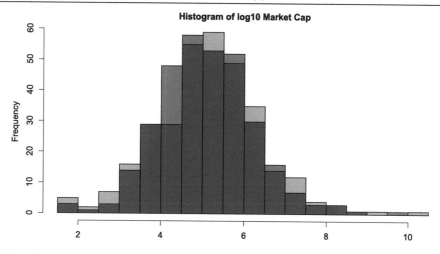

Figure 7.1: *Histogram of market capitalizations.* **Frequency of market capitalization on a log scale on 2016-07-24 (shaded red) and in the time period 2015-07-25 until 2016-07-24 (shaded blue) for all crypto-currencies. The overlapping area is displayed in purple. (For interpretation of the references to color in this figure legend, the reader is referred to the web version of this chapter.)**

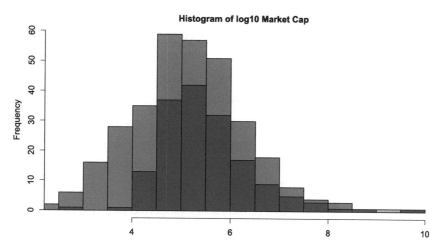

Figure 7.2: *Histogram of market capitalizations over time.* **Frequencies cover the periods 2014-03-30 to 2014-08-01 (shaded red) and 2016-01-01 to 2016-07-24 (shaded blue), with overlapping areas in purple. Time intervals cover periods of high market capitalization, compare Fig. 7.4. (For interpretation of the references to color in this figure legend, the reader is referred to the web version of this chapter.)**

Fig. 7.1 shows that in the last year most of the crypto-currencies exhibited aggregate market valuations in the range of 1,000 to 10,000,000 USD. Comparing distribution at the end of our sample with the mean over the last year, a shift of mass in the direction of the tails becomes

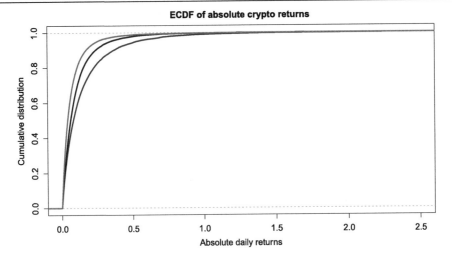

Figure 7.3: *Empirical distribution of absolute returns.* **The figure shows the empirical cumulative distribution of the absolute returns of all crypto-currencies in the data set, divided into three groups depending on their mean market value. Group1 has a mean market value below or equal 50,000, group2 between 50,000 and 500,000, and** group3 **above 500,000. Excluded were returns where the daily trading volume was below 10 USD. (For interpretation of the references to color in this figure legend, the reader is referred to the web version of this chapter.)**

visible. Mostly crypto-currencies with market capitalization between 10,000 and 32,000 USD either gained or lost in value or vanished from the market.

To analyze structural shifts in the market, a closer look over certain time horizons is called for. For instance, Fig. 7.4 reveals that the aggregate crypto-currency market exhibited fairly high market capitalization in the beginning of the observed time period, declined subsequently, and achieved again similar values at the end of the time period.

Fig. 7.2 shows the surprising result that in the earlier subperiod in 2014, more crypto-currencies with high market capitalization were present in the market, as compared to the later subperiod in 2016. In the latter period, the recovery of the aggregate market value was driven mainly by crypto-currencies with smaller valuations having become more frequent in the market.

Assets with differences in certain features, like market value, often exhibit differences in the behavior of their returns. Stocks have an often-observed size effect, see e.g., Gabaix (2009). Fig. 7.3 shows the empirical cumulative distribution function (ecdf) of the absolute returns of all crypto-currencies for different sizes of market value. Apparently, crypto-currencies with smaller mean market value exhibit higher returns; crypto-currencies therefore share the size effect with stocks.

Figure 7.4: *Aggregate market capitalization and trading volume.* **Evolution of aggregate market capitalization on** $\log_{10}$ **scale over the period 2014-03-30 to 2016-07-24. The width of the line (spanned in red) indicates the daily trading volume of the aggregate market. (For interpretation of the references to color in this figure legend, the reader is referred to the web version of this chapter.)**

7.3.2 The Evolution of the Crypto-Currency Universe Over Time

As detailed, the relative ease of constructing a new crypto-currency and the diversity of objectives regarding their desired properties lead to a dynamic environment with new currencies being introduced and some established ones fading out of usage over often short intervals of time. At the same time, the distribution of trading volumes attracted by various currencies is highly skewed, with BTC generally still generating the dominating fraction of aggregate daily trading volume.

The entire market showed a high increase in daily trading volume over the observed time period 2014-03-30 to 2016-07-24. Fig. 7.4 shows that the relatively thin trading volume in 2014 was accompanied by a frequent change in the market capitalizations. After a strong decline of capitalization in early 2015, market cap increased until the end of the observation period while showing deepening liquidity.

7.3.3 Liquidity of Crypto-Currencies

Fig. 7.5 displays the evolution of daily trading volume for the 10 major crypto-currencies, using a logarithmic scale due to the high skewness of volumes across crypto-currencies.

More results on standard liquidity measures are reported by Fink and Johann (2014).

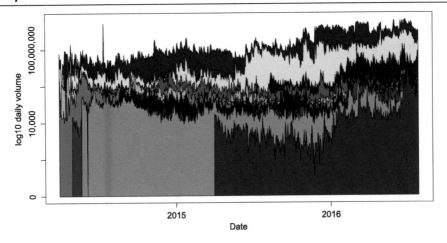

Figure 7.5: *Crypto-currencies' volume evolution.* **Daily USD trading volume of the ten major crypto-currencies over 2014-03-30 to 2016-07-24, on log scale. Color code is** BTC, ETH, XRP, LTC, DASH, DOGE, MAID, BTS, XEM, XMR. **Crypto-currencies entering the data set display a spike. The volume per crypto-currency is depicted by the height of its colored area; hence the upper contour describes aggregate volume over all 10 crypto-currencies. (For interpretation of the references to color in this figure legend, the reader is referred to the web version of this chapter.)**

7.3.4 Financial Returns on Investing in Crypto-Currencies

7.3.4.1 Summary Statistics

Compared to standard financial assets, crypto-currencies exhibit remarkably higher dispersion in their returns. Table 7.2 displays summary statistics for the currently most important (in terms of market capitalization) 10 crypto-currencies.

The first interesting fact which these crypto-currencies share can be inferred from the mean and median. The means are – except for LTC – positive while the medians are mostly negative. Obviously most of the returns are negative but with a smaller absolute degree than the positive ones. The row 'percent negative' shows the extent of this implication. Notice that BTC is the only crypto-currency with more positive returns than negative ones, a fact which strengthens its special role in the crypto-currency market.

Crypto-currencies thus lose value more frequently than they gain, but gain in stronger movements. The quantiles, maximal and minimal values support this result. Mostly the maximal simple return is higher than the minimal one, where LTC is the exception again. Also the upper deciles are mostly greater than or at least very close to the lower ones in absolute value. These two findings imply that the returns in the positive tails are sizably bigger than the ones in the negative tails, measured in absolute values.

Table 7.2: Descriptive statistics on simple daily returns (in percent) of the 10 crypto-currencies with the largest final market capitalizations over the time period 2014-03-30 to 2016-07-24.

	BTC	ETH	XRP	LTC	DASH	MAID	DOGE	XEM	XMR	BTS
maximum	22.31	55.24	86.02	41.82	114.24	72.91	61.65	69.50	123.93	64.31
upper decile q_{90}	3.37	11.88	4.92	4.12	7.85	9.02	5.15	10.09	9.03	6.65
upper quartile q_{75}	1.32	4.95	1.73	1.29	2.76	4.07	1.74	3.88	3.42	2.40
median	0.09	−0.07	−0.22	−0.18	−0.20	−0.07	−0.39	−0.13	−0.09	−0.61
mean	0.09	1.07	0.10	−0.01	0.66	0.54	0.08	1.10	0.38	0.18
lower quartile q_{25}	−1.21	−3.39	−1.97	−1.60	−2.82	−3.55	−2.35	−3.41	−3.56	−3.34
lower decile q_{10}	−3.07	−7.29	−4.73	−4.41	−6.39	−7.66	−4.90	−8.00	−7.63	−6.58
minimum	−22.26	−48.33	−34.22	−42.14	−40.80	−31.20	−28.62	−24.87	−29.43	−23.74
percent negative	47.85	50.57	53.24	52.98	52.73	51.19	56.90	51.98	50.51	55.71
volatility	3.34	9.28	6.03	5.34	9.07	8.44	6.10	10.04	8.77	7.70
N	848	351	848	848	848	817	848	479	794	733

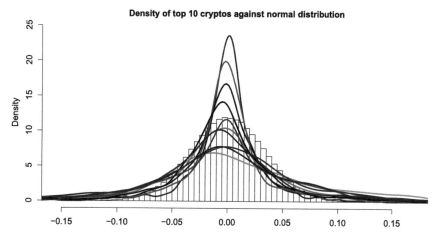

Figure 7.6: *Probability density of daily returns.* The probability density functions of the distributions of daily returns for the main 10 crypto-currencies with the following color code: BTC, ETH, XRP, LTC, DASH, DOGE, MAID, BTS, XEM, XMR. A normal distribution with the same mean and standard deviation as the returns on BTC is displayed as a histogram in the background. The observation period is 2014-03-30 to 2016-07-24. (For interpretation of the references to color in this figure legend, the reader is referred to the web version of this chapter.)

Fig. 7.6 shows the densities of the returns of the top 10 crypto-currencies by market capitalization (and for comparison the normal distribution). Apparently the crypto-currencies with higher market cap have more weight around zero. All of the crypto-currencies show devi-

Table 7.3: Risk measures, including value at risk, expected shortfall, and the CAPM β, for daily log returns of the 10 crypto-currencies with highest final market capitalizations and for three crypto-currency portfolios over the time period 2014-03-30 to 2016-07-24. The portfolios are investments into the crypto-currency index CRIX, into an equally-weighted portfolio (EW), or a value-weighted portfolio (VW) of all crypto-currencies in our data set.

	BTC	ETH	XRP	LTC	DASH	MAID	DOGE	XEM	XMR	BTS	CRIX	EW	VW
volatility	0.034	0.092	0.057	0.054	0.083	0.081	0.058	0.092	0.081	0.071	0.032	0.045	0.062
skewness	−0.564	−0.612	1.152	−0.805	1.268	0.500	1.062	1.334	1.164	1.774	−0.680	2.495	0.614
excess kurtosis	8.617	9.550	22.953	20.637	16.581	6.603	11.059	6.357	14.511	10.549	8.990	28.897	29.354
VaR at 1%	0.072	0.207	0.064	0.117	0.104	0.170	0.069	0.124	0.121	0.119	0.064	0.103	0.068
exp. shortfall at 1%	0.098	0.306	0.085	0.194	0.138	0.231	0.101	0.134	0.148	0.147	0.089	0.135	0.093
VaR at 5%	0.034	0.107	0.036	0.042	0.063	0.116	0.038	0.086	0.078	0.082	0.031	0.058	0.034
exp. shortfall at 5%	0.056	0.178	0.055	0.082	0.092	0.172	0.061	0.107	0.107	0.111	0.052	0.089	0.055
CAPM β	0.103	−0.519	0.436	−0.098	0.614	0.032	0.052	−0.501	0.374	0.605	0.009	−0.099	−0.270
N	838	350	819	840	842	717	840	479	792	727	724	724	723

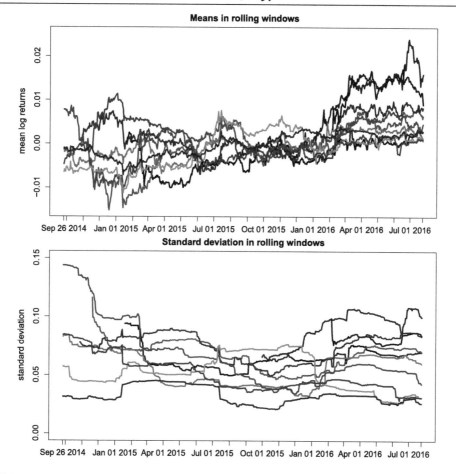

Figure 7.7: *Measures over time in rolling windows.* **Calibrated parameters in rolling windows of 180 days. The upper panel displays means, the lower panel displays the standard deviations in the respective windows. Colors denote** BTC, ETH, XRP, LTC, DASH, DOGE, MAID, BTS, XEM, XMR. **(For interpretation of the references to color in this figure legend, the reader is referred to the web version of this chapter.)**

ations from the Gaussian distribution. Especially the tails are heavier. This visual result is supported by the measures of skewness and kurtosis, see Table 7.3.

7.3.4.2 Returns and Their Stability Over Time

Having established that crypto-currencies, unlike most fiat currencies, exhibit sizable fluctuations in their market value even over short time horizons, the question arises how the risk inherent in an altcoin position and the related expected returns evolve over time. Fig. 7.7 displays the evolution of the main parameters of the return distribution of the crypto-currencies over time, evaluated in rolling windows of 180 trading days. Since crypto-currencies are traded on all days including weekends, this corresponds to half a year. The upper panel shows the means; standard deviation serves as a risk measure and is depicted in the lower panel. The figure showcases the high instability of crypto-currencies' risk and return properties over time: Some, like BTC, even have a lower mean when the standard deviation is higher. Others, like LTC, exhibit the opposite pattern. Apparently, the higher standard deviations result from opposing reasons: for some crypto-currencies from higher positive and for others from higher negative returns. However, since idiosyncratic risk will not be priced, we need to turn to risk compensation in the following.

At this point the analysis has showed that even simple properties of the return process as means and standard deviations are unstable over time. In the following, we investigate the risk of investment in the crypto-currency market further.

7.3.4.3 Risk Measures

The measures of value at risk (VaR) and expected shortfall (ES) are given in Table 7.3, both at a risk level of 1% and 5%. Definitions and calculation details are in Section A.1.

XRP bears the lowest risk in terms of the two risk measures, but must still be considered highly risky in comparison to standard financial assets. Its ES at the 1% level is 8.53%, which means that the expected loss over the days which are the worst with a 1 in 100 chance is 8.53%. ETH exhibits the highest value with 30.57% of daily expected loss at the same risk level. Clearly, these crypto-currencies are not stable investments but entail high risk. However, due to their low correlations especially with established assets (see Section 7.3.4.4) they provide strong diversification benefits in a portfolio.

Next we investigate βs in the context of the CAPM, with the S& P500 as the market index. The βs, see Table 7.3, show very different sensitivities of crypto-currencies to the market excess rate. This measure implies that movements of the top 10 crypto-currencies are little correlated with the stock market.

In the following, we investigate the question of the co-movement of crypto-currencies deeper by means of correlations and PCA.

7.3.4.4 Diversification in a Crypto-Currency Portfolio

In light of the similarity of many crypto-currencies and the fact that their implementations often share large parts of their source code (and arguably the investor base), it may be expected that the returns among the class of altcoins exhibit a high degree of co-movement. This intuition, however, is wrong. Table 7.4 shows that among the top 10 crypto-currencies, most pairs

Table 7.4: The upper triangular displays the correlations of the crypto-currencies BTC, ETH, XRP, LTC, DASH, DOGE, MAID, BTS, XEM, XMR against each other. Missing values were pairwise omitted. The lower triangular shows the corresponding p-values.

	BTC	ETH	XRP	LTC	DASH	MAID	DOGE	XEM	XMR	BTS
BTC		0.08	0.17	0.58	0.33	0.24	0.43	0.32	0.31	0.27
ETH	0.13		0.03	0.05	0.10	0.29	0.05	−0.01	0.12	0.19
XRP	0.00	0.61		0.12	0.07	0.19	0.13	0.10	−0.02	0.16
LTC	0.00	0.33	0.00		0.20	0.08	0.43	0.23	0.21	0.20
DASH	0.00	0.06	0.03	0.00		0.11	0.17	0.11	0.15	0.11
MAID	0.00	0.00	0.00	0.02	0.00		0.12	0.02	0.14	0.14
DOGE	0.00	0.37	0.00	0.00	0.00	0.00		0.20	0.15	0.28
XEM	0.00	0.82	0.03	0.00	0.02	0.73	0.00		0.04	0.12
XMR	0.00	0.02	0.65	0.00	0.00	0.00	0.00	0.38		0.22
BTS	0.00	0.00	0.00	0.00	0.00	0.00	0.00	0.01	0.00	

exhibit low return correlations. More importantly, Table 7.8 displays the results of a principal-component analysis of the altcoins' daily returns: the single-strongest factor only explains 26% of the variation of crypto-currency returns. Moreover, each subsequent factor is providing only slowly declining additional information content, so that seven factors are needed in order to account for 90% of the variation from these ten crypto-currencies, visualized in Fig. 7.8.

This result already shows a distinct movement of the crypto-currencies. The rotation matrix – upper part of the Table 7.8 – shows that the returns are adequately displayed by different factors of the PCA. For explanation, consider the two most important crypto-currencies in terms of market value in the data set, ETH and BTC. While ETH shows strong representation in the first factors, BTC is represented by the latter factors. This observation is supported by the low correlation of the two crypto-currencies, see Table 7.4.

However, the question arises whether the return co-movements are only this low unconditionally, and are subject to spikes for (strong) negative-return times as is common for stocks? We thus calculate pairwise correlations separately for days on which CRIX moves up vs. down and report the results in Table 7.5. Clearly, correlations indeed are stronger on days of negative movements; however, most crypto-currency pairs still exhibit surprisingly low correlations after all. Results are qualitatively similar if we partition the days into positive and negative ones by following the S&P500 index instead of CRIX.

Focusing on correlations of volatilities, and restricting the days of positive/negative market movements to the tenth/first decile of the market's return distribution yields the results in Table 7.6. Here correlations are somewhat higher, and again differences between positive and negative conditions pertain. However, correlations are still lower than in public stock markets.

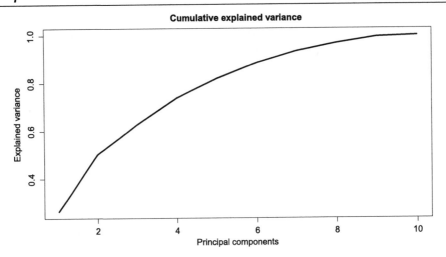

Figure 7.8: *Principal components of crypto-currency returns.* **Representation of the cumulated fraction of explained variance by the PCA components of** BTC, ETH, XRP, LTC, DASH, DOGE, MAID, BTS, XEM, XMR.

Table 7.5: **Pairwise crypto-currency correlations of returns separately for positive (upper triangular matrix) and negative (lower triangular matrix) market-movement days, as defined by returns on CRIX.**

	BTC	ETH	XRP	LTC	DASH	MAID	DOGE	XEM	XMR	BTS
BTC		0.02	0.07	0.31	0.25	0.11	0.30	0.25	0.25	0.11
ETH	−0.08		−0.03	0.03	0.05	0.22	0.02	−0.03	0.17	0.19
XRP	0.16	0.02		0.05	0.07	0.11	0.14	0.09	−0.01	0.16
LTC	0.69	−0.11	0.08		0.12	−0.05	0.23	0.15	0.08	0.13
DASH	0.36	0.09	0.08	0.32		0.05	0.17	0.08	0.17	0.05
MAID	0.28	0.35	0.12	0.13	0.20		0.08	−0.06	0.12	0.11
DOGE	0.40	−0.01	0.05	0.39	0.20	0.09		0.15	0.04	0.23
XEM	0.32	−0.07	0.03	0.27	0.04	0.11	0.16		−0.09	0.08
XMR	0.41	−0.01	0.10	0.29	0.15	0.18	0.18	0.14		0.16
BTS	0.30	0.17	0.10	0.16	0.07	0.10	0.25	0.14	0.22	

It can be concluded that various crypto-currencies are not close substitutes. Rather, their different technical properties give rise both to different usability as media of exchange and stores of value as well as different price dynamics.

This fact also strengthens the rationale for capturing the aggregate crypto-market movement via an index like CRIX, proposed by Härdle and Trimborn (2015), further investigated by Trimborn and Härdle (2016) and available at `crix.hu-berlin.de`. Table 7.3 shows that an investment strategy based on CRIX also exhibits the lowest risk in terms of Value-at-Risk

Table 7.6: Pairwise crypto-currency correlations of volatilities separately for days with returns in the highest decile (upper triangular matrix) and lowest decile (lower triangular matrix) of market movements, as defined by returns on the S&P500.

	BTC	ETH	XRP	LTC	DASH	MAID	DOGE	XEM	XMR	BTS
BTC		0.15	0.22	0.65	0.32	0.14	0.56	0.47	0.34	0.23
ETH	−0.06		0.01	0.11	0.19	0.37	0.19	0.06	0.04	0.23
XRP	0.11	−0.04		0.16	0.18	0.17	0.21	0.17	0.03	0.26
LTC	0.52	−0.03	0.07		0.26	0.02	0.55	0.43	0.15	0.25
DASH	0.41	−0.01	0.04	0.21		0.12	0.21	0.19	0.04	0.18
MAID	0.27	0.26	0.21	0.09	0.13		0.14	0.04	0.11	0.10
DOGE	0.41	−0.06	0.06	0.45	0.24	0.11		0.38	0.16	0.43
XEM	0.26	−0.08	0.08	0.11	0.07	−0.02	0.12		0.12	0.22
XMR	0.29	0.16	−0.08	0.23	0.15	0.16	0.17	−0.03		0.15
BTS	0.28	0.18	0.07	0.19	0.13	0.25	0.23	0.01	0.30	

Table 7.7: Correlations between BTC, ETH, XRP, LTC, DASH, DOGE, MAID, BTS, XEM, XMR and conventional financial assets: 3 exchange rates, gold, 3 stock indices, real estate and the US Treasury Bills Rates.

	BTC	ETH	XRP	LTC	DASH	MAID	DOGE	XEM	XMR	BTS
USD/EUR	−0.05	−0.04	0.04	−0.06	−0.01	−0.03	−0.06	−0.01	−0.05	−0.03
JPY/USD	0.02	−0.04	−0.03	−0.04	0.09	0.02	0.05	−0.05	0.02	0.06
USD/GBP	−0.06	−0.09	0.04	−0.09	−0.01	−0.01	−0.02	−0.17	−0.04	−0.03
Gold	0.05	0.04	0.04	0.05	−0.01	0.07	0.01	0.09	0.02	−0.01
SP500	0.00	−0.05	0.05	−0.05	0.02	0.00	0.01	−0.05	0.03	0.04
XWD	0.01	−0.03	0.02	−0.07	0.03	0.03	0.01	−0.07	0.05	0.07
EEM	0.00	−0.09	0.04	−0.09	0.00	−0.01	0.02	−0.04	0.02	0.04
REIT	0.03	−0.09	0.04	0.05	0.00	−0.03	0.01	0.05	−0.01	−0.05
DTB3	0.02	0.09	0.00	0.02	0.03	0.04	0.04	0.07	0.03	0.05
DGS10	−0.02	−0.08	0.00	−0.02	0.01	−0.03	−0.01	−0.01	−0.02	−0.01

(VaR) and Expected Shortfall (ES), the risk measure currently proposed by the Basel Committee on Banking Supervision (BCBS, 2014). This holds despite the fact that equally-weighted (EW) and value-weighted (VW) portfolios are rebalanced daily for all crypto-currencies in the data set (Section A.2), while CRIX is rebalanced monthly, with a quarterly selection of index constituents; and even though BTC has a high influence in CRIX (and naturally the VW portfolio) due to its high market value.

So far, we have addressed the potential for diversification of a portfolio consisting exclusively of crypto-currencies. Prior studies, in particular Eisl et al. (2015) and also Briere et al. (2013), have shown that, at least for BTC, including the digital asset in a standard financial portfolio provides a sizable effect on diversification as well. Table 7.7 shows the correlation of the

Table 7.8: PCA of the crypto-currencies BTC, ETH, XRP, LTC, DASH, DOGE, MAID, BTS, XEM, XMR. **Due to the late market entry of** ETH **and** XEM, **the reported results are based on an analysis starting in August 2015.**

	PC1	PC2	PC3	PC4	PC5	PC6	PC7	PC8	PC9	PC10
BTC	−0.13	−0.04	0.11	−0.07	0.19	−0.23	0.03	0.05	0.46	0.81
ETH	−0.44	0.70	−0.46	−0.32	0.07	−0.01	−0.04	0.02	−0.02	−0.01
XRP	−0.08	−0.01	0.08	0.02	−0.01	−0.08	0.09	0.97	−0.15	−0.02
LTC	−0.14	−0.05	0.12	−0.10	0.17	−0.32	0.00	0.05	0.70	−0.58
DASH	−0.12	0.02	0.15	−0.09	0.12	−0.33	0.86	−0.17	−0.26	−0.04
MAID	−0.28	0.34	0.16	0.87	−0.10	−0.08	0.00	−0.05	0.05	0.00
DOGE	−0.18	−0.02	0.32	−0.15	0.00	−0.65	−0.49	−0.11	−0.41	−0.01
XEM	−0.74	−0.60	−0.25	0.06	−0.03	0.15	−0.01	−0.04	−0.07	−0.02
XMR	−0.18	0.11	0.49	−0.07	0.69	0.45	−0.09	−0.02	−0.13	−0.05
BTS	−0.25	0.14	0.55	−0.30	−0.65	0.27	0.06	−0.03	0.13	0.03
Standard deviation	0.10	0.10	0.07	0.07	0.06	0.05	0.05	0.04	0.03	0.02
Proportion of Variance	0.26	0.24	0.12	0.11	0.08	0.07	0.05	0.03	0.03	0.01
Cumulative Proportion	0.26	0.50	0.63	0.74	0.82	0.88	0.93	0.97	0.99	1.00

top 10 crypto-currencies by market value and 10 standard financial assets. The correlations between these assets and the crypto-currencies are very close to zero, which is especially surprising for the fiat-currency returns on USD/EUR, USD/JPY, USD/GBP. This result hints that the findings by Eisl et al. (2015) and Briere et al. (2013) for BTC may hold for other crypto-currencies, too.

7.3.5 The Power Law in Crypto-Currency Returns

To investigate the evolution of the return dynamics of crypto-currencies from their emergence in the market as they mature, we study the power-law parameter of their absolute-returns distributions over time. We divide each time series of returns into periods of 90 days, compute the scaling parameter alpha per period for every crypto-currency in our data set, and then average over the cross-section in the corresponding periods, taking into account the size of the crypto-currencies in terms of market value. For the definition of the power law and the specifications of the estimation, see Section A.3.

Fig. 7.9 shows the results, partitioned into three distinct groups by mean market value. Thus the three alphas for period one display the means over all first periods of the crypto-currencies in the three respective groups. Clauset et al. (2009) state that α, referred to as the scaling

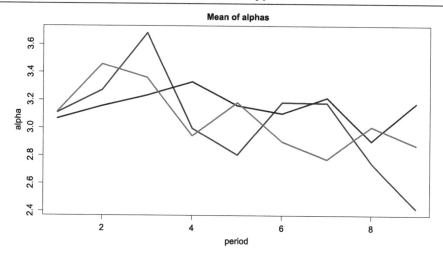

Figure 7.9: *Scaling parameters of the power-law distribution.* **Power-law alphas of all crypto-currencies in the data set, divided into three groups: Group1 has a mean market value ≤ 50,000 USD, group2 between 50,000 and 500,000 USD, and group3 > 500,000 USD. Crypto-currencies with daily trading volume < 10 USD were excluded. Each alpha is calculated in time windows of 90 days.**

parameter, typically lies in the range $2 < \alpha < 3$ for stocks. Interestingly, the mean over the alphas for the crypto-currencies in the first periods is higher than 3.

The mean alpha levels of group2 and group3 are less volatile than those of group1 with low-market-value crypto-currencies. Higher alpha implies a narrower distribution, i.e. more prevalence of lower absolute returns. Therefore, the higher alphas for the less successful crypto-currencies in terms of market capitalizations in the first periods indicate that they show lower absolute returns compared to the other two groups. After the first year, the returns increase for group1, while the medium-value crypto-currencies show smaller absolute returns. After 1.5 to 2 years, the three groups converge to alphas as known from standard financial assets. Since the analysis is performed based on event time, common market shocks should not drive the results. Also, as shown before, movements of crypto-currency returns share little common variation.

For results about power-law parameters regarding the wealth distribution of crypto-currencies, see Li and Xiangjun (2017).

7.4 Conclusion

From the perspective of an investor into the alternative asset class of crypto-currencies, we document that returns of crypto-currencies are weakly correlated both in their cross-section and with established assets, and thus interesting investments for diversifying portfolios. An investment strategy based on the CRypto-currency IndeX (CRIX) bears lower risk than any single of the most liquid crypto-currencies.

Furthermore, we show that crypto-currencies exhibit a size effect like stocks. The market's deepening liquidity is accompanied by increases in market valuations. At the same time, the structure of the market has evolved over the past years. For instance, more crypto-currencies with comparatively smaller market valuations exist today.

We conclude that this still new alternative asset market can provide valuable contributions to portfolio allocation: crypto-currencies display high expected returns with large volatilities and at the same time remarkably low correlations with each other and with standard financial assets, allowing for diversification benefits. Thus, investors in alternative assets should keep a close eye on further developments in the crypto-currency market.

Appendix A   Technical Appendix

A.1 Value at Risk and Expected Shortfall

We calculate Expected Shortfall (ES) and Value-at-Risk (VaR) among our risk measures. Following Artzner et al. (1999) and Franke et al. (2015), the VaR is specified as follows:

Definition. Given $\alpha \in (0, 1)$, the VaR_α for a random variable X with distribution function $F(\cdot)$ is determined as

$$VaR_\alpha(X) = \inf\{x \,|\, F(x) \leq \alpha\}. \quad \square$$

ES is then determined as

$$E[X \,|\, X > VaR_\alpha] \tag{7.1}$$

A common approach to determine (7.1) was investigated in McNeil and Frey (2000). The authors define $\{\varepsilon_t^{neg}\}_{t \in \mathbb{Z}}$ as a strictly stationary time series which represents the negative log returns of the underlying. It is assumed that the negative log returns follow the process

$$\varepsilon_t^{neg} = \mu_t + \sigma_t Z_t \tag{7.2}$$

with Z_t a strict white-noise process. They propose an ARMA-GARCH approach to obtain the realizations of Z_t.

Here, we employ a GARCH(1,1) model, defined as

$$\sigma_t^2 = \beta_0 + \beta \varepsilon_{t-1}^{2,neg} + \gamma \sigma_{t-1}^2$$

with $\beta_0 > 0$, $\beta, \gamma \geq 0$ and $\varepsilon_t^{neg} | (\varepsilon_{t-1}^{neg}, \sigma_{t-1}^2, \ldots) \sim N(0, \sigma_t^2)$.

A pseudo-ML approach is used to obtain the parameters of the model. Afterwards a threshold u is chosen and a General Pareto Distribution (GPD) is fitted to the data beyond this threshold. McNeil and Frey (2000) state that it is assumed that the tails begin with the threshold u. Hence the choice of u is critical for the analysis.

The GPD has the following distribution function, as given in McNeil and Frey (2000):

$$G_{\xi,\zeta}(z_t) = \begin{cases} 1 - (1 + \xi \frac{z_t}{\zeta})^{-1/\xi} & \xi \neq 0 \\ 1 - \exp(-\frac{z_t}{\zeta}) & \xi = 0 \end{cases}$$

where $\zeta > 0$, the support is $z_t \leq 0$ when $\xi \leq 0$ and $0 \geq z_t \geq -\frac{\zeta}{\xi}$ when $\xi < 0$. McNeil and Frey (2000) further show that for a random variable W with an exact GPD distribution with parameter $\xi < 1$ and ζ it can be shown that

$$E[W|W > w] = \frac{w + \zeta}{1 - \xi},$$

where $\zeta + w\xi > 0$.

McNeil and Frey (2000) also show that in case the excesses of the threshold have exactly this distribution, it follows that

$$E\left[Z_t|Z_t > z_{t,\alpha}\right] = z_{t,\alpha} \left(\frac{1}{1 - \xi} + \frac{\zeta - \xi u}{(1 - \xi)z_{t,\alpha}} \right)$$

with $z_{t,\alpha}$ as the $VaR_{t,\alpha}$, where t indicates dependence on time.

A.2 Portfolios

In order to contrast the results we find for investments into a single crypto-currency, we also perform the same analyses on portfolios of crypto-currencies. We consider three portfolios: first, an investment according to the market index CRIX, as well as two portfolios of investment into all crypto-currencies: one equally-weighted portfolio (EW), and one value-weighted (VW) by market capitalization.

The log returns on the equally-weighted portfolio are defined as the log return on an investment of equal amount into all crypto-currencies i, each yielding ε_{it}:

$$\epsilon_t^{EW} = \frac{1}{n} \sum_{i=1}^{n} \varepsilon_{it} \tag{7.3}$$

where n is the number of assets in the portfolio.

The value-weighted portfolio is constructed similarly to the CRIX index (Trimborn and Här-dle, 2016). Denote by MV_{it} the market value of a single crypto-currency at time t; the log return on the value-weighted portfolio VW_t is then defined as the log return to a portfolio with invested amounts proportional to the MV_{it}:

$$\epsilon_t^{VW} = \frac{1}{\sum_{i=1}^{n} MV_{it}} \sum_{i=1}^{n} MV_{it}\varepsilon_{it} \tag{7.4}$$

A.3 Power Law

In Section 7.3.5 we investigated the behavior of groups of crypto-currencies (clustered by market capitalization) with a power-law analysis. Following Clauset et al. (2009), the defini-tion of the probability density function of a power law in the discrete case is

$$p(x) = Cx^{-\alpha} \tag{7.5}$$

where x is the observed value, α the power law parameter and C a normalizing constant. Since the distribution would diverge at 0, a lower bound $x_{min} > 0$ has to be chosen. Solving for C, it follows that

$$p(x) = \frac{x^{-\alpha}}{\zeta(\alpha, x_{min})}$$

with

$$\zeta(\alpha, x_{min}) = \sum_{i=0}^{\infty}(i + x_{min})^{-\alpha}$$

the Hurwitz zeta function, see Clauset et al. (2009).

To compute the αs, we use the R-package by Csardi and Nepusz (2006). The x_{min} and α are computed as proposed by Clauset et al. (2009). We have not fixed x_{min}; it was chosen by comparing the p-values of a Kolmogorov–Smirnov test between the fitted distribution and the original sample, see Csardi and Nepusz (2006). The x_{min} was chosen such that the p-value is largest. More details are in the cited articles.

References

Artzner, P., Delbaen, F., Eber, J.-M., Heath, D., 1999. Coherent measures of risk. Mathematical Finance 9 (3), 203–228.

Back, A., Corallo, M., Dashjr, L., Friedenbach, M., Maxwell, G., Miller, A., Poelstra, A., Timón, J., Wuille, P., 2014. Enabling Blockchain Innovations with Pegged Sidechains. Technical report. blockstream.com. Available at https://blockstream.com/sidechains.pdf.

BCBS, 2014. Fundamental Review of the Trading Book: Outstanding Issues – Consultative Document. Technical report. Bank for International Settlements (BIS). Basel Committee on Banking Supervision. Available at http://www.bis.org/bcbs/publ/d305.pdf.

Böhme, R., Christin, N., Edelman, B., Moore, T., 2015. Bitcoin: economics, technology, and governance. Journal of Economic Perspectives 29 (2), 213–238.

Briere, M., Oosterlinck, K., Szafarz, A., 2013. Virtual Currency, Tangible Return: Portfolio Diversification with Bitcoins. Available at SSRN: http://ssrn.com/abstract=2324780 or http://dx.doi.org/10.2139/ssrn.2324780.

Clauset, A., Shalizi, C.R., Newman, M.E.J., 2009. Power-law distributions in empirical data. SIAM Review 51 (4), 661–703.

Csardi, G., Nepusz, T., 2006. The igraph software package for complex network research. InterJournal, Complex Systems, 1695.

Duffield, E., Diaz, D., 2015. Dash: A Privacy-Centric Crypto-Currency. Technical report, dash.org. Available at https://www.dash.org/wp-content/uploads/2015/04/Dash-WhitepaperV1.pdf.

Eisl, A., Gasser, S., Weinmayer, K., 2015. Caveat Emptor: Does Bitcoin Improve Portfolio Diversification? Working Paper WU. Available at SSRN: http://ssrn.com/abstract=2408997 or http://dx.doi.org/10.2139/ssrn.2408997.

Fink, C., Johann, T., 2014. Bitcoin Markets. Available at SSRN: http://ssrn.com/abstract=2408396 or http://dx.doi.org/10.2139/ssrn.2408396.

Franke, J., Härdle, W.K., Hafner, C.M., 2015. Statistics of Financial Markets: an Introduction. Springer Science & Business, Media.

Gabaix, X., 2009. Power laws in economics and finance. Annual Review of Economics 1, 255–293.

Härdle, W., Trimborn, S., 2015. Crix or Evaluating Blockchain Based Currencies. Oberwolfach Report No. 42/2015 "The Mathematics and Statistics of Quantitative Risk".

Houy, N., 2014. It Will Cost You Nothing to 'Kill' a Proof-of-Stake Crypto-Currency. Available at SSRN: http://ssrn.com/abstract=2393940 or http://dx.doi.org/10.2139/ssrn.2393940.

King, S., Nadal, S., 2012. Ppcoin: Peer-to-Peer Crypto-Currency with Proof-of-Stake. Technical report, peercoin.net. Available at https://peercoin.net/assets/paper/peercoin-paper.pdf.

Li, G., Xiangjun, L., 2017. The risk analysis of cryptocurrency as an alternative asset class. In: Chen, C., Härdle, W.K., Overbeck, L. (Eds.), Applied Quantitative Finance. Springer Verlag.

McNeil, A.J., Frey, R., 2000. Estimation of tail-related risk measures for heteroscedastic financial time series: an extreme value approach. Journal of Empirical Finance 7 (3), 271–300.

Schwartz, D., Youngs, N., Britto, A., 2014. The Ripple Protocol Consensus Algorithm. Technical report, ripple.com. Available at https://ripple.com/files/ripple_consensus_whitepaper.pdf.

Trimborn, S., Härdle, W.K., 2016. CRIX an Index for Blockchain Based Currencies. SFB 649 Discussion Paper 2016-021, Sonderforschungsbereich 649. Humboldt Universität zu Berlin, Germany. Available at http://sfb649.wiwi.hu-berlin.de/papers/pdf/SFB649DP2016-021.pdf.

Yermack, D., 2015. Chapter 2 – Is bitcoin a real currency? An economic appraisal. In: Chuen, D.L.K. (Ed.), Handbook of Digital Currency. Academic Press, San Diego, pp. 31–43.

Note

1. Financial support from the Deutsche Forschungsgemeinschaft via CRC 649 "Economic Risk" and IRTG 1792 "High Dimensional Non Stationary Time Series," Humboldt-Universität zu Berlin, is gratefully acknowledged.

CHAPTER 8

Econometric Analysis of a Cryptocurrency Index for Portfolio Investment

Shi Chen, Cathy Yi-Hsuan Chen, Wolfgang Karl Härdle, T.M. Lee, Bobby Ong

Contents

The CRIX (CRyptocurrency IndeX) has been constructed based on approximately 30 cryptos and captures high coverage of available market capitalization. The CRIX index family covers a range of cryptos based on different liquidity rules and various model selection criteria. Details of ECRIX (Exact CRIX), EFCRIX (Exact Full CRIX) and also intraday CRIX movements may be found on the web page hu.berlin/crix.

In order to price contingent claims one needs to first understand the dynamics of these indices. Here we provide a first econometric analysis of the CRIX family within a time-series framework for portfolio investment. The key steps of our analysis include model selection, estimation and testing. Linear dependence is removed by an ARIMA model, the diagnostic checking resulted in an ARIMA(2, 0, 2) model for the available sample period from Aug 1st, 2014 to April 6th, 2016. The model residuals showed the well-known phenomenon of volatility clustering. Therefore a further refinement leads us to an ARIMA(2, 0, 2)-t-GARCH(1, 1) process. This specification conveniently takes care of fat-tail properties that are typical for financial markets. The multivariate GARCH models are implemented on the CRIX index family to explore the interaction. This chapter is practitioner oriented, and four main questions are answered:

1. What's the dynamics of CRIX?
2. How to employ statistical methods to measure their changes over time?
3. How stable is the model used to estimate CRIX?
4. What do empirical findings imply for the econometric model?

A large literature can be reached for further study, for instance, Hamilton (1994), Franke et al. (2015), Box et al. (2015), Lütkepohl (2005), Rachev et al. (2007), etc. All numerical procedures are transparent and reproduced on **Q** www.quantlet.de.

8.1 Econometric Review of CRIX

8.1.1 Introductory Remarks

The CRyptocurrency IndeX **CRIX** developed by Härdle and Trimborn (2015) is aimed to provide a market measure which consists of a selection of representative cryptos. The index fulfills the requirement of having a dynamic structure by relying on statistical time series techniques. The following Table 8.1 are the 30 cryptocurrencies used in the construction of CRIX index.

Table 8.1:   30 cryptocurrencies used in construction of CRIX.

No.	Cryptos	Symbol	Description
1	Bitcoin	BTC	Bitcoin is the first cryptocurrency. It was created by the anonymous person(s) named Satoshi Nakomoto in 2009 and has a limited supply of 21 million coins. It uses the SHA-256 Proof-of-Work hashing algorithm.
2	Ethereum	ETH	Ethereum is a Turing-completed cryptocurrency platform created by Vitalik Buterin. It raised US$18 million worth of bitcoins during a crowdsale of ether tokens in 2014. Ethereum allows for token creation and smart contracts to be written on top of the platform. The DAO (No. 30) and DigixDAO (No. 15) are two tokens created on the Ethereum platform that is also used in the construction of CRIX.
3	Steem	STEEM	Steem is a social-media platform that rewards users for participation with tokens. Users can earn tokens by creating and curating content. The Steem whitepaper was co-authored by Daniel Larimer who is also the founder of BitShares (No. 16).
4	Ripple	XRP	Ripple is a payment system created by Ripple Labs in San Francisco. It allows for banks worldwide to transact with each other without the need of a central correspondent. Banks such as Santander and UniCredit have begun experimenting on the Ripple platform. It was one of the earliest altcoin in the market and is not a copy of Bitcoin's source code.
5	Litecoin	LTC	Litecoin is branded the "silver to bitcoin's gold". It was created by Charles Lee, an ex-employee of Google and current employee of Coinbase. Charles modified Bitcoin's source code and made use of the Scrypt Proof-of-Work hashing algorithm. There is a total of 84 million litecoin with a block time of 2.5 minutes. Initial reward was 50 LTC per block with rewards halving every 840,000 blocks.
6	NEM	NEM	NEM, short for New Economy Movement is a cryptocurrency platform launched in 2015 that is written from scratch on the Java platform. It provides many services on top of payments such as messaging, asset making and naming system.
7	Dash	DASH	Dash (previously known as Darkcoin and XCoin) is a privacy-centric cryptocurrency. It anonymizes transactions using PrivateSend (previously known as DarkSend), a concept that extends the idea of CoinJoin. PrivateSend achieves obfuscation by combining bitcoin transactions with another person's transactions using common denominations of 0.1DASH, 1DASH, 10DASH and 100DASH.

The Research Data Center ▍▍RDC supported by Collaborative Research Center (CRC) 649 provides access to the data set. At time of writing, Bitcoin's market capitalization as a percentage of CRIX total market capitalization is 83%.

Table 8.1: (*Continued*)

No.	Cryptos	Symbol	Description
8	Maid-SafeCoin	MAID	MaidSafeCoin is the cryptocurrency for the SAFE (Secure Access For Everyone) network. The network aims to do away with third-party central servers in order to enable privacy and anonymity for Internet users. It allows users to earn tokens by sharing their computing resources (storage space, CPU, bandwidth) with the network. MaidSafeCoin was released on the Omni Layer.
9	Lisk	LSK	Lisk is a Javascript platform for the creation of decentralized applications (DApps) and sidechains. Javascript was chosen because it is the most popular programming language on Github. It was created by Olivier Beddows and Max Kordek who were actively involved in the Crypti altcoin before this. Lisk conducted a crowdsale in early 2016 that raised about US$6.15 million.
10	Dogecoin	DOGE	Dogecoin was created by Jackson Palmer and Billy Markus. It is based on the "doge", an Internet meme based on a Shiba Inu dog. Both the founders created Dogecoin for it to be fun so that it can appeal to a larger group of people beyond the core Bitcoin audience. Dogecoin found a niche as a tipping platform on Twitter and Reddit. It was merged-mined with Litecoin (No. 5) on 11 September 2014.
11	NXT	NXT	NXT is the first 100% Proof-of-Stake cryptocurrency. It is a cryptocurrency platform that allows for the creation of tokens, messaging, domain name system and marketplace. There is a total of 1 billion coins created and it has a block time of 1 minute.
12	Monero	XMR	Monero is another privacy-centric altcoin that aims to anonymize transactions. It is based on the Cryptonote protocol which uses Ring Signatures to conceal sender identities. Many users, including the sender, will sign a transaction thereby making it very difficult to trace the true sender of a transaction.
13	Synereo	AMP	Synereo is a decentralized and distributed social network service. It conducted its crowdsale in March 2015 on the Omni Layer where 18.5% of its tokens were sold.
14	Emercoin	EMC	Emercoin provides a key-value storage system, which allows for a Domain Name System (DNS) for .coin, .emc, .lib and .bazar domain extensions. It is inspired by Namecoin (No.26) DNS system which uses the .bit domain extension. It uses a Proof-of-Work/Proof-of-Stake hashing algorithm and allows for a maximum name length of 512.
15	Digix-DAO	DGO	DigixDAO is a gold-backed token on the Ethereum (No. 2) platform. Each token represents 1 gram of gold and each token is divisible to 0.001 gram. The tokens on the Ethereum platform are audited to ensure that the said amount of gold is held in reserves in Singapore.

Table 8.1: (*Continued*)

No.	Cryptos	Symbol	Description
16	BitShares	BTS	BitShares is a cryptocurrency platform that allows for many features such as a decentralized asset exchange, user-issued assets, price-stable cryptocurrencies, stakeholder approved project funding and transferable named accounts. It uses a Delegated Proof-of-Stake consensus algorithm.
17	Factom	FCT	Factom allows businesses and governments to record data on the Bitcoin blockchain. It does this by hashing entries before adding it onto a list. The entries can be viewed but not modified thus ensuring integrity of data records.
18	Siacoin	SC	Sia is a decentralized cloud storage platform where users can rent storage space from each other. The data is encrypted into many pieces and uploaded to different hosts for storage.
19	Stellar	STR	Stellar was created by Jed McCaleb, who was also the founder of Ripple (No. 4) and Mt. Gox, the previously-largest bitcoin exchange which is now bankrupt. Stellar was created using a forked source code of Ripple. Stellar's mission is to expand financial access and literacy worldwide.
20	Bytecoin	BCN	Bytecoin is a privacy-centric cryptocurrency and is the first cryptocurrency created with the CryptoNote protocol. Its codebase is not a fork of Bitcoin's.
21	Peercoin	PPC	Peercoin (previously known as PPCoin) was created by Sunny King. It was the first implementation of Proof-of-Stake. It uses a hybrid Proof-of-Work/Proof-of-Stake system. Proof-of-Stake is more efficient as it does not require any mining equipments to create blocks. Block creation is done via holding stake in the coin and therefore resistant to 51% mining attacks.
22	Tether	USDT	Tether is backed 1-to-1 with traditional US Dollar in reserves so $1 USDT = 1 USD$. It is digital tokens formatted to work seamlessly on the Bitcoin blockchain. It exists as tokens on the Omni protocol.
23	Counter-party	XCP	Counterparty is the first cryptocurrency to make use of Proof-of-Burn as a method to distribute tokens. Proof-of-Burn works by having users send bitcoins to an unspendable address, in this case: $1 Counterparty XXXXXXXXXXXXXXX UWLpVr$. A total of 2,125 BTC were burnt in this manner, creating 2.6 million XCP tokens. The Proof-of-Burn method ensures that the Counterparty developers do not enjoy any privilege and allows for fair distribution of tokens. Counterparty is based on the Bitcoin platform and allows for creation of assets such as Storjcoin X (No. 25).

8.1.2 Statistical Analysis of CRIX Returns

In the crypto market, the CRIX index was designed as a sample drawn from the pool of cryptos to represent the market performance of leading currencies. In order for an index to work

Table 8.1: (*Continued*)

No.	Cryptos	Symbol	Description
24	Agoras	AGRS	Agoras is an application and smart currency market built on the Tau-Chain to feature intelligent personal agents, programming market, computational power market, and a futuristic search engine.
25	Storjcoin X	SJCX	Storjcoin X is used as a token to exchange cloud storage and bandwidth access. Users can obtain Storjcoin X by renting out resources to the network via DriveMiner and they will be able to rent space from other users by paying Storjcoin X using Metadisk. Storjcoin X is an asset created on the Counterparty platform (No. 23).
26	Name-coin	NMC	Namecoin is one of the earliest altcoin that has been adapted from Bitcoin's source code to allow for a different use case. It provides a decentralized key-value system that allows for the creation of an alternative Domain Name System that cannot be censored by governments. It uses the .bit domain extension. It was merge-mined with Bitcoin from September 2011.
27	Ybcoin	YBC	Ybcoin is a cryptocurrency from China that was created in June 2013. It uses the Proof-of-Stake hashing algorithm.
28	Nautilus-coin	NAUT	Nautiluscoin uses DigiShield difficulty retargeting system to safeguard against multi-pool miners. It has a Nautiluscoin Stabilization Fund (NSF) to reduce price volatility.
29	Fedora-coin	TIPS	Fedoracoin is based on the Tips Fedora Internet meme. Fedoracoin is also used as a tipping cryptocurrency.
30	The DAO	DAO	The DAO, short for Distributed Autonomous Organization, ran one of the most successful crowdfunding campaigns when it raised over US$160 million. The DAO is a smart contract written on the Ethereum (No. 2) platform. The DAO grants token holders voting rights to make decision in the organization based on proportion of tokens owned. In June 2016, a hack occurred resulting in the loss of about US$60 million. The Ethereum Foundation decided to reverse the hack by conducting a hardfork of the Ethereum platform.

as an investment benchmark, in this section we first focus on the stochastic properties of CRIX. The plots are often the first step in an exploratory analysis. Fig. 8.1 shows the daily values from 01/08/2014 to 06/04/2016. We can observe that the values of CRIX fell down substantially until the mid of 2015, CRIX did poorly, perhaps as a result of the cool off of the cryptocurrency. After a few months moving up and down, the CRIX was, however, sloped up till now as a better year for crypto market. It is worthwhile to note here that the CRIX index were largely impacted and/or influenced by the crypto market, therefore, makes it a better indicator for the market performance.

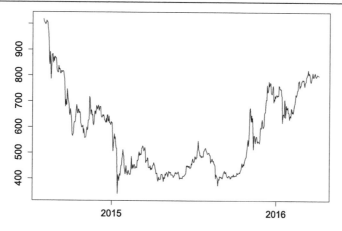

Figure 8.1: CRIX Daily Price from Aug. 1st, 2014 to April 6th, 2016.
(🔍 *econ_crix*)

To find out the dynamics of CRIX, we would first look closer to stationary time series. A stationary time series is one whose stochastic properties such as mean, variance, etc. are all constant over time. Most statistical forecasting methods are based on the stationary assumption, however the CRIX is far from stationary as observed in Fig. 8.1. Therefore we need first to transform the original data into stationary time series through the use of mathematical transformations. Such transformations includes detrending, seasonal adjustment, etc., the most general class of models amongst them is ARIMA fitting, which will be explained in the next section 8.2.

In practice, the difference between consecutive observations was generally computed to make a time series stationary. Such transformations can help stabilize the mean by removing the changes in the levels of a time series, therefore removing the trend and seasonality. Here the log returns of CRIX are computed for further analysis, we remove the unequal variances using the log of the data and take difference to get rid of the trend component. Fig. 8.2 shows the time series plot of daily log returns of the CRIX index (hence after CRIX returns), with the mean of -0.0004 and volatility of 0.0325.

We continue to investigate distributional properties. We have the histogram of CRIX returns plotted in the left panel of Fig. 8.3, compared with the normal density function plotted in blue. The right panel is QQ plot of CRIX daily returns. We can conclude that the CRIX returns is not normal distributed. Another approach widely used in density estimation is kernel density estimation. Furthermore, there are various methods to test if sample following a specific distribution, for example Kolmogorov–Smirnoff test and Shapiro-Test.

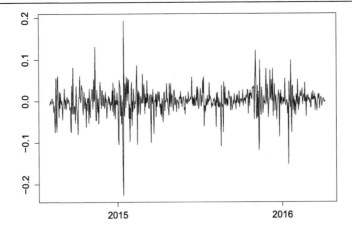

Figure 8.2: The log returns of CRIX index from Aug. 2nd, 2014 to April 6th, 2016.
(🅀 *econ_crix*)

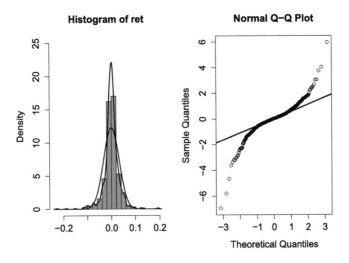

Figure 8.3: Histogram and QQ plot of CRIX returns.
(🅀 *econ_crix*)

8.2 ARIMA Models

The ARIMA(p, d, q) model, with p standing for the lag order of the autoregressive model, d for the degree of differencing and q for the lag order of the moving average model, is given by (for $d = 1$)

$$
\begin{aligned}
\Delta y_t &= a_1 \Delta y_{t-1} + a_2 \Delta y_{t-2} + \ldots + a_p \Delta y_{t-p} \\
&+ \varepsilon_t + b_1 \varepsilon_{t-1} + b_2 \varepsilon_{t-2} + \ldots + b_q \varepsilon_{t-q}
\end{aligned}
\tag{8.1}
$$

or

$$a(L)\Delta y_t = b_L \varepsilon_t \tag{8.2}$$

where $\Delta y_t = y_t - y_{t-1}$ is the differenced series and can be replaced by higher order differencing $\Delta^d y_t$ if necessary. L is the lag operator and $\varepsilon_t \sim N(0, \sigma^2)$.

There are two approaches to identify and fit an appropriate ARIMA(p, d, q) model. The first one is the Box–Jenkins procedure (subsection 8.2.1), another one to select models is selection criteria like Akaike information criterion (AIC) and Bayesian or Schwartz Information criterion (BIC), see subsection 8.2.2.

8.2.1 Box–Jenkins Procedure

The Box–Jenkins procedure comprises the following stages:

1. Identification of lag orders p, d and q.
2. Parameter estimation
3. Diagnostic checking

A detailed illustration of each stages can be found in the textbook of Box et al. (2015).

In the first identification stage, one needs first to determine the degree of integration d. Fig. 8.2 shows that the CRIX returns are generally stationary over time. As well as looking at the time plot, the sample autocorrelation function (ACF) is also useful for identifying the non-stationary time series. The values of ACF will drop to zero relatively quickly compared to the non-stationary case. Furthermore, the unit root tests can be used more objectively to determine if differencing is required. For instance, the augmented Dickey–Fuller (ADF) test and KPSS test, see Dickey and Fuller (1981) and Kwiatkowski et al. (1992) for more technical details.

Given d, one identifies the lag orders (p, q) by checking ACF plots to find the total correlation between different lag functions. In an MA context, there is no autocorrelation between y_t and y_{t-q-1}, the ACF dies out at q. A second insight one obtains is from the partial autocorrelation function (PACF). For an AR(p) process, when the effects of the lags $y_{t-1}, y_{t-2}, \ldots, y_{t-p-1}$ are excluded, the autocorrelation between y_t and y_{t-p} is zero. Hence a PACF plot for $p = 1$ will drop at lag 1.

8.2.2 Lag Orders

We exhibit the discussion thus far by analyzing the daily log return of CRIX introduced in subsection 8.1.2. The stationarity of the return series is tested by ADF (null hypothesis: unit

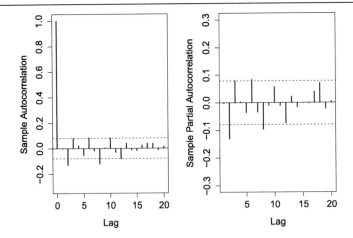

Figure 8.4: The sample ACF and PACF plots of daily CRIX returns from Aug. 2nd, 2014 to April 6th, 2016, with lags = 20.

(Q econ_arima)

root) and KPSS (null hypothesis: stationary) tests. The p-values are 0.01 for ADF test, 0.1 for KPSS test. Hence one concludes stationarity on the level $d = 0$.

The next step is to choose the lag orders of p and q for the ARIMA model. The sample ACF and PACF are calculated and depicted in Fig. 8.4, with blue dashed lines as 95% limits. The results suggest that the CRIX log returns are not random. The Ljung–Box test statistic for examining the null hypothesis of independence yields a p-value of 0.0017. Hence one rejects the null hypothesis and suggests that the CRIX return series has autocorrelation structure.

The ACF pattern in Fig. 8.4 suggests that the existence of strong autocorrelations in lag 2 and 8, partial autocorrelation in lag 2, 6 and 8. These results suggest that the CRIX return series can be modeled by some ARIMA process, for example ARIMA(2, 0, 2).

In addition to ACF and PACF, several model selection criteria are widely used to overcome the problem of overparameterization. They are Akaike Information Criterion (AIC) from Akaike (1974) and Bayesian or Schwartz Information Criteria (BIC) from Schwarz et al. (1978); the formulas are given by

$$AIC(\mathcal{M}) \ = \ -2\log L(\mathcal{M}) + 2p(\mathcal{M}) \tag{8.3}$$

$$BIC(\mathcal{M}) \ = \ -2\log L(\mathcal{M}) + p(\mathcal{M})\log n \tag{8.4}$$

where n is the number of observations, $p(\mathcal{M})$ is the number of parameters in model $\mathcal{M}$ and $L(\mathcal{M})$ represents the likelihood function of the parameters evaluated at the Maximum Likelihood Estimation (MLE).

The first term $-2 \log L(\mathcal{M})$ in each equations (8.3) and (8.4) reflects the goodness of fit for MLE, while the second terms stand for the model complexity. Therefore AIC and BIC can be viewed as measures that combine fit and complexity. The main difference between two measures is that the BIC is asymptotically consistent while AIC is not. Compared with BIC, AIC tends to overparameterize.

8.2.3 ARIMA Model Estimation

We start with ARIMA(1, 0, 1). As an example, fit the ARIMA(1, 0, 1) model derived from equation (8.1),

$$y_t = a_1 y_{t-1} + \varepsilon_t + b_1 \varepsilon_{t-1}$$

The estimated parameters are: $\hat{a}_1 = 0.5763$ with standard deviation of 0.5371, $\hat{b}_1 = -0.6116$ with standard deviation of 0.5205; y_t represents the CRIX returns.

In the third stage of Box–Jenkins procedure one evaluates the validity of the estimated model. The results of diagnostic checking are reported in the three diagnostic plots of Fig. 8.5. The upper panel is the standardized residuals, the middle one is the ACF of residuals and the lower panel is the Ljung–Box test statistic for the null hypothesis of residual independence. One observes that the significant autocorrelations of the model residuals appear at lag of 2, 3, 6 and 8, and the low p-values of the Ljung–Box test statistic after lag 1. We cannot reject the null hypothesis at these lags, hence ARIMA(1, 0, 1) model is not sufficient to get rid of the serial dependence. A more appropriate lag orders are needed for better model fitting.

Nevertheless, model diagnostic checking is often used together with model selection criteria. In practice, these two approaches complement each other. Based on the discussion results of Fig. 8.4 in subsection 8.2.2, we select a combination of (p, d, q) with $d = \{0, 1\}$ and $p, q = \{0, 1, 2, 3, 4, 5\}$. A calculation of the AIC and BIC for each model yields the best six models listed in Table 8.2. In general, an ARIMA(2, 0, 2) model

$$y_t = c + a_1 y_{t-1} + a_2 y_{t-2} + \varepsilon_t + b_1 \varepsilon_{t-1} + b_2 \varepsilon_{t-2} \tag{8.5}$$

performs best. Its diagnostic plots are given in Fig. 8.6 and look very good, the significant p-values of Ljung–Box test statistic suggest the independence structure of model residuals. Furthermore, the estimate of each element in equation (8.5) is reported in Table 8.3.

With the identified ARIMA model and its estimated parameters, we predict the CRIX returns for the next 30 days under the ARIMA(2, 0, 2) model. The out-of-sample prediction result is shown in Fig. 8.7. The 95% confidence bands are computed using a rule of thumb of "prediction $\pm 2 *$ standard deviation".

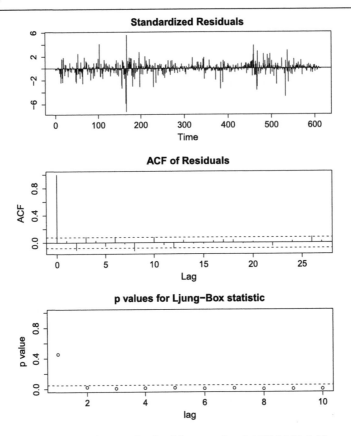

Figure 8.5: Diagnostic checking result of ARIMA(1,0,1).
(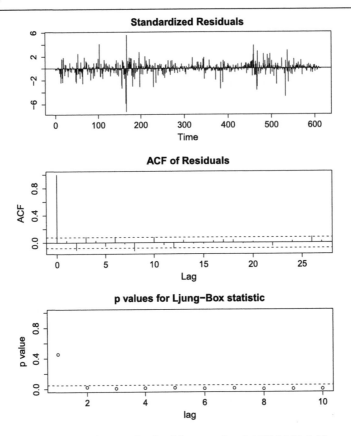 econ_arima)

Table 8.2: The ARIMA model selection with AIC and BIC.
Source: econ_arima

ARIMA model selected	AIC	BIC
ARIMA(2,0,0)	−2468.83	−2451.15
ARIMA(2, 0, 2)	−2474.25	−2447.73
ARIMA(2,0,3)	−2472.72	−2441.78
ARIMA(4,0,2)	−2476.35	−2440.99
ARIMA(2,1,1)	−2459.15	−2441.47
ARIMA(2,1,3)	−2464.14	−2437.62

8.3 Model with Stochastic Volatility

Homoskedasticity is a frequently used assumption in the framework of time series analysis, that is, the variance of all squared error terms is assumed to be constant through time, see

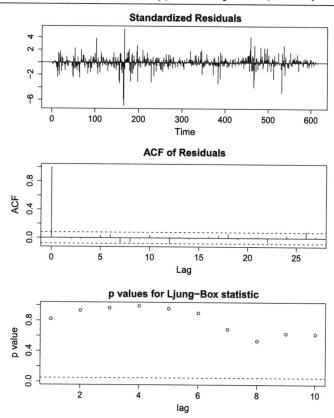

Figure 8.6: Diagnostic checking result of ARIMA(2, 0, 2).
(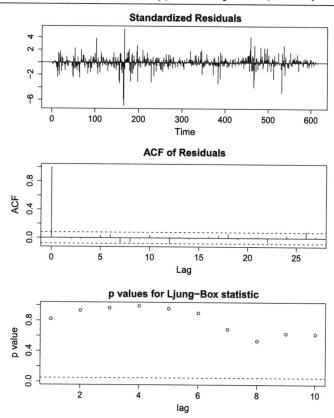 *econ_arima*)

Table 8.3: Estimation result of ARIMA(2, 0, 2) model.
Source: *econ_arima*

Coefficients	Estimate	Standard deviation
intercept c	−0.0004	0.0012
a_1	−0.6989	0.1124
a_2	−0.7508	0.1191
b_1	0.7024	0.1351
b_2	0.6426	0.1318
Log likelihood	1243.12	

Brooks (2014). Nevertheless we can observe hetero skedasticity in many cases when the variances of the data are different over different periods.

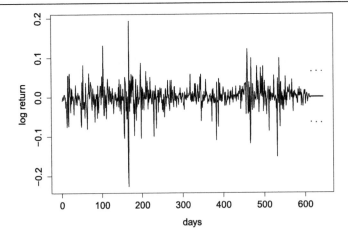

Figure 8.7: CRIX returns and predicted values. The confidence bands are red dashed lines.
(⬛ *econ_arima*)

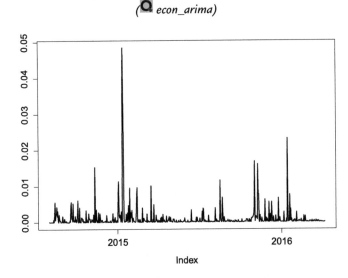

Figure 8.8: The squared ARIMA(2, 0, 2) residuals of CRIX returns.
(⬛ *econ_vola*)

In subsection 8.2.3 we have built an ARIMA model for the CRIX return series to model intertemporal dependence. Although the ACF of model residuals has no significant lags as evidenced by the large p-values for the Ljung–Box test in Fig. 8.6, the time series plot of residuals shows some clusters of volatility. To be more specific, we display the squared residual plot of the selected ARIMA(2, 0, 2) model in Fig. 8.8.

To incorporate the univariate heteroskedasticity, we first fit an ARCH (AutoRegressive Conditional Heteroskedasticity) model in subsection 8.3.1. In subsection 8.3.2, its generalization, the GARCH (Generalized AutoRegressive Conditional Heteroskedasticity) model, provides even more flexible volatility pattern. In addition, a variety of extensions of the standard GARCH models will be explored in subsection 8.3.3.

8.3.1 ARCH Model

The ARCH(q) model introduced by Engle (1982) is formulated as

$$
\begin{aligned}
\varepsilon_t &= Z_t \sigma_t \\
Z_t &\sim N(0,1) \\
\sigma_t^2 &= \omega + \alpha_1 \varepsilon_{t-1}^2 + \ldots + \alpha_p \varepsilon_{t-p}^2
\end{aligned}
\tag{8.6}
$$

where ε_t is the model residual and σ_t^2 is the variance of ε_t conditional on the information available at time t. It should be noted that the parameters should satisfy $\alpha_i > 0, \forall i = 1, \ldots, p$. The assumption of $\sum_i^p \alpha_i < 1$ is also imposed to assure the volatility term σ_t^2 is asymptotically stationary over time.

Based on the estimation results of subsection 8.2.3, we proceed to examine the heteroskedasticity effect observed in Fig. 8.8. The model residual ε_t in equation (8.5) is used to test for ARCH effects using ARCH LM (Lagrange Multiplier) test, the small p-value of $2.2e - 16$ cannot reject its null hypothesis of no ARCH effects. Another approach we can use is the Ljung–Box test for squared model residuals, see Tsay (2005). These two tests show similar result as the small p-value of Ljung–Box test statistic indicates the dependence structure of ε_t^2.

To determine the lag orders of ARCH model, we display the ACF and PACF of squared residuals in Fig. 8.9. The autocorrelations display a cutoff after the first two lags as well as some remaining lags are significant. The PACF plot in the right panel has a significant spike before lag 2. Therefore the lag orders of ARCH model should be at least 2.

We fit the ARCH models to the residuals using candidate values of q from 1 to 4, where all models are estimated by MLE based on the stochastic process of equation (8.6). The results of model comparison are contained in Table 8.4. The log likelihood and information criteria jointly select an ARCH(3) model, with the estimated parameters presented in Table 8.5. All the parameters except for the third one are significant at the 0.1% level.

8.3.2 GARCH Model

Bollerslev (1986) further extended ARCH model by adding the conditional heteroskedasticity moving average items in equation (8.6); the GARCH model indicates that the current volatility depends on past volatilities σ_{t-i}^2 and observations of model residual ε_{t-j}^2.

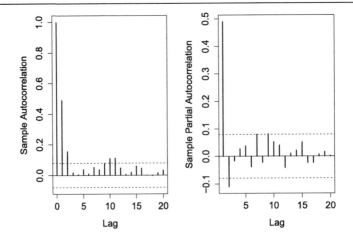

Figure 8.9: **The ACF and PACF of squared residuals of ARIMA$(2, 0, 2)$ model.**
(⊙ *econ_vola*)

Table 8.4:   Estimation result of ARIMA-ARCH models.

Source: ⊙ *econ_arch*

Model	Log Likelihood	AIC	BIC
ARCH(1)	1281.7	−2567.4	−2558.6
ARCH(2)	1283.4	−2560.8	−2547.6
ARCH(3)	1291.6	−2575.2	−2557.5
ARCH(4)	1288.8	−2567.5	−2545.4

Table 8.5:   Estimation result of ARIMA$(2, 0, 2)$-ARCH(3) model, with significant level at 0.1%.

Source: ⊙ *econ_arch*

Coefficients	Estimates	Standard deviation	Ljung–Box test statistic
ω	0.001	0.000	16.798*
α_1	0.195	0.042	4.589*
α_2	0.054	0.037	1.469
α_3	0.238	0.029	8.088*

The standard GARCH(p, q) is written as

$$
\begin{aligned}
\varepsilon_t &= Z_t \sigma_t \\
Z_t &\sim N(0, 1) \\
\sigma_t^2 &= \omega + \sum_{i=1}^{p} \beta_i \sigma_{t-i}^2 + \sum_{j=1}^{q} \alpha_j \varepsilon_{t-j}^2
\end{aligned}
\tag{8.7}
$$

Table 8.6: Comparison of GARCH model, orders up to $p = q = 2$.

Source: *econ_garch*

GARCH models	Log likelihood	AIC	BIC
GARCH(1, 1)	1305.355	−4.239	−4.210
GARCH(1, 2)	1309.363	−4.249	−4.213
GARCH(2, 1)	1305.142	−4.235	−4.199
GARCH(2, 2)	1309.363	−4.245	−4.202

Table 8.7: Estimation result of ARIMA(2, 0, 2)-GARCH(1, 2) model. $*$ represents significant level at 5% and $***$ at 0.1%.

Source: *econ_garch*

Coefficients	Estimates	Standard deviation	Ljung–Box test statistic
ω	9.906e−05	4.753e−05	2.084*
α_1	1.654e−01	3.719e−02	4.448***
β_1	8.074e−02	8.244e−02	0.979
β_2	6.513e−01	8.202e−02	7.940***

with the condition that

$$\omega > 0; \quad \alpha_i \geq 0, \beta_i \geq 0; \quad \sum_{i=1}^{p} \beta_i + \sum_{j=1}^{q} \alpha_j < 1 \tag{8.8}$$

The conditions in equation (8.8) ensure that the GARCH model is strictly stationary with finite variance. Normally up to GARCH(2, 2) model is used in practice. Particularly, the orders of $p = q = 1$ are sufficient in most cases.

The comparison of different GARCH models is reported in Table 8.6, the selection of lag orders up to $p = q = 2$. It shows that a GARCH(1, 2) model performs slightly better than the other ones through the comparison of log likelihood and information criteria. Using the GARCH(1, 2) model as selected,

$$\sigma_t^2 = \omega + \beta_1 \sigma_{t-1}^2 + \alpha_1 \varepsilon_{t-1}^2 + \alpha_2 \varepsilon_{t-2}^2 \tag{8.9}$$

We obtain the estimation results presented in Table 8.7. The conditions $\omega > 0$ and $\alpha_1 + \beta_1 + \beta_2 = 0.897 < 1$ are fulfilled to obtain a strictly stationary solution. However β_1 is not significantly different from the Ljung–Box test statistic.

Aforementioned GARCH(1, 1) is sufficient in most cases. We proceed further to fit the model residuals of ARIMA to the GARCH(1, 1) model and present the estimation result in

Table 8.8: Estimation result of ARIMA$(2, 0, 2)$-GARCH$(1, 1)$ model. $*$ represents significant level at 5% and $***$ at 0.1%.

Source: 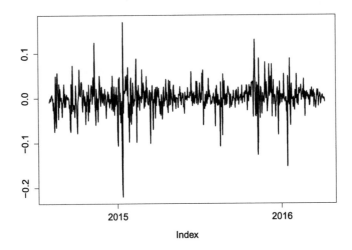 *econ_garch*

Coefficients	Estimates	Standard deviation	Ljung–Box test statistic
ω	5.324e−05	2.251e−05	2.365*
α_1	1.204e−01	2.785e−02	4.324***
β_1	8.322e−02	3.992e−02	20.847***

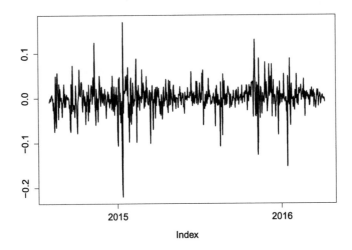

Figure 8.10: The ARIMA$(2, 0, 2)$-GARCH$(1, 1)$ residuals.
(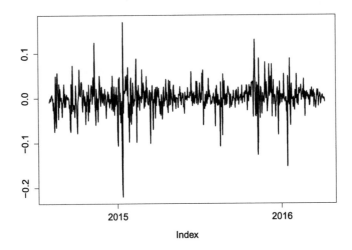 *econ_garch*)

Table 8.8. The GARCH$(1, 1)$ outperforms the ARCH(3) model with all the estimated parameters being significant. The estimated parameters $\omega > 0$ and $\alpha_1 + \beta_1 = 0.953 < 1$ fulfill the stationary condition as well. Although the model performance of GARCH$(1, 2)$ is better than that of GARCH$(1, 1)$, all parameters of GARCH$(1, 1)$ are significant. Since the level of $\sum_{i=1}^{p} \beta_i + \sum_{j=1}^{q} \alpha_j$ reveals the persistence of volatility, we know that the GARCH$(1, 1)$ is more persistent in volatility compared to GARCH$(1, 2)$. Therefore for simplicity, GARCH$(1, 1)$ is suggested for further analysis in CRIX dynamics.

We have the model residuals of ARMA-GARCH process plotted in Fig. 8.10. Fig. 8.11 displays the ACF and PACF plots for model residuals of ARIMA$(2, 0, 2)$-GARCH$(1, 1)$ process. We can see all the values are within the bands, which suggests that the model residuals have no dependence structure over different lags. Therefore GARCH$(1, 1)$ model is sufficient to explain the heteroskedasticity effect discussed in subsection 8.3.1.

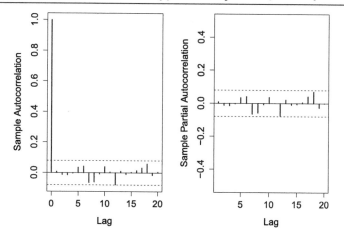

Figure 8.11: The ACF and PACF plots for model residuals of ARIMA$(2, 0, 2)$-GARCH$(1, 1)$ process.
(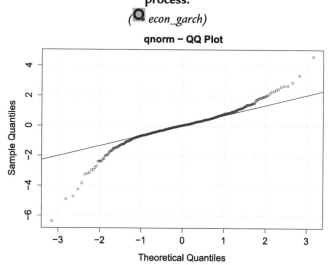 econ_garch)

Figure 8.12: The QQ plots of model residuals of ARIMA-GARCH process.
(econ_garch)

8.3.3 Variants of the GARCH Models

As we observed in Fig. 8.2, the return series of CRIX exhibits leptokurtosis. We further check the QQ-plot in Fig. 8.12, which suggests the fat tail of model residuals using ARIMA$(2, 0, 2)$-GARCH$(1, 1)$ process. The Kolmogorov distance between residuals of the selected model and normal distribution is reported in Table 8.9. With the small p-value of Kolmogorov–Smirnov test statistic, we reject the null hypothesis that the model residuals are drawn from the normal distribution.

Table 8.9:   Test of model residuals of ARIMA-GARCH process.

Source: 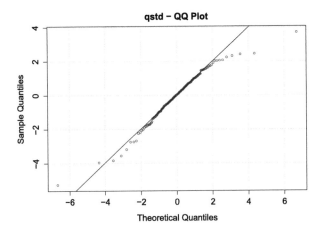 *econ_garch*

Model	Kolmogorov distance	P-value
ARIMA-GARCH	0.495	2.861e−10

Table 8.10:   Estimation result of ARIMA($2, 0, 2$)-t-GARCH($1, 1$) model. . represents significant level at 10% and $***$ at 0.1%.

Source: 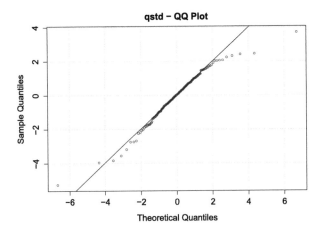 *econ_tgarch*

Coefficients	Estimates	Standard deviation	t test
ω	8.391e−05	5.451e−05	1.539
α_1	2.816e−01	1.461e−01	1.928$\cdot$
β_1	7.896e−01	6.116e−02	12.910***
ξ	2.577e+00	3.623e−01	7.113***

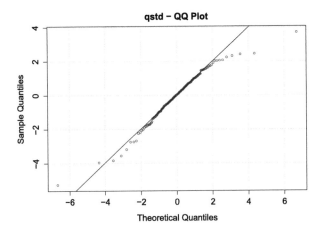

Figure 8.13: The QQ plot of t-GARCH($1, 1$) model.
(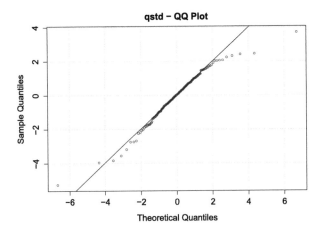 *econ_tgarch*)

We impose the assumption on the residuals with student distribution, that is, applying the non-normal assumption on Z_t in equation (8.7). With $Z_t \sim t(d)$ to replace the normal assumption of Z_t in GARCH model, the MLE is implemented for model estimation. The results for ARIMA-t-GARCH process are represented in Table 8.10. The shape parameter ξ controls the height and fat-tail of density function, therefore different shapes of distribution function. It is obvious that the shape parameter is significantly different from zero. The QQ plot in Fig. 8.13 indicates that the residuals are quite close to student-t distribution. The ACF and PACF plots for ARIMA-t-GARCH are given in the following Fig. 8.14, with all values staying inside the bounds. Hence the residuals and their variance are uncorrelated.

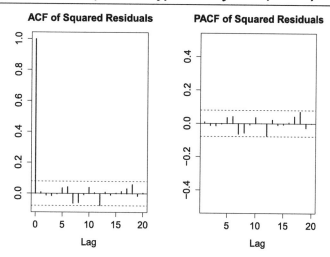

Figure 8.14: The ACF and PACF plots for model residuals of ARIMA(2, 0, 2)-*t*-GARCH(1, 1) process.

(Q econ_tgarch)

In addition to the property of leptokurtosis, leverage effect is commonly observed in practice. According to a large literature, such as Engle and Ng (1993), the leverage effect referring to the volatility of an asset tends to respond asymmetrically with negative or positive shocks, declines in prices or returns are accompanied by larger increase in volatility compared with the decrease of volatility associated with rising asset market. Although the introduced GARCH model successfully solves the problem of volatility clustering, the σ_t^2 cannot capture the leverage effect.

To overcome this, the exponential GARCH (EGARCH) model with standard innovations proposed by Nelson (1991) can be expressed in the following nonlinear form,

$$
\begin{aligned}
\varepsilon_t &= Z_t \sigma_t \\
Z_t &\sim N(0, 1) \\
\log(\sigma_t^2) &= \omega + \sum_{i=1}^{p} \beta_i \log(\sigma_{t-i}^2) + \sum_{j=1}^{q} g_j \left(Z_{t-j} \right)
\end{aligned}
\tag{8.10}
$$

where $g_j (Z_t) = \alpha_j Z_t + \phi_j (|Z_{t-j}| - \mathrm{E}|Z_{t-j}|)$ with $j = 1, 2, \ldots, q$. When $\phi_j = 0$, we have the logarithmic GARCH (LGARCH) model from Geweke (1986) and Pantula (1986). However LGARCH is not popular due to the high value of the first few ACFs of ε^2.

Based on the results shown in Fig. 8.12, we fit a EGARCH(1, 1) model with student-*t* distributed innovation term. The estimation results using the ARIMA(2, 0, 2)-*t*-EGARCH(1, 1) model are reported in Table 8.11.

Table 8.11: Estimation result of ARIMA$(2, 0, 2)$-t-EGARCH$(1, 1)$ model. $*$ represents significant level at 5% and $* * *$ at 0.1%.

Source: 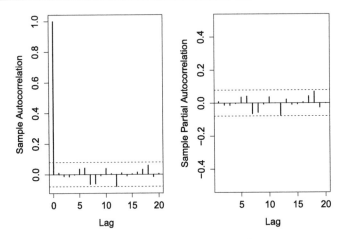 *econ_tgarch*

Coefficients	Estimates	Standard deviation	Ljung–Box test statistic
ω	9.906e−05	4.753e−05	2.084*
α_1	1.654e−01	3.719e−02	4.448*
β_1	8.074e−02	8.244e−02	0.979
ϕ_1	6.513e−01	8.202e−02	7.940*

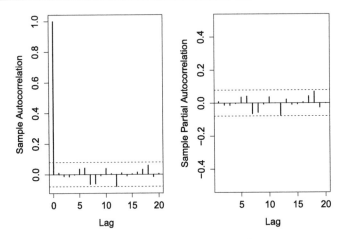

Figure 8.15: The ACF and PACF for model residuals of ARIMA-t-EGARCH process. (*econ_tgarch*)

The ACF and PACF of ARIMA-t-EGARCH residuals are plotted in Fig. 8.15. The small values indicate independent structure of model residuals. We further check the QQ plot in Fig. 8.16: the model residuals fit better to student-t distribution compared with normal case of Fig. 8.12.

We compare the model performance of selected GARCH models in Table 8.12, where the log likelihood and information criteria select the t-GARCH$(1, 1)$ model. With the selected ARIMA$(2, 0, 2)$-t-GARCH$(1, 1)$ model, we conduct a 30-step-ahead forecast. The forecast performance is plotted in Fig. 8.17 with the 95% confidence bands marked in blue.

8.4 Multivariate GARCH Model

While modeling volatility of CRIX returns has been the center of attention, understanding the co-movements of different indices in CRIX family are of great importance. In this subsection

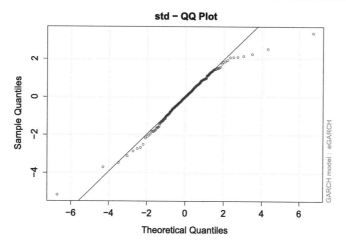

Figure 8.16: The QQ plot of t-EGARCH$(1, 1)$ model.
(🔍 *econ_tgarch*)

Table 8.12: Comparison of the variants of GARCH model.

Source: 🔍 *econ_tgarch*

GARCH models	Log likelihood	AIC	BIC
GARCH$(1, 1)$	1305.355	−4.239	−4.210
t-GARCH$(1, 1)$	1309.363	−4.249	−4.213
t-EGARCH$(1, 1)$	1305.142	−4.235	−4.199

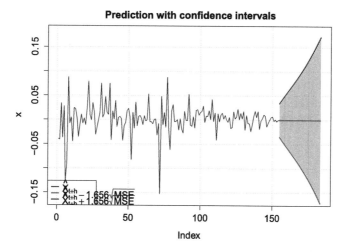

Figure 8.17: The 30-step-ahead forecast using ARIMA-t-GARCH process.
(🔍 *econ_tgarch*)

we proceed further to MGARCH (multivariate GARCH) model, whose model specification allows for a flexible dynamic structure. It provides us a tool to analyze the volatility and co-volatility dynamic of asset returns in a portfolio.

8.4.1 Formulations of MGARCH Model

Consider the error term ε_t with $E(\varepsilon_t) = 0$ and the conditional covariance matrix given by the $(d \times d)$ positive definite matrix H_t; we assume that

$$\varepsilon_t = H_t^{\frac{1}{2}} \eta_t \tag{8.11}$$

where $H_t^{\frac{1}{2}}$ can be obtained by Cholesky factorization of H_t. The η_t is an iid innovation vector such that

$$\begin{aligned} E(\eta_t) &= 0 \\ \mathsf{Var}(\eta_t) &= E(\eta_t \eta_t^\top) = \mathcal{I}_d \end{aligned} \tag{8.12}$$

with $\mathcal{I}_d$ the identity matrix of order d.

So far the standard MGARCH framework is defined, different specifications of H_t yield various parametric formulations. The first MGARCH model was directly a generalization of univariate GARCH model proposed by Bollerslev et al. (1988), which is called VEC model. Let $vech(\cdot)$ denote an operator that stacks the columns of the lower triangular part of its argument square matrix. The VEC model is formulated as

$$vech(H_t) = c + \sum_{j=1}^{q} A_j vech\left(\varepsilon_{t-j}\varepsilon_{t-j}^T\right) + \sum_{i=1}^{p} B_i vech\left(H_{t-i}\right) \tag{8.13}$$

where A_j and B_i are parameter matrices and c is a vector of constant components.

However it is difficult to ensure the positive definiteness of H_t in VEC model without strong assumptions on parameter. Engle and Kroner (1995) proposed the BEKK specification (defined by Baba et al., 1990) that easily imposes positive definite under-weak assumption. The form is given by

$$H_t = CC^\top + \sum_{k=1}^{K}\sum_{j=1}^{q} A_{kj}^\top \varepsilon_{t-j}\varepsilon_{t-j}^T A_{kj} + \sum_{k=1}^{K}\sum_{i=1}^{p} B_{ki}^\top H_{t-i} B_{ki} \tag{8.14}$$

where C is a lower triangular parameter matrix.

Other than the direct generalization of GARCH models introduced above, the nonlinear combination of univariate GARCH models are more easily estimable. This kind of MGARCH model is based on the decomposition of the conditional covariance matrix into conditional

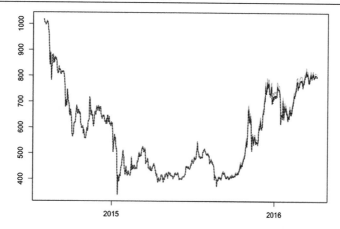

Figure 8.18: The price process of CRIX (black), ECRIX (grey) and EFCRIX (dotted).
(⌨ *econ_ccgar*)

standard deviations and correlations. The simplest is Constant Conditional Correlation (CCC) model introduced by Bollerslev (1990). The conditional correlation matrix of CCC model is time invariant and can be expressed as

$$H_t = D_t P D_t \qquad (8.15)$$

where D_t denotes the diagonal matrix with the conditional variances along the diagonal. Therefore $\{D_t\}_{ii} = \sigma_{it}^2$, with each σ_{it}^2 being a univariate GARCH model.

To overcome this limitation, Engle (2002) proposed a Dynamic Conditional Correlation (DCC) model that allows for dynamic conditional correlation structure. Rather than assuming that the conditional correlation ρ_{ij} between the i-th and j-th components is constant in P, it is now the ij-th element of the matrix P_t which is defined as

$$
\begin{aligned}
H_t &= D_t P_t D_t \\
P_t &= (\mathcal{I} \odot \mathcal{Q}_t)^{-\frac{1}{2}} \mathcal{Q}_t (\mathcal{I} \odot \mathcal{Q}_t)^{-\frac{1}{2}}
\end{aligned}
\qquad (8.16)
$$

with

$$\mathcal{Q}_t = (1 - a - b)\mathcal{S} + a\varepsilon_{t-1}\varepsilon_{t-1}^{\top} + b\mathcal{Q}_{t-1} \qquad (8.17)$$

where a is positive and b is a non-negative scalar such that $a + b < 1$. $\mathcal{S}$ is unconditional matrix of ε_t, $\mathcal{Q}_0$ is positive definite.

8.4.2 DCC Model Estimation

Fig. 8.18 presents the time path of price series for each indices of CRIX family. As observed, the price processes are slightly different after October of 2015. Before that, three indices presented similar trend over time. This indicates that the ARIMA(2, 0, 2) model selected for

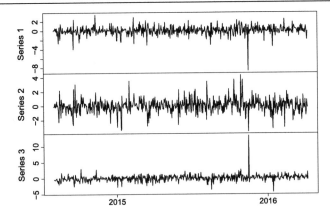

Figure 8.19: The standard error of DCC-GARCH model, with CRIX (upper), ECRIX (middle) and EFCRIX (lower).

(🔍 *econ_ccgar*)

Table 8.13: Estimation result of DCC-GARCH$(1, 1)$ model coefficients.

Source: 🔍 *econ_ccgar*

Index type	Coef.	Estimates	Std Error	t test	p-value
CRIX	μ	0.000	0.000	0.759	0.448
	ω	0.000	0.000	0.874	0.382
	α_1	0.123	0.037	3.360	0.001
	β_1	0.832	0.091	9.155	0.000
ECRIX	μ	0.001	0.001	0.775	0.438
	ω	0.000	0.000	0.942	0.346
	α_1	0.123	0.044	2.807	0.004
	β_1	0.832	0.092	9.026	0.000
EFCRIX	μ	0.001	0.001	0.802	0.422
	ω	0.000	0.000	0.946	0.344
	α_1	0.124	0.042	2.960	0.003
	β_1	0.831	0.091	9.153	0.000
DCC	a	0.268	0.018	15.189	0.000
	b	0.571	0.015	38.966	0.000

CRIX return to remove the intertemporal dependence can be implemented to ECRIX and EFCRIX as well, the model selection and estimation procedures are similar to the way of CRIX. In this section, the ARIMA fitting residuals for each index are used in the following analysis.

The DCC-GARCH$(1, 1)$ model estimation is employed by the QMLE based on the stochastic process of equations (8.16) and (8.17). One of the assumptions is the iid innovation term of η_t

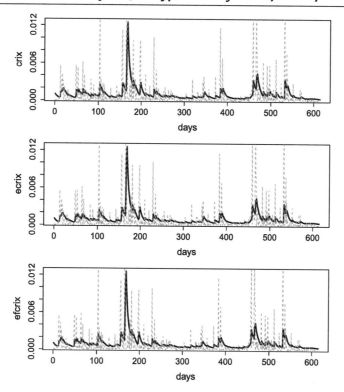

Figure 8.20: The estimated volatility (black) and realized volatility (gray) using DCC-GARCH model, with CRIX (upper), ECRIX (middle) and EFCRIX (lower).

(*econ_ccgar*)

in equation (8.11). We check the standard residuals of DCC-GARCH(1, 1) in Fig. 8.19, which displays white noise pattern to some extent.

The estimation results are contained in Table 8.13.

All the estimated parameters are statistically significant except for the constant terms: mean μ and the constant ω from equation (8.7). Each σ_{it}^2 is a univariate GARCH(1, 1) model,

$$\sigma_{CRIX,t}^2 = 0.123\varepsilon_{CRIX,t-1}^2 + 0.832\sigma_{CRIX,t-1}^2$$
$$\sigma_{ECRIX,t}^2 = 0.123\varepsilon_{ECRIX,t-1}^2 + 0.832\sigma_{ECRIX,t-1}^2$$
$$\sigma_{EFCRIX,t}^2 = 0.124\varepsilon_{EFCRIX,t-1}^2 + 0.831\sigma_{EFCRIX,t-1}^2$$

The matrix $\mathcal{Q}_t$ of equation (8.17) is

$$\mathcal{Q}_t = (1 - 0.268 - 0.571)\mathcal{S} + 0.268\varepsilon_{t-1}\varepsilon_{t-1}^\top + 0.571\mathcal{Q}_{t-1}$$

with the unconditional covariance matrix $\mathcal{S}$,

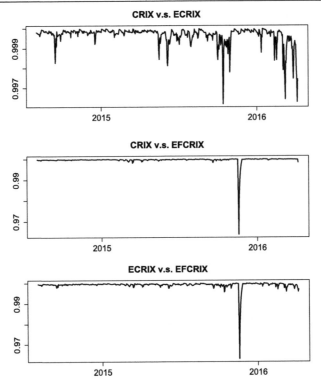

Figure 8.21: The dynamic autocorrelation between three CRIX indices: CRIX, ECRIX and EFCRIX estimated by DCC-GARCH model.

(🅠 econ_ccgar)

$$S = \begin{pmatrix} 0.994 & 0.994 & 0.994 \\ 0.994 & 0.994 & 0.993 \\ 0.994 & 0.993 & 0.994 \end{pmatrix}$$

8.4.3 DCC Model Diagnostics

Based on the estimation of DCC-GARCH(1, 1) model, the estimated and realized volatility are shown in Fig. 8.20. The volatility clustering feature is seen graphically from the presence of the sustained periods of high or low volatility, the large changes tend to cluster. In general, the DCC-GARCH(1, 1) fitting is satisfactory as it captures almost all significant volatility changes.

Fig. 8.21 presents the estimated autocorrelation dynamics for each of the following series (CRIX vs. ECRIX, CRIX vs. EFCRIX and ECRIX vs. EFCRIX) respectively. We can ob-

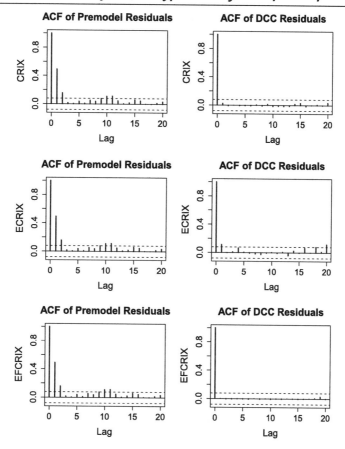

Figure 8.22: The comparison of ACF between premodel squared residuals and DCC squared residuals.

serve that three autocorrelation dynamics are similar as we expect. To be more specific, three indices are highly positive correlated during the whole sample period. As evidenced in Fig. 8.18, the time period after the third semester of 2015 is characterized by relatively lower correlation between three indices, which in turn explains the slight declines in the autocorrelation dynamics.

To check the adequacy of MGARCH model, we compare the ACF and PACF plots between the pre-model squared residual ε_t and the DCC-GARCH(1, 1) squared residuals. Fig. 8.22 and Fig. 8.23 show the GARCH effect is largely eliminated by DCC-GARCH model. Most of the lags are within the 95% confidence bands marked in blue.

Moreover, we conduct a 100-step-ahead forecast of estimated volatility as illustrated in Fig. 8.24; the forecast behavior generally follows the estimated dynamics (black line).

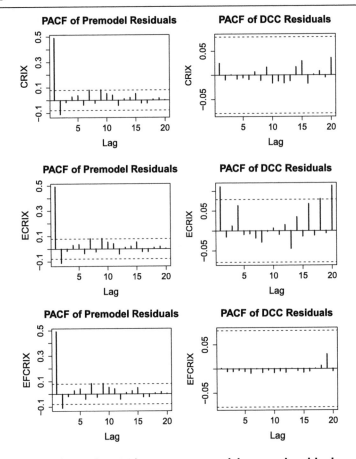

Figure 8.23: The comparison of PACF between pre-model squared residuals and DCC squared residuals.

8.5 Nutshell and Outlook

Understanding the dynamics of asset returns is of great importance, it is the first step for practitioners to proceed with analysis of cryptocurrency markets, like volatility modeling, option pricing and forecasting, etc. The motivation behind trying to identify the most accurate econometric model, to determine the parameters that capture economic behavior arises from the desire to produce the dynamic modeling procedure.

In general it is difficult to model asset returns with basic time series model due to the features of heavy tail, correlated for different time periods and volatility clustering. Here we provide a detailed step-by-step econometric analysis using the data of CRIX family: CRIX, ECRIX and EFCRIX. The time horizon for our data sample is from 01/08/2014 to 06/04/2016.

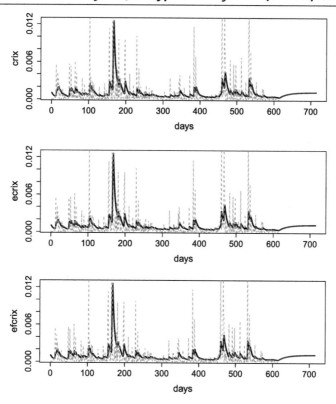

Figure 8.24: **100-step-ahead forecasts of estimated volatility using DCC-GARCH**($1, 1$) **model.**

At first, an ARIMA model is implemented for removing the intertemporal dependence. The diagnostic checking stage helps to identify the most accurate econometric model. We then observe the well-known volatility clustering phenomenon from the estimated model residuals. Hence volatility models such as ARCH, GARCH and EGARCH are introduced to eliminate the effect of heteroskedasticity. Additionally, it is observed that the GARCH residuals show fat-tail properties. We impose the assumption on the residuals with student-t distribution, t-GARCH($1, 1$) is selected as the best fitted model for all our samples of data based on measures of log likelihood, AIC and BIC. Finally, a multivariate volatility model, DCC-GARCH($1, 1$), is introduced in order to show the volatility clustering and time varying covariances between three CRIX indices.

With the econometric model in the hand, it facilitates the practitioners to make financial decisions, especially in the context of pricing and hedging of derivative instruments.

References

Akaike, H., 1974. A new look at the statistical model identification. IEEE Transactions on Automatic Control 19 (6), 716–723.

Baba, Y., Engle, R., Kraft, D., Kroner, K., 1990. Multivariate Simultaneous Generalized Arch, Department of Economics. Technical report, Working Paper. University of California at San Diego.

Bollerslev, T., 1986. Generalized autoregressive conditional heteroskedasticity. Journal of Econometrics 31 (3), 307–327.

Bollerslev, T., 1990. Modelling the coherence in short-run nominal exchange rates: a multivariate generalized arch model. The Review of Economics and Statistics, 498–505.

Bollerslev, T., Engle, R.F., Wooldridge, J.M., 1988. A capital asset pricing model with time-varying covariances. The Journal of Political Economy, 116–131.

Box, G.E., Jenkins, G.M., Reinsel, G.C., Ljung, G.M., 2015. Time Series Analysis: Forecasting and Control. John Wiley & Sons.

Brooks, C., 2014. Introductory Econometrics for Finance. Cambridge University Press.

Dickey, D.A., Fuller, W.A., 1981. Likelihood ratio statistics for autoregressive time series with a unit root. Econometrica: Journal of the Econometric Society, 1057–1072.

Engle, R., 2002. Dynamic conditional correlation: a simple class of multivariate generalized autoregressive conditional heteroskedasticity models. Journal of Business & Economic Statistics 20 (3), 339–350.

Engle, R.F., 1982. Autoregressive conditional heteroskedasticity with estimates of the variance of United Kingdom inflation. Econometrica: Journal of the Econometric Society, 987–1007.

Engle, R.F., Kroner, K.F., 1995. Multivariate simultaneous generalized arch. Econometric Theory 11 (01), 122–150.

Engle, R.F., Ng, V.K., 1993. Measuring and testing the impact of news on volatility. The Journal of Finance 48 (5), 1749–1778.

Franke, J., Härdle, W.K., Hafner, C.M., 2015. Statistics of Financial Markets: An Introduction. Springer.

Geweke, J., 1986. Modelling the persistence of conditional variances: a comment. Econometric Reviews 5 (1), 57–61.

Hamilton, J.D., 1994. Time Series Analysis, vol. 2. Princeton University Press, Princeton.

Härdle, W.K., Trimborn, S., 2015. Crix or Evaluating Blockchain Based Currencies. Technical report, SFB 649 Discussion Paper.

Kwiatkowski, D., Phillips, P.C., Schmidt, P., Shin, Y., 1992. Testing the null hypothesis of stationarity against the alternative of a unit root: how sure are we that economic time series have a unit root? Journal of Econometrics 54 (1), 159–178.

Lütkepohl, H., 2005. New Introduction to Multiple Time Series Analysis. Springer Science & Business, Media.

Nelson, D.B., 1991. Conditional heteroskedasticity in asset returns: a new approach. Econometrica: Journal of the Econometric Society, 347–370.

Pantula, S.G., 1986. Comment. Econometric Reviews 5 (1), 71–74.

Rachev, S.T., Mittnik, S., Fabozzi, F.J., Focardi, S.M., Jašić, T., 2007. Financial Econometrics: From Basics to Advanced Modeling Techniques, vol. 150. John Wiley & Sons.

Schwarz, G., et al., 1978. Estimating the dimension of a model. The Annals of Statistics 6 (2), 461–464.

Tsay, R.S., 2005. Analysis of Financial Time Series, vol. 543. John Wiley & Sons.

CHAPTER 9

Financial Intermediation in Cryptocurrency Markets – Regulation, Gaps and Bridges

Immaculate Dadiso Motsi-Omoijiade

Contents

Abbreviations

AML Anti-Money Laundering
BTC a unit of Bitcoin (also denominated in lower case bitcoin)
CDD Customer Due Diligence
CFT Countering the Financing of Terrorism
CFPB United States Consumer Financial Protection Bureau
DLT Distributed Ledger Technology
EBA European Banking Authority
FATF Financial Action Task Force
FCA Financial Conduct Authority (United Kingdom)
FinCen Financial Crimes Enforcement Network (United States Treasury)
FinTech Financial Technology
FINTRAC Financial Transactions and Reports Analysis Center of Canada
KYC Know Your Customer (requirements)
MAS Monetary Authority of Singapore
MSB Money Services Business
NYDFS New York Department of Financial Services
P-2-P Peer-to-Peer
SAR Suspicious Activities Reporting

9.1 Introduction

Initially seen as niche and parochial, the cryptocurrencies industry, dominated by Bitcoin, came to the regulatory fore after the seminal cases of Mt. Gox and Silk Road. These two incidents, where billions of dollars' worth of Bitcoin was lost (Mt. Gox) and where the extent of the criminal network using Bitcoin for the sale and purchase of illicit goods and services over the Tor Network was exposed (Silk Road), led regulators around the world to start considering how best to oversee their use. This regulatory attention has focused on preventing the use of cryptocurrencies for nefarious purposes and preventing the use of cryptocurrencies as conduits and facilitators of criminal activity. Regulation has also been concerned with consumer protection and putting in place mechanisms to ensure that those who use cryptocurrencies for legitimate purposes, such as investment, commercial transactions and remittances, are protected. These regulatory initiatives, arguably, more in some jurisdictions than in others, are tempered by an awareness of the need to ensure that the innovative gains of cryptocurrencies, with a focus on the near ubiquitous efficiency gains of Distributed Ledger Technology (DLT), are nurtured, harnessed and exploited.

Despite the variation in the locus and concentration of regulatory approaches across and sometimes within different jurisdictions, the common feature of regulation of cryptocurrencies has been the almost exclusive concentration of regulatory attention on the financial intermediaries that facilitate cryptocurrencies-based transactions. This is because apart from the few countries where the use of cryptocurrencies has been banned altogether, 'regulating cryptocurrencies' per se is problematic due that that they are a form of digital and virtual currency generated and traded autonomously and pseudonymously online. What is within the grasp and ambit of supervisory authorities is the ability to regulate, to a certain extent, how cryptocurrencies are used at the point where the value generated in the digital sphere moves into the physical fiat-based economy. At this point, regulators can engage with a tangible known, often, with a physical rather than digital presence, that is the financial intermediary. This chapter will provide an overview of financial intermediation in cryptocurrency markets through an analysis of the activities, risks and regulation of the key services currently offered by key cryptocurrency intermediaries, through an introduction to less-regulated intermediation activities and, finally, through the consideration of the possible direction of future regulatory interventions in this market.

9.2 Financial Intermediation in Cryptocurrency Markets

Financial intermediaries are generally defined as being "entities that intermediate between providers and users of financial capital" (Greenbaum et al., 2015). This intermediation hinges upon the ability to leverage information in order to match transactors, manage risk and transform assets. This brokerage function fuels financial markets and industry by matching and bringing together transactors with complementary needs, such as lenders and borrowers, due to the informational asymmetries that exist prior to entering into a contractual arrangement. Being well positioned to pool data, intermediaries are able to process risk and transform assets, for example changing maturity of claims, in order to broker optimal outcomes for their clients. Although financial intermediaries are often distinguished as either depository or non-depository in nature, this distinction has become blurred as non-depository institutions, such as mutual funds, have been offering products and services similar to those of commercial banks and vice versa. The same can be said of intermediation within the cryptocurrency market. Here, intermediation takes place mainly through exchanges which offer products and services that other intermediaries in the same market, such as wallet providers and remittance services, provide exclusively.

In cryptocurrency markets, the simplest form of transactions takes place using Distributed Ledger Technology (DLT) on the blockchain. However, the movement of cryptocurrencies off the blockchain requires intermediation. Here, intermediaries "act as custodians of cryptocurrency or cryptocurrency credentials originally belonging to their clients and may facilitate and clear transactions for clients without updating the public ledger" (Hughes and Middlebrook, 2015). More generally, as adapted from the NYDFS (2015) intermediaries in cryptocurrency markets are mainly entities involved in (a) receiving cryptocurrency for transmission or transmitting it, (b) holding cryptocurrency for others, (c) buying and selling cryptocurrency, and

(d) exchanging services in the conversion or exchange of fiat currency or other value into cryptocurrency.

Of regulatory significance is the fact that financial intermediation is often characterized by vulnerability to risks specific to the products and services they provide. Generally speaking, deposit-taking financial intermediaries are either highly leveraged or subject to the weaknesses of fractional reserve banking, whereas non-deposit taking intermediaries need to hedge for the vagaries of markets. The same can be seen in the cryptocurrency market where each intermediary is subject to a range of risk-factors endemic to the services and products it offers. What follows is an examination of the activity, risk profile and regulation of exchanges and electronic wallet providers respectively.

9.3 Exchanges

9.3.1 Activity

Exchanges are a pivotal component of the cryptocurrency ecosystem with the primary role of converting cryptocurrencies into fiat currency or trading one form of cryptocurrency into another. Some exchanges are large operations geared towards institutional traders whilst others offer simpler services with limited buying and selling capabilities (Coindesk, 2015). In addition to this, exchanges are also the primary hub for cryptocurrency trading activities (including derivatives) with some offering limited storage facilities for cryptocurrency-denominated investments to their customers. There are currently 170 cryptocurrency exchanges in operation (Bitcoinx.io, 2016) with the largest by transaction volume being based in China where, over the past two years, almost 92% of the volume of Bitcoin trading activity took place across China-based Okcoin, Huobi and BTC China and the Chinese Yuan's market share being 90.46% compared to the United States' Dollar's 7.65% market share during the same two-year time-frame (Bitcoininty.org, 2016).

Despite the dominance of Chinese exchanges, explained in part due to China being a major mining hub, Chinese investors hedging against Yuan devaluation, low fees and limited regulation (Pel, 2015), some insights of regulatory significance can be gleaned from examining localized exchange activity. A case in point here would be the United Kingdom (UK) where data showed that only 18% of surveyed users acquired their bitcoin through mining. The remaining 82% of UK bitcoin users acquire their bitcoin directly through exchanges, with Bitstamp and Coinfloor being the most popular sites (Coinjournal, 2015). This statistic further highlights the significance of intermediation in this market and the prevalent need for exchange services which play the vital role of connecting buyers to sellers in the exchange cryptocurrency to fiat and cryptocurrency to cryptocurrency.

9.3.2 Risk Profile

Buying or selling cryptocurrency through an exchange entails the depositing of cryptocurrency into a wallet provided by the exchange service provider. In order to ensure constant and adequate liquidity to execute transactions in near real-time, exchanges have access to the private keys assigned to each customer, enabling them to partake in a form of fractional reserve banking, a fact that sometimes pushes them to act "more like a margin-taking balance-sheet deploying broker-dealers" (Kaminska, 2016) instead of a simple exchange service – an activity for which Bitfinex was sanctioned for by United States (US) regulators prior to its August 2016 hack. The act of depositing bitcoin in an exchange and ceding exclusive use of private key to a third party invokes fiduciary duties and the need for trust between the exchange and the customer. In addition to this, the exchange requests and has access to customer's bank details and other identity markers again invoking a duty of trust in the protection of customer's data. Similarly, the removal of the safety found in the immutable digital seal of transactions on the blockchain, as a result of transactions between customers being recorded only on exchanges' trade history with only the exchanges' wallet transactions being recorded on the blockchain (Bhaskar and Lee, 2015), further adds to the risks faced by consumers. Where exchange services are provided by brokerages or facilitated by peer-to-peer platforms (P-2-P), further risk arises from the need for customers to verify for themselves the legitimacy of a trading partner as well as the risk of delivery of funds either via bank transfer or in person.

However, the most frequent manifestation of risk in exchange services has to do with the loss of funds held in escrow by hacking. According to Bitcoinx.io (2016) at least ten exchanges have been hacked in 2016 alone. More historically, Moore and Christin (2013, 1) found that 18 out of 40 Bitcoin exchanges tracked between 2010 and 2013 had closed down after being breached showing the failure rate of Bitcoin exchanges to be 45% with a median lifetime of only 381 days. Interestingly, their study found that high-volume exchanges are less likely to close but more likely to experience a breach meaning that exchanges face a paradoxical challenge whereby "the continued operation of an exchange depends on running a high transaction volume, which makes the exchange a more valuable target to thieves" (Moore and Christin, 2013). An additional risk factor lies in the irrevocability of transactions where, in this case, "irrevocability makes any Bitcoin transaction involving one or more intermediaries subject to added risk, such as if the intermediary becomes insolvent or absconds with customer deposits" (Moore and Christin, 2013). In addition to these customer-centric risks, regulators are concerned with the possibility of exchange services being the conduit for money laundering, terrorist financing and tax avoidance. These risks stem from the ability to transfer and deposit cryptocurrency in some cases, anonymously and in all cases "globally, rapidly and irrevocably" whilst also "undermining the ability of enforcers to obtain evidence and recover criminal assets" (European Banking Authority, 2014) due to the difficultly, albeit increasingly less so, of tracing transactions. This risk profile of exchange services has informed the nature and structure of their regulation.

9.3.3 Regulation

The regulation of cryptocurrency intermediaries involved in exchange services has been dominated by concerns around the use of cryptocurrencies in the committing of financial crimes and fueled by the need to prevent the compromising national security (terrorist financing) and state revenue generation (tax evasion and money laundering). The main response to these threats has been the use of licensing and registration obligations. Cryptocurrency exchanges are generally required to obtain Money Services Business (MSB) and Money Transmitter licenses in order to operate in most jurisdictions. Embedded in these licenses is the legal compulsion, on pain of license revocation, to conform to Anti-Money Laundering (AML) and Countering the Financing of Terrorism (CFT) requirements mainly consisting of Know-Your-Customer (KYC) customer identity verification, record-keeping rules and Suspicious Activity Reporting (SAR).

An example of how this form of regulation is operationalized can be seen in the United States. Here, at the federal level, the Department of Treasury Financial Crimes Enforcement Network (FinCEN) invokes the Bank Secrecy Act of 1970 (BSA) and the USA Patriot Act of 2011 to require cryptocurrency exchanges to register as MSBs and comply with the accruing AML and CTF requirements. According to FinCEN (2013), this licensing requirement applies to any "administrator or exchanger that (1) accepts and transmits a convertible virtual currency or (2) buys or sells convertible virtual currency for any reason" and, in so doing, meets the FinCEN definition of a Money Transmitter, a category of MSB. In addition to FinCEN MSB licensing and registration, some states require additional Money Transmitter Licensing with more locally-defined legal obligations.

Several enforcement actions based on these regulations have already been taken. In 2015, Ripple Labs Inc. settled criminal and civil allegations for BSA violations. Ripple Labs violated several requirements of the BSA "by acting as a Money Services Business (MSB) and selling its virtual currency without first registering with the Financial Crimes Enforcement Network (FinCEN) and by failing to implement an adequate AML and CFT programming (FinCEN, 2015). Further cases in which BSA violations took place include *United States v Murgio* and *United States v Lebedev* where Murgio and Lebedev "allowed customers to exchange cash for bitcoins, knowing that their customers were transacting in the proceeds of criminal activity" and "exchanged cash for bitcoins for victims of cyber-attacks in which criminals had blocked access to a victim's computer system until a bitcoin ransom was paid" (FinCEN, 2015).

Similar emphasis of regulation in other jurisdictions on CFT and AML is evident. In Canada, exchanges are required to register with the Financial Transactions and Reports Analysis Centre of Canada (FINTRAC) in line with the 2014 amendment of the Proceeds of Crime (Money Laundering) and Terrorist Financing Act, SC 2000 to include "regulating those dealing in digital currencies as money services businesses, so that they are subject to record keeping verification procedures, suspicious transaction reporting, and registration requirements" (FINTRAC, 2014). Other jurisdictions are still in the formulation stages in the application of similar laws. In the European Union (EU), plans are being made by the EU Commission to push forward implementation of 4th Anti-Money Laundering Directive (4AMLD) with tabled amendments to include the regulation of cryptocurrency exchanges under both 4AMLD and the Payment Services Directive (European Commission, 2016). A similar AML/CTF position has been taken by the Monetary Authority of Singapore (MAS) and the UK's Financial Conduct Authority (FCA) application of AML/CTF regulations under Electronic Money Licensing and HM Treasury's plan to do the same (HM Treasury, 2016). A notable exception to this rule is Australia where the Anti-Money Laundering and Counter Terrorism Financing Act 2006 does not apply to Bitcoin as it is not backed by precious metal or bullion as per the definition of e-currency (Marshall, 2015) although this position is currently under review (Rizzo, 2016).

Beyond regulations targeted at AML and CFT, further regulation to do with consumer protection have also been put in place to address the risks involved with cryptocurrency exchange services. In the United States, these concerns are addressed more at the state-level, with the most robust requirements having been issued by the New York Department of Financial Services (NYDFS)'s Bitlicense. In order to obtain a Bitlicense, cryptocurrency intermediaries must, amongst other requirements, ensure that they have a board-approved cybersecurity program which includes the employment of a qualified Chief Information Security Officer (CIO); the protection of consumers by providing initial and per transaction disclosures of risks, terms and conditions, complaints policies and disclosures, advertising and marketing requirements; the safeguarding of assets through the holding of capital, surety bonds and full reserves for custodial assets; and the becoming subject to exams, reports and oversight including reporting of transactions exceeding a certain amount and a customer identification program (NYDFS, 2015). A similar state-based, in this case province-based, approach is taken in Canada where, in particular, Ontario and British Columbia have applied the Ontario Consumer Protection Act and the British Columbia Business Practices and Consumer Protection Act respectively, to cryptocurrency-related activities (Burgoyne, 2013).

As has been previously alluded to, exchanges in cryptocurrency markets are also the site for trading activity for investment and speculative purposes. The act of buying and selling currency is fueled by various motives one of which is to generate revenue by taking advantage of price fluctuations. The ability to execute these forms of trades via exchanges has put these intermediaries under the spotlight of regulators concerned with standards in securities and commodity trading. An example of the application of Securities and Commodity Trading Laws involves the United States Securities Exchange Act of 1934. Here, the United States Securities and Exchange Commission brought cases against Erik T. Voorhees and BTC Trading Corporation and Ethan Burnside for failure to register bitcoin-related securities offerings. In *SEC v. Erik T. Voorhees*, Voorhees admitted to publicly offering securities in two ventures without registering offerings where investors paid for their shares in FeedZe-Birds and SatoshiDICE securities offerings in bitcoin with Voorhees raising 50,600 bitcoins worth US$722,659 at the time by selling 13 million shares to the public (SEC, 2014a, 2014b). Similarly, in *SEC v. BTC Corporation and Ethan Burnside*, the SEC brought administrative charges against programmer Ethan Burnside for the unlawful operation of two online platforms used to trade securities using virtual currencies essentially operating a "virtual stock exchange" without registration in violation of Section 5 of the Exchange Act (SEC, 2014a, 2014b). With the totality of enforcement action using securities and commodity trading laws having occurred in the United States, the efficacy of this source of law elsewhere is yet to be seen.

Overall, the regulation of cryptocurrency intermediaries has drawn from laws governing the functioning of payment systems (such as Visa and MasterCard); laws governing the functioning of Money Service Businesses (MSB's) including Money Transmitters (such as Western Union and MoneyGram); securities and commodity trading laws; and Anti-Money Laundering (AML) and Countering the Financing of Terrorism (CFT) Laws. At the international level, the regulatory responses comprise of the issuance of reports, guidance and manuals in the areas of expertise of specific organizations. These have included the Financial Action Task Force (FATF), the United Nationals Office on Drugs and Crime (UNODC), the International Monetary Fund (IMF), the Committee on Payments and Market Infrastructure (CPMI), as well as the Organization of Economic Co-operation and Development (OECD), the European Banking authority and the Commonwealth Secretariat who have each issued opinions and provided forums for the discussion of issues to do with VC and regulation

9.4 Electronic Wallet Providers

9.4.1 Activity

Electronic Wallet Providers are exclusively concerned with the storage of cryptocurrency and as such have theoretically more liability than exchanges. This distinction is sometimes blurred as most exchanges offer wallet services although they tend to discourage the dormant storage of cryptocurrency for protracted lengths of time. In the simplest of terms, wallets are for storing cryptocurrency whereas exchanges are mainly for buying and selling cryptocurrencies from and into other cryptocurrencies or fiat. Wallet services are either accessed through mobile applications, web interfaces, desktop clients (which requires the downloading of software) or a combination of the three. As shall be further discussed below, wallet services offer storage facilities either online or offline with most offline storage services being offered at a fee and online storage often taking place at no direct cost to customers. In addition to this, some wallets are independent (cannot be controlled or accessed by the service providers) whilst others are not independent. An example of the former is Coinbase's Vault service which denies the company access to consumer funds and examples of the latter are MyCelim and Exodus Blockchain Assets, a recently launched wallet service that also allows for the trading of cryptocurrency within wallets (99 Bitcoins, 2016).

9.4.2 Risk Profile

Firstly, it must be noted that cryptocurrency wallet services are less prone to the instability and liquidity vulnerabilities of fractional reserve banking that can technically extend to exchange services. This means that their main risk factor has to do with the possibility of loss or theft of stored cryptocurrency mainly through hacking.

As has been previously noted, cryptocurrency wallet provision services range from those providing hot (online) and/or cold (offline) storage services. Cold storage services store client's cryptocurrencies in a manner that is not connected to the Internet through various techniques such as the provision of paper wallets, flash drives and bespoke hardware devices such as Trezor device or brain wallets. Having cryptocurrency stored online is risker than cold storage due to the possibility of the wallet service provider being hacked. Examples of hacked wallet providers are Blockchain.info where $101,000's worth of bitcoin was stolen in December 2014 and $800,000's worth of the same was stolen in December 2013 and Flexcoin where $738,240's worth of bitcoin was stolen in March 2014 (SatoshiLabs, 2016). Between November and December 2013, three cryptocurrency wallet services Input.io, BIPS and Blockchain.info were almost simultaneously attacked at a time when the price Bitcoin had risen by sixty times to almost $600. At the time, prior to the fall of Mt. Gox, it was noted that the increase in the value of the cryptocurrency led to cybercriminals targeting companies with large holdings of Bitcoins in their servers (Franceshi-Bicchierai, 2013). Since then, cyberattacks have occurred almost exclusively on wallets of exchange services with intermediaries exclusively offering wallet services reporting no new incidents of breaches in the past two years. This might possibly be attributed to higher security measures including the general exodus from internet connectivity and the cold storage of customer's wallets becoming standard practice. This practice is complemented by additional security measures including the use of multi-signature features, AES-256 encryption and back-up facilities.

9.4.3 Regulation

In most cases, e-wallet providers are likely to be similarly defined as MSBs (Money Trans-mitters) or subject to similar licensing rules as providers of pre-paid access (FinCEN, 2013). Money Transmitter Licensing in the US is targeted at non-bank entities that receive and hold consumer funds, with promise of making funds available later or sending funds elsewhere as well as entities that issue of sell payment instruments. Here, the main requirements for this license in the US are minimum capitalization of $50,000–$1 million, background check on principals, holding 100% of consumer funds in permissible investments, as well as regular reports, filings and audits (FinCEN, 2013). This application of capital requirements to cryp-tocurrency wallet providers has been problematized by several authors and pundits including Hughes and Middlebrook (2015, 23). Of note is the fact that there is no interest gained on de-posits made in wallet services. A fee is paid to safely store depositor's cryptocurrency. In this way, they can be considered to be akin to safety deposit box facilities. The only factor that places them under the ambit of financial regulation is the financial nature of the deposits. But in actual fact, given the basic storage functions of wallet services (without deposits accruing interest and without deposits being lent forward) means they can be treated as any other safety deposit or brick and mortar storage facility. The latter is usually considered as an 'ancillary banking service' where it is the responsibility of the service provider to ensure the safety of the premises and the responsibility of the customer to insure the content of their deposit box (Ombudsman News, 2013). This means there need to be regulations in place for recourse and like-to-like compensation when cryptocurrencies stored in cold storage or hardware format are lost or stolen, similarly to when this is the case in storage units or safety deposit boxes. In 2015, BitGo joined other cryptocurrency exchanges Xapo and Coinbase in offering an opt-in insurance product for its customers developed by XL Group and Innovation Insurance Group LLC to provide "robust cyber and professional liability policy" tailored to the bitcoin industry (Carruthers, 2015). This development might offer a sensible option for deposit insurance in the regulation of wallet provision services in lieu of bank security level capital requirements.

9.5 Other Intermediaries

Other relevant but less widely regulated intermediaries in cryptocurrency markets can be ob-served. Of particular interest is the use of hybrid institutional arrangements and the rise in cryptocurrency-based lending platforms and remittance services.

9.5.1 Hybrid Models

Hybrid models combine blockchain-based service provision with existing traditional bank-ing and finance institutions. An example of this is Circle Pay. Having recently acquired an e-money license in the UK and being fully registered as a MSB across all US states, including being one of the few to acquire a NYC Bitlicense, Circle's operations in the UK are based on a partnership with Barclays bank which allows them to hold pound sterling on behalf of their customers. Circle operates on the bitcoin blockchain in order to facilitate near instantaneous transactions; however, it does not participate in trading activities so it cannot be fully classified as an exchange. It does however provide limited wallet services and high frequency, low-volume remittances (Allison, 2016; Circle.com, 2016). This hybrid model follows on for the 2013 partnerships between the German bank Fidor Bank AG and Bitcoin.de (providing liability for Bitcoin.de's parent company, Bitcoin Germany GmbH) and the exchange Kraken in the first cooperation between the banking sector and the cryptocurrency industry (Mullan, 2014). This fiat-focused, over-the-blockchain model which also allows for bitcoin transactions in partnership with the traditional banking industry is potentially a signpost for the future of intermediation of cryptocurrencies and the blockchain. Despite the growing interest of the banking sector in DLT, the intersections delineation of the regulations in these hybrid models remain opaque.

9.5.2 Cryptocurrency Lending Platforms

Based on crowd-funding models, cryptocurrency lending platforms are fast growing in popularity. In disintermediating banks, the platforms themselves play a crucial role in P-2-P financing where for example relationship lending and traditional credit scoring are replaced with algorithms based on Big Data mining in order to assess creditworthiness and trustworthiness through analysis of variables such as buying habits, lifestyle choices and memberships (Greenbaum et al., 2015). These platforms not only connect potential lenders to borrowers, they provide a space in which borrowers can 'pitch' their business plans to lenders directly and, in so doing, reducing the information asymmetries evident in traditional banking, all without geographical barriers. In addition to this, cryptocurrency lending platforms facilitate transactions by transmitting and exchanging cryptocurrency and remitting interest repayments in the lender's cryptocurrency of choice. Examples of cryptocurrency lending platforms include BTCJam, BitLendingClub and BitBond. Regulation is this space is largely yet to be defined.

9.5.3 Cryptocurrency Remittance Services

Similarly, there is a plethora of Financial Technology (FinTech) start-ups leverage cryptocurrency and DLT to provide remittance services. These services exploit the technology's ability to transfer and exchange value in near real time to and from anywhere in the world, leveraging the exchangeability of any cryptocurrency into any fiat currency across the world. The website Let's Talk Payments (2016) offers a comprehensive list of remittance start-ups with the common feature being the use of blockchain as a settlement trail. Often with a geographical focus on the developing world, these cryptocurrency remittance services connect remitters to receivers using bespoke Automated Teller Machines (ATM's), mobile and smart phones, and local exchangers. Examples of these forms of service providers include BitPesa (Sub-Saharan Africa), BitSpark (APAC region), and Coin.ph (South-East Asia). In this instance, Money Transmitter regulations, similar to those applicable to Western Union and MoneyGram, are likely to be applicable.

9.6 Future Directions – Filling Gaps and Building Bridges

Thus far, this chapter has provided an overview of the activities, risks and regulation of the key intermediation services of cryptocurrency exchanges and wallet providers as well as given an introduction to other currently less comprehensively regulated intermediaries operating in this market. What follows is an overview of further issues for regulators to consider in the future governance of the cryptocurrency market. These include the filling in of gaps in the areas of P-2-P platforms and the resolution of exchanges, and creating bridges between current regulation and alternative sources of law including the consideration of implications of industry self-regulation.

9.6.1 Gaps

The first notable area falling between the cracks of the regulation of cryptocurrency intermediaries has to do with exchange services that take place through peer-to-peer platforms and services. These services allow for the purchase, selling and exchange of cryptocurrencies to fiat directly between two parties over an online platform. An example of such a platform is Local Bitcoins, a peer-to-peer cryptocurrency exchange where "you can still buy Bitcoins without verifying your ID" and, in instances where traders do request for identification (ID) verification before buying, this requirement changes "from country to country and trader to trader" (Local Bitcoins, 2016). This lack of, where it does occur, loose requirements for customer identification effectively means that any person intent on acquiring or selling cryptocurrency anonymously can do so by forum shopping and targeting traders who waive ID requirements undermines and essentially void the AML and CFT regulations currently in place for cryptocurrency exchange services. This fact is particularly significant when the volumes of transactions and trades occurring through P-2-P platforms are considered. In the United Kingdom alone, survey data showed that of the 47% of respondents acquired their bitcoin primarily through P-2-P and Brokerage services, with 41.7% of these doing so through

Local Bitcoins (Coinjournal, 2015). Along with the regulatory implications, particularly for AML, of local trades being conducted in cash, these are also often carried out face-to-face, and without any escrow facility in place, further jeopardizing consumer protection.

A further area in need of further regulatory consideration is that of resolution mechanisms for exchanges. Upon its collapse, Mt. Gox announced that over $450 million worth of Bitcoin was missing or stolen (McMillan, 2014). Although a formal claims process was initiated by Mt. Gox's bankruptcy trustees and although security consultancies have been appointed to attempt to trace the missing bitcoins, most customers have still been left out of pocket. In the more recent hack of Bitfinex, the exchange resorted to bankruptcy resolution techniques seen in traditional financial institutions through a bail-in process in which the customers whose wallets were not hacked were obliged to pay 36% or their own deposits in order to reimburse the 36% of customers whose wallets were hacked into (Maras, 2016). Similarly, the placing of Mt. Gox into receivership where its remaining customers where effectively taken over by other exchanges follows models evident in traditional bank resolution. The inclusion of resolution strategies in the licensing agreements of exchanges and the drafting of industry guidelines by regulators, taking into account the unique nature of the operation of cryptocurrency exchanges, should perhaps be considered.

9.6.2 Bridges

In addition to these two areas of oversight, there remains scope for the application of alternative sources of existing law. Firstly, it has been suggested that fuller regulation of exchanges would be possible should they be redefined as payment institutions. This reclassifcation would make exchanges subject to Payment Services Regulations which more robustly considers consumer protection issues such as governance, safe-guarding measures, internal controls and risk management procedures (Vaziri, 2014). This proposal is in line with recent initiatives within Europe where in addition to the inclusion of cryptocurrencies in the 4th AMLD, the Council called for a similar amendment in the 2nd Payment Services Directive (Council of the European Union, 2016). In the United States, the same gap in the regulation of payment systems brought about by the advent of cryptocurrency and mobile payments can be seen. It has been shown that "private contract law (might need to be) expanded to fill the gaps where payment technology has exceeded the scope of public law" through the use of the Uniform Commercial Code (Burge, 2016; Hughes and Middlebrook, 2015). Similarly, calling for the application of alternative existing sources of law is Hody (2016), who proposes the application of laws on custody, authorization and possession noting that "possession of your keys by someone else (intermediaries) does not, in the eyes of the law, negate your ownership of those keys", leaving scope and precedent to apply legal consideration of topics to do with custody, possession and authorization similar to the laws on car accidents or other instances involving custodial relationships.

Also, to be taken into consideration is the well-developed nature of self-regulation in this industry. Numerous examples in which self-enforced compliance drawing upon industry expertise, such as the recent ethereum-based Decentralized Autonomous Organization's (DAO) hard fork and mining pools voluntarily preventing a 51% attack on the Bitcoin network, can be cited. This industry of self-regulation is based on an internal market discipline stemming from issues of reputation and potential loss of business and discontinuation of operation. The leveraging of expertise towards compliance can be seen by the growing number of start-ups with enforcement-orientated business models. The most prolific of these are Elliptic and Chainanalysis which have developed compliance and fraud detection systems and software designed to track and monitor illicit activity over the Blockchain. With Chainanalysis already working in partnership with Europol and various leading exchanges having adopted Elliptic's risk assessment system (Redman, 2016), growing advances in regulation technology ('RegTech') geared at the cryptocurrency industry are likely to shape and define the trajectory of regulation in this industry.

In sum, it is important to consider the fact that intermediaries have a vested interest in maintaining the integrity of their networks and ensuring compliance when drafting regulation specific to this industry. Repeated hacks are an existential crisis to cryptocurrency intermediaries due to the accruing loss of confidence and cooperation with regulatory authorities grants them access to larger markets. An example of this is Gemini which was one of the first exchanges to meet all the requirements needed to obtain a Bitlicense in the State of New York and formalized partnerships with the banking industry with an eye on capturing the interest of institutional investors. It remains to be seen whether or not there will be a return in the investment of the hefty compliance costs paid. The key question for regulators to consider is whether or not compliance cost and requirements should be lowered in order to harness the innovative potential of cryptocurrencies, or whether or not they should be maintained to ensure a 'thinning of the herd' and a scaling up of robustness cryptocurrency markets and safety and soundness of intermediaries.

9.7 Conclusion

This chapter has shown that the loci of issues of regulatory concern in the cryptocurrency industry are the intermediaries operating in this market, particularly exchanges and electronic wallet providers. These intermediaries are the channel through which money can be laundered, taxes can be evaded, gains from the sale of illicit goods can be integrated into the real economy, ill-informed consumers can be exploited, investments can be lost and should the cryptocurrency market grow systemically significant through gaining critical mass, exchanges would be the main conduits of systemic risk. In this way, cryptocurrency financial intermediaries are both the key tool and main target of supervisory authorities' approaches to the regulation of cryptocurrencies. The need for regulation is ideally not only to deter negative outcomes but also to promote positive ones. Having cryptocurrency intermediaries operating in a regulated environment would facilitate capital inflows and allow for the harnessing of the benefits of innovation by the Fintech sector. It also means that rogue elements intent on criminal activity would be regulated-out of this space, allowing for increased security and, along with it, increased adoption of cryptocurrency and pursuing exchange services. Addressing gaps and oversights in current regulation as well as exploring the options that present themselves in existing laws and regulatory models should be further considered.

References

Allison, I., 2016. Bitcoin graduate Circle launches free social payment app in UK with Barclays. International Business Times [online], available: http://www.ibtimes.co.uk/bitcoin-graduate-circle-launches-free-social-payment-app-uk-barclays-1553353. Accessed 22 August 2016.

Bitcoinx.io, 2016. Exchanges [online], available: http://bitcoinx.io/exchanges/. Accessed 5 August 2016.

Bitcoininty.org, 2016. Market data [online], available: http://bitcoinity.org/markets. Accessed 5 August 2016.

Bhaskar, N., Lee, D., 2015. Bitcoin exchanges. In: Lee, David, K.C. (Ed.), Handbook of Digital Currency: Bitcoin, Innovation, Financial Instruments, and Big Data. Elsevier.

Burge, M., 2016. Apple pay, bitcoin and consumers: the ABC's of future public payments law. Hastings Law Journal 67 (5).

Burgoyne, M., 2013. Canadian Provincial Bitcoin Law: it's all about protecting the consumer. Coindesk [online], available: http://www.coindesk.com/canadian-bitcoin-law-consumer-protection/. Accessed 7 June 2016.

Carruthers, W., 2015. BitGo unleashes FDIC-like insurance ushering in a new era of Bitcoin security. Bitcoin Magazine [online], available: https://bitcoinmagazine.com/articles/breaking-news-bitgo-unleashes-fdic-like-insurance-ushering-new-era-bitcoin-security-1424894391. Accessed 7 June 2016.

Circle.com, 2016. About [online], available: https://www.circle.com/en-gb/about. Accessed 22 August 2016.

Coindesk, 2015. How can I buy Bitcoins? [online], available: http://www.coindesk.com/information/how-can-i-buy-bitcoins/. Accessed 20 May 2016.

Coinjournal, 2015. Bitcoin usage in the UK [online], available: http://coinjournal.net/bitcoin-usage-in-the-uk/. Accessed 4 May 2016.

Council of the European Union, 2016. Press Release 50/16 'Council conclusions on the fight against the financing of terrorism' [online], available: http://www.consilium.europa.eu/en/press/press-releases/2016/02/12-conclusions-terrorism-financing/. Accessed 19 August 2016.

European Banking Authority, 2014. Opinion on virtual currencies [online], available: http://www.eba.europa.eu/documents/10180/657547/EBA-Op-2014-08+Opinion+on+Virtual+Currencies.pdf. Accessed 20 May 2016.

European Commission, 2016. Communication from the commission to the European Parliament and the Council on an Action Plan for strengthening the fight against terrorism financing (COM 50/2 2016) [online], available: http://ec.europa.eu/justice/criminal/files/com_2016_50_en.pdf. Accessed 7 June 2016.

FinCEN, 2013. Guidance: application of FinCEN's regulations to persons administering, exchanging, or using virtual currencies [online], available: https://www.fincen.gov/statutes_regs/guidance/html/FIN-2013-G001.html. Accessed 23 August 2016.

FinCEN, 2015. FinCEN Fines Ripple Labs Inc. in first civil enforcement action against a virtual currency exchanger [online], available: https://www.fincen.gov/news_room/nr/html/20150505.html. Accessed 7 June 2016.

Financial Transactions Reports and Analysis Centre of Canada, 2014. FINTRAC advisory regarding money services businesses dealing in virtual currency [online], available: http://www.canafe-fintrac.gc.ca/new-neuf/avs/2014-07-30-eng.asp. Accessed 7 June 2016.

Franceshi-Bicchierai, L., 2013. Cyberattack leads to $1million bitcoin heist. Mashable.Com [online], available: http://mashable.com/2013/11/25/cyberattack-leads-to-heist-of-1-million-in-bitcoin/#rSGF28HniuqO. Accessed 19 August 2016.

Greenbaum, S., Thakor, A., Boot, A., 2015. Contemporary Financial Intermediation. Academic Press, London.

Hody, S., 2016. Ownership does not require possession [online], available: https://medium.com/@SHodyEsq/ownership-doesnt-require-possession-5eac8e29e460#.itw4rw4f7. Accessed 19 August 2016.

Hughes, S., Middlebrook, S., 2015. Advancing a framework for regulating cryptocurrency payments intermediaries, Articles by Maurer Faculty. Paper 2025.

HM Treasury, 2016. Action plan for anti-money laundering and counter terrorist finance. April 2016 [online], available: https://www.gov.uk/government/uploads/system/uploads/attachment_data/file/517992/6-2118-Action_Plan_for_Anti-Money_Laundering__web_.pdf. Accessed 04/05/16.

Kaminska, I., 2016. Time to re-evaluate blockchain hype. FTAphaville, August 3, 2016 [online], available: http://ftalphaville.ft.com/2016/08/03/2171799/time-to-reevaluate-blockchain-hype/. Accessed 22 August 2016.

Let's Talk Payments, 2016. 19 bitcoin remittance startups that won't let the cryptocurrency die [online], available: https://letstalkpayments.com/19-bitcoin-remittance-startups-that-wont-let-the-cryptocurrency-die/. Accessed 22 August 2016.

Local Bitcoins, 2016. About LocalBitcoins.com [online], available: https://localbitcoins.com/about. Accessed 23 August 2016.

Maras, E., 2016. Bitfinex 'bail-in' – new financial system offers laboratory for handling unexpected losses [online], available: https://www.cryptocoinsnews.com/bitfinex-bail-new-financial-system-offers-laboratory-handling-unexpected-losses/. Accessed 22 August 2016.

Marshall, R., 2015. Bitcoin: where two worlds collide. Bond Law Review 27 (1), 89–112.

McMillan, R., 2014. The inside story of Mt. Gox, Bitcoins $460 million disaster. *Wired.Com* [online], available: http://www.wired.com/2014/03/bitcoin-exchange/. Accessed 20 May 2016.

Moore, T., Christin, N., 2013. Beware the middleman: empirical analysis of bitcoin-exchange risk. In: International Conference on Financial Cryptography and Data Security. Springer, Berlin, Heidelberg, pp. 25–33.

Mullan, P., 2014. The digital currency challenge [online], available: http://0-www.palgraveconnect.com.pugwash.lib.warwick.ac.uk/pc/doifinder/10.1057/9781137382559.0001. Accessed 8 August 2016.

NYDFS, 2015. Proposed New York codes, rules and regulations: regulations of the superintendent of financial services: virtual currencies. New York State Department of Financial Services [online], available: http://dfs.ny.gov/legal/regulations/revised_vc_regulation.pdf. Accessed 06 August 2016.

Ombudsman News, 2013. Banking: safe deposit boxes [online], available: http://www.financial-ombudsman.org.uk/publications/ombudsman-news/30/30-box.htm. Accessed 23 August 2016.

Pel, A., 2015. Money for Nothing and Bits for Free: The Geographies of Bitcoin'. Master's Thesis. University of Toronto. Unpublished Manuscript.

Redman, J., 2016. Law Enforcement continues to invest in Bitcoin tracking services. Bitcoin.com [online], available: https://news.bitcoin.com/law-enforcement-continues-invest-bitcoin-tracking-services/. Accessed 23 August 2016.

Rizzo, P., 2016. Australia nearing decision on bitcoin exchange regulation. Coindesk [online], available: http://www.coindesk.com/australia-near-decision-bitcoin-exchange-aml-ctf/. Accessed 23 August 2016.

SatoshiLabs, 2016. Bitcoin hacks [online], available: http://satoshilabs.com/news/bitcoin-thefts/. Accessed 23 August 2016.

SEC, 2014a. Press Release: SEC charges bitcoin entrepreneur with offering unregistered securities [online], available: https://www.sec.gov/News/PressRelease/Detail/PressRelease/1370541972520. Accessed 23 August 2016.

SEC, 2014b. Press Release: SEC sanctions operator of bitcoin-related stock exchange for registration violations [online], available: https://www.sec.gov/News/PressRelease/Detail/PressRelease/1370543655716. Accessed 23 August 2016.

Vaziri, A., 2014. Bitcoin exchanges as payment institutions. Neopay [online], available: http://neopay.co.uk/site/wp-content/uploads/Diacle-Bitcoin-Regulation.pdf. Accessed 19 August 2016.

99 Bitcoins, 2016. Who is the best bitcoin wallet for 2016? [online], available: https://99bitcoins.com/best-bitcoin-wallet-2015-bitcoin-wallets-comparison-review/. Accessed 7 September 2016.

CHAPTER 10

Legal Risks of Owning Cryptocurrencies

Kelvin F.K. Low[#] , Ernie Teo[#]

Contents

10.1 Introduction

On 18 July 2016, economists at the Bank of England published a research paper studying the macroeconomic consequences of issuing central bank digital currencies (Barrdear and Kumhof, 2016).[1] The following day, *The Wall Street Journal* gave an account of the study under the headline 'The Central Bankers' Bold New Idea: Print Bitcoins' (Sindreu, 2016), making a connection between the idea of a central bank digital currency to Bitcoin, the original cryptocurrency conceived by the mysterious[2] Satoshi Nakamoto. One week later, in a column lauding the benefits of electronic money, a *Financial Times* columnist (Sandbh, 2016) astutely observed that the report had mistakenly conflated two quite distinct questions: 'One is whether individuals and companies should have access to electronic cash that is official money (in essence, claims on the central bank) rather than private money (as in today, claims on private banks, or non-bank private claims, as in bitcoin). The other question is whether

---

[#] The authors would like to thank Professor Mark Findlay and Professor Yeo Tiong Min for helpful comments on an early draft of the paper. The usual caveats apply.

official e-money should be implemented by central banks' adopting bitcoin-style technology (so-called "distributed ledgers" where a network of computers verifies transactions and holdings) or as it is today, through centralized registers held by the money issuers.' From an economics perspective, the distinction drawn by the *Financial Times* may perhaps be correct. However, as a matter of legal analysis (and perhaps more importantly, the risks associated with the legal analysis), the classification between official money and private money needs to be more carefully examined. This is because the different forms of money, broadly defined, expose their holders to different risks depending on their legal nature.

In the next two sections, we discuss the various legal treatments of (both non-digital and digital) money before cryptocurrencies came about. This is followed by an introduction to Bitcoin/cryptocurrencies and how they work differently from money as we know it. We then look at the legal risks associated with cryptocurrencies and associate them with some real-life examples.

10.2 Money Before Bitcoins

Since we are proposing to analyze the consequences (in terms of risks) of a *legal* classification, it is necessary to ground our study in a particular legal system. For our purposes, we will do so with reference to the English common law.[3] The absolute core instances of money, of which there can be no controversy, are of course corporeal money (Fox, 2008). In England, this takes the form of metallic coins issued by the Royal Mint and banknotes issued by the Bank of England. Historically, metallic coins are the earliest form of money asset still in use today (Fox, 2008). The standard weights and composition of coinage, as well as the amount of debt for which they pass as legal tender,[4] is today regulated by the Coinage Act 1971.[5] The other indisputable form of money takes the form of banknotes issued by the Bank of England. Banknotes take the form of promissory notes that are made payable to bearer. They were part of a group of property known as documentary intangibles in which the paper form embodies a legally enforceable promise to pay. They were considered documentary intangibles because the promise to pay is regarded by the English common law as a form of intangible property, also known as a chose in action,[6] but the law regarded the promise as being embodied in a corporeal, documentary form. Today, the promise is primarily symbolic rather than real, the right of a holder of banknote to redeem it for payment in metallic coin having been abolished in 1914 (Fox, 2008). While they continue to take the form of promissory notes payable on demand by the bearer, 'a banknote presented for payment at the offices of the Bank of England would nowadays only entitle the bearer to be paid an equivalent amount of notes in a different denomination,' Fox (2008). They are therefore effectively pure fiat money.

Somewhat more controversial is the place of incorporeal assets as property, in large part because of the Roman classification of legal rights into rights *in rem* and rights *in personam*. 'If the argument [against treating incorporeal assets as property] were correct, it would drive a wedge through any unified treatment of money since it would require an entirely different explanation of money in its corporeal and incorporeal forms,' Fox (2008). This is particularly significant because the 'de-physicalization' of money is a very real phenomenon. In 2011, corporeal money in the form of coins and banknotes amounted to only about 3.6% of the British economy (Burda and Wypolz, 2013). In Sweden, not only has the ratio of corporeal money to deposits held at banks and other financial institutions been diminishing, the amount of actual corporeal money in circulation appears to have shrunk in a phenomenon christened 'peak cash' (see Editorial, 2015 and JP Koning, 2015). Whilst it is probably premature to write off corporeal money as outdated,[7] incorporeal money[8] in the form of bank deposits therefore is indisputably gaining in economic significance. The question whether such bank deposits are also properly regarded as money and whether there is property in bank money is somewhat trickier. This is because:

> [i]n legal terms, incorporeal money consists in the customer's legal right to enforce the chose in action entitling him or her to draw upon the credit balance with the bank or any overdraft facility, or to instruct the bank to make payments from the fund in his or her account as his or her agent. ... Incorporeal money is therefore a claim to be paid money in primary corporeal form, even though in all likelihood the customer will rarely seek to reduce his or her claim to payment in coins. The customer's transferable balances on the account become media of exchange in their own right. (Fox, 2008)

While economists distinguish between different grades of bank money, we can gloss over these quite cursorily since we are primarily concerned with the risks arising out of the *legal* classification of money. Thus, classifications by economists according to their liquidity and yield into M1, M2 and M3 grades are not significant for our purposes (Fox, 2008; Burda and Wypolz, 2013). For the purposes of this paper, it is also unnecessary to consider in detail whether such bank money is properly regarded as property as a matter of legal classification.[9] This is because we are primarily concerned with risks arising out of *holding* particular assets, whether they are regarded as property (however defined).

However, without analyzing the issue in too much detail, it suffices to observe that choses in action, whether they take the form of bank debts (money) or otherwise (non-money), have traditionally been regarded as property under English law (Blackstone, 1765). The rejection of incorporeal assets as property is largely premised upon an artificial distinction drawn between rights *in rem* (rights in relation to things) and rights *in personam* (rights against persons). The former is said to comprise the law of property whereas the latter comprises the law of obligations. Fox rightly criticizes the distinction as artificial (Fox, 2008). One of the chief proponents of this Roman classificatory system in English law, the late Professor Birks, conceded that 'the subdivision of rights between *in rem* and *in personam* is not exhaustive ... The category which is omitted is the category of rights which are good against all people but do not follow any *res*. All of these are superstructural rights ...' (Birks, 2000, xxxviii).[10] This view of property, as one of us has previously observed, requiring as it does near universal enforceability of a right, confuses exclusivity with exigibility (Low and Lin, 2015).

This is not to say that the Roman classificatory system is wholly without value. Whilst it may be an outmoded means of identifying property in the digital age, it is ironically a very useful starting point for our identification of risks inherent in different forms of legal rights. We begin with the two different forms of money before the advent of cryptocurrencies. While we agree with Fox that they are both properly regarded as property, they happen to fall on either side of the Roman classificatory divide. Rights to corporeal money are protected by the law through *in rem* rights.[11] Rights to incorporeal money are debts owing by the relevant financial institution[12] and hence indisputably protected as *in personam* rights. In terms consistent with the Roman classification, the difference may crudely[13] be described as the distinction between owning something (in the case of corporeal money) and being owed something (in the case of incorporeal money). This exposes holders of corporeal money to completely different risks from those holding incorporeal money. The object of this paper is to demonstrate starkly the different risks that stem from holding different forms of money but before we begin in earnest, we must emphasize that risk is unavoidable. This is the case even with respect to cryptocurrencies, which came to be popularized in part because of the vaunted security of their ledgers. Some of these risks stem from fraud and it bears reminder that, in relation to a different attempt to set up a definitive register of rights (in this case land), the learned Starke J remarked that '[n]o definition of fraud can be attempted, so various are its forms and methods.'[14] The enactment of the Fraud Act 2006[15] in the UK can also be seen as an acknowledgment of the boundless creativity of the criminal mind. As the Law Commission remarked in its Report that led to the reform: 'A general offence of fraud would be aimed at encompassing fraud in all its forms. It would not focus on particular ways or means of committing frauds. Thus it should be better able to keep pace with developing technology.'[16]

Rights to corporeal money are *in rem* rights in the traditional Roman sense of the term. A right *in rem* is a right in or against a thing. It is generally enforceable against all persons, securing its holder freedom from interference by others of the thing concerned. In the case of corporeal money, the thing (or *res*) will either be banknotes or coins. The advantage of such a right is that it is enforceable against (almost) all comers. Provided the thing can be located, the law will generally permit its recovery or at least recovery of its value. The insolvency of its current holder is thus of no concern to the true owner. Rights to incorporeal money, on the other hand, are classical *in personam* rights. A right *in personam* is a right against a person (or specified persons). Bank money, being simply a particular species of debt, is in legal terms a right to repayment from the particular bank. As the right does not relate to a tangible thing, it is pointless to attempt to locate that thing. Corporeal money deposited with HSBC may be subsequently located in the vaults of Barclays Bank but the actual location of the corporeal money is irrelevant because a deposit involves a transfer of the right *in rem* of the depositor to the coins or banknotes to HSBC in return for a corresponding promise to repay (typically with interest) on the part of HSBC. If HSBC becomes insolvent, the depositor cannot demand repayment by Barclays Bank. At first glance, it may appear that a right *in rem* is obviously superior to a right *in personam* since it is enforceable against multiple parties rather than a single (or limited) party (parties). However, careful reflection reveals that exchanging one form of right for another involves exchanging one form of risk for another. While an *in rem* right may indeed be almost universally enforceable, one needs to locate the thing itself (or at least demonstrate that a particular defendant had indeed interfered with the thing) before an action can be brought. If you cannot identify the thief of your coins or banknotes, your right to sue the thief is largely theoretical. Provided the debtor is solvent, an *in personam* right frees the holder of the right from concerns over the theft or destruction of any particular thing since the right does not relate to any particular thing.[17] Therefore, risk is inevitable though its form will differ depending on the nature of the right.

10.3 'Digital Money' Before Bitcoins

It may come as a shock to economists, technologists, businessmen and consumers but there is no such thing as digital money as a matter of law. At least that was almost certainly true before the invention of cryptocurrencies. References to digital money, so far as legal rights are concerned, represent sloppy thinking and a failure to distinguish the legal right held by holders of such money from the manner in which they were recorded. The distinction is crucially important to our understanding of the risks involved in holding both bank money and earlier iterations of digital money. It is useful to begin our analysis with bank money because the legal analysis of bank money is clearer. Today, electronic banking allows us to view our bank balances digitally over the Internet. Yet the fundamental legal nature of bank money has not changed from the early days of banking when ledger entries were made in ink on paper, whether by hand on vellum or by printing on a passbook. Just as a ledger entry on paper did not, except in the case of banknotes,[18] transform bank money render the incorporeal corporeal, neither does a digital entry render it digital. This is an easy mistake to make, for both lawyers and non-lawyers. In *Armstrong DLW GmbH v Winnington Networks Ltd.*, for example, EU carbon credits (technically European Union Allowances or EUAs) recorded in electronic registries were regarded by the trial judge as existing 'only in electronic form' (Low and Lin, 2015). This, one of us has observed, is 'not strictly accurate' and reflects 'a failure to distinguish between a right and its record' (Low and Lin, 2015). 'Registration systems serve as *records* of rights. They do *not* represent the rights themselves' (Low and Lin, 2015). Thus, in the context of carbon credits, it is not the carbon credits but their 'inconclusive *record* that exists in electronic form' (Low and Lin, 2015). The carbon credits themselves were, like bank money, entirely without form. From the perspective of risk, this distinction is crucial. Where there has been an unauthorized transfer out of a customer's account, and the account is adjusted to reflect the unauthorized transfer, '[t]he basic answer in English law is that, in the absence of fraud, the customer is not precluded by the bank statement or the passbook from disputing an error or an incorrect debit made by the bank or from insisting upon its correction' (Ellinger et al., 2011). If such errors stem from fraud, provided they are detected quickly, before money is withdrawn, reversing such transfers is often simply an exercise in reversing a data entry.

Consider the recent Bangladesh Central Bank cyberheist. On 4 February 2016, unknown hackers used the SWIFT credentials of employees of the Bangladesh Central Bank to send transfer requests to the Federal Reserve Bank of New York requiring the latter to transfer millions of the Bangladesh Bank's money to bank accounts in, *inter alia*, the Philippines and Sri Lanka. In this way, $81m was transferred to Rizal Commercial Banking Corporation in the Philippines and $20m was transferred to Pan Asia Banking Corporation in Sri Lanka. It is necessary to explain how such money 'transfers' work in legal terms before delving further into the facts of the cyberheist. As Fox explains, '[t]he explanation of how property in incorporeal money is transferred has very little to do with the law governing the transfer of chattels by delivery. Far more relevant are the principles of the law of contract and agency, and the enforcement of title to choices in action.' There is in truth no 'transfer' of property, only a transfer of value (Fox, 2008):

> The choice in action representing the money transferred to the recipient's bank account is a distinct item of property from the choice in action representing the funds which were originally in the payer's account. The payer's title to the money is not strictly transferred. Instead, the title to the value represented in the transfer passes to the recipient because the payer's bank extinguishes (wholly or partially) the debt which it owes the payer, and the recipient's bank creates a new debt owed by itself to the recipient.

Unlike a transfer of corporeal money, which involves the simultaneous extinction of the transferor's rights to the banknotes or coins and the vesting of the transferee's rights to the same, 'transfers' of incorporeal bank money involve no such simultaneous vesting and extinction.[19] The time when the transferee acquires irrevocable rights to the transferred sum, in the form of a debt owing by its bank, is dependent on the terms of its contract with its bank and the rules of banking practice governing the particular transfer (Fox, 2008). It is clear, however, that this is neither the time its bank receives the payment instruction, the time its bank receives the funds transferred (typically in the form of incorporeal money it holds with a correspondent bank), nor the time a credit entry is made in the bank's ledger for the transferee's account (Fox, 2008). The only way to be absolutely sure of a secure receipt is for the transferee to withdraw the funds transferred. The timing of the Bangladesh heist appears to have been chosen carefully to take advantage of the weekend when no one at the New York Fed was available to respond to attempts by the Bangladesh Bank to halt the transfer orders (Zetter, 2016), probably in the hopes that this will permit the hackers sufficient time to withdraw the funds from the accounts to which they had been transferred. This was true of the transfers to Rizal Commercial Banking Corporation.[20] However, the transfer to Pan Asia Banking Corporation, though receiving far less media attention, is more instructive for our purposes. Although the transfer had already been cleared by the Fed, the recipient bank had not released the funds to the account holder and so the transfer could simply be, and was indeed, reversed once the fraud was clearly established. In this case, it appears that Pan Asia Banking Corporation had contacted its routing counterpart, Deutsche Bank, because, according to an official (Quadir, 2016), '[t]he transaction was too large for a country like [ours].' Upon checking, Deutsche Bank 'came back and said it was a suspect transaction.' This was because the request had misspelt the recipient's name as Shalika *Fandation* instead of Shalika *Foundation*. Thus, 'the typo was caught in time to freeze the funds, which were returned to Bangladesh Bank's account in New York via Deutsche Bank on Feb 17' (Allison, 2016). In legal terms, the Bangladesh Central Bank's statement of accounts with the Federal Reserve Bank of New York was corrected to reflect the wrongly debited $20m.

Even in respect of money that has been withdrawn by the transferee, the loss does not necessarily fall on the account holder because the statement of accounts is not authoritative and normally, barring contractual terms to the contrary, losses stemming from any unauthorized 'transfers' fall on the bank rather than its customers. The contract between the bank and the customer may attempt to shift these losses onto customers. In some jurisdictions, such as Canada, this has taken the form of the practice of inserting verification clauses into their contracts with customers. Such clauses would 'impose on the customer a duty to peruse his account statements promptly and to notify the bank of any errors or irregularities within a specified time. Failure so to notify the bank should be deemed to constitute a verification by the customer of the balance struck' (Ellinger et al., 2011). However, as Ross Anderson, Professor of Security Engineering at the Computer Laboratory at the University of Cambridge observed, 'Since the late 1990s the move to phone banking and then the Internet has led to contract terms and conditions along the lines of "You agree to be liable for any transactions which, according to our records, were made using your password, whether you actually made them or not" (Brignall, 2015; see also Becker et al., 2016). Drafted in extremely broad and all-encompassing terms, it should be observed that such clauses are subject to statutory control. Although directed towards verification clauses, the following statement applies equally to clauses that purport to transfer liability for unauthorized online transactions onto customers (Ellinger et al., 2011; also see Bohm et al., 2000):

> *Where the bank's customer is a consumer, or a non-consumer dealing on the bank's written standard terms of business, [such clauses] run the risk of being held unreasonable and, therefore, ineffective under the [Unfair Contract Terms Act] 1977. Under section 13(1)(c) of UCTA 1977, clauses that exclude or restrict rules of evidence or procedure are treated in the same way as those that exclude or restrict liability. Where the customer is a consumer, the clauses are also at risk of being held to be unfair and, therefore, unenforceable under the [Unfair Terms in Consumer Contracts Regulations] 1999. Schedule 2, paragraph 1(q) of the Regulations indicates that a term may be unfair where it has the object and effect of unduly restricting the evidence available to a customer against his bank or imposes a burden of proof on the customer that should, by law, be on the bank.*

Clauses that are as widely drafted as those referred to by Professor Anderson are unlikely to survive judicial scrutiny and it is likely that banks will shoulder the losses rather than pass them onto customers if litigation is simply threatened unless the sums involved are large and/or they are able to demonstrate gross negligence on the part of their customers. First, banks make substantial savings through Internet banking and if customers stopped using these services because they feel that the system cannot be trusted, these savings would be lost.[21] Secondly, litigation, as already observed, is likely to lead to such clauses being pronounced ineffectual, especially since they seem to contradict the standards set out in the 'Banking: Conduct of Business Sourcebook' issued by the Financial Conduct Authority.[22]

Consider then the precursors of Bitcoin that are *not* bank money. In the early nineties, a product called DigiCash was launched which openly touted itself as digital money (Levy, 1994). There were two problems with the product, one of which proved fatal. As its inventor, David Chaum, observed, 'It was hard to get enough merchants to accept it, so that you could get enough consumers to use it, or vice versa' (Pitta, 1999). This practical problem resulted in DigiCash Inc., the company, being declared bankrupt in 1998. However, it is the lesser of the two problems that interest us. Digital money, it turns out, is not money in digital form after all. Rather, similarly to bank money recorded digitally, digital money (sometimes also called electronic money) is an *in personam* claim on the issuer (chose in action) that is stored digitally (or electronically, including magnetically).[23] While the accounts may be recorded digitally and may perhaps be more secure (one of the vaunted attributes of DigiCash was its use of cryptography to secure the records) than banks' statements of accounts, such digital money, if it is even legally money at all, is completely incorporeal as a matter of law. The records may take on a digital form. The right itself has no form whatsoever. It therefore exposes holders to the same sort of risks as bank money – primarily the insolvency of the issuer. Where the issuer is regulated under the Electronic Money Regulations 2011,[24] this risk is diminished (though not eliminated) through regulations such as the imposition of capital requirements.[25] Regulated electronic money is always 'redeemable' and is thus best construed as debts against the issuer (much like bank money). The rights conferred by issuers to holders of non-regulated electronic money will vary depending on the terms of the contract but they likely remain *in personam* claims against their issuers, though the claim may not take the form of a debt (i.e. a claim for a sum of money). It may instead be a claim for services of a certain monetary value but the claim is always an *in personam* against the issuer. As such, it will always expose holders to the insolvency risk of the issuer. We posit therefore that the risk of 'theft' through hacking is likely to treated similarly to hacks of bank accounts.

While there are some suggestions in the literature which attempt to assign proprietary or quasi-proprietary status to the electronic token that represents the value of the electronic money,[26] all such accounts nonetheless resort to a personal obligation against the issuer as the means by which such electronic money attains its commercial value. Furthermore, all accounts that seek to reify (i.e. reduce to the nature of a thing) the electronic token, as opposed to treating it merely as a record of a right (as we have suggested), have failed to properly account for how such electronic tokens are transferred nor have they explained the nature of their legal protection in any detail. Such accounts are analogous to the original form which banknotes (sometimes privately issued) took where the value in the banknotes lies in the obligation of their issuers to pay an equivalent value in fiat currency (or coins in the case of banknotes issued by Central Banks). However, the analogy breaks down because for banknotes, as promissory notes, the *in personam* obligation was reduced to corporeal form and the banknotes were essentially protected and transferred similarly to other corporeal property. Electronic tokens, on the other hand, are fundamentally distinct and incorporeal. In the first place, it is not clear if they are capable of transfer in the property law sense of the word. When we speak of transferring digital files, for example, the process is distinct from that of delivery of a corporeal thing by one person to another. Rather, the 'transfer' process involves the creation of a copy in a new medium before the 'original' copy is deleted in the original medium. This process simulates, but is not identical to, a transfer properly so called (Low and Llewelyn, 2016). Likewise, there is no account of what forms of interferences 'holders' of electronic tokens will be protected from as a matter of law since a basic understanding of property law reveals that the owner of any property is not always entitled to protection from all forms of unwelcome activity. A landowner, for example, cannot complain of neighbors looking over into their land because there is no such thing as visual trespass.[27] Finally, even if correct, treating such electronic tokens as electronic embodiments of incorporeal *in personam* rights simply exposes 'holders' of such tokens to *both* the risk of loss/destruction *and* the risk of their issuer's insolvency since all issuers to date have been private issuers rather than State issuers.

10.4 Bitcoins: A Primer

In his/her/their white paper, Nakamoto describes a cryptographic system for 'electronic cash' in which payment transactions are verified on the basis of group consensus rather than through financial institutions serving as trusted third parties. According to Nakamoto, the inherent weakness of a trust based model was that transactions are not completely non-reversible. As such, financial institutions cannot avoid mediating disputes which 'increases transaction costs, limiting the minimum practical transaction size and cutting off the possibility for small casual transactions' (Nakamoto, 2008). If payment transactions are reversible, it also entails merchants undertaking the risk of non-performance on the part of their counterparties since apparent payments can be subsequently rescinded. Bitcoin was envisaged as 'an electronic payment system based on cryptographic proof instead of trust, allowing any two willing parties to transact directly with each other without the need for a trusted third party' (Nakamoto, 2008). As a result of the central role played by cryptography in the system, bitcoin and its derivatives are known as cryptocurrencies. Once properly validated, bitcoin transactions are irreversible.[28]

Unlike DigiCash, the absence of an issuer or trusted third party means that bitcoin and other cryptocurrencies cannot be regarded as an *in personam* claim on an issuer and so must be analyzed differently from bank money and earlier forms of digital money. It also obviously differs in nature from corporeal money in the form of banknotes and coins since there is no corporeal thing (*res*) for any legal right to relate to. If legal protection in the form of property rights to attach to bitcoins, it is likely to be in the form of universal abstract rights akin to intellectual property, which do not neatly fall into either Roman classification.[29] It is not entirely clear what, if any legal rights, attach to bitcoins and other private cryptocurrencies like bitcoin. It has thus been argued that '[t]here is ... a good policy reason for the conclusion that one cannot, in a private law sense, "own" bitcoin,' Cutts and Goldstone QC (2015). Among cryptocurrency enthusiasts, a not insignificant segment subscribes to the idea of immutability, even in the face of demonstrable fraud, as if it were some sort of code of law. This can be seen in the aftermath of a hack of a curious 'fund' called the DAO (or Decentralized Autonomous Organization). Set up as an investment fund which would allow all the investors to have a say in the investments made (as opposed to fund managers) (Metz, 2016), the DAO attracted more than US\$168m worth of a cryptocurrency called Ether; Popper (2016a). Unfortunately, on 17 June 2016, a hacker managed to siphon off some US\$50m worth of the invested Ether; Finley (2016). The hack tested the immutability of the Ethereum ledger. The core developers of Ethereum eventually decided on a hard fork of the ledger, in effect a sort of reset that rolled back the entire Ethereum network to its state before the hack, Wong and Kar (2016). The hard fork was approved by 97% of the Ethereum network, Quentson (2016). This in effect created two versions of the ledger. The original intent of the developers (and those voting for the hard fork) was for the compromised ledger to wither away, while the original compromised ledger refused to go away, van Wirdum (2016). The survival of this zombie chain that refuses to die, now styled as Ethereum Classic to distinguish it from the hard forked Ethereum which is now called Ethereum One, demonstrates that there is a significant segment of the cryptocurrency community who 'would like to see a strict adherence to the original concept of code as law,' Torpey (2016).

10.5 Cryptocurrency Risks

Professor Eugene Howard Spafford, a leading computer security expert, was once quoted as saying, 'The only truly secure system is one that is powered off, cast in a block of concrete and sealed in a lead-lined room with armed guards – and even then I have my doubts,' Spafford (1989). A cryptocurrency network is vulnerable at several levels. Some of these vulnerabilities are theoretical but many have in fact been exploited in practice. At the personal level, a person's private cryptographic key can be 'stolen.' If it is stored electronically on his personal computer or mobile device, this 'theft' or hack can be achieved using malicious e-mail attachments or applications or by using keystroke logging devices or software to trace the private cryptographic key as it is typed in. Even if the private cryptographic key is not stored electronically but offline, for example using a so-called paper wallet, access to the private cryptographic key will still allow a 'thief' to make off with one's bitcoins, as happened to the CEO of a financial services company who left his account information in his car while having it valet parked, Maras (2015). At the exchange level, security loopholes may allow hackers to gain access to an exchange's hot wallet. The most famous case of such a hack is that of Mt Gox, one of the earliest and biggest bitcoin exchanges where US\$460 million worth of bitcoins were apparently 'stolen' by hackers, McMillan (2014a). More recently, roughly US\$72 million worth of bitcoins were 'stolen' by hackers from Bitfinex, an exchange based in Hong Kong. At least, they were worth US\$72 million before the hack. The price of bitcoins plunged on news of the hack, Tsang (2016). There are also security flaws at the network level though the threat here has mostly remained theoretical. Technically, if a person or more likely group of persons gains control of more than 50% of the total network hash power of the bitcoin network, they can invalidate transactions and/or double spend bitcoins from their own bitcoin addresses. Such an attack is unlikely to occur for a number of reasons. First, it is extremely expensive to amass sufficient computing power to launch such an attack. Secondly, such an attack will lead to widespread reluctance to accept bitcoins as payment, causing its value to plummet; a counterproductive effect for persons controlling sufficient nodes to launch such an attack as they are likely to hold a lot of bitcoins.[30] However, coding vulnerabilities in 'smart' contracts[31] that employ cryptocurrencies could also expose holders of cryptocurrencies to hacks such as that carried out against the DAO. It appears that the vaunted security of cryptocurrencies, through the use of cryptography, is limited to 'preventing double spending attacks or the forging of coins' (Kaminska, 2016b). This is confirmed on a careful reading of Satoshi Nakamoto's White Paper, the object of which was to 'propose a solution to the double-spending problem using a peer-to-peer distributed timestamp server to generate computational proof of the chronological order of transactions' (Nakamoto, 2008). The cryptographic protocols of the blockchain only promise to prevent double-spending. They provide *zero* protection from other forms of fraud, such as hacking, which is not only possible but commonplace. As the *Financial Times* reported, '[o]nline lists curated by bitcoin community members suggest bitcoin exchanges have been involved in up to 60 high-profile hacking incidents since the digital asset class was created in 2009. The true scale of the hacking problem, however, is hard to estimate' (Kaminska, 2016b). This is despite bitcoin's (and other cryptocurrencies) current miniscule scale in terms of transaction volume as compared to other payment services; Grossman et al. (2014). More generally, it has been observed that, '[o]n an almost daily basis it seems major companies with whom citizens share their precious financial data and identities have been hit by external and internal attackers. Many have simply not had adequate basic protection measures in place; others have been caught short by the ever-changing inventiveness of hackers with which they cannot keep pace,' The Cambridge Security Initiative (2016). Thus, 'while antivirus software preciously detected most malware, it now detects only a minority of it.' Online crime, leading computer security experts say, 'has taken off as a serious industry since about 2004' (Moore et al., 2009). According to these experts (Moore et al., 2009 and Wall, 2008):

> *In the old days, electronic fraud was largely a cottage industry, local and inefficient: a typical card fraudster ran a vertically-integrated small business. For example, he might buy a card-encoding machine, get a job in a shop where he could copy customers' cards, and then go out at night to steal cash from automatic teller machines (ATMs). . . .*
> *But now criminal networks have emerged – online black markets in which the bad guys trade with each other, with criminals taking on specialized roles (Thomas and Martin, 2006). Just as in Adam Smith's pin factory, specialization has led to impressive productivity gains, even though the subject is now bank card PINs rather*

than metal ones. [S]omeone who can collect bank card and PIN data or electronic banking passwords can sell them online to anonymous brokers at advertised rates of $0.40–$20.00 per card and $10–$100 per bank account (Symantec, 2008). The information needed to apply for credit in someone else's name, such as name, social security number, and birthday, fetches $1 to $15 per set. The brokers in turn sell the credentials to specialist cashiers who steal and then launder the money.

The Anti-Phishing Working Group, in its latest quarterly report, notes that the number of unique phishing websites detected per month rose from 48,114 in October 2015 to 123,555 in March 2016, a 250% increase over six months; the number of unique phishing e-mail reports increased from 99,384 in January 2016 to 229,265 in March 2016; and that there is an average of 227,000 new malware samples per day in the 4th Quarter of 2015, rising from an average of 225,000 per day a year ago.[32] While these statistics should be taken with a pinch of salt, as some members of the group have a vested interest in exaggerating the scale of the problem (Wall, 2008), there is a distinct upward trend in cases of online fraud and even experts alive to the difficulties with statistics from the security industry acknowledge that the frauds are increasing in sophistication, see also Moore et al. (2009). Fraudsters, it appears, are endlessly inventive. No system is immune from fraud. Often, they will target the weakest link in a system. As computer security expert, Bruce Schneier once remarked, 'Only amateurs attack machines; professionals target people,' Schneier (2000). In the case of bitcoins and other cryptocurrencies, running off blockchain technology, the weakest link will often be the end users (including cryptocurrency exchanges) rather than the integrity of their ledgers, which appear to remain largely secure. In 2014, Ciaran Martin, the Director General for Cyber Security at GCHQ observed that, apart from the threat from cybercrime, cyber risk in the financial sector can also arise from terrorism, a major conflict between states that draws in the UK, and a major accident or natural event; Martin (2014). Presumably, such attacks are aimed not so much at financial gain but at destabilizing the economy of the victim state. If holders of cryptocurrencies (fiat or otherwise) are not protected from hacking, then any economy that is dependent on such cryptocurrencies (presumably greater in the case of fiat cryptocurrencies) will be vulnerable to such exceptional attacks.

The increasing concern over cybercrime stands in marked contrast to the '[m]arked reductions [that] have been seen in property crime since peak levels in the 1990s' (Office for National Statistics, 2015). Some of the theories on why property crime has fallen include 'significant improvements in forensic and other crime scene investigation techniques and record keeping, such as fingerprinting and DNA testing' as well as 'changes (real or perceived) in technology such as CCTV,' both of which may have a deterrent effect as they are perceived to increase the likelihood of conviction (Office for National Statistics, 2015). By contrast, cyber criminals are, at least presently, at an advantage compared to the law enforcement agencies. '[O]nline crime usually crosses national boundaries. Existing mechanisms for international police co-operation are expensive and slow – designed to catch the occasional fugitive murderer, but not for dealing with millions of frauds at a cost of a few hundred dollars each.' Furthermore, whereas 'conventional crime is generally committed by marginal members of society,' cyber criminals 'tend to be educated and capable, but they live in societies with poor job prospects and ineffective policing' (Moore et al., 2009). Cybercrime, as with so much activity related to the Internet, is perceived by the criminals as being relatively anonymous.[33] It has even been suggested that another barrier to deterrence lies in 'the inability of key stakeholders in criminal justice systems to grasp fundamental aspects of technology aided crime.' Thus, although reports of serious cybercrime are escalating, there has not been a corresponding increase in conviction rates, 'with many investigations and prosecutions failing to get off the ground' (Brown, 2015).

It is against this factual backdrop that we must examine the legal risk that follows from holding cryptocurrency. The Bitfinex hack is instructive in terms of our study. As a lawyer explained to the *Financial Times*, 'With Bitfinex, user wallets were segregated. As a result, the relationship was seemingly more custodial in nature. In other words, the hack resulted in the theft of users' property.'[34] This particular *Financial Times* report is in equal parts tantalizing and frustrating. It drew an analogy to a thief stealing contents from users' safety deposit boxes rather than the contents of their bank accounts. Quoting the same unnamed lawyer, the report added, '[t]his matters because in the bank account situation, losses are necessarily socialized whereas socializing deposit box losses would be theft.' Whilst the result is mostly correct (losses are not always socialized)[35] *if* indeed the 'stolen' bitcoins were held on trust,[36] it fails to explain why the legal analysis would lead to a different result than the 'theft' of bank money from an ordinary bank account. A custodial relationship, in common law jurisdictions, would either take the form of a bailment or a trust. In the case of cryptocurrencies, which are incorporeal property if they are property at all, it would seem that this relationship cannot be explained as a bailment,[37] which leaves the trust analysis. If trust property is 'stolen,' then it is its beneficial owner that bears the loss, subject to possible claims against the trustee for breach of duty (in this case, a duty of care). The reason why money 'stolen' from a bank account is not treated this way is, as we have seen, that the statement of accounts does not represent the legal rights of the bank customers (or any rights at all). It is merely an imperfect record of the customers' rights. It is only upon withdrawal of the 'stolen' money that a cyber-theft is effective and the money so withdrawn belongs not to the customer but the bank. When a customer deposits money (in whatever form) with a bank, any legal rights to *that* money is transferred to the bank in exchange for an *in personam* claim against the bank. Account holders thus do not hold any property rights to any particular assets belonging to the bank. Rather, they all have *in personam* claims (debt claims) against the bank (reflected as its liabilities, not assets). As they do not hold any particular assets in the bank, nothing can be stolen from them in the conventional sense of the word.

Consider a bank with four customers: Alan, Beatrice, Charles and Diana. Just as Alan's account with the bank is merely a debt claim against it, the same is true of Beatrice, Charles and Diana. These accounts represent liabilities owing by the bank; they do not represent claims on any particular assets belonging to the bank. Hence, the bank is free to use the £50 deposited by Diana to repay Alan if his account has been hacked. This is because, upon deposit, the £50 belongs to the bank, not Diana. It is for this reason that a bank *may* (not must or will) socialize losses among account holders. It may not do so in two circumstances. First, depending on the terms of its banking contract and the circumstances surrounding a particular hack, a bank may try to transfer the loss to the particular customer, perhaps on the grounds of the customer's gross negligence. Secondly, provided its assets still exceed its liabilities, there is simply no cause to 'socialize' the loss. It is only in the event that the bank is insolvent and unable/unwilling to transfer the loss to the particular affected customer that the loss is 'socialized' or 'shared' with unaffected customers. This 'socialization' of loss is in effect the flipside of not having any legal interest *in* an asset belonging to the bank which can be stolen. While no particular asset held by the bank belongs to the customer, the customer runs the risk that the bank may become insolvent. While the risk of insolvency is minimized through banking regulation, including, inter alia, reserve ratios or capital requirements and deposit insurance,[38] it is not and cannot be eliminated.[39] Where an exchange 'holds' bitcoins for its customers in the way that a bank holds money for its account holders, the bitcoin holders are exposing themselves to the insolvency risks of the exchange. Interestingly, by preferring to socialize the losses, Bitfinex appears to have taken the view that this is the legal arrangement they had with their customers, contrary to the assessment of the lawyer quoted in the Financial Times.[40] Where, however, an exchange holds bitcoins in a custodial capacity, the bitcoin holders exchange the insolvency risk of the exchange for risk of loss/destruction of *their* bitcoins. If the exchange were to become insolvent, they can simply 'withdraw' *their* bitcoins without suffering any loss. Nevertheless, as we have already observed, it is not true that a customer of Bitfinex is entirely without remedy against Bitfinex even if their bitcoins were held on trust rather than simply owed to them. If it can be demonstrated that Bitfinex was negligent in its custody of the relevant bitcoins, it will be liable to its customers who suffered a loss through the hack. Whether it will have sufficient assets to reimburse these customers is, of course, an entirely different matter. This is because it must be recalled that if a trust analysis is correct, most if not all of the other bitcoins it holds will also likely belong beneficially to its other customers (whose wallets were not hacked). A direct holder of cryptocurrencies would be in a similar position to an account holder at Bitfinex whose account has been hacked. Indeed, this holder would be even more vulnerable (legally as a matter of risk) because there would simply be no entity at all to pursue a negligence claim against. If the loss was the result of careless-ness, it was the holder's own carelessness.

For such direct holders of cryptocurrencies, there are nevertheless a number of parties that it may wish to pursue, provided they can be identified. First, it is likely that any hack would in-volve acquiring the holder's private key. This would expose the hacker, provided he/she/they can be identified, to a claim for breach of confidence. Secondly, they may wish to trace their stolen bitcoins or other cryptocurrency in the hopes of recovering them or at least their value. With the passage of time, this party is unlikely to be the hacker. Whether this can be done will depend in part on the cryptocurrency concerned and in part on how the law chooses to re-spond to cryptocurrency as property. The traceability of subsequent holders of cryptocurrency will depend on the anonymity protocols of the particular cryptocurrency. Bitcoin, it should be remembered, is not completely anonymous but only pseudo-anonymous. While the identity of the address holder is not known, all transactions related to the address are in fact transparent and tracked in the blockchain. With the appropriate information, including publicly available information, it is possible to track some bitcoin transactions (Greenberg, 2015). It has been estimated that 'almost 40% of users can be, to a large extent, recovered even when users adopt privacy measures recommended by Bitcoin' (Androulaki et al., 2013). Some cryptocurrencies, such as darkcoin (Greenberg, 2014), are designed to offer far greater anonymity than bitcoin. This will make tracking 'stolen' darkcoins far more difficult than tracking 'stolen' bitcoins. Even assuming they are successfully tracked, holders face great uncertainty in terms of the protection that the law will afford them. At one extreme, though we consider this unlikely, es-pecially if cryptocurrencies achieve mainstream adoption, the law may adopt the attitude of the adherents to Ethereum Classic. In other words, the code is law and immutability means immutability. There is no known property law regime that operates in this fashion – to a prop-erty lawyer, this is indefeasibility on steroids. At the other extreme, the common-law courts could apply the principle of *nemo dat quod non habet*[41] strictly so that subsequent holders of the 'stolen' cryptocurrencies are liable to their 'true owners' for their value in an action em-ulating the tort of conversion that exists for corporeal money, regardless of whether they are bona fide purchasers of the same. This is possible because the key attribute of money in the legal system is its attribute of currency. This involves 'the creation of a fresh indefeasible title in a person who receives money as a bona fide purchaser for value' (Fox, 2008). By tempering the harsh *nemo dat* rule with such a robust defense, the law indirectly supports the economic function of money as a medium of exchange (Fox, 2008). Its applicability to cryptocurrencies may be doubted, and thus the harsh *nemo dat* rule may be applied in full (at least in some in-stances), for two reasons. First, 'the question whether the law should treat a certain kind of asset as money ... can only be answered by observing whether the community where it cir-culates treats it as such' (Fox, 2008). It is far from clear that bitcoin, to say nothing of all its competing cryptocurrencies, has come to be generally acceptable as a medium of exchange.

Secondly, even where a particular class of asset has acquired the attribute of currency, the bona fide purchase rule 'would not apply when money was transferred as a specific good or as a commodity' (Fox, 2008). Thus, in *Moss v Hancock*, a second-hand jewelry shop bought a stolen five-pound gold piece for five sovereigns. In determining whether the shop was liable to restore the coin, the court rejected the shop's invocation of the bona fide purchase defense because the gold piece had been sold to the shop as a dealer in curios rather than paid as money for goods or services. A significant segment of the cryptocurrency community treats bitcoins and similar cryptocurrencies as investments rather than as a medium of exchange. This explains in part the Chinese dominance of bitcoin computing power. As Bobby Lee, chief executive of BTCC, explained to *The New York Times*, 'For one thing, the Chinese government had strictly limited other potential investment avenues, giving citizens a hunger for new assets. Also, ... the Chinese loved the volatile price of Bitcoin, which gave the fledgling currency network the feeling of online gambling, a very popular activity in China' (Popper, 2016b). Such cryptocurrency investors may find that, even if some cryptocurrencies achieve the legal status of currency, they may not take advantage of the bona fide purchase rule that comes with that status. This means that, for pure investors in bitcoin, their investment carries the risk that they become liable to the 'true owners' of any 'stolen' bitcoin that they may acquire, even if they did so bona fide at full market price.

10.6 Conclusion

It is early days yet in the development and adoption of cryptocurrencies. While a number of central banks have expressed interest in cryptocurrencies, including fiat varieties of the same, their suitability for wide adoption and/or eventual replacement of either corporeal money or bank money is a matter that deserves closer reflection. Particularly disconcerting are the frequency of hacks of cryptocurrency exchanges and the lack of information of hacks at the level of individual holders. This is despite the fact that cryptocurrencies remain very much a niche product. It is thus difficult to estimate the scale of the problem should fiat cryptocurrencies be adopted, or worse mandated, as replacement for corporeal money. Presumably, the property status of fiat cryptocurrency will not then be in issue since Parliament can simply enact laws to confirm its status. However, differing in nature as it does from bank money, which many laypersons also regard as digital money, losses stemming from cybercrime in the form of hacking will hit individual holders particularly hard whereas hacks of bank accounts are typically borne by banks and spread to its other depositors in the form of fees and bank charges. Mandatory fiat cryptocurrencies will provide an opportunity for large scale lucrative fraud. The risk of loss through 'ownership' of what may be the first true form of digital money would also be difficult to guard against because unlike theft of corporeal money, cyber theft is an unbounded crime and there is no requirement of physical proximity between perpetrator and victim. Cybercrime not only removes the need for proximity between perpetrator and victim, the nature of the Internet gives perpetrators a far wider reach. Whilst there are only so many burglaries a skilled burglar can commit in any given time, automation allows the perpetrator of a cybercrime to reach a significantly greater number of victims so that relatively few offenders can reach a very large number of victims in a very short amount of time (Wall, 2008). Not only is there likely to be an explosion of cybertheft, considering current trends in cybercrime,[42] it is likely that the elderly are likely to be disproportionately exposed to such losses from a switch to cryptocurrency. This is unsurprising since they are likely to have the most wealth whilst at the same time being among the least tech savvy of all users (Carlson, 2007). This means that any central bank which is serious about issuing fiat cryptocurrency must consider seriously the problem of cybersecurity at the individual user level (a problem that may well prove intractable) or instituting some form of insurance for loss through hacking, or both. It must also seriously consider phasing in any cryptocurrency whilst maintaining the continued use of coins and banknotes, though this will somewhat diminish the appeal of cryptocurrencies as a tool for the easy application of negative interest rates as compared to corporeal money.[43] Perhaps even more importantly, the relevant officials looking into developing fiat cryptocurrencies should beware the hype surrounding the blockchain technology that underpins bitcoins and other cryptocurrencies. While promoters vigorously proclaim the security of ledgers operated using the blockchain, they often fail to mention that the blockchain's system of cryptographic proof is directed *exclusively* towards the problem of double spending. The blockchain technology provides *zero* protection against any other kinds of fraud. In other words, the blockchain protects the network from user fraud but does not protect users from other frauds. However, unless such other frauds are suitably addressed, presumably through the use of other technological innovations, the issue of fiat cryptocurrency must be regarded as extremely foolhardy. In the meantime, the only proper advice for persons looking to invest in/use private cryptocurrencies must surely be *caveat emptor*.

References

Allison, Chelsea, 2016. Anatomy of a bank heist. Fin. https://fin.plaid.com/articles/anatomy-of-a-bank-heist. 2 June 2016.

Androulaki, Elli, Karame Ghassan, O., Roeschlin, Marc, Scherer, Tobias, Capkun, Srdjan, 2013. Evaluating user privacy in bitcoin. In: Sadeghi, Ahmad-Reza (Ed.), Financial Cryptography and Data Security, p. 34.

Baldwin, Clare, 2016. Bitfinex exchange customers to get 36 percent haircut, debt token. Reuters. http://www.reuters.com/article/us-bitfinex-hacked-hongkong-idUSKCN10I06H. 6 August 2016.

Barrdear, John, Kumhof, Michael, 2016. Staff working paper No. 605: the macroeconomics of Central Bank issued digital currencies. http://www.bankofengland.co.uk/research/Pages/workingpapers/2016/swp605.aspx. 18 July 2016.

Becker, Ingolf, et al., 2016. International comparison of bank fraud reimbursement: customer perceptions and contractual terms. In: Workshop on the Economics of Information Security (WEIS). 13–14 June 2016, Berkeley, CA, USA.

Birks, Peter, 2000. English Private Law, vol. 1. OUP.

Blackstone, William, 1765. Commentaries on the Laws of England Volume 2 of the Rights of Things. Clarendon Press 1765–69, p. 442.

Bohm, Nicholas, et al., 2000. Electronic commerce: who carries the risk of fraud? Journal of Information, Law and Technology 3. https://www2.warwick.ac.uk/fac/soc/law/elj/jilt/2000_3/bohm/.

Brignall, Miles, 2015. So you think you're safe doing internet banking? The Guardian. https://www.theguardian.com/money/2015/nov/21/safe-internet-banking-cyber-security-online. 21 November 2015.

Brown, Cameron S.D., 2015. Investigating and prosecuting cyber crime: forensic dependencies and barriers to justice. International Journal of Cyber Criminology 9, 55, 56.

Burda, Michael, Wypolz, Charles, 2013. Macroeconomics: a European Text, 6th edn. Oxford.

Calomiris, Charles W., 2014. Bank failures, the great depression, and other "contagious" events. In: Berger, Allen N., Molyneux, Philip, Wilson, John O.S. (Eds.), The Oxford Handbook of Banking, 2nd edn., p. 721.

Carlson, Eric L., 2007. Phishing for elderly victims: as the elderly migrate to the internet fraudulent schemes targeting them follow. The Elder Law Journal 14.

Chawki, Mohamed, et al., 2015. Anonymity, privacy and security issues in cyberworld. In: Cybercrime, Digital Forensics and Jurisdiction (Chap 7).

Cutts, Tatiana, Goldstone, David Q.C., 2015. Bitcoin ownership and its impact on fungibility. Coindesk. http://www.coindesk.com/bitcoin-ownership-impact-fungibility/. 14 June 2015.

Devnath, Arun, 2016. Printer error triggered Bangladesh race to halt cyber heist. Bloomberg News. http://www.bloomberg.com/news/articles/2016-03-16/printer-error-set-off-bangladesh-race-to-halt-illicit-transfers. 16 March 2016.

Douglas, Simon, McFarlane, Ben, 2013. Defining property rights. In: Penner, James, Smith, Henry E. (Eds.), Philosophical Foundations of Property Law, p. 219.

Editorial, 2015. The case for retiring another 'barbarous relic'. Financial Times. 24 August 2015.

Ellinger, E.P., Lomnicka, E., Hare, C.V.M., 2011. Ellinger's Modern Banking Law, 5th edn. OUP.

Finley, Klint, 2016. A $50 million hack just showed that the DAO was all too human. The Wired. http://www.wired.com/2016/06/50-million-hack-just-showed-dao-human/. 18 June 2016.

Fox, David, 2008. Property Rights in Money.

Green, Sarah, 2012. Conversion and theft – tangibly different? (2012) 128 LQR 564.

Greenberg, Andy, 2014. Darkcoin, the shadowy cousin of bitcoin, is booming. Wired. 21 May 2014.

Greenberg, Andy, 2015. Prosecutors trace $13.4m in bitcoins from the silk road to Ulbricht's Laptop. Wired. 29 January 2015.

Grossman, Robert, Mitropoulos, Atanasios, Boise, Jonathan, 2014. Sizing up bitcoin. The Why? Forum. http://thewhyforum.com/articles/sizing-up-bitcoin. 2 April 2014.

Haldane, Andrew, 2015. How low can you go? http://www.bankofengland.co.uk/publications/Documents/speeches/2015/speech840.pdf. 18 September 2015.

Higgins, Stan, 2016. China's Central Bank discusses digital currency launch. CoinDesk, 20 January 2016. http://www.coindesk.com/peoples-bank-of-china-discusses-plans-to-issue-digital-currency/. Accessed: 1 August 2016.

Hooley, Richard, 1998. Payment in a cashless society. In: Rider, Barry AK (Ed.), The Realm of Company Law: A Collection of Papers in Honour of Professor Leonard Sealy, p. 233.

Kaminska, Izabella, 2016a. Bitcoin: identity crisis. Financial Times. 7 May 2016.

Kaminska, Izabella, 2016b. Bitcoin Bitfinex exchange hacked: the unanswered questions. Financial Times. https://next.ft.com/content/1ea8baf8-5a11-11e6-8d05-4eaa66292c32. 4 August 2016.

Kaminska, Izabella, 2016c. Legal tussle looms for bitcoin holders in hacked Bitfinex. Financial Times. https://next.ft.com/content/c3b9f89c-5b18-11e6-9f70-badea1b336d4. 5 August 2016.

Koning, J.P., 2015. Sweden and peak cash. Moneyness: the blog of JP Koning. 26 February 2015.

Kreltszheim, David, 2003. The legal nature of "electronic money". 14 JBFLP 161, 261.

Kroll, Joshua A., Davey, Ian C., Felten, Edward W., 2013. The economics of bitcoin mining, or bitcoin in the presence of adversaries. In: The Twelfth Workshop on the Economics of Information Security, pp. 11–12.

Levine, Matt, 2016. Blockchain company's smart contracts were dumb. Bloomberg. http://www.bloomberg.com/view/articles/2016-06-17/blockchain-company-s-smart-contracts-were-dumb. 17 June 2016.

Levy, Steven, 1994. E-money (that's what I want). The Wired. http://www.wired.com/1994/12/emoney/. 1 December 1994.

Low, Kelvin F.K., Lin, Jolene, 2015. Carbon credits as EU like it: property, immunity, tragiCO$_2$medy? Journal of Environmental Law 27.

Low, Kelvin F.K., Llewelyn, David, 2016. Digital files as property in the New Zealand Supreme Court: innovation or confusion? Law Quarterly Review 132, 394. 396.

Maras, Elliot, 2015. Researcher has bitcoin stolen off his back in a public experiment. Crypto Coins News. https://www.cryptocoinsnews.com/researcher-bitcoin-stolen-off-back-public-experiment/. 11 November 2015, Accessed: 17 March 2016.

Martin, Ciaran, 2014. Speech at the Financial Services Summit 2014. https://www.gchq.gov.uk/speech/director-general-cyber-security-gchq-speaks-financial-services-summit-2014. 15 July 2014.

McMillan, Robert, 2014a. The inside story of Mt Gox, bitcoin's $460 million disaster. Wired. 3 March 2014.

McMillan, Robert, 2014b. Why bitcoin doesn't want a real Satoshi Nakamoto. The Wired. 7 March 2014.

Metz, Cade, 2016. The biggest crowdfunding project ever – the DAO – is kind of a mess. The Wired. http://www.wired.com/2016/06/biggest-crowdfunding-project-ever-dao-mess/. 6 June 2016.

Moore, Tyler, Clayton, Richard, Anderson, Ross, 2009. The economics of online crime. Journal of Economic Perspectives 23.

Nakamoto, Satoshi, 2008. Bitcoin: a peer-to-peer electronic cash system. https://bitcoin.org/bitcoin.pdf. Accessed: 14 March 2016.

National Fraud Intelligence Bureau and City of London Police, 2016. Cyber Crime – Victimology Analysis. https://www.cityoflondon.police.uk/news-and-appeals/Documents/Victimology%20Analysis-latest.pdf.

O'Hagan, Andrew, 2016. The Satoshi affair. London Review of Books. 30 June 2016.

Office for National Statistics, 2015. Statistical Bulletin, Focus on Property Crime: 2014–2015, '5. Existing Theories on Why Property Crime Has Fallen'. http://www.ons.gov.uk/peoplepopulationandcommunity/crimeandjustice/bulletins/focusonpropertycrime/2014to2015. 26 November 2015.

Popper, Nathaniel, 2016a. Ethereum, a virtual currency, enables transactions that rival bitcoin's. The New York Times. http://www.nytimes.com/2016/03/28/business/dealbook/ethereum-a-virtual-currency-enables-transactions-that-rival-bitcoins.html. 27 March 2016.

Popper, Nathaniel, 2016b. How China took centre stage in bitcoin's civil war. The New York Times. http://www.nytimes.com/2016/07/03/business/dealbook/bitcoin-china.html. 29 June 2016.

Quadir, Serajul, 2016. How a hacker's typo helped stop a billion dollar bank heist. Reuters. http://www.reuters.com/article/us-usa-fed-bangladesh-typo-insight-idUSKCN0WC0TC. 10 March 2016.

Quentson, Andrew, 2016. Ethereum reaches unanimous agreement to hardfork. Crypto Coins News. https://www.cryptocoinsnews.com/ethereum-reaches-unanimous-agreement-hardfork/. 8 July 2016.

Pitta, Julie, 1999. Requiem for a bright idea. Forbes. http://www.forbes.com/forbes/1999/1101/6411390a.html. 1 November 1999.

Sandbh, Martin, 2016. Free lunch: electronic money is a public good. Financial Times. 26 July 2016.

Schneier, Bruce, 2000. Semantic attacks: the third wave of network attacks. Crypto-Gram. https://www.schneier.com/crypto-gram/archives/2000/1015.html#1. 15 October 2000.

Simester, A.P., Sullivan, G.R., 2005. On the nature and rationale of property offences. In: Duff, R.A., Green, Stuart P. (Eds.), Defining Crimes: Essays on the Special Part of the Criminal Law, p. 168.

Sindreu, Jon, 2016. The central bankers' bold new idea: print bitcoins. The Wall Street Journal. 19 July 2016.

Spafford, Eugene H., 1989. In: AK Dewdney, "Computer Recreations: Of Worms, Viruses and Core War". Scientific American 110. March 1989.

Stafford, Philip, 2016. Canada experiments with digital dollar on Blockchain. Financial Times. 17 June 2016.

Swadling, William, 2000. Property: general principles. In: Birks, Peter (Ed.), English Private Law Volume I. OUP [4.52].

Swadling, William, 2013. Property: general principles. In: Burrows, Andrew (Ed.), English Private Law, 3rd edn. OUP [4.03].

The Cambridge Security Initiative, 2016. Cash is King – The Digital Revolution: The Future of Cash.

Torpey, Kyle, 2016. Ethereum experts debate merits of two ethereum chains. Bitcoin Magazine. https://bitcoinmagazine.com/articles/ethereum-experts-debate-merits-of-two-ethereum-chains-1470432064. 5 August 2016.

Tsang, Amie, 2016. Bitcoin plunges after hacking of exchange in Hong Kong. The New York Times. 3 August 2016.

Tyree, Alan L., 1999. The legal nature of electronic money, 10 JBFLP 273.

van Wirdum, Aaron, 2016. Rejecting today's hard fork, the Ethereum classic project continues on the original chain: here's why. Bitcoin Magazine. https://bitcoinmagazine.com/articles/rejecting-today-s-hard-fork-the-ethereum-classic-project-continues-on-the-original-chain-here-s-why-1469038808. 20 July 2016.

Wall, David S., 2008. Cybercrime, media and insecurity: the shaping of public perceptions of cybercrime. International Review of Law Computers & Technology 22.

Wong, Joon Ian, Kar, Ian, 2016. Everything you need to know about the Ethereum 'Hard Fork'. Quartz. http://qz.com/730004/everything-you-need-to-know-about-the-ethereum-hard-fork/. 18 July 2016.

Zetter, Kim, 2016. That insane, $81m Bangladesh bank heist? Here's what we know. The Wired. https://www.wired.com/2016/05/insane-81m-bangladesh-bank-heist-heres-know/. 17 May 2016.

Notes

1. The Bank of England is not alone in exploring such an initiative. See also Stafford (2016) and Higgins (2016).

2. The true identity of Satoshi Nakamoto has been much speculated but remains unknown. See, for example, McMillan (2014b), Kaminska (2016a) and O'Hagan (2016).

3. This decision is in very large part the result of the availability of an excellent modern treatise examining money from the perspective of English private law by Fox (2008). While some or even most of our analysis may apply to other legal systems, particularly common law systems derived from English law, the jurisdictional nature of law as a discipline means that there will inevitably be variations in analysis.

4. The definition of tender is irrelevant for our purposes. Readers who are interested should refer to Fox (2008).

5. Coinage Act 1971, ss 2, 6 and 7.

6. Chose being French for thing.

7. See The Cambridge Security Initiative (2016). According to the Chief Cashier of the Bank of England, 'Cash is now used in 52% of UK transactions.' (at 5) This is a measure of volume, not value.

8. This is the generic expression coined by David Fox comparable to the expression 'bank money' found in economic writings (Fox, 2008).

9. Our forthcoming paper, "Bitcoins as Property?", considers both this question and the question of how cryptocurrencies would conceivably fit within a broadly defined property regime.

10. The late Professor Birks attempts to salvage the Roman classificatory system by suggesting that it is perhaps exhaustive of 'rights realizable in court.' Birks opines, at xxxix: "Thus the right to bodily integrity is protected through the torts which are committed against the body, and the right to reputation is protected by the torts of defamation. Such primary rights are 'superstructural' in that they provide the superstructure over the wrong:

every wrong is the infringement of a primary right." However, this cannot be correct. Superstructural rights are realizable in court through the grant of an injunction protecting the primary right.

11. Ignoring for present purposes the token right, almost never exercised, by a holder to compel the issuing bank of a banknote by action to pay him or her an equivalent value of notes of a smaller denomination.

12. *Foley v Hill* (1848) HLC 28.

13. While this may be inconsistent with the wider definition of property earlier proposed, the Roman classification is better suited to our understanding of risk arising out of the differing nature of the rights.

14. *Stuart v Kingston* (1923) 32 CLR 309, 359.

15. Chapter 35.

16. The Law Commission Report on Fraud 2002 (Law Comm 276), 3.

17. Despite s 4(1) of the Theft Act 1968 defining property broadly as including "money and all other property, real or personal, including things in action and other intangible property," it remains a matter of some controversy whether an *in personam* right itself should be regarded as capable of being the subject-matter of theft. See, for example, Simester and Sullivan (2005), *Contra* Green (2012).

18. The nature of banknotes in their original form is complicated and would be distracting for our purposes. They fall within a category of property called 'documentary intangibles,' a name that reveals the tensions and contradictions within this concept.

19. 'A payment instruction may become irrevocable before the point is reached where a payment to the beneficiary becomes complete. There may be a hiatus during which neither the originator nor the beneficiary has a complete title to the money which is being transferred between them. This marks a significant difference from payments made by the physical delivery of corporeal money where the transfer of title from the payer and to the recipient happens simultaneously. It is a consequence of the fact that a payment of incorporeal money is always made through a bank acting as intermediary between the parties to the payment transaction, and of the distinct identity of the choices in action by which the money is represented' (Fox, 2008).

20. 'It turns out that the four-day lapse before the fraud was uncovered was plenty of time for $81 million to be transferred from the Bangladesh Bank account at the New York Fed to Wells Fargo Mellon Bank, Citibank, and Bank of New York, to Rizal Commercial Banking Corporation's Settlement Division, to bank accounts for a Chinese businessman at a local branch at RCBC, and then on to casinos in the Philippines,' Allison (2016). It should be noted that even so, of the $81m, some $68,305 funds that had not been withdrawn were eventually put on hold, Devnath (2016).

21. Cf. 'Banks choose not to advertise the number of electronic attacks taking place on their systems but instead prefer to pay back the lost amount and then raise the general service charges': The Cambridge Security Initiative (2016).

22. 'Banking: Conduct of Business Sourcebook' (Release 9: August 2016), paras 5.1.11–5.1.12. The 'Banking: Conduct of Business Sourcebook' replaces 'The Banking Code: Setting Standards for Banks, Building Societies and Other Banking Service Providers' (March 2005), paras. 12.5, 12.9, 12.11–12.12, 12.14–12.16. See also Becker et al. (2016).

23. Reg. 2(1) of The Electronic Money Regulations 2011 (SI 2011/99) defines 'electronic money' as 'electronically (including magnetically) stored monetary value as represented by a claim on the electronic money issuer …'

24. Reg 3 of The Electronic Money Regulations 2011 (SI 2011/99) sets out exclusions.

25. See reg 19 of The Electronic Money Regulations 2011 (SI 2011/99).

26. Cf. Hooley (1998), Tyree (1999), Kreltszheim (2003).

27. *Victoria Park Racing and Recreation Grounds Co. Ltd. v Taylor* (1937) 58 CLR 479.

28. This is not strictly speaking true. They are not unilaterally irreversible but a payee can always repay a payor. This is not technically a reversal in the sense of erasing the initial transfer but it is in substance a reversal through the addition of a further transaction in reverse.

29. It is possible to classify intellectual property as *in rem* rights if one does not insist on a strict requirement of a *res* (thing) that is separable from the legal right. Compare Swadling (2013) with Swadling (2000), cf. Douglas and McFarlane (2013).

30. See Kroll et al. (2013).

31. 'Smart' contracts are not really smart in the sense that artificial intelligence is smart. They are simply the digital world's equivalent of vending machines and are perhaps more accurately labeled called 'automated' contracts. The manner of their automation is entirely dependent on human coding and therefore a smart contract is as dumb as its code: Levine (2016).

32. APWG Phishing Activity Trends Report, 1st Quarter 2016 (published 23 May 2016).

33. QC, Marr and Parker (2015). See also (Chawki et al., 2015). Strictly speaking, this is not so much anonymity but the lack of resources available to follow the digital trail: see Wall (2008). In relation to bitcoin, see Greenberg (2015).

34. Kaminska (2016c) *Contra* Baldwin (2016).

35. Cases involving gross negligence on the part of the customer are not socialized. Consider the scenarios derived from decisions of the UK Financial Ombudsman chosen by the authors of this international comparative report on bank fraud reimbursement (Becker et al., 2016).

36. Segregation and non-segregation are merely indicators of the legal relationship (in this case, trust or personal obligation) between the exchange and its customers. The correct classification will always turn on a careful examination of the contract between the parties. Cf. Baldwin (2016).

37. Norman Palmer et al., *Palmer on Bailment* (3rd edn., 2009), 1-006. But see Chap 30.

38. Section 213 of the Financial Services and Markets Act 2000 (c 8) requires the Financial Services Authority to set up a Financial Services Compensation Scheme.

39. See, for example, Calomiris, 2014.

40. See Baldwin (2016). If its assessment of the legal effect of its arrangement with its customers is wrong, then Bitfinex is exposing itself to lawsuits from customers whose wallets were *not* hacked.

41. No one gives what he does not have.

42. Carlson, 2007. See also National Fraud Intelligence Bureau and City of London Police, 2016.

43. It is notable that one of the earliest mentions of cryptocurrencies, specifically bitcoins, by a Bank of England official was that by Andrew Haldane, the Chief Economist, as a speech given at the Portadown Chamber of Commerce, Northern Ireland (Haldane, 2015).

CHAPTER 11

InsurTec15h and FinTech: Banking and Insurance Enablement

Tan Choon Yan, Paul Schulte, David LEE Kuo Chuen

Contents

11.1 Introduction

This chapter surveys the landscape of insurance technology and its potential from the perspective of enablement for financial and insurance services (Schulte, 2015; Tan, 2016). Digital revolution is occurring in a sector that has hardly changed over the last 300 years. Surprising to many, recent innovation in China's digital finance space has shown that emerging entities can and will disrupt the multitrillion-dollar industry. With big data and Blockchain, the impact on insurance sector is going to be a lot faster and more significant than most people will anticipate.

The lack of innovation in the product space of insurance sector and the failure to cater to market needs have created a situation of disappointing experience for many. With advancement in technology, it is now known that "The person is now the product" in the insurance space. By that, it means that InsurTech, a shorter technical name for Insurance Technology, offers individual, bespoke, customized solutions to life risks using data analytics, sensors, wearables and cell phone data in ways that were impossible only a few years ago. It is conjectured that agent-like insurance brokers may disappear slowly, then suddenly, as in insurance disruption that we have seen so far in China.

11.2 InsurTech Activities

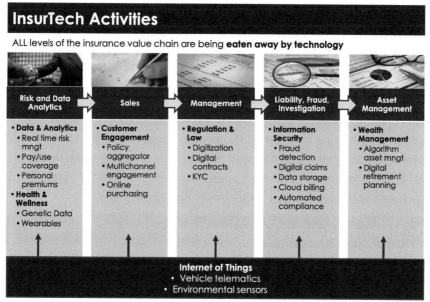

Source: CB Insights, Schulte Research

There are two main reasons for the lack of innovation in the insurance sector. The first is the complexity and the heavily regulated nature of the industry. The second is the profitability of incumbents that provides few incentives to change. There is simply no reason for any change to take place within the organization or the industry while it is doing well and plain sailing. But that may have changed recently (Schulte, 2015).

Despite few innovations, new products are constantly introduced to the market created with new hardware, software and techniques. While new, it is not innovative nor productive with characteristics of inflated prices, more confusing consumer experience and poor claims processes. These new products lack the application of technology to address the long list of problems that the insurance companies face. It is hardly surprising that there is no improvement in user experience.

What is Insurtech? It is the application of technology to address the long list of problems currently facing insurance industry. In customer engagement, it involves the use of technology to improve CRM, price aggregation, Omni channel acquisition, Digital Claims Process and online policy purchasing. For IoT, technology can assist insurers in new revenue areas by using vehicle telematics, environmental sensors, provenance, asset trading and home security. For the health industry, wearables, genetic data, chronic conditional management and preventive healthcare can alter the way insurance services their clients. As for information security, technology can be used in areas such as claims fraud detection, cyber breach insurance, risk management and personal data storage. Using data analytics, insurers can engage in real time risk mitigation, pay per use insurance, dynamic underwriting and personalized premium. Wealth management is another area that can employ algorithm asset management, digital saving plans and pension management. Finally, in the space of regulation and the law, digital smart contracts, KYC identity verification and automatic compliance processes will lower operating costs.

Insurers need to rethink their business models to meet changing consumer demand and switch from product centric to customer centric by leveraging on technology such as big data, analytics, AI and IoT. According to report by Capgemini (Capgemini, 2015), the global customer experience level has dropped nearly 4% with 10 countries dropping more than 5 percentage points in 2014. There was a rebound in consumer experience in 2015 (Capgemini, 2016) but positive experience levels lag for Gen Y customers across the globe.

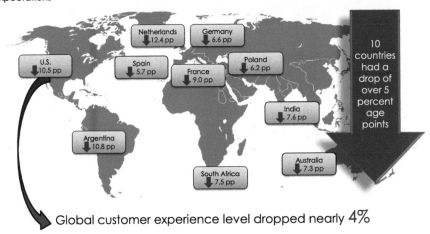

Declining Customer Experience

Customer experience declined globally, indicating insurers are not keeping pace with rising expectations

Global customer experience level dropped nearly 4%

Source: Capgemini, Schulte Research (2014)

There is a massive change in behavior especially from the young with nearly a quarter of millennials likely to buy insurance from technology firms. According to KPMG, only 6% of surveyed insurers have their strategy focusing on "wholly new" products, with 31% focusing on enhancing existing products and services. New distribution and introduction of new products were cited by only 29% and 18% of executives respectively, the latter down from 39% in 2013 (KPMG, 2014). Most of the insurers are focusing on sustaining business rather than focusing on digital disruptive innovation. Eighty-three percent of insurers see the Internet of Things bringing about complete transformation or significant change in the industry

(Accenture, 2016). Less than half of the surveyed insurers target IoT as an important growth opportunity in another survey.

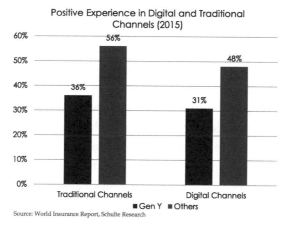

Source: World Insurance Report, Schulte Research

In fact, as described in Schulte (2015), the six areas to succeed in digital era are:

1. Strategy
2. Digitize Business Processes
3. Organize for Digital
4. Digital Analytics and Decision Making
5. Customer-centricity
6. Technology

Six Areas to Succeed in Digital Era

1. Strategy
Imagine processes from a zero base; reduce costs and errors; boost customer satisfaction

2. Digitize Business Processes
Corporate culture of digital excellence (talent + organization)

3. Organize for Digital
Internal and external real-time data mined from actionable insight

The Digital Insurer

4. Digital Analytics & Decision Making
Adapts to rapid industry change while supporting overall business aspirations

5. Customer-Centricity
Improve customer experience

6. Technology
Two-speed IT allows for digital development and safely maintained systems

Source: Mckinsey, Schulte Research

11.3 The 4 Most Disruptive Technology

InsurTech allows continuous interaction between insurers and customers so that insurers can encourage customers to reduce their risk. With Internet of Things, activity trackers encourage customers to exercise and then offering reduced premiums when they hit health goals. The driving trackers provide immediate feedback and automatic "on-demand" change to insurance cover based on the data collected by the trackers. Adding on data analytics, insurers can better target underwriting and tailor premiums to specific needs. These are made possible by natural language processing, deep learning, and machine learning that allow for sophisticated modeling and analytics to generate risk profiles and insights. The new technology Blockchain can provide transparent, responsive and irrefutable claims management process. With smart contracts, publicly known data automatically trigger policy claim, thereby reducing claims processing costs and disputes. Finally, P2P insurance allows family and friends to form groups of policyholders online. Those groups with low claims gain discount on policy premiums thereby minimizing moral hazard issues that are common in the industry.

Internet of Things is Neglected by Insurers

Less than half of insurers surveyed by Accenture target "Internet of Things" (IoT) as an important growth opportunity

 44% Insurers who rank connected devices as a "Top 5" priority to drive revenue growth in the next 3 years

 46% Those who have launched/tested personalized and real-time digital services

 30% Carriers who include products based on the "Internet of Things" among their top investment priorities

Source: Accenture, Schulte Research

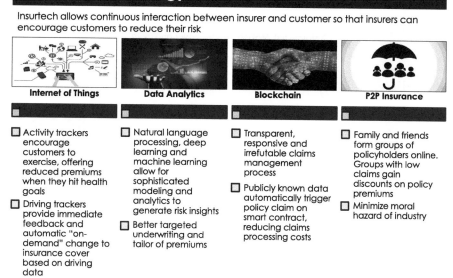

The Big 4 Technology

Insurtech allows continuous interaction between insurer and customer so that insurers can encourage customers to reduce their risk

Internet of Things	Data Analytics	Blockchain	P2P Insurance
☐ Activity trackers encourage customers to exercise, offering reduced premiums when they hit health goals ☐ Driving trackers provide immediate feedback and automatic "on-demand" change to insurance cover based on driving data	☐ Natural language processing, deep learning and machine learning allow for sophisticated modeling and analytics to generate risk insights ☐ Better targeted underwriting and tailor of premiums	☐ Transparent, responsive and irrefutable claims management process ☐ Publicly known data automatically trigger policy claim on smart contract, reducing claims processing costs	☐ Family and friends form groups of policyholders online. Groups with low claims gain discounts on policy premiums ☐ Minimize moral hazard of industry

Source:, Schulte Research

11.4 The 3 Fundamental Trends

There are likely to be three clear trends: Personalization, Connectivity and Simplification. Services will become more personalized made easy by technology. Services provided will be more relevant to the customers making customers' needs the main focus. With APIs, IoTs and Telematics and connectivity inclusion, anyone or anything is able to interact, trade or exchange information anywhere and anytime. Blockchain will enable simplification with transparency of processes thereby reducing complexity.

Three Fundamental Trends

Personalization
- Customer first. Making services easier and more relevant for the user
- Technologies: **Big Data**, Cognitive Computing, Machine Learning

Connectivity
- Anyone or anything is able to interact, trade or exchange information anywhere and anytime
- Technologies: APIs, **Internet of Things**, **Telematics**

Simplification
- Technologies and processes that reduce complexity
- Technologies: **Blockchain**

Source: Insly,, Schulte Research

11.5 Benefits of InsurTech

Technology allows insurers to gain insight on changing consumer behavior and creates new, personalized and on-demand coverage of risks. The use of Blockchain smart contract, AIs, autonomous transportation, cyber security can protect consumer identity and allow for new coverage of risks. Given that consumers are always connected, they can always be insured on demand with personalized coverage with IoT, data analysis and mobile innovation. With the emerging sharing economy, such as Airbnb and Uber, different participating agents can leverage and scale on each other's expertise to anticipate changing consumer behavior. As a result, additional on-demand services that were not previously anticipated can be met, made convenient by the use of smart devices.

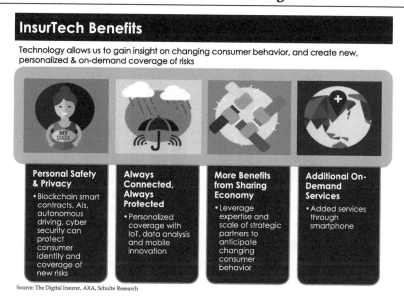

Source: The Digital Insurer, AXA, Schulte Research

11.6 InsurTech Deal Activities

Funding for Insurtech amounted to $2.65nm in 2015 from $740mn in 2014 with an increase of 45% in the number of deals in the US. US Insurtech deal flow has seen more activity in non-health insurance related startups. Globally, in Q1 206, 60% of deals are in the US and 53% of deals at deed-stage.

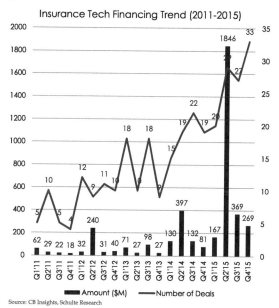

Source: CB Insights, Schulte Research

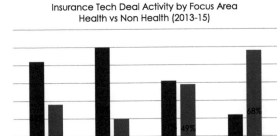

Insurance Tech Deal Activity by Focus Area
Health vs Non Health (2013-15)

38%   30%   49%   68%

2013   2014   2015   Q1 2016

■ Health insurance tech   ■ Non-health insurance tech

Source: CB Insights, Schulte Research

InsurTech Deals by Insurance Companies

Strategic tech investments by corporate insurance investors grew 43% YoY in 2015. Wide majority of investments **have NOT gone** to insurance tech startups

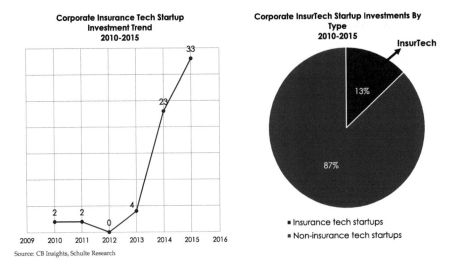

Corporate Insurance Tech Startup
Investment Trend
2010-2015

Corporate InsurTech Startup Investments By
Type
2010-2015

InsurTech

13%

87%

■ Insurance tech startups
■ Non-insurance tech startups

Source: CB Insights, Schulte Research

11.7 From FinTech to InsurTech: Mobile Revolution

Finance is brewing a new wave of entrepreneurial people using technology to hyper grow and scale their startups. This industry has always been seen as highly sensitive, highly technical and highly regulated industry dominated by several mega-banks. What have changed? Computing and telecommunications have made the world far more connected today than a decade ago. Ingredients to build tech startups are available: cheaper computing, powerful analytics, low interest capital and frustrated talented individuals who prefer to do something other than toiling inside the banking corporations. People are also more receptive to dealing with their financial assets in both personal and business ways. This is perhaps due to the rise of number of smartphones.

Mobile is changing how people work, travel, read, communicate, shop and many other lifestyle behaviors. In the Internet Trends 2015 report by KPCB (Mary Meeker, 2016), mobile engagement is better than ever, with three hours of time per day spent on mobile devices in 2015 compared to an hour per day five years ago (a 300-percent increase). Adding to this, there was 69 percent and 23 percent annual worldwide growth in mobile data traffic and smartphone subscribers (2.1 billion) in 2014, respectively.

It is no surprising. Hip and young consumers are already soaked in the world of emerging service landscapes through mobile. Near-magical push-button on-demand services like Grab and Airbnb have provided a new form of consumer empowerment and increased expectations. As the millennials move on to their first jobs, they are going to expect the same or something better, from setting up accounts to getting their first investment and credit card.

Because of the legacy banking infrastructure that dates back to the 1970s, it is not an easy feat for current brick-and-mortar banks to introduce a new stack of technology to improve experiences. Apps on smartphones have made consumers' lives better, but current banking apps have failed to catch up to them.

Despite banks in all major developed markets providing mobile options, there is a new wave of emerging startups building digital, mobile and online-only banks from scratch. It makes sense when you imagine the man-hours lost to handling paperwork to open an account or apply for a loan, the exorbitant fees for using your credit card abroad, having onerous overdraft charges and non-responsive mobile apps that can only transfer money and check balances.

The idea behind these mobile banking startups is to influence how retail banking works in the 21st century by eliminating the extra costs of running physical branch operations and maintenance of legacy infrastructure, and passing on the savings to share with their digital-savvy consumers. There are several unique selling points offered by mobile banking, and it presents many amazing opportunities.

11.8 Mobile First

London's office rental prices can be exorbitant. Tandem, the second digital-only bank to be licensed by the Bank of England this year, understands that physical infrastructure costs can be reduced. Instead of opening retail stores, it utilizes call centers to help consumers go through the bigger transactions and still preserve a service-oriented experience.

A common trait among these mobile banks are slick and beautiful app interfaces to open accounts and manage various financial activities. The Danish firm Lunar Way decided to take this up a notch by partnering with local banks for regulatory strengths, so as to focus on technology and user experiences.

11.9 Cross-Sell and Up-Sell

A look at the fees section on a traditional banking account page spells out lots of complex situations that will cost consumers. In contrast, banks should provide value first – account holders can be monetized, in the long run, with other financial products, but not on a per-transaction basis. For example, Monese, allows new arrivals to have a current account in the U.K. regardless of citizenship and to hold multiple currency balances, which help to avoid foreign exchange fees for trips. Leveraging this, it attacks the segment on international remittances, which is 10 times cheaper than traditional bank offerings.

Another instance is Mondo, valued at $43 million before launch. Mondo understands the power of context in helping their consumers. The startup recognizes consumers might need to borrow when their balance is low. Loans can be communicated to consumers in real time through instant messaging, just before they overdraft. It is no surprise; their experienced team members were the former heads at Allied Irish Bank and Mizuho International.

11.10 Virtual Financial Advisor

Don't you feel like having an intelligent Siri as a financial advisor instead of one that keeps pestering you to buy irrelevant financial products? Mobile banks are evolving to make money work for you through their platforms (minus the voice, for now).

Blockchain-inspired Secco wants to offer its consumers a marketplace that will consolidate best offers from various financial providers and serve them based on personalized intent. Another excitement that Secco brings is to help you reclaim and monetize your data based on how interested you are in a tokenized method; for example, tweeting or other non-financial actions to receive a voucher in return.

Fidor, a German mobile banking startup that just launched in the U.K., reimagined the concept of financial advisor with its online community, where the community can be financially incentivized to provide financial advice, as well as evaluate and review financial products to other members. This greatly injects trust and transparency in the purchase process of financial products.

11.11 Data Driven

From the cyberattack on JPMorgan Chase, which resulted in close to 76 million household accounts being compromised two years ago, to HSBC's two days down time on online banking systems after DDOS attacks earlier this year, it is no doubt the banks are still struggling with the hardening of their legacy infrastructure, which was layered over the decades. With its own brand new stack of banking software, Peter Thiel-backed Number26 and $70 million-funded Starling put their hearts into reliability through data.

Consumers are notified in real time about new transactions so as to take action in fraud situations and instantly disable debit cards if the card is suspected to be lost. Data science can be useful in detecting fraud: If the consumer's phone location is in London and a card is being used in Berlin, verification can be solicited. BBVA-backed Atom's CEO Mark Mullen, former CEO of first direct, HSBC' telephone/online bank, intends to use gamification to make banking fun, and a mix of biometric data (such as selfies, voice and fingerprint) to increase security after being the first digital bank to secure a license in the U.K.

With these benefits, more and more people are going to start engaging banking apps that can fit in every part of their lives. Developing markets like Southeast Asia fit the prerequisites for this to kick off, given their large amount of underbanked and unbanked consumers who have access to smartphones as well as low rates of home broadband and urbanization that make traditional methods inaccessible to them. Beside Singapore in the region, the digital banking penetration is depressingly low, ranging from 13–44 percent in 2014 – even though consumers in their 20s are 50 percent more willing than their parents to try mobile banking.

If banks are unable to continue to rapidly innovate and create new, user-friendly and differentiated mobile offerings and effectively advertise and distribute on these platforms, they could lose market share to existing competitors or new entrants, and their future growth and bottom line could adversely take a hit. In other words, banks have to start disrupting themselves by acquiring new technologies and/or partnering with technopreneurs before they become a part of history.

Another disrupting force is aiming at Insurance. Insurance policies can be complex, and some policyholders may not understand all the fees and coverages included in a policy.

Indeed, people typically buy policies on unfavorable terms from both banks and insurers. In 2014, two major insurers, Blue Shield and Cigna of California, were sued for misrepresentation of the coverage network, which caused delays for their consumers in accessing needed health care. Yet, insurance should help societies and individuals mitigate catastrophes' impact through the way it changes who bears the cost of losses.

"There are 46 insurance companies in Fortune 500, with an average age of 95 years. Cumulative market cap is more than $1T," said Spencer Lazar of General Catalyst Partners. However, according to Morgan Stanley/BCG consumer's survey (Morgan Stanley, 2015), half of policyholders have one or less interactions per year with their insurers – and less than 60 percent of those who made the contact are satisfied with the experience.

Underwriting and closing a policy may take several days, even several weeks. Once the policy is underwritten, claims management and customer service are cumbersome due to the insurer-centric and paper-based structure. The commission structure of the status quo is such that agents and insurers make the process a misalignment of interest between the insurers and policyholders.

Fortunately, it is not a lost war for insurer incumbents, as they have their competitive advantages. Incumbents have the consumers' trusted brand perception and existing coverage network, regulator's policed compliance and licenses, as well as the most analytical actuarial talents.

An insurance premium paid currently provides coverage for losses that might arise many years in the future. The financial stability and strength of an insurance company is a major consideration when buying an insurance contract.

To understand the insurance business better, it has to start from their business model. Insurers' business profit can be reduced to a simple equation: Insurer's profit = sum of earned premiums and investment income on premiums after underwriting cost and claim expenses.

With the dawn of the pension scheme and a changing workforce that has increased the number of freelancers, startups are exploring the nexus of technology and insurance in an attempt to wake the dinosaurian industry.

In 2014, insurance tech startups raised just over $740 million in venture and equity funding. Just a year later, funding to insurtech companies rose by 350 percent, to $2.65 billion in annual funding, according to CB Insights (CB Insights, 2016). These insurtech startups may open new streams of premiums, encourage investment income, find a leaner method to underwrite costs or effectively manage claim expenses.

11.12 Earned Premiums

The emergence of digital-first insurers has created a new business model on delivering value to consumers. The world's biggest insurtech startup is Zhong An, valued at $8 billion after being invested in by three Ma (Alibaba's Jack Ma, Tencent's Pony Ma and China's second largest insurer, Ping An's Ma Mingzhe).

It opened new segments of insurance, where traditional insurers did not touch: Zhong An partnered with Alibaba for coverage on returned goods' delivery charges and even drone/mobile phone damage policies tailored to the new digital economy. Besides tackling the new digital frontier, Zhong An is essentially innovating on distribution, with a more integrated sales channel embedded as part of the e-commerce shopping process rather than depending on the traditional third-party agent distribution model.

Anthemis-backed Trov creates customization of home insurance by allowing coverage of individual key items rather than a predefined set with an average payout. An app-based mobile platform helps easily collect information about the things users bought through photos, market values, receipts and other product details.

With Trov, users can always see the total value of the things they own and have stored on Trov and track their value over time. With detailed records close at hand, it can be used as information to decide on the level of insurance coverage with Trov's partnered insurers serving in the backend. A one-stop shop like this can capture a use case and add more value with protective insurance products.

11.13 Investment Income

Insurtech such as Friendsurance, Guevara and stealth Sequoia-backed Lemonade are banging big on P2P insurance models. Using a sharing economy approach, users are invited to form small groups of policyholders who pay partial premiums into a pool to use for small claims. Policyholders can get back the remaining pool of money at the end of the year, after claims. Claims-free policyholders can obtain higher cash back, which is a clear financial benefit for fair behavior to reduce fraud and claims expenses.

Most importantly, these P2P models can possibly rethink how to make short-term liquid investments on the pooled money and higher returns bet on other premiums.

11.14 Underwriting Cost

With distribution channels being increasingly digital, will insurance agents end up in the same fate as the local bank branch? Despite huge commissions, traditional insurance agents fail to provide significant added value. Thus, new intermediaries are welcomed, especially online tools that are scalable.

SaleMove brings in-person customer experience online by offering website surfers an option to talk to live representatives via video, which aims to give potential leads more meaningful information than just poking around randomly. Furthermore, it allows insurers to mitigate the effects of not having the human touch in insurance sales, and tailor products for possible completion of micro-insurance online.

With Big Data and AI, there are lots of new opportunities with low cost by use of technology on marketplace and micro-insurance models, especially in developing economy like Asia with growing mobile penetration. The core competence of insurance is ready for a big leap, thanks to all sorts of new technologies, such as machine learning and data analytics.

AdviceRobo solutions make use of a machine learning platform that combines data from structured and unstructured sources to score and predict risk behavior of consumers. For instance, it provides insurers with preventive solutions, applying big behavioral data and machine learning to generate the best predictions on default, bad debt, prepayments and customer churn resulting in individualized risk assessment.

11.15 Claims Expenses

Insurers must see themselves in the prevention business on top of the protection business that they are already in.

Data is going to drive healthcare, which indirectly impacts insurance. Data can be leveraged to individually underwrite and personalize insurance for people. Metromile innovates in the preventive business by rewarding car owners with lower premiums for fewer miles driven (through a plugged-in car sensor).

There are going to be more insurers leveraging IoT devices, such as fitness tracker Fitbit and environment sensor uHoo. Perhaps the speed and ease with which self-automating smart contracts could be changed within the blockchain could see more insurance policies that reflect actual personalized risk in a real-time manner. However, the industry has to make good strides in not creating subsectors of the society that can't buy insurance due to big data rendering them as less attractive risks.

There is now an experimental P2P insurance platform called Teambrella that uses bitcoin wallets and multi-signature to allow users to manage the flow of funds in a trustless, decentralized way (Paperno et al., 2016). It will offer supplementary coverage for collision car insurance and pet veterinary insurance with more to offer.

In addition, Bauxy, Claim Di and Snapsheet are all about mobile solutions that help insurers make a leap in customer engagement to become much more effective every step of the new digital journey. Claims adjusters obtain the tools to enjoy an automated experience; a mobile solution enables consumers of insurers to settle a claim completely virtually. The solution simplifies claims, reduces the operation costs and increases touch points between insurer and customer, leading to better satisfaction.

Gone are the days when insurers were the perfect intermediaries to underwrite decisions or own the narrative of how insurance products get pushed to end users. IoT with inexpensive sensors will have a transformational impact on how insurance policies are underwritten. New digital entrants with strong customer relationships can formulate personalized policies and distribute more efficiently.

11.16 Mutual Aid Industry in China

Many of the successful Fintech companies started as social enterprises in emerging markets and scaled successfully to be unicorns. Notable examples are Ant Financial in China and M-PESA in Kenya. Alipay of Ant Financial and M-PESA both exhibit the LASIC (Lee and Teo, 2015) characteristics. Alipay has more than 800 m users globally with more than 300 m Chinese mobile users and M-PESA accounts is four times more than all the traditional bank accounts in aggregate in Kenya. LASIC startups are those with low profit margin business, asset light balance sheet, scalable business, innovative technology and operate in a compliance light regime. Ant Financial and M-PESA have all the LASIC characteristics.

When it comes to insurance in China, Zhong An will rank the highest in terms of innovation and valuation given its association with Alipay as a digital (online and mobile) micro insurance provider (Fintech News, 2016). It is not surprising that Zhong An exhibits the LASIC characteristics too. But a new class of LASIC insurtech model may be emerging in China. These new insurtech business models originated from the concept of Mutual Aid and started operation in the last two years. In organization theory, the term mutual aid is used to describe a voluntary reciprocal exchange of services and resources for mutual benefits. In America, the fraternity societies existed during the Great Depression providing their members with insurance and benefits for health, life and funeral. In the 1930s, the English "workers' clubs" also provided health insurance. Yet as early as in 18th and 19th centuries, forms of mutual aid organizations such as the Friendly Societies and medieval craft guilds provided their members with insurance, funeral expenses, pensions, care for sickness, and even dowries for poor girls. The intellectual abstraction has its roots in mutualism, labor insurance system, trade unions, cooperatives and other civil society movements.

Typically, mutual aid is a term used to describe a structure or organization that everyone is free to join and free to participate. The participants in mutual aids groups and all their activities are voluntary. It emphasizes the open and voluntary cooperation as opposed to induced cooperation (Kropotkin, 2008). The idea of mutual aid flourishes in entities that support participatory, democracy, equality of member status and decentralization of decision making at the structure level. Status of the group is determined or conferred mainly by participation. External societal status is irrelevant within the group.

Platform	Number of users	Website
众托帮 Zhongtuobang	1867373	Zhongtuobang.com
水滴互助 Shuidihuzhu	1381435	Shuidihuzhu.com
夸克联盟 Quarker	1078323	BaoBaoji.cn
e 互助 ehuzhu	708076	ehuzhu.com
抗癌公社 Kangaikongshe	605961	Kags.com
17 互助 17Huzhu	506475	chinamuxie.com
壁虎互助 Bihuhuzhu	387911	ibehoo.cn
同心互助 Tongxinhuzhu	126895	tongxinclub.com
蚂蚁互保 Mayihubao	52175	mayihubao.com
斑马社 Banmashe	11001	banmahz.com

Figure 11.1: Mutual Aid Platforms in China (as reported at end September 2016).
(Source: http://www.huzhuzj.com/)

On the Internet, Mutual Aid Platform is seen as a mutual financial assistance and risk sharing platform. It is a class of platforms that members can lower their aid threshold and raise their aid limitation through mutual financial assistance and risk sharing. Members can join a mutual assistance plan with an advance deposit of only RMB10. As a member, one may apply for an aid of up to a maximum of RMB300,000. The maximum deduction from the member's account for each application is RMB3. The more members there are, the lower the contribution. When there is zero balance in the member's account, there will be a call for payments. If the member's account keeps zero balance more than 30 days, he/she will quit the plan automatically. It is estimated that the yearly contribution is between RMB60 and RMB90. When there is an application for RMB300,000 as mutual aid amount and if there are 1m participants, each user contributes only RMB0.30 (PR Newswire, 2016).

The largest mutual aid platforms are listed in Fig. 11.1.

11.17 Zhongtuobang and Shuidihuzhu

Started in July 2016 with a Blockchain platform, Shanghai based with RMB100m registered capital Zhongtuobang (ZTB) has reached two million users as at 1 Oct 2016 and it is the first mutual aid company to have a double A rating from the Chinese Internet Association iTrust. On August 19, Shuidihuzhu was the largest with over a million users before being taken over by Zhongtuobang in the second half of 2016. The growth in this sector is exponential. The founders of these platforms have insurance experience and bridge the gap in serving the underserved.

Column1	Subscribers	Outstanding Amount (RMB)	Deposits	Insured Amount	Age
Cancer Plan for the Young	450083	3005157	9	300000	30 days-17
Youth Health Plan	27822	320760	9	30000	18-50
Cancer for the Mid and Old	42224	421553	9	10000	51-65
Comprehensive Accident	87925	1047977	9	10000	Jan-65
Total	608054	4795447			

Figure 11.2: Four different Mutual Aid Plans at Shuidihuzhu (for August 2016).
(Source: Shuidihuzhu.com)

Date	New Subscribers	Outstanding Amount (RMB)
May-June	116350	638613
July	357765	1752901
Aug	608054	4795447
Total	1082169	7186961

Figure 11.3: Number of subscribers and outstanding amount at shuidihuzhu (as reported at end August 2016).
(Source: Shuidihuzhu.com)

ZTB main business is in medical mutual aid and lower the barrier entry for micro enterprises and farmers that are deterred from buying insurance of high entry premiums. It is a form of insurance inclusion scheme where the risk is pooled with low contribution. Zhongtuobang has launched multiple mutual aid products including Anti-Cancer & Disease, Travel Accident, Dad & Mom Mutual Aid, Women's Health and a Students Comprehensive Plan. According to ZTB, the average age of members is 31 and 27 for male and female respectively. To cater to those who are above 55 and not eligible for traditional insurance, ZTB rolled out mutual aid product for those between 51 and 65 years old. They have launched products specifically designed for medical care personnel and diabetes sufferers. There are plans to launch smart contract insurance products using the Blockchain technology. Blockchain with analytics also has certain features that will minimize false claims and frauds because the data are transparent and permanent.

However, according the reported figures in the table, the figures remain insignificant (Figs. 11.2, 11.3). The total investment by Venture Capital into Beijing based Shuidihuzhu is RMB55m by IDG, Tencent, and others. They have launched four programs so far. The numbers in Fig. 11.2 are new subscriptions for Aug 2016.

11.18 Blockchain Use Cases

There are two Blockchain use cases that we know of in the mutual aid industry in China, ZTB and Tongxinhuzhu. Tongxinhuzhu blockchain (https://www.tongxinclub.com/pc/blockchain/

Figure 11.4: Number of subscribers at ZTB.

index) has 124,858 members, 90 nodes and around 971,533H/s, equivalent to computing power of 4 MacBook Pro and 2.7 GHz Intel Core i5 8G storage. There are 537345 blocks as at 4 Oct 2016. Both cases are using Blockchain for identification and verification purposes for the members.

Above is a demonstration of the Blockchain application of ZTB.

The website shows the number of subscribers as 1,064,568. When the subscriber number is keyed in, the information will be shown in the e-wallet as in Fig. 11.4. In Fig. 11.5 below, we can see that the person is the 4th subscriber (您是第 4 位). By requesting the information for the private key (个人密钥), the key will be shown together with the public key or Blockchain address (您的区块链地址). With the membership number, further information can be provided such as the joining date/time (2016-08-27 11:11:23) and the plan (抗癌互助医疗, cancer treatment mutual aid).

The advantage of this Blockchain application is that historical information can be obtained for every account at low cost. Given that the information is permanent and public (it prevents the service provider from changing the records), it solves the issues of trust in a mutual aid platform (see Fig. 11.6). It is easy to match, execute, monitor with the potential use of smart contracts at low cost as compared to a centralized system. At present, claims are not verified or executed by smart contracts and Blockchain is only utilized to address the issue of trust in the mutual aid industry.

This ZTB use case has demonstrated that mutual aid is scalable by solving the issue of trust among potential subscribers who are strangers to each other (see Fig. 11.7). This is scalable to 1.3b population from all over China with potential use of smart contracts. Insurance inclusion is achievable for specialized risk pooling in areas of insatiable demand, especially in rural areas and critical illnesses. With big data, such risk will be better understood and allowing for mass adoption and efficient pricing of insurance services. Network effect of risk sharing will enable mutual aid platforms to scale across a large number of members.

Figure 11.5: eWallet of ZTB with multiple functions.

Figure 11.6: eWallet showing the user number, private key and blockchain address.

Figure 11.7: Account information in ZTB.

11.19 Are Mutual Aid LASIC?

Are these new Mutual Aid business models a form of LASIC InsurTech? This class of business model has low profits margin with no requirement of heavy investment in assets. It has been scaling as seen in the last few months with the help of low premium. Some of them are using Internet with Blockchain as an innovative technology to lower cost and increase trust. There are hardly any compliance rules at this moment for the industry. It remains to see if the use of new technology can detect and reduce fraudulent claims and whether the industry can increase its scope of services to a larger base of sticky customers. Ant Financial has only 1 fraud in 100,000 transactions and like M-PESA, offers services beyond payments of daily purchases and utilities. Users can buy insurance, funds, tickets, movie bonds, obtain loans, and even get a credit rating. The latest innovation Alipay Everywhere is to purchase household services such as cooking and caregiving from neighbors for a fee (Horowitz, 2016 and Jain, 2016). These are all made possible because of data analytic, location services and mobile technology. Big data, smart contract and artificial intelligence risk analytic remains an area that the mutual aid InsurTech industry need to take advantage of. There are LASIC unicorns such as Ant Financial to emulate and if the industry can harness the right technology to serve the masses, mutual aid startups such as Zhongtuobang will become the new unicorns.

11.20 Conclusion

According to World Bank (World Bank, 2015), the global population is set to reach 9.7 billion in 2050 and 34 percent of global growth in worker population (aged 15–64) lies in South Asia. Although B2B insurtech CXA and many financial comparison sites are operating in the underinsured and uninsured region, much of the insurtech innovations and targeted consumers are still primarily located in Western and China markets.

The next generation of Fortune 500 banks and insurers will have to partner with various stakeholders, including the unmentioned regulators, to drive cost low and premium acquisition high on the equation in a consumer-centric way, as well as replicating successes in high-growth emerging markets.

11.21 Technology Disruptions

Slide Disruption 1

Disruption 1 – Risk and Data Analytics

Technology give insurers **real-time** data specific to an individual risk. This allows them to accurately price risk and lead to cheaper premiums for consumers

- Traditional insurers use single point in time assessment of risk based on **static data points**
- Wearables, internet of things and smartphones brings real-time data, allowing **pay/use coverage**
- This leads to **personalized & variable** premiums over policy terms to incentivize better behaviors
- More sophisticated data modeling and predictive analytics solutions being developed

Insurance Type	Factors	Insurtech Factors	Technology
Auto	• Type of car • How much you drive • Age, sex, marital status • Driving record • Credit History	• Acceleration • Rotation • Location • Hard brakes • Time eyes leave the road	**Telematics**
Health	• Body mass index • Tobacco Use • Pre-existing medical condition • Age, sex, marital status • Family history	• Heart rate • Glucose level • Blood pressure • Sleep pattern • Calories burned	**Wearables**
Home	• Security and alarm system • House structure and age • Square footage of home • Roof type • Fire protection	• Water leak detection • Window sensors • Smart Thermostats • Smoke detector • Smart locks	**Smart Homes**

Source: Insly, Schulte Research

Examples

Auto	Health	Home
Okchexian	**Manulife MOVE**	**Nest Safety Rewards**

Auto — Okchexian

- Analyzes driving speed and behavior using telematics and sensors inside smartphone
- Driving 20km/hr for 5min due to traffic rewards 5rmb of oil discount voucher
- Reward good drivers with lower auto insurance premiums
- Uber can do this!

Health — Manulife MOVE

- Members get ~40% discount for fitness tracker linked to ManulifeMOVE app
- Rewards members with premium discounts based on avg daily steps
- Members enjoy offers for health products
- Engagement Insurance and gamification

Home — Nest Safety Rewards

- Partnered with American Family & Liberty Mutual
- Nest Protect smoke and carbon monoxide detector sends data to insurer on whether detector is working
- If so, customers get 5% discount on home insurance

Source: Schulte Research

Drones can be used at disaster sites or in industries where survey work is inherently risky (telecom, oil & gas) to get risk and loss engineers out of harm way

- Aerial information platform for rapid and safe operation of commercial drones
- Provide enterprise software and drone solutions to conduct risk and loss
- Enables enterprises to plan, capture and analyze data all within an enterprise workflow

High Definition Photos Taken by Drones at a Construction Site

Source:,Schulte Research

Slide Disruption 2

Disruption 2 – Sales

Digitalization and multi-channel engagement are increasingly important role in distribution

Traditional Channels	Description	Example
Broker / Financial Advisors	Client consults broker, explains needs. Broker approaches insurer and present options to client	**Willis AON**
Direct Insurance	Client approaches insurer directly via telephone or online	Manulife

New Channels		
Insurance Aggregator	Website portal or search utility that enable client to gain several comparative quotes based on specified needs	CoverHound
Integrated Third Party	Selling related insurance products as part of the shopping process. e.g. Return goods insurance when shopping on Taobao	众安保险
Engagement Insurance	Insurers connect with customers throughout life of the policy, not just at renewal or claim	MOVE

Source: Insly, Schulte Research

Slide Disruption 3

Disruption 3 – Management

Insurance companies are slow to upgrade antiquated systems

- Digitizing business processes (esp. claims & servicing) can deliver significant near-term gains i.e. reduced costs, lower error rates and increased customer satisfaction
- One UK insurer eliminated around 20 million calls per year by introducing an app that allowed customers to make changes to their policies

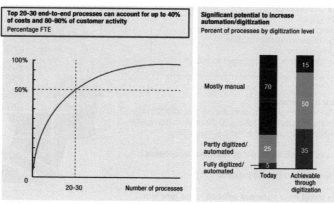

Source: Mckinsey, Schulte Research

Digitized insurers can cut non-commission operating costs by 30-50%, reduce compensation costs by 1-3% and increase collected premiums by 1-3%

Digitization Approach		
Online purchase	Policies purchased online in just a few minutes due to automatic algorithms that instantly calculate premiums	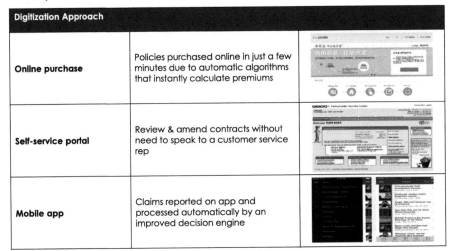
Self-service portal	Review & amend contracts without need to speak to a customer service rep	
Mobile app	Claims reported on app and processed automatically by an improved decision engine	

Source: Mckinsey, Schulte Research

KYC is the expensive part of onboarding a new client; every financial institution must do it

Know Your Customer (KYC)
- Acquiring personal information
- Acquiring proofs of personal information
- Storage of personal information
- Background checks
- Ongoing monitoring of changes to clients

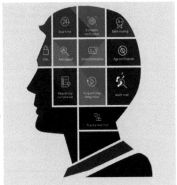

Compliance Is Expensive
- USD10 bn is spent on AML compliance globally (2014)
- KYC delays transactions, taking 30-50 days to complete
- Substantial duplication of effort between firms

For businesses, this is a **high cost of customer acquisition**

For customers, this is a **painful process**

Blockchain could be a potential solution to the problem

Source: Deloitte, Schulte Research

Blockchain could unlock advantages by automating processes and reduce compliance errors

What is a Blockchain?
- Public ledger of all transactions that is shared to each computer connected to the network
- Can be used to **track the movement of assets** throughout supply chains or **electronically initiate/enforce contracts**
- Allows companies to make and verify transactions on a network **instantaneously without a central authority** using cryptography

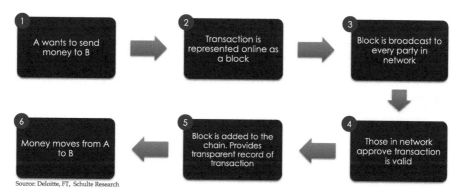

Source: Deloitte, FT, Schulte Research

Blockchain registry can remove duplication of effort in KYC checks and enable encrypted updates on client details to be distributed to all banks in real-time

- KYC burden can be reduced through shared database of client background documents
- SWIFT established its **KYC Registry**, where 1125 member banks share KYC documentation
    - Ledger provide historical record of all documents shared and compliance activities taken
    - Cement real-world identities to cryptographic identities in database
    - Transactions only permitted for parties with adequate KYC evidence in blockchain

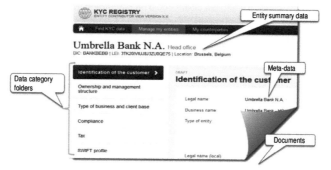

Source: Deloitte, FT, Schulte Research

Slide Disruption 4

Disruption 4 – Liability, Fraud & Investigation

Smart contracts powered by **blockchain** could provide customers and insurers with the means to manage claims in a transparent, responsive and irrefutable manner

Current Bottlenecks/Issues
- Claim frauds such as "crash for cash" scams are very costly for the insurance industry

Solution
- Digital contracts can be recorded on a blockchain and validated by the network, ensuring that only valid claims are paid

Smart Contracts
- **Oracles** are trusted entities that provide information about outside world and execute code which contracting parties agreed on

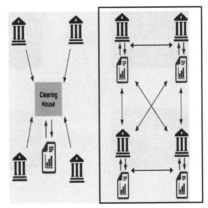

Blockchain Network

Source: Schulte Research

Blockchain can help insurers in customer identification procedures, monitoring of transactions and risk management

Blockchain Applications in Insurance

	Automated Compliance • Automatically trigger payments when conditions on smart contracts are met • Streamline processing and offer better user experience for filing claims • Crop insurance claims could be automated through a smart contract on a blockchain linked with a trusted weather data feed
	Fraud Prevention • Wide range of personal data can be managed and stored on blockchain • Can help prevent identity theft, financial fraud, money laundering and terrorist financing • Smart contracts can reject multiple "crash for cash" claims for one accident because network knows that claim has already been made

- Provides P2P supplementary unemployment insurance using the Etherium Blockchain and Linkedin as reputation system
- **Current policy holders** rather than employees of **decentralized autonomous organization (DAO)** underwrite new policies and evaluate new claims

Source: Deloitte, Dynamis, Schulte Research

Smart contracts can prevent error, ensure accountability, minimize fraud and lower costs

Benefits of Smart Contract
- **Enforce rules** which hold, transfer, receive & spend digital assets
- **Prevents human error** and coercion
- **Ensures accountability** since beneficiaries of claims are public on auditable ledger (operations can be examined re unfair result occurrence)
- **Minimize insurance fraud** at every level, from fund management to individual claims
- **Lowers cost** due to less overhead required to maintain and operate the system

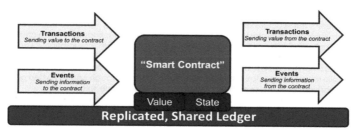

Source: Schulte Research

Slide Disruption 5

Disruption 5 - Asset Management

Robo-advisors offer sound financial advice for small fraction of the price of real life advisors

Problem
- Millionaires pay 1-3% annual fee for investment advice. Worth it?

Solution
- Automated wealth managers employ textbook techniques, mathematical formulas and high speed computers to construct tailored investment portfolios based on customer's risk appetite

Fee structure
- Fees comprises of annual service cost to use robo-advisor and fees of the funds customers buy

Market Size
- Robo-advisers are doubling their AUM every few months but AUM is still less than $20 bn (traditional asset managers have $17 tn in AUM)

Source: Economist, Schulte Research

Robo advisors are registered investment advisers – required put customers ahead of all else

Benefits	Pitfalls

• Transparent fee structure and low costs
• Prevents conflict of interest
  • Banks tend to recommend in house investment products
• Portfolios monitored 24/7, optimizing portfolio rebalancing & tax-loss harvesting
• Automatically evolve & search for new patterns, adjusting to what works in markets
• Asset managers can use them as tools to enhance investment process
	• **Overfitting** – overly complex or badly coded algorithm finds false correlations from data. E.g. margarine consumption linked with divorce rates in Maine
	• Could collapse in real market situations
	• Not thorough enough when gather information about investors
	  • Cannot notice subtleties in conversations
	  • Does not ask about5 money held outside its services
	• Can't think as creatively as human, especially in a crisis

Source: Goldman Sachs, Economist, Schulte Research

"The challenge facing the investment world is that the human mind has not become any better than it was 100 years ago, and it's very hard for someone using traditional methods to juggle all the information of the global economy in their head"
- David Siegel, co-head of Two Sigma

Notable Robo Wealth Managers

	Year founded	Minimum investment, $	Advisory fee (based on investment of $100K), %	AUM ($m)	Investors served
Wealthfront	2011	5,000	0.25	2,000	17,400
Betterment	2008	0	0.15	1,400	65,000
Personal Capital	2009	100,000	0.89	1,000	2,500
FutureAdvisor Premium	2010	10,000	0.50	240	1,700
Nutmeg	2011	1,500	0.75	N/A	N/A

Source: Goldman Sachs, Economist, Schulte Research

Aidyia is a hedge fund startup based in HK that is completely managed by AI

- **Ben Goertzel** – Cofounder and Chief Scientist
- **Two Funds** – US equity long/short, Global Macro
- **Predict long term stock movements** (Most quantitative fintechs forecast short-term movements)
- **Machine learning** – learn what works and what doesn't to manage its portfolio
- Predict price changes based on price, volume, news, social media data in various languages, economic and accounting data at national & company levels
- Historical testing between 2003-2014 yielded **annualized returns of 29%**
- Returns are consistent in real-time simulation

Source: Schulte Research

11.22 InsurTech Ecosystem

Useful Links

www.schulte-research.com

https://blog.wearesosure.com/what-is-insurtech-94a84b177a37#.3ph64yxps

http://www.mckinsey.com/~/media/McKinsey/dotcom/client_service/Financial%20Services/Latest%20thinking/Insurance/Making_of_a_digital_insurer_2015.ashx

https://www.linkedin.com/pulse/how-incumbents-responding-insurtech-evolution-rick-huckstep

http://www.slideshare.net/capgemini/infographic-world-insurance-report-2015-from-capgemini-and-efma

https://www.linkedin.com/pulse/how-incumbents-responding-insurtech-evolution-rick-huckstep

http://ins.accenture.com/rs/897-EWH-515/images/Reimagining-insurance-distribution-Distribution-and-Agency-Management-Survey.pdf

http://www.kwm.com/en/au/knowledge/insights/10-things-you-need-to-know-insurtech-insurance-industry-data-blockchain-20160712

https://www.insly.com/en/blog/what-are-the-insurtech-trends-for-2016

http://www.the-digital-insurer.com/axa-infographic-insurtech-china/

https://www.cbinsights.com/blog/insurance-tech-startup-funding-2015/

https://www.cbinsights.com/blog/insurance-tech-overview-q1-2016/

http://iireporter.com/after-telematics-what-smart-homes-mean-for-insurance-product-innovation/

https://www.insly.com/en/blog/what-are-the-insurtech-trends-for-2016

http://carinsurance.arrivealive.co.za/what-is-an-insurance-aggregator.php

https://www2.deloitte.com/content/dam/Deloitte/uk/Documents/Innovation/deloitte-uk-blockchain-app-in-banking.pdf

https://assets.weforum.org/editor/_DRLsawgrOCG3OwH3VP4o9VuR4HMAsBeRGFZSo_7RPk.png

https://assets.weforum.org/editor/_DRLsawgrOCG3OwH3VP4o9VuR4HMAsBeRGFZSo_7RPk.png

http://www.comtelcommunications.com/blog/cio-explainer-what-is-blockchain52016

https://www2.deloitte.com/content/dam/Deloitte/ch/Documents/innovation/ch-en-innovation-deloitte-blockchain-app-in-insurance.pdf

http://www.economist.com/news/special-report/21650292-human-wealth-advisers-are-going-out-fashion-ask-algorithm

https://www.cbinsights.com/blog/insurance-tech-periodic-table/

https://www.cbinsights.com/blog/insurance-tech-corporate-investment-record/

https://www.cbinsights.com/blog/insurance-startup-investing/

https://www.linkedin.com/pulse/how-incumbents-responding-insurtech-evolution-rick-huckstep

http://pinnacle.smu.edu.sg/demo

http://www.the-digital-insurer.com/the-digital-insurer-reviews-the-ninety-consulting-white-paper-on-the-omnichannel-insurer/

http://www.the-digital-insurer.com/dia/metlife-infinity-digital-vault-memories-today-tomorrow/

http://www.the-digital-insurer.com/axa-infographic-insurtech-china/

Acknowledgments

Appreciation to Ge Long, Co-founder, Eric Yu, CTO of Zhongtuobang and James Gong of Chainb.com.

References

Accenture, 2016. Accenture technology vision for insurance, people first: the primacy of people in the age of digital insurance. https://s3.amazonaws.com/assets.accenture.com/PDF/Accenture-Technology-Vision-for-Insurance-2016-Full-Report.pdf.

Biznews, 2016. Mutual aid rising in China. http://www.biznews.in/article/mutual-aid-rising-in-china.

Capgemini, 2015. World insurance report 2015. https://www.worldinsurancereport.com/.

Capgemini, 2016. World insurance report 2015. https://www.worldinsurancereport.com/.

CB Insights, 2016. Insurnace tech startup funding hits $2.65B in 2015 as deal activity heats up. https://www.cbinsights.com/blog/insurance-tech-startup-funding-2015/.

Jain, Aman, 2016. New Alibaba App allows you to ask strangers do anything for a fee. Valuewalk. http://www.valuewalk.com/2016/09/alibaba-app-strangers-anything-fee/.

Fintech News, 2016. Top50 fintechs in China. http://fintechnews.sg/5639/fintech/top-50-fintechs-china-kpmg/.

Horowitz, Josh, 2016. With Alipay, China's most popular payments app, you can now ask total strangers to do anything for a fee. http://qz.com/795732/alipay-everywhere-from-alibaba-and-ant-financial-lets-you-ask-total-strangers-to-do-anything-for-a-fee/.

Huzhuzhijia, 2016. 互助之家. http://www.huzhuzj.com/.

KPMG, 2014. 2014 Insurance industry outlook survey: revolution, not evolution. http://www.kpmginfo.com/industryoutlooksurveys/2014/pdfs/284763_InsuranceIndustrySurveyReportV8.pdf.

Kropotkin, Peter, 2008. Mutual Aid: A Factor of Evolution. Forgotten Books, Charleston, SC.

Lee Kuo Chuen, David, Teo, Ernie, 2015. Emergence of fintech and the LASIC principles. Journal of Financial Perspective 3, 3.

Meeker, Mary, 2016. "Internet Trends 2016", Code Conference, Kleiner Perkins Caufield Byers. http://www.kpcb.com/internet-trends.

Paperno, Alex, Kravchuk, Vlad, Porubaev, Eugene, 2016. Teambrella: a peer-to-peer insurance system. White Paper. https://teambrella.com/WhitePaper.pdf.

PR Newswire, 2016. Mutual aid rising in China: inclusive aid catches up with new opportunities after the G20 summit. http://en.prnasia.com/story/159264-0.shtml.

Schulte, Paul, 2015. The InsurTech Asteroid: Is Extinction of Traditional Insurance Inevitable? Schulte Research.

Stanley, Morgan, 2015. Insurance and technology, insight: the emerging role of ecosystems in insurance. https://www.bcgperspectives.com/Images/Insurance-Tech-Ecosystems-April-2015.pdf.

World Bank, 2015. Year in review: 2015 in 12 charts. https://medium.com/world-of-opportunity/year-in-review-2015-in-12-charts-a2aeffc5f593#.4r5xkqphh.

Yan, Choon Tan, 2016. The insurance equation. https://startupsventurecapital.com/how-is-technology-affecting-insurance-the-insurance-equation-76fd91ccf976#.lp8hguith.

CHAPTER 12

Understanding Interbank Real-Time Retail Payment Systems

Roy Lai

Contents

Handbook of Blockchain, Digital Finance, and Inclusion, Volume 1
DOI: 10.1016/B978-0-12-810441-5.00012-9

12.1 Introduction

This writing is organized into four sections and introduces the reader to the concept of real-time retail payment systems.

- **The Overview of Interbank Payment Landscape**. The reader will learn about the plethora of interbank payment services and their purposes. This will lead the reader into understanding how Real-Time Retail Payment Systems fit in.
- **The Case for Real-Time Retail Payment Systems**. The reader will learn about the rising trends in global implementations of such systems as well as the drivers behind this trend.
- **The Characteristics of Real-Time Retail Payment Systems**. The reader will learn about what constitutes real-time payment systems that make them unique from other systems.
- **The Architecture and Design of Real-Time Retail Payment Systems**. The reader will learn about how different are designs of such systems and how they are implemented.

Finally, the writing will end with a conclusion that looks into developments in financial industry that can influence the evolution of real-time retail payment systems.

12.2 The Overview of Interbank Payment Landscape

In this section, the reader is introduced to the plethora of payment systems that can exist in a country. As one's perception of payment instruments and payment habit is shaped by what is available in one's country, it will help the reader to understand the subtle differences between payment systems and their purpose for existence. It will also look behind the scenes on how these systems work in general so as to give the reader greater appreciation of their utility and limitations. Ultimately, the objective for this section is to help the reader understand how RTPS fit in overall and how it addresses the gap due to the shortcomings of existing systems (Fig. 12.1).

12.2.1 Wholesale Payment Systems

A country's domestic interbank **payment system**[1] can be classified as either a wholesale payment system or a retail payment system. **Wholesale payment systems**[2] (also known as **large-value payment systems**) are usually operated by a country's central bank for the transfer of high-value funds between banks and large corporations. There are generally two types of wholesale payment systems but most systems are hybrid that contain features of both using special techniques in minimizing liquidity risks and credit risks.

- A **Real-Time Gross Settlement (RTGS)** system is used for settling funds between accounts on a per transaction basis in real-time.

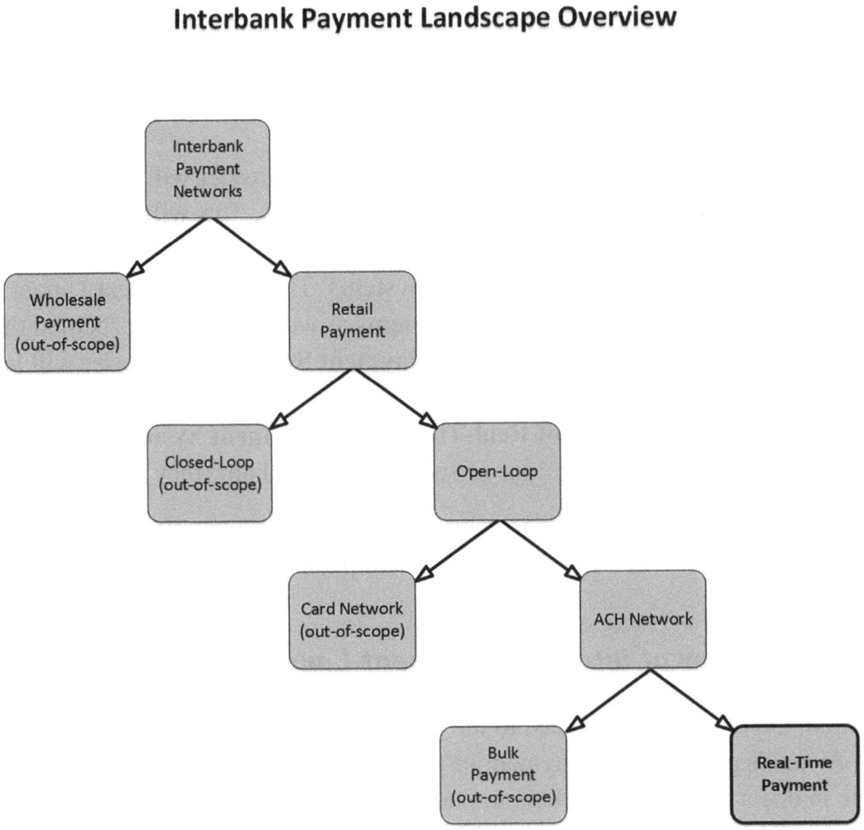

Interbank Payment Landscape Overview

Figure 12.1: Interbank payment landscape overview.

- A **Deferred Net Settlement** system is used for settling funds between accounts at designated times of the day on a net basis. This is done by consolidating batch of transactions between accounts and instead of settling them individually, only the net positions are settled after offsetting the batches.

Due to the sheer scale in the total value of funds transferred, such systems are classified as **Systemically Important Payment Systems**[3] (SIPS) which can impact the entire financial well-being of a country in the event of a failure. To understand the criticality of such systems, UK's RTGS called CHAPS processed 3.3 million payments worth 6.6 trillion GBP over 22 settlement processing days in September 2016 (CHAPS, 2016). An average CHAPS transaction value is around 2.11 million GBP based on 2012 statistics. When CHAPS suffered an outage in 2014 that impacted the processing of 142,759 transactions totaling 276 billion GBP (Deloitte, 2015). The outage delayed 82% of housing transactions for the day and created downstream impact to international cross-currency settlements even though it lasted only

Three-Party Model

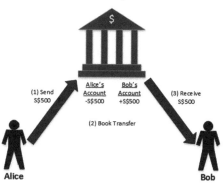

Figure 12.2: Three-party model.

9 hours. This is the reason why non-urgent and low-value retail payments are usually cleared by a separate retail payment systems to minimize impact to the critical transactions while the wholesale payments are reserved for deferred net settlement of retail payments only.

12.2.2 Retail Payment Systems

The **retail payment system**[4] (also known as a **low-value payment system**) is used for processing non-urgent, low-value transactions such as consumer payments and is typically conducted in huge volumes. Retail payment systems can exist in two forms – closed-loop and open-loop.

Closed-Loop Retail Payment Systems

A closed-loop system requires both payer and payee to be on the same platform, therefore it is also known as a "three-party" payment system. Settlement is a lot more simpler and can be achieved in one step via internal book-transfer as transactions are managed by one entity. Most closed-loop systems are operated end-to-end by **non-bank** entities. However, non-bank entities are fast becoming open-loop systems integrating with bank's payment processes in the back-end (BIS, 2014) (Fig. 12.2).

Open-Loop Retail Payment Systems

An open-loop system is used to facilitate the transfer of funds between a payer and payee belonging to different banks. Therefore, it is also known as a "four-party" system. Although payments can be settled **bilaterally** between banks, that is not common and efficient involving

Four-Party Model

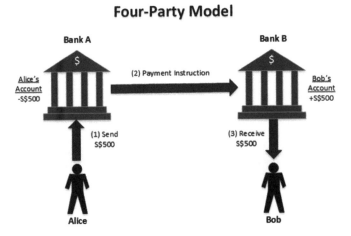

Figure 12.3: Four party model.

a network of banks. Therefore, in an open-loop payment system, a trusted centralized third party is appointed by the banks and regulated by the financial authorities to be responsible for processing and coordinating the transactions. This can be achieved with either using a **card payment system** or via an **automated clearing house (ACH) batch payment system**. Because a transaction can only be completed by involving multiple intermediaries, therefore settlement is a lot more complicated than a closed-loop system and involves multiple steps (Fig. 12.3).

The following sections will explain the difference between closed-loop systems, card payment systems and ACH batch payment systems in more detail.

12.2.3 Closed-Loop Payment Systems

Closed-loop system is a single vendor system that requires customers to deposit funds as a pre-payment for the goods and services offered by the vendor. The funds that are deposited usually exist in the form of electronic money[5] that cannot be withdrawn as cash but usually can be transferred to customers of the same vendor. Because transactions are controlled by the same vendor, therefore transfers can happen very quickly with low overhead and therefore reduced cost. Such systems are usually designed for a single purpose and are very difficult to achieve ubiquity coming from a single vendor.

However, there are some well-known success stories that have demonstrated the successful use of closed-loop systems but these are usually the exceptions rather than the norm.

- Octopus card in Hong Kong for example was originally created in 1997 for public transportation use and has since been evolved from a single-purpose card into multi-purpose cash card with 24 million in circulation that can be used in convenient stores, restaurants and supermarkets supporting over 13 million transactions per day.
- In China, the largest social messaging company Tencent has successfully turned its single-purpose mobile social app WeChat into a multi-purpose mobile wallet. With 700 million active monthly users, WeChat Payment has the advantage of economy of scale and is estimated by Reuters to support $556 billion transactions from P2P payments alone in 2016.
- M-PESA (Jack and Suri, 2010) is a good example where cash is substituted with airtime transferred between mobile phones to facilitate remittance and mobile payments in Kenya.

12.2.4 Card Payment Networks

A card payment network, for example VISA and Master, is an open-loop payment system that is commonly used for electronic fund transfer point-of-sale systems (**EFTPOS**) internationally. The merchant (accepting party) holds an account with its bank (acquirer) for receiving payments. The consumer (cardholder) holds a credit or debit card account with its bank (issuer) for making card payments. This is originally designed for point-of-sale scenarios whereby the merchant and consumer that are in close physical proximity during the transaction and card signature can be visually verified or a card-based terminal is available for PIN verification. However, card payment can also be used in "card not present" situations such as online e-commerce, but they are not originally designed for such use cases (DB, 2015) and can be costly to maintain and difficult to use.

Although the settlement of card payment involves three distinct steps – authorization, clearing and settlement – authorization and clearing are generally combined into one step for more recent networks. Although this section explains how a card payment is processed from a credit card's perspective, the process is similar for debit card with key difference being that funds are immediately deducted from a payer's bank account as opposed to being billed for payment later.

Card Payment Authorization

Card Payment Authorization is the process whereby merchant is authorized by the card's issuing bank to accept payment using the card presented by consumer. This happens at the point of purchasing when the cardholder's card is swiped. Upon authorization approval, the payment amount is deducted from the card's credit limit (or bank account funds put on hold in debit card transaction) until clearing happens. This process may give the impression of payment being immediate but, in reality, fund is not transferred to the merchant yet (Fig. 12.4).

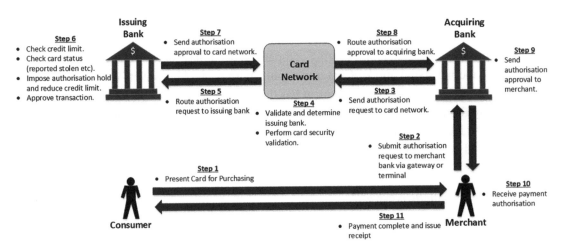

Figure 12.4: Credit card payment authorization.

Card Clearing

Card Clearing is the process by which acquiring bank and issuing bank exchange transaction information but funds are not actually transferred yet. This process works by all acquiring banks sending payment instructions to the credit card network in a batch and the credit card network distributing each transaction to each issuing banks for collection (Fig. 12.5).

Card Settlement

Card Settlement is the process by which funds are actually transferred from the card issuing bank to the acquiring bank based on the net settlement position advised by the credit card network. Issuing bank will transfer the net settlement amount to the acquiring bank after deducting the interchange fees. Acquiring bank will then credit the received amount to the merchant's bank account after deducting the discount fee (Fig. 12.6).

As it can be seen, every intermediary from acquiring bank, to credit card network, to issuing bank takes a cut out of the merchant revenue which makes card transactions not suitable for use by merchants offering low margin purchases.

12.2.5 Automated Clearing Houses (ACH) Payment Networks

An automated clearing house payment network is another open-loop retail payment system besides card payment that facilitates domestic fund transfer directly between banks (also

Credit Card Clearing

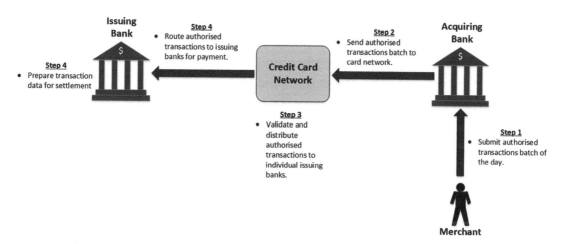

Figure 12.5: Credit card clearing.

Card Settlement

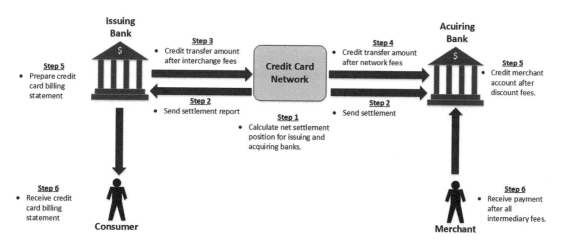

Figure 12.6: Card settlement.

known as **Account-to-Account** or **A2A** transfer). The original purpose of clearing houses is to provide clearing services for paper checks between banks. With the increasing use of paperless transactions, clearing houses have taken on the role of processing electronic payment instruments in general hence the term "automated." ACH payment networks are designed for batch processing only[6] and are cheaper than card networks. However, such networks like

Credit Transfer

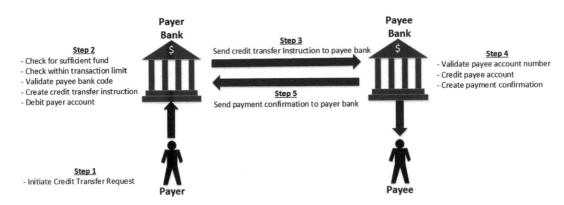

Figure 12.7: Credit transfer.

wholesale payments only operate during normal working days and since they process transactions in batches, payments can take days to settle, especially over weekends and public holidays. They can cater very well to scheduled batch payments use cases such as payrolls and bill payments but are not feasible for real-time payments. There are two types of payment instruments that are supported by ACH – credit transfer and direct debit.

Credit Transfer

A **credit transfer** is a payment service that is originated by the payer of one bank to send money to a payee of a different bank (Fig. 12.7).

Direct Debit

Conversely, a **direct debit** is a payment service that is originated by the payee of one bank to collect money from a payer of another bank (Fig. 12.8).

ACH Clearing

ACH batch payment systems operate only during normal working day. A specific clearing window of the day known as the outward clearing window is open for banks to submit payment instructions from their account holders to the ACH for validation and processing. A different clearing window known as the inward clearing window is used by the clearing house to distribute the payment instructions to the receiving banks for processing payments to their account holders.

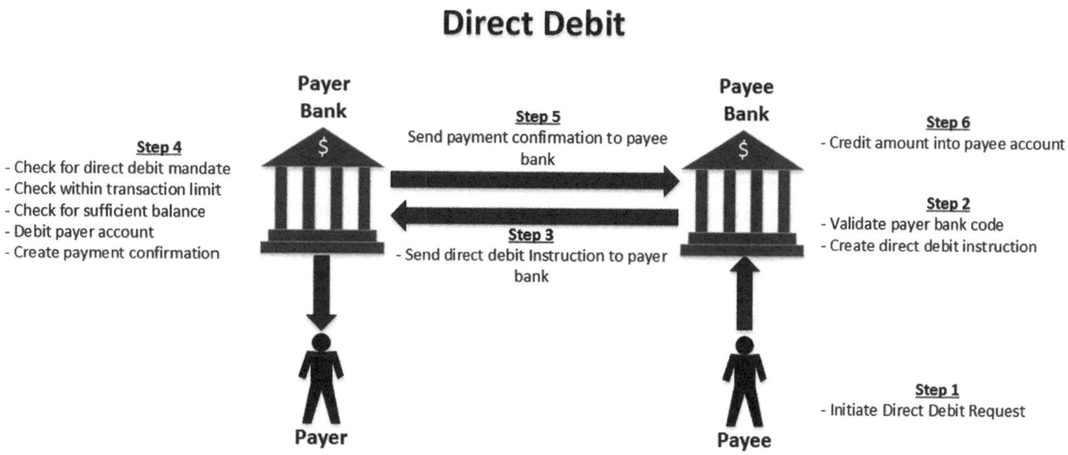

Direct Debit

Figure 12.8: Direct debit.

Deferred Net Settlement

Settlement usually takes place immediately after the outward clearing window by submitting a batch settlement file to the central bank. Because the central bank also operates only during normal working days, file submission must take place before a cut-off time. Due to the high volume of transactions involved, settlement processing is usually performed on a deferred net settlement basis. The inward clearing window usually happens after the settlement for the following day. That is why it can take more than one day for funds to be settled and sometime even longer over weekends and public holidays.

12.2.6 Conclusion

In a study conducted by the Reserve Bank of Australia, it was found that consumers would like payment services to be timely, accessible, easy to use and easy to integrate into existing processes and systems (RBA, 2012). To sum it up, modern day payment systems must be able to support low value fund transfer securely and the service must be available anytime, any-where, at a low cost. The systems described earlier have their limitations and are usually not fit for purpose in fulfilling these needs:

- Wholesale systems, although can operate in real-time, are not accessible and are too ex-pensive for low value payments.
- Card payment networks, although they operate in real-time and are designed for retail purposes, are expensive to the merchant and are best suited for use when both payer and payee are in close proximity during the transaction. It can take days for funds to be made available to merchant accounts.

- Closed-loop systems, although the most cost-effective and efficient, are ubiquitous in most countries. It requires a brand that is more trusted than the bank, card and government institutions. It must be dominant in their market and reach the critical mass to be adopted by both payers and payees.
- ACH payment networks are ubiquitous and lower in cost than card payment networks. They facilitate account-to-account transfers but can only support batch processing and operate only during working days.
- Cash is still the best way to make low-cost payment such as bill splitting or thrift stores in face-to-face situations but is not efficient in other cases.

	Availability	Clearing	Settlement	Scalability	Costs	Ubiquitous
Wholesale Payment	Working Days	NA	Fast	Low	High	Low
Card Payment	24 / 7	Fast	Slow	High	High	High
Closed-Loop Payment	24 / 7	NA	Fast	Maybe	Low	Low
ACH Bulk Payment	Working Days	Slow	Medium	High	Low	High

Due to these limitations, Real-Time Payment Systems can be seen as the modernization of ACH network's batch payment systems in addressing new payment needs that cannot be readily addressed by existing systems. The following diagram summarizes the characteristics of payment systems described earlier (Fig. 12.9).

Interbank Payment Landscape Overview

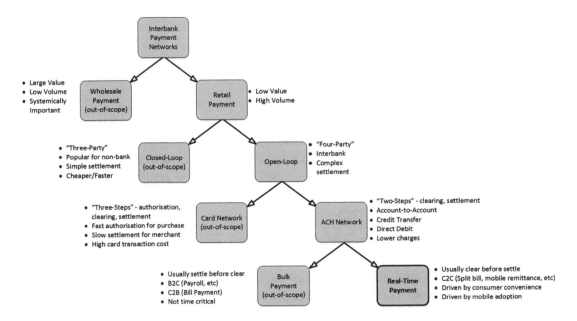

Figure 12.9: Interbank payment landscape overview.

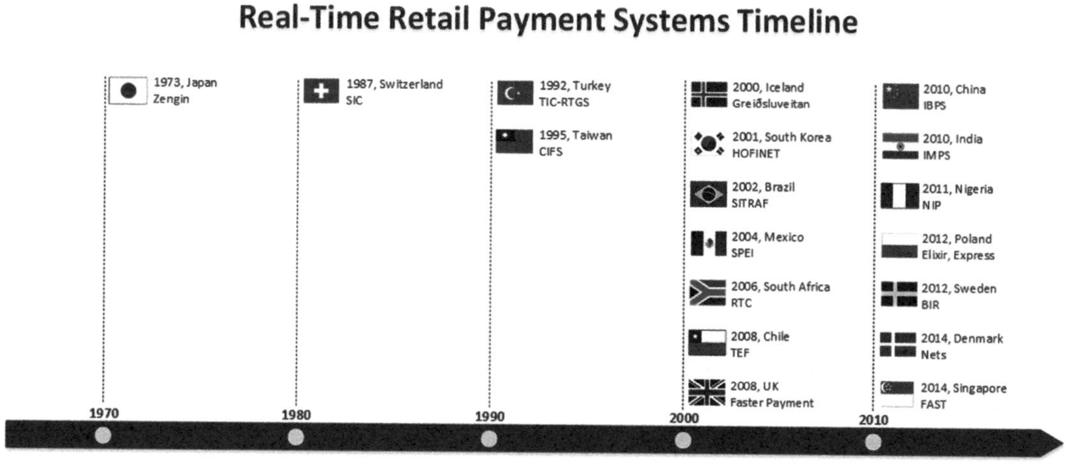

Real-Time Retail Payment Systems Timeline

1973, Japan Zengin	1987, Switzerland SIC	1992, Turkey TIC-RTGS	2000, Iceland Greiðsluveitan	2010, China IBPS
		1995, Taiwan CIFS	2001, South Korea HOFINET	2010, India IMPS
			2002, Brazil SITRAF	2011, Nigeria NIP
			2004, Mexico SPEI	2012, Poland Elixir, Express
			2006, South Africa RTC	2012, Sweden BIR
			2008, Chile TEF	2014, Denmark Nets
			2008, UK Faster Payment	2014, Singapore FAST
1970	1980	1990	2000	2010

Figure 12.10: Real-time retail payment systems timeline.

12.3 The Case for Real-Time Retail Payment Systems

RTPS is not a new concept and has started way back when Japan created the Zengin Systems in 1973. However, recent years have seen a rise in RTPS implementations in various countries especially towards the end of 2010 (BIS, 2012b). This phenomenon is largely attributed to consumers becoming accustomed to the high-speed and readily accessible information brought on by the mobile revolution. With e-commerce and m-commerce purchases taking place in real-time, and in some countries where deliveries can be made on the same day, the expectations are for the banks and businesses to be able to provide services that can cater for faster payment needs anytime and anywhere (Fig. 12.10).

One of the most commonly publicized examples of RTPS is UK's Faster Payment System (FPS) that was implemented in 2008. It has most of the characteristics of what most countries will expect out of having an RTPS. In 2014, FPS has handled more than 1 billion transactions worth over $1 billion (Accenture, 2015).

12.3.1 Reasons for Real-Time Retail Payment Systems

There are many reasons for implementing an RTPS system and it comes generally from regulatory, consumer and business perspectives. However, banking industry in general does not find RTPS a compelling business case especially with its potential to cannibalize existing revenue stream such as card and float revenue. As highlighted by RBA, benefits to RTPS are for serving a public good in fostering a better risk control, promoting efficiency and competition in the payment services market. The following points illustrate some of the motivations in implementing RTPS.

Regulator's Perspective

- **Adherence to their mandates.** Maintaining stability and efficiency of the financial system is part of the mandate given to the financial regulations and central banks of countries. As such, it is in the central banks' interest to foster payment innovation and competition in payment sector to improve overall payment effectiveness (RBA, 2012). In UK's Faster Payment, main driver for RTPS came from Office of Fair Trading to remove the float from regular fixed amount payments which can take as long as $T + 3$ (Greene et al., 2015).
- **Financial Inclusion.** Kenya, Nigeria and India are examples of countries whose primary objective is to improve the financial inclusion situation through the use of RTPS.
- **Controlling high-inflation rate.** SITRAF was implemented by Brazil in 2002 to combat the hyperinflation problem (as high as 4000% in 1990) that has resulted in severe loss of confidence for the Brazilian Real. Implementing a real-time payment system is for the purpose of enabling payment as soon as possible avoiding the use of the slow paper check payment instrument to counter the effect of its sliding currency value (McIntosh et al., 2015).
- **Improving Economy.** Faster payments can speed up cash conversion cycle, generate working capital, reduce short-term interest rate expenses. In the United States, the interest has been there since 2002 (Greene et al., 2015) but it has only just commissioned a new RTPS in 2016 to be implemented by Vocalink, operator for UK's Faster Payment. RTPS is also used as a motivation to drive down the use of cash and check payments which is a more costly and ineffective payment instrument. It is estimated that once a paper-based payment system if fully transitioned to electronic payment, a country can save more than 1% of its annual GDP (Humphrey et al., 2003).

Consumer's Perspective

- **Availability of fund.** Existing electronic payment methods usually imply a delay of at least one day. This becomes an issue when urgent payment needs to be made. RTPS is available around the clock and can address urgency payment very well such as late payment of bills.
- **Proximity Person-to-Person payment.** There is no easier way to make payment to someone face-to-face apart from the use of cash. This problem can be solved electronically in consumer-to-business transactions through the use of EFTPOS.
- **Instant confirmation.** When a payment is made, payer will usually want to know if the payment is transferred successfully rather than waiting for the following day to receive a confirmation.

Merchant's Perspective

- **Card is expensive.** The biggest issue with card payment is the card charges that merchants have to pay.
- **Availability of fund.** Being able to receive payment faster can improve the cash position of businesses and contributed to the economy overall.
- **Ability to support more payment information.** One of the advantages of paper check is the ability to carry additional payment information (RBA, 2012) either as a separate attached paper document or additional account payment information written at the back of the check. This can help businesses improve payment reconciliation for handling of account receivables.

Reasons Against Real-Time Retail Payment Systems

Reserve Bank of Australia in its Strategic Review of Innovation in the Payment Systems has indicated that depending on cooperative innovation alone from the banking industry is not likely to succeed without public sector initiatives as RTPS implementations may encounter coordination problems and lack of bank motivations due to lack of compelling business case (RBA, 2012). This is an accurate view as seen with other successful implementations of RTPS worldwide. Banks are generally against the adoption of RTPS and this is more so in the developed countries as explained in the points below.

High Implementation and Support Cost

The most notable problem is the cost associated with implementing and supporting RTPS. The cost depends on how entrenched and developed the countries' existing retail payment system is and therefore developed versus developing countries may face different cost issues (DB, 2015).

- In developed markets, banks have lesser motivation to change. An established ACH network may already have been operating efficiently for some time. The whole industry including banks and ACH may have its processes and systems optimized for batch processing. Therefore, implementing real-time may come at substantial cost of change for incumbents that have invested substantially in batch systems.
- In emerging markets, banks may be more receptive to change. A mature payment infrastructure may not be in existence yet and banks do not have as high a sunk cost. As BIS has pointed out in their report (BIS, 2012a), innovations in retail payments may represent only incremental improvements of established payment services whereas large leaps can occur in countries where payment infrastructure is underdeveloped. This is especially so when banks are expected to improve their banking rate involving large pool of unbanks.

However, the implementation of RTPS assumes that the country has a solid market infrastructure foundation that is compliant with the systemic risk mitigation recommendations issued by CPMI (SWIFT, 2015). This is generally not the case for emerging countries and ability to implement such technologies may not be within the immediate budget or reach.

- There will be substantial upfront cost involved for the implementation of RTPS and it will not be economically viable without sufficient banks' participation. For the ACH, the upfront cost will involve paying for the new RTPS infrastructure and major part of project implementation costs. For the banks, the investment will likely involve upgrading of existing financial message format to a universal standard like ISO20022, upgrading their core banking software to support straight-through-processing (STP) for real-time, upgrading their network infrastructure to support high throughput and high-availability and, in addition to that, upgrading their own customer facing application to utilize the new infrastructure. According to Accenture's 2015 report (Accenture, 2015), UK banks each spent close to $300 million for Faster Payments Service access and more than $1 billion for internal systems upgrade. Cost estimated by Accenture for each bank to implement RTPS ranges from $50 million to $250 million. According to US Federal Reserve Bank and The Clearing House, implementing RTPS for US can cost about $5 billion.
- There will be ongoing support cost and enhancement investments that are critical to ensure no down-time to RTPS operations in a 24/7/365 setup. It will be challenging to maintain the centralized support capabilities, domain expertise and human resources as ACH's operator revenue model will not be as high as the bank's. Central operation can experience high turnover upon completion of the implementation resulting in loss of domain know-how critical to the central operations.

Unclear Revenue Potential

The upfront cost in upgrading existing bank systems combined with low margin from RTPS and potential impact to profitable revenue stream will mean longer time to achieve return on investment. In some of the major implementations of RTPS such as Singapore's FAST and UK's FPS, consumer transactions are free with the view that savings from paper-based payment will offset the cost of transaction, introduction of new innovative overlay services may create new revenue opportunities but this is still too early to be proven.

- **Loss of competitive advantage.** Larger banks especially those that have achieved a dominant position in the markets have more to lose in implementing RTPS as it levels the playing field for the industry and neutralizes their competitive advantage from information asymmetry (RBA, 2012).
- **Cannibalization of card revenue.** Card revenue is an important revenue source to banks performing the roles of acquirer and/or issuer. This revenue can be significantly impacted

if payments by cards are overly substituted by RTPS without reasonable revenue transfer (Greene et al., 2015). However, it is also worth noting that regardless of RTPS implementations, the same competition will be faced by new entrants offering cheaper payment alternatives to cards. On the other hand, in developing countries where card penetrations are not high, the impact may not be as significant.

- **Loss of float revenue.** RTPS will remove the time for cash to be outside of consumers' bank accounts and reduce revenue opportunities of float from the banks. Any float revenue opportunity is a constraint to what the paying bank can earn from the time between clearing and settlement. This has less implications in a low interest rate environment.
- **Fraud.** Making transactions faster and irrevocable also means making it harder to manage fraud. Banks will need to invest in better fraud detection mechanisms as well as risk management procedures.

Project Implementation Risks

- Implementations of RTPS even by some of the more successful examples are often plagued with delays including UK's FPS, Singapore's FAST and Australia's NPP (McIntosh et al., 2015).
- The Polish national clearing house, Krajowa Izba Rozliczeniowa S.A. (KIR), introduced Express ELIXIR, Poland's RTPS, in June 2012 but is not successfully adopted. This is due to the lack of central bank mandate, and as a result there are only 11 out of 49 banks participating in the network. KIR was created out of the need to compete against a strong third-party competitor, BlueCash.
- In South Africa, only 27% of the banks participated in RTC.
- In Brazil, banks are reluctant to use SITRAF because of the loss of float.
- Difficult to apply is "Baby-Step Giant-Step" as the cost for operating the central infrastructure is high and investment will need to be maximized involving as many banks as possible to share the cost.

This explains why take-up rate of RTPS in developing countries is not high since RTPS technologies are too costly for them to implement and developing countries stand the most to lose from the inability to unlock the economic potential from the rise in digitalization. On the other hand, banks in developed countries are not motivated to change due to lack of compelling business case and seemingly incremental benefit can only be materialized in longer terms. Therefore, implementation of RTPS usually requires a regulatory push and is not entirely driven by market forces. SWIFT's studies have shown that regulatory initiatives formed 73% of the factors driving RTPS adoption (SWIFT, 2015). Slow adoption in Poland, South Africa and Brazil can be attributed to lower government involvement and/or higher industry resistance (less than 10% since its implementation against other electronic payment instruments) compared to more typical circumstances such as UK, South Korea, Switzerland and Japan (achieving between 30% and 90% of adoption rate).

12.4 The Characteristics of Real-Time Retail Payment Systems

There is no standard definition to the term RTPS. It is being used very broadly in different countries and is constantly evolving with new features that support new type of payment services. It is also worth noting that simply because it is called "Real-Time" does not mean that being able to make payment faster is all there is to RTPS. To observe what sets various implementations of RTPS apart, it is important to understand the characteristics that are generally expected in new generations of such systems. For the purpose of this writing, a real-time retail payment system is defined to be a domestic interbank payment system that is used for the transfer of funds from a payer's bank account to a payee's bank account of a different bank with near instant confirmation and availability of funds. Settlement of transferred funds between the payer's and payee's bank need not be real-time.

12.4.1 Timeliness

The term "real-time" cannot be defined definitively because it is highly subjective and can be interpreted differently depending on implementations. There is no quantitative and authoritative definition for how fast should transactions be processed in order to qualify as real-time. It is generally used by the industry to mean a faster mechanism of processing payments. Payment processing is "near instantaneous" but not instantaneous because latencies can occur when involving multiple parties and will require time for validation, confirmation and transaction posting within banks.

A real-time payment transaction can involve processing for clearing, posting and settlement. For real-time to take place, posting and clearing must at least be able to operate in real-time.

- **Payer's Bank**
  - Must be able to immediately forward a payment instruction from payer to the RTPS.
  - Must be able to debit the payer's account after receiving a successful payment confirmation from RTPS.
- **Payee's Bank**
  - Must be able to immediately credit the payee's account after receiving the payment instruction from RTPS.
  - Must be able to respond immediately to the RTPS with a successful payment confirmation.
- **ACH**

- Must be able to receive payment instruction from any originating member bank and process the instruction within a very short timeframe that is collectively agreed by all participants.
- Must be able to route the payment instruction to the corresponding receiving member bank immediately after processing it.
- Must be able to receive payment confirmation from any receiving member bank and process the instruction immediately.
- Must be able to route the payment confirmation to the corresponding originating member bank immediately after processing it.

However, the settling of funds between banks does not have to take place in real-time and can be aggregated as a batch for netting and settlement at a later time.

12.4.2 Availability

RTPS is primarily driven by online and mobile consumer needs and, therefore, the service must be made available round the clock throughout the year. Most systems that operate 24/7/365 include Denmark's RealTime24/7, India's IMPS, Korea's HOFINET, Singapore's FAST, South Africa's RTC, Sweden's BIR and UK's FPS. Some RTPS, however, only operate on working days, for instance, Mexico's SPEI, Brazil's SITRAF and Japan's Zengin.

12.4.3 Universal Financial Messaging Standards

The types of financial messaging standards used by RTPS are an important part of the design consideration. In general, the financial messaging standards should be:

- **Interoperable.** Based on an open standard that is widely understood and adopted by various countries and interoperable to support future cross-border payment needs.
- **Can carry richer information.** Facilitate the inclusion of payment related information such as payer's detail for KYC/AML check, payee's detail such as bill account number to facilitate account receivables reconciliation and support for unicode.
- **Ease of Straight-Through-Processing (STP) Integration.** Because transaction processing has to take place in real-time, therefore transaction being sent to payee's bank must be automatically processed immediately by the payee's bank the moment that payment instruction is received without human intervention. To facilitate this integration effort, the messaging standard must be implemented in a form that is easy to program, make changes and verified.

Based on these considerations, the industry will have to collectively agree on the messaging standard and will usually choose from one of the following options:

- Industry can also create their own bespoke and proprietary message format. Some may use legacy SWIFT FIN message format that is commonly used in telegraphic transfer. The benefit is that the domain knowledge is more readily available but this standard is in the process of being phased out by the newer ISO20022 standard.
- ISO20022 is a new international financial messaging format not specific to payments only. It is the preferred standard for new generations of RTPS due to its more open and extensible XML-based design, able to support for cross-border usage and support larger payload. However, ISO20022 is relatively new and evolving, industry adoption is still at early stage. The cost to change can be high and require heavy investments for systems upgrade and applications integration. Countries using ISO20022 include Singapore's FAST, Australia's NPP, Denmark's RealTime24/7, Sweden's BIR.
- ISO8583 is the international message standard for card originating transactions used by ATM and EFTPOS. As such networks are usually already in existence in most countries, it is therefore easier to consider piggybacking onto this standard for RTPS. However, ISO8583 has its limitations as each implementation may use its own proprietary binary format and is constraint by the amount of data it can carry. However, this is usually a choice when a country has deep investment on ISO8583 network and switching to ISO20022 may require change and cost. Countries using ISO8583 include UK's FPS, India's IMPS.

12.4.4 Overlay Services

RTPS is only a means to an end because just being able to process transactions faster will not be enough to create a compelling case for widespread adoption. It is generally expected in most implementations that banks and payment service providers will develop new and innovative services that overlay on the platform that provides new value-adds to the consumers. This is a somewhat "If you built it, they will come" mentality that is predominantly assumed.

One of the most common overlay services that is implemented together with RTPS is known as the addressing service. It is the ability to allow payer to make payments to a payee using an alternative form of identification without the need to use bank account numbers. For instance, instead of sending money to a bank account, payer can send money to the payee's phone number instead. From a payees' perspective, they may not be comfortable with sharing their bank account details to payer to receive payment due to fear of fraud and scams. From a payer's perspective, it is more convenient to send using the payee's phone number and is less likely to make a mistake in sending funds. It makes the payment experience simpler and much like a check where the sender is only required to know the addressee but up to the receiver to bank into their own account. This is the reason why in the case of Australia's NPP, addressing is identified as a part of the core function integral to the platform. In the case of UK's FPS, it is operated as a separate service known as PayM. India's IMPS uses a seven-digit Mobile Money Identifier (MMID) to link a customer's bank account to their mobile phone number.

Other examples may include the application of overlay services in mandate management and e-Invoicing (McIntosh et al., 2015).

12.5 Architecture and Design of Real-Time Retail Payment Systems

12.5.1 Architecture Models

SWIFT has identified three models that RTPS can adopt – hub-centric model, RTGS-centric model, and decentralized model (SWIFT, 2015).

Hub-Centric Model

Hub-centric model is the most common approach of all three. The clearing is performed centrally at the clearing house in near real-time and usually involves four legs, i.e. payment request from originating bank to clearing house, payment request from clearing house to receiving bank, payment confirmation from receiving bank to clearing house and payment confirmation from clearing house to the originating bank. Clearing house is responsible for validating, calculating the settlement positions and routing payment instructions between banks. Payee banks will post the transaction and update payee account upon successful processing of payment instruction. Payer banks will post the transaction and update payer account upon successful receipt of payment confirmation. Settlement is usually carried out on a deferred net settlement basis multiple times a day to minimize counterparty risks (Fig. 12.11).

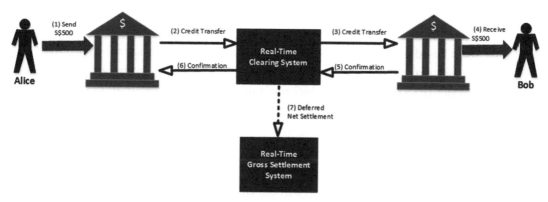

Figure 12.11: Hub-centric real-time retail payment model.

This is the model adopted by Singapore's FAST payment network and UK's Faster Payment System.

RTGS-Centric Model

As mentioned in the previous section, RTPS is different from the wholesale payment system called Real-Time Gross Settlement system (RTGS). RTPS transactions are generally settled on a deferred net settlement basis at least once a day using the hub-centric model. However, in some countries, an RTGS system may be extended to process both low-value and high-value transactions because retail payment volume is low or because of the way it has evolved (Fig. 12.12).

Figure 12.12: RTGS-centric real-time retail payment model.

Switzerland's SIC uses RTGS for both retail and high-value payments. Japan's Zengin system clears high-value and low-value transactions on the same clearing system but transactions are routed to either an RTGS for large value (amount equal or larger than 100 million JPY) or a DNS for low value (amount lesser than 100 million JPY). Mexico's SPEI runs multilateral netting every few seconds for both high-value and retail payment processing.

Distributed Model

The final model adopts a distributed model whereby payments are cleared bilaterally between payer and payee banks (Fig. 12.13).

This is the model used by Australia's New Payment Platform. Unlike normal approach of using deferred net settlement system, Australia's architecture includes a component called Fast Settlement Service (FSS) that provides 24/7 settlement in complementing RTGS's function.

12.5.2 Design Approach

Implementation of RTPS is not usually something that can come right out of the box. Although most countries generally would like to use some form of a reference point by looking at how others have implemented similar strategies, it is very unlikely to have an apple-to-apple comparison as too many similar factors will need to be involved. Therefore, the design approach can be based on the extension of existing systems, developing of new system, or a combination of both.

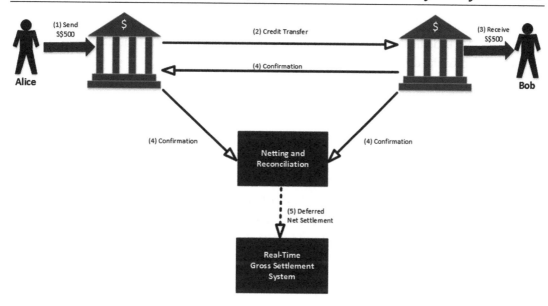

Figure 12.13: Distributed real-time retail payment model.

Extending From RTGS

One way to implement RTPS is to upgrade the existing RTGS to support high volume of retail payment. This is the approach adopted in Switzerland, Turkey and Mexico. On the other hand, Qatar and Saudi Arabia are going from an RTGS-centric model to a Hub-centric model by creating a new ACH system to offload retail payments from RTGS. Another variant of this approach is to take in both high-value and low-value for clearing but route them to different settlement systems based on the transaction size, which is the approach adopted by Japan.

Extending From ACH Payment

Since ACH payment systems are already supporting the existing interbank network, one way to approach real-time is to increase the frequency of DNS cycles so that rather than settling once a day, the system can settle every few minutes or several times a day. This is the approach adopted by Brazil, Denmark and South Korea.

Implementing a Fresh Build

Finally, a new RTPS can be implemented entirely standalone from the existing payment systems. The most common approach is to implement real-time for ACH clearing and transaction posting at the banks while settlement remains as deferred net settlement. This is the approach adopted by UK and Singapore. To take this one step further, both clearing and settlement can be implemented in real-time. This can be done by creating a separate real-time settlement component that is dedicated for settling funds cleared through the real-time clearing system. This is the approach adopted by Australia.

12.5.3 Risk Management Principles

Because funds are cleared between banks in real-time but settled later, payer bank is exposed to counterparty risk between time of clearing and time of settlement. One of the ways to mitigate this risk is to increase the frequencies of settlement, for instance Singapore's FAST payment network is settled twice a day, UK's Faster Payment settles three times a day whereas Australia's NPP is designed to cater for 24×7 real-time settlement. Besides increasing settlement frequencies, the network can also adopt certain risk management measures such as collateral management, debit cap, daily transaction limit and loss sharing.

Collateral Posting

Banks are required to create special collateral accounts for holding funds that can be used for settlement of real-time payments. The disadvantage is that this can lock in the bank's funds in a reserve and limiting the bank's liquidity.

Imposing a Daily Debit Cap

Banks can be imposed with a cap that limits the net debit settlement position (i.e. the amount to be paid out by the bank during settlement). Sending of funds cannot take place until either the bank receives incoming payments to reduce its net debit position or after settlement cutover takes place.

Imposing a Daily Maximum Account Transfer Limit

A daily limit can be imposed by a bank to control the maximum value of funds that can be sent by an individual account for a single day to limit the bank's credit exposure. UK's Faster Payment impose a limit of 100,000 GBP per day and Singapore's FAST impose a limit of 50,000 SGD.

Loss Sharing

In the event of member's default, the collateral put up by the defaulted member will be disbursed to the remaining members on the network. In return, all other members on the network will be obligated to provide liquidity to fund the shortfall due to the member's default.

12.6 Conclusion

To sum it up, this writing has sought to give readers an understanding of RTPS. It begins by illustrating the role that RTPS plays in the existing interbank payment landscape and the problems it is designed to solve. This is followed by providing a description of what constitutes RTPS by inferring its characteristics from real world examples. Finally, it considered ways that RTPS can be designed and built. The writing thus far is based on RTPS that has already been implemented and known to the world.

As a conclusion, this writing will look into the future possibilities of RTPS evolution.

Major Implementations Rollout

While the writing is based on the countries that already have publicly known implementations of RTPS, there are some major implementations that are in the pipeline for rolling out over the next few years. These are all ambitious and large scale projects happening in some of the most developed countries in the world. These implementations have a strong commonality and that they are all geared for cross-border payment transfers and imply a future of great competitions and innovations in cross-border payment space.

- Pan-European Instant Payment

The European Central Bank (ECB) is driving the development of a pan-European Instant Payment scheme to be adopted by Euro-based national retail payment system operators of SEPA countries (34 as of 2015). This is to prevent any fragmentation of European instant payment system as a result of individually developed systems that cannot interoperate with one another. The standardized Pan-European instant payments infrastructure may represent an important development for the world as it will be the first to create a true cross-border real-time retail payment network. The mandate is given to the European Retail Payments Board (ERPB), comprised of supply and demand side representatives of the European retail payments market, to come up with an instant payment scheme to be ready for implementation by November 2017.

- NPP

The implementation of Australia's RTPS referred to as the New Payments Platform (NPP) started in December 2014 and is slated to be operational in 2017. Once completed, NPP will be among the most advanced RTPS in the world with ability to perform real-time clearing and settlement with new addressing capabilities.

- United States

The Clearing House (TCH) has embarked on the development of an ambitious US real-time payment implementation in late 2015 and according to its CEO, James Aramanda, will connect leading 24 banks that have 60% of the market with the existing 14,000 financial institutions with a target to go-live in late 2017.

Real-Time Payments in Emerging Countries

Although cross-border payments seem to be the focus for innovations in developed countries, domestic retail payment remains to be a major hurdle in emerging countries, especially those with high unbanked populations. While benefits of implementing RTPS may be incremental for the developed countries, the benefits to the emerging countries may be a lot more substantial. These countries are experiencing the highest growth rate in digitalization and are in urgent need for payment infrastructure that can help them unlock the economic potentials. It should come as no surprise that some of these countries may have a higher population of social media users than bank account holders. Even when their e-commerce and m-commerce are experiencing a boom, the economy is still very much cash-based.

In Vietnam, for instance (IFC, 2014), it is not uncommon for online users to make purchases over the Internet but payment is done via cash-on-delivery. This results in third party logistic providers with better reach into rural areas becoming a more strategic e-commerce partner than even the banks. It is estimated that more than 90% of e-commerce payments are paid through cash (Viet, 2015). Dependency on cash for e-commerce is largely due to consumers appreciating the convenience but cannot trust the quality of purchases made online. Consumers are also concerned about fraud and security risks from making online payments. Card penetration in Vietnam is still very low and complicated for online use. This creates an opportunity whereby underdeveloped payment infrastructure may result in a large leap in payment innovation over retail payment instruments (BIS, 2012a). With one of the largest e-tailer in Vietnam, Lazada, being acquired by Alibaba in April 2016 (Bloomberg, 2016), the banks will be facing even stronger competition in the near future from Alibaba's mobile wallet and microfinancing play (Bales, 2016).

Can RTPS be viable a solution for financial inclusion in emerging country? Maybe.

In India, similarly to Vietnam, only an estimated 10–15% of Indians have ever used any kind of non-cash payment instrument compared to 40% in China and Brazil (Creehan, 2016). Having adopted a common strategy to drive up financial inclusion by combining the use of their biometric identification cards (Aadhaar Cards) with the use of Real-Time Payment (IMPS), they are poised to launch a new service called Unified Payment Interface (UPI) to gradually encourage adoption of cash-less payments. Once the infrastructure is properly in place, India's welfare payment can be issued to the populations via their identity cards and encourage them to open bank accounts to receive the funds. The same strategy is adopted by Thailand's RTPS implementation called PromptPay (BOT, 2016). It is still early to tell how successful these schemes will be but it is certainly a prod in the right direction with a strong regulatory support.

The challenges, however, are largely associated with incentives. Larger banks enjoying a dominant market position will not be keen to adopt RTPS whereas smaller banks will find strength in numbers leveraging on the network effect. The cost aspect will be extremely important as RTPS systems are not known to be cheap as explained in the earlier sections and have dependencies on the maturity of a country's financial infrastructure foundations. Therefore, the traditional approach and design of RTPS may be out of the reach for most emerging countries but with the advent in distributed ledger technologies, it can be a viable alternative to warrant further considerations. This is certainly a one design option that the United States have not entirely ruled out in their plans for implementation of RTPS as highlighted in their paper "Strategies for Improving the U.S. Payment System" (Federal Reserve System, 2015). Payments can be cleared via a distributed ledger system with a central authority responsible for settlement via DNS.

References

Accenture, 2015. Real-time payments A roadmap for banks. s.l.: s.n.

Bales, S., 2016. Banks, you should be scared [online]. Available at: http://fintechnews.sg/2198/fintech/scott-bales-banks-you-should-be-scared/.

BIS, Bank for International Settlements, 2003. A glossary of terms used in payments and settlement systems, s.l.: s.n.

BIS, Bank for International Settlements, 2012a. Innovations in retail payments, s.l.: s.n.

BIS, Bank for International Settlements, 2012b. Payment, clearing and settlement systems in Japan, s.l.: s.n.

BIS, Bank for International Settlements, 2014. Non-banks in retail payments, s.l.: s.n.

Bloomberg, 2016. Alibaba expands in Southeast Asia with $1 billion Lazada deal. s.l.: s.n.

BOT, Bank of Thailand, 2016. A new funds transfer service – "PromptPay", Bangkok: s.n.

CHAPS, 2016. CHAPS statistics [online]. Available at: http://www.chapsco.co.uk/about-chaps/chaps-statistics.

Creehan, S., 2016. How modernizing India's payment system can drive financial inclusion. San Francisco: s.n.

DB, Deutsche Bank, 2015. Instant revolution of payments, s.l.: s.n.

Deloitte, 2015. Independent review of RTGS outage on 20 October 2014 [online]. Available at: http://www.bankofengland.co.uk/publications/Documents/news/2015/rtgsdeloitte.pdf.

Federal Reserve System, 2015. Strategies for improving the U.S. payment system, s.l.: s.n.

Greene, C., Rysman, M., Schuh, S., Shy, O., 2015. Costs and Benefits of Building Faster Payment Systems: The U.K. Experience and Implications. Federal Reserve Bank of Boston, Boston.

Humphrey, D., Willeson, M., Lindblom, T., Bergendahl, G., 2003. What does it cost to make a payment? Review of Network Economics 2 (2).

IFC, 2014. E- and M-commerce and payment sector development in Vietnam. s.l.: s.n.

Jack, W., Suri, T., 2010. The economics of M-PESA [online]. Available at: http://www.mit.edu/~tavneet/M-PESA.pdf.

McIntosh, G., et al., 2015. Flavors of fast – a trip around the world in immediate payments. Brussels, Belgium: Clear2Pay.

RBA, Reserve Bank of Australia, 2012. Strategic review of innovation in the payment systems: conclusions, s.l.: s.n.

SWIFT, 2015. The global adoption of real-time. s.l.: s.n.

Viet, T.Q., 2015. E-payments in Vietnam: an emerging market with great potential [online]. Available at: http://www.thepaypers.com/expert-opinion/e-payments-in-vietnam-an-emerging-market-with-great-potential/762417.

Notes

1. A **payment system** consists of a set of instruments, banking procedures and, typically, interbank funds transfer systems that ensure the circulation of money (BIS, 2003).

2. A **wholesale payment system** is a funds transfer system through which large-value and high-priority funds transfers are made between participants in the system for their own account or on behalf of their customers (BIS, 2003).

3. A payment system is systemically important where, if the system were insufficiently protected against risk, disruption within it could trigger or transmit further disruptions amongst participants or systemic disruptions in the financial area more widely (BIS, 2003).

4. A **retail payment system** is a funds transfer system which handles a large volume of payments of relatively low value in such forms as cheques, credit transfers, direct debits, ATM and EFTPOS (Electronic Funds Transfer at Point of Sale) transactions (BIS, 2003).

5. Electronic money is defined by BIS as value stored electronically in a device such as a chip card or a hard drive in a personal computer (BIS, 2003).

6. Before the use of RTPS.

CHAPTER 13

Real-Time Inbound Marketing: A Use Case for Digital Banking

Alan Megargel, Venky Shankararaman, Srinivas K. Reddy

Contents

13.1 Introduction

In this era of digital banking, customers are becoming increasingly more sophisticated, expecting personalized banking services to be delivered to them anytime, anywhere, and across any channel. Customers are now unresponsive to banks' direct marketing tactics that target whole demographic segments rather than to them individually. Rather customers expect banks to know their situational needs, predict a next best offer, and deliver that offer to them at the right time and place.

Let's say you are shopping for cologne for yourself. Your credit card is swiped, and 2 seconds later you receive an SMS from your bank saying "we know it's your wife's birthday in 2 days, and we know she likes Gucci products, and we offer 15% discount on Gucci if you use our credit card, and there is a Gucci shop right across the corridor from you" (Ranadivé and Bilski, 2013). Your first reaction might be that you are thankful for the reminder because you indeed forgot about your wife's upcoming birthday, and your second reaction might be to go across the corridor to Gucci and buy something for your wife. Furthermore, you would be delighted that your bank really knows you. The offer was delivered to you at precisely the right time, because you were just leaving one shop having purchased your cologne. If you had received the SMS 20 minutes later, already in your car, it would have been too late.

So how would a bank accomplish such a feat? In fact, only a few banks do it well, and many other banks are trying to follow their lead. This capability to deliver real-time personalized offers, at the customer point of interaction with the bank or merchant, is becoming increasingly strategic. Banks that fall behind will certainly lose market share. For the solution, you will need to look deep into the bank's architecture at the enterprise platform layer. There you will find enterprise platforms such as: messaging middleware, process orchestration engines, in-memory data grids, and complex event processing (CEP) engines. These are the architectural building blocks that make real-time inbound marketing happen.

This chapter proposes the usage of real-time inbound marketing as an important use case for a digital bank. The chapter will first discuss the evolution of marketing in retail banking along with the IT systems that support it, followed by an analysis of marketing strategies in today's digital banking era. The chapter will then provide a conceptual view of the various technology enablers of the enterprise platform layer of a bank's architecture. Finally, it will present a novel set of CEP patterns for implementing real-time inbound marketing, along with business scenario use cases for each pattern.

13.2 Evolution of IT Systems and Marketing Methods in Retail Banking

Marketing methods in retail banking are highly dependent on IT systems capability. The evolution of marketing methods can therefore be best understood in relation to the evolution of IT systems in retail banking. The evolution of IT systems can be explained in three separate eras: the "data processing era", the "client–server era", and the "predictive era". As IT systems evolved over these three eras, marketing methods evolved from batch mode outbound marketing to mass consumers without segmentation, followed by outbound marketing with customer segmentation, and finally to real-time personalized inbound marketing to individual consumers.

Data Processing Era. The "data processing era" (or "mainframe era") took place in the 1960s through 1980s. In this era, banking transactions were typically made over the counter, during normal office hours – 8 by 5. A typical bank with 10 million customers, for example, would interact with customers in person at the branch, and the number of customer interactions per day could be measured in the thousands.

A transaction was the only record of an interaction with a customer. A business day's transactions were processed overnight in batch mode (Martin, 2012), which meant that any potential marketing opportunities associated with customer transactions could only be assessed on the next day. In this era, customers had little or no access to information technology, and therefore products and services offered to customers were limited and unsophisticated relative to today. Furthermore, banking systems in this era were focused around accounting (Martin, 2012), and did not accommodate customer segmentation for the purposes of marketing. Banking was mostly relationship based, and with a relatively low level of sophistication, the speed of doing business was slow.

Client–Server Era. The "client–server era" took place in the 1980s through 2000s. The client–server architecture was meant to enable a bank's IT infrastructure to scale more cost effectively as compared to the mainframe, and it enabled more users to access their business systems. "Thick" client applications led to "thin" client web applications, and products and services were then offered over the Internet. With the advent of the Internet and other self-service channels, customers became more sophisticated and demanded better products and faster service, 24 by 7. As a result, the speed of doing business increased, in order to stay competitive. The number of customer interactions per day could be measured in the millions.

Self-service channels like the Internet resulted in more customer touch points, but these events did not necessarily get captured as a transaction. For example, if a customer logged in and browsed a bank's web site and showed interest in a product or service (e.g., used a simple mortgage calculator), no transaction took place, and therefore there was no record of the customer's interest.

In this era, banking operations were still transaction based. A transaction was still the only record of an interaction with a customer. But with the speed of business increasing, more transactions were being stored. Relational databases became popular for operational systems that processed a day's transactions. Enterprise data warehouses (EDWs) became popular to store historical transactions, but as a carryover from batch-style thinking, EDWs would only be updated during end-of-day batch processing.

To gain competitive advantage, banks began to mine their EDWs to generate marketing leads based on historical customer transaction behavior. Business Intelligence (BI) software became popular to help segment customers, and to identify opportunities (e.g., cross-sell, up-sell) as well as threats (e.g., late payments, fraud). However, an EDW-based BI could only access transaction data that was one day old at best, and therefore real-time business decisions were not possible due to "information latency" (TIBCO, 2006a).

In the client–server era, it was not possible for a bank to predict in real-time what products or services a customer might be interested in. Nor was it possible for a bank to predict in real-time if they were going to lose a customer. This era could also be described as the "wish I knew era," because once a critical business event had passed then it was too late to do anything about it.

Predictive Era. We are currently in the "predictive era" or the "we know what's about to happen era" (Ranadivé, 2005). The speed of doing business demands that events from multiple sources be captured and correlated in real-time, so that the bank can know ahead of time what is about to happen, and do something about it before it is too late. In the previous era, banking operations were transaction based, and decisions were made based on historical data-at-rest sitting in a database or EDW. In the current era, decisions are also made based on data-in-motion which can be either transactions or business events that are evaluated in real-time, in memory. To a predictive bank, data-in-motion is an order of magnitude more valuable than data-at-rest (Ranadivé and Maney, 2011).

Business Events can originate from a multitude of different sources, including: customer interactions (self-service and assisted), process milestones, system notifications, etc. Events can be temporal in nature also: for example, if something occurs earlier or later than expected, then that is useful information. Or if something doesn't occur at all, then that is an event (e.g., if a person starts an online loan application, but does not submit it). When assessed in isolation, a single event might not be enough information to predict something is about to happen. However, when events from different sources are correlated, patterns can be formed that lead to a prediction. For example, if a person is late renewing their credit card membership, and this person logs a complaint with the bank's call center, and within a week this person transfers a large sum of money to another bank, then a prediction can be made that the bank will lose this customer unless they do something about it.

When customer interaction events, such as: a credit card swipe, a web page visit, an ATM transaction, a bill payment, etc., are correlated with life-stage events, such as: getting married, moving house, having children, retiring, etc. (Bailey et al., 2009), there arise opportunities to effectively cross-sell or up-sell specific products targeting specific customers in real-time at the point of customer interaction with the bank (TIBCO, 2006b). Decisions made in real-time on these opportunities enable banks to intelligently sell the right products to the right customers via the right channels (Kamakura, 2008). The real-time execution of a perfectly customized and personalized "next best offer" (NBO) is the holy grail of inbound marketing (Davenport et al., 2011). Banks that do this well will have a competitive advantage.

Table 13.1 summarizes the key attributes for each era.

Table 13.1: Comparison of the different era's.

	Period	Customer Interaction	Marketing Strategy	IT Architecture	Transaction Processing
Data Processing Era	1960s–1980s	Face-to-Face over the counter. Around 1000 interactions/day through face-to-face over the counter.	Relationship based	Internally focused infrastructure with mostly the bank officers using systems	End of day batch processing of transactions
Client–Server Era	1980s–2000s	Many touch points for customer interaction. However not all interactions are captured as transactions and correlated.	Marketing leads based on historical customer data and segmentation	Internally and externally focused infrastructure with both bank officers and customers accessing services over the internet 24 by 7	Transactions in real-time but analytics and decision making are not real-time
Predictive Era	Now	Many touch points for customer interaction. All interactions are captured as transactions and correlated in real-time	Marketing leads based on historical and data in motion, segmentation, current context	24 by 7 open but secure infrastructure across the business ecosystem of bank, partners and customers	Transactions, analytics and decision making are in real-time

13.3 Marketing Strategies in Today's Digital Banking Era

Digital Banking. "A digital bank uses a broad range of technology-centric capabilities that enable new methods of interaction and service delivery to augment the customer experience and potentially transform the business. These capabilities are supported by a robust, dynamic and accessible digital infrastructure and open banking system that transform the analog environment" (Gartner Research, 2013b).

In the digital banking market, retail banks can no longer compete solely based on products which have become commoditized, rather they must compete based on customer experience driven service differentiation (Drotskie, 2009). Digital natives, who have been immersed in technology their entire lives (Prensky, 2001), are unresponsive and even annoyed with mass marketing promotions that are irrelevant to them personally, rather they expect technologically sophisticated and personalized treatment (Cotton and Walker, 2011; Drotskie, 2009).

Cross-Selling Strategy. Brand loyalty based on relationships is not sufficient. As banking customers are exposed to increasingly more innovative self-service channels, these now sophisticated customers tend to shop around and do business with every bank that offers the best service, which usually means the fastest delivery (Cotton and Walker, 2011). Cross-selling products to existing banking customers is more cost effective, roughly one-fifth the cost of selling to new customers (Kona and Surti, 2010), and also improves customer loyalty as the number of products per customer increases. Cross-selling therefore, as a means to both increase revenue and retain customers, has become a key strategic initiative for many retail banks (Dass, 2006; Kamakura, 2008; Mann and Kumar, 2014).

Traditionally, cross-selling required person-to-person interaction at the branch and relied on the skill and intuition of the bank officer. However, in the digital banking market, self-service online channels have largely supplanted human interactions at the branch, and therefore IT systems and analytics tools are now central to cross-selling (Kamakura, 2008).

Cross-selling has implications on a bank's channel integration strategy, as increasingly more customers do their banking across multiple channels, and expect consistent treatment across all channels (Cotton and Walker, 2011; Stone, 2009). The effectiveness of product offers delivered across multiple channels needs to be understood and optimized, and marketing content needs to be designed and optimized specifically for each channel. Customer interaction management is needed as well which: a) enables customers to opt-in to receive promotions and select their preferred mode of delivery, and b) enables the bank to track whether or not a customer has expressed interest in the offer in order to avoid irritating the customer with repeated offers for a product they are not interested in.

Cross-sell offers can be delivered via assisted channels such as branch and call center, provided that the branch teller or call center operator is prompted with an auto-generated "Next Best Offer" (NBO) tailored for the customer (Hesse, 2009). This is typically the first form of inbound marketing capability implemented by banks, although the reach to customers is limited as increasingly more customers prefer to do their banking through online channels. Still, it is an important milestone for a bank to achieve, since the capability to deliver tailored offers across multiple channels implies that the bank has a 360-degree view of customers supported by predictive analytics (Cognizant, 2011).

In the current predictive era, a bank's inbound marketing strategy must include online channels and payments as the predominant sources of customer interaction. In Asia, 40% of mass affluent customers and 50% of customers under the age of 40 prefer to use Internet and mobile banking channels (McKinsey & Company, 2014). In the US, 80% of all customer interactions with the bank are for payment-related activities such as making payments, checking payment status, or paying bills (Denecker et al., 2014). Therefore, banks must invest in technology that enables cross-sell offers to be delivered via online channels in real-time, i.e., at the moment of customer interaction with the bank.

Simple Message Service (SMS) text messaging is a cost-effective and reliable channel for delivering targeted cross-sell offers to customers at the point-of-sales (POS) in real-time just after a credit card swipe (Riley et al., 2011). If the merchant has a tie-in with the bank, the cross-sell offer might be related to that merchant and offer a discount coupon. The merchant may not have a tie-in with the bank however, and the customer interaction might then be used to cross-sell another nearby merchant's offer which is relevant to the customer. Either way, it is a NBO that is delivered in real-time.

A Framework for NBO. Davenport et al. (2011) propose a four-step framework for enabling NBO, namely defining objectives, by gathering data, analyzing and executing, and learning and evolving. In the defining objective step, the bank must define what it intends to achieve as the end goal, for example, increased revenues, increased customer loyalty, increased customer purchase or new customers. In the gathering data step, the bank must collect and integrate detailed data about their customers, product and service offerings, and the context in which customer purchases the products. In the analyzing and executing step, the bank must identify the right technology for analyzing and predicting the offer to be offered, and also the channel (e.g. call center, online in real-time) through which the NBO is to be delivered. In the learning and evolving step, the bank must put in place mechanisms to monitor and learn from their NBO performance and evolve their strategy and implementation.

Organizational Challenges. Cross-selling effectively requires a change in marketing method; from traditional outbound campaign-driven mass marketing based on customer segmentation, to inbound marketing which delivers personalized offers targeted to individual customers based on their situational needs. This presents several organizational challenges:

Firstly, traditional outbound marketing is very much product-centric, aligning to traditional product-centric organizational silos (Kamakura, 2008). A marketer designs an offer for a banking product, selects a segment of customer's to target, and then delivers the same offer through the same channel to all customers in the selected segment (Hesse, 2009). Banks will need to unlearn what they have learned in order to break down their product-centric mentality. Inbound marketing requires a customer-centric mindset (Kamakura, 2008). A customer interacts with the bank using their preferred channel, the customer's profile and current situation determine which one of many possible product offers is best suited for the customer at that point in time, and the offer is delivered in real-time via the customer's preferred delivery channel.

Secondly, there may be management resistance to implementing a customer-centric inbound marketing strategy, due to existing sales incentives which are traditionally tied to product performance (Kamakura, 2008). New creative incentive schemes are needed, possibly tied to customer value or cross-sell related metrics.

Thirdly, banks may lack the right mixture of expertise. Inbound marketing requires a combination of: data analytics expertise, banking domain knowledge, and decision support systems expertise. Marketing activities would need to be supported by a cross-functional team of business users having product knowledge and customer experience knowledge, as well as data analysts skilled in analyzing and interpreting large amounts of data from various sources (Kona and Surti, 2010). Actionable cross-sell decisions in the form of business rules would then be deployed by decision support systems specialists.

Citibank Example. The capability to deliver real-time personalized offers, at the customer point of interaction with the bank or merchant, is becoming increasingly strategic. Only a few banks do it well, and many other banks are trying to follow their lead. One example of a successful real-time inbound marketing implementation is at Citibank, where they have developed a real-time marketing engine they call Centralized Offer Pallet System (COPS).

"COPS is able to instantaneously consider a number of customer events, including banking events, such as credit card purchases or ATM transactions, and life events, such as customer birthdays or overseas travel, when determining the bank's response. The system deploys complex event processing technology to evaluate static and dynamic events against a customer profile and 'propensity model', to determine in real-time the next best offer the bank can extend to the customer" (The Banker, 2009).

13.4 Technology Enablers for Real-Time Inbound Marketing NBO

It the present predictive era, the speed of doing business demands real-time decision making. Predictive capability requires massively scalable highly resilient event-driven architecture, complex event processing, and high performance in-memory analytics. Massive scale, in some cases, means millions of events per second originating from a multitude of different event sources need to be collected and correlated in real-time, so that the bank can know ahead of time what is about to happen, and do something about it before it is too late to take advantage of an opportunity or avert a threat.

With massive amounts of events being captured, data volumes are increasing (see Fig. 13.1). However, the time to react to opportunities or threats is decreasing. After it is too late to react, the data becomes less useful (Fülöp et al., 2012, September). At the same time, the cost of solid state storage and the cost of memory are decreasing rapidly. While events (data-in-motion) are becoming business critical, databases (data-at-rest) are becoming less relevant

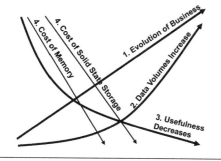

Speed of Business
1. The speed of business is increasing
2. In order to compete increasingly more events (data) are being captured
3. Since shorter time is available to react to opportunities or threats, the usefulness of data decreases with time
4. Cost of solid state storage and memory is decreasing

What This Means
- Events (data-in-motion) are becoming business critical
- Databases (data-at-rest) are becoming less relevant
- In-Memory Event-Driven Architectures will become mainstream

Figure 13.1: Shift towards In-Memory Event-Driven Architectures.

(Ranadivé and Maney, 2011). Databases will always be required to store historical transaction data. But as the cost of memory is decreasing, massive scale high performance in-memory analytics and real-time decision systems will become mainstream.

An Event-Driven Architecture (EDA) is one in which business events, indicating a change in state, are detected and automatically trigger business processes to activate (Shankararaman and Megargel, 2013). For example, a creditworthy customer changing their mailing address online might trigger a business process to cross-sell a furniture promotion, whereby the furniture store has a merchant tie-in with the bank. The essential enterprise platform components of an EDA, given in the typical order of adoption by banks, are as follows:

Message-Oriented Middleware. A means by which applications share information across the network, message-oriented middleware (MOM) is typically the first integration technology adopted by banks. Middleware vendors offer MOM software that is compliant to the Java Message Service (JMS) standard as ratified by the World Wide Web Consortium (W3C). JMS is preferred by banks as it is robust, secure, high performing, and guarantees delivery of messages which often contain customer sensitive financial information. In an EDA, JMS messages are an "event source" which trigger real-time inbound marketing offers.

Service-Oriented Standards. Services are reusable software components that expose functionality via a defined interface, for example, a balance inquiry service. An enterprise service bus (ESB) exposes the functionality of an enterprise as reusable services. A service oriented architecture (SOA) enables new applications to be "assembled" rapidly by invoking existing reusable services via an ESB. The rapid construction and assembly of reusable services requires a high degree of consistency in interface design, which is why most banks comply with

W3C standards for SOA including, Simple Object Access Protocol (SOAP), and Web Services Description Language (WSDL). As a bank's level of SOA maturity increases, so does its business agility.

Established banks that are still using monolithic legacy core banking systems, which are inflexible to change, have a higher barrier to entry into the digital banking market currently lead by FinTech and other IT companies. "Legacy core banking platforms across the industry, traditionally dependent on mainframes, are now giving way to platforms based on service-oriented architectures" (Cognizant, 2011).

Business Process Orchestration. Business Process Management (BPM) platforms are used by banks to model, simulate, execute and monitor complex business processes such as customer on-boarding, credit evaluation, and loan origination. BPM platforms orchestrate business processes that include human steps as well as machine steps. For each machine step, the BPM platform will invoke a reusable service via an ESB, based on the WSDL that defines the interface of that service. In an EDA, a JMS message as an event source might activate a BPM process which orchestrates an inbound marketing offer to the customer.

Complex Event Processing. "Complex-event processing (CEP) is a kind of computing in which incoming data about events is distilled into more useful, higher level 'complex' event data that provides insight into what is happening. CEP is event-driven because the computation is triggered by the receipt of event data. CEP is used for highly demanding, continuous-intelligence applications that enhance situation awareness and support real time decisions" (Gartner Research, 2013a). A mid-size bank might have thousands of simple events occurring every second, forming an "event cloud" (Luckham, 2008), consisting of deposits or withdrawals, fund transfers or bill payments, credit card swipes or online purchases.

At the core of a CEP is a rule engine capable of composing context-sensitive complex events (or rules) out of the thousands of simple events that occur every second (Adi et al., 2006). Context-sensitive rules encompass: historical customer banking behavior and credit worthiness, elapsed time between related events, proximity or location of events, as well as algorithmic measurement or aggregation of numeric event data (Adi et al., 2006; Luckham, 2008; Lundberg, 2006). Rules are externalized or decoupled from the business process execution such that the rules are independently managed and reusable across multiple business processes (Adi et al., 2006).

In a bank, there are typically two business units which are involved in setting up a real-time inbound marketing NBO. A decision support unit will use a CEP designer tool to: a) model the context-sensitive threshold, variance, temporal and spatial constraints, algorithms and data aggregations which constitute a complex event (or rule), and b) deploy the rule onto a CEP runtime execution environment (TIBCO, 2006a). A marketing team will then: a) design a promotion for a banking product or merchant product associated with the bank, and b) use the CEP designer tool to select a set of rules which will trigger the promotion to be delivered to targeted customers whom have opted-in to receive such promotions. The NBO will then be deployed onto an in-memory data grid, queued up to be delivered in real-time to each individual targeted customer upon their next interaction with the bank (TIBCO, 2006b), ergo the NBO delivered in real-time.

See the Appendix for CEP patterns and use cases for real-time inbound marketing.

The term "real-time" in the context of inbound marketing means roughly "less than 2 seconds" as a key performance benchmark, which means that the targeted customer will receive a relevant NBO within 2 seconds of their next interaction with the bank, typically via SMS. If NBOs were to be retrieved from a customer analytics data mart situated downstream from a large data warehouse, the overhead of "seek" access-times while reading data from physical disk drives would inhibit the 2 second performance benchmark. Disk drive access times are measured in milliseconds, whereas memory access times are measured in nanoseconds. Therefore, real-time NBOs are more effective when stored in memory rather than on disk.

From 1956–2015, the cost per megabyte of disk drives has fallen from $9,200.00 to $0.0000317 (McCallum, 2015a). From 1957 to 2015, the cost per megabyte of random access memory (RAM) has fallen from $411,014,792 to $0.0056 (McCallum, 2015b). The price of disk drives has leveled off since 2006, whereas the price of RAM has halved since 2011 (McCallum, 2015a, 2015b). The cost of RAM is decreasing faster than the cost of disk drives.

In-Memory Data Grid (IMDG). "In-memory data grids are distributed, in-memory data stores aimed at high performance/high-scale, data-intensive applications. IMDGs are moving into mainstream adoption, driven by their versatility, including support for cloud architectures, and bundling in various software products and services" (Gartner Research, 2012). IMDGs provide a virtual shared memory by replicating data elastically across any number of active–active fault tolerant nodes (servers) in a peer-to-peer style of architecture. IMDGs store and retrieve in-memory data using key-value pairs, and can "push" or "listen" to events in support of event driven architectures and CEP. IMDGs are therefore well placed to store millions of NBOs in memory, queued up to deliver inbound marketing offers in real-time. Memory access-times are around a million times faster than disk drive access-times, and the low cost of memory is catching up with the lower cost of disk drives. In the context of real-time inbound marketing, databases are becoming less relevant. Hence, there is a shift towards in-memory event driven architectures. "Memory is the new disk, disk is the new tape", coined by Jim Gray (Robbins, 2008).

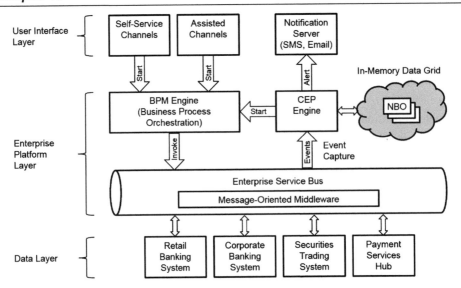

User Interface Layer

Figure 13.2: Layered Architecture to support Real-time In-Bound Marketing.

Layered Architecture for Real-time Inbound Marketing. The various technology components collaborate to support real-time inbound marketing. Fig. 13.2 shows the interactions between the technology components. In order to understand the interactions, let us use the following CEP Pattern 4: Life-stage event – merchant product cross-sell (use case 4.3 from the appendix):

"Customer John Tan is moving house. He logs into bank's website and changes mailing address."

The customer initiates the "address change" service through the self-service channel. This triggers the corresponding business process in the BPM engine, and through the enterprise service bus (ESB) the appropriate service, for example, "change_address" is invoked in the Retail Banking System. Simultaneously, this business event is captured by the complex event processing (CEP) engine. Within the CEP engine, the following marketing business rule is triggered:

"IF business event = "change_address" THEN send "furniture_cross_sell SMS to customer"

From the In-Memory Data Grid data, an affiliated furniture store nearest to the customer's new mailing address is selected, and a SMS is sent with the following data"

"Dear Mr John Tan we have updated your address in the bank system. We are glad to offer you a credit card discount of 15% for purchases above $200 at the Myfurniture store located at 20 Queen Street".

13.5 Summary

This chapter first examined the evolution of marketing methods in retail banking, as a function of IT systems capability across three separate eras; the "data processing era", the "client–server era", and the "predictive era". The chapter then discussed banks' marketing strategy in the context of today's digital banking market, with emphasis on cross-selling and its related benefits and organizational challenges. Finally, the chapter covered the banking industry shift towards in-memory event-driven architectures which enable the real-time delivery of personalized "next best offers" targeting individual customers based on their profile and situational needs.

In the digital banking market, retail banks can no longer compete solely based on products which have become commoditized, rather they must compete based on service differentiation. Digital natives who expect technologically sophisticated and personalized service are unresponsive to traditional campaign-based outbound marketing methods. Inbound marketing processes implemented at assisted channels such as branch and call center have a limited reach as increasingly more customers prefer to do their banking through online channels. Therefore, banks must invest in technology that enables cross-sell offers to be delivered via online channels in real-time, i.e. at the moment of customer interaction with the bank. Banks that do this well will have a competitive advantage. Banks that do not adopt this new paradigm will not survive.

Appendix – CEP Patterns and Use Cases for Real-Time Inbound Marketing

Assumptions for the below use cases:

- Customers have opted-in to receive real-time offers.
- Offers occur roughly within 2 seconds of the event, i.e. a customer interaction.
- Offers are not repeated, or the frequency of repeated offers is otherwise optimized.
- "[NBO]" indicates offer is queued up in memory, to be triggered at the next customer interaction.

See Tables 13.2–13.6.

Table 13.2: CEP Pattern 1.

CEP Pattern 1: Life-stage event – banking product cross-sell		
Use Case	**Event**	**Offer**
1.1	Customer enters university. Pays application fee using the bank's credit card.	An SMS is sent to the customer with education loan rates, a link to the bank's web page, 3 possible appointment times at the branch nearest the customer's address, and the phone number of a relationship manager (RM).
1.2	Customer's firstjob. First payroll direct deposit for a customer having no credit card.	[NBO] An SMS is sent to the customer with credit card rates, and a link to the bank's web site. A credit card application form is sent to the customer via regular mail.
1.3	Customer is buying a house. Logs into bank's website and uses a mortgage calculator.	A robo-chat box pops up providing credit terms computed based on the customer's credit worthiness. Dialog leads to connection with a human to facilitate loan application.
1.4	Customer has first child. Pays for a crib or high chair using the banks credit card.	An SMS is sent to the customer offering a "Baby Bonus" savings plan. A loan application form is sent to the customer via regular mail.
1.5	Customer reaches middle age.	[NBO] An SMS is sent to the customer offering wealth management advisory services, and the phone number of an RM. A wealth management brochure is sent to the customer via regular mail.
1.6	Customer reaches retirement age.	[NBO] An SMS is sent to the customer offering an annuity based on the customers accumulated wealth, and the phone number of an RM. An annuity plan is sent to the customer via regular mail.

Table 13.3: CEP Pattern 2.

CEP Pattern 2: Financial event – banking product cross-sell		
Use Case	**Event**	**Offer**
2.1	Dormant account. Customer has a large balance in a demand deposit account which has been dormant for an extended period.	[NBO] An SMS and/or email is sent to the customer offering a higher yielding structured deposit product. The dormant account is mentioned in the communications, and the phone number of an RM is provided.
2.2	Mortgage full repayment inquiry. Customer uses the bank's website to compute the full repayment of existing mortgage.	A robo-chat box pops up to inquire if the customer is planning to refinance with another bank, or is planning to sell and reinvest in another property. Dialog leads to connection with a human to offer competitive rates.
2.3	Direct debit authorization with a competitor. Insurance company is authorized to debit your customer's account directly.	[NBO] An SMS and/or email is sent to the customer to inform them of your bank assurance products that they may not be aware of. A link to the bank's relevant web page is included in the communications.
2.4	Salary bonus. Customer's direct payroll deposit is much larger than normal.	[NBO] An SMS and/or email is sent to the customer mentioning their bonus and offering an investment product featuring a lump sum premium based on the customer's value/portfolio with the bank.
2.5	Large credit card transaction. Customer who is a "transactor" (not a "revolver") makes a large credit card transaction.	An SMS is sent to the customer offering to convert their credit card debt to a lower interest personal loan, providing rates computed according to the customer's credit worthiness, and the phone number of an RM.
2.6	Time Deposit renewal. A customer's TD maturity is approaching.	[NBO] An SMS and/or email is sent to the customer offering a renewal of their TD, with more attractive rates if they increase the deposit amount.
2.7	Flight Insurance. Customer purchases a budget airline ticket using the bank's credit card, while at the airport.	An SMS is sent to the customer offering cheap flight insurance, and a link to the bank's relevant web page where they can purchase the insurance online.
2.8	ATM insufficient balance. Customer attempts an ATM withdrawal but has insufficient funds in their account.	An SMS is sent to the customer offering a short term personal loan, with rates based on the customer's credit worthiness, and a link to the bank's relevant web page to apply for the loan online.

Table 13.4: CEP Pattern 3.

CEP Pattern 3: Point-of-sales (POS) event – merchant product cross-sell		
Use Case	**Event**	**Offer**
3.1	Customer makes a POS purchase at an affiliated merchant, using the bank's credit card.	An SMS is sent to the customer offering a credit card discount for the next purchase at the same merchant, redeemable one time only via a QR code. The customer receives merchant loyalty points.
3.2	Customer makes a POS purchase within walking distance of an affiliated merchant where the customer has an affinity.	An SMS is sent to the customer offering a credit card discount at the nearby affiliated merchant. The bank establishes customer affinity for the merchant at the originating POS.

Table 13.5: CEP Pattern 4.

CEP Pattern 4: Life-stage event – merchant product cross-sell		
Use Case	**Event**	**Offer**
4.1	Birthday or anniversary. Family member has an approaching birthday or anniversary.	[NBO] An SMS is sent to the customer offering a credit card discount at an affiliated merchant where the customer's family member has an affinity.
4.2	Customer changes jobs. The customer's direct payroll deposit has changed to originate from a new employer's account.	[NBO] An SMS is sent to the customer offering a credit card discount at an affiliated clothing store where the customer has an affinity.
4.3	Customer is moving house. Logs into bank's website and changes mailing address.	An SMS and/or email is sent to the customer offering a credit card discount at an affiliated furniture store in the proximity of the customer's new mailing address.
4.4	Customer is taking a trip. Books a hotel using the bank's credit card.	An SMS and/or email is sent to the customer offering a credit card discount with an affiliated airline, where the loyalty programs of the bank and airline are linked.

Table 13.6: CEP Pattern 5.

CEP Pattern 5: Location-based event – merchant product cross-sell		
Use Case	**Event**	**Offer**
5.1	Customer retrieves ATM card from the machine, and the time of day is around 11am or 5pm.	An SMS is sent to the customer offering a credit card discount at an affiliated restaurant where the customer has an affinity, and is within walking distance of the ATM.
5.2	GPS tracking is enabled on the customer's mobile phone, and the customer is on foot in a downtown area.	An SMS is sent to the customer offering a credit card discount at an affiliated merchant where the customer has an affinity, and the merchant is within walking distance of the customer's current location.

References

Adi, A., Botzer, D., Nechushtai, G., Sharon, G., 2006. Complex Event Processing for Financial Services. In null. IEEE, pp. 7–12.

Bailey, C., Baines, P.R., Wilson, H., Clark, M., 2009. Segmentation and customer insight in contemporary services marketing practice: why grouping customers is no longer enough. Journal of Marketing Management 25 (3–4), 227–252.

Cognizant, 2011. Cognizant reports: how analytics can transform the U.S. retail banking sector. Retrieved December 15, 2015, from http://www.cognizant.com/InsightsWhitepapers/How-Analytics-Can-Transform-the-U.S.-Retail-Banking-Sector.pdf.

Cotton, B., Walker, C., 2011. Smarter customers, smarter commerce: innovations for the banking industry.

Davenport, T.H., Mule, L.D., Lucker, J., 2011. Know what your customers want before they do. Harvard Business Review 89 (12), 84–92.

Dass, R., 2006. Data Mining in Banking and Finance: A Note for Bankers. Indian Institute of Management Ahmedabad.

Denecker, O., Gulati, S., Niederkorn, M., 2014. The Digital Battle that Banks Must Win. McKinsey & Company, Washington, DC. http://www.mckinsey.com/insights/financial_services/the_digital_battle_that_banks_must_win.

Drotskie, A., 2009. Customer Experience as the Strategic Differentiator in Retail Banking. Doctoral dissertation. University of Stellenbosch, Stellenbosch.

Fülöp, L.J., Beszédes, Á., Tóth, G., Demeter, H., Vidács, L., Farkas, L., 2012, September. Predictive complex event processing: a conceptual framework for combining complex event processing and predictive analytics. In: Proceedings of the Fifth Balkan Conference in Informatics. ACM, pp. 26–31.

Gartner Research, 2012. What IT leaders need to know about in-memory data grids. Publication G00231619, March 6, 2012. Retrieved December 18, 2015, from https://www.gartner.com/doc/1942417/it-leaders-need-know-inmemory.

Gartner Research, 2013a. Gartner IT Glossary: Complex-Event Processing. Retrieved December 18, 2015, from http://www.gartner.com/it-glossary/complex-event-processing.

Gartner Research, 2013b. What is digital banking? Publication G00255405, September 30, 2013.

Hesse, A., 2009. Case study: ING delivers personalized product offers across channels in real time.

Kamakura, W.A., 2008. Cross-selling: offering the right product to the right customer at the right time. Journal of Relationship Marketing 6 (3–4), 41–58.

Kona, Y.A., Surti, B.C., 2010. Analytics in cross selling – a retail banking perspective.

Luckham, D., 2008. Complex event processing in financial services.

Lundberg, A., 2006. Leverage complex event processing to improve operational performance. Business Intelligence Journal 11 (1), 55.

Mann, P.K., Kumar, R., 2014. Effectiveness of E-CRM in banking sector.

Martin, I., 2012. Too far ahead of its time: Barclays, Burroughs, and real-time banking. IEEE Annals of the History of Computing 34 (2), 5–19.

McCallum, J.C., 2015a. Disk drive prices (1955–2015). Retrieved December 18, 2015, from http://www.jcmit.com/diskprice.htm.

McCallum, J.C., 2015b. Memory prices (1957–2015). Retrieved December 18, 2015, from http://www.jcmit.com/memoryprice.htm.

McKinsey & Company, 2014. 2014 Digital banking in Asia – winning approaches in a new generation of financial services. Retrieved November 23, 2015, from http://www.google.com.sg/url?sa=t&rct=j&q=&esrc=s&source=web&cd=6&ved=0ahUKEwihjarL6aXJAhXi26YKHVuqDekQFghBMAU&url=http%3A%2F%2Fwww.mckinsey.com%2F~%2Fmedia%2Fmckinsey%2520offices%2Fsingapore%2F2014%2520digital%2520banking%2520in%2520asia%2520%2520winning%2520approaches%2520in%2520a%2520new%2520generation%2520of%2520financial%2520services.ashx&usg=AFQjCNFed4vE2ub6wyt2ajok5SidadAeBw.

Prensky, M., 2001. Digital natives, digital immigrants part 1. On the Horizon 9 (5), 1–6.

Ranadivé, V., 2005. The Power to Predict: How Real Time Businesses Anticipate Customer Needs, Create Opportunities, and Beat the Competition. McGraw-Hill Pub. Co.

Ranadivé, V., Maney, K., 2011. The Two-Second Advantage: How We Succeed by Anticipating the Future–Just Enough. Crown Business.

Ranadivé, V., Bilski, D., 2013. Real-time seer: Vivek Ranadivé. Outlook business, February 2013. Retrieved December 15, 2015, from http://blogcms.outlookindia.com/article_v3.aspx?artid=283868.

Riley, B., Schmidt, A., Tubin, G., 2011. SMS in financial services: accessing your customers on their terms. TowerGroup. Research is available on the Internet at www.towergroup.com.

Robbins, S., 2008. RAM is the new disk. . . . InfoQ News. Retrieved December 25, 2005, from http://www.infoq.com/news/2008/06/ram-is-disk.

Shankararaman, V., Megargel, A., 2013. Enterprise integration: architectural approaches. Service-Driven Approaches to Architecture and Enterprise Integration, 67.

Stone, M., 2009. Staying customer-focused and trusted: Web 2.0 and Customer 2.0 in financial services. Journal of Database Marketing & Customer Strategy Management 16 (2), 101–131.

The Banker, 2009. Innovation In Technology Awards 2009. The Chair's Choice & Innovation in Customer Service and Marketing Technology. Winner: Citibank Hong Kong. Project: Real-time marketing. The Banker, June 2009, p. 44.

TIBCO, 2006a. Complex event processing: framework for operational visibility and decisions.

TIBCO, 2006b. Predictive Customer Interaction Management: an architecture that enables organizations to leverage real-time events to accurately target products and services.

CHAPTER 14

Regulation and Supervision in a Digital and Inclusive World

Loretta Michaels, Matthew Homer

Contents

Digital technologies are transforming the delivery of financial services everywhere. Among its many benefits, "fintech" offers new opportunities to widen access to financial services. The potential for improving people's lives through financial inclusion is enormous, and many of the gains are already being realized. There are risks as well, though, and making the most of these opportunities will require skillful regulation. At the moment, regulators and policymakers alike are struggling to keep up.

This chapter reviews where the effort to regulate fintech for financial inclusion stands, and tries to draw guidance from the experience to date. One of the most important lessons may be something of a challenge to traditional thinking, and one that many regulators will resist – namely, that in some respects they should cooperate more closely with the enterprises they oversee, communicating more freely in an exchange of information that goes both ways.

14.1 Fintech Meets Financial Inclusion

This book and countless papers and reports over the last few years attest to the surge of interest in the use of digital technologies for financial services. The topic has moved beyond Silicon Valley start-ups and African mobile-money operators to global policymakers and financial regulators – who are concerned not only with the potential benefits of new technology but also with the risks.

At the same time, governments have been asking how to widen access to financial services. Studies show that financial inclusion can reduce income inequality, boost job creation, accelerate consumption, increase investments in human capital, and directly help poor people manage risk and absorb financial shocks.[1] Financial inclusion, in other words, is both an important goal in its own right and a way to promote economic development more broadly: Financial *exclusion* can prevent countries from achieving their full economic potential.

These two trends come together in a very powerful way. Many of the new financial technologies make it possible to connect people with financial services – over distances and under circumstances that would once have made it prohibitively expensive.

There are other synergies as well. Financial inclusion supports other important global policy goals, including action against money laundering and terrorist financing. Global Anti-Money Laundering and Countering the Financing of Terrorism (AML/CFT) safeguards, which nearly all countries agree to and follow as part of the Financial Action Task Force (FATF[2]), are undermined when large groups of people remain outside the regulated financial system. Making the domestic and global financial systems safer requires services that regulators can see and, where necessary, monitor.

Especially in emerging markets, fintech also serves other development priorities. Off-grid solar technology is supplying power to many African households for the first time. This would not be possible without digital payments. The technology uses an embedded mobile-money SIM card that enables consumers to spread payments over time; this in turn makes the business feasible for solar companies, because they are assured that the underlying loan for the solar panel can be serviced cost-effectively. Similarly, potent innovations are emerging in other sectors as well. Digital payments are facilitating entirely new business models, enabling the private sector to meet the needs of the poor in new ways.

This technological revolution – the marriage of fintech and financial inclusion – is already well under way. Underpinned in large part by ubiquitous mobile networks, it is rapidly changing the face of financial services across the globe, allowing the financial sector to reach more people in more remote places than ever before. It is expanding the reach and scale of financial services, at lower cost than traditional branch-based services, and creating new business models, new kinds of service provider and new distribution channels. It offers the prospect of more convenient, tailored, and responsive services that traditionally underserved users find easier to understand and are thus more likely to adopt. The ability to offer low-cost, convenient and confidential financial services is particularly important for women in the developing world, giving them more control, helping them save, and increasing their economic participation.

14.2 Policy Is Struggling to Keep up With the Market

The recent pace of innovation has left the current policy and regulatory environment struggling to keep up. Laws and regulations governing financial services evolve, but the basic framework and many of the most important rules were developed decades ago, when financial services were offered only by banks, and maybe post offices, and people signed up in person at their local branch office. Customers opened basic checking and savings accounts, made payments mostly by cash or check, and had no choice but Western Union (or an envelope and a bus driver) for emergency long-distance payments. Credit cards and ATMs came along, but these were banking services so the same basic rules applied. This world has gone. Today, a teeming variety of online, mobile and card-based services are offered by a plethora of providers, many of them unrecognizable as financial-services companies to policymakers and regulators.

In coping with all this, regulators face five main difficulties. First, many new fintech firms aren't financial institutions as traditionally defined, and so may not fall cleanly under the regulators' oversight. Sometimes, on the other hand, they fall within the jurisdictions of several different regulators, and it's unclear how to proceed. Second, regulators are rarely experts in technology, which makes it hard for them to assess new business models and practices. Third, central banks and other financial regulators have traditionally been conservative, tending to frown on new types of providers. This is changing, but regulatory culture still tends toward caution, valuing stability over innovation. Fourth, there's the question of resources: New fintech firms present regulators with added responsibilities, but no corresponding increase in capacity. Finally, in many instances, the old – and sometimes new – businesses are well connected politically, which makes it harder for regulators to discharge their duty of independent oversight.

So perhaps it's unsurprising that most regulations bearing on fintech and inclusion, most of the training that regulators receive, and most of their monitoring tools have changed too slowly: Overall, systems stand many years behind the times. Financial regulators aren't alone in this, to be sure. Government more broadly is struggling to catch up. As one set of authors recently put it, the state is everywhere trying to "govern the world of Google and Facebook with a quill pen and an abacus".[3] Policymakers are aware, and to their credit are trying to adapt, but digital innovation is outrunning them.

Policy work on inclusion and technology is now under way at both the national and international levels. The Group of Twenty (G20), founded in 1999 with the aim of promoting cooperation on financial stability, is a forum of governments and central-bank governors from 20 major economies. In 2010, it recognized financial inclusion as one of the main pillars of the global development agenda, endorsed a Financial Inclusion Action Plan and created the Global Partnership for Financial Inclusion (GPFI[4]) to drive all work in this area. The GPFI has produced reports on various aspects of inclusion and fintech.

Multilateral organizations such as the World Bank and the Consultative Group to Assist the Poor (CGAP[5]), the International Monetary Fund (IMF), and the United Nations are involved. An area of particular interest is the catalytic role that digitized government payments can play in expanding access to and use of formal financial accounts. In developed economies, electronic transactions are taken for granted; in most of the developing world, bills and wages are still typically paid in cash, with all the attendant risks of theft, loss and bribery. The Better Than Cash Alliance (BTCA), housed within the UN, is a partnership of governments, companies, and international organizations seeking to accelerate the transition from cash to digital payments for financial transactions of all kinds – salaries, bill payments, taxes. The aim is to reduce poverty and drive inclusive growth.[6] Encouraging the use of formal accounts will also benefit the governments and organizations, by reducing costs, leakage and corruption.

Global regulators are engaged. The Global Standard Setting Bodies (SSBs) have begun to address the intersection of fintech and inclusion, with help from the GPFI. In 2011, the GPFI issued a White Paper, "Global Standard-Setting Bodies and Financial Inclusion for the Poor: Toward Proportionate Standards and Guidance".[7] In 2016 another paper, "Global Standard-Setting Bodies and Financial Inclusion: The Evolving Landscape",[8] looked at the implications of fintech for consumer protection; competition and interoperability (transactions straddling different financial networks); customer identity and privacy; crowdfunding; and management of risk, or "derisking."

Other initiatives are under way. The Alliance for Financial Inclusion (AFI) was founded in 2008 as the first global knowledge-sharing network designed exclusively for developing-country policymakers concerned with financial inclusion. The AFI network now includes members from more than 90 countries "working together to advance its mission of accelerating the adoption of proven and innovative financial-inclusion policy solutions with the ultimate aim of making financial services more accessible to the world's 2 billion unbanked people".[9] Its remit includes balancing inclusion, integrity and stability; consumer empowerment and market conduct; digital financial services; financial-inclusion strategies; measuring financial inclusion; small and medium-scale enterprise (SME) finance; and other growing areas of interest such as targeting underserved groups like women and youth, use of alternative data for credit monitoring, and widening the scope of deposit insurance.

Donors and think tanks are weighing in. Organizations such as the US Agency for International Development (USAID), the UK's Department for International Development (DfiD), the Bill and Melinda Gates Foundation, the Center for Global Development, the Center for Financial Inclusion, the Brookings Institution and many others are publishing research and conducting programs. The Cash Learning Partnership,[10] an alliance of individuals and humanitarian organizations promoting cash transfers for emergency relief, has studied the use of digital payment technologies in conflict zones, refugee camps and remote drought-stricken areas.

Industry associations are working on the issues too. The Groupe Speciale Mobile Association (GSMA), representing the bulk of the world's mobile network operators, runs the Mobile Money for the Unbanked program. This promotes the use of mobile money for underserved users, in part through the support of other industry groups, such as the MasterCard Foundation and Omidyar Network. The Institute of International Finance (IIF), a global finance-industry association, is researching financial inclusion and advising members on how to best address the issue. Last year the Wall Street Journal issued a "Financial Inclusion Challenge," inviting enterprises around the world – for-profit and not-for-profit alike – to showcase innovations in financial access for the poor in the Asia Pacific region.[11]

This is only a partial list. Clearly there's broad global agreement on both the importance of financial inclusion and on the great potential for new digital technologies to advance welfare – whether it's by delivering financial services to the poor through mobile phones or by streamlining government payments through digitization, to name just two. There's growing acknowledgment, as well, that the traditional approach to financial regulation isn't suited to these innovations.

14.3 A New World for Policymakers, Regulators and Supervisors

Financial regulators have a demanding mandate. Although they have historically focused mostly on safeguarding the stability of financial systems, there is growing awareness and commitment among regulators and standard setting bodies to four key priorities, collectively referred to as I-SIP: financial inclusion (I), financial stability (S), financial integrity (I) and financial consumer protection (P).[12] The characteristics of the typical unbanked consumer – with limited and unpredictable income, and little financial or technological sophistication – introduce risks that are new to many regulators. Policymakers everywhere, but especially in the developing world, are struggling to design policy and regulatory environments that work for existing financial institutions, while encouraging innovations and market entry by new players and addressing the unforeseen risks that new approaches may bring. They also need to devise systems and tools for safely supervising new service providers, recognizing that a one-size-fits-all approach is no use in a constantly evolving environment. The formula needs to be measured, flexible, and capable of responding immediately to potential crises.

A dual mandate – to expand financial services while ensuring their safety – has directed attention to several key building blocks, critical for establishing sound, stable and accessible financial systems. Some of these are mainly concerned with establishing an easily accessible, inclusive physical environment for adoption and use of digital financial services, such as customer-identity systems and broadband infrastructure. Others focus on promoting the uptake of digital financial services, with programs aimed at digitizing government payments and developing a larger ecosystem of digital payments, particularly through retail networks. And finally, regulators are aiming to establish regulatory frameworks and supervisory regimes that can foster innovation without compromising safety and stability. Here are some of the key areas:

14.3.1 Digital Identity (ID) Programs

Customer-identity systems play a critical role in both financial inclusion and anti-money-laundering schemes. Consumers need proof of identity to participate in formal financial systems. Central banks and FATF agree on the importance of verifiable ID – yet central banks are rarely responsible for ID systems. Policymakers need to work together to develop identity systems that incorporate existing local, regional and national identity mechanisms, such as birth certificates and voter IDs, alongside new forms of identity verification such as digital and biometric data. It is essential to ensure that all citizens have easy access to some form of legal identity, allowing them to access public and financial services. In many parts of the world getting a birth certificate is not straightforward; in others, many births, especially of girls, aren't registered at all. And the challenges aren't limited to birth certificates. In many countries, street addresses aren't used in rural areas, making proof of address virtually impossible. In others, getting proof of a change of residency (from your place of birth, say, to the city where you're now working) can be difficult and time-consuming; in the meantime, you can't open a bank account to receive your pay.

Global policymakers are beginning to acknowledge the importance of digital identity information. Some countries are trying to institute broad national identity programs using digital and biometric data; India's Aadhar program is one example. Others are trying to establish a national database that links all relevant existing identity systems and is accessible to authorized parties such as service providers. Meanwhile technology companies that provide services in the share economy, such as Uber and Airbnb, are employing new ways to verify identities, including through online social media.

14.3.2 Digital Broadband Infrastructure and Payment-Acceptance Networks

Providing data and communications networks has typically been left to the private sector, but policymakers are coming to see that developing digital broadband highways is fundamental to economic and social development. Both the public and private sectors are relying more heavily on broadband data networks for delivering important public and private services, from health and education to communications and financial services.

It's especially important to expand the retail payments infrastructure to give all users access to convenient, reliable points of service for sending and receiving payments as well as converting cash to digital and vice versa. Real-time, openly accessible digital-payments platforms can radically reduce the cost of transactions for both service providers and consumers. They can make processing small payments – which represent the bulk of the world's financial transactions – commercially feasible, and at the same time encourage innovation and new entrants. Open digital platforms will improve interoperability and consumer choice.

Enabling consumers to pay digitally wherever they shop is challenging in contexts where cash is still king. But designing policies and incentives to encourage merchants to accept digital payments and consumers to pay digitally is increasingly seen as crucial: Building an ecosystem of cheap and reliable digital payments won't be possible otherwise. Branches and agents are important access points in the short term, but the industry recognizes that digital opportunities such as ATMs, point of sale (POS) devices, mobile phones and Internet applications must start to replace them. Supply of broadband networks in urban areas can mostly be left to the private sector, but more can be done to encourage expansion into rural, unserved regions. Tools under consideration include public–private partnerships, tax incentives, shared infrastructure subsidies and targeted procurement policies.

14.3.3 Digitizing Government Payments

As noted above, countries are increasingly seeing the value of digitizing their public payment streams – to cut costs, promote transparency, curb corruption and encourage citizens to open accounts in the formal financial system. The Government of India, for example, recently digitized their subsidy program for propane gas, and in less than two years managed to save 25 percent, or $2 billion, in lower program costs and reduced corruption. But digitizing public-sector payments is a more complex undertaking than many governments had supposed. The Government of Mexico undertook a program to digitize and centralize all its payments, but the plan took some fifteen years to complete. The government estimates that it's saving $1.27 billion per year[13] and considers the program a success, but the project was far more difficult than expected. Policymakers recognize the scale of the challenge but haven't been deterred: The Better Than Cash Alliance continues to announce commitments by many governments to digitize social payments. Success will require sustained effort, broad political support, and specialized technical expertise and human resources, demand for which currently outstrips supply.

14.3.4 Establishing an Enabling Regulatory Framework

Regulators are working on the new rules and guidelines that financial innovation will demand, and considering how to move smoothly from frameworks devised for commercial banks to systems encompassing banks, non-banks, and non-financial regulators such as those responsible for communications networks, consumer protection, data privacy and competition law. It's a daunting and time-consuming task, complicated by politics and vested interests, often requiring legislatures to agree. Meanwhile the industry is clamoring for progress.

According to a recent report,[14] fintech start-ups and investors rank regulation number one of the top ten challenges facing the industry. The GPFI, global SSBs, multilateral development banks and various thinks tanks (including some that don't typically focus on the financial sector) are all looking at the issue. The Center for Global Development recently convened an industry task force which issued a report, "Financial Regulations for Improving Financial Inclusion,[15]" asking how regulators might reconcile the goal of financial inclusion with the traditional dual mandate of systemic safety and consumer protection. The report made 26 recommendations under four main headings: how to make competition policy favor inclusion; how to level the playing-field for providers; how to design know-your-customer rules; and how to tailor each of those approaches to retail payments specifically.

As new kinds of provider come forward, regulators are also prompted to think more about rules based on function or product, rather than on type of institution, the traditional approach. The idea is that all companies offering a specific type of product or service would be regulated in the same way, regardless of whether they have a banking license or fall outside the definition of "financial institution." Banks in some countries favor this approach, believing that it could help limit regulatory arbitrage and require their upstart competitors to follow the same rules.

14.3.5 Supervision of Digital Payments Service Providers

Central banks and supervisors traditionally concentrate on banks rather than payment providers, and their processes and monitoring systems reflect this historical focus. The scope of oversight needs to widen. At the same time, regulators learned from the rapid growth of the microfinance industry in the 1970s and 1980s that relying on manual reports and onsite inspections of hundreds of small institutions required more resources than they had. Fintech raises the same issue, only more so. New entrants such as e-money providers, mobile-money operators, payment banks and non-bank agents, not to mention traditional non-bank players such as microfinance institutions, credit unions, and postal banks operating in the same markets, make it necessary to design new regulatory systems and tools. Otherwise, comprehensive and coherent oversight of all the new players and technologies won't be possible.

Regulators are recognizing that an environment of new and diverse providers and technologies will also require fresh emphasis on quality of service and market conduct. For instance, they will need to review exclusivity demands, and practices concerning access and pricing for channels such as mobile USSD networks. Again, this will add to their workload, particularly when you factor in having to coordinate with other agencies such as communications and competition regulators.

Global policymakers increasingly recognize, on the one hand, the macroeconomic benefits of financial inclusion and, on the other, the need for stronger supervision as the number of new users grows. IMF Managing Director Christine Lagarde recently said that "greater financial inclusion has tangible economic benefits, such as higher GDP growth and lower income inequality. By providing access to accounts, credit, infrastructure, women and low-income users, financial inclusion helps make growth more inclusive... Good supervision can play an important role in promoting financial stability even as access to credit reaches a broader population, raising growth rates and reducing inequality.[16]"

14.4 A Risk-Based Approach to Know-Your-Customer

KYC is the process by which banks verify the identity of their customers, and typically includes name, date of birth, address, and in some cases proof of income. As policymakers have tried to draw more low-income users into the financial system, it's become apparent that many lack the necessary documentation to fulfill standard KYC requirements. One way that policymakers are addressing this gap is by reducing the documentation required for KYC in low-risk, typically low-value, transactions. FATF supports this approach, but governments in many countries are uncertain how to apply it, and unsure how much latitude they have in designating different risk tiers for financial services. This may incline national regulators to take an unduly conservative one-size-fits-all approach, which in turn will discourage banks and other service providers from extending services to low-income customers. FATF has begun issuing guidance papers on how national authorities might conduct their risk-based approaches to national KYC rules, but many countries will need further technical advice.

14.4.1 Protecting the Consumer

This means full transparency and disclosure on costs such as fees and interest rates, making sure that consumers understand their rights, and providing fast and accessible recourse when problems occur. It's a particular challenge when multiple service providers are involved in a single transaction. Policymakers are especially concerned about the ability of traditionally unbanked users, with low levels of financial and technological literacy, to navigate the new digital-finance marketplace. They are also keenly aware that the new technologies may pose greater risk of fraud. While penetration of digital financial services is certainly growing, evidence suggests that it would be growing even faster if it weren't held back by a lack of consumer trust and confidence.[17] Consumer protection thus becomes even more important, a prerequisite for the industry's long-term success.

14.4.2 Blockchains

Some in the industry believe that no aspect of fintech has greater transformative potential than distributed-ledger technology, or "blockchains." At its core, a blockchain is just a secure database for recording transactions. Individual banks and settlement systems use electronic ledgers to track assets and transactions, often relying on manual entry that can be slow, inefficient and open to hacking and fraud. Blockchain technology shares the task of amending and verifying the ledger amongst all the participants in the network. Proponents say a ledger maintained in this way could reduce collateral and settlement costs dramatically, while allowing banks' creaky and expensive back-office systems to be automated. Blockchain technology might also reduce the costs of global remittance transactions, which are vital for many developing countries (and which are currently threatened by banks' efforts to derisk). The Financial Stability Board (FSB[18]), an international body that monitors and makes recommendations about the global financial system, has deployed a working group to review the potential uses and financial-stability implications of distributed-ledger technology.

While blockchain technology holds great promise in various applications, its prospects as a way to create private virtual currencies – which is where it began, with bitcoin – are uncertain. The early hype around bitcoin and its role in supporting illegal marketplaces such as the Silk Road website have tainted the concept of private virtual currencies, particularly in the minds of regulators and law enforcement.

Nonetheless the basic concept of digital currency itself isn't in question. This seems a likely if not inevitable evolution, and many central banks are investigating the idea of issuing their own digital fiat money, or legal tender. The People's Bank of China says it intends[19] to issue a digital currency. Central banks in Ecuador,[20] the Philippines,[21] the U.K.[22] and Canada[23] are mulling similar ideas. At least one company[24] in the US has sprung up to help them. The success of these efforts depends on the details, of course. But overall this is a welcome trend. In theory, digital legal tender combines the innovation of private virtual currencies with the stability and consumer protection afforded by a government mint. Again in theory, digital legal tender would also resolve questions concerning e-money issuance, conversion and interoperability, since all service providers would be using the same digital currency.

14.5 Emerging Responses to Supervising Digital and Inclusive Markets

Some of the topics just mentioned call for close cooperation between public and private sectors, and within and between governments, especially around infrastructure, identity and digitizing government payments. Regulators have a stake in these issues, but are rarely the driving force. In other cases, the issues are directly under the purview of regulators, and especially supervisors – and the pace of change is forcing them to rethink their methods. While innovators are busy transforming what it means to be a financial services company, many regulators are realizing that supervising the new digital marketplaces will demand no less a transformation of them.

In broad terms, this challenge applies as much to wealthy nations as to developing economies, but regulators in emerging markets face additional problems. Staff with the necessary skills and industry knowledge, especially around non-bank payments, may be hard to find. Additionally, regulators may lack adequate enforcement capabilities.

The disruption of traditional supervision is an opportunity for regulators to redesign their supervisory toolkit. The task is not just to supervise current services and emerging innovations effectively, although that is critical; what's needed is an approach that can also accommodate future, as yet unknown, innovations. How might that be done? Some of the thinking that drives fintech innovation can also be applied to supervision. Up to a point, this is already happening. This spirit of regulatory innovation can be organized into three broad themes: technology as a regulatory tool, a renewed focus on learning, and new modes of engagement with industry and consumers.

14.5.1 Technology as a Regulatory Tool

While using technology to improve supervision is not new, particularly with regard to prudential supervision, vastly more data is now available to enable a more digital-first approach.

This is particularly true in emerging markets, where mobile phones are becoming the most common way for consumers to use financial services. As the availability of data increases, regulators can access additional sources of information for supervisory purposes – and new analytical tools, such as visualization software that can help regulators better monitor and spot patterns (e.g. heat maps that show regulators where consumer complaints are most prevalent), in turn, can help regulators make sense of it all.

More data and new analytical methods are also allowing regulators and entrepreneurs to develop new compliance tools, in a market segment known as regtech. These innovations, developed by a small but growing group of enterprises, have focused up to now on making it easier for financial institutions to comply with regulatory requirements. This has included, for instance, real-time risk analysis tools to help institutions spot fraud more quickly. Investment and commercial banking have been the main targets so far, but over time regtech will likely extend to retail banking, including consumer protection. As this industry emerges, regulators should explore using similar tools to assist with market oversight and supervision. Regulators are accustomed to interacting with technology innovators as potential regulated institutions; they should also see them as solution providers and partners.

As fintech and digital-finance products make up a greater share of the marketplace, a digital-first approach to supervision will become increasingly necessary and likely inevitable. This is for several reasons. First, consumer-facing digital-finance products can scale much more quickly than traditional brick-and-mortar financial services, straining the capacity of regulatory staff to monitor them adequately, especially in previously unserved rural areas. Second, existing methods such as on-site supervision and periodic reporting requirements aren't well suited to an industry whose shape is rapidly shifting. Third, the amount of data to be analyzed will grow exponentially, and regulators will need sophisticated data analytics to help them visualize and make sense of it. Digital supervision tools will not completely replace traditional regulatory techniques, but should be viewed as a complimentary, and critical, component of oversight. Yes, they will supplant some traditional approaches, but they will also free up regulator bandwidth to more quickly identify and focus on critical priorities.

Technology-led supervision could be an important enabler of a risk-based regulatory approach that promotes consumer trust. Crucially, it could help regulators monitor risk more effectively, allowing them to concentrate on the most serious threats to consumers and the system. Faster and more direct communication with consumers, for instance, would serve this purpose. Interactive voice response (IVR) and SMS technology could enable regulators to conduct periodic consumer surveys at a relatively low cost. Similarly, regulators could provide channels for consumers to make real-time complaints about their experiences with agents or with specific products or services. Using this input along with other data, perhaps collected automatically from mobile phones (geo-location and transaction data, for example), regulators could identify issues and providers that warrant increased scrutiny. For regulators with limited human resources, this type of information would be especially valuable, allowing them to prioritize intelligently.

Similarly, technology can facilitate a tiered approach to regulatory requirements, such as the one recommended by FATF for KYC – allowing participation in the system by previously unserved consumers without compromising effective oversight. A binary (yes or no) process for opening new accounts is easier to implement and supervise than a system that allows for varying types of accounts based on the identification documents available, but simple technology makes a better, multiple-option system feasible. It could help guide agents and providers through the process and link directly to regulatory databases, giving regulators a window in real time on accounts being opened and the supporting documents. Technology can help regulators shift from high-touch on-site supervision to off-site supervision, which is important as financial services reach increasingly distant and remote localities.

Perhaps most critical for financial inclusion is the potential for regulatory technology to promote transparency and public confidence. As regulators use technology to track and detect bad actors and abuses, and to make more information available to consumers, they will make the market more open, more competitive, and better incentivized to correct itself when necessary.

Promising as these many opportunities for improving supervision may be, technology is no panacea. As a tool, it can help regulators collect and rapidly analyze new types of information. But regulators are still going to need a foundational level of knowledge of business models, technology platforms, and products and services in the marketplace.

14.5.2 Renewed Focus on Learning

Building knowledge about fintech and digital finance among regulators is essential to effective supervision. A fast-moving marketplace requires more iterative and opportunistic learning opportunities so that regulators can adapt quickly and dynamically.

Several models are starting to meet this need. One is peer learning. This enables regulators to learn from their counterparts in other countries. It's effective, and regulators often find such lessons especially compelling. The AFI has several peer-learning schemes in place. Study tours give regulators a chance to learn first-hand from other regulators and see how they are tackling specific challenges; study groups bring regulators with similar interests together to explore specific topics and share experiences; toolkits and other resources help regulators stay on top of current and emerging issues. Peer learning can help regulators broaden their skills in a safe and supportive environment – important for organizations that are often reluctant to betray their unfamiliarity with industry practices or market dynamics.

Other new types of training are appearing. Specialized digital-finance training courses, such as the Digital Frontier Institute[25] and the Fletcher School Leadership Program in Financial Inclusion,[26] are creating blended learning opportunities that bring together regulators and other participants to learn from digital-finance and financial-inclusion experts. These learning platforms include online and in-person discussions.

Technical assistance remains a valuable part of building knowledge, but the new learning models tend to take a more collaborative and less top-down approach. One reason for this may be that fintech and digital finance are topics that regulators from all countries, regardless of geography and other circumstances, are grappling with at the same time. This increases the premium on information sharing, as regulators experiment to see what works.

Although the knowledge required has a strong foundational component, learning about fintech and digital finance is not a once-and-for-all task for regulators. The rapidly evolving market demands continuous training. In addition to learning from experts and each other, engaging more directly with industry and consumers can also help address this challenge.

14.5.3 New Modes of Engagement With Industry and Consumers

The rapid pace of change is leading to new ways of engaging with consumers and industry for the purpose of supervision. Financial regulators have historically been more interested in prudential regulation than consumer protection – partly because consumer protection has typically been conducted by other agencies, if at all – but the global financial crisis has caused a cultural shift. Regulators have come to see consumer protection and the safety and soundness of financial institutions as related and mutually reinforcing objectives.

As protecting consumers has assumed a higher priority, regulators have tried new ways to engage with them. In the United States, for example, the Consumer Financial Protection Bureau (CFPB) is redesigning consumer-disclosure information, and testing extensively to understand how consumers use disclosures. The agency has also developed a user-friendly complaint-reporting tool, with the aim of encouraging providers to resolve issues quickly. Verified complaint data is shared publicly, holding all providers publicly accountable for their consumer performance. The CFPB feeds this consumer data into its rule-making and supervision efforts.

As regulators struggle to keep up with innovations that strain methods designed for traditional business models, some are developing programs that enable innovators to conduct limited and controlled testing of new ideas in coordination with regulators. These regulatory "sandboxes" can allow innovators to test new services, including some that may test the limits of existing regulation, in a way that limits the risks for consumers and lets regulators learn from the experiments. Innovators benefit from being able to test and prove new ideas with the consent of regulators; regulators benefit by learning about emerging business models in real time and by gaining familiarity with marketplace trends.

Other initiatives concentrate on making it easier for innovators to learn about regulatory requirements. One approach is "office hours" that let innovators meet with regulators and ask questions in a safe, off-the-record environment. Another way is to form teams to consult with innovators around licensing and other regulation. A variant is to establish specific product-based teams that are responsible for providing deep domain expertise related to specific product trends.

The CFPB in the United States and Financial Conduct Authority (FCA) in the United Kingdom provide two useful case studies. The CFPB's Project Catalyst "encourage[s] consumer-friendly innovation in markets for consumer financial products and services" by providing several unique engagement opportunities for innovators.[27] For example, the CFPB regularly conducts informal "office hours," and lets innovators conduct pilot programs in a sandbox-like setting, so new ways of meeting regulatory or disclosure requirements can be studied jointly by both the agency and the company. The pilot program is also viewed as a valuable learning mechanism for the CFPB. As part of the pilots, they are provided significant amounts of pilot data. This has spillover effects to other policy efforts by advancing the CFPB's understanding of consumer behavior and financial innovation, including whether or which aspects of innovations may be beneficial to certain segments of consumers. Recently, the CFPB also announced a new "no-action letter" policy – allowing companies to request a CFPB opinion on whether the CFPB has an "intention to recommend enforcement or supervisory action with respect to the particular aspects of the company's product".[28] The CFPB says "the policy could be appropriate in a case where an innovative product is being developed that involves technology that did not exist and may not have been contemplated at the time existing regulations were adopted." The Office of the Comptroller of the Currency, another US financial regulator, is also exploring approaches to engaging with fintech innovators and to supporting what it calls "responsible innovation."[29]

The UK's FCA is also leaning forward in this area. Its Project Innovate initiative works to promote innovation in the interests of consumers. Through its Innovation Hub it offers a dedicated team to help innovators with regulatory questions and authorization requirements.[30] Although still young, the program worked with over 270 innovators in its first 18 months. It also works to ensure that the regulations themselves are supportive of innovation. As part of the initiative, the FCA is launching a Regulatory Sandbox, which is a set of regulatory tools to provide a safe space for firms to test out innovative ideas for new products, services, and business models with real consumers in a real environment. The hope is that this will support more innovative products coming to market and help firms build in customer safeguards at an early stage. The FCA has also been signing Co-operation Agreements with overseas regulators to facilitate the referral of innovative firms between their respective markets, in order to reduce the regulatory barriers to entry involved in overseas expansion. The FCA also conducts workshops, roundtables, and "themed weeks" that engage industry on specific topics, such as regtech and robo advice, described by the FCA as "automated investment advice business models".[31]

In developing markets where regulatory capacity is weaker, an industry-led approach to self-supervision is emerging. Sensitive to the fact that some regulators aren't knowledgeable about mobile digital finance and lack the resources to supervise effectively, Mobile Network Operators (MNOs) have established a voluntary code of conduct[32] both for mobile operators and for agents delivering mobile-money services. Focused particularly on consumer protection, this model seeks to prevent instances of consumer harm that could be a setback to an industry that hasn't traditionally operated within the robust regulatory framework of commercial and retail banking. The idea of self-supervision isn't new in developed markets: Various self-regulatory organizations (SROs) exercise some degree of regulatory authority over an industry or profession. In the US, for example, the Securities and Exchange Commission (SEC) approved a merger in 2007 of the enforcement arms of the NYSE and the National Association of Security Dealers (NASD), to form a new SRO, the Financial Industry Regulatory Authority (FINRA). National payment associations can be found around the world, most of them representing service providers, and several with their own codes of conduct. Promoting these models in developing markets where they're less common would help regulators and enterprises alike.

In a sector that has traditionally relied on a "Chinese wall" between regulators and the companies they oversee, exchanging information and cooperating in other ways across the divide is a radical departure. The new approaches nonetheless are essential in the face of digitization. In particular, if innovators engage more closely with regulators in the development of new products, both sides will gain. Correctly done, stronger cooperation between regulators and regulated institutions can promote innovation while helping to protect consumers and safeguard financial stability.

Notes

1. http://gpfi.org/sites/default/files/documents/FINAL_The%20Opportunities%20of%20Digitizing%20Payments.pdf.

2. http://www.fatf-gafi.org.

3. Micklethwait, J., Wooldridge, A. 2014. The Fourth Revolution: The Global Race to Reinvent the State. Penguin Books.

4. http://gpfi.org.

5. http://www.cgap.org.

6. https://www.betterthancash.org/about.

7. http://www.gpfi.org/sites/default/files/documents/White-Paper-Global-Standard-Setting-Bodies-Oct-2011.pdf.

8. http://www.gpfi.org/sites/default/files/documents/GPFI%20White%20Paper%20final%20prepublication%20version%20March%202016.pdf.

9. http://www.afi-global.org/who-we-are.

10. http://www.cashlearning.org.

11. http://www.wsj.com/public/resources/documents/financialinclusion.html.

12. http://www.gpfi.org/sites/default/files/documents/GPFI%20SSBs%20Conference%20%20Issues%20Paper%203%20Financial%20Inclusion%20%20E2%80%93%20A%20Pathway%20to%20Financial%20Stability_1.pdf.

13. https://www.betterthancash.org/news/blogs-stories/digitization-of-payments-in-mexico-saves-billions.

14. http://www.businessinsider.com/fintech-ecosystem-and-financial-technology-research-and-business-opportunities-2016-2.

15. http://www.cgdev.org/publication/financial-regulations-improving-financial-inclusion.

16. https://www.imf.org/external/np/speeches/2016/041116.htm.

17. http://www.cgap.org/publications/doing-digital-finance-right.

18. http://www.fsb.org.

19. http://www.bloomberg.com/news/articles/2016-01-21/chinese-central-bank-studies-prospect-of-own-digital-currency.

20. http://www.bbc.com/news/world-latin-america-28992589.

21. http://www.philstar.com/business/2014/10/05/1376516/solon-pushes-e-peso-act.

22. http://www.bankofengland.co.uk/publications/Documents/speeches/2015/speech840.pdf.

23. http://www.cbc.ca/news/canada/kitchener-waterloo/bank-of-canada-looking-into-issuing-digital-currency-1.2834759.

24. http://www.wsj.com/articles/central-bankers-explore-response-to-bitcoin-their-own-digital-cash-1449657001.

25. http://digitalfrontiersinstitute.org.

26. http://fletcher.tufts.edu/FinancialInclusion.

27. http://www.consumerfinance.gov/about-us/project-catalyst/.

28. http://www.consumerfinance.gov/about-us/newsroom/cfpb-finalizes-policy-to-facilitate-consumer-friendly-innovation/.

29. http://www.occ.treas.gov/publications/publications-by-type/other-publications-reports/pub-responsible-innovation-banking-system-occ-perspective.pdf.

30. https://innovate.fca.org.uk/.

31. https://innovate.fca.org.uk/innovation-hub/project-innovate-next-steps.

32. http://www.gsma.com/mobilefordevelopment/programmes/mobile-money/policy-and-regulation/code-of-conduct.

CHAPTER 15

Singapore Approach to Develop and Regulate FinTech

Pei Sai Fan

Contents

15.1 MAS Organizational Support for FinTech

The financial regulator in Singapore - the Monetary Authority of Singapore (MAS) is one of the regulators worldwide that respond early to the development of FinTech. As FinTech has the potential to fundamentally transform the financial industry, MAS actively seeks to frame the appropriate regulatory approach in order to support as well as supervise the development of FinTech.

In this regard, MAS formed of a new FinTech & Innovation Group (FTIG) with effect from 1 August 2015.[1] The FTIG is given the same level of hierarchy as Financial Supervision Group within MAS' organization structure, signaling the importance attached to the Group. FTIG will be responsible for regulatory policies and development strategies to facilitate the use of technology and innovation to better manage risks, enhance efficiency, and strengthen competitiveness in the financial sector.

In order to seek expert advice on the international developments in Fintech and how Singapore can harness new technologies worldwide to enhance the provision of financial services, MAS also established an International Technology Advisory Panel (ITAP).[2] The ITAP comprises international chief innovation and science officers in major financial institutions, FinTech business leaders, venture capitalists, and thought leaders in technology and innovation. One of the likely contributions from the Panel is to provide inputs and feedback to MAS in framing a regulatory regime that facilitates innovation and adoption of new technologies while maintaining trust and confidence in the financial system.

At the national level, MAS and the National Research Foundation (NRF) in Prime Minister Office of Singapore jointly established a FinTech Office on 3 May 2016 to serve as a one-stop virtual entity for all FinTech matters and to promote Singapore as a FinTech hub.[3] The FinTech Office is co-led by MAS and SG-Innovate, with representatives from The Economic Development Board, Infocomm Investments Pte Ltd., Info-communications Media Development Authority, National Research Foundation and SPRING Singapore.

The objectives of the FinTech Office are: (i) to review, align and enhance FinTech-related funding schemes across government agencies, (ii) to identify gaps and propose strategies, policies, and schemes in industry infrastructure, talent development and manpower requirements, and business competitiveness, and (iii) to manage the branding and marketing of Singapore as a FinTech hub through FinTech events and initiatives. According to MAS, the FinTech Office will enable a whole-of-government approach to develop the FinTech ecosystem in Singapore and support MAS' vision of fostering a Smart Financial Center. Through the FinTech Office, MAS will be able to go beyond the financial industry to help nurture a wider FinTech ecosystem and engage the FinTech community more actively.

15.2 MAS Existing Regulatory Regime

The mission of the Monetary Authority of Singapore (MAS) is *"to promote sustained and non-inflationary economic growth, and a sound and **progressive financial services sector"**.* For the financial services sector to be progressive, innovation and entrepreneurship of the financial institutions and the necessary conducive environment to support such innovation and entrepreneurship are the necessary elements.

The current guiding principles of financial supervision in Singapore, namely *"Risk-Focused"*, *"Disclosure-Based"*, *"Stakeholder-Reliant"* and *"Supportive of Enterprise"*[4] – are indeed in general helpful in creating conducive environment to support innovation and entrepreneurship in the financial markets.

Briefly speaking, the current *"Risk-Focused"* instead of old "one-size-fits-all" supervisory approach allows greater business latitude to financial firms that do not pose significant risks to the financial system and to financial firms that are well-managed. *"Disclosure-Based"* regime means that MAS requires financial firms to disclose accurate, meaningful and material information that consumers could rely on in making decisions on the selection and use of financial products and services offered by these financial firms, instead of the regulator assessing the suitability of a financial product or service before it is allowed to be introduced in the marketplace. This encourages more innovation of financial products and services to be made available to the consumers. *"Stakeholder-Reliant"* seeks to reinforce the responsibility of the financial firms' board and management in self-regulating and self-supervising their firms' risk-taking activities so as to minimize the need for the regulator to interfere with financial firms' business decisions. And lastly, *"Supportive of Enterprise"* means that MAS takes a consultative approach to regulating the industry and undertakes supervision in a way not to hinder enterprise and innovation or impair the competitiveness and dynamism of individual financial firms and the financial services sector.

15.3 Shaping Regulatory Approach for Fintech

For many years, financial institutions have been applying technological innovations in their products and services. MAS encourages and welcomes financial firms to develop and apply new technologies into the financial ecosystem to enhance value for customers, increase efficiency, manage risks better, create new opportunities and improve people's lives.

Under the MAS existing regulatory regime, the technology risk, together with other risks, of each of the significant activities of a financial institution are systematically identified and the control factors, oversight and governance to manage such risks are assessed under the MAS' risk assessment system for financial institutions known as Comprehensive Risk Assessment Framework and Techniques (CRAFT). Such a risk assessment approach is in response, firstly, to the need for sharper focus on the risk and threat analysis associated with increasingly complex activities, products and delivery mechanisms of financial institutions where multiple risks are taken and/or bundled together and, secondly, to the advancement in activity-specific risk management and control practices in the financial services industry.

In assessing the quality of technology risk management by the financial institutions within the CRAFT, MAS had since March 2001 been issuing a set of Internet banking and technology risk management guidelines (today known as "Technology Risk Management Guidelines" with its latest revision in March 2013[5]) as benchmarks for such assessment. The guidelines cover areas such as oversight by board of directors and senior management; technology risk management framework (risk identification, risk assessment, risk treatment and risk monitoring and reporting); management of IT outsourcing risks; acquisition and development of information systems; IT service management, system reliability, availability and recoverability; operational infrastructure security management; data centers protection and controls; access control; online financial service; payment card security; and IT audit. After several revisions, the existing guidelines are very comprehensive and crafted with very detailed standards expected of financial institutions in their technology risk management.

In recent time, the fast emerging FinTech start-ups are showing great potential of creating disruptive innovation with the use of new technology that may emerge as genuine competitors to the existing incumbents. However, these FinTech start-ups are not likely to have the financial strength nor the business and management track record that meet the existing regulatory requirements for the necessary license to offer financial services. Here lie the difficult issues facing the regulators: How can regulation foster innovation from these start-ups and promote competition in financial services for the good of financial consumers? How to ensure regulation is not a front-runner and not stifling innovation? How can regulators ensure a regulatory environment fit for the disruptive innovation?

At current stage, it's uncertain to tell how financial innovation will play out in the financial landscape in the future and whether the FinTech start-ups – the disrupters – will indeed disrupt the existing financial business models in a significant way that poses macro-prudential concerns. Is it therefore important that regulators strike the delicate balance between encouraging financial innovation and not creating unnecessary barriers to the many opportunities to improve efficiency in the financial markets, and on the other hand ensuring financial stability?

MAS recognized that at this stage of the development, the disrupters are still experimenting how the new technology could improve and in what areas of the financial services, and also the disrupters and incumbents are still exploring and strategizing whether they should treat each other as friends or enemies, or in some areas of financial services they should combine strength for mutual gain by collaborating and cooperation, hence the terms **"Friendnemy"** and **"Co-opetition"** came about.

At this transition stage, MAS wants to allow for this experimentation, but at the same time foremost in MAS' minds is that it must be done in a way that preserves trust and credibility in financial system. MAS will adopt the following policy approach in regulating this new wave of innovation in financial services[6]:

Firstly, MAS will take a differentiated approach to different technologies and their applications. It is worth noting that unlike a full-fledged financial firm such as banks, which provide comprehensive services and products, the current wave of FinTech start-ups by themselves individually are developing technology to improve **a particular** financial service or product, hence the risks embedded in their activities or due to the nature of their technology are different. A "one-size-fits-all" regulatory approach will clearly not be appropriate. For example, digital payments and digital currencies pose issues of authentication and identity; P2P lending platforms and crowdfunding have implications for consumer protection and fraud risk; and cloud computing and big data face the risk of cyber security, etc. MAS will develop regulatory policy after evaluating the merits of each technology and considering which financial activity it is being applied to and the likely implication and impact.

Secondly, MAS will adopt a risk-based approach to FinTech innovation in the unregulated sector. MAS is clearly aware that introducing regulation prematurely may stifle innovation and potentially derail the adoption of useful technology, therefore it always ensures that regulation must not be a front-runner of innovation. Instead, MAS applies a **materiality** and **proportionality** test. This means that when the risk posed by new technology becomes material, then regulation comes in. Also, the regulation must be proportionate to the risk posed. Take, for example, that MAS regulates banks chiefly because they take deposits from ordinary people. Securities (debt or equity) crowdfunding platforms are not allowed to take deposits, and where investors are limited to accredited or sophisticated investors, MAS generally regulates such platforms lightly. However, when some crowdfunding platforms are looking to help companies to raise business loans from retail investors, MAS steps in to require such platforms to be licensed by the MAS and impose licensing requirements such as minimum capital and disclosure requirement. The purpose is to strike the right balance between improving access to securities crowdfunding for business start-ups and small and medium-sized enterprises and protecting investor interests. MAS also declares that if such financing platforms get very large and pose concerns to the stability of the financial markets, then MAS may consider macro-prudential regulations such as capital adequacy, credit rating and fund solvency, etc. to strengthen the individual player and other measures to solidify the resilience of the entire market.

Thirdly, with regard to FinTech experiment as mentioned above, MAS on 16 November 2016 issued "FinTech Regulatory Sandbox Guidelines"[7] in which MAS proposed a "Regulatory Sandbox" for trials by both FinTech start-ups and large financial companies to experiment with financial technology (FinTech) solutions. MAS is keenly aware that the speed at which the burgeoning FinTech landscape is fast evolving and that the friction caused by the existing regulations can slow down the innovation process. Also, according to MAS, "there may be circumstances where it is less clear whether a particular FinTech solution complies with regulatory requirements or poses unacceptable risks. The uncertainty may stifle promising innovations, and may result in missed opportunities".

15.4 "Regulatory Sandbox"

MAS recognizes that failure is often a feature of such FinTech experiments and the purpose of the "Regulatory Sandbox" is to provide appropriate safeguards to contain the consequences or cost of failure for customers and the market as a whole, rather than to prevent failure altogether.

The Regulatory Sandbox will therefore enable FinTech start-ups or financial institutions to experiment with proposed financial services leveraging on innovative FinTech solutions, after being tested in a "laboratory environment", in an environment where actual products or services are provided to the customers ("production environment") but within a well-defined space and duration where the consequences of failure can be contained. The Sandbox cannot remove all risks, as failure is an inherent characteristic of innovation. But the Sandbox helps carve out a safe and conducive space to experiment with FinTech solutions, and if an experiment fails, its impact on consumers and on financial stability will be limited.

For the duration of the regulatory sandbox, a risk-based approach will be adopted by MAS in determining the most appropriate and effective form of regulatory support to facilitate experimentation in the sandbox. MAS will, on a case-by-case basis, relax specific regulatory requirements which an applicant would otherwise be subject to. Examples of requirements which can be relaxed include credit rating, financial soundness, management experience, track record, and MAS Guidelines, such as technology risk management guidelines and outsourcing guidelines, etc. MAS will not compromise on requirements in areas such as confidentiality of customer information, fit and proper criteria particularly on honesty and integrity of people operating the Sandbox, handling of customer's moneys and assets by third-party intermediaries, and anti-money laundering and countering the financing of terrorism.

Apart from the above **regulatory support**, MAS encourages applicants to engage MAS FinTech Office to discuss other possible forms of support from MAS such as financial support, cross-agency support, mentorship, training on regulatory framework, access to Application Programming Interfaces (APIs), business partnerships, manpower, co-working space, and introductory services and provisioning of a cloud environment for sandbox experimentation, and MAS will explore the most appropriate ways in which such **non-regulatory support** can be rendered.

MAS stipulates that applications for proposed financial services leveraging on innovative FinTech solutions to be tested in the regulatory sandbox be assessed on the following evaluation criteria:

(1) The proposed financial service includes new or emerging technology, or uses existing technology in an innovative way. For example, secondary research should show that few or no comparable offerings are available in the Singapore market;

(2) The proposed financial service addresses a problem, or brings benefits to consumers or the industry. For example, these could be supported by evidence from relevant consumer or industry research;

(3) The applicant has the intention and ability to deploy the proposed financial service in Singapore on a broader scale after exiting the sandbox. If there are exceptional reasons why the proposed financial service cannot be deployed in Singapore, for example it is not commercially viable to deploy in Singapore, the applicant should be prepared to continue contributing to Singapore in other ways, such as continuing the developmental efforts of the proposed financial service in Singapore;

(4) The test scenarios and expected outcomes of the sandbox experimentation should be clearly defined, and the sandbox entity should report to MAS on the test progress based on an agreed schedule;

(5) The appropriate boundary conditions should be clearly defined, for the sandbox to be meaningfully executed while sufficiently protecting the interests of consumers and maintaining the safety and soundness of the industry;

(6) Significant risks arising from the proposed financial service should be assessed and mitigated. For example, providing evidence of preliminary testing of the proposed financial service as part of the sandbox application, identifying the risks discovered from the preliminary testing and the proposal for mitigating the risks; and

(7) An acceptable exit and transition strategy should be clearly defined in the event that the proposed financial service has to be discontinued, or can proceed to be deployed on a broader scale after exiting the sandbox.

In addition, MAS states that the sandbox may not be suitable under the following circumstances:

(a) The proposed financial service is similar to those that are already being offered in Singapore, unless the applicant can show that either:
    (i)   a different technology is being applied; or
    (ii) the same technology is being applied differently.

(b) The applicant has not demonstrated that it has done its due diligence, including testing the proposed financial service in a laboratory environment and knowing the legal and regulatory requirements for deploying the proposed financial service.

An illustration by way of flow chart on how the MAS' "Regulatory Sandbox" can encourage experimentation of innovative FinTech solutions to improve the authentication to secure the customer data and transactions against cyber-attacks is appended below:

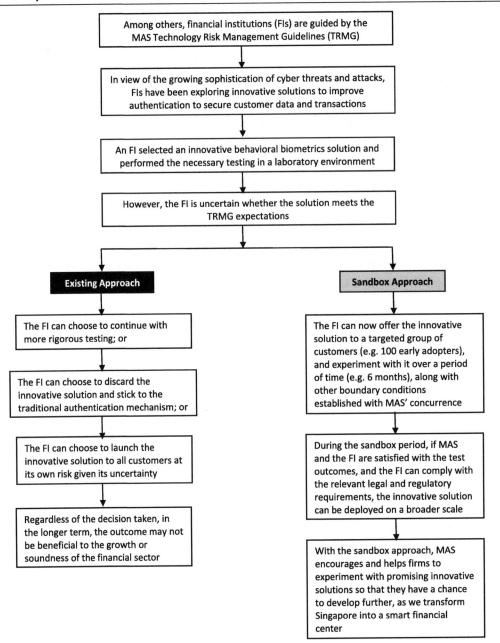

Among others, financial institutions (FIs) are guided by the MAS Technology Risk Management Guidelines (TRMG)

In view of the growing sophistication of cyber threats and attacks, FIs have been exploring innovative solutions to improve authentication to secure customer data and transactions

An FI selected an innovative behavioral biometrics solution and performed the necessary testing in a laboratory environment

However, the FI is uncertain whether the solution meets the TRMG expectations

Existing Approach

The FI can choose to continue with more rigorous testing; or

The FI can choose to discard the innovative solution and stick to the traditional authentication mechanism; or

The FI can choose to launch the innovative solution to all customers at its own risk given its uncertainty

Regardless of the decision taken, in the longer term, the outcome may not be beneficial to the growth or soundness of the financial sector

Sandbox Approach

The FI can now offer the innovative solution to a targeted group of customers (e.g. 100 early adopters), and experiment with it over a period of time (e.g. 6 months), along with other boundary conditions established with MAS' concurrence

During the sandbox period, if MAS and the FI are satisfied with the test outcomes, and the FI can comply with the relevant legal and regulatory requirements, the innovative solution can be deployed on a broader scale

With the sandbox approach, MAS encourages and helps firms to experiment with promising innovative solutions so that they have a chance to develop further, as we transform Singapore into a smart financial center

According to MAS, applications for the sandbox initiative if approved would be limited to certain number of customers and allowed to run their tests for certain period, during which they could measure customer experience and assess the product's risk exposure and mitigation measures.

The Sandbox would be deployed and operated by the applicant, with MAS providing the appropriate regulatory support by relaxing specific legal and regulatory requirements. However, it is noteworthy that no specific legal form or structure for the sandbox entity has been specified.

In the event that the sandbox entity requires an extension of the sandbox period, the sandbox entity should apply to MAS at least **1 month** before the expiration of the sandbox period and provide reasons to support the application for extension. For example, additional time is needed to make changes to the financial service under experimentation after taking into account customer feedback or to rectify flaws, or the sandbox entity requires more time in order to fully comply with the relevant legal and regulatory requirements. MAS will review the application and approval will be granted on a case-by-case basis.

The Sandbox will be discontinued when:

(1) MAS is not satisfied that the sandbox has achieved its intended purpose, based on the latest test scenarios, expected outcomes and schedule mutually agreed with the sandbox entity;
(2) the sandbox entity is unable to fully comply with the relevant legal and regulatory requirements at the end of the sandbox period. If such a situation is anticipated, the sandbox entity is encouraged to engage MAS earlier;
(3) a flaw has been discovered in the financial service under experimentation where the risks posed to customers or the financial system outweigh the benefits of the financial service under experimentation, and the sandbox entity acknowledges that the flaw cannot be resolved within the duration of the sandbox;
(4) MAS terminates the sandbox due to reasons such as the sandbox entity breaching any condition imposed for the duration of the sandbox; or
(5) the sandbox entity has informed MAS of its decision to exit the sandbox at its own discretion.

The sandbox entity should ensure that any existing obligation to its customers of the financial service under experimentation must be fully fulfilled or addressed before exiting the sandbox or discontinuing the sandbox.

On the other hand, upon successfully exiting the Sandbox, the applicant can proceed to deploy the financial service on a broader scale, provided that:

(1) both MAS and the sandbox entity are satisfied that the Sandbox has achieved its intended test outcomes; and
(2) the sandbox entity can fully comply with the relevant legal and regulatory requirements.

The sandbox entity is encouraged to engage MAS early if it anticipates that it cannot comply with the legal and regulatory requirements upon exiting the sandbox and can apply to MAS for an extension of the sandbox period if it helps the sandbox entity to fully comply with the relevant legal and regulatory requirements subsequently. MAS will assess such situations on a case-by-case basis in the interest of encouraging FinTech innovation, protecting consumers and maintaining a level-playing field.

Lastly, while the FinTech Regulatory Sandbox Guidelines describe the application and approval process, and inform and guide applicants in their preparation for a sandbox application, they are principle-based so as to allow MAS the flexibility to facilitate experimentation of a wide range of financial services by a broad range of firms. MAS also does not rule out the possibility of applying other supervisory tools where appropriate and where legally permissible.

15.5 Closing

While the FinTech Regulatory Sandbox Guidelines has been issued, the exact implementation details of the Regulatory Sandbox, such as the sandbox testing period, size of sample set of customers to be tested, etc., which are likely to be determined on a case-by-case basis, remain to be seen. The case-by-case approach is entirely understandable, given that all kinds of FinTech solutions might be presented and it would be difficult for the regulator to know beforehand what sort of Sandbox scenarios and FinTech solutions might be presented for consideration.

Also in writer's view, what will be interesting to watch is whether, upon successfully exiting the Sandbox, the applicant could fully comply with the relevant legal and regulatory requirements in order to proceed to deploy the FinTech solution on a broader scale. This is because by their nature, many of the FinTech start-ups are strong in technological innovations but lack the financial strength, resources and track record, and it is unlikely for them to be able to build up these prudential requirements imposed by the regulator during the duration of the Sandbox implementation. Hence, one possible and likely outcome is that MAS may design regulatory requirements around the types or categories of FinTech solutions, akin to the "activity-based" regulatory approach currently applicable to capital market activities adopted by MAS, or that we may well see more collaboration and cooperation between the FinTech start-ups and the large and established financial institutions which then allow the FinTech solutions to be deployed on a broader scale under the umbrella of the large and established financial institutions which are better able to comply with the relevant legal and regulatory requirements.

In any case, what is clear so far based on MAS' responses on its stated policy approach towards Fintech is that MAS recognizes financial technology is fast evolving and can be disruptive, but it can also be a means that has the potential to eventually improve the end – the efficiency of financial markets. Therefore, MAS understands a responsive and forward-looking regulatory approach is needed to further enhance the ability of promising FinTech innovations to develop and flourish, and hence the need for regulator to be innovative in developing "Smart Regulation" such as the proposed "Regulatory Sandbox", so as to allow for quick experimentation of innovative FinTech solutions, and improve "time to market" for innovative FinTech solutions if the solution is proven successful, and on the other hand help to minimize cost of failure if the solution fails. This aligns with the vision to make Singapore a "Smart Financial Center" of which a key driver is the provision of a regulatory environment that is conducive for the innovative and safe use of technology.

Notes

1. MAS website – http://www.mas.gov.sg/news-and-publications/media-releases/2015/mas-sets-up-new-fintech-and-innovation-group.aspx.

2. MAS website – http://www.mas.gov.sg/News-and-Publications/Media-Releases/2016/MAS-sets-up-International-Technology-Advisory-Panel.aspx.

3. MAS website – http://www.mas.gov.sg/News-and-Publications/Media-Releases/2016/New-FinTech-Office.aspx.

4. "Objectives and Principles of Financial Supervision in Singapore", MAS Monograph, April 2004.

5. "Technology Risk Management Guidelines" issued by MAS in March 2013. http://www.mas.gov.sg/~/media/MAS/Regulations%20and%20Financial%20Stability/Regulatory%20and%20Supervisory%20Framework/Risk%20Management/TRM%20Guidelines%20%2021%20June%202013.pdf.

6. "FinTech – Harnessing its Power, Managing its Risks" – Panel Remarks by Mr. Ravi Menon, Managing Director, Monetary Authority of Singapore, at Singapore Forum on 2 April 2016.

7. MAS FinTech Regulatory Sandbox – MAS Media Release, 16 November 2016. http://www.mas.gov.sg/Singapore-Financial-Centre/Smart-Financial-Centre/FinTech-Regulatory-Sandbox.aspx.

CHAPTER 16

RegTech: Building a Better Financial System[1]

Douglas W. Arner, Jànos Barberis, Ross P. Buckley

Contents

16.1 Introduction

Since the 2008 Global Financial Crisis ('GFC'), regulatory and technological developments have changed financial markets, services and institutions in unexpected ways.[2] 'FinTech', the use of technology to deliver financial solutions, is one aspect of these changes. Its rapid evolution demands a similar evolution of RegTech.[3] 'RegTech', a contraction of the terms 'regulatory' and 'technology', describes the use of technology in the context of regulatory monitoring, reporting and compliance.[4] Automation of processes allows for better, more efficient risk identification and regulatory compliance.[5]

Recently two pain points have arisen in the financial services industry, which drive the development of RegTech and support our vision. On the expense side, post-crisis fines have exceeded US$200 billion,[6] and the ongoing cost of regulation and compliance has become an industry-wide concern.[7] On the revenue side, competition from FinTech companies threatens up to US$4.7 trillion of revenues.[8] As with FinTech,[9] the GFC represented a turning point in RegTech development.[10] However, the factors underlying, and beneficiaries of, RegTech are quite different. Start-ups (increasingly partnering with, or being acquired by, traditional financial institutions)[11] have led FinTech growth, whilst RegTech has arisen from the huge costs of complying with new institutional demands by regulators and policy-makers.[12] In one survey, 87% of banking CEOs considered these costs disruptive.[13] This provides a strong economic incentive for more efficient reporting and compliance systems to better control risks and reduce costs. Furthermore, massive increases in the volume and types of data reported to regulatory authorities[14] represent a major opportunity for the automation of compliance and monitoring processes. For the financial services industry, the application of technology to regulation and compliance could massively increase efficiency.

For regulators, RegTech enables a move towards a proportionate risk-based approach where access to and management of data enables more granular, effective supervision of markets and market participants.[15] This can minimize risks of the regulatory capture witnessed prior to the GFC and respond to the increasingly digital nature of finance.[16] Furthermore, applying technology to regulation facilitates the monitoring of financial markets participants that are increasingly fragmented by the emergence of FinTech start-ups.[17]

Enhanced reporting accuracy and decreased compliance costs are not new incentives.[18] However, with the digitization of the financial services industry, the gap between the accuracy, and costs, of manual and automatic compliance and monitoring has widened. Combined with recent advances in data science and analytics, RegTech's growth can be understood as process automation to substantially decrease both compliance costs and the potential for regulatory actions and fines.[19]

Early signs of real-time, proportionate and efficient regulatory regimes are emerging. However, automating and streamlining regulatory processes is only an incremental evolution toward a more efficient regulatory framework.

16.2 RegTech: A Framework of Analysis

The GFC and post-crisis financial regulatory reforms transformed the way financial institutions operate, reducing their risk-taking, profitability and spectrum of operations.[20] Extensive post-crisis regulation has dramatically increased the compliance burden on financial institutions, adding to the direct cost of regulatory penalties.[21] These changes were intended by the post-crisis regulatory reform agenda,[22] which has driven RegTech's emergence; we return to this issue in Section 16.3.

With this dramatically altered environment has come the rapid evolution of FinTech. While this term has only gained popularity in the past three years,[23] the interaction between finance and technology has a long history.[24]

Today, FinTech impacts every area of the financial system globally, most dramatically in China, where technology firms Alibaba, Baidu and TenCent ('BATs') have transformed finance and posed new regulatory challenges.[25] Furthermore, since 2016 regulators in the United States, UK, Australia and Singapore have attempted to better understand FinTech market dynamics and develop new regulatory approaches.[26]

According to the FCA: 'RegTech is a subset of FinTech that focuses on technologies that may facilitate the delivery of regulatory requirements more *efficiently* and *effectively* than *existing* capabilities' (emphasis added).[27] This pragmatic assessment of RegTech today underestimates RegTech's true potential.[28] RegTech is not only an efficiency tool. It is a pivotal change that could trigger a paradigm shift in regulation. Viewed holistically, RegTech represents the next logical evolution of financial services regulation and should underpin the entire financial services sector.

In the near future, the application of technology to monitoring and compliance offers massive cost savings to established financial companies and opportunities to emerging FinTech start-ups, IT and advisory firms.[29] For regulators, RegTech enables continuous monitoring that improves efficiency by both liberating excess regulatory capital,[30] and making it faster to investigate non-compliant firms.[31] RegTech however offers more: the potential of continuous monitoring capacity, providing close to real-time insights, through deep learning and AI filters, which identify problems in advance rather than enabling enforcement action after the fact. This would be a profound transformation in the approach to both finance and its regulation.

While FinTech has an inherently financial focus, RegTech has the potential for application in various contexts from monitoring corporations for environmental compliance to monitoring trucking companies for speeding infractions. As our financial system moves from one based on Know-Your-Customer ('KYC') principles to a Know-Your-Data ('KYD') approach, a new regulatory paradigm dealing with everything from digital identity to data sovereignty, extending beyond the financial sphere, must evolve.

It is therefore critical to distinguish RegTech from FinTech. The conception that RegTech is a subset of FinTech may come from the fact that the GFC catalyzed both. However, their underlying causes were different.

RegTech's emergence is attributable to: (1) post-crisis regulation requiring additional data disclosure from supervised entities[32]; (2) data science developments (particularly AI and deep learning), which can structure unstructured data[33]; (3) economic incentives to minimize rising compliance costs; and (4) regulators' efforts to make supervisory tools more efficient to foster competition and uphold their mandates of financial stability and market integrity.[34]

FinTech's emergence is attributable to: (1) financial market deficiencies caused by the GFC and resulting regulatory responses; (2) public distrust in the financial services industry; (3) political pressure for alternative sources of finance for small and medium enterprises; (4) unemployed financial professionals looking to apply their talents; and (5) the commoditization of technology and market penetration of the Internet and mobile phones.[35]

FinTech post-GFC has grown organically as a bottom-up movement led by start-ups and IT firms, whilst RegTech has grown in response to top-down institutional demand and encompasses three distinct, but complementary groups.

Firstly, financial institutions and the financial industry are increasingly applying technology to meet regulatory demands.

Secondly, regulators need to use technology to address challenges of monitoring and enforcing new regulatory requirements in rapidly developing cross-border markets. They must also deal with rapidly emerging FinTech technologies and entrants. Regulators must develop regulatory approaches that allow innovation but limit risks to consumers and financial stability.[36]

Thirdly, policy-makers and regulators will face the challenge of rapidly transforming financial systems, and building the necessary infrastructure to support their regulation, which will necessitate the increasing use of RegTech and close cooperation with industry participants.

To date, RegTech development has primarily been driven by the financial services industry wishing to decrease costs.[37] Increasingly, going forward, it is likely to be driven by regulators seeking to increase their supervisory capacity. We therefore expect RegTech to focus more on business-to-business ('B2B') solutions in contrast to FinTech which focuses on business-to-consumer ('B2C'), as well as B2B, solutions.[38]

16.3 RegTech in the Financial Services Industry

Financial institutions applied technology intensively to risk management and compliance in the 1990s, with regulators relying heavily on such systems. However, the GFC fundamentally altered that paradigm. Regulators globally have since implemented extensive regulatory reforms, which have driven global firms to develop global centralized risk management and compliance functions.[39]

RegTech's emergence can be largely attributed to the *complex, fragmented* and *ever-evolving* post-GFC regulatory regime. Financial supervision, in response to growing regulatory complexity, inevitably required greater granularity, precision and frequency in data reporting, aggregation, and analysis.[40]

Examples appear in capital and liquidity regulations under Basel III, stress testing and risk assessments in the UK, US and EU, and reporting requirements imposed on OTC derivatives transactions resulting from Group of 20 ('G20')/Financial Stability Board ('FSB') agreed approaches and as implemented – in conflicting fashions – in the context of Dodd–Frank or the EU's EMIR.[41] Rising compliance costs made innovative technologies a natural solution to compliance requirements.[42] As reported, '[t]he annual spending by financial institutions on compliance is estimated to be in excess of US $70 billion.'[43] It is no wonder the industry turned to RegTech for cost-effective solutions.

Second, deepening regulatory fragmentation has given rise to an additional layer of compliance burdens for financial institutions. Regulatory overlaps and contradictions between markets led financial institutions to turn to RegTech to optimize compliance management.[44]

Third, the rapidly evolving post-crisis regulatory landscape introduced uncertainty on future regulatory requirements, placing a premium on financial institutions enhancing their *adaptability*.[45] RegTech may have taught financial institutions how to ensure compliance in a changing environment through iterative modeling and testing.

Finally, regulators are motivated to become familiar with RegTech to ensure financial institutions comply with regulations in a responsive manner.[46] RegTech adds value to regulators by helping them understand, in closer to real-time, innovative products and complex transactions, market manipulation, internal fraud and risks.[47] New technological developments additionally allow for new forms of market monitoring or reporting processes.[48] The Bank of England is closely observing RegTech development, stating that (emphasis added):

> *Firms have started to make progress in response to the limitations of existing surveillance solutions, including the use of* new technology and analytics which go beyond *the key-word surveillance and simple statistical checks previously used by firms to detect improper trading activity...*[49]

As noted, this was initially driven by post-crisis regulatory reforms, with the application of technology the enabling factor.

In 2014, Goldman Sachs established what is now its second largest office in Bangalore (Bengaluru), India, with capacity for 9,000 staff.[50] Other major financial institutions, including

JP Morgan, Citibank, Barclays, and HSBC, have many staff in centralized support operations in India, especially in Bangalore, Mumbai, New Delhi and Chennai. Rather than traditional back office or call center operations, these are focused on integrated global risk management and regulatory compliance. In the context of customer on-boarding/account opening and KYC operations, these functions may be centralized in India (or elsewhere) for all operations of a global financial services firm.[51]

Likewise, with respect to extensive reporting requirements, financial institutions now look to centralized operations to gather necessary data globally on a real-time basis so that they have a clearer picture of operations and risks and can repackage the information to meet regulatory requirements.[52] Ironically, these operations resemble pre-2008 trading floors, with rows of desks with telephones and multiple screens to allow continuous monitoring and communication across the institution.

From a regulatory standpoint, these separately incorporated subsidiaries are not regulated as banks in their host jurisdiction, as they are not conducting 'banking' activities requiring licensing and regulation. Rather, they are subject to domestic outsourcing rules of the jurisdictions of the group entities they support.[53]

Consequently, an entirely different way of addressing compliance is emerging – one driven by technology and regulatory change and comprising the most sophisticated level of RegTech today, the first element of a new post-crisis RegTech 2.0. RegTech's increasing prevalence in industry requires regulators to adapt and adopt technology within their own internal processes, which comprises the second element of post-crisis RegTech 2.0 discussed in Part IV.

16.4 Data Driven Regulation

While regulators' lack of financial and human resources is generally a barrier to RegTech development (particularly in developing countries), regulators have had notable successes combining technology and regulation.[54]

Relative to the private sector there has however been a lag in regulator adoption of RegTech. Nonetheless, large market incidents have prompted regulatory (re)action. Regulators have used technology since the 1980s to monitor and enforce market integrity in exchange-traded securities markets, with the US Securities and Exchange Commission ('SEC') leading globally.[55] Regulators and the financial industry have long worked closely in the evolution of robust technological and regulatory solutions to issues regarding cross-border electronic payment systems and securities trading and settlement systems. However, with the increasing information reported to regulators and new technology such as AI and deep learning, there is potential for more to be done in terms of automating market supervision, consumer protection and prudential regulation.[56] The pace of FinTech innovation has also proven challenging.

RegTech's evolution in the financial industry highlights the rate of change within industry. However, regulators themselves provide an example of the relatively wide gap between IT-enabled systems in the industry and the lack of IT-enabled solutions among regulators. Regulators are becoming aware of this due to the simple necessity of dealing with the masses of data which industry is required to deliver.[57] Given these data streams are designed to ensure financial stability and market integrity, it is essential that regulators develop systems to appropriately monitor and analyze these data sets.

16.4.1 Big Data

AML/KYC has so far provided a fertile area for RegTech development in the post-crisis financial services industry. However, the information produced by the financial services industry – particularly suspicious transactions reports – is an area where regulators are beginning to consider technological solutions to assist monitoring and analysis. Failure to develop the IT capabilities to use new data provided will undermine underlying policy objectives.[58] This also provides an opportunity for collaboration between regulators and academia to produce a greater understanding of market behavior and dynamics.[59]

Regulators have successfully used technology in reporting transactions in public securities markets. Today, regulators rely heavily on the trade reporting systems of securities exchanges to detect unusual behavior which can trigger potential regulatory investigation and enforcement.[60] Such systems illustrate the use of RegTech 1.0 in the pre-crisis period.

Since 2008, such systems have proven to be limited by their lack of information on activities taking place off the exchange, which is concerning given the majority of trading in many markets occurs off-exchange via ECNs and 'dark pools'.[61] US and EU regulatory reforms are set to change this by mandating reporting of all transactions in listed securities, regardless of where those transactions take place. Regulators must match this with IT systems that monitor and analyze information and apply this approach across their regulatory roles. This is the second element of an emerging RegTech 2.0. However, we need to move beyond this to develop a new approach.

16.4.2 Cybersecurity

Cybersecurity concerns highlight the necessity of further regulatory development.[62] As the financial services industry becomes digitized and data-based, there is an increasing risk of attack, theft and fraud from hackers. The 2016 Bangladesh central bank heist, implemented via SWIFT, exposed the vulnerabilities of existing frameworks. Unsurprisingly, this is a focus area for regulators and organizations including the FSB and Basel Committee.[63] This adds to the natural attention placed on the issue by financial institutions themselves: cybersecurity is among the most significant risks they face.[64] Cybersecurity should be a key concern for data intensive FinTech start-ups, who may fail to comprehend the need for security because they live in a digital, data-abundant world. Whilst the scarcity of money drove the development of secure vaults and payment systems, data abundance may not create the right incentive for firms (beyond reputation risks) and can clearly harm consumers.

Cybersecurity is the clearest example of how FinTech demands RegTech. However, RegTech's greatest potential is in the area of macroprudential policy.

16.4.3 Macroprudential Policy

Pre-2008 regulation focused on the soundness of individual financial institutions, assuming that if each bank was financially sound, then the whole financial system would likewise be stable. The GFC fundamentally altered this view and since the crisis there has been a new focus on macroprudential policy, with the G20 tasking the IMF, FSB and BIS with the development of related early warning systems to prevent the build-up of risks which lead to financial crises, thereby ultimately either preventing crises or minimizing their severity. Macroprudential policy focuses on overall financial system stability, based on holistic analysis and focusing on interconnections and evolution over time.[65]

Numerous jurisdictions have implemented new institutional frameworks to support macroprudential policy, including the Financial Stability Oversight Council (FSOC) in the US and the European Systemic Risk Board (ESRB) in the EU. These have also been tasked to develop and implement macroprudential policies to support financial stability. Macroprudential policy thus seeks to use the extensive data reported to regulators to identify patterns and reduce the severity of the financial cycle.

Some progress is being made in identifying potential leading indicators for future financial instability.[66] It involves quantitative analysis of large volumes of data searching for interconnections and implications. The ever-increasing volumes of data being reported can feed into these analytical processes. Already, central banks such as the Federal Reserve, the European Central Bank and the Bank of England are using data 'heat maps' to highlight potential issues arising from automated analyses of data (such as stress tests).[67]

These early efforts highlight the likely future direction of RegTech with respect to macroprudential policy. Simultaneously, regulators are continually identifying needs for even more data.[68] Ever-increasing reporting requirements further drive the need for RegTech processes and the necessity of centralized support services to collect and produce the required data at the required frequency and in the required format. In particular, the Basel Committee has set requirements for risk data aggregation and reporting which are driving internal processes in financial institutions and regulators, with an increasing focus on near real-time delivery, with near real-time analysis hoped to follow.[69] Significantly, the FSB and IMF have identified the need to harmonize reporting templates for systemically important financial institutions and simplify data analysis.[70]

These developments show the first important steps on the way to better regulation through technology, but highlight challenges for other regulators regarding expertise, access to technology and financial constraints. They also set the stage for the application of more sophisticated big data tools including deep learning and AI.

16.5 Looking Forward

The speed of FinTech innovation, combined with the dramatic progress witnessed in some developing countries warrants that RegTech be used not only to make financial regulation more effective and affordable, but to reconceptualize and redesign financial regulation in line with the transformation of financial market infrastructure.[71] As FinTech gradually moves from digitization of money to the monetization of data, the regulatory framework must be rethought to cover notions previously unnecessary such as data sovereignty and algorithm supervision. At this stage, the sustainable development of FinTech will need to be built around a new RegTech framework. This requires a sequenced approach.

First, a holistic approach that focuses on building twenty-first century infrastructure to support market functions is required. This is clearest in the context of SWIFT, with efforts now focusing on developing an improved structure to support global payments. On the technological side, blockchain allows the replacement of clearing and settlement methods devised in the nineteenth century.[72] India's recent introduction of a multi-level strategy to support FinTech evolution and innovation demonstrates how RegTech 3.0 could look in emerging markets.

Second, appropriate regulatory responses to FinTech innovation must be developed. This core aspect of RegTech 3.0 has been challenging for regulators.[73] One group of participants argue for a laissez-faire approach, so as to only put regulations in place once FinTech has developed.[74] This was largely China's approach until 2015. Because of numerous negative experiences, since mid-2015, China has instead focused on implementing a complete regulatory framework for FinTech.[75] The traditional financial services industry – arguably fearful of competition from new entrants unhindered by complex and expensive regulatory and compliance requirements – typically argues in favor of similar treatment for all.

In our view, the key is to balance risk and potential innovation by working closely to understand industry developments while making sure similar activities are regulated in similar ways to prevent regulatory arbitrage.[76] Regulatory arbitrage together with excessive reliance on financial institutions' internal quantitative risk management systems were two factors underlying the GFC.[77] It underlies the post-crisis focus on addressing risks of shadow banking.

Simultaneously, there should be a multi-level approach which applies graduated regulatory requirements to firms based upon their level of risk, and often correlating with size. Recent FinTech experience – particularly in Africa and China – highlights the challenge of rapid development and the potential to move from 'too small to care' to 'too big to fail' very quickly.[78] This prompted China to reevaluate its regulatory approach.[79] This also highlights the necessity of monitoring new developments across the financial system, in order to understand both what is happening and its implications. This is now taking place internationally through the FSB in conjunction with the IMF and BIS, to identify and raise awareness of new developments that may quickly arise in other markets.[80]

Third, regulatory sandboxes have been a central focus in the context of appropriate FinTech regulation. Perhaps the greatest potential for the sandbox tool is the testing of new RegTech approaches by industry and regulators.

The transformative potential of RegTech is for it to be used to reconceptualize the future of financial regulation by leveraging new technology. We are beginning to see elements of RegTech 3.0 emerge, with technological progress changing both market participants and infrastructure, with data as the common denominator. The practical consequence of this is a transformation from a KYC to a KYD approach.

As our financial system moves beyond KYC to KYD, we will move into an entirely new regulatory paradigm that must deal with everything from digital identity to data sovereignty and that has the potential to extend beyond the financial sphere.[81]

For regulators, this implies that: data security and use will be vital for consumer protection; prudential regulation will focus on algorithm compliance; and financial stability will be concerned with financial and information networks. The shift represents a market-wide reform which must be sequenced. The emergence of FinTech companies, combined with wider use of regulatory sandboxes, offers a unique opportunity to pilot this regulatory architecture that is proportionate, efficient and data-driven before market-wide implementation. FinTech requires RegTech.

Notes

1. This chapter is derived from a much longer article: Douglas W. Arner, Janos N. Barberis & Ross Buckley, "FinTech, RegTech and the Reconceptualization of Financial Regulation", 47 *Northwestern Journal of International Law and Business* (2017).

The authors gratefully acknowledge the financial support of the Hong Kong Research Grants Council Theme-based Research Scheme (Enhancing Hong Kong's Future as a Leading International Financial Centre) and the Australian Research Council Linkage Grant Scheme (Regulating a Revolution: A New Regulatory Model for Digital Finance); the substantial input of Dr Cheng-Yun Tsang, and the research assistance of Sarah Webster and Jessica Chapman.

2. *See* Douglas W. Arner, Janos Barberis & Ross P. Buckley, *The Evolution of FinTech: A New Post-Crisis Paradigm?*, GEORGETOWN J. INT'L L. (forthcoming 2016); ROSS P. BUCKLEY & DOUGLAS W. ARNER, FROM CRISIS TO CRISIS: THE GLOBAL FINANCIAL SYSTEM AND REGULATORY FAILURE (2011).

3. *See* INSTITUTE OF INTERNATIONAL FINANCE, REGTECH IN FINANCIAL SERVICES: TECHNOLOGY SOLUTIONS FOR COMPLIANCE AND REPORTING 5–8 (March 2016).

4. *See* Christophe Chazot quoted in INSTITUTE OF INTERNATIONAL FINANCE, REGTECH: EXPLORING SOLUTIONS FOR REGULATORY CHALLENGES 2 (Oct. 2015).

5. *See* SANTIAGO FERNANDEZ DE LIS, ET AL., REGTECH, THE NEW MAGIC WORD IN FINTECH 1 (March 2016).

6. *See* Jeff Cox, *Misbehaving banks have now paid $204B in fines*, CNBC (Oct. 30, 2015), http://www.cnbc.com/2015/10/30/misbehaving-banks-have-now-paid-204b-in-fines.html.

7. *See, Thomson Reuters Annual Cost of Compliance Survey Shows Regulatory Fatigue, Resource Challenges and Personal Liability to Increase throughout 2015*, THOMSON REUTERS (May 13, 2015), http://thomsonreuters.com/en/press-releases/2015/05/cost-of-compliance-survey-shows-regulatory-fatigue-resource-challenges-personal-liability-to-increase.html.

8. *See, The Fintech Revolution*, THE ECONOMIST (May 9, 2015), http://www.economist.com/news/leaders/21650546-wave-startups-changing-financefor-better-fintech-revolution.

9. Arner, Barberis & Buckley, *supra* note 1.

10. *See* Institute of International Finance, *supra* note 2: at 1.

11. *See, Banks Rushing to Collaborate with FinTech Startups*, FINEXTRA (Sep. 16, 2016), https://www.finextra.com/newsarticle/29443/banks-rushing-to-collaborate-with-fintech-startups; EY, FINTECH: ARE BANKS RESPONDING APPROPRIATELY? (2015); Andrew Meola, *1 in 5 European Banks Would Buy FinTech Startups*, BUSINESS INSIDER (July 17, 2016), http://www.businessinsider.com/1-in-5-european-banks-would-buy-fintech-startups-2016-6/?r=AU&IR=T.

12. *See* Gregory Roberts, *FinTech Spawns RegTech to Automate Compliance*, BLOOMBERG (June 28, 2016), https://www.bloomberg.com/enterprise/blog/fintech-spawns-regtech-automate-compliance-regulations/.

13. Fernandez de Lis, et al., *supra* note 4: at 1.

14. *See* Institute of International Finance, *supra* note 2: at 5–8.

15. *See* IMRAN GULAMHUSEINWALA, SUBAS ROY & ABIGAIL VILJOEN, INNOVATING WITH REGTECH – TURNING REGULATORY COMPLIANCE INTO A COMPETITIVE ADVANTAGE 10 (2015).

16. *See* Douglas Arner and Janos Barberis, *FinTech in China: From The Shadow?*, 3(3) J. FIN. PERSPECTIVES 23 (2015).

17. GPFI, G20 HIGH-LEVEL PRINCIPLES FOR DIGITAL FINANCIAL INCLUSION 12 (2016).

18. Institute of International Finance, *supra* note 4: at 1; *Thomson Reuters Annual Cost of Compliance Survey Shows Regulatory Fatigue, Resource Challenges and Personal Liability to Increase Throughout 2015*, *supra* note 9.

19. DELOITTE, REGTECH IS THE NEW FINTECH: HOW AGILE REGULATORY TECHNOLOGY IS HELPING FIRMS BETTER UNDERSTAND AND MANAGE THEIR RISKS 4 (2015).

20. *See* Ross P. Buckley, *Reconceptualizing the Regulation of Global Finance*, 36 OXFORD J. LEGAL STUD. 242 (2016).

21. *See* Cox, *supra* note 5.

22. *See* FINANCIAL STABILITY BOARD, IMPLEMENTATION AND EFFECTS OF THE G20 FINANCIAL REGULA-TORY REFORMS: REPORT TO THE G20 (Aug. 2016); Buckley & Arner, *supra* note 2; RECONCEPTUALIS-ING GLOBAL FINANCE AND ITS REGULATION (Ross P. Buckley, Emilios Avgouleas and Douglas W. Arner (eds.), 2016).

23. *See, Fintech: Interest over Time*, GOOGLE TRENDS, https://www.google.com/trends/explore#q=fintech (accessed Sep. 19, 2016).

24. *See* Arner, Barberis & Buckley, *supra* note 1; Andrew Lo, *Moore's Law vs. Murphy's Law in the Financial System: Who's Winning?* (Bank for International Settlement, Working Paper No. 564, May 2016).

25. *See* Weihuan Zhou, Douglas W. Arner & Ross P. Buckley, *Regulation of Digital Financial Services in China: Last Mover Advantage*, 8 TSINGHUA CHINA L. REV. 25 (2015); Arner & Barberis, *supra* note 15.

26. *See* ASIC, *Fintech: ASIC's Approach and Regulatory Issues* 10–12 (Paper submitted to the 21st Melbourne Money & Finance Conference, July 2016); ASIC, *Further Measures to Facilitate Innovation in Financial Services* (Consultation Paper No. 260, June 2016).

27. Feedback Statement, Financial Conduct Authority, Call for Input on Supporting the Development and Adopters of RegTech, 3 (July 2016) emphasis added.

28. *Id. See* Arner, Barberis & Buckley, *supra* note 2.

29. Adrian Shedden & Gareth Malna, *Supporting the Development and Adoption of RegTech: No Better Time for a Call for Input*, BURGES SALMON 2 (Jan. 2016), https://www.burges-salmon.com/-/media/files/publications/open-access/supporting_the_development_and_adoption_of_regtech_no_better_time_for_a_call_for_input.pdf.

30. *See* Citigroup, Comment Letter on Regulatory Capital Rules: Enhanced Supplementary Leverage Ratio Standards for Certain Bank Holding Companies and Their Subsidiary Insured Depository Institution, 3 (Oct. 21, 2013), https://www.federalreserve.gov/SECRS/2013/October/20131030/R-1460/R-1460_102113_111420_579523237031_1.pdf. *See* John Heltman, *Long-Term Liquidity Plan Is Costly and Redundant, Banks Argue*, AMERICAN BANKER (Aug. 12, 2016), http://www.americanbanker.com/news/law-regulation/long-term-liquidity-plan-is-costly-and-redundant-banks-argue-1090708-1.html.

31. Daniel Gutierrez, *Big Data for Finance – Security and Regulatory Compliance Considerations*, INSIDE BIG DATA (Oct. 20, 2014), http://insidebigdata.com/2014/10/20/big-data-finance-security-regulatory-compliance-considerations/.

32. *See* Institute of International Finance, *supra* note 2: at 5–8.

33. *Id.*, at 12–14.

34. *See, e.g.,* BASEL COMMITTEE ON BANKING SUPERVISION, CORE PRINCIPLES FOR EFFECTIVE BANKING SUPERVISION 30–31 (Sep. 2012).

35. Arner, Barberis & Buckley, *supra* note 1.

36. *See* OFFICE OF THE COMPTROLLER OF CURRENCY, SUPPORTING RESPONSIBLE INNOVATION IN THE FEDERAL BANKING SYSTEM: AN OCC PERSPECTIVE (March 2016).

37. *See* Institute of International Finance, *supra* note 2: at 1.

38. *See generally* WARREN MEAD, RICHARD IFERENTA & ROBERT HIBBERT, A NEW LANDSCAPE: CHAL-LENGER BANKING ANNUAL RESULT (May 2016).

39. *See* EY, CENTRALIZED OPERATIONS – THE FUTURE OF OPERATING MODELS FOR RISK, CONTROL AND COMPLIANCE FUNCTIONS (Feb. 2014).

40. Institute of International Finance, *supra* note 2: at 5–8.

41. *Id. See also* FINANCIAL STABILITY OVERSIGHT COUNCIL, STUDY ON THE EFFECTS OF SIZE AND COM-PLEXITY OF FINANCIAL INSTITUTIONS ON CAPITAL MARKET EFFICIENCY AND ECONOMIC GROWTH CARRIED OUT AT THE DIRECTION OF THE CHAIRMAN OF THE FINANCIAL STABILITY OVERSIGHT COUNCIL (March 2016).

42. *See* Eleanor Hill, *Is RegTech the Answer to the Rising Cost of Compliance?*, FX-MM (June 13, 2016), http://www.fx-mm.com/50368/fx-mm-magazine/past-issues/june-2016/regtech-rising-cost-compliance/; Andrew Cornell, *AgTech, ResTech, RegTech, FinTech – Actual Solutions or Techno-Babble?*, ANZ BLUE NOTES (Feb. 23, 2016), https://bluenotes.anz.com/posts/2016/02/is-regtech-the-answer-to-billions-being-spent-on-compliance-and-reporting/; James Eyers, *Welcome to the New World of RegTech*, FINANCIAL REVIEW (June 20, 2016), http://www.afr.com/technology/welcome-to-the-new-world-of-regtech-20160619-gpmj6k.

43. Kate, *A Report on Global RegTech: A $100-Billion Opportunity – Market Overview, Analysis of Incumbents and Startups*, LET'S TALK PAYMENTS (April 18, 2016), https://letstalkpayments.com/a-report-on-global-regtech-a-100-billion-opportunity-market-overview-analysis-of-incumbents-and-startups/.

44. *See* Hill, *supra* note 41.

45. *See id.*

46. *See* Eyers, *supra* note 41.

47. *See* Hannah Augur, *Regtech: The 2016 Buzzword is Turning Heads*, DATACONOMY (May 3, 2016), http://dataconomy.com/regtech-the-2016-buzzword-is-turning-heads/.

48. *See* Institute of International Finance, *supra* note 2: at 11–14.

49. CHARLES ROXBURGH, MINOUCHE SHAFIK & MARTIN WHEATLEY, FAIR AND EFFECTIVE MARKET REVIEW: FINAL REPORT (June 2015).

50. *See, Goldman Sachs to Invest Rs 1,200 Crore in Bangalore*, THE TIMES OF INDIA (Sep. 25, 2014), http://timesofindia.indiatimes.com/business/india-business/Goldman-Sachs-to-invest-Rs-1200-crore-in-Bangalore/articleshow/43383998.cms.

51. *See* BEARING POINT, SURVEY: SHARED SERVICES INDUSTRY SPECIFICS AND TRENDS IN THE EURO-PEAN FS MARKET 7–10 (2011).

52. *See* EY, CENTRALIZED OPERATIONS – THE FUTURE OF OPERATING MODELS FOR RISK, CONTROL AND COMPLIANCE FUNCTIONS (Feb. 2014).

53. *See generally* DELOITTE, SHARED SERVICES HANDBOOK: HIT THE ROAD (2011).

54. Chris Brummer, *Disruptive Technology and Securities Regulation*, 84 FORDHAM L. REV. 977 (2015).

55. *See, e.g.*, US SECURITIES AND EXCHANGE COMMISSION, REPORT TO THE CONGRESS: THE IMPACT OF RECENT TECHNOLOGICAL ADVANCES ON THE SECURITIES MARKETS (1997); *see also* TECHNICAL COMMITTEE OF THE INTERNATIONAL ORGANIZATION OF SECURITIES COMMISSIONS, REGULATORY ISSUES RAISED BY THE IMPACT OF TECHNOLOGICAL CHANGES ON MARKET INTEGRITY AND EFFICIENCY (Oct. 2011).

56. *See* Maryam Najafabadi, et al., *Deep Learning Applications and Challenges in Big Data Analytics*, 2 J. BIG DATA 1 (2015).

57. UK GOVERNMENT CHIEF SCIENTIFIC ADVISER, FINTECH FUTURES – THE UK AS A WORLD LEADER IN FINANCIAL TECHNOLOGIES, 48 (March 2015), https://www.gov.uk/government/uploads/system/uploads/attachment_data/file/413095/gs-15-3-fintech-futures.pdf.

58. Ravi Kalakota, *RegTech – Regulatory/Risk Data Management, AML and KYC Analytics*, PRACTICAL ANALYTICS (Jan. 17, 2013), https://practicalanalytics.co/2013/01/17/data-management-aml-and-kyc-analytics/; see also in Australia: KPMG, TEN KEY REGULATORY CHALLENGES FACING THE BANKING & CAPITAL MARKETS INDUSTRY IN 2016 2 (2015).

59. *See* UK Government Chief Scientific Adviser, *supra* note 119: at 56.

60. THE BOARD OF THE INTERNATIONAL ORGANIZATION OF SECURITIES COMMISSIONS, TECHNOLOGICAL CHALLENGES TO EFFECTIVE MARKET SURVEILLANCE ISSUES AND REGULATORY TOOLS: CONSULTATION REPORT 14–15 (August 2012).

61. Public Statement, U.S. SEC Commissioner Luis A. Aguilar, Shedding Light on Dark Pools (Nov. 18, 2015), http://www.sec.gov/news/statement/shedding-light-on-dark-pools.html#_edn5.

62. *See* FINANCIAL STABILITY OVERSIGHT COUNCIL, FSOC 2016 ANNUAL REPORT (2016).

63. *See, e.g.*, THE BOARD OF THE INTERNATIONAL ORGANIZATION OF SECURITIES COMMISSIONS, CYBER SECURITY IN SECURITIES MARKETS – AN INTERNATIONAL PERSPECTIVE (2016).

64. *See* Sarah Dahlgren, Executive Vice President of the Federal Reserve Bank of New York, Speech at the OpRisk North America Annual Conference, New York City: The Importance of Addressing Cybersecurity Risks in the Financial Sector (March 24, 2015).

65. *See* INTERNATIONAL MONETARY FUND, FINANCIAL STABILITY BOARD & BANK FOR INTERNATIONAL SETTLEMENTS, ELEMENTS OF EFFECTIVE MACROPRUDENTIAL POLICY (Aug. 2016).

66. *Id. See* BIS Committee on the Global Financial System, *Experiences with the Ex Ante Appraisal of Macro-Prudential Instruments* (CGFS, Paper No. 56, July 2016); Blaise Gadanecz & Kaushik Jayaram, *Macroprudential Policy Frameworks, Instruments and Indicators: A Review* (BIS Irving Fisher Committee on Central Bank Statistics, Paper, Dec. 2015).

67. *See* IMF, FSB & BIS, *supra* note 64.

68. *See* FINANCIAL STABILITY BOARD & INTERNATIONAL MONETARY FUND, THE FINANCIAL CRISIS AND INFORMATION GAPS: SECOND PHASE OF THE G-20 DATA GAPS INITIATIVE (DGI-2) – FIRST PROGRESS REPORT (Sep. 2016).

69. With thanks to Kevin Nixon of Deloitte and formerly of the Institute of International Finance for this point. BASEL COMMITTEE, PRINCIPLES FOR EFFECTIVE RISK DATA AGGREGATION AND RISK REPORTING (Jan. 2013).

70. *Id.*

71. *See* WEF, THE FUTURE OF FINANCIAL INFRASTRUCTURE (Aug. 2016).

72. ACCENTURE, BLOCKCHAIN TECHNOLOGY: PREPARING FOR CHANGE (2015).

73. Arner, Barberis & Buckley, *supra* note 1; Zhou, Arner & Buckley, *supra* note 50.

74. *See, e.g., FinTech Regulation in China, Hong Kong, and Singapore*, NORTON ROSE FULBRIGHT (May 10, 2016), http://www.nortonrosefulbright.com/knowledge/publications/139380/fintech-regulation-in-china-hong-kong-and-singapore; Deborah Ralston, *Let's Not Regulate Away the Competition Fintech Can Bring*, THE CONVERSATION (Aug. 6, 2015), https://theconversation.com/lets-not-regulate-away-the-competition-fintech-can-bring-45496.

75. Andrew Meola, *China Just Hinted It Could Increase Fintech Regulation*, BUSINESS INSIDER (June 29, 2016), http://www.businessinsider.com/china-just-hinted-it-could-increase-fintech-regulation-2016-6/?r=AU&IR=T.

76. *See* G20, HIGH-LEVEL PRINCIPLES FOR DIGITAL FINANCIAL INCLUSION (2016).

77. *See also* US FINANCIAL CRISIS INQUIRY COMMISSION, THE FINANCIAL CRISIS INQUIRY REPORT – FINAL REPORT OF THE NATIONAL COMMISSION ON THE CAUSES OF THE FINANCIAL AND ECONOMIC CRISIS IN THE UNITED STATES (2011).

78. Arner, Barberis and Buckley, *supra* note 2.

79. Zhou, Arner and Buckley, *supra* note 24.

80. *See* Huw Jones, *Global Regulators Move Closer to Regulating Fintech*, REUTERS (March 31, 2016), http://www.reuters.com/article/us-g20-regulations-fintech-idUSKCN0WX21J.

81. *See e.g.*, WEF, A BLUEPRINT FOR DIGITAL IDENTITY – THE ROLE OF FINANCIAL INSTITUTIONS IN BUILDING DIGITAL IDENTITY (Aug. 2016).

CHAPTER 17

Ambient Accountability

Shared Ledger Technology and Radical Transparency for Next Generation Digital Financial Services

David G.W. Birch, Salome Parulava

Contents

17.1 Introduction

The blockchain, the distributed shared ledger technology that underpins Bitcoin (Wood and Buchanan, 2015), is a consensus database that everybody can copy and access but by clever design cannot subvert: a permanent record of transactions that no-one can go back and change. The key characteristics of the blockchain that make it an interesting (but not the only) kind of *shared ledger* and that are particularly appealing to financial services markets are that it is distributed, decentralized, transparent, time-stamped, persistent, and verifiable (DuPont and Maurer, 2015).

Many people think that this technology has considerable promise for financial services beyond payments. Indeed, R3CEV consortium of 60 international financial institutions has announced multiple tests and developments of the technology and the noted Wall Street financier Blythe Masters has raised $60m[1] for her Digital Asset Holdings blockchain-based business. The high hopes for the shared ledgers have also been evidenced by the Hyperledger project, Linux Foundation-led initiative with more than 80 members including IBM, Intel and Samsung SDS.[2] Recently, UBS, BNY Mellon, Deutsche Bank, Icap and Santander in cooperation with the blockchain start-up Clearmatics have announced a "Utility Settlement Coin" initiative that is claimed to facilitate trading in digital assets.[3]

17.2 Why Now?

A ledger is a view of the current state of a marketplace, and all of the transactions that led to that current state. A *shared* ledger provides a *shared* view of the "truth" about current state of the marketplace. In the old days, we used to have to trust someone to maintain this ledger of transactions. Then we started to adopt a federated approach in which each organization maintains its own part of the ledger. Today, technological advances in networks and storage mean that it has become possible for all market participants to be able to store everything and to resolve, in a reasonable time, discrepancies between the different copies (Fig. 17.1). Such replication of data across devices and organizations is the core principal of the shared ledger technology (SLT) because errorless replication assures each party that its opinion (view) of the state of the marketplace is in fact consistent across participants. *The Economist* puts it this way (The great chain of being sure about things, 2015):

> *"It offers a way for people who do not know or trust each other to create a record of who owns what that will compel the assent of everyone concerned. It is a way of making and preserving truths."*

Such massively replicated shared ledgers promise a new solution to the old problem of maintaining a transaction ledger across multiple organizations.

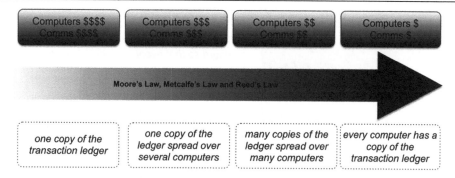

Figure 17.1: The technology drivers.

17.3 Shared Ledger Building Blocks

A simple way to see how shared ledgers might work in practice is to start by considering the basic building blocks of the shared ledger. We see these comprising the four main layers, shown in the Fig. 17.2 below. These are the communications, contents, consensus and contracts layers, each of which leads to a different key driver for the use of a shared ledgers rather than a database.

We begin with the **communications** layer, where shared ledgers use consistent cryptographic rules to create transactions and propagate them across networks, which ensure the security and robustness of the system. Above this is the **content** layer that records the ownership of assets (put to one side what these assets might be for a moment) in the immutable ledger of transactions in an appropriately standardized way.

Above the content layer we need a **consensus** layer, a mechanism to reach system-wide agreement over the things that are written into the ledger, to maintain integrity of the transaction history across organizations. Since copies of the ledger are held by the some or all of the participants, there must be a mechanism for determining which copies are true in the event of discrepancies that might be caused by delays, errors or fraud. This is known as a "consensus mechanism" and it varies according to the type of ledger. For example, Bitcoin is an instance of a shared ledger that uses a "proof-of-work" protocol as a way to constantly achieve consensus among network participants. And "blockchain" is an implementation choice which records new transactions connecting them to the old ones in a particular "chain of blocks" way.

Differences in the consensus layer across different implementations of SLT lead to very different kinds of shared ledgers, and thus different ways of settling between individuals or doing business between organizations.

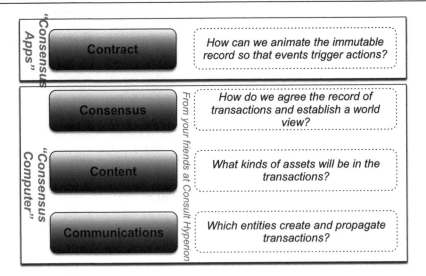

Figure 17.2: A layered model for ledger architecture (four main layers).

The **contract** layer (aka "smart contracts") serves to add enhanced business logic to the shared ledger. Smart contracts are pre-arranged agreements that self-execute after the relevant conditions have been made, that can also be called *shared ledger application programs* (SLAPs, or "Consensus Apps"). The model (Fig. 17.2) suggests the useful new paradigm of the *"consensus computer"* (Bouvier, 2015), the shared ledger as a platform for running SLAPs. As we will see, this ability to execute an entirely new kind of programs is where the potential for disruption is concentrated.

Financial services will be paying particular attention to the idea of adding business logic to the shared ledger: so that the "facts" being recorded aren't just who owns what but actual agreements between parties (Birch et al., 2016). This opens up the intriguing possibility of a world where counterparties agree that a SLAP represents the agreement they have made with each other and they execute it on the consensus computer, perhaps completely eliminating the need to build, maintain, operate and reconcile their own proprietary platforms. It is entirely possible to introduce concepts of moral agency and personhood, allowing the code to take custody of assets on the ledger, to manage cashflows and margin automatically (Kaplan, 2015).

These assets need not be limited to finance and when smart contracts are paired with "smart property" – where deeds, titles and other certifications of ownership are put in digital form to be acted on by software – these contracts could allow for the automatic transfer for ownership of a physical asset (Vigna and Casey, 2015). Hence the implications are significantly greater than efficient financial services.

17.4 Shared Ledger as Infrastructure: Bank of England Example

We will explore how financial organizations can benefit from using shared ledger technology looking at the particular case of Bank of England. We choose this case study because a deputy governor of the Bank of England gave a notable speech that mentioned the replicated decentralized shared ledger (Shafik, 2016):

> *"Instead of settlement occurring across the books of a single central authority (such as a central bank, clearing house or custodian), strong cryptographic and verification algorithms allow everyone in a DLT [SLT] network to have a copy of the ledger and give distributed authority for managing and updating that ledger to a much wider group of agents."*

But why would the Bank of England and market participants want to do this?

Before analyzing the reasons, we should remind ourselves of the background. Deputy Governor Shafik was speaking in the context of the review of the Real-Time Gross Settlement System (RTGS). This is operated by the Bank of England, whose role as a settlement agent emerged in the mid-nineteenth century with the provision of settlement accounts for the commercial banking sector. Since 1996, these accounts have been held in RTGS, which provides for real-time posting, with finality and irrevocability, of debit and credit entries to participants' accounts. This system, which is an element of vital national infrastructure in United Kingdom, is used for several purposes.

- It is used settle in real-time for the Clearing House Automated Payment System (CHAPS).
- It is also used to settle in real-time for payments within the CREST (Certificateless Registry for Electronic Share Transfer) securities settlement system.
- It is used to settle several times per day on deferred, net basis for the Faster Payments Service (FPS).
- It is also used to settle on a deferred, net basis for a variety of other retail payment systems (BACS, Cheque & Credit, LINK and Visa).

Crucially, it is used by CHAPS, the real-time settlement to any limit in "central bank money," which means that all transfers are final If RTGS were to fall over, it would mean that large value payments throughout United Kingdom would be totally knackered and that would have an immediate and very serious impact (on, for example, people buying and selling houses). It is therefore a piece of vital national infrastructure. The current system itself dates back to 1984, so it is not the very latest in technology but Bank of England cannot afford to deal with anything but tried, tested and sound technology. Nevertheless (Giles et al., 2014):

Table 17.1: Potential benefits of shared ledger approach.

Contract *Flexibility*	It may well be that the RTGS-SLT members might want to add shared ledger application programs (SLAPs) to the ledger in order to create new kinds of financial markets. Current centralized systems (such as RTGS) are inflexible and difficult to change and SLAPs give markets tools to build customized self-enforceable agreements across the balances and new kinds of assets introduced at the content layer. In a SLAPs world built upon the distributed "consensus computer," business rules could be invented and implemented with relative ease.
Consensus *Integrity*	A very fast consensus protocol can be used to ensure the near-immediate integrity of the copies held by each participant so that counterparty risk would be down at the same level that it is today using the centralized system. This integrity is crucial especially for delivery versus payment (DvP) settlement as is used for CREST. The integrity of the ledger would, in this case, represent finality of payment (and the reduction of counterparty risk) because of the legal status that the Bank of England would confer on the RGTS-SLT.
Content *Innovation*	The member banks might decide to hold balances in new assets so that final settlement might be in something other than central bank money. Because of technological and economic change, settlement could be in corporate paper, energy, Islamic e-Dinars, water, land, gold, or London Lucre, all of them appearing as content on a shared ledger.
Communications *Robustness*	If every bank had an RTGS gateway but there was no actual central RTGS system, and each gateway had a full copy of the Bank of England's ledger (the Bank of England would have a copy, too) holding the participants' central bank balances, there would be no single central RTGS to go down.

"Mark Carney, Bank of England governor, launched an independent review on Monday into the worst disruption of Britain's banking payment system in seven years... The breakdown meant the CHAPS payment system, which last year processed £277 billion of transactions a day, was down for more than nine hours. The bank was forced to start processing the most important payments manually."

So: why would a conservative and practical financial institution such as the Bank of England think about the very latest in replicated decentralized shared ledger technology for real-time gross settlement (RTGS-SLT) in this context? Table 17.1 shows potential benefits of the shared ledger associated with each of the architectural layers set out in Fig. 17.2.

Looking at this case, Bank of England's RTGS, we can see there are a number of reasons for financial participants to explore the shared ledger technology. However, there are potentially millions of different kinds of shared ledgers depending on the ledger architecture and the design requirements and the choices that are made at each architectural layer. For the purposes of analysis and business planning, we can proceed simply by considering two main subcategories of shared ledger architectures, public and private ledgers.

17.5 Types of Shared Ledgers

17.5.1 Permissionless (Public) Ledgers

Despite being the most widely known kind of shared ledger, Bitcoin is a very special case, an instance of a so-called "permissionless" shared ledger. A permissionless ledger is open to everyone to use, there is no need for any individual or organization to permit or allow anyone to be a part of the ledger: to view, transact or maintain it. Bitcoin addresses a very specific problem (a problem which no banks have, incidentally), which might be summarized as "I don't trust anyone to maintain a truthful copy of the ledger" whereas the more general shared ledger problem might be categorized as "I can trust someone to maintain the truthful copy but I don't want them to be able rewrite history" (Levin and Pannifer, 2015). A ledger whose contents cannot be rewritten but which is still reliant on trusted entities to maintain it is one that can be censored. So, in building a system that does not rely on trusted entities, the breakthrough of Bitcoin was to create the closest system yet to "digital cash," a digital asset that you can own outright and transfer to anybody else without permission. Its design follows directly from its objectives. It is a replicated, distributed shared ledger designed to enable the existence of a censorship-resistant digital bearer asset. It is, therefore, hardly surprising that bankers and regulators look at it with deep suspicion! However, there is also a good reason why the smart observers do not dismiss it: censorship-resistance implies an open, neutral platform that could be a driver of permissionless innovation.

17.5.2 Permissioned (Private) Ledgers

There are problems with the way that bitcoin works, however. The operational risks, generated by Bitcoin's most fundamental structures strongly undermine the Bitcoin blockchain's suitability to serve as financial market infrastructure (Walch, 2015). For permissionless ledgers in general, allowing anyone to take part in the consensus-forming process means that that process is susceptible to forms of attack (such as the much-discussed "51% attack" on Bitcoin). Hence for this and other reasons relating to privacy and data protection, many financial firms are looking closely at permissioned (i.e., private) ledgers. All parties to the transactions in such a system are known, identified ("permitted" to use it) and thus legally accountable for their actions. This, for example, is the view of one of the most powerful voices on Wall Street, the former JP Morgan investment banker Blythe Masters, who says (Robinson and Leising, 2015):

> *"With private chains, you can have a completely known universe of transaction processors... That appeals to financial institutions that are wary of the bitcoin blockchain."*

There is a fundamental question to ask about this focus though: why? If you do not have protection from censorship as your business objective, and therefore need a private ledger, why look at a shared ledger at all? As indicated in Table 17.1, rather than those bodies maintaining a central database or network of interconnected databases, a replicated shared ledger means we can build more robust solutions where database attacks or corruption do not stop the replicated shared ledgers from working. Further, replicated shared ledgers can solve another problem: if marketplace participants all run similar systems to keep track of records (whether account balances or derivatives positions or securities orders or whatever) then all participants are paying to maintain these duplicated undifferentiated record systems. And, because they are all slightly different, each participant needs to reconcile them with others all the time to make sure they agree. So, one argument for using private shared ledgers is that you can mutualize the cost of running and securing a single logical ledger, with relevant data copied across organizations so that each has its own copy and is not reliant on a powerful central entity for access.

The permissioned ledger also provides a cross-organizational transparency, integrity and accountability that are appealing to regulators as well as participants, and most importantly (as we shall see) allows for further innovation around automation through SLAPs. This would bring the famous Lawrence Lessig maxim "Code is Law" into the realm of the Financial Conduct Authority (FCA). It seems to use that the worlds of shared ledgers – private and public – might actually be leading financial services to the same place: a world where business logic in regulated financial markets – the FCA (Financial Conduct Authority) as an OS (operating system), if you like – is deployed to shared ledgers and executes agreements autonomously.

17.6 Shared Ledger Governance

Once we begin talking about the private (permissioned) ledger and how it may look like in practice, we add a new, fifth, layer to our model to manage identities of the participants and "permissions" given to them on the ledger (Fig. 17.3). Such **control** layer is a main point of governance for shared ledger: it manages the admission to use the ledger, distribution of roles and permissions, resolutions of disputes, validation of smart contracts code and integration with other systems. The control layer is especially important in the context of SLAPs that are executed autonomously after the conditions are pre-established and agreed upon between parties.

Fig. 17.4 depicts some of the key developments in the SLT space by date against the five-layer model that includes governance. It shows that while most of the developments embrace the "consensus computer" concept (i.e. they use the three main layers: *communication*, *content*, and *consensus*), the *contract* and *control* layers are unevenly developed across platforms.

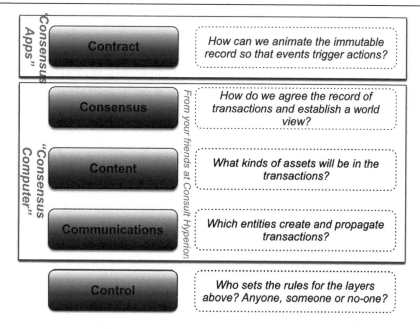

Figure 17.3: A layered model for ledger architecture (complete).

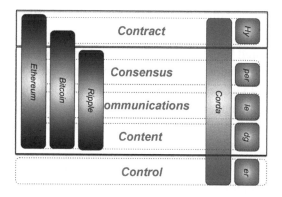

Figure 17.4: Examples of shared ledger platforms.

Fig. 17.4 also emphasizes the modularity of the open-source *Hyperledger* architecture, as it is a stack of different software, a "fabric," rather than plug and go platform, or just another shared ledger. It is a collective name of several codebases, which makes its modularity a key principle.

There are a number of ways to implement shared ledger solutions using this stack but key to understanding the potential are the business drivers behind technology choices that need to be made at each layer.

17.7 The New Infrastructure

Having looked at the replicated, distributed shared ledger as a new way to deliver financial market infrastructure, a new platform for banking that can solve a number of problems, it is natural to wonder why market participants would not just pay somebody (e.g., SWIFT or VocaLink or Google) to run a big database that stores all of the transactions on a big computer that can run all of the applications under the control of their central authority that sets all of the rules? That's a good question, and answering it will take us to this chapter's conclusion (which is that lower costs and higher efficiency may not be the drivers for change).

We think that using an "hierarchical double-permissioned" ledger (Birch et al., 2016) will be the choice of the banking world here. Customers can use it, provided their bank gives them permission, but they are not responsible for maintaining its integrity. The banks and the regulators are. If we return to the potential benefits set out in Table 17.1 and assess them against this kind of industry-wide shared ledgers for banking, we can see two broad advantages.

There are *fintech* advantages to the reliability, innovations, integrity and the flexibility that come from the combination of the shared ledger and the shared ledger applications. And we are sure that innovators in this space will continue to surprise us all, since we are at only the earliest stages of the evolution of the new family of shared ledger technologies.

There are also, however, potentially greater *regtech* advantages. With a shared ledger, banks would not potentially need to declare anything to anyone anywhere as long as their regulators are "subscribed" to the shared ledger. A permissioned shared ledger could erase the boundaries between compliance and auditing, thus benefiting each party of the bank–regulator relationship. And this is not just about sharing access to transactional data, but also about letting regulators have the permanent effortless oversight over more complex automatic procedures and execution of agreements. Thus, we think that regulators are also key stakeholders in the shared ledger enabled world.

Having described the logic of using a hierarchical double-permissioned shared ledger with regulator-approved smart contracts, precisely *which* consensus mechanism and shared ledger technology banks should use, which hierarchies they should establish, what kinds of contracts might be allowed (and so on) is, of course, another matter. UBS, for one example, has a London-based crypto-currency research laboratory that has put forward the idea of some kind of "utility coin" (Irrera, 2015) for settlement between banks and this provides a useful case study should the reader want to explore these trade-offs in more detail.

17.7.1 Translucency

We think that the combination of fintech and regtech advantages mean that a shared ledger can provide a more efficient and effective way to manage a financial services marketplace. It provides the right solution to problems that banks actually have. But note one important and practical implication of sharing transaction details. Some of the information in the ledger is confidential to the customers, the banks involved in the transactions, the market where the transactions take place. There are many applications where the transactions must be private. Therefore we need mechanisms to exploit the beneficial transparency of the shared ledger in such a way as to preserve necessary privacy. We use the term "translucent" to illustrate the case where observers could look through a list of bank deposits and loans to check that the bank is solvent, but not be able to see who those depositors are (although they will want third-party verification that they exist!). This is why further development is needed to deliver publicly-verifiable private records on such a ledger.

Does the technology for translucent transactions exist? We think it does. Many years ago, Eric Hughes, the author of the "cypherpunk manifesto" in the early 1980s, wrote about "encrypted open books," a topic that now seems fantastically prescient. His idea was to develop cryptographic techniques so that you could perform certain kinds of public operations on private data: in other words, you could build "glass organizations" where anyone could run software to check your accounts without actually being able to read every item of data in them (Birch et al., 2016). Nick Szabo later referred back to the same concepts when talking about the specific issue of auditing.

We can see that for financial markets this kind of controlled transparency will be a competitive advantage for both permissioned and permissionless ledgers: as an investor, as customer, as a citizen, I would trust these organizations far more than "closed" ones. Why wait for quarterly filings to see how a public company is doing when you could go on the web at any time to see their sales ledger? Why rely on management assurances of cost control when you can see how their purchase ledger is looking (without necessarily seeing what they're buying or who they are buying it from)?

A market built up from glass organizations that are trading with each other, serving their customers, working with regulators in entirely new ways is a very attractive prospect and suggests to us that new financial market infrastructure may be on the horizon and that the lasting impact of shared ledger technology will not be to implement existing banking processes in a new way but to create new kinds of markets and therefore new kinds of institutions.

17.7.2 Ambient Accountability

We appear to have an architecture that benefits banks, regulators and customers. We appear to have some promising technology options to deliver those benefits. We conjecture that the use of shared ledgers in financial services even with no cost benefits and no innovation will still bring a degree of transparency and accountability to the markets that will have very significant benefits. The transparency and the automation associated with smart contracts, application programming interfaces (APIs) and the ability to constantly monitor the ledgers means that we will no longer need to wait until the end of the reporting period to conduct an audit and produce the results with the help of skilled financial professionals. Instead we will find ourselves in an era of **ambient accountability**, where the technological architecture means constant verification and validation. It will simply not be possible to write a smart contract that is beyond the bounds of regulation (back to "code is law")[4] and if you want to check whether a bank is solvent before you deposit your life savings there you will do it using an app on your smart phone not by looking at a year-old auditor's report covering some figures from a year before filtered through levels of management.

This framework takes us beyond fintech to the combination of fintech and regtech because the processes of the regulators will be revolutionized as much as the process of the market participants. Since the regulators will be able to see the state of the ledger at all times they will be able to spot unusual or inappropriate activity. Since the information stored in the ledgers, albeit in an encrypted form, has been put there by regulated institutions, then should there be a need to investigate particular transactions because of, for example, criminal activity, then law enforcement agencies will be able to ask the relevant institutions to provide the keys necessary to decrypt the specific transactions.

Ambient accountability is a term that we borrowed from architecture. It describes perfectly how the replicated decentralized shared ledger will transform the financial services industry and serves as a rallying cry for the next generation of financial services technology innovators, giving it a focus and raison d'être beyond shifting private profits from banks to technology companies and other third parties.

Authors

David G.W. Birch is Director of Innovation at Consult Hyperion, the secure electronic transactions consultancy. He is an internationally-recognized thought leader in digital identity and digital money; was named one of the global top 15 favorite sources of business information (Wired magazine) and one of the top ten most influential voices in banking (Financial Brand); was listed in the top ten Twitter accounts followed by innovators, along with Bill Gates and Richard Branson (PR Daily); was ranked in the top three most influential people in London's FinTech community (City A.M.), was voted one of the European "Top 40" people in digital financial services (Financial News) and was rated Europe's most influential commentator on emerging payments (Total Payments). He graduated from the University of Southampton with a B.Sc. (Hons) in Physics.

Salome Parulava is a Consultant at Consult Hyperion. In this role, she has worked on a variety of projects covering payments, Internet-of-Things and digital identity. As a recognized expert on the blockchain and its applications, Salome has spoken and chaired at the industry's key events. She holds an M.Sc. in Information Systems Management and Innovation from the Warwick Business School, where her thesis was on the potential of blockchain technology in securities settlement. Salome has a degree with Distinction in Mathematical Economics from the Saint-Petersburg State University of Economics and Finance. Her research interests include shared ledger technology, artificial intelligence, financial technology, securities markets, information and knowledge sharing across financial systems.

References

Birch, D., Brown, R., Parulava, S., 2016. Towards ambient accountability in financial services: shared ledgers, translucent transactions and the legacy of the great financial crisis. Payment Strategy and Systems 10 (2), 118–131.

Bouvier, P., 2015. A new framework for Distributed Ledgers or dare I say Consensus Computers (CC) in FiniCulture at http://finiculture.com/a-new-framework-for-distributed-ledgers-or-dare-i-say-consensus-computers-cc/.

DuPont, Q., Maurer, B., 2015. Ledgers and law in the blockchain. In: King's Review (22nd Jun... 2015).

Giles, C., Dunkley, E., Fleming, S., 2014. Mark Carney launches review after BoE payment system crash. Financial Times (20th Oct. 2014).

Irrera, A., 2015. UBS building virtual coin for mainstream banking. Digits. The Wall Street Journal (3rd Sep. 2015).

Kaplan, J., 2015. Officer, arrest that bot. In: Humans Need Not Apply. Yale University Press, Yale, pp. 78–92.

Levin, J., Pannifer, S., 2015. Demystifying cryptocurrency and the blockchain for the uninitiated. Cryptocurrency, London, Payments Forward (11th May 2015).

Robinson, E., Leising, M., 2015. The blockchain changes everything. Bloomberg Markets (31st Aug. 2015).

Shafik, M., 2016. A New Heart for a Changing Payments System. Bank of England (27th Jan. 2016).

The great chain of being sure about things, 2015. The Economist (31st Oct. 2015).

Vigna, P., Casey, M., 2015. The everything blockchain. In: The Age of Cryptocurrency—How Bitcoin and Digital Money Are Challenging the Global Economic Order. St. Martin's Press, New York, NY, pp. 219–245.

Walch, A., 2015. The bitcoin blockchain as financial market infrastructure. NYU Journal of Legislation and Public Policy 18 (4), 837–893.

Wood, G., Buchanan, A., 2015. Advancing egalitarianism. In: Chen, D.L.K. (Ed.), Handbook of Digital Currency. Academic Press, San Diego, CA, pp. 385–402.

Notes

1. https://digitalasset.com/press/goldman-sachs-and-ibm-invest-in-digital-asset.html.

2. https://www.hyperledger.org/news/announcement/2016/08/hyperledger-project-grows-170-percent-six-months.

3. http://www.ft.com/cms/s/0/1a962c16-6952-11e6-ae5b-a7cc5dd5a28c.html#axzz4IwFvuxxe.

4. It is necessary to mention that there has been a precedent for unintentional behavior by a smart contract called "DAO," created on the Ethereum platform. In Ethereum's "DAO" case it was possible to write and deploy a smart contract that turned out to be exploitable by attackers because Ethereum is a permissionless platform with no defined "control layer," and thus no governance procedures around testing, approving or certifying smart contracts.

CHAPTER 18

Peer-To-Peer Lending

Anju Patwardhan

Contents

18.1 Banking in the Digital Age

Banking is at an inflection point. Most people think that banking is being reshaped by regulations since the global financial crisis but that is only half the story. The other half is about technology. Banking is an entirely digital business and innovation using technology is an obvious choice. Financial innovation is the dominant theme at financial centers around the world. The multi-trillion-dollar financial services industry is being digitally disrupted and digitally re-imagined.

Most banks today are under regulatory pressure to simplify their business models but are unable to move as fast as their shareholders or boards would like them to because of legacy systems. They are facing a tsunami of competition from several non-traditional competitors that are offering everything including loans, wealth management products, insurance, funds transfers and much more. The field is filled with born-in-the-cloud financial technology upstarts, known as "fintech" companies that are leveraging advanced technologies and data analytics to offer a host of alternatives to the public.

Investments in "fintech" companies have grown rapidly in the past decade rising from USD 1.8 billion in 2010 to USD 19 billion in 2015, with over 70 percent of the investment focusing on the "last mile" of user experience in the consumer space.[1] In 2015, there were more than 1500 fintech companies that had received over USD 31 billion in cumulative funding.[2]

Enabling customers to manage their money and conduct basic banking services on their smartphones or personal computers is helpful and adds marginal value to the existing banking customers. However, the nimble fintech disruptors are working to revolutionize current business models and user experience from the ground up.

The rapid growth of online alternative lending models in China, United States, United Kingdom and other countries is an example of that.

Alternative lending refers to financial instruments and distribution channels that have emerged outside the traditional financial system. Online alternative lending refers to businesses that operate primarily in the digital space and includes peer-to-peer lending, marketplace lending, equity-based crowdfunding and online balance sheet lending.

This chapter focuses mainly on peer-to-peer lending and marketplace lending which have been the fastest growing business models. Companies such as Lending Club and Funding Circle belong to this category. Online balance sheet lending is the next largest component of online alternative lending and includes companies such as Kabbage and OnDeck Capital.

18.2 Peer-to-Peer (P2P) Lending: Democratization of Finance

P2P lending platforms began over a decade ago in 2005 with the objective of democratizing consumer financial services by dynamically matching individual borrowers and lenders, using technology as the enabler. The platforms employ technology for more efficient distribution and credit underwriting. They fund 100 percent of the loans off-balance-sheet through "peers", a new kind of funding model. In this model, the individuals can make their pitches to borrow money and investors can offer credit without the involvement of financial institutions.

The banks were originally cut out of the lending equation. However, as the industry grew, it became a magnet for institutional investors in the United States such as hedge funds, asset managers, private equity funds, investment banks and insurers searching for higher yield. The investor profile changed from "peers" to mostly institutional investors. Consequently, the peer-to-peer lending platforms morphed into Marketplace Lending Platforms (MPL).

The marketplace lending platforms are an online marketplace for individuals or institutional investors to fund the borrowers. In this chapter, the terms P2P lending and marketplace lending are used interchangeably. The process of loan origination, distribution, credit underwriting, risk pricing and servicing is broadly similar in both models. The primary differentiation is in the type of investors and the risks associated with wholesale funding versus retail funding. These risks have been covered separately in subsequent sections.

Some of the earliest P2P lending platforms include Zopa in UK (founded in 2005), Lending Club and Prosper in the US (2006), and CreditEase in China (2006).

P2P platforms can evaluate borrowers and give a credit decision in minutes or hours, unlike most banks that can take several days or weeks. They compete with the banks on digital marketing prowess, automated credit underwriting, proprietary product creation and other areas where financial institutions have historically been weak.

Balance sheet lenders like Kabbage and OnDeck Capital, in contrast to the marketplace lenders, directly fund the loans originated on their platforms and book them on their balance sheet. They assume the associated credit risk which makes their business model more akin to bank lending except that they finance their loans with equity and debt, and do not have access to retail consumer deposits.

18.3 Rapid Growth After the Global Financial Crisis

China is presently the largest P2P lending market in the world with CreditEase and Lufax leading the charge. The cumulative P2P lending volume of RMB 440 billion (USD 67 billion) in 2015 amounts to about 3 percent of the system retail loans. Total outstanding loans were RMB 104 billion in 2014 and RMB 27 billion in 2013.[3]

China's cumulative P2P lending volume in 2015 of USD 67bn is close to four times that of the United States (USD 17bn) and over 10 times that of the United Kingdom (USD 6bn).[4] These numbers refer to the 'loan balances outstanding'.

The industry reports also often quote statistics on new loans issued or originated. This refers to the amount of new loans granted at the time of booking. Most P2P loans are booked as amortizing personal loans with durations ranging from six months to a few years which means that the loan balances begin with 'loan amount issued' and eventually reduce to zero as the loans are paid off. The outstanding balances in a loan portfolio at any time are therefore significantly lower than the loan amounts issued at the time of origination.

The global financial crisis resulted in several large American and European banks scaling back their lending operations, as they reduced their on- and off-balance sheet credit exposures. That, combined with ensuing lack of trust in the banking system, helped the nascent P2P industry gain traction in these markets.

Since the crisis, SME lending as a percentage of all bank business loans in the United States has fallen from 35 percent to 24 percent. Small business loans from banks are down 20 percent while loans to larger businesses have risen 4 percent in the same period.[5] According to bank regulatory filings, the 10 largest US banks lent USD 45 billion in 2014, which was down 38 percent from its peak of USD 72.5 billion in 2006.[6] Another reason for withdrawal of bank lending to this sector has been the regulatory framework and higher capital requirements for small business finance. In the Eurozone, borrowing costs for SMEs as spread over larger loans increased by 150 percent.[7]

Since the global financial crisis, the interest rates have been at a record low. In the United States, real interest rates, adjusted for inflation, have been about 0.2 percent for the last 10 years, which should have been great for any business that needs a loan, and any bank that wants to lend.

The global financial crisis resulted in several discussions on the 'too-big-to-fail' banks but it has also created a 'too-small-to-care' crisis about lending to small businesses.

The credit needs of SMEs are high in complexity and low in scale, leading to the traditional banks viewing financing to this segment as low-end and unprofitable. The credit underwriting process is manual, time-consuming and expensive for a variety of reasons, such as lack of credit bureaus, stringent regulatory know-your-customer requirements and the fact that many SMEs lack an audited financial history.

Small businesses are the Goldilocks of digital banking; corporate applications are too complex for them and retail ones are way too simple. They often end up being offered retail credit products, though their diverse needs call for a more customized service. Lending in this area by banks is often pursued under regulatory pressures or as part of philanthropic ambitions.

In the United States, other factors supporting the rapid growth of peer-to-peer lending were the historically low yield environment and a massive amount of high interest rate credit card debt that had accumulated in prior years. Participation of institutional investors searching for higher yield provided the required liquidity. P2P companies started out making unsecured personal loans, mostly to help consumers pay off the higher-priced revolving credit card debt through lower-priced unsecured loans, but have since expanded into other products such as student loans, housing loans, small-business loans, micro-financing and commercial real estate.

Unsecured consumer loans dominate P2P lending in the United States and in that category, Lending Club and Prosper together have over 90 percent market share. While this form of lending has grown rapidly in recent years, it remains a small part of overall consumer lending at less than one percent of total retail loans.

Social Finance, or SoFi, is another large online lending platform that started with refinancing student loans and has expanded into housing loans and other products.

The growth of P2P industry in Asia has been driven mainly by the rise of China as a major alternative lending region. The number of active online lending platforms in China was estimated at over 3000 at its peak in 2014. The main driver of the boom in China was a state controlled banking system that directed credit mainly towards State Owned Enterprises and large corporates in the last couple of decades and did not focus on individuals. Other factors included a relatively underdeveloped consumer credit market, a tightly regulated banking sector that capped interest rates on deposit, and individuals looking for higher returns than bank deposits.

Technology giants in China have moved into consumer financial services and gained considerable market share in e-commerce and third-party payments. Fintech companies, referred to as "internet finance" companies in China, often have as many, if not more, clients than the top banks. Lufax and CreditEase are two of the largest P2P companies in China. CreditEase started with student loans and expanded into lending products but has since diversified into wealth management and asset management products and services in recent years.

Some of the lending platforms have had successful listings on major stock exchanges. Lending Club listed on the New York Stock Exchange (NYSE) in December 2014 and became the first major P2P company to be listed. Yirendai, a subsidiary of CreditEase China, listed on the NYSE in 2015 and became the first public P2P company from China.

In the United Kingdom, growth in this sector was driven mainly by a supportive government and a streamlined regulatory approach. Decline in lending by big banks to small businesses since the global financial crisis prompted the government to take a series of decisive actions to support small business finance by P2P lenders. The United Kingdom is the largest P2P lending market in Europe, constituting 75 percent of Europe's alternative lending sector and the largest platforms are Funding Circle, Zopa and RateSetter.

In the United States and the United Kingdom, although P2P fintech companies are growing, incumbent financial institutions still have the upper hand in terms of scale. Unlike China, digital disruption has not yet reached the tipping point in either of these markets.

In Asia, excluding China, peer-to-peer lending is still at a nascent stage. China accounts for over 95 percent of Asian peer-to-peer lending business. Asian banks have shown an incredible resilience post the global financial crisis and the customers continue to favor banks over the financial technology companies. Asian financial regulators have also been more cautious in allowing expansion of lending and payment businesses outside the established financial services industry.

The other reason is the product range offered by the banks themselves in Asia. The earliest P2P business models in the United States were focused on proposed consolidation of revolving card debt into amortizing unsecured personal loans. While this product works in the United States, it is not likely to work in Asia as most banks already offer this as a standalone product as well as a feature linked to credit cards that allow card customers to convert the revolving card balances into lower priced personal loans at the click of a button via online banking or through the call enters.

An area where P2P lending can play a significant role in Asian and Latin American emerging markets is in serving the segments underserved by traditional banks. These include small businesses, self-employed individuals and micro-businesses that find it difficult to acquire financing from banks in most countries.

18.4 Supporting Financial Inclusion and Economic Growth

A significant factor driving the initial growth of unsecured P2P lending in the United States was consolidation and refinancing of credit card debt. As per information released by Lending Club, close to 60 percent of the borrowers state using their loans for this purpose and the average borrower can get a 33-percent reduction in interest rate compared to a traditional credit card rate for revolving balances. However, it is unproven whether the loans are replacing the existing card debt or increasing consumer leverage by facilitating incremental unsecured credit to the same customer at a cheaper rate.

The area where lending by these platforms undoubtedly plays a significant is in supporting financial inclusion by providing access to credit to the unbanked and underbanked individuals and self-employed borrowers running the micro-, small, and medium enterprises ("SMEs"). This has filled a huge gap in the economy and provided them with the much-needed access to capital.

Financial inclusion means having universal access to reasonably priced financial services, provided by sound and sustainable institutions. It includes saving, investing, borrowing, and insurance. Billions of people in developed and emerging markets are financially excluded and have no access to financial services.

As per the World Bank Global Findex Report of 2014, the number of unbanked adults globally is 2 billion or 38 percent of all adults. They do not have access to a basic bank account or mobile money account. The percentage of individuals and businesses globally that don't have access to credit facilities is significantly higher.

In recent years, a lot of progress has been made in promoting financial inclusion for individuals for their saving needs through new mobile money accounts and increased access to bank accounts. In the three years to 2014, the number of unbanked adults globally has dropped 20 percent to 2 billion.[8] They now have a basic bank account or mobile wallet but progress for access to credit has been much slower.

SMEs are a major driver of economic growth and job creation, accounting for more than half of the world's GDP and two-thirds of its work force.[9] And yet, they have difficulty securing financing, limiting their ability to grow and thrive. More than 200 million SMEs in emerging markets lack access to finance. This inability to raise working capital is particularly a concern for small businesses as well as for start-ups and professionals branching out into entrepreneurship. Most end up borrowing from family and friends, or at exorbitant rates from money lenders and payday lenders. Many risk falling into cycles of bad credit.

The International Finance Corporation estimates that financially excluded SMEs face a significant credit gap of over USD 2.1 trillion[10] in developing economies. This represents a major constraint for SMEs and a massive missed revenue opportunity for the traditional financial sector.

Another study by CARE International and Accenture estimates that bringing today's excluded small businesses into the formal banking sector could generate annual revenues of about USD 270 billion[11] for banks by 2020, by closing the credit gap at average lending spreads and adding fee-based services. The greatest revenue potential is estimated to be in Asia-Pacific region at USD 95 billion.

Helping these businesses get access to finance is key not just to their growth, but also to the growth of the overall economy.

The alternative lenders use technology and data science that helps leverage existing and new data sources to assess credit and fraud risk. This enables them to lend to borrowers that banks consider too risky, which could be as much as 30 to 40 percent of consumer lending, and up to 75 percent of small-business loans.

The online alternative lending has become a game changer for small businesses. Because fintech solutions are efficient and effective at lower scale, small businesses are one of the main beneficiaries of these lending platforms. The platforms offer a range of products tailored to their needs including working capital facilities, merchant and e-commerce finance, invoice finance, online supply chain finance, and online trade finance.

18.5 Peer-to-Peer Lending Business Models

The online lending platforms started over a decade ago in the United States, the United Kingdom and China. The business models across these countries are similar is several ways but also have their own unique features.

P2P lending in the United States is dominated by online platforms that have become significantly dependent on institutional funding. The regulatory landscape is evolving and remains unclear. P2P lending in the United Kingdom is also an online model but funding is primarily from retail investors. Growth in the United Kingdom has been driven by decisive government actions and regulatory support that has helped build retail investor confidence. The largest expense for platforms in the United States and the United Kingdom is on digital marketing to acquire new customers.

China is a hybrid online-offline lending model funded mostly by retail investors. The platforms typically partner with third parties to identify new borrowers. Large Chinese platforms have expanded beyond lending into wealth management and insurance products to build an inclusive financial services business that caters to all customer segments.

The marketplace lending platforms provide the underlying technology to match borrowers and investors but are not the actual lenders or investors. They do not take any credit risk; nor do they hold loans on their balance sheet. In the United States, they use a bank in the middle to write loans and sell them to investors while this is done directly by the platforms in the United Kingdom and China.

For borrowers, the lending platforms have been very beneficial. The basic structure of unsecured loans offered to individual borrowers is not that different from the banks. The benefits to borrowers, however, are many. The platforms are fast and efficient. They have an easy-to-use, intuitive design and leverage cloud and other technologies to best serve customers.

Most loans are granted at fixed rates, which can be beneficial to the borrowers in a rising interest rate environment. Once the loans are granted, the borrowers must start making monthly repayments within 30 to 45 days. These repayments are computed as equal monthly installments covering principal and interest using a standard amortization schedule.

The investor interest in the platforms has been growing from both retail and institutional investors as they offer better returns than a bank deposit. Investors fall into two broad categories: those who plan to hold the loans to maturity (typically retail investors) and those that buy the loans with the aim of securitizing them, using leverage to multiply their returns (typically institutional investors). Retail investors generally invest their own money while institutional investors invest money on behalf of a company.

A single loan can be funded by fractional amounts from a pool of investors. In the United States, an investor can put in as little as USD 25 towards a loan. The retail investors aim to make higher returns than bank deposits by investing in this form of lending but they take significantly higher risks than bank deposits. The investments carry risks like buying securities and are not covered under retail banking deposit guarantee schemes. The investors can lose their entire investment if a borrower they funded defaults or the platform goes bust. Investors lower this risk through diversification by investing in several loans with different risk profiles across multiple platforms. However, unlike equity investments, the investor upside remains capped.

Most lending platforms have reasonably comprehensive risk disclosures but the disclosures are lengthy and confusing. Investors need to ensure that they have read and understood the terms and conditions and consumer education for retail investors is critical.

Platforms generate income through commission from borrowers and investors. Borrowers for new loans accounts pay an unfront fees that accounts for a significant portion of income for the platforms and ranges from one to five percent of the loan amount issued, based on a range of factors including the borrower's credit rating. The investors typically pay the platform an annual servicing fee of one percent of the amount invested.

To mitigate the credit risk for investors, P2P platforms in some countries offer unique features in the form of reserve funds or offer credit guarantees. In the United Kingdom, most large platforms maintain 'provision funds' or reserves designed to compensate investors exposed to loan defaults. The reserves function like a privately funded deposit insurance scheme. The platforms set aside a portion of the loan origination fees paid by the borrowers into the reserve pool which is common for the entire portfolio and an investor's risk is therefore spread across the entire loan book. The monies are held in a trust and are segregated from business assets.[12] If a borrower defaults and the loan is unpaid for a certain period, funds are withdrawn from the reserve fund to repay investors. This can continue until the reserve fund is depleted.

In China, P2P model was originally based on loan guarantees. The platforms would originate a high interest rate loan, offer a lower but guaranteed rate of return to the investors, and make money on the spread. Some Internet finance companies, however, have started switching from a guarantee model to a credit risk reserve fund model, like that in the United Kingdom.

The concept of a reserve fund that mitigates credit risk for investors makes sense and helps build investor confidence. Conceptually, this is similar to portfolio impairment provisions that traditional banks are required to hold for their loan portfolios as per regulatory requirements.

18.6 Credit Risk Assessment and Credit Defaults

Some believe that success in marketplace lending means maximizing lending volumes. However, other considerations like risk management and getting loans back are equally, if not more, important factors of success.

While the platforms have no skin-in-the-game to ensure credit quality of loans, their overall business sustainability and future funding from investors depends on providing sustainable returns to investors. The returns in turn are closely linked to credit performance of their loan portfolios.

Credit underwriting is an important part of P2P lending. To establish a borrower's creditworthiness, most platforms use credit bureau data, credit scores that reflect past financial behavior history, and other alternate data sources. Credit risk assessment remains challenging in markets that do not have a credit bureau or where platforms target new customer segments that do not have adequate credit history.

P2P lenders in the United States and the United Kingdom use a combination of credit bureau scores and custom-developed application scores. They use the credit bureau data as a starting-point in the same way as banks and credit-card companies and complement this with additional data sources and fraud checks. However, the mechanism to access the bureau information varies. P2P lenders in the United States have partnered with FDIC-regulated banks to access the bureau data while in the United Kingdom, the regulations enable the platforms to access bureau information directly.

P2P lenders use risk-based pricing for loans. They classify borrowers into a range of credit risk grades based on criteria such as borrower's credit history, bureau score, income and employment data. Interest rates are determined for each loan depending on the borrower's credit grade, loan amount requested and loan duration. The borrowers with a better credit history are likely to get a better loan grade and therefore a lowest interest rate.

Lending platforms in countries such as China and India remain excluded from the credit bureaus and rely on alternate data sources to establish creditworthiness.

Historically, one of the biggest inhibitors of growth in the Chinese consumer lending industry has been the lack of a national consumer credit bureau with long consumer credit history like an Trans-Union or Experian bureau in the US. A national centralized credit bureau, the Credit Reference Center ("CRC"), was set up in 2006 under the supervision of People's Bank of China ("PBOC"). The CRC database contains personal identification information and positive and negative credit information about consumers, including data on credit limit, payment history, utility and telecommunications payments, social security fund payments, tax arrears records and court records. The banks have a mandatory obligation to report credit information to the bureau and can access customer credit history. However, the P2P lenders are outside the banking system and do not have access to the CRC database.

The platforms use technology better than traditional lenders and have lower underwriting and origination costs. However, from a credit risk perspective, lower underwriting cost can be an issue. For example, in the United States, many P2P lenders do not verify most of the information supplied by borrowers. This lack of verification may lower the underwriting cost but it can also adversely impact the loan quality and predictive ability of credit risk models.

This is worrisome as the platforms do not have "skin in the game" from a credit default perspective. Majority of their revenue is from origination fee on new loans and only a tiny fraction of revenues is tied to repayment performance of loans. The divorce between credit analysis and exposure to loan performance is widely thought to have fuelled the market collapse in mortgage-backed securities during the global financial crisis. An important lesson learned from the crisis was that mortgage originators should hold some credit risk in the product they create to distribute or sell. The same argument can be extended to other forms of lending like P2P lending.

18.7 Divergence in Business Models Across Countries

The business models have several similarities globally as outlined in the previous section but also have key differences based on local financial infrastructure, regulations, customer needs and the history of evolution. This section covers P2P lending models in different countries in detail, highlighting the benefits and risks, and explores the evolving regulatory landscape.

18.7.1 P2P Lending in the United States

The key online alternate lending players in the US are Lending Club, Prosper, OnDeck Capital, SoFi, Avant, Kabbage and Funding Circle. Goldman Sachs estimated that over the next five years, USD 11 billion out of USD 150 billion in annual US bank profits could be threatened by non-traditional lending such as the peer-to-peer platforms.

The online lending industry originated USD 23 billion of loans in 2015, up from USD 12 billion in 2014 and USD 1 billion in 2010.[13] The influx of additional liquidity from the institutional investors since 2012 has enabled online lenders to grow faster and compete more directly with traditional banks.

As of mid-2016, Lending Club has funded new loan originations of over USD 20 billion since launch while Prosper has funded loans of over USD 7 billion. SoFi started in 2011 with refinancing of student loans and has since expanded into personal loans and mortgage loans. In June 2016, SoFi crossed the milestone of USD 10 billion in total new loans issued, of which USD 5.3 billion were funded in 2015 and USD 3.5 billion in the first half of 2016.

P2P unsecured consumer loans typically have annual interest rates ranging from 6 percent to as much as 30 percent, higher than many other fixed-income assets. The loan durations range from a few months to three years but most are repaid after just over a year. Attractive yield and short duration in a yield-starved world is what makes them interesting for the Wall Street.

A look at the funding composition of Lending Club and Prosper shows that 100 percent of their loans in 2008 were funded by individual investors. Between 2013 and 2015, over 72 percent of business loans and 53 percent of consumer loans on marketplace lending platforms were funded by institutional investors in the US.[14]

The platforms in the United States partner with FDIC-member banks such as Web Bank and Cross River Bank to conduct credit bureau checks, obtain loan documentation, and do loan disbursals. This symbiotic relationship with the banks allows the platforms to operate with much less capital than the traditional lenders, which means they can generate more loans for every dollar of equity on their balance sheet. Since the platforms do not originate loans directly, they are not subject to prudential bank regulations for consumer lending. The FDIC-insured partner banks, however, must comply with those regulations including the Truth in Lending Act, Equal Credit Opportunity Act, Fair Credit Reporting Act, and Fair Debt Collection Practices Act.

For a borrower, receiving funding for a loan on the platform is a result of many steps that include pre-screening, creating a listing, investors viewing the listing, and committing to fund the listing. The platforms pre-screen the application and conduct some level of verification. They apply advanced analytics to evaluate borrower credit risk and to mitigate fraud risk. They also set the loan interest rate based on borrower's creditworthiness and their internal credit models. Applications that pass verifications and meet the credit criteria are listed online.

Going online and creating a listing is just a request for a loan. It does not guarantee approval and requires commitment from enough investors to fund the application. If an application is fully funded by the investors, the loan is issued. If the application fails to be fully funded, it is deleted from the platform and any investments received to partially fund the loan are returned to the investors.

A loan application can typically stay on the platform for up to 14 days, although most get funded much faster than that. Once funding is complete, approved borrowers receive the funds, after deducting the origination fee, in two to three business days.

Platforms like Lending Club and Prosper are regulated by the Securities and Exchange Commission ("SEC"). They need to register the loans they originate as securities or Notes with the SEC and file regular reports. The platforms must conduct Know-Your-Customer checks on borrowers and investors. These include verifications that they are US citizens or legal residents who are at least 18 years old with a valid bank account and a valid Social Security number. Other anti-fraud and identity verification checks are also conducted.

The Notes are treated the same way as securities of public companies requiring the platforms to make detailed disclosures regarding investor risks on their websites. For example, the Lending Club website highlights to investors that they need to be cautious participants in this innovative business model. Investments are not guaranteed or insured by governments or other sources, and investors are at risk of losing their entire capital if credit defaults increase beyond the expected levels. It also states that investing in Lending Club Notes[15] involves risks, including the risk that borrowers may not repay their loans and the risk of Lending Club discontinuing loan servicing.

18.7.2 P2P Lending in China

The massive size and scale of the Chinese lending market is awe-inspiring. The US and China are the clear market leaders globally in P2P lending. Both countries started at about the same time in 2006 but have followed different trajectories, based on market needs and national infrastructure.

Internet finance in China started to grow rapidly in 2013 after it received explicit government support when the People's Bank of China ("PBOC") expressed support for technology companies promoting online consumer financial services. In recent years, Chinese Premier Li Keqiang has made multiple calls of support in the Report on the Work of the Government over 2014/15, stating that "Internet-based finance has swiftly risen to prominence" with the imperative "to encourage the healthy development of . . . Internet banking". Premier Li has also spoken at the World Economic Forum in 2015 and 2016, encouraging start-ups and citing 'mass entrepreneurship and innovation' as engines for future growth and domestic economic development in China.

Most P2P platforms in China service a client base that has traditionally not been serviced by the banks and are therefore not seen as a threat to the consumer loan business of large Chinese banks. Lufax, CreditEase and Renrendai are some of the most competitive Chinese P2P platforms.

The P2P lending model in China is mostly a hybrid offline/online ("O2O") model where investors are sourced online but loan applications are acquired offline. Most large P2P lenders have physical branch networks across the country and employ their own sales and credit underwriting staff. Some P2P lenders partner with small credit institutions or guarantee companies that recommend applicants offline. The platforms review the project or applicant information offline relying on traditional credit assessment methods to assess credit risks. Applications that meet the criteria are posted online for funding by the investors. The primary focus of platforms is on building an investor base and managing the technology platform.

Several O2O platforms in China are also directly subject to credit risk. They guarantee a certain level of return to investors and mitigate this credit risk in several ways including taking guarantees from third party companies for principal and interest or requiring borrowers to provide collateral. Although third party guarantees can help mitigate borrower credit risk to some extent, the counterparty risk is transferred to the guarantee companies and the number of high quality guarantee companies is limited. At times, the guarantee company may be indirectly owned by the P2P platform.

If a loan defaults, investors can transfer the claim to the platforms. Platforms repay the investors first and then pursue recovery of non-performing loans from the guarantee companies or through debt collections.

Many large P2P companies in China use a credit assignment model. Under this model, a specialized creditor is established that lends money to borrowers and transfers the debt to investors. Borrowers and investors do not have a direct claim debt contract. The advantage of this model is that it can meet different needs of borrowers and investors. Deals are not done reactively as matches occur, but proactively, resulting in faster expansion.

China also has a few traditional online P2P lending platforms such as Yirendai that match borrowers and investors online.

Some of the newer fintech companies, such as Dianrong in China and Wolaidai under WeLab from Hong Kong, offer their technology platform and related services to help the traditional banks build their P2P lending infrastructure. The platforms originate, underwrite and service loans which are booked by the banks on their balance sheet. In this model, banks provide the funding but credit risk is underwritten by the platform. In return, the platforms are paid a percentage of the loan amount or may have profit-sharing arrangements.

Many large professional P2P companies have expanded into other forms of lending such mortgage lending, automobile loans and consumer finance loans for purchases of travel packages and electronic goods. Some have additionally diversified into wealth management for their investor base.

The scale of market leaders such as Lufax and CreditEase is much larger than most people in the industry realize.

Lujiazui International Financial Asset Exchange Co. Ltd. (commonly referred to as Lufax and now rebranded as Lu.com), based in Shanghai, is one of the largest online financial services company and P2P lender in China. It was founded in 2011 as the Internet finance arm of Ping An Group, one of China's largest insurance companies. Lufax started with P2P but has expanded into other financial service verticals. In 2015, Lufax claimed that it had over 23.3 million users.

CreditEase is arguably the largest P2P lending, wealth management and asset management company in China. Launched in 2006 with student loans, it now provides inclusive finance across a range of lending products including auto loans, rural loans, mortgages, small business loans, and consumer loans. Its focus on 'inclusive finance' means that the company offers products to borrowers across the entire credit spectrum ranging from prime quality borrowers to near prime and sub-prime borrowers. It has a network of over 230 physical locations in China and originated loans of over USD 10 billion in 2016.[16] CreditEase introduced wealth management products and services for its investor base in 2011 and these include equities, real estate, fixed income, private equity, alternative investments and insurance.

In December 2015, CreditEase became the first non-US P2P lender to complete a successful initial public offering when Yirendai, its majority owned subsidiary that offers online unsecured consumer lending, listed on the NYSE. This was an important milestone for the industry as it marked the first major IPO of a Chinese P2P company and third overall after Lending Club and OnDeck.

The P2P model in China was originally based on loan guarantees. Some companies have switched from a guarantee model to a credit risk reserve fund. Despite loan guarantees and reserve funds, investor risk is high. Investor disclosures by many P2P platforms in China were non-existent or vague until 2015. There was also limited transparency on end-use of investments.

With the economic slowdown in China since 2014, hundreds of online lending platforms have reportedly failed, some due to fraud or liquidity concerns and others due to rising delinquency and credit default rates. Ezubao, one of the largest P2P platforms, turned out to be a classic Ponzi scheme, with approximately 95 percent of loan applications on the platform being false.

	2015 Loans originated (USD billions)[1]	Number of borrowers	Number of employees[2]	Market Cap[3]
CreditEase[4]	10[3]	2,000,000[5]	45,000	n/a
Lending Club	8.4	756,000	1382	$2.4 billion
OnDeck	1.9	45,000[6]	638	$388 million
Yirendai	1.5	146,390[1]	608	$1.8 million

[1] Public filings for the year ended Dec. 30, 2015.
[2] Most recent data available from Sec Filings.
[3] As of Oct. 6, 2016.
[4] Estimated.
[5] Historical cumulative data.
[6] Total number of small businesses served based on investor presentation as of Feb. 2016.

The platform closed its operations in early 2016 and the one million investors lost over USD 7.6 billion.

Big professional companies like Lufax and CreditEase that have reached scale will survive and thrive but there also will be several more failures. Consolidation will benefit larger platforms that are already well-funded and have significant market share. Companies that have learnt the appropriate lessons of the past will survive and become global giants.

18.7.3 P2P Lending Model in United Kingdom

In the United Kingdom, P2P platforms market themselves to retail investors as an alternative to bank deposits and not as a risky investment vehicle. The objective is to provide a low, stable return to retail investors and provide reasonably priced loans to individual borrowers and small businesses. Some of the largest P2P lending platforms are Funding Circle, Zopa, Lend-Invest, and RateSetter. Investors can invest as little as £10 with no maximum cap.

The world's first P2P lender, Zopa, was founded in the United Kingdom in 2005. The real growth in this sector began in 2014 as consumer awareness grew and the government introduced P2P specific regulations that helped build consumer confidence. A streamlined regulatory approach and a supportive government have been major drivers behind the industry growth and have given confidence to both borrowers and investors.

The United Kingdom is an innovative leader in alternative finance and is also the first market in the world to impose self-regulation. In 2011, the industry created its own regulatory body, the Peer-to-Peer Finance Association, with the stated goal of "ensuring high minimum standards of protection" for lenders and borrowers in the industry.

In 2014, the United Kingdom became the first country in the world to create a regulatory framework specifically for P2P lenders platforms. Under this framework, they are licensed by the Financial Conduct Authority ("FCA"). The license enables them to issue loans and be a member of national credit bureaus. Unlike the United States, P2P lenders in the United Kingdom do not need to partner with banks to issue loans or conduct credit bureau checks. Having a partner bank adds an extra step in the origination process and can be confusing for both borrowers and investors.

The United Kingdom Government also invests money in small businesses via P2P lenders, and offers tax incentives to consumers who want to invest via P2P lenders. To encourage more retail investments in this sector, the Government also launched the Innovative Finance Individual Savings Account ("IFISA") in April 2016 which enables consumers to invest up to £15,000 per annum in P2P platforms and pay no interest on their returns.

18.7.4 P2P Lending Models in Other Countries

P2P transactions are gaining momentum in the United States, the United Kingdom, and China but remain at a nascent stage in other parts of the world.

Europe (excluding UK): A European Alternative Finance Benchmarking Report published by the University of Cambridge and Ernst & Young in early 2015 noted that the United Kingdom was the undisputed leader in Europe, followed by France and Germany.

The crowdfunding industry in France had almost 70 platforms in 2015, with Younited Credit as the industry leader. In October 2014, the French government issued a set of P2P lending rules and regulations that allow the platforms to operate within a bespoke framework. In Germany, P2P companies are obliged to acquire a banking license or partner with banks, which hinders the development of the industry. The largest platform in Germany is Auxmoney.

The Cambridge report analyzed the comparative volume of alternative finance transactions in Europe in 2014 by country per capita and using that measure, the dynamics of the European markets alter considerably. The United Kingdom remained in the first place with an alternative finance volume per capita of €36 but Estonia, with a small population of just over 1.3 million, took second place (€17 per capita), followed by Sweden (€10.9), France (€2.39) and Germany (€1.72).

Some French and German P2P lenders are planning international expansion within Europe. The regulation of cross-border loans is untested and there is no common European framework for oversight of crowdfunding activities. The European Commission is in the process of carrying out research in this sector. The European policy makers and regulators are also studying this sector at both national and supranational levels.

Australia: Banks in Australia have almost AUD 250 billion in consumer finance and SME loans. P2P lending industry is eyeing a part of that and is slowly picking up momentum. The platforms are regulated by the Australian Securities and Investments Commission ("ASIC") but are not subject to prudential regulations as they don't take deposits. Leading industry players include SocietyOne, ThinCats, Moula, and DirectMoney.

Asia (excluding China): P2P lending in these remains small. While some countries such as Singapore and Hong Kong have opted to regulate alternative lending within the existing regulatory frameworks, others such as Malaysia, New Zealand, and South Korea have created bespoke regulation.

Most lending platforms in Hong Kong, Singapore, and South Korea are focused mainly on unsecured consumer lending. Some Hong Kong platforms are trying to expand into China as the current trade agreements offer preferential treatment to Hong Kong companies in Chinese services market, including lesser restrictions for setting up operations in the mainland.

In underbanked countries like the Philippines, India, and Indonesia where consumer credit penetration is very low at 10 to 20 percent of GDP, the addressable market is large. For SMEs, raising working capital is a cumbersome process and many digital players have emerged to bridge the gap.

P2P lending as seen in the United States or China is less common in these underbanked markets and the deterrents include lack of clear regulations, low commissions, and high credit risk. Thin spreads between loan demand and funding supply rates, combined with small loan ticket sizes, do not overcome the operating costs of credit underwriting, fraud verifications, collections and other variable expenses. Hence the platforms need to reach massive scale to achieve profitability.

In India, there has been a surge of online lending platforms in recent years for consumer lending and working capital finance to SMEs. Several fintech companies also provide related supporting services such as loan product comparisons and credit score improvement tools that facilitate rehabilitation of those with adverse credit history.

18.8 Arrival of Institutional Investors and Securitization

Arrival of institutional investors in this sector provided additional capital and liquidity to support rapid growth. However, it also introduced new risks associated with any form of lending that is largely dependent on wholesale funding. Sharp changes in interest rates, an economic slump or unexpectedly high rates of credit default can prompt the institutional investors to withdraw as quickly as they arrive, leaving the industry suddenly starved of funds to lend.

History has taught us several lessons about finance companies that raise majority of their funding from capital markets. The model works well in good times but a finance company can quickly hit the wall when institutional funding is tight or prohibitively expensive.

For platforms that become overly reliant on institutional funding, a market disruption can force them to scale back on loan originations. We have seen evidence of that in early 2016 in the United States. To mitigate this risk, marketplace lenders should ensure a balance in funding mix from institutional and retail investors.

Securitization provides another source of capital and liquidity for the platforms to support growth. The loans can be packaged into higher-yield bonds for investors. Making securities out of the debt paves the way for investors such as pension funds and insurers to hold the loans.

In the United States, New York-based hedge fund Eaglewood Capital became the first fund to securitize marketplace loans in 2013 with a USD 53m unrated deal.

In July 2014, SoFi became the first marketplace lender to receive an investment grade Single-A rating from S&P for a securitization of student loans that was also rated by DBRS. SoFi had earlier done its first USD 150m securitization of student loans that was rated by DBRS, but participation of S&P was an important milestone as many large investors are restricted to buying securities that have been rated by one or more of the big three rating agencies. Participation by DBRS opened the insurance market but S&P opened the money manager universe which holds bulk of the capital. In early 2015, a portfolio of consumer loans from Prosper was rated by Moody's, the first time a major rating agency evaluated a securitization deal of P2P consumer loans.

Securitization provides liquidity but also exposes the industry to interest rate risk. If yields on other types of debt increase, that can make the P2P loans offering less attractive to investors. Marketplace securitizations also carry an extra element of risk and can be harder to rate.

The lower returns in the United Kingdom make investing in P2P loans less attractive to institutional investors. While the United States has migrated to marketplace lending platforms, dominated by institutional investors, the United Kingdom has largely stayed closer to the original P2P model in which retail investors supply majority of the industry's capital.

Securitization has also been less commonly used in the United Kingdom. As of mid-2016, Funding Circle was the only P2P lender in that market to have done this. A large share of Funding Circle's least risky tranche was bought by KfW, a German Government-backed bank, and it was guaranteed by the European Investment Fund ("EIF"). The EIF is owned by the European Investment Bank whose aim is to increase small business lending investment across Europe.

The government in the United Kingdom has also invested money in promoting lending to small businesses via RateSetter and Funding Circle. While the Government is an institutional investor, it is likely to behave differently than banks and hedge funds in the event of an interest rate hike or liquidity squeeze. This is because its aim is to fund small businesses and facilitate the economic growth in the country through the P2P industry, and not to seek the largest possible return. Investments by the European Investment Bank have also been made with a similar intent.

Given the growth of marketplace loans and its positive impact of small business lending and overall economic growth, more securitizations and participation by quasi-government entities can be expected in select segments that support financial inclusion and economic growth.

18.9 Credit Bureaus and Credit Scoring

Consumer credit bureaus are organizations that collect, manage and distribute positive and negative information on creditworthiness of borrowers. The collection, reporting and sharing of consumer credit data have been strongly encouraged by both the World Bank and the International Monetary Fund (IMF) as a means of facilitating economic growth and ensuring a stable consumer lending environment. Information disseminated by credit bureaus helps lenders assess and monitor the inherent risks associated with consumer lending and make informed credit decisions.

Credit bureaus are relatively new in several emerging markets. In most Asian countries, credit bureaus were established in early 2000s after the Asian Financial Crisis. Many countries in Africa and Middle East are still in the process of setting up bureaus. Only 7 percent of Africans and 13 percent of South Asians are covered by private credit bureaus,[17] compared to over 85 percent of adults in the United States.[18]

This lack of credit bureau data has forced many P2P lending platforms in emerging markets to explore use of alternate data sources and alternate techniques to establish borrower creditworthiness. P2P lenders in mature markets like the United States are also exploring better use of existing data and use of new data sources for expanding into the unbanked or underbanked customer segments such as micro and small businesses.

Alternate data sources can include telco data, utilities payment information, invoices, sales data from e-commerce sites, shipping data from logistics companies, data from business checking accounts, data from payment processors, as well as accounting platforms and social media data. All these can be good proxies to estimate income and business revenues and hence facilitate decision making.

Numerous articles cite the use of alternate data sources by P2P lenders as a credit advantage. The hypothesis that alternate data sources and credit-scoring algorithms enable better credit assessment and hence lower credit defaults compared to data used by conventional financial institutions is plausible but unproven so far.

The innovation has been in using existing data better than traditional lenders by using automation and machine learning. The opportunity of innovation with alternate data sources is more in assessing income and cash flows than in credit decision making. New data sources and use of technology have also been helpful in detecting and mitigating fraud risk.

Building new credit models is hard, time-consuming and expensive. The credit models fundamentally rank risk from low to high and discriminate between the 'goods' and the 'bads' by using historical experience. Good customers are defined as those who repay on time while bad customers include those that default repeatedly or have been charged off. A credit model cannot be built without sufficient 'bads'. The number of different types of data sources or amount of data is not the most important indicator; what matters is the ability to identify variables that provide the largest discrimination. Credit losses can also vary depending on the customer segment, asset class and the macroeconomic conditions. Unless a model has been built using large data sets that include different segments with default history through different parts of the economic cycle, it is unlikely to be very predictive or very accurate.

For those applicants without an adequate credit history or bureau score, offering relatively small loans for short durations can be a good starting point to assess creditworthiness and repayment behavior. These loans can then be scaled up to larger amounts and longer durations for the 'goods'. After large enough data sets of 'goods' and 'bads' are available, a reliable predictive model can be built.

Some P2P lenders use machine learning effectively to build and rebuild credit risk models rapidly to enhance their credit assessment capability. Most large financial institutions tend to be slow in their ability to rebuild and implement newer credit models and the time taken to implement a new credit model can range from several months to a few years.

Models built on verified information rank credit risk better than those built on unverified information. In the United States, much of the information supplied by borrowers is not verified by the P2P lenders. This can include a borrower's income, employment status, home ownership status, and debt-to-income ratio. This can limit the ability of credit models to discriminate risk properly.

Most balance sheet lenders, defined earlier in this chapter as another form of online alternative lenders, and financial institutions verify the information through multiple sources and use technology to triangulate the information. This is because they have 'skin-in-the-game' and their financial performance is very closely tied to the credit quality of their portfolio and loan repayments.

18.10 Incumbents and Challengers

The critical components of any lending process are customer acquisition, credit risk assessment or credit underwriting, funding, servicing and ongoing portfolio management including collections. Non-bank lenders have innovated one or more of those components and differentiated themselves in ways that are harder for banks to replicate quickly.

The biggest advantage that banks have is low-cost funding through retail deposits. But big banks also have underwriting processes and legacy technology systems that create cost inefficiencies. Operating expenses for unsecured loans in banks can be 5 to 8 percent of loan balances. A large part of cost base in banks is in fixed expenses like branches, people and technology systems which make the cost structure largely inflexible.

In contrast, the platforms create efficiencies using automation and rely less on people and physical distribution channels. They use technology to significantly lower their cost for sourcing loans, underwriting and loan servicing. This provides them with an opportunity to refinance the credit card balances or bank loans at a lower interest rate, despite the higher funding cost.

The biggest spend for P2P lending platforms tends to be on marketing activities to acquire new customers. Customer acquisition is harder than it might appear. The real advantage for P2P platforms lies in reaching segments underserved by the banks in a cost-effective manner. These include small businesses, self-employed individuals, immigrants or those without sufficient credit history. Many may not have adequate credit bureau history or income proof in the form of tax returns or audited cash flow statements to get a bank loan and hence represent a large pool of potential customers for the platforms.

18.11 Evolving Regulatory Landscape

P2P lending industry in most countries has operated relatively untouched by government oversight for several years. But the rapid growth in this sector is now starting to get regulatory attention and scrutiny. Regulators are wary of new risks being introduced. Digital revolution is challenging the regulators as much as the banks and the regulatory views and policies vary significantly across countries.

Some regulators are treating the activity of P2P platforms as banking while others view them as intermediaries. In some countries, the P2P lending platforms are regulated by the securities regulators but do not have to follow the prudential regulations that apply to traditional bank lending.

Many securities regulators and consumer protection agencies primarily look out for unsophisticated individual investors. If an institutional investor is somehow taken advantage of, it is considered okay as they are expected to understand the risk. If several retail investors get burnt, there will be questions around who regulated this area, who was responsible and who was looking out for them. Consequently, some countries have chosen to ban P2P lending, while others such as Singapore and Hong Kong have adopted a more cautious approach to protect retail investors, starting with participation from institutional investors and accredited investors only.

18.11.1 Regulatory Developments in the United States

P2P lending initially was not regulated at all in the beginning in 2006. A pivotal point in the evolution came in 2008 when the two large players – Lending Club and Prosper – came under the scrutiny of the SEC and were temporarily forced to curtail their operations. The investor notes issued by them were subsequently classified as securities and they were required to go through the expensive and time-consuming SEC registration process to be able to sell to retail investors going forward.

The SEC registration process is costly and newer competitors have chosen not to follow suit. Instead many have opted to go with accredited[19] and institutional investors.

In July 2015, the US Treasury Department issued a 12-page request for information (RFI) soliciting comments, data and recommendations on how or to what extent regulators should set more stringent standards on the fast growing peer-to-peer lending industry. The RFI laid out specific questions, including the impact of marketplace lending on market segmentation, implications for anti-money-laundering and fraud, and the considerations for traditionally underserved demographics. The Treasury also asked how marketplace lenders protect consumers against scams or default and whether the lenders should be required to have "skin in the game" by having to put up their own capital to back loans they originate or underwrite.

This move has raised the possibility of new rules for the P2P industry. The officials have struck a positive tone by wanting to know more about the business models and product offerings of online marketplace lenders, the potential for online marketplace lending to expand access to credit to historically underserved market segments, and how the financial regulatory framework should evolve to support the safe growth of this industry.

18.11.2 Regulatory Developments in China

The initial expansion of marketplace or P2P lending in China happened with light regulation. The government has taken significant steps in recent years towards codifying the largely unregulated Internet finance space. In July 2015, the first set of rules governing Internet finance was released and framework classified this sector into seven segments: Internet payments, online lending, equity crowdfunding, Internet fund sales, online trusts, insurance services, and Internet consumer finance. Different segments were placed under the remit of different regulators.

P2P online lending is now the responsibility of China Banking Regulatory Commission ("CBRC") while equity crowdfunding is controlled by the China Securities Regulatory Commission.

CBRC issued detailed guidelines for P2P industry in August 2016. These require platforms to register with the local finance authorities for obtaining appropriate business licenses, to maintain a certain minimum level of capital and to use banks as custodians for customer funds. Platforms are banned from taking deposits from the public, setting up asset pools and offering guaranteed returns. The platforms also need to submit routine reports detailing loan turnover and default rates to a government established central database for online lending.

The platforms are also being encouraged to reduce concentration risk and issue mainly small loans and set single borrower limits. For individual borrowers, caps have been proposed for borrowing from a single platform and cumulative borrowing across all P2P platforms.

The government is encouraging financial institutions to provide custodian services for online transactions. These custodian arrangements bring online lending transactions within the official banking system, reassuring investors.

The increased regulation will be beneficial for the long-term healthy development of the sector which is an important player in promoting mass entrepreneurship in China and provides the much-needed capital to its micro- and small businesses. It will result in consolidation in the sector and help market leaders compliant with the new regulations to take further market share.

18.11.3 Regulatory Developments in the United Kingdom

The UK Government has created a clear set of laws tailored to the industry and has taken several steps to bolster the retail market.

From April 2014, the P2P platforms are overseen by the FCA which has introduced a disclosure-based regulatory regime to provide protection for retail investors. It requires platforms to ensure that all financial promotions are fair, clear and not misleading.

The FCA also requires platforms to keep client monies separate from their own and to be held in a third-party account to prevent co-mingling of client funds. It requires platforms to follow certain prudential regulations such as holding capital to weather financial shocks. This is separate from the provision fund or credit reserves, which some platforms have created voluntarily.

Apart from mandating minimum capital requirements and ongoing reporting requirements, the platforms are also required to have arrangements or resolution plans in place to ensure loan servicing continues in the event the platform ceases to exist and ensure that investors do not lose out.

After it was highlighted in a research by the Department for Business in 2014 that half of all small firms that applied for a bank loan were rejected, the Government started working on several additional measures to push banks to refer such rejected applications to alternative lenders. It established the British Business Bank in 2013 which has put funds through several P2P platforms to support small business lending. It also included investing in P2P lending in the popular UK tax-free Individual Savings Account ("ISA") scheme to give consumers more choice of investments.

In 2015, the finance ministry introduced referral plans that will mandate the nation's largest banks to offer information on alternative financing options to SMEs that are not approved for a traditional business loan. The law related to Bank Referral Scheme was passed by the parliament in late 2016 and requires high street banks to refer declined SME finance applications to designated online finance platforms. Three platforms have been designated so far and more are likely to be added in future.

18.11.4 The Future of Regulation

Regulators around the world are reflecting on appropriate measures for fintech companies conducting banking businesses as they try to balance financial stability and consumer protection with economic growth. Regulations today are designed one-size-fits-all, for most part.

Peer-to-peer lending sector is an ideal case for introducing proportionate regulation; i.e. instead of applying the same regulations for all entities, they should be much more differentiated based on contribution to systemic risk and usefulness for the real economy.

Fintech start-ups are innovating faster than the regulators can adapt the rules. Some of the progressive regulators, such as the FCA in the United Kingdom and the Monetary Authority of Singapore are introducing regulatory sandboxes to address the risks and support innovation.

The banking industry trade groups argue that the online industry's rise is at least partially due to regulatory arbitrage or its exploitation of gaps in regulation. It is true that the marketplace lenders are not supervised or examined by regulators in the way the banks are. Unlike banks, they are not required to hold portfolio impairment provision on their books for expected future credit losses. They are also not required to periodically conduct rigorous stress tests to prove that they can survive a severe downturn scenario as outlined by the regulators. They escape all this because of the clever business model of not holding any loans on their own balance sheet and therefore not needing any retail deposits on the balance sheet.

While the authorities are alert to the risks, a regulatory crackdown looks unlikely at this stage. The platforms are a promising source of finance for small businesses that can't always access a bank loan. Several governments and regulators are welcoming the extra competition as a win for customers.

The likely forms of increased legislation could include risk retention requirements, minimum capital requirements to help alternative lending platforms withstand financial shocks (like what is required in the United Kingdom), and heightened disclosure and reporting requirements.

Regulations could raise online lenders' costs, but could also benefit the industry in the long term by encouraging stronger lending standards and consumer protection, thereby encouraging stronger participation from retail investors.

18.12 Growing Pains – The Shakedown in May 2016

As the industry matures, it is starting to get its share of turmoil and May 2016 will be remembered as an important marker in the short history of online alternative lending industry in the United States.

Lending Club Founder and CEO resigned amid accusations of improprieties and the company also announced its plans to tighten the lending standards for certain high-risk segments. Prosper announced that it was laying off 28 percent of its staff due to reduced growth expectations. OnDeck Capital announced a larger than expected loss in the earlier quarter due to flat loan volumes, narrowing spreads and rising expenses.

These events have hastened regulatory scrutiny of the sector. There was a temporary retreat by the institutional investors and the securitization market. The reasons are hard to pin down, but are likely a combination of factors including concerns over credit quality, loan performance in a stressed environment, regulatory uncertainty, and spread compression.

Institutional investors fuelled the marketplace lending industry's astounding growth in the United States in 2014 and 2015, and their waning interest in 2016 is forcing the industry to take a hard look at its liquidity and funding options. The funding market appears to be getting disrupted even though the macro-economic environment in the United States is still good, interest rates remain low and the job market is strong. This should be an early warning indicator of what could follow if the macro-economic environment worsens.

China's P2P sector experienced a shakedown in 2015 and has started to stabilize since then. P2P industry in the United Kingdom has not been impacted much by these events as the platforms depend mainly on retail investors and the industry has strong government and regulatory support.

Alternative lenders are learning what generations of nonbank finance companies have learnt in the past: liquidity is everything, institutional money cannot be relied on, unusually high rates of loan growth are not sustainable and a business model based on volatile gain on sale margins is inherently unstable.

The peer-to-peer lenders digressed from their original business model of investing by peers and moved rapidly towards institutional money over the last few years. A course correction for the funding model was needed.

Rapid growth also attracted several new players and competition intensified. Platforms faced the pressure to show explosive growth amidst increasing institutional funding and declining spreads, while attempting to reduce acquisition costs and manage credit losses. This is a difficult balancing act.

The unsecured loan industry cannot continue to grow exponentially while maintaining credit quality. To maintain that level of growth, it has to start looking at newer, riskier customer segments. And for those segments, arguably at higher risk-adjusted pricing, the credit losses can be unpredictable and higher than anticipated. The credit risk models using newer data sources have also not yet been tested in stress conditions and may or may not work.

But this recent disruption should be viewed in the wider context of P2P industry's disruptive innovation and significant benefits to the broader economy. The role played by the platforms in providing SMEs with access to finance and its impact on economic growth and creating employment opportunities is significant and should be encouraged.

18.13 The Future of Peer-to-Peer Lending

The P2P lenders have been around for only a decade. The business model is yet to be tested through the credit cycle. Fixed rate nature of these loans also exposes the investors to market risks and the current uncertainty over the future of regulation adds to investor anxiety.

It isn't yet clear whether this boom is a structural change in the financial services industry or a temporary response to the combination of banks shrinking their balance sheets and ultra-low real interest rates.

While the risk factors need to be considered, at the micro- and macro level, the transformative power of marketplace lending is evident, especially in providing access to credit to micro-, small, and medium enterprises that are underserved by the banks and in supporting global inclusive economic growth. Acceptance of online lending platforms by consumers and small businesses continues to grow because they work well and provide a great customer experience.

Platforms and banks are also starting to forge partnerships with the online lenders thereby increasing adoption. Forward looking banks are recognizing the potential of online lending platforms and the larger ecosystem of fintech start-ups. Banks have liquidity and low-cost retail deposits while the platforms have better technology and faster processing capability.

The alternate lenders can forge partnerships with banks to either offer their superior technology or sell loans to banks or both. Some of this collaboration is already underway. JPMorgan Chase has partnered with OnDeck in the United States to offer loans to small businesses that are funded by its balance sheet but processed by OnDeck. In the United Kingdom, Santander refers to small businesses it has rejected for financing to Funding Circle. Other examples of collaboration include those between Kabbage and Santander in the United Kingdom, and Dianrong and Bank of Suzou in China.

P2P lending offers opportunities to international banks on multiple fronts. The United States and China may provide sufficient scale for P2P companies to spread their wings on their own but most emerging markets lack scale, are fragmented and have varying credit infrastructure and regulatory complexities. Established banks in emerging markets with a large customer base and a deep understanding of the credit and regulatory environment can take an active role in shaping the future by supporting growth of new entrants and forming win–win relationships.

Incumbent banks and technology disruptors are destined to be in a symbiotic relationship where each benefits the other, thereby enhancing the overall value proposition for customers.

In 2016, we saw a shift in focus by the lending platforms from rapid growth to stabilization and sustainability. We also saw increased regulatory scrutiny. Regulation is beneficial for long-term healthy development of this sector but a materiality and proportionality test must be applied to regulations based on contribution to systemic risk and significance to the real economy. Most regulations today are designed one-size-fits-all. Regulation must not front-run innovation as premature regulation can stifle innovation and potentially derail the adoption of useful technology. But it is also important to assess the risks and continually evaluate the need to regulate or leave things to evolve further.

Peer-to-peer lending sector is an ideal case for introducing proportionate regulation. The industry is working actively with the regulators to create appropriate standards. Consumer education and regulation have a role to play to protect the retail investors. The more informed and financially literate individuals become, the better it is for the future of this industry.

To ensure ongoing growth in this sector, several enabling factors are critical. These include a supportive regulatory environment, the provision of sufficient investor capital, greater transparency by the platforms and financial education among the retail investors.

Opportunities exist for national governments, regulators and policy makers, incumbent financial institutions, technology entrepreneurs and investors to support the sector and, at the same time, benefit from this trend.

References

Anon, 2016a. [online] Ifc.org. Available at: http://www.ifc.org/wps/wcm/connect/ 4d6e6400416896c09494b79e78015671/Closing+the+Credit+Gap+Report-FinalLatest. pdf?MOD=AJPERES (Accessed 12 Mar. 2016).

Anon, 2016b. About Us | Prosper. [online] Prosper. Available at: https://www.prosper.com/plp/about/ (Accessed 11 Oct. 2016).

Anon, 2016c. Banks Have a $380 Billion Market Opportunity in Financial Inclusion, Accenture and CARE International UK Study Find | Accenture Newsroom. [online] Newsroom.accenture.com. Available at: https://newsroom.accenture.com/news/banks-have-a-380-billion-market-opportunity-in-financial-inclusion-accenture-and-care-international-uk-study-find.htm (Accessed 22 Oct. 2016).

Anon, 2016d. CFPB Report Finds 26 Million Consumers Are Credit Invisible | Consumer Financial Protection Bureau. [online] Consumer Financial Protection Bureau. Available at: http://www.consumerfinance.gov/about-us/newsroom/cfpb-report-finds-26-million-consumers-are-credit-invisible/ (Accessed 30 Mar. 2016).

Anon, 2016e. Press | SoFi. [online] SoFi. Available at: https://www.sofi.com/press/ (Accessed 11 Oct. 2016).

Anon, 2016f. Tests of character. The Economist. [online] Available at: http://www.economist.com/news/finance-and-economics/21707978-how-personality-testing-could-help-financial-inclusion-tests-character?frsc=dg%7Ca (Accessed 17 Oct. 2016).

Fleisher, C., 2016. Small businesses increasingly seeking online lenders. [Blog] Available at: http://triblive.com/business/headlines/9825140-74/lenders-businesses-banks (Accessed 14 Apr. 2016).

Ghose, R., Dave, S., Levin, J., 2016. Digital Disruption – How FinTech is Forcing Banking to a Tipping Point. [online] Available at: https://ir.citi.com/AI2lJSeuRUcB4wxuFyAt38KmnNXDpSNL11b63B6NuLTIAZ caz4V9sYSgJhCrONR83E60vfWtw9c%3D (Accessed 11 Oct. 2016).

Kocianski, S., 2016. THE UK P2P LENDING REPORT. BI Intelligence.

Patwardhan, A., 2015. Peer-to-peer lending: banking's wake-up call. [Blog] LinkedIn Pulse. Available at: https://www.linkedin.com/pulse/peer-to-peer-lending-bankings-wake-up-call-anju-patwardhan (Accessed 6 Oct. 2015).

Patwardhan, A., 2016a. CIO-Asia – Financial inclusion for small businesses in the digital economy. [online] Cio-asia.com. Available at: http://cio-asia.com/blogs/blogs/financial-inclusion-for-small-businesses-in-the-digital-economy/ (Accessed 22 Oct. 2016).

Patwardhan, A., 2016b. Financial Inclusion for Small Businesses in the Digital Economy. [Blog] CIO Asia. Available at: http://cio-asia.com/blogs/blogs/financial-inclusion-for-small-businesses-in-the-digital-economy/ (Accessed 7 Jul. 2016).

Renton, P., 2013. The World's Largest P2P Lending Company That You Have Never Heard Of – Lend Academy. [online] Lend Academy. Available at: http://www.lendacademy.com/the-worlds-largest-p2p-lending-company-that-you-have-never-heard-of/ (Accessed 10 Dec. 2015).

Renton, P., 2016. Lend Academy. [online] Lend Academy. Available at: http://www.lendacademy.com/?s=creditease (Accessed 4 Sep. 2015).

World Economic Forum, 2015. The Future of FinTech – A Paradigm Shift in Small Business Finance. [online] Available at: http://www3.weforum.org/docs/IP/2015/FS/GAC15_The_Future_of_FinTech_Paradigm_Shift_Small_Business_Finance_report_2015.pdf (Accessed 11 Oct. 2016).

Zhang, B., Deer, L., Wardrop, R., Grant, A., Thorp, S., 2016. Harnessing Potential – The Asia-Pacific Alternative Finance Benchmarking Report. [online] Cambridge, UK. Available at: https://www.jbs.cam.ac.uk/faculty-research/centres/alternative-finance/publications/harnessing-potential/#.V_xMDeArI2w (Accessed 10 Apr. 2016).

Zhang, Y., Zhang, N., 2014. China: The Different Categories of Peer to Peer Lending Platforms – Crowdfund Insider. [online] Crowdfund Insider. Available at: http://www.crowdfundinsider.com/2014/11/57456-china-different-categories-peer-peer-lending-platforms/ (Accessed 15 Mar. 2015).

Notes

1. Citi Digital Disruption Report, 2016.

2. Venture Scanner Sector Maps, 2015 https://venturescannerinsights.wordpress.com/venture-scanner-sector-maps/.

3. March 2016: China's Internet Finance: Full article saved as pdf under folder called China.

4. Citi Digital Disruption report, May 2016.

5. http://triblive.com/business/headlines/9825140-74/lenders-businesses-banks.

6. https://techcrunch.com/2016/01/30/the-state-of-p2p-lending/.

7. European Central Bank 2014.

8. http://www.worldbank.org/en/programs/globalfindex.

9. Stein et al. 2010; ACCA 2010 (Peter Stein of World Bank Group).

10. http://www.ifc.org/wps/wcm/connect/4d6e6400416896c09494b79e78015671/Closing+the+Credit+Gap+Report-FinalLatest.pdf?MOD=AJPERES.

11. https://newsroom.accenture.com/news/banks-have-a-380-billion-market-opportunity-in-financial-inclusion-accenture-and-care-international-uk-study-find.htm.

12. Peer-to-peer lending – The Wisdom of Crowds (FT 19 May 2014, Elaine Moore and Tracy Alloway).

13. https://www2.deloitte.com/content/dam/Deloitte/uk/Documents/financial-services/deloitte-uk-fs-marketplace-lending.pdf.

14. Cambridge study of 2016.

15. From Lending Club website in Jan 2015.

16. http://www.lendacademy.com/?s=china+p2p; Article by Jason Jones.

17. The Economist 1 Oct 2016.

18. http://www.consumerfinance.gov/about-us/newsroom/cfpb-report-finds-26-million-consumers-are-credit-invisible/.

19. Defined as those who have a net worth of USD 1 million or more (excluding their primary residence) or make at least USD 200,000 per annum. In March 2015, definition was expanded for crowd-funded investments to include investors who meet a sophistication test, regardless of their income or net worth.

CHAPTER 19

EU VAT Implications of Crowdfunding

Aleksandra Bal[#]

Contents

19.1 Introduction

Innovations in the financial sector have broadened access to finance and changed the way capital is raised nowadays. One of the fastest-growing financial innovations resulting from the digital revolution is crowdfunding. Crowdfunding is a way of financing new ideas or projects by soliciting funds from large numbers of people via the Internet. It represents a significant shift in the way entrepreneurs and start-up companies raise capital.

[#] PhD, LLM, MSc, Manager of the Current Awareness and Tables (CAT) Knowledge Group, IBFD, and Managing Editor of the Bulletin for International Taxation.

Just like any other digital innovation, crowdfunding raises plenty of legal questions. For tax lawyers, the most interesting ones are those about the tax consequences of crowdfunding activities for people who participate in crowdfunding campaigns (entrepreneurs and contributors). The aim of this chapter is to examine the EU VAT treatment of crowdfunding transactions. The chapter first briefly describes the concept of crowdfunding (section 19.2) and the current situation of this alternative form of financing in the European Union (section 19.3). Next, it provides a short introduction to the EU VAT system (section 19.4) and proceeds with a detailed examination of the VAT implications of crowdfunding arrangements (section 19.5). The final section summarizes the chapter.

19.2 The Concept of Crowdfunding

In simple terms, crowdfunding can be defined as an open call to the public to raise funds for a project. Usually, the call is launched for a limited period of time and small contributions from a large number of parties are expected. Any type of project can be financed through crowdfunding. Small and medium-sized enterprises (SMEs), artists, innovative start-ups, social entrepreneurs may all benefit from this form of funding.

The expression "crowdfunding" refers merely to a channel of financing that can take many different forms. In general, two main crowdfunding models can be distinguished: (1) non-financial return models, where the return may range from nothing (donation-based model) to goods or services (reward-based model); and (2) financial return models, where a financial return is expected, either in the form of revenues from securities or intellectual property rights (crowd-investing, equity-based model) or interest on loans (crowd-lending).

In a donation-based model, individuals donate amounts to meet the larger funding aim of a specific project while receiving no financial or material return. This form is frequently used by charities and by individuals who ask for donations to their cause. Reward-based crowdfunding means that contributors are rewarded with a non-financial compensation, such as goods or services, in exchange for their participation in the funding campaign. Rewards can take multiple forms, for example, a copy of a product that the campaign aims at developing. In some cases, the reward may be of symbolic value, compared to the contribution that is given in exchange. This form has been very successful with films, new technology and products ideas that need funding to launch.

In equity-based models, contributors receive a financial remuneration in exchange for the funds provided. The financial reward may take the form of dividends derived from shares, revenue received from bonds or royalties received from the ownership of intellectual property rights. Lending-based crowdfunding (also known as debt crowdfunding, crowd-lending, peer-to-peer or marketplace lending) means that companies or individuals seek to obtain funds in the form of a loan agreement. Contributors expect the entrepreneur to repay the money lent, often with a fixed interest rate: some debt crowdfunding is interest free or carries low interest rates, whereas other applies interest rates at commercial level. Debt crowdfunding is very attractive for investors who desire a fixed return. Debt investments that are secured against the company assets are seen as less risky but provide a lower yield than the unsecured instruments.

Due to its flexibility, community engagement and variety of models, crowdfunding can offer many benefits to entrepreneurs. Small companies, especially young and innovative ones, often have difficulty getting the funding they need. Given their dependence on intangible assets and high uncertainty of market demand, they may not qualify for traditional loans. Some sectors of the economy (social and creative enterprises) may not find many financing offers tailored to their needs either. Crowdfunding can foster entrepreneurship not only in terms of increased access to finance, but also as an additional market testing and marketing tool that can help entrepreneurs acquire relevant knowledge of customers and media exposure. It can give a proof of concept and idea validation to the project seeker, help attract other sources of funding, such as venture capital and business angels, and provide the entrepreneur with insights and information from a large number of people.

In this chapter, the term "contributor" is consistently used to refer to the party that provides funds, whereas "entrepreneur" means the recipient of the funds. In other publications, "entrepreneurs" are also called "investees" or "borrowers". For "contributors", the expressions "donator" or "investor" are sometimes used.

19.3 Crowdfunding in the European Union

Crowdfunding is growing fast in the European Union. In 2012 about EUR 735 million was raised through crowdfunding (European Commission, 2014a). In 2015, this number increased to EUR 4.2 billion, whereby EUR 4.1 billion was raised through models that entail a financial return. During 2013 and 2014, there were 510 crowdfunding platforms operating in the European Union. The United Kingdom had the largest number of platforms (143), followed by France (77), Germany (65), the Netherlands (58) and Italy (42). Crowdfunding projects were present in all Member States. While coverage varies significantly among Member States, the five largest markets by total amounts raised were France, Germany, the Netherlands, Spain, and the United Kingdom (European Commission, 2015a).

Some Member States have already adopted special crowdfunding regulations or proposed policy initiatives affecting the crowdfunding market (for example, the Italian regulation of equity crowdfunding by the *Commissione Nazionale per le Societa la Borsa* or the UK regulation of crowdfunding by the FCA under a new dedicated regime).

The European Commission has taken an active interest in crowdfunding and has been closely monitoring its development. In the Commission's view, "supporting innovative ways of connecting savings to growth and diversifying the funding sources for European businesses is crucial to improving growth and job creation in Europe" (European Commission, 2016). On 27 March 2014, the Commission adopted a communication on crowdfunding. The objective of this communication was to unleash the potential of crowdfunding within the European Union by developing, in cooperation with stakeholders, a common understanding at EU level and preparing the ground for possible future actions (European Commission, 2014b). The next step was the establishment of the "European Crowdfunding Stakeholders Forum" (ECSF) on 25 June 2014. The main task of the group was to assist the Commission in developing policies for crowdfunding to flourish while taking into account the interest of contributors. On 30 September 2015, the Commission adopted an Action Plan on Building a Capital Markets Union (CMU). The CMU Action Plan pledged that the Commission would publish a report on the development of European crowdfunding to assess national regimes, identify best practice, and present the results of the Commission's monitoring of the evolution of the crowdfunding sector. In November 2015, the European Commission published a study that analyzes data on crowdfunding markets across the European Union in 2013 and 2014 as well as examines how national legislations may have impacted the markets (European Commission, 2015a). On 3 May 2016, the Commission published a report that explains the market and regulatory landscape in the crowdfunding field (European Commission, 2016). The report concluded that if crowdfunding is appropriately regulated, it has the potential to be a key source of financing for SMEs over the long term.

19.4 EU VAT System

VAT is an important pillar in the tax and economic system of the European Union. Apart from being a significant revenue source, it contributes to a non-distortive trade policy and respects the fundamental freedoms. VAT legislation in the European Union has been harmonized to a large extent to ensure the proper functioning of the internal market. The VAT Directive (112/2006) lays down the fundamental concepts of the VAT system. Decisions of the Court of Justice of the European Union (CJEU) play a fundamental role in the application of the EU VAT rules. The CJEU is "the supreme court" in EU VAT matters, as it has the main responsibility for ensuring that VAT law is interpreted and applied in the same way in all EU countries.

In simple terms, the functioning of the VAT system can be described as follows. All supplies of goods and services carried out for consideration by a taxable person in the EU territory are subject to VAT, unless a specific exemption applies. VAT charged by the supplier to his customers is known as "output VAT". The supplier is generally responsible for the remittance of output VAT to the tax authorities. VAT paid by the supplier to other businesses on goods and services that he receives is known as "input VAT". A taxable person is generally able to recover input VAT attributable to his taxable transactions by setting it off against the output VAT in his VAT return, provided that all the requirements for an input VAT deduction are met.

As the EU VAT legislation is silent on the issue of crowdfunding, there was a risk that this phenomenon might be treated differently by various Member States. In February 2015, the European Commission presented its views on the VAT treatment of crowdfunding in a report to the VAT Committee (European Commission, 2015b). In response, the VAT Committee issued guidelines in which the main VAT implications of crowdfunding are explained (VAT Committee, 2015).

19.5 VAT Treatment of Crowdfunding Transactions

19.5.1 Introductory Remarks

EU VAT is levied on supplies of goods and services made for consideration by a taxable person acting as such as long as such supplies are not subject to an exemption. Therefore, the following four basic questions need to be investigated in order to determine the VAT consequences of crowdfunding activity:

- does the entrepreneur, or in some cases also the contributor, qualify as a taxable person;
- is there a supply of goods and services for consideration (i.e. can the funds provided by contributors be seen as consideration for EU VAT purposes);
- when does VAT become chargeable;
- can a crowdfunding transaction fall within the scope of an exemption, meaning that no VAT needs to be levied?

19.5.2 Taxable Person

19.5.2.1 Entrepreneur

For a VAT liability to arise, the entrepreneur must be considered a taxable person. "Taxable person" is an autonomous VAT concept. It does not exist in civil or trade law. Under article 9 of the VAT Directive (112/2006), a taxable person is anyone who independently carries out in any place any economic activity, whatever the purpose or result of that activity. Thus, the definition of "taxable person" is very broad: it is not limited to EU residents ("any person in any place") or to persons acting for profit motives ("whatever the purpose"). This is in line with the objective of VAT as a general consumption tax. The characterization as a taxable person depends on two factors: the existence of economic activities and the independent pursuit of such activities.

The concept of economic activity is very broad. Article 9 of the VAT Directive (112/2006) makes it clear that an activity may be considered an economic one, irrespective of its purpose or result. Thus, an activity does not cease to be an economic one because it is loss-making or carried out for a charitable or philanthropic purpose. The CJEU held in *Hotel Scandic Gåsabäck AB* (CJEU, C-412/03) that the fact that the price paid for an economic transaction is higher or lower than the cost price is irrelevant. In *Enkler* (CJEU, C-230/94), the CJEU stated that the hiring out of the caravan could be an economic activity despite that fact that it resulted in losses. The indifference towards profit making is consistent with the nature of VAT: whether a profit is made is irrelevant, it is private expenditure made for consumption what counts.

Under article 11 of the VAT Directive (112/2006), "the condition in Article 9(1) that the economic activity be conducted 'independently' shall exclude employed and other persons from VAT in so far as they are bound to an employer by a contract of employment or by any other legal ties creating the relationship of employer and employee as regards working conditions, remuneration and the employer's liability". In general, entrepreneurs starting a crowdfunding campaign do not perform this activity in an employment relationship. Thus, they act independently.

Given the fact that crowdfunding is mostly used by start-ups and individuals who intend to carry out a particular project in the future and may not perform any economic activity yet, a question arises whether they can qualify as taxable persons. The CJEU ruled that a person may acquire the status of a taxable person long before he first performs a taxable transaction. It held in *Rompelman* (CJEU, C-268/83) that economic activity begins "with the first preparatory act, i.e. with the first transaction on which input tax may be charged". Thus, preparatory activities, such as the acquisition of operating assets, must be treated as economic activities. It is not relevant that the acquired assets are immediately used for taxable transactions (CJEU, C-97/90, *Lennartz*). Even if the project that is being financed by means of crowdfunding has never materialized, the preparatory acts would retain the character of economic activity (CJEU, C-110/94, *INZO*). Nevertheless, the tax authorities may require that the declared intention to perform taxable supplies is supported by objective evidence.

In the equity-based model, the entrepreneur issues shares, bonds or grants intellectual property rights to the contributor in exchange for the funds received. The granting of intellectual property rights may constitute a taxable transaction subject to VAT provided that the entrepreneur meets the general requirements to qualify as a taxable person. In contrast, the CJEU clarified in *Kretztechnik* (CJEU, C-465/03) that the issuing of shares is not an economic activity as it is made with the aim of raising capital and not providing services. The same applies to bonds. Thus, the entrepreneur will not qualify as a taxable person as a result of these activities. However, he may acquire the status of taxable person due to undertaking preparatory work for the project that he intends to carry out using the funds collected via crowdfunding arrangements.

In summary, the entrepreneur will qualify as a taxable person if he independently carries out economic activities, the purpose and result of which is irrelevant. The entrepreneur's status as a taxable person must be determined on a case-by-case basis, taking into consideration his current and future activity.

19.5.2.2 Contributor

In the context of crowdfunding, it also needs to be investigated whether the contributor may qualify as a taxable person due to his participation in the financing of the project. This question is generally to be answered in the negative. Donating money to a project is not an economic activity. In the case of reward-based crowdfunding, donations in kind may trigger VAT consequences only if the contributor has already the status of a taxable person since under articles 16 and 26 of the VAT Directive (112/2006) a disposal of goods and provision of services free of charge is deemed a supply of goods/services.

In a lending-based model, the contributor grants a loan to the entrepreneur. According to the settled CJEU case law, making capital available constitutes an economic activity only if capital is exploited with a view to obtaining income by way of interest therefrom on a continuing basis, the granting of loans is not carried out merely on an occasional basis and is not confined to managing an investment portfolio (CJEU, C-142/99, *Floridienne*). Thus, only institutional investors whose activities go beyond investment portfolio management and who provide capital for commercial purposes will be considered taxable persons in respect of their crowdfunding activity.

In an equity based-model, the contributor is rewarded with shares, bonds or intellectual property rights. The mere acquisition and holding of shares and bonds do not qualify as economic activity (CJEU, C-60/90, *Polysar*). They may however qualify as such if the contributor carries out a commercial share-dealing activity or if the holding of shares and bonds can be seen as a necessary, direct and permanent extension to economic activities of the contributor (CJEU, C-306/94, *Régie dauphinoise*). Similarly, the mere holding of intellectual property rights does not constitute an economic activity. According the article 9(1) of the VAT Directive (112/2006), only the exploitation of intangible property for the purposes of obtaining income therefrom on a continuing basis may be seen as an economic activity. Thus, if the contributor exploits the intellectual property right granted to him by the entrepreneur and obtains revenue for a longer period of time, he may acquire the status of a taxable person.

In summary, the contributor is very unlikely to qualify as a taxable person as a result of his participation in the financing of the entrepreneur's project. His crowdfunding activity may trigger VAT consequences if he is already considered a taxable person or if his activities are carried out for a commercial purpose for a sufficiently long time period.

19.5.3 Consideration

To fall within the scope of VAT, the supply must be carried out for consideration. In *Hong Kong Trade Development Council* (CJEU, C-89/81), the CJEU held that a person who habitually provides services free of charge is not a taxable person at all. Such a person must be assimilated to a final consumer. There must be a direct link between the service provided and the consideration received (CJEU, C-102/86, *Apple and Pear Development Council*). A supply is taxable only if there is a legal relationship between the service provider and the recipient (a reciprocal performance) (CJEU, C-267/08, *SPÖ Landesorganisation Kärnten*). However, VAT liability does not depend on the existence of an enforceable and binding obligation according to domestic law of a Member State. This would be contrary to the principle of VAT neutrality. Decisive is the mutual agreement, i.e. that the parties agree to exchange some items and not a valid legal relationship between them (CJEU, C-498/99, *Town & County Factors*). In the context of crowdfunding, a legal relationship and reciprocal performance seem to exist between the contributor and the entrepreneur since they agree that the reward will be provided only if a contribution to the project is made.

It frequently happens that the reward received by the contributor does not reflect the value of the contribution provided. It may be of a symbolic value and thus lower than what would have been paid for similar goods or services if they had been provided outside the crowdfunding framework. This mismatch between the value of the reward provided by the entrepreneur and the contribution to the project is irrelevant for VAT purposes. The CJEU clarified that the consideration is a subjective concept. It does not have to reflect the actual value of the supply or a value estimated according to objective criteria (CJEU, C-154/80, *Coöperatieve Aardappelenbewaarplaats*).

19.5.4 Time of Taxation

In general, VAT becomes chargeable when the goods or the services are supplied (article 63 of the VAT Directive (112/2006)). The application of this general rule would be difficult in the context of crowdfunding since contributors provide financing to the entrepreneur well before he is able to supply goods or services. The VAT Directive (112/2006) provides for a special rule applicable to payments made on account. According to article 65 of the VAT Directive

(112/2006), where a payment is to be made on account before the goods or services are supplied, VAT shall become chargeable on receipt of the payment and on the amount received. The CJEU clarified that in order for the tax to become chargeable when payments on account are made, all the relevant information concerning the chargeable event, namely the future delivery or future performance, must already be known and, in particular, the goods or services must be precisely identified (CJEU, C-419/02, *BUPA*). During a crowdfunding campaign, it is made clear to contributors what rewards they can expect in the future. Thus, their contribution can be seen as payments on account, meaning that VAT is due when the payment is received. This view has also been endorsed by the VAT Committee. The VAT Committee also unanimously agreed that the contribution can be considered a donation if the reward received by the contributor is negligible or totally unrelated to the amount of the contribution. In such as case, the VAT rules on donation-based crowdfunding will apply.

19.5.5 Exemption

The term "exempt supplies" describes supplies that do not bear output tax: the supplier does not have to collect and remit any tax in respect of the supply and the recipient is not entitled to any input tax deduction. There is an extensive use of VAT exemptions across the European Union. Member States exempt some categories of goods and services considered as essential for social reasons: healthcare, education and supplied by charities. In addition, they also use exemptions for practical reasons (e.g. in the case of financial and insurance services due to the difficulties in assessing the taxable amount).

In the lending-based model, if the provision of capital by the contributor is considered economic activity, the supply of funds is within the scope of EU VAT. Consequently, the contributor would have to charge VAT on his contribution to the project. However, article 135(1)(d) of the VAT Directive (112/2006) exempts "the granting and the negotiation of credit and the management of credit by the person granting it". Thus, the crowdfunding transaction remains VAT free.

In the equity-based model, contributors receive remuneration in the form of securities (shares or bonds) or intellectual property rights. The issuing of shares and bonds by the entrepreneur is not an economic activity and thus remains outside the scope of VAT (*see* section 19.5.2.1). In the rare circumstances that the holding of shares and bonds by the contributor is considered economic activity and falls within the scope of VAT (*see* section 19.5.2.2), the exemption of article 135(1)(f) of the VAT Directive (112/2006) will apply. Pursuant to that provision, transactions in shares, interest in companies and other securities are exempt from VAT. The CJEU clarified in *Granaton Advertising* (C-461/12) that this exemption also applies to securities representing a debt (i.e. bonds). In contrast, the supply of intellectual property rights that qualifies as economic activity (i.e. when the general requirements for the existence of an economic activity are met) is subject to VAT and not covered by any exemption.

19.6 Summary

Crowdfunding is still a young and evolving form of finance. It is growing fast in the European Union although the level of activity and the rate of growth vary significantly across the Member States. To ensure uniform treatment of crowdfunding arrangements for VAT purposes across the European Union, the European Commission and the VAT Committee clarified the most important VAT aspects of crowdfunding transactions.

The main VAT consequences of the different crowdfunding models are as follows. Donation-based crowdfunding does not have any VAT consequences as nothing is received in exchange for the contribution provided. The mere giving of money is outside the scope of EU VAT. Reward-based crowdfunding, where goods or services are promised to contributors in exchange for their funds, may give rise to taxable transactions. There is usually a supply of goods or services by the entrepreneur to the contributor. For a VAT liability to arise, the entrepreneur must carry out economic activities and qualify as a taxable person. This must be determined on a case-by-case basis. A contribution that is made well before the reward is received is treated as payment on account provided that the goods or services to be supplied are precisely identified when the payment is made. VAT is due when the payment is received. It is irrelevant that the contribution does not correspond to the open market value of goods or services.

In the lending-based model, the contributor lends money to the entrepreneur and expects a financial return in the form of interest. The granting of a loan constitutes an economic activity if it is done with a view to obtaining income by way of interest on a continuing basis and is not confined to managing an investment portfolio. However, even if the contributor qualifies as a taxable person, the granting of a loan is exempt from VAT.

In the equity-based model, the contributor receives shares, bonds or intellectual property rights in exchange for his contribution. For the entrepreneur, the granting of intellectual property rights may constitute a taxable transaction subject to VAT provided that he qualifies as a taxable person. The issue of shares or bonds is generally outside the scope of VAT. In the rare circumstances in which it constitutes an economic activity, it is exempt from VAT. For the contributor, the mere acquisition and holding of shares, bonds and intellectual property rights is not an economic activity. He can be regarded as a taxable person only if he carries out a commercial share-dealing activity, the holding of shares and bonds is seen as a necessary, direct and permanent extension to his other economic activities or if exploits intangible property for the purposes of obtaining income therefrom on a continuing basis.

References

CJEU, C-154/80, 5 Feb. 1981. Staatssecretaris van Financiën v Association coopérative Coöperatieve Aardappelenbewaarplaats GA.

CJEU, C-89/81, 1 Apr. 1982. Staatssecretaris van Financiën v. Hong Kong Trade Development Council.

CJEU, C-268/83, 14 Feb. 1985. D. A. Rompelman and E. A. Rompelman-Van Deelen v. Minister van Financiën.

CJEU, C-102/86, 8 Mar. 1988. Apple and Pear Development Council v. Commissioners of Customs and Excise.

CJEU, C-60/90, 20 June 1991. Polysar Investments Netherlands BV tegen Inspecteur der Invoerrechten en Accijnzen.

CJEU, C-306/94, 11 Jul. 1996. Régie dauphinoise – Cabinet A. Forest SARL v Ministre du Budget.

CJEU, C-230/94, 26 Sep. 1996. R. Enkler v. Finanzamt Homburg.

CJEU, C-142/99, 14 Nov. 2000. Floridienne SA and Berginvest SA v Belgian State.

CJEU, C-498/99, 17 Sep. 2002. Town & County Factors Ltd v Commissioners of Customs & Excise.

CJEU, C-412/03, 20 Jan. 2005. Hotel Scandic Gåsabäck AB v. Riksskatteverket.

CJEU, C-465/03, 26 May 2005. Kretztechnik AG v Finanzamt Linz.

CJEU, C-419/02, 21 Feb. 2006. BUPA Hospitals Ltd and Goldsborough Developments Ltd v Commissioners of Customs & Excise.

CJEU, C-267/08, 6 Oct. 2009. SPÖ Landesorganisation Kärnten.

European Commission, 2014a. European Commission, Communication from the Commission to the European Parliament, the Council, the European Economic and Social Committee and the Committee of the Regions Unleashing the Potential of Crowdfunding in the European Union, COM/2014/0172 final, http://eur-lex.europa.eu/legal-content/EN/TXT/?uri=COM:2014:172:FIN.

European Commission, 2014b. European Commission, Commission roadmap to meet the long-term financing needs of the European economy (27 March 2014), http://europa.eu/rapid/press-release_IP-14-320_en.htm?locale=en;%20http://eur-lex.europa.eu/legal-content/EN/TXT/?uri=COM:2014:172:FIN.

European Commission, 2015a. European Commission, Crowdfunding: Mapping EU markets and events study (30 September 2015), http://ec.europa.eu/finance/general-policy/docs/crowdfunding/20150930-crowdfunding-study-executive-summary_en.pdf.

European Commission, 2015b. European Commission, Working Paper No 836, Question Concerning the Application of EU VAT Provisions, taxud.c.1(2015)576037.

European Commission, 2016. European Commission, Capital Markets Union: Commission supports crowdfunding as alternative source of finance for Europe's start-ups (3 May 2016), http://europa.eu/rapid/press-release_IP-16-1647_en.htm?locale=en.

VAT Committee, 2015. VAT Committee, Guidelines resulting from the 102nd meeting of 30 March 2015, Document H–taxud.c.1(2015)5528628–870.

CHAPTER 20

Automated, Decentralized Trust: A Path to Financial Inclusion

Andreas Freund[#]

Contents

20.1 Setting the Stage

Financial exclusion is a byproduct of centralization as expressed through centralized entities such as governments or banks in all societies. Centralization *was and still is* the most important concept in our societal development. Why is that? The answer is quite simple, evolution made us quasi linear beings because for millions of years nothing changed for us. Normally nothing happening outside a couple of days walk or ride impacted us. Change was slow and steady, if it occurred at all. Families and small tribes dominated through the formative millennia of Homo-Sapiens. Homeostasis was the norm, not the exception. The best visual of this is the picture of the evolution of the world population and the world social development index and its components over time in Fig. 20.1.

As one can easily see, nothing really changed much during the millennia of human existence until the development of the steam engine as the largest driver of global change in our history. This started the exponential evolution of mankind. As one can see, we are evolving exponentially but since evolution made us quasi linear, humans are singularly inept to recognize

---

[#] Head Blockchain Advisory, Tata Consultancy Services.

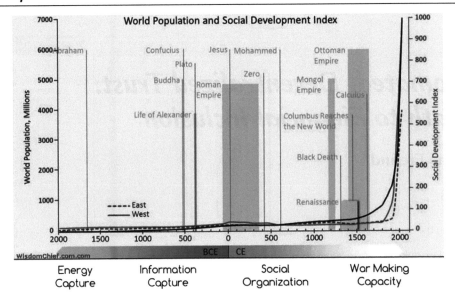

Figure 20.1: **World population and social development index.**

exponential changes until it is too late. Exponential behavior cannot be readily detected by the software and hardware of our bodies that nature gave us. We desperately need a software and hardware upgrade. And this is what the promise of exponential technologies such as Artificial Intelligence, Big Data, the Internet of Things, Blockchain, 3D printing, Drones, Synthetic Biology and Nanotechnologies hold for the human race; to help us recognize and effectively harness exponential behavior and changes.

In addition to being linear beings, humans did not come together into larger groups until the invention of agriculture which prompted the formation of villages, a centralization concept similar to the family, but at a larger scale. Villages then grew into towns and cities as trade between villages picked up. However, because most of our evolutionary time was spent in very small units, evolution in its attempt to optimize our bodies for our environment gave us what behavioral scientists now call the *Dunbar limit* (*Dunbar, 1992*). The Dunbar limit is the number of stable and trusted social relationships an individual can maintain, and is typically assessed to be between 100 and 250, depending on study. This means that *any* level of trust beyond, say 150 people, the number originally proposed by Dunbar, is impossible for an individual without additional trust arbiters. Therefore, when many humans come together, they need a trust authority, a 3rd party that they themselves trust such as a government or a bank to ensure order. Therefore, order is nothing but trust that individuals will behave in a certain way. For example, we rely on the fact that laws are in place and enforced such that people will not kill one another, because there are sever punishments in place for such an order violation.

The introduction of 3rd party trust arbiters to allow the size of human groups to go beyond the Dunbar limit was a fundamental shift in how humans organized. Furthermore, since participants of those trusted 3rd party entities were and are humans too, the Dunbar limit applies as well. And, typically, the limit of stable and trusted social relationships for an individual in a group of less well known people is significantly lower than 150. This fact gave rise to hierarchies such as kingdoms and later on large companies. It is still present in virtually all organizations large and small on this planet. This organizing principle of centralized trust agents has not changed for thousands of years, since mankind had no way to automate and decentralize trust, until today. More about that statement later on.

An immediate consequence of such a centralized trust model, as just described, is that if one has not been bestowed by an agreed upon trust entity the tag of "I trust this individual" through an agreed upon attestation process, one will be left out of all the benefits others enjoy that are "on the inside". Of course, such a system is not binary, but has many layers of trust, and, therefore, the more trusted one is, the more benefits one enjoys – a bank account, a driver's license, a registered deed to one's house, a loan to buy a car, access to exclusive information giving an individual economic advantages and so forth. Given that the 3rd party arbiters of trust are governed by humans, they are imminently fallible and corruptible. The more one has, the more access one has, the more one can influence decisions of those 3rd party trust arbiters to one's own or a group's benefit. The inverse, therefore, is also true leading to financial exclusion.

This is why billions of people, their human potential and the assets they hold, have been systematically shut out of the financial and economic workings of the global economy. They can be exploited without repercussions because they, economically and financially speaking, do not exist within a reliable legal framework. The question that comes immediately to mind is, why are we behaving this way? The answer to this question will enable us to understand not only the motivation behind the current state of affairs but also developments that we are seeing around us right now; exponential changes in society and technology, where one is reinforcing the other. The understanding and harnessing of these developments holds the key to including the billions of people that have been shut out from advancement and economic growth.

20.2 Spiral Dynamics & Human Social Development

Most of us will probably be familiar with Maslow's Hierarchy of Needs from our College courses. Another model that describes human social development significantly better with a wealth of empirical data behind it, is called Spiral Dynamics and was created by Clare Graves

Technology & Societal Progress

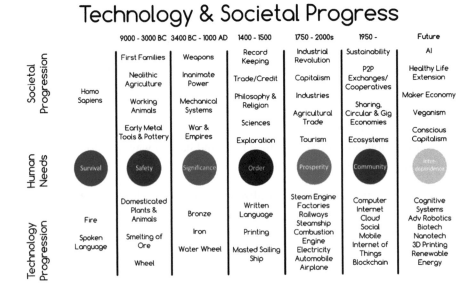

Figure 20.2: Technology & Social Progress within Spiral Dynamics.

(Graves, 2005). Spiral Dynamics explains human social development over time by correlating it to the developmental phases of an individual from infancy to adulthood. David Kish (Kish, 2015) was able to extend the model and correlate development of technologies with societal progression and the psychological developmental phases as expressed through needs or memes (see Fig. 20.2).

As we can see, at the dawn of time, just like an infant, humanity was all about survival. Centralization started with Safety & Significance, as we breached the Dunbar limit in the size of human groups congregating. This is equivalent to adolescence and early adult years of an individual. As societies formed and became larger, order became the most important meme, as early as 4000 years ago in China and most recently with the British Empire. This represents early adulthood of an individual with the founding of family and first workplace experiences. Then as individuals go into middle age, Prosperity becomes more important. This is represented on a global scale by the rise of Capitalism and the Industrial Revolution and had its height during the 20th and the early 21st century. We are currently primarily in the Prosperity meme on a global scale, though all memes can be found on this planet across societies and geographies.

However, something important happened just recently. As we see often in middle aged adults, there is the need for meaning and purpose and belonging to something greater, often referred to as Midlife Crisis. Very successful people, for example, often become philanthropists to give back to communities. Something similar also started on a societal scale and is exemplified

Platforms are enabling emerging communities ...

... that embody a cultural shift toward decentralization.

Figure 20.3: Shift towards decentralization.

by terms like the Sharing or Gig economy and the rise of P2P businesses such as AirBnB, MechanicalTurk, TopCoders, Friendsurance, and so forth. This shift is enabled on a massive scale by emerging technology platforms (see Fig. 20.3). This represents a shift away from centralization of societies towards their decentralization.

Though Uber and Airbnb still represent centralized platforms enabling P2P exchanges, more and more, completely decentralized entities such as LaZooz, Couchsurfing, K or Bitcoin are emerging. They represent, politically and economically speaking, post-capitalistic cooperatives, massively enabled through platforms built on Social, Mobile, Analytics, Cloud and Blockchain. These developments can be summarized in and explained through the 7 Ds of our digital time (Freund, 2015) based on the 6 Ds as described by Diamandis and Kotler (Diamandis and Kotler, 2015)

Digitize: Everything that can be digitized will be digitized to enable near zero marginal supply costs

1. Deceptive: Disruptive waves start deceptively small, but become Tsunamis, for example the digital camera or the Smart Phone.
2. Disrupt: Exponential technologies brought together enable exponential business models for example Uber and AirBnB which disrupt entire industries.
3. Dematerialize: Existing goods, services and business models dematerialize through digitization – the video recorder, the camera, the Walkman etc. all disappeared into the Smart Phone.
4. Demonetize: Near zero marginal supply costs through digitization means that prices and margins are shrinking dramatically – see Kodak's demise in 2012 due to digital photography.

5. Democratize: Goods, services and business models are democratized by opening them to "the wisdom of the crowd" and empower individuals and communities to shape and refine them see for example DIY Drones or Local Motors as powerful DIY communities that exist today.

6. Decentralize: New business models and organizations change how value is delivered to ecosystem participants through new decentralized technologies and loosely-coupled lean/agile thinking. For example, true P2P Lending or Insurance networks such as Kiva and Friendsurance or fully distributed autonomous organizations such as Bitcoin or Ethereum have emerged.

With Spiral Dynamics and the 7 Ds, we are now equipped to analyze recent developments in more detail. The first question that arises is, who is adopting these (partially) decentralized models? As it is to be expected, it is not the Baby Boomers or Gen X. The vanguard in adoption of decentralized structures are millennials, both in the developed and the developing world. Mostly well educated, digitally savvy, yet disillusioned and disenfranchised with societies which are not giving them opportunities to thrive, that favor an ever shrinking group of rich individuals and families, and that are devoid of purpose and fractured both politically and socially.

Despite the clear empirical evidence of the movement towards decentralization, the path towards decentralization will not be a straight line. As was summarized in the article series about the Societal Consequences of the Digital Revolution (Freund, 2015):

- New technologies and their combinations which create more and faster innovations are the key enablers of the Digital Revolution.
- Wage depression, underemployment and wealth concentration are exacerbated, and in part driven by, the Digital Revolution.
- Digital services will be the accelerators of large scale movements and one of its key success factors.
- Large scale, effective movements will organize as digital ecosystems as the network effect of connecting millions at the same time increases their impact and the time for a movement to be effective will be significantly shortened.
- The Digital People's reporter and its power to report anything, from anywhere, at any time has created global transparency – nothing stays hidden for long!
- Digital Movements will collapse, quickly, after their massive, transformative purpose has been fulfilled.
- The Digital Revolution will not only give rise to peaceful innovations and changes but also to violent ones.
- The Digital Revolution will bring about a new, highly effective kind of army: a truly digital, ecosystem driven army.

Despite this somewhat gloomy, or at least ambivalent, picture, I believe that there is a way towards financial inclusion at a massive scale for billions of people. The key lies in providing a trusted legal digital identity for everyone. The absence of such a legal identity for those who do not have it, were best summarized by De Soto (De Soto, 2016b).

He reminds us that

"The formal, legal world is one most of us in the West know. It is a world where the majority of people enjoy the rule of law—where property, identity, and businesses all are legally defined and documented. This system is responsible for our staggering prosperity. It is a system in which:

- *citizens can prove who they are,*
- *people and businesses have legal addresses and identities,*
- *property titles and registries allow everyone to know who owns what,*
- *articles of incorporation enable investors and customers to know who they are buying and selling from,*
- *legal contracts are binding and enforceable.*

This is the world we move in daily. We never think about the vast invisible architecture that lets us live, work, and prosper as few in human history ever have."

From the same source, De Soto makes the point that *"Four billion of the world's six billion, many of them with assets – homes and businesses – and eager to improve their life chances in the larger markets are outside the rule of law. Those four billion have little chance of success because discriminatory burdensome, and costly legal systems have kept them from the legal tools they need to cooperate economically on a national basis, never mind a global one."*

He states that *"As a result, the poor exist outside the legal system. They are in an extralegal place, a place in which:*

- *the poor's assets cannot be represented in such a way to be economically useful;*
- *people are not easily held accountable for their commitments;*
- *assets are not liquid and cannot be used to create credit or capital;*
- *people are not as interconnected across distances and transactions cannot easily be tracked from one owner to the next;*
- *the poor do not have the means to divide labor and control risks through limited liability and asset partitioning, or associate freely in forms such as corporations and cooperatives, and*
- *people cannot be identified, and contracts are unable to reach a market outside the limited confines of acquaintance."*

De Soto believes, and I concur, that the reach of the legal economy in our world is still too limited. He, therefore, believes that this is the primary reason why globalization has not yet delivered on its promise.

From the above it is clear that financial inclusion starts with identity. Everything else is derived from it. That is why the UN supported ID2020 project is aiming to give 1.8 Billion people a verifiable and irrevocable legal identity by 2030 to realize the UN Sustainable Development Goal 16.9 (United Nations, 2015).

As I just explained, the impact of the availability of legal (digital) identities to those that have none or not a sufficient identity is tremendous. However, if we continue to rely on centralized trust authorities which are, as we have seen many times before, both fallible and corruptible, there are too many incentives not to grant or to revoke identities. Therefore, legal digital identities should not be granted through a centralized trust entity but through a decentralized autonomous organization, an Identity Federation. I will discuss such a Federation in more detail below.

In addition, once a legal identity is granted, it can never be revoked, irrespective of nationality, gender, sex, religion or political orientation. Furthermore, it should be self-sovereign. In other words, anyone needs to be able to associate their assets and transactions related to those assets to one's own identity as long as that relationship can be proven. In the following, I will discuss how this can be achieved through probably the most transformative technology since the Steam Engine: Blockchain Technology.

20.3 Automated, Decentralized Trust Through Blockchain

What is a Blockchain and why is it important? Let me try to explain the What as succinctly as possible on a high level:

1. A Blockchain is a cryptographically-secured database that is append-only.
2. This database is shared by all computers, also known as nodes, running a Blockchain protocol encoding the rules of the Blockchain. This creates a giant record book that no-one owns but all agree on through a consensus mechanism. There are no more middlemen or trust agents necessary.
3. Therefore, trust is decentralized and automated and rests with a Blockchain Protocol not any 3rd party such as Banks or Governments.
4. A full copy of a Blockchain contains every asset and asset transactions ever executed and all account balances at any point in history and sits on *each* Blockchain node.
5. Only the account number can be identified on a Blockchain, not the account holder – like a Swiss numbered bank account – unless the individual wants to reveal his or her identity which would be required for most financial transactions.

As the reader might have realized already, the above are statements with significant implications for all industries. However, before I go into those implications and what it means for financial inclusion in more detail, let me explain how a Blockchain works in a bit more detail in order to illustrate the decentralized, automated trust that it provides. To keep things simple, let's assume that you want to pay a bill at a restaurant for $50 and that you and the restaurant are connected to a Blockchain network. You might have heard of some of the more popular ones, namely Bitcoin (Wikipedia, 2016) and Ethereum (Ethereum, 2016). These are what are called public Blockchains. This means that anyone in the world can connect to and do business through those Blockchains. There are no entry barriers, no rules for identification, except that one needs to be able to be connected to the internet and download and run the Blockchain protocol software. There are also private Blockchains which have entry barriers such that you need to identify yourself through an identity attestation process to be able to participate. Examples of such private Blockchains are the NASDAQ Linq Platform (NASDAQ, 2015) to trade private equities such as shares of private companies or the trading platform t0 is majority owned by Overstock.com. But now on with our example where it does not matter if the Blockchain is private or public.

What you need in order to pay your bill at the restaurant through a Blockchain is the Blockchain account number of the restaurant, also known as its public address or its public key. This could be found for example encoded in something known as a QR-code, similar to the well-known barcode you find on most items in a super market, shown on your bill, as some restaurants already do. You can scan the QR code with your Blockchain Payment App on your Smart Phone, such as for example the Airbitz wallet, and enter the amount you want to transfer. You digitally sign the payment transaction with your private address also known as a private key that only you know and that was created when you signed up for your Blockchain Payment App. This private key is securely stored on your Smart Phone and is backed up in a secure location, in case you lose your phone. The digital signature you create when you make the payment marks the transaction as authenticated by you just as your signature on a check or credit card payment slip would. Then your payment – it is actually a payment and not a payment request that you would send to a bank – is submitted to your Blockchain network of choice, for example Bitcoin or Ethereum through your Blockchain Payment App. What happens now is key to understand the concept of automated, decentralized trust.

Your transaction is sent to *all* the computers, the Blockchain nodes, which run the protocol of the Blockchain you chose. *Each* node checks that you actually have the money to pay the restaurant in your account and that the restaurant has a valid account by scanning the node's copy of the Blockchain, the distributed ledger that no one owns and not a single entity controls. Once your payment is validated – remember that each node has to validate that transaction – your payment is packaged with other submitted transactions in what is known as a Block by *each* node. Think of a Block as a section of the larger ledger with a header summarizing all transactions of the ledger in that section and then a list of all transactions in the block and, very important, the unique identifier, known as a Block hash, of the previous block. The inclusion of that unique identifier is what chains Blocks together into a Blockchain, because one creates a unique link between two blocks of the chain by including this hash in what happens next. Now the cryptographic magic happens, and different Blockchains use different methods to make this happen. Since this is not a chapter on Cryptography or Consensus Models and their algorithms, let me explain the best known example of a Blockchain which is Bitcoin. Each Bitcoin node, also commonly known as a miner, applies a cryptographic function to each block that needs to produce a Block hash which has a large number of leading zeros – at least 19 at the writing of this chapter – which is known as the Difficulty. In order to find this Block hash, *each* node has to repeat the hashing of the block many, many, many times by adding a number to the block content starting with one and increasing it by one unit each time until the Block hash has at least 19 leading zeros.

A node needs to do this hashing so many times in fact that you need purpose built computers that *only* do this hashing calculation really, really fast in order to solve this riddle in a reasonable amount of time – in the case of Bitcoin about 10 minutes. These special computers, also known as ASICS, use a very large amount of electricity since they have to be so fast. They use so much electricity in fact that all the Bitcoin nodes combined use the same amount of electricity a year as the country of Denmark!

Once a node, which actually consists of many of these special, super-fast computers, has found the Block hash, it sends this unique identifier, together with the block content and the number, also known as the nonce, it had to add to the block in order to produce the unique identifier to *all* other nodes. What the node has done is to produce a Proof-of-Work; it validated all the transactions and it spent a lot of energy, and thus money, to find the nonce that produced the unique identifier, the Block hash. The nice thing about the Proof-of-Work is that it is easy to validate that the nonce is correct and, therefore, the miner was *honest* and actually did the work. Another node just needs to hash the block that it received together with the nonce and compare the result to the Block hash the node received; that takes a few milliseconds. If the two hashes match, everything is ok. If not, then the node knows right away that the other node lied and the block the other node sent will be rejected. Once a block has been included by the majority of the nodes in the network as the latest block, this block is now part of the longest, and therefore, valid Blockchain – this is called consensus. Since there is a constant transaction flow, there are multiple blocks in the race to become the latest block in the Blockchain. In fact, it can take quite a while, over an hour, before the network has finally agreed upon the latest block with a high probability of finality. That does not mean that your transaction has not been completed. It just means that the transaction has not finally settled yet. If you think that an hour is a long time, compare this to the time it takes to clear a check or to send money through a wire or through ACH. Even though credit and debit card transactions appear to be real time, they are in fact not. Visa, Mastercard or Amex just vouch that the transaction is final, just like the Blockchain protocol does, even though the recipient will not receive the money for at least 24 hours. Knowing that 1 hour does not seem so bad. There are faster consensus protocols than the Bitcoin one but for a public Blockchain such as Bitcoin or Ethereum, Proof-of-Work is still a very robust trust mechanism, even though other models such as Proof-of-Stake are faster and as robust, but not as wildly adopted yet. Given the asset and energy intensive nature of Proof-of-Work, other models will most likely dominate in the future as Blockchain is adopted more wildly and for different use cases.

The observant reader will by now probably ask why are the nodes doing all this work and spending all this money to produce the Proof-of-Work. The answer is simple: Money. In the case of Bitcoin, it is Bitcoin. At the moment, the node which wins the race to have produced the latest block in the Blockchain is rewarded with currently 12.5 Bitcoin plus the transaction fees associated with the transactions in a Block. A transaction fee can vary greatly depending on the amount of data and how quickly the transaction should be finalized. At a USD to Bitcoin exchange rate of over $2300 give or take a few hundred dollars at the time of writing, a Block reward is on the order of $29,000 for the Bitcoin Blockchain. A quite lucrative business opportunity given a Block rate of about 10 minutes in other words about 144 blocks or nearly $41.4 million a day.

There is a little long term catch though, the Block reward is halved every 210,000 blocks. Why is the block reward halved? The goal of the Bitcoin protocol is to both keep Bitcoin scarce and to stretch out the limited supply of new Bitcoin as long as possible and increase competition at the transaction fee level.

Where do the Bitcoin come from? The supply of Bitcoin was determined at its inception to be 21 million and not more in order to avoid inflationary scenarios. This means that unless the Bitcoin network will go under, Bitcoin will appreciate over time as Bitcoin will become scarce compared to demand.

All good and well you might say, but can a node not simply change the content of the ledger to its own or someone else's benefit. The answer to that is no, at least not easily. In fact, it is virtually impossible to do so. Remember that a miner has to do all this massive computational work for just 1 block. If you want to change history, say 100 blocks back, you will have to have more compute power than what was put into the Blockchain for these 100 Blocks. How much work? Well, do the math. The Bitcoin Blockchain's compute power is over 5.6 Eta Hashes a second, at the time of this writing that is over 5.6 Billion Giga Hashes a second, that is a number with 18 zeros! 100 Blocks are about 10,000 minutes of compute power or 600,000 seconds that means you need more than a few thousand Zeta hashes a second to subvert the Bitcoin Blockchain 100 Blocks back! Unless you have the compute power of the

NSA, good luck in changing the Bitcoin Blockchain. The work required to solve the cryptographic riddle, the nonce, is protecting the Blockchain history and its authenticity and the consensus ensures decentralization of decision making. Again, this is done automatically through the protocol. Therefore, one could also call a Blockchain, a decentralized, automated trust engine!

What does this mean for you who sent the payment to the restaurant? You and the restaurant will get a simple notification in your app upon submission, and once the Block containing your transaction is confirmed by the network. That is it! All the complexities we just talked about stay hidden from you. You paid your restaurant bill and the restaurant will get its money after about 1 hour, much better than the next day as we already discussed, and without a single point of failure as banks currently are.

This is already quite a remarkable feat. You paid someone, just like as you would with cash, but electronically and without having to know who or what they are and without relying on a bank as a provider of trust. It is getting even better, once you bring Smart Contracts into the picture. Smart Contracts were first described in the literature by Nick Szabo in 1997 (Szabo, 1997). Smart Contracts on a Blockchain are effectively just like legal contracts in real life with verified counterparty signatures. For example, you sign a contract to buy or sell a car or a house to or from someone or pay money in exchange for services such as a massage. The difference to Smart Contracts on a Blockchain is that those Smart Contracts are actual computer code. And since they are on the Blockchain, these Smart Contracts work exactly the same way each and every time they are executed because their code is secured and made immutable through the Blockchain protocol; it cannot be altered by anyone once the Smart Contract has been saved on a Blockchain. That means one can *trust* the Smart Contract to run properly, even if you do not really trust the counterparty. Since all counterparties agreed upon and should have digitally signed the Smart Contract upon deployment, all counterparties need to abide by its rules whether they want to or not – again decentralized, automated trust through a Blockchain. This then opens up the door to an infinite number of possibilities. Combine Smart Contracts and smart devices such as smart locks and you can rent a house or a car in a paperless, automated fashion where you know that the renter cannot enter the house anymore or open or start the car after the lease period is over since the smart devices – the house lock and the car lock & ignition – are controlled by Smart Contracts which are incorruptible and censorship resistant!

The first implication of a Blockchain with Smart Contracts is that the technology can function as a smart value exchange protocol for the internet similar to what the TCP/IP protocol does for data exchange on the internet. This realizes and goes beyond the wish by Milton Freedman in 1999, *"One thing that's missing* (on the Internet: inserted by the author) *but will soon be developed is a reliable e-cash, a method whereby on the Internet you can transfer funds from*

A to B without A knowing B or B knowing A – the way I can take a $20 bill and hand it over to you, and you may get that without knowing who I am".

In addition to smart value exchanges, any data exchange can be facilitated through a Blockchain in a trusted, decentralized and safe manner. This means the emergence of a decentralized internet which, together with 50 billion plus devices by 2020 based on Cisco's predictions from 2011 (Cisco, 2011), will disrupt every industry once adopted broadly. We are just at the beginning of the Blockchain revolution given that Bitcoin is only about 8 years old and Ethereum less than 2 years with private Blockchains even less than that. Just as during the early days of the internet, people are experimenting with many different approaches and models and the strongest ones will survive through consensus of adoption. Once that happens, the transformative effect will reach every human being on this planet providing never before seen opportunities for the individual or small groups to make a big impact; especially those individuals and groups that have so far been systematically excluded from the global economy.

20.4 Financial Inclusion Through Decentralized, Automated Trust on Blockchains

After we discussed Blockchain's role as a decentralized, automated trust engine, how can this be now applied to improve financial inclusion?

Let's start with a real world example. The company Abra[1] (Abra, 2016) allows people to transfer and hold funds in any currency worldwide, even if people do not have a bank account. The funds are held and secured on the Bitcoin Blockchain and the Bitcoin holdings of individuals are protected against currency fluctuations through smart hedging contracts run by Abra. Abra's customers only see fiat currency holdings, never Bitcoin. And this is not all. If someone wants to deposit funds or send funds, one does not need to go to a bank or even to a Western Union, MoneyGram or Xoom office. The person just looks on the Abra app where the nearest human teller is, makes an appointment to meet through the app, give the teller for example US dollars and sees how the funds appear in their wallet inside the Abra app and/or are transferred to another person of choice. In case of a transfer, the individual receiving the money is then notified and can pick up all or a portion of the funds any time and wherever and whenever a human teller is available. This network of ondemand human tellers with their own money that Abra operates follows the same principle as Uber which operates a network of ondemand car drivers with their own cars. Abra combines two innovations to create a new experience for the financially excluded, Blockchain and ondemand resources. How is that achieved? First, no bank account is required, which means anyone, anywhere in the world can participate as long as they have internet access through a smart phone. Furthermore, people do not have to carry around larger amounts of cash in areas where they could be robbed. Also, people receiving money transfers do not have to withdraw the entire amount, potentially having to walk around with a large amount of cash making them potential targets. Note, that this is a pure Peer-to-Peer (P2P) transaction system. The trust and security of funds is ensured by the Bitcoin Blockchain. The integrity of the human tellers is ensured by Abra, similar to what Uber does in vetting their drivers. Hence, Abra is not fully decentralized but has made a significant step towards fully automated decentralized trust in a business model.

Obviously, the Abra approach has its limitations, and it is only meant as an illustrative example of what is already reality with regard to financial inclusion. Going beyond the Abra example, Blockchain offers more opportunities for financial inclusion through automated, decentralized trust. First and foremost, Blockchain makes it possible for the first time in human history to give every human being on this planet a legal digital identity that can never be lost and can never be taken away in alignment with the UN Sustainable Development Goal 16.9 (United Nations, 2015). As was discussed before, a legal identity is the foundation for being included in reliable legal frameworks that form the basis of our prosperity in the West. Before I go on to discuss how this can be achieved through Blockchain, it is worth discussing the term legal identity.

A legal identity means different things depending on the jurisdiction one is in. For example, a legal identity in Germany is different from a legal identity in the USA. What does that mean? For example, a 16 year-old in the US is legally allowed to drive, however, not so in Germany where the legal driving age is 18. This means that even though both countries verify that the 16 and the 18 year-old are unique in their identities, the societal trust in individuals as represented by the things that people legally can or cannot do in the two countries differ. Common to the US and German definition of legal identity, in fact common to all definitions of legal identity across all nations is the expression of uniqueness of the individual that has been attested by a *national* trust agent imbued with government authority as expressed through the International Civil Aviation Organization, a UN special agency, (ICAO, 1944) founded in 1944 with 191 member countries and which outlays mutually accepted passport requirements to its members. The mutual recognition of national governments as trust agents across the world allows, therefore, at least the proof of uniqueness of an individual to be universally recognized because the majority of governments across the world recognize each other as legitimate representatives of nation states. This has far reaching consequences. It means that an attested uniqueness of an individual is not necessarily bound to citizenship of a nation state. For example, children born in Germany are not necessarily automatically German, if both parents are not German. The parents have the opportunity to choose which nationality the child has, German, or one of the countries of origin of the parents, or none. Therefore, a child could remain stateless if its parents were stateless, and yet it would still have a legal identity in Germany, possibly even as an adult, with a right of residency under certain circumstances. Such an individual has the right to own property or drive a car or have a bank account or be eligible for state retirement funds. All very important aspects of one's life. In particular, one's economic life, at least within the country of *legal* residence. This has significant ramifications with regard to legal identity. If the minimal definition of a legal identity that a majority of countries could agree on is being attested by a recognized trust entity to be unique then it would be possible to create a universally recognized legal identity. Such a legal identity could serve as the basis for further inclusion of individuals into the legal frameworks of stable nation states; the key requirement for financial inclusion.

How can this be achieved through Blockchain? Blockchain Smart Contracts, the immutability of transactions and data on the Blockchain itself and biometric data together allows one to establish a unique legal identity, independent of citizenship, through an identity attestation process that could be underwritten by a globally recognized institution such as the United Nations and their delegated trust agents. Even broader, and a probably quicker way to adoption, would be the creation of an Identity Federation made up of large global corporations under the sponsorship of the United Nations. The Federation members could bring in their customers as first users of such a digital identity system allowing their customers to have seamless digital business and customer experiences with Federation members given the automated, decentralized trust afforded by the Blockchain platform. There are additional benefits for customers of Federation members to voluntarily participate

- Data privacy through the cryptographic capabilities of a Blockchain
- Better cyber security through the safe and secure transaction mechanism of a Blockchain as explained before
- Identity validation without having to reveal Personal-Identifiable-Information or PII through the automated, decentralized trust given to the identity data during the identity attestation process

Establishing traction on digital identity this way at a large scale – 100 million plus identities at launch – would give legitimacy to the effort; it would launch the initiative above the line of super-credibility as Peter Diamandis explains in his book Bold (Diamandis and Kotler, 2015). Governments which might have been reluctant to participate initially, will then be more inclined to join the Federation. This would make the Identity Federation the largest public-private partnership on this planet to the benefit of all.

After having discussed how a legal digital identity could be launched, we need to specify what such an identity should have as minimum requirements. A legal digital identity requires a minimal set of identifying criteria which has to contain at least one if not two biometric markers that prove uniqueness such as digitized forms of finger prints or retinal scans or DNA patterns, together with ownership and control characteristics which could be expressed through public keys associated with the individual. The distinction between ownership and control as key characteristics is necessary since minors, even though they own themselves, are legally controlled by others such as their parents or other legal guardians. Such a core digital identity for individuals can be created on the Blockchain where it can be changed but not deleted and is attested to by trusted agents from an Identity Federation in an irrevocable manner using cryptographic digital signatures. Such a legal digital identity could be accessed from anywhere at any time by the individual the identity belongs to and by individuals or organizations that require proof of legal identity from the individual in a particular situation. This access can be achieved in a seamless, yet real time manner through virtually any device, streamlining processes and making legal identity both portable, convenient to use, highly secure and irrevocable. Of course, in order to prevent identity theft and subsequent impersonation or to enable recovery in case of loss, the private key that is related to the legal identity and is needed to attest through a cryptographic digital signature that the legal identity belongs to a specific individual, needs to be secured. The requirements for safe and secure storage and recovery of a private key given the realities of most people that do not have a legal digital identity can be summarized as follows:

- Secure storage in an encrypted form on any real or virtual device used by an individual such as a phone
- Secure and encrypted online recovery storage either at one or more 3rd party trust agents such as the United Nations or a Blockchain system such as the Inter Planetary File System (IPFS) (IPFS, 2016) in Zero Knowledge. Zero Knowledge means that the trust agent cannot decode the encrypted private key. Access is only possible through a secret such as a password or passphrase only the individual knows and, additionally, multi-factor authentication such as additional secret questions, biometric authentication or multiple-digital signatures of trusted individuals. All access data has to be also stored in Zero Knowledge.
- Secure and encrypted offline recovery storage that allows for final disaster recovery in a manner similar to the online solution. Offline storage could be provided by a computer system that is not connected to the Internet and secured in for example a vault and administered by trusted 3rd parties such as the United Nations.
- Access to recovery needs to be provided globally through for example a webpage and through trust agent services such as the United Nation offices and offices of United Nations delegates that can facilitate a recovery process such as the Red Cross or other NGOs
- Identity recovery also requires forward recovery. That means that impersonation activities after the loss of a private key such as selling of property with false documents and using the private key to forge a digital signature cannot take effect immediately or require multiple digital signatures to be provided by previously designated trusted individuals. And that once identity theft has been reported and validated through a similar attestation process as the creation of a legal identity, the legal identity is updated through the same attestation process as during its creation to invalidate the compromised private/public key pair.

These requirements seem very complex, and they are. However, their Blockchain implementation through Smart Contracts is imminently doable as evidenced by multiple, though still relatively simple Blockchain based identity systems which are already in use today such as ShoCard (ShoCard, 2016), Onename (Onename, 2016) or Bitnation (Bitnation, 2016) that has partnered with the Estonian government to provide legal identities to non-Estonians (Allison, 2015) to name but a few.

In addition to a legal core identity as described above, one can now create and link additional identity dimensions to the core identity which represent different aspects of one's life such as social, financial, commercial etc. For example, using a similar Blockchain based attestation process as described above, banks could run a Know-Your-Customer (KYC) check on a new customer, as they are required by financial regulation almost everywhere and then publish that result on the Blockchain for anyone to see and link it to the core identity. This publishing could take the form of a simple attestation transaction digitally signed by the bank and the requesting legal identity that states that for example the name, address, social security or other national ID number, over 18 years of age, has more than $100,000 in annual income etc. associated with the public key of the requesting legal core identity were successfully validated. That means that anyone or any organization in the world can check that the KYC process for a particular legal identity was successfully completed by a known and trusted 3rd party agent such as a bank while personal identifiable information (PII) is not made public. In other words, the KYC check by another party can be done in Zero Knowledge. This can greatly reduce the dissemination of PII data, significantly improving privacy and reducing the risk of identity theft at a global scale. This trust process can be expanded further such as to national security clearances or to attestation of one's property. The latter one is of great importance for financial inclusion and I will discuss it next.

As I just described, a digital legal core identity together with digital "trust stamps" from other organizations such as KYC from banks that can be validated by anyone from anywhere at any time could rapidly bring formerly excluded individuals, in particular refugees, into stable legal frameworks that would enable them to participate in legal economic activities.

Another important roadblock to financial inclusion can now also be remedied, namely the lack of clear, legal titeling of property, especially of larger assets such as real-estate, in many parts of the world. The lack of such clear legal titeling makes these assets "dead capital" in Hernando De Soto's words. He estimated this "dead capital" to be about $10Tn globally in 2000 (De Soto, 2016a). How can this "dead capital" be brought into stable legal frameworks? Leveraging the attestation processes that were described above for the legal digital identity and associated "trust stamps" together with Blockchain Smart Contracts and the ledgers immutability of transactions allows one to use a similar process to attest the ownership of for example a house or a plot of land and its potential distribution amongst multiple owners.

Once ownership has been attested to through 3rd party trust agents, either locally, nationally or supranationally and recorded in for example a tamper-proof and censorship resistant Blockchain property registry and be given an identity itself, the asset can now be leveraged as collateral in a loan to finance a new or existing business or some other economic endeavor. This is true not only for individuals but communities as well. They could pool assets as collateral for local improvement projects etc. The possibilities for activating currently dead capital of $10Tn+ are significant, if one is willing to go to smaller, less valuable and more mobile assets such as phones. These could form the basis of micro-loans through organizations such as micro-lender Kiva (Kiva, 2016) to build more grass-roots economic activity in a legal framework that is now no longer bound to a national framework alone! That means, for example, that even if the owner of an asset would be displaced through disasters such as war, or would lose the asset, he or she can always prove ownership of the asset, even given contradicting documentation by others since the initial ownership attestation process is trusted and the Blockchain cannot be altered. This enables refugees for example to return to something that they can prove is still theirs despite war or natural disaster, and build upon that ownership a new life. First attempts to create such a Blockchain based titeling system are made by Factom together with Honduras (Chavez-Dreyfuss, 2015), or Bitland (Redman, 2016) and others and more advanced approaches are under way.

The ultimate power to drive financial inclusion is the combination of legal identity, "trust stamps" and asset registries tied to legal identities based on Blockchain technology that will start overcoming the financial exclusion of the vast majority of mankind.

20.5 Summary

To summarize, we have shown that the key to understanding the root causes of financial exclusion is to understand the origin of centralization of human societies based on

- individual and societal psychological development as explained through Spiral Dynamics,
- evolution having made human beings quasi-linear in their perception and thinking and
- the Dunbar limit which constrains the number of stable and trusted social relationships an individual can maintain at the same time.

We then went on to show that the tamper-proof and censorship resistant nature of Blockchain technology holds the key to provide an automated, decentralized trust engine that human kind has been lacking so far in order to create

- a legal, universally recognized and readily verifiable, digital identity similar to a passport as the foundation for inclusion in stable legal frameworks
- public "trust stamps" by organizations such as banks to provide some form of assurances for economic exchanges between counterparties and

- a method by which assets can be publicly recorded and made visible for all time without the possibility of losing proof of ownership to unlock $10Tn+ of "Dead Capital" of the world's poor

such that we can rapidly improve financial inclusion of those amongst us that have been systematically excluded from economic opportunity.

The opinions expressed here are my own and do not reflect the views of my employer, Tata Consultancy Services. No intellectual property or content belonging to Tata Consultancy Services were used in the creation of this chapter.

References

Abra, 2016. Abra. Retrieved from Go Abra: https://www.goabra.com.

Allison, I., 2015. Bitnation and Estonian government start spreading sovereign jurisdiction on the blockchain. Retrieved from International Business Times: http://www.ibtimes.co.uk/bitnation-estonian-government-start-spreading-sovereign-jurisdiction-blockchain-1530923.

Bitnation, 2016. Bitnation. Retrieved from Bitnation: Governance 2.0: https://bitnation.co/.

Chavez-Dreyfuss, G., 2015. Honduras to build land title registry using bitcoin technology. Retrieved from Reuters: http://in.reuters.com/article/usa-honduras-technology-idINKBN0O01V720150515.

Cisco, 2011. The internet of things. Retrieved from Cisco: http://www.cisco.com/c/dam/en_us/about/ac79/docs/innov/IoT_IBSG_0411FINAL.pdf.

De Soto, H., 2016a. Dead capital. Retrieved from The Power of the Poor: http://www.thepowerofthepoor.com/concepts/c6.php.

De Soto, H., 2016b. Informality and extralegality. Retrieved from The Power of the Poor: http://www.thepowerofthepoor.com/concepts/c3.php.

Diamandis, P., Kotler, S., 2015. Bold: How to Go Big, Create Wealth and Impact the World. Simon & Schuster.

Dunbar, R., 1992. Neocortex size as a constraint on group size in primates. Journal of Human Evolution 22 (6), 469–493.

Ethereum, 2016. Ethereum. Retrieved from Ethereum: https://www.ethereum.org/.

Freund, A., 2015. Digital revolution and its social consequences: some case studies. Retrieved from Linkedin: https://www.linkedin.com/pulse/digital-revolution-its-social-consequences-some-case-freund-phd?trk$=$pulse_spock-articles.

Graves, C., 2005. The Never Ending Quest. ECLET.

ICAO, 1944. ICAO. Retrieved from ICAO: http://www.icao.int/about-icao/Pages/default.aspx.

IPFS, 2016. IPFS. Retrieved from IPFS: https://ipfs.io/.

Kish, D., 2015. The next evolution. Retrieved from Ecosystem Of You: http://www.thenextevolution.com/presentations-2/ecosystem-of-you-presentation/.

Kiva, 2016. Kiva. Retrieved from Kiva: https://www.kiva.org/.

NASDAQ, 2015. NASDAQ Linq. Retrieved from NASAQ Linq: http://ir.nasdaq.com/releasedetail.cfm?releaseid=948326.

Onename, 2016. Onename. Retrieved from Onename: https://onename.com/.

Redman, J., 2016. Bitland: blockchain land registry against 'corrupt government'. Retrieved from Bitcoin.com: https://news.bitcoin.com/bitland-blockchain-land-registry/.

ShoCard, 2016. ShoCard. Retrieved from ShoCard: https://shocard.com/.

Szabo, N., 1997. Formalizing and securing relationships on public networks. Retrieved from First Monday: http://journals.uic.edu/ojs/index.php/fm/article/view/548/469.

t0, 2016. Retrieved from t0: https://www.t0.com/.

United Nations, 2015. Sustainable development goals. Retrieved from UN Sustainable Development Knowledge Platform: https://sustainabledevelopment.un.org/sdgs.

Wikipedia, 2016. Bitcoin – Wikipedia, the free encyclopedia. Retrieved from Wikipedia: https://en.wikipedia.org/wiki/Bitcoin.

Note

1. Please, note that the author is not affiliated with Abra and does not want to promote their services. Abra merely serves as a real world example of how Blockchain can improve financial inclusion.

Index

Edwards Brothers Malloy
Ann Arbor MI. USA
August 30, 2017